Economic Theory of
Natural Resources

Economic Theory of
Natural Resources

Edited by
W. Eichhorn, R. Henn, K. Neumann, and R.W. Shephard
at the Universities of Karlsruhe/Germany and Berkeley/U.S.A.

Physica-Verlag · Würzburg — Wien
1982

CIP-Kurztitelaufnahme der Deutschen Bibliothek

Economic theory of natural resources / ed. by
W. Eichhorn . . . − Würzburg ; Wien : Physica-
Verlag, 1982.
  ISBN 3-7908-0274-3

NE: Eichhorn, Wolfgang [Hrsg.]

©Physica-Verlag, Rudolf Liebing GmbH + Co., Würzburg 1982
Composed and printed by repro-druck „Journalfranz" Arnulf Liebing GmbH + Co., Würzburg

Printed in Germany

ISBN 3 7908 0274 3

Preface

As a consequence of the ever increasing economic problems connected with the depletion of natural resources, the literature on the subject has grown rapidly within the past decade. Since this literature is scattered throughout a great number of international journals, it is very difficult to obtain an impression of the present state of the art. Therefore it is desirable that from time to time books should appear that offer a representative part of the newest results of research on the subject.

This book offers such material, in addition to some excellent earlier monographs. It contains 42 hitherto unpublished articles written by 56 authors from four of the five continents. Each paper has been reviewed by two anonymous referees. Consequently, the articles of this book are revisions or, in many cases, revised revisions of the original papers.

The contributions are organized in six parts. Part I contains six papers on resource extraction, substitute production and recycling. Special interest is concentrated on learning in planning with exhaustible resources and on aggregation in resource economics.

Five papers on locational aspects of resource search and depletion and on the production and management of marine fisheries have been included in Part II.

Turning next to markets and prices in the context of natural resources, Part III consists of ten contributions involving national and international markets as well as oligopolistic and competitive ones. In this connection, problems of efficiency and nonefficiency of markets and prices are treated.

Part IV contains seven articles on production or growth models with special emphasis on natural resources.

The six papers of Part V are devoted to topics concerning environment and welfare that are influenced by problems emerging from natural resources.

The concluding Part VI consists of eight studies on energy-modeling and methodology.

We take this opportunity to acknowledge indebtedness to Stifting Volkswagenwerk (Volkswagen Foundation), Alfried Krupp von Bohlen und Halbach-Stiftung (Krupp Foundation) and Fritz Thyssen Stiftung (Thyssen Foundation) for providing the financial means to conduct a symposium on *Natural Resources and Production* (University of Karlsruhe, June 23 – July 4, 1980) at which oral presentations and discussions of several of the topics of this book first took place. In addition, the Alfried Krupp von Bohlen und Halbach-Stiftung provided the funds that made publication of this book possible. To all sponsors we express our sincere appreciation for their support.

Karlsruhe and Berkeley

October 1981

W. Eichhorn, R. Henn
K. Neumann, R.W. Shephard
Editors

Contents

Part I
Depletion and Substitution

Economic Theory of Natural Resources. ©Physica-Verlag, Würzburg—Wien, 1982.

The Importance of Learning in Planning with Exhaustible Resources[1])

Gautam Bhattacharya

1. Introduction

A large number of papers discussing optimal depletion policies for an exhaustible resource assume the stock of the resource is known with certainty to the society [for instance, *Dasgupta/Heal; Dasgupta/Heal/Majumdar; Hotelling; Kamien/Schwartz; Koopmans; Manne; Pindyck; Stiglitz; Smith; Solow*]. Some of these papers consider possibility of arrival of an advanced technology at some unknown future date and examine the effect of this uncertainty on optimal depletion policy for an exhaustible resource [e.g. *Dasgupta/Heal; Dasgupta/Heal/Majumdar; Kamien/Schwartz*; etc.]. However, there have been relatively few studies of optimal depletion of an *uncertain* resource stock. *Kemp* [1976] and *Loury* [1978] consider optimal depletion of an uncertain stock of a resource in a centrally planned economy where the planner possesses an initial probability distribution about the resource. There is no feasibility constraint in the sense that the society might plan to consume any amount of resource at any time. The social welfare obtained from any program is the discounted sum of instantaneous utility levels weighted at each moment by the probability of the resource not being exhausted up to that instant.

Another group of papers [*Gilbert; Deshmukh/Pliska; Arrow/Chang*] make a distinction between the known (proven) stock of the resource and the unknown actual stock. In this approach, the maximum amount that can be extracted at any point of time is the known stock of the resource. Further, exploration activities are considered in these studies as a means of augmenting the amount of the known stock and gaining new information about the unknown actual stock. Following this approach, this paper considers the process of learning through exploration and its effect on the optimal extraction program. Section 2 describes the resource extraction problem in the form of a discrete time dynamic programming model with incomplete state observation [discussed by *Yushkevich* and *Rhenius*].

To emphasize on the informational aspect of the model, a partial equilibrium approach is adopted. The planner is assumed to know the instantaneous social welfare function dependent on the amount of extraction of the resource in one period and to maximize the expected value of discounted sum of utilities by choosing an extraction program.

---

[1]) This paper contains material from Chapter I of my Ph. D. Dissertation submitted to the University of Rochester. I am indebted to my advisors, Professor L.W. McKenzie and Professor J.W. Friedman for helpful comments and suggestions. Discussions with Professor M. Majumdar have been extremely helpful in different stages of writing this paper.

Thus the effect of interaction between different sectors of the economy, of the production technology and of supply functions of other factors of production are ignored in this paper. It is also assumed that the decisions about exploration activity have already been made. The planner observes the results of exploration every period (which are random in nature) and learns new information from these observations. In a subsequent paper, a general equilibrium model will be developed incorporating several sectors and considering decisions about exploration as endogenous.

It is shown in section 2 that an optimal extraction policy exists and is stationary in the sense that it depends only on the current known stock and the current information about the unknown actual stock, when the current information is obtained by Bayesian revision of the previous period's information after observing the results of exploration in the current period. In section 3, some properties of the optimal extraction policy are examined in a simple example.

2. The Model

A centrally planned economy is considered here with the unknown actual stock of the resource denoted by s and known (proven) reserves denoted by m. No distinction is made between proven reserves in the ground and reserves already extracted and being held in the inventory. Thus extraction of an amount (a) implies use of the extracted amount for production or consumption so that the instantaneous utility accruing to the society is $u(a)$. In the beginning of the planning period (period zero), the information about the unknown actual stock s_0 is described by a probability distribution ϕ_0. Of course, s_0 is not less than the known stock m_0. s_0 is also believed to be possibly at most as large as $\bar{s}$, when $\bar{s}$ is an arbitrarily large number (e.g. if the resource is oil, $\bar{s}$ may be the largest stock of oil reserves that might possibly exist on earth). Therefore, the support or the range of ϕ_0 is $[m_0, \bar{s}]$.

The decision about extraction at each period a_t is taken by the planner for $t = 0, 1, 2, 3, \ldots$ Therefore although s_t is unknown, it is known that for every $t = 0, 1, 2, \ldots$

$$s_{t+1} = s_t - a_t. \tag{2.1}$$

As mentioned before, the determination of exploration activities is exogenous to our model. However, even after the level of exploration activities have been decided upon, the results of exploration, namely discovery of new reserves, are random in nature. Let Δ_t be the amount of discovery through exploration in period t. If the results of exploration conducted in period t become known in period $t + 1$, then

$$m_{t+1} = m_t + \Delta_t - a_t \qquad \text{for } t = 0, 1, 2, 3, \ldots \tag{2.2}$$

The minimum possible value of Δ_t is zero, when no additional reserves are discovered. The maximum possible value is $(s_t - m_t)$. When $\Delta_t = s_t - m_t$, all of the existing actual stock becomes known. Thus $\Delta_t \in [0, s_t - m_t]$ and for every $t = 0, 1, 2, \ldots$

$$m_{t+1} \in [m_t - a_t, s_t - a_t]. \tag{2.3}$$

The approach taken here is to treat m_{t+1} as a random variable that has a probability distribution q^m for each value of $[m_t, s_t, a_t]$. $q^m(m_{t+1} \mid s_t, m_t, a_t)$ is the conditional distribution of m_{t+1}, given m_t, s_t, a_t. The range of q^m $(\cdot \mid s_t, m_t, a_t)$ is, for every s_t, m_t, a_t

$$\text{supp } q^m (\cdot \mid s_t, m_t, a_t) = [m_t - a_t, s_t - a_t]. \tag{2.4}$$

The planner is assumed to have complete knowledge of the whole family of these conditional distributions given by (2.4).[2] Given a discount factor β, he chooses a feasible extraction program a_t, $t = 0, 1, 2, 3, \ldots$ (such that $0 \leqslant a_t \leqslant m_t$ for all t) to maximize the expected value of $\sum\limits_{t=0}^{\infty} \beta^t u (a_t)$.

This problem can be set up as a dynamic programming problem with incomplete state observations. The following notation is required. If X is a metric space, $B(X)$ is the Borel σ-field of X. $(X, B(X), \mu)$ is a probability space when μ is a probability measure defined on the Borel-measurable space $(X, B(X))$. $f: X \to Y$ is a Borel-measurable (or simply, measurable) function if $f^{-1}(B) \in B(X)$ for each $B \in B(Y)$. The set of all probability measures on $(X, B(X))$ is denoted as $M(X)$. $M(X)$ is endowed with the topology of weak convergence. If X is a metric space $M(X)$ is a metric space [see *Parthasarathy*]. A probability measure is sometimes abbreviated as p.m.

A dynamic programming problem with incomplete state observations consists of an unobservable state, an observable state, an action or decision taken every period, a transition mechanism, initial conditions, a return function and a discount factor. These are defined formally below for the resource extraction problem (problem Z).

The actual amount of the resource, s, is the *unobservable state*. The unobservable state space is

$$S = [0, \bar{s}] \subset R. \tag{2.5}$$

As a subset of R, S is a compact metric space. Hence, S is a complete and separable metric space.

The amount of known stock of the resource, m, is the *observable state*, $m \in M = S$.

The amount of extraction of the resource, a, is the action variable. A is the *action space*, $A = S$. The *set of feasible actions* is given by a correspondence α

$$a \in \alpha (m) \text{ for every } m \in M, \text{ when } \alpha (m) = [0, m]. \tag{2.6}$$

It is easy to check $\alpha (m) \in B(A)$ for all $m \in M$, and α is a compact-valued, upper- and lower-semi-continuous correspondence.

The *transition mechanism* describes the movement from the current period's state to next period's state. In this case q^s and q^m are transition mechanisms for s and m, respectively.

$$q^s: S \times A \times M \to M(S)$$

such that for all $m \in M$, $s \in S$ and $a \in \alpha (m)$,

$$q^s (\cdot \mid s, m, a) = \delta_{(s-a)} \tag{2.7}$$

---

[2] Although exploration activities are assumed to have been decided beforehand, this formulation does not imply that the exploration process is stationary. In fact, for each value of the known stock m_t and the unknown actual stock s_t, there exists a particular $q^m (m_{t+1} \mid \cdot)$ giving the distribution of the results of explorations.

when $\delta_{(s-a)}$ is a p.m. degenerate on the point $(s-a)$. Thus $s_{t+1} = s_t - a_t$ with probability one.

$q^m : S \times M \times A \rightarrow M (M)$ gives the transition mechanism for the known stock, m. q^m is a probability measure on M for every value of the previous period's state $(s_t, m_t) \in S \times M$ for $t = 0, 1, \ldots$ and previous period's extraction $a_t \in A$ for $t = 0, 1, 2, \ldots$

$$\text{supp } q^m (\cdot \mid s, m, a) = [m-a, s-a] \quad \text{for all } (s, m, a). \tag{2.8}$$

In addition, we make two assumptions on q^m.

Assumption 1. q^m satisfies the following

a) q^m is a function measurable with respect to $B (S \times M \times A)$ (2.9)

b) q^m is weakly continuous with respect to (s, m, a) (2.10)

(2.9) ensures that the family of measures $q^m (\cdot \mid s, m, a)$ becomes eligible as a transition mechanism for a dynamic programming problem. (2.10) implies if $(s_n, m_n, a_n) \rightarrow$ $\rightarrow (s, m, a), q^m (\cdot \mid s_n, m_n, a_n) \rightarrow q^m (\cdot \mid s, m, a)$ in the topology of weak convergence on $M (M)$. This assumption means the planner's expectation about the next period's known stock (or equivalently, expectations about the result of this period's exploration) does not change drastically if the current period's state and extraction are changed by small amounts. The return function u is the utility function depending on extraction in a single period, a. The following standard assumption is made.

Assumption 2. $u : A \rightarrow R$ is a continuous, monotonically increasing, bounded and strictly concave function. The initial conditions are $- m_0$ is the known stock in period zero, $\phi_0 \in M (S)$ is the planner's initial information on S, supp $\phi_0 = [m_0, \bar{s}]$.

The objective is to choose $a_t, t = 0, 1, 2, \ldots$ such that $a_t \in \alpha (m_t)$ for all $t = 0, 1, 2, \ldots$ to maximize

$$v = E (\sum_{t=0}^{\infty} \beta^t u (a_t)) \tag{2.11}$$

when the expectation is conditioned on the transition probability measures and the initial conditions.

Problem Z can be transformed to a problem where all state variables are observable (problem $\bar{Z}$). In problem $\bar{Z}$, the state in period t is the pair (ϕ_t, m_t) when m_t is the known stock, ϕ_t is the planner's current information about s_t. Given $\phi_t, m_t, a_t,$ and m_{t+1}, ϕ_{t+1} can be constructed for each $t = 0, 1, 2, \ldots$ The procedure is described below.

Lemma 1. Assume that to each (ϕ_t, m_t, a_t) in the measurable space $\Phi \times M \times A$ there corresponds a probability measure $q (ds_{t+1}, m_{t+1} \mid \phi, m, a)$ on the direct product of Borel spaces $S \times M$ which is measurable with respect to (ϕ, m, a). Then to each $(\phi_t, m_t, a_t, m_{t+1}) \in \Phi \times M \times A \times M$, one can associate a probability measure $\phi (ds_{t+1} \mid \phi_t, m_t, a_t, m_{t+1})$ on S such that

(a) ϕ is measurable with respect to $(\Phi \times M \times A \times M)$ (2.12)

(b) for each (ϕ_t, m_t, a_t), $q \, (ds_{t+1}, dm_{t+1} \mid \phi_t, m_t, a_t) =$

$\bar{q} \, (dm_{t+1} \mid \phi_t, m_t, a_t) \times \phi \, (ds_{t+1} \mid \phi_t, m_t, a_t, m_{t+1})$ (2.13)

when $\bar{q}$ is a p.m. on M induced by q.

The lemma is a direct consequence of a theorem in *Parthasarathy* [1967] (Theorem 8.1) which says any probability measure on a product of two spaces can be expressed as a product of two probability measures, one of which is a conditional probability measure.

To apply this lemma, let

$$q \, (ds_{t+1} \, dm_{t+1} \mid s_t, m_t, a_t) = q^s \, (ds_{t+1} \mid s_t, a_t) \times q^m \, (dm_{t+1} \mid s_t, m_t, a_t).$$

For each $(s_t, m_t, a_t) \in S \times M \times A$, q is a p.m. on $S \times M$. Let $\phi_t \in \Phi \, (= M \, (S))$ be any p.m. on S. Then define, for every $\phi_t \in \Phi$, $(m_t, a_t) \in M \times A$

$$q \, (ds_{t+1}, dm_{t+1} \mid \phi_t, m_t, a_t) = \int_S q \, (ds_{t+1}, dm_{t+1} \mid s_t, m_t, a_t) \, \phi_t \, (ds_t).$$ (2.14)

By applying lemma 1, we get

$q \, (ds_{t+1}, dm_{t+1} \mid \phi_t, m_t, a_t) = \bar{q} \, (dm_{t+1} \mid \phi_t, m_t, a_t) \times$

$\phi \, (ds_{t+1} \mid \phi_t, m_t, a_t, m_{t+1})$ (2.15)

when

$$\bar{q} \, (dm_{t+1} \mid \phi_t, m_t, a_t) = \int_S q \, (ds_{t+1}, dm_{t+1} \mid \phi_t, m_t, a_t).$$ (2.16)

Also, $\phi \, (ds_{t+1} \mid \phi_t, m_t, a_t, m_{t+1})$ is a p.m. on S measurable with respect to $\phi_t, m_t, a_t, m_{t+1}$.

Define for every $(\phi_t, m_t, a_t, m_{t+1}) \in (\Phi \times M \times A \times M)$, $\phi_{t+1} \in \Phi$ such that

$$\phi_{t+1} \, (ds) = \phi \, (ds \mid \phi_t, m_t, a_t, m_{t+1}).$$ (2.17)

We are now able to set up a transition mechanism for problem $\bar{Z}$, for going from the current period's state and action (ϕ_t, m_t, a_t) to (ϕ_{t+1}, m_{t+1}). For each (ϕ_t, m_t, a_t), we get a p.m. on m_{t+1} given by (2.16). Thus, for each (ϕ_t, m_t, a_t) we get a pair $(m_{t+1}, \phi \, (\cdot \mid \phi_t, m_t, a_t, m_{t+1}))$ with the joint distribution of the pair given by $\bar{q} \, (m_{t+1} \mid \phi_t, m_t, a_t)$. Using this transition mechanism, problem $\bar{Z}$ is described below.

The state space is $\Phi \times M$ when $\Phi = M \, (S)$. Φ is a compact metric space [see *Parthasarathy*]. Thus $\Phi \times M$ is a compact metric space. The action space, the return function, the set of feasible actions and the initial conditions (ϕ_0, m_0) are the same as in Problem Z. The transition function is $q^{\phi m} : \Phi \times M \times A \to M \, (\Phi \times M)$ when

$$q^{\phi m} \, (d\phi_{t+1}, dm_{t+1} \mid \phi_t, m_t, a_t) = \bar{q} \, (dm_{t+1} \mid \phi_t, m_t, a_t)$$ (2.18)

and

$$\phi_{t+1} = \phi \, (\cdot \mid \phi_t, m_t, a_t, m_{t+1}).$$ (2.19)

The objective is to choose feasible a_t, $t = 0, 1, 2, \ldots$ to maximize

$$\bar{v} = \bar{E} \, (\sum_{t=0}^{\infty} \beta^t \, u \, (a_t))$$ (2.20)

when $\bar{E}$ denotes expectation conditioned on transition probabilities $q^{\phi m}$ and initial conditions (ϕ_0, m_0). In problem $\bar{Z}$, under the usual concept of probability distributions

q $(ds_{t+1}, dm_{t+1} \mid \cdot)$ is the joint distribution on $S \times M$ and $\bar{q}$ $(dm_{t+1} \mid \cdot)$ is the marginal distribution on M obtained from q. Therefore

$$\phi (ds_{t+1} \mid \cdot) = q (ds_{t+1}, dm_{t+1} \mid \cdot) / \bar{q} (dm_{t+1} \mid \cdot) \tag{2.21}$$

which is the well-known Bayes' rule for constructing posterior distributions. Applying (2.21) recursively after m_t is observed, a new posterior is obtained every period.

An *admissible observable history* up to time t for problem Z is given by $h_t = (\phi_0, m_0, a_0, m_1, a_1, \ldots, m_t)$ such that $a_j \in \alpha (m_j)$ for all $j = 0, 1, \ldots, t$. The set of all admissible observable histories up to time t for problem Z is denoted by H_t. For problem $\bar{Z}$, we define an *admissible history* up to time t as $\bar{h}_t = (\phi_0, m_0, a_0, \phi_1, a_1, \ldots, m_t, \phi_t) \in \bar{H}_t$.

Definition 1. An admissible policy for problem Z is given by $\pi = (\pi_1, \pi_2, \pi_3, \ldots)$ such that $\pi_t : H_t \to A$ is $\mathcal{B} (H_t)$ measurable for all t and $\pi_t \in \alpha (m_t)$ for every $t = 0, 1, \ldots$ The set of all admissible policies is denoted by Π. For problem $\bar{Z}$, $\bar{\pi}$ and $\bar{\Pi}$ are defined in the same way.

Problems Z and $\bar{Z}$ are obviously related to each other. In fact, there exists an onto mapping i by which a policy for $\bar{Z}$ can be transformed into a policy for Z. Define $i : \bar{\Pi} \to \Pi$ by

$$i \, \bar{\pi}_{t+1} (\phi_0, m_0, a_0, m_1, \ldots, m_t, a_t, m_{t+1})$$
$$= \bar{\pi}_{t+1} (\phi_0, m_0, a_0, m_1, \phi_1, \ldots, m_t, \phi_t, a_t, m_{t+1}, \phi_{t+1})$$

when for $t > 0$, ϕ_t are computed recursively with respect to the observed past and formulas (2.17) and (2.15).

Yushkevich [1976] and *Rhenius* [1978] show that problems Z and $\bar{Z}$ are equivalent in the following sense.

Lemma 2. Problem $\bar{Z}$ has an optimal policy $\bar{\pi}^*$ if and only if problem Z has an optimal policy $\pi^* = i \, \bar{\pi}^*$ with equal values of expected returns, i.e.

$$\bar{v} (\phi_0, m_0, \bar{\pi}^*) = v (\phi_0, m_0, \pi^*).$$

Proof: See *Yushkevich* [1976, 155–156].

Thus it suffies to consider problem $\bar{Z}$ as the resource extraction problem. If the following assumption is made, it is possible to show that the optimal value function exists for $\bar{Z}$ and satisfies the "optimality equation". Further, there exists a stationary policy for $\bar{Z}$ depending only on ϕ and m.

Assumption 3. M is a countable subset of S.

Assumption 3 implies that it is possible to observe only a countable number of values as known stock. This assumption is necessary to prove the following.

Theorem 1.
(i)   problem $\bar{Z}$ has an optimal value function $w : \Phi \times M \to R$ such that
$$w (\phi_0, m_0) = \sup_{\bar{\pi} \in \bar{\Pi}} \bar{v} (\phi_0, m_0, \bar{\pi}).$$

(ii)   Problem $\bar{Z}$ has an optimal stationary policy $\bar{\pi} = (f^{\alpha})$ such that, a) $\pi_t = f$ for all $t = 0, 1, 2, \ldots$; b) $f \colon \Phi \times M \to A$ is a measurable function; c) $f(\phi, m) \in \alpha(m)$ for all (ϕ, m).

(iii) w is continuous in (ϕ, m) and satisfies the following "Optimality Equation".

$$w(\phi_0, m_0) = \max_{0 \leqslant a_0 \leqslant m_0} [u(a_0) +$$

$$\beta \sum_{m_1} w(\phi(ds \mid \phi_0, m_0, a_0, m_1), m_1) \bar{q}(m_1 \mid \phi_0, m_0, a_0)]. \tag{2.22}$$

Proof. It is shown in Yushkevich [1976] that under assumption 1 and 3 $\bar{q}(m_{t+1} \mid \phi_t, m_t, a_t)$ is weakly continuous. This fact will be used below. The proof uses the standard methods developed by Blackwell [1965], Maitra [1968] and others.

Let $\bar{S} = \Phi \times M = B(S) \times M$. $\bar{S}$ is a compact metric space. Let $B(\bar{S})$ (resp. $C(\bar{S})$) be the space of bounded measurable real-valued functions (resp. bounded continuous real-valued functions) on $\bar{S}$. A metric on $B(\bar{S})$ is given by $\mu(a, b)$ for any $(a, b) \in B(\bar{S})$

$$\mu(a, b) = \sup_{\bar{s} \in S} |a(\bar{s}) - b(\bar{s})|.$$

Define $T \colon B(\bar{S}) \to B(\bar{S})$ by

$$Tw(\phi_0, m_0) = \sup_{0 \leqslant a_0 \leqslant m_0} (u(a_0) + \beta \sum_{m_1} w(\phi(\cdot \mid \phi_0, m_0, a_0, m_1), m_1)$$

$$\times \bar{q}(m_1 \mid \phi_0, m_0, a_0)). \tag{2.23}$$

As $\bar{q}(\cdot \mid \phi_0, m_0, a_0)$ is weakly continuous, $T \colon C(\bar{S}) \to C(\bar{S})$ and it can be shown that T is a contraction mapping [Blackwell], thus, T has a unique fixed point w^* such that $Tw^* = w^*$.

Next, define $T_f \colon B(\bar{S}) \to B(\bar{S})$ as

$$T_f w(\phi_0, m_0) = u(f(\phi_0, m_0)) + \beta \sum_{m_1} w(\phi(\cdot \mid \phi_0, m_0, a_0, m_1), m_1) \bar{q}(m_1 \mid \cdot) \tag{2.24}$$

when $a_0 = f(\phi_0, m_0)$.

T_f is defined for all $f \colon \bar{S} \to A$ such that $f(\phi, m) \in [0, m]$. Using the same arguments, T_f is a contraction mapping and has a fixed point. Denote the fixed point as $I(f^{\alpha})$. It can be shown that $T_f I(f^{\alpha}) = I(f^{\alpha}) = \lim_{n \to \alpha} T_f^n(0)$. This proves that $I(f^{\alpha})$ is a $B(\bar{S})$-measurable function. The following lemma is stated from Maitra [1968] without proof.

Lemma 3. Let $\bar{S}, A$ be compact metric spaces, α a continuous, compact-valued correspondence from $\bar{S}$ to A, and $g \colon S \times A \to R$ be a bounded continuous function. Then there exists a $B(\bar{S})$ measurable function f from $\bar{S}$ into A such that,

a) $f(\bar{s}) \in \alpha(\bar{s})$ for all $\bar{s} \in \bar{S}$;
b) for every $\bar{s} \in \bar{S}$, $g(\bar{s}, f(\bar{s})) = \max_{a \in \alpha(\bar{s})} g(\bar{s}, a)$.

From before, w^* is the unique fixed point of T. Define g as

$$g(\phi_0, m_0, a_0) = u(a_0) + \beta \sum_{m_1} w^*(\phi(\cdot \mid \phi_0, m_0, a_0, m_1), m_1) \bar{q}(m_1 \mid \cdot). \tag{2.25}$$

$g: \bar{S} \times A \to R$ is a bounded real-valued continuous function. $\alpha(\bar{s}) = \alpha(m_0) = [0, m_0]$ is a continuous compact-valued correspondence from $\bar{S}$ to A. Using Lemma 2.2, there exists a $B(\bar{S})$ measurable function f from $\bar{S}$ into A such that

a) $f(\phi_0, m_0) \in \alpha(m_0) = [0, m_0]$ for all $(\phi_0\ m_0) \in \bar{S}$.
b) For every $(\phi_0, m_0) \in \bar{S}$,

$$g(\phi_0, m_0, f(\phi_0, m_0))$$

$$= \max_{0 \leqslant a \leqslant m_0} (u(a_0) + \beta \sum_{m_1} w^*(\phi(\cdot \mid \phi_0, m_0, a_0, m_1), m_1) \bar{q}(m_1 \mid \cdot)).$$

$$(2.26)$$

But the right-hand-side of (2.26) is Tw^* from (2.23). (2.26) is also equal to $T_f w^*$ (see (2.24)). Thus, there exists a stationary policy f such that $Tw^* = T_f w^* = w^*$. But T_f has a unique fixed point $I(f^\alpha)$. Therefore $w^* = I(f^\alpha)$ when $I(f^\alpha)$ is the return from following a stationary policy f. From (2.23), it was already shown w^* satisfied the "optimality equation" $Tw^* = w^*$. Thus, we have proved w^* is the return from following a stationary policy. From *Blackwell* [1965, Theorem 6(f)] it follows that w^* is the optimal value function for problem $\bar{Z}$.   Q.E.D.

3. Nature of Optimal Extraction Policy

In general, the nature of optimal extraction policy depends on (ϕ_0, m_0) and the conditional distributions $q^m(m_{t+1} \mid \cdot)$. To find out specific properties of a, it is necessary to specify ϕ_0 and q^m explicitly. Information obtained from exploration has two effects in this model. Firstly, the known stock is augmented and the support of ϕ_t changes every period. Thus supp $\phi_t = [m_t, \bar{s}]$ but supp $\phi_{t+1} = [m_{t+1}, \bar{s} - a_t]$. Secondly, as the Bayesian updating method is used, the form of ϕ_t also changes over time. The following example will clarify the role of information in a simple situation.

Suppose $M = S = [0, s^2]$, $m_0 = s^1 \in S$ when $s^1 < s^2$. The planner starts with only two possible values of s,

Prob. $(s_0 = s^1) = 1 - p$, prob. $(s_0 = s^2) = p$.

In every period, exploration activities are carried out to discover the unknown part of the resource, $(s^2 - s^1)$. q^m is given by

$$q^m(m_{t+1} = m_t - a_t \mid s^1) = 1 \qquad (3.1)$$

$$q^m(m_{t+1} = m_t - a_t \mid s^2) = q \qquad (3.2)$$

$$q^m(m_{t+1} = m_t - a_t + s^2 - s^1 \mid s^2) = 1 - q. \qquad (3.3)$$

If the starting stock is s^2, probability of not finding $(s^2 - s^1)$ is q in every period. If the starting stock is s^1, however, no discoveries can be made through exploration. The functional equation for the infinite horizon problem in this case is found as

$$w(p, s^1, s^2) = \max_{0 \leqslant a \leqslant s^1} \left[u(a) + \beta((1-p) + pq) \times \right.$$

$$w\left(\frac{pq}{1-p(1-q)}, s^1 - a, s^2 - a\right) + \beta p (1-q) w (1, s^2 - a, s^2 - a)\Big].$$ (3.4)

In the right-hand-side of (3.4), if in period 1, $m_1 = s^1 - a$,
prob. $(s_1 = s^2 - a \mid m_1 = s^1 - a) = (pq)/(1 - p(1-q))$. If $m_1 = s^2 - a$,
prob. $(s_1 = s^2 - a \mid m_1 = s^2 - a) = 1$.

This situation can be contrasted with three other possible situations.

a) Here, prob. $(s_0 = s^2) = 1$ and the functional equation is

$$w (1, s^2, s^2) = \max_{0 \leqslant a \leqslant s^2} [u (a) + \beta w (1, s^2 - a, s^2 - a)].$$ (3.5)

b) Here, prob. $(s_0 = s^1) = 0$ and we have

$$w (0, s^1, s^1) = \max_{0 \leqslant a \leqslant s^1} [u (a) + \beta w (0, s^1 - a, s^1 - a)].$$ (3.6)

c) Here, the planner sticks to his original probability belief p over time instead of revising if the additional amount $(s^2 - s^1)$ is not discovered. Here, the relevant functional equation is

$$\bar{u} (p, s^1, s^2) = \max_{0 \leqslant a \leqslant s^1} [u (a) + \beta (1 - p(1-q)) \bar{u} (p, s^1 - a, s^2 - a)$$

$$+ \beta p (1-q) \bar{u} (1, s^2 - a, s^2 - a)].$$ (3.7)

Let the optimal initial extraction policy in case of (3.4) be denoted by $a^* (p, s^1, s^2)$.

Proposition 1. If u is twice continuously differentiable with

$$u' (a) > 0, u'' (a) < 0, \text{ and } \lim_{a \to 0} u' (a) = \infty,$$

then $a^* (p, s^1, s^2)$ is strictly monotonically increasing in p, s^1, s^2.
Let the optimal initial extraction in case of (3.7) be $\bar{a} (p, s^1, s^2)$.

Proposition 2. Under the same assumptions as in Proposition 1

$$a^* (p, s^1, s^2) \leqslant \bar{a} (p, s^1, s^2).$$

Propositions 1 and 2 have the following implications. The initial extraction is highest for (3.5) when it is known with certainty that the higher stock exists and lowest for (3.6) when it is known that only the lower stock exists. If $0 < p < 1$, the optimal extraction policy is such that

$$a^* (0, s^1, s^1) < a^* (p, s^1, s^2) < a^* (1, s^1, s^2).$$

Also, proposition 3.2 implies that if the planner does not revise his initial information when additional resource is not discovered, optimal extraction policy cannot be more conservative.

Further, keeping in mind that $u' (a^*)$ can be interpreted as the starting price for the resource stock the society is willing to pay, we can see that the starting price is a decreasing function of s^1, s^2 and p (which is the belief that the higher stock exists). From (3.4), it can be seen that the price of the stock of the resource will rise at an expected rate $(1/\beta - 1)$ which is equal to the social rate of discount or the rate of interest. The actual rate of price increase will depend on whether new discoveries are made. If no new discoveries are made, the rate of rise in price will be rising over time and asymptotically approaching the rate of interest as the society becomes more pessimistic about existence of the higher stock. If the higher stock is discovered, the price of the resource will have a discrete jump at the time of discovery and then will rise at the social rate of discount. *Arrow/Chang* [1978], *Dasgupta/Stiglitz* [1976] and *Deshmukh/Pliska* [1980] have discussed the behavior of price of the resource stock under uncertainty (without considering any learning mechanism) in similar situations.

Propositions 1 and 2 can be proved by using standard dynamic programming techniques. A sketch of proof of proposition 1 is given below. Proposition 2 can be proved using the same techniques.

Proof of Proposition 1 (Sketch).

Define a truncated *T*-period problem as

$$W^T (p, s^1, s^2) = \max_{0 \leqslant a \leqslant s^1} G^T (p, s^1, s^2, a) \tag{3.8}$$

when

$$G^T = u (a) + \beta (1 - p (1 - q)) w^{T-1} \left(\frac{pq}{1 - p (1 - q)}, s^1 - a, s^2 - a \right)$$

$$+ \beta p (1 - q) W^{T-1} (1, s^2 - a, s^2 - a). \tag{3.9}$$

Let $a^T (p, s^1, s^2)$ be the optimal solution to (3.8). The following can be proved. For all $T = 1, 2, \ldots$

(i) G^T is twice differentiable in p, s^1, s^2, a
(ii) w^T exists and is twice differentiable in p, s^1, s^2
(iii) a^T is the unique solution to $\partial G^T / \partial a = 0$. a^T is differentiable in p, s^1, s^2
(iv)   The partial derivatives are

$$\frac{\partial w^T}{\partial p} = w_1^T, \frac{\partial w^T}{\partial s^1} = w_2^T, \frac{\partial w^T}{\partial s^2} = w_3^T, w_i^T > 0, \quad \text{for all } i = 1,2,3.$$

$$w_{11}^T > 0, w_{22}^T < 0, w_{33}^T < 0, w_{12}^T < 0, w_{13}^T > 0, w_{23}^T > 0.$$

Similarly, $a_p^T > 0, a_{s^1}^T > 0, a_{s^2}^T > 0.$

(i) – (iv) above may be proved by using an induction argument and by using the relation,

$$w^T (p, s^1, s^2) = G^T (p, s^1, s^2, a^T (p, s^1, s^2)) \tag{3.10}$$

when a^T is the solution to $\partial G^T / \partial a = 0$.

Next, $a^T (p, s^1, s^2)$, $T = 1, 2, \ldots$ can be considered as a sequence of functions with compact domain $[0, 1] \times S \times S$.

It can be shown that

(v) a^T is monotonic, i.e. $a^T (p, s^1, s^2) > a^{T+1} (p, s^1, s^2)$ for all $T = 1, 2, \ldots$
(vi) a^T is uniformly bounded
(vii) a^T is equicontinuous.

(v), (vi), and (vii) imply, by Arzela-Ascoli theorem, $a^T \overset{u}{\to} a^*$. [See *Hille*, p. 98.] By a standard result in dynamic programming [*Blackwell*] $w^T \overset{u}{\to} w$. It can be shown that a^* is the solution to the equation

$$w (p, s^1, s^2) = \max_{0 \leqslant a \leqslant s^1} G (p, s^1, s^2, a). \tag{3.11}$$

Thus a^* is the unique optimal policy for the infinite horizon problem. By uniform convergence $a^* (p, s^1, s^2)$ is continuous. Also, as $a^T (p, s^1, s^2)$ is strictly increasing in (p, s^1, s^2), a^* is non-decreasing in p, s^1, s^2. But it can be directly checked that a^* is not constant. Therefore $a^* (p, s^1, s^2)$ is strictly increasing in (p, s^1, s^2). Q.E.D.

Proposition 3.2 can be proved using the same kind of arguments as proposition 3.1. Defining a truncated problem for (3.7) and denoting the solution as $\bar{a}^T$, it can be shown that $a^T (p, s^1, s^2) \leqslant \bar{a}^T (p, s^1, s^2)$ and $\bar{a}^T \overset{u}{\to} \bar{a} (p, s^1, s^2)$, which shows that $a^* (p, s^1, s^2) \leqslant \bar{a} (p, s^1, s^2)$.

4. Concluding Remarks

Many economic phenomena involve decision-making under an unknown state of the world along with a changing structure of information. The theory of controlled Markov process gives a general method of solving these problems. The problem of optimal extraction of an uncertain resource stock has been shown in this paper to be an useful application of this theory. Other possible applications are optimal fishing [*Majumdar*], two-armed bandit theory of pricing [*Rothschild*] and consumption of a commodity with uncertain effectiveness [*Grossman/Kihlstrom/Mirman*].

In this paper, we have solved the non-trivial problem of showing that an optimal extraction policy exists and depends on current information which is updated by the Bayesian method every period. However, it has not been possible to obtain explicit closed-form solutions of the optimal policy. Further, the determination of exploration activities has not been considered explicitly. Some efforts in this direction are made in *Bhattacharya* [1980].

References

Arrow, K., and *S. Chang*: Optimal Pricing, Use and Exploration of Uncertain Natural Resource Stocks. Discussion Paper No. 675, Harvard Institute of Economic Research, Harvard University, 1978.

Bhattacharya, G.: Two essays in the economics of Uncertainty: The Importance of Learning in Planning with Exhaustible Resources and Optimality of Equilibrium with Incomplete Markets. Ph. D. Dissertation, University of Rochester, 1980.

Blackwell, D.: Discounted Dynamic Programming. Annals of Math. Stat. 36, 1965, 226–235.

Dasgupta, P., and *G. Heal*: The Optimal Depletion of an Exhaustible Resource. Review of Economic Studies Symposium, 1974, 3–28.

Dasgupta, P., G. Heal, and *M. Majumdar*: Resource Depletion and Research and Development. Frontiers of Quantitative Economics, vol. 3. Ed. by M. Intrilligator. Amsterdam 1977, 483–506.

Dasgupta, P., and *J. Stiglitz*: Uncertainty and the Rate of Extraction under Alternative Institutional Arrangements. Technical Report No. 179. Institute of Math. Studies in Social Sciences. Stanford University, 1976.

Deshmukh, S., and *S. Pliska*: Optimal Consumption and Exploration of Nonrenewable Resources under Uncertainty. Econometrica **48**, 1980, 177–200.

Gilbert, R.: Optimal Depletion of an Uncertain Stock. Review of Economic Studies **46**, 1979, 47–57.

Grossman, S., R. Kihlstrom, and *L. Mirman*: A Bayesian Approach of the Production and Information of Learning by Doing. Review of Economic Studies **44**, 1977, 533–47.

Hille, E.: Methods in Classical and Functional Analysis. Reading, Mass., 1972.

Hotelling, H.: The Economics of Exhaustible Resources. Journal of Pol. Economy **39**, 1931, 137–175.

Kamien, M., and *N. Schwartz*: Optimal Exhaustible Resource Depletion with Endogenous Technical Change. Review of Economic Studies **44**, 1977, 179–196.

Kemp, M.C.: How to Eat a Cake of Unknown Size. Three Topics in the Theory of International Trade. Ed. by M.C. Kemp. Amsterdam 1976.

Koopmans, T.: Proof for a Case Where Discounting Advances the Doomsday. Review of Economic Studies Symposium Issue, 1974, 117–120.

Loury, G.: The Optimum Exploitation of an Unknown Reserve. Review of Economic Studies **45**, 1978, 621–636.

Maitra, A.: Discounted Dynamic Programming on Compact Metric Spaces. SANKHYA **30**, Part II, 1968.

Majumdar, M.: A Note on Learning and Optimal Decisions with a Partially Observable State Space. Working Paper No. 220, Department of Economics, Cornell University, 1980.

Manne, A.: Waiting for the Breeder. Review of Economic Studies Symposium Issue, 1974, 47–66.

Parthasarathy, K.R.: Probability Measures in Metric Spaces. New York 1967.

Pindyck, R.: Optimal Exploration and Production of a Nonrenewable Resource. Journal of Political Economy **86**, 1978, 841–862.

Rhenius, D.: Incomplete Information in Markovian Decision Models. The Annals of Statistics **2**, 1978, 1327–1331.

Rothschild, M.: A Two-Armed Bandit Theory of Market Pricing. Journal of Economic Theory **10**, 1974, 185–220.

Smith, V.: An Optimistic Theory of Exhaustible Resources. Journal of Economic Theory **9**, 1974, 384–396.

Solow, R.: Intergenerational Equity and Exhaustible Resources. Review of Economic Studies Symposium, 1974.

Stiglitz, J.: Growth with Exhaustible Resources: Efficient and Optimal Growth Paths. Review of Economic Studies Symposium, 1974, 139–152.

Yushkevich, A.A.: Reduction of a Controlled Markov Problem with Incomplete Data to a Problem with Complete Information in Case of Borel State and Control Spaces. Theory of Probability **22**, 1976, 153–158.

Economic Theory of Natural Resources. ©Physica-Verlag, Würzburg–Wien, 1982.

Rationalizing the Use of Aggregates in Natural Resource Economics[1])

Charles Blackorby and *William Schworm*

1. Introduction

In natural resource economics as in many other areas it is a frequent practice to treat entire industries or even economies as if they were a single firm extracting from a single resource. It is further assumed that there is an aggregate technology set and that the optimization of the present value of net receipts of a firm subject to the technology set characterizes the optimal movement over time of the aggregate extraction rate and the resource stock.

The uses to which such aggregative models have been put are many. In the seminal *Hotelling* paper [1931], *Levhari/Liviatan* [1977], and in *Dasgupta/Heal* [1979], a model of a single extracting firm is used to analyze price and output paths over time and the effects of taxation on these paths. In *Dasgupta/Heal* [1974], single firm optimizing models are used to characterize general equilibrium growth paths for capital goods and the resource stock. In addition to these theoretical uses of aggregative resource models, there has also been the frequent use of such models for estimation, numerical calculations, and policy prescriptions.

The reasons for being concerned about aggregation assumptions in natural resource problems are quite obvious. Various deposits of a single type of resource can differ in the location of the deposit, the owner of the capital equipment associated with the deposit, or the quality of the deposit. Also, there are many different types of exhaustible resources that a researcher might want to treat as a single resource stock. The properties of optimal extraction paths from a set of heterogeneous resource deposits may be quite different from the properties of the optimal extraction path from a single homogeneous resource. Therefore, the implications of aggregate models may be misleading.

Several aggregation problems have been posed and solved in static production theory. One of the most important results is that if all factors or production are freely variable and purchased in competitive markets, then there exists an aggregate technology for any set of technologies for the firms in the industry, *Bliss* [1975]. *Gorman* [1968] has derived the restrictions on the firm technologies that are necessary and sufficient for the existen-

---

[1]) In preparing this we have benefited from our conversations with Bob Allen, Erwin Diewert, Pierre Lasserre, Tracy Lewis and Phil Neher.

ce of an aggregate technology and an aggregate capital stock when capital is a fixed factor that is used with freely variable factors. *Nataf* [1948] solved the problem posed by *Klein* [1946] of finding the technologies that are consistent with aggregating inputs, outputs, and technology sets when there is no presumption of a competitive allocation of the inputs among the firms.

The known solutions to these static aggregation problems, however, can not be applied to aggregation issues in natural resource economics. The optimal exploitation of a nonrenewable resource is necessarily a dynamic optimization problem and the static results are not valid in a dynamic context. In a previous paper, we have derived necessary and sufficient conditions for the existence of an aggregate investment function when each firm in an industry or economy has adjustment costs associated with the rate of investment. The techniques developed in that paper for solving an aggregation problem in an intertemporal optimization model appear to be the appropriate techniques for investigating aggregation issues in natural resource problems.

In this paper, we present the solutions to several different aggregation problems hat arise in nonrenewable resource models. In the first problem analyzed in section 2, we assume there is a set of firms in an industry or economy and that each firm is extracting from a deposit of a natural resource. The resource deposits of different firms can be in different locations, of different grades, or even different types of resources. In addition, we assume that capital is used in the resource extraction process and that investment can alter the capital stock over time. The firms have adjustment costs associated with investment. The joint determination of optimal extraction and investment paths has been investigated by *Puu* [1977], *Burt/Cummings* [1970], and *Clark/Clarke/Munro* [1979].

The aggregation problem is to find conditions under which the aggregate extraction and investment behavior of the firms can be represented as the solution to a single, intertemporal optimization problem. The aggregate problem is represented by a technology set that has as elements, the aggregate net output vector, an aggregate capital stock and investment rate, and an aggregate resource stock and extraction rate. The aggregate wealth is the present value of net revenues when the time paths of aggregate investment and aggregate extraction are chosen optimally. The consistency requirement we impose, analogous to the usual static one, is that the wealth achieved in the aggregate problem is equal to the sum of the wealth of each firm for any admissible price paths and initial sizes of the resource and capital stocks. The solution to this problem is given in Theorem 2.1.

In section 3, we investigate aggregation issues in a quite different model. We assume there are a number of different firms extracting from a single resource deposit. Necessary and sufficient conditions are found under which there is an aggregate technology and an aggregate extraction rate that replicates the depletion of the common pool by all the firms. It is assumed that each firm engages in Cournot-Nash behaviour in choosing its optimal extraction path. The consistency requirement imposed on the aggregate problem is that the aggregate problem mirror the micro problems only for equilibrium-configurations of extraction paths by all the firms. We obtain the surprising result that aggregation places no restrictions on the technologies of the firms extracting from the common pool.

In the conclusion, we comment on some lessons to be learned from the results in this paper by examining the original Hotelling model.

2. Aggregation with Firms Extracting from Separate Resource Deposits

The industry or economy which is to be represented by an aggregate model is assumed to consist of F firms which have a capital stock, K^f, and a resource stock, S^f, for $f = 1, \ldots, F$. The resource stocks can be different deposits of a single, homogeneous resource, different grades of the same resource, or even different resources.

Each firm has a technology set, T^f, which contains the feasible production vectors $(X^f, K^f, i^f, S^f, q^f)$ where X^f is a vector of variable net outputs, i^f is the investment rate, and q^f is the extraction rate for firm f. We assume that the technology of each firm is independent of the production vector of the other firms. All variables are treated as functions of time.

A net revenue function for firm f is defined by

$$a^f(t) = A^f(P, K^f, i^f, S^f, q^f) = \max_{X^f} \ \{P \cdot (X^f, q^f, -i^f) \mid (X^f, K^f, i^f, S^f, q^f) \in T^f\}$$
$$\text{(2.1)}$$

where P is a vector of present-value prices of $(X^f, q^f, -i^f)$. Under suitable regularity conditions, A^f is an equivalent representation of the technology set, T^f [see *Gorman* or *Diewert*, 1974]. We assume the net revenue functions satisfy the following conditions:

A^f for $f = 1, \ldots, F$, is a) twice continuously differentiable,
nondecreasing, convex, and linearly homogeneous in $P \geqslant 0$;
b) twice continuously differentiable, increasing, and
concave in $(K^f, -i^f, S^f, q^f)$ for all points at which
$A^f(P, K^f, i^f, S^f, q^f) > 0$. $\qquad$ (2.2)

The firm chooses an investment path, denoted $\{i^f\}$, and an extraction path, denoted $\{q^f\}$, that maximizes the present value of the net revenues of the firm given the initial state, (K^f, S^f), and subject to the dynamic relations between (i^f, q^f) and the motion of the stocks (K^f, S^f). The wealth function W^f for $f = 1, \ldots, F$ is defined by

$$W^f(\{P\}, K^f, S^f) = \max_{\{i^f, q^f\}} \int_0^\infty a^f(t)\, dt \qquad \text{(2.3a)}$$

subject to

$$\dot{K}^f = i^f, \qquad \text{(2.3b)}$$

and

$$-\dot{S}^f = q^f, \qquad \text{(2.3c)}$$

$$K^f \geqslant 0, q^f \geqslant 0, S^f \geqslant 0 \qquad \text{(2.3d)}$$

where $\{P\}$ is the time path of the vector of prices.

We restrict the analysis to a set of admissible price paths P with the following properties:

If $\{P\} \in P$, then a) $\{P\}$ is a continuous function of time;
b) $W^f(\{P\}, K^f, S^f)$ is finite for all $(K^f, S^f) \geqslant 0$; and

c) $\displaystyle \lim_{t \to \infty} \frac{\partial}{\partial K^f} W^f(\{P\}, K^f, S^f) = \lim_{t \to \infty} \frac{\partial}{\partial S^f} W^f(\{P\}, K^f, S^f) = 0$
for all $(K^f, S^f) \geqslant 0$. $\qquad$ (2.4)

If the net revenue functions satisfy (2.2), then the wealth functions as defined in (2.3) satisfy the following properties:

W^f for $f = 1, \ldots, F$ is a) continuously differentiable, nondecreasing, convex, and linearly homogeneous in $\{P\} \in P$;

b) continuously differentiable, increasing, and concave in (K^f, S^f) for all $\{P\} \in P$, $(K^f, S^f) \geqslant 0$ for which $W^f (\{P\}, K^f, S^f) > 0$. (2.5)

An aggregate model is characterized by a technology set T specifying feasible production vectors (X, k, i, s, q) where X is a vector of variable net outputs, i is the aggregate investment rate, q is the aggregate extraction rate, and k and s are the aggregate capital and resource stocks, respectively. The aggregate capital stock, k, and the aggregate resource stock, s, are scalars that depend on the vector of firm capital stocks and resource stocks, respectively:

$$k = K (K^1, \ldots, K^F) = \Sigma \alpha^f K^f, \tag{2.6a}$$

$$s = S (S^1, \ldots, S^F) = \Sigma \beta^f S^f. \tag{2.6b}$$

The aggregate technology is represented by an aggregate net revenue function, A, defined by

$$a (t) = A (P, k, i, s, q) = \max_X \ \{P \cdot (X, q, -i) \mid (X, k, i, s, q) \in T\}. \tag{2.7}$$

The aggregate net revenue function is required to satisfy conditions (2.2).

In the aggregate problem, the aggregate investment path, $\{i\}$, and the aggregate extraction path, $\{q\}$, are chosen to maximize the present value of the aggregate net revenue given the initial stocks, (k, s), and subject to the dynamic relations between (i, q) and (k, s). The aggregate wealth function, W, is defined by

$$W (\{P\}, k, s) = \max_{\{i,q\}} \int_0^\infty a (t) \, dt \tag{2.8a}$$

subject to

$$\dot{k} = i, \tag{2.8b}$$

$$-\dot{s} = q, \tag{2.8c}$$

and

$$k \geqslant 0, q \geqslant 0, s \geqslant 0. \tag{2.8d}$$

The consistency requirement we impose between the firm optimization problems and the aggregate problem is that

$$W = \sum_{f=1}^{F} W^f. \tag{2.9}$$

That is, we require that the wealth achieved in the aggregate problem by the optimal control of the single investment rate and the single extraction rate is equal to the wealth achieved in the sum of the firm problems by optimal control of the F investment rates and the F extraction rates. This equality is required to hold for all initial values of the capital stock vector, $(K^1, \ldots, K^F)$, and the resource stock vector, $(S^1, \ldots, S^F)$, and all admissible price paths, $\{P\} \in P$.

The aggregation problem is to find conditions on the firms' technologies that are necessary and sufficient for the existence of an aggregate net revenue function, A, an aggregate capital stock function, K, and an aggregate resource stock function, S, for which (2.9) is satisfied. The first theorem characterizes the technologies that are consistent with aggregation in terms of the Hamiltonian functions. The Hamiltonian functions for the firms are defined by

$$h^f(t) = H^f(P, K^f, S^f, \lambda^f, \gamma^f) =$$

$$= \max_{i^f, q^f} \{A^f(P, K^f, i^f, S^f, q^f) + \lambda^f i^f - \gamma^f q^f\} \tag{2.10}$$

for $f = 1, \ldots, F$. The aggregate Hamiltonian function is defined by

$$h(t) = H(P, k, s, \lambda, \gamma) = \max_{i, q} \{A(P, k, i, s, q) + \lambda i - \gamma q\}. \tag{2.11}$$

The following theorem is proved in the appendix.

Theorem 1. There exists an aggregate net revenue function, A, defined by (2.7), an aggregate capital stock function K and an aggregate resource stock function S, defined by (2.6), and an aggregate wealth function, defined by (2.8), such that $W = \sum\limits_{f=1}^{F} W^f$ if and only if the aggregate Hamiltonian is given by

$$h(t) = H^k(P, \lambda, \gamma) k + H^s(P, \lambda, \gamma) s + \overset{\circ}{H}(P, \lambda, \gamma) \tag{2.12}$$

and the firm Hamiltonians are given by

$$h^f(t) = H^k\left(P, \frac{\lambda^f}{\alpha^f}, \frac{\gamma^f}{\beta^f}\right) \alpha^f K^f + H^s\left(P, \frac{\lambda^f}{\alpha^f}, \frac{\gamma^f}{\beta^f}\right) \beta^f S^f + \overset{\circ}{H}^f\left(P, \frac{\lambda^f}{\alpha^f}, \frac{\gamma^f}{\beta^f}\right) \tag{2.13}$$

where

$$\lambda^f = \alpha^f \lambda \tag{2.14a}$$

and

$$\gamma^f = \beta^f \gamma \tag{2.14b}$$

for $f = 1, \ldots, F$ and where

$$k = \sum_{f=1}^{F} \alpha^f K^f \tag{2.15a}$$

$$s = \sum_{f=1}^{F} \beta^f S^f \tag{2.15b}$$

and

$$\overset{\circ}{H} = \sum_{f=1}^{F} \overset{\circ}{H}^f. \tag{2.15c}$$

It is necessary and sufficient for consistent aggregation that the aggregate Hamiltonian function be affine in the aggregate capital and resource stocks and that the aggregate capital and resource stocks are weighted sums of the firms' capital and resource stocks,

respectively. The aggregate Hamiltonian has this structure if and only if each firms'
Hamiltonian is affine in (K^f, S^f) and the derivatives of the Hamiltonian with respect to
$K^f, \alpha^f H^k$, and with respect to $S^f, \beta^f H^s$, are common to all firms except for a multiplicative constant.

An important aspect of the technologies that are consistent with aggregation is
revealed by the shadow present values of the capital stocks and the resource stocks; in
both the aggregate model and the firm models, the shadow values of capital and the
shadow values of the resources are independent of the capital stocks and the resource
stocks. In addition the shadow values of capital and the resource stocks are the same for
all firms except for a multiplicative constant.

The intertemporal behaviour of economies that are consistent with aggregation is
immediate from Theorem 1. By using the relations

$$\frac{\partial h(t)}{\partial \lambda} = \overset{*}{i} \quad \text{and} \quad \frac{\partial h(t)}{\partial \gamma} = \overset{*}{q} \tag{2.16}$$

one finds that the aggregate investment and extraction functions must be affine in the
capital and resource stocks. In addition, the effect on firm investment or extraction of an
increase in an efficiency unit of capital, $\alpha^f K^f$, or in an efficiency unit of a resource,
$\beta^f S^f$, is the same for all firms. Finally, it is easy to show that aggregate investment and
extraction are weighted sums of the firms' investment and extraction rates, respectively:

$$\overset{*}{i} = \sum_{f=1}^{F} \alpha^f \overset{*}{i}^f, \tag{2.17a}$$

and

$$\overset{*}{q} = \sum_{f=1}^{F} \beta^f \overset{*}{q}^f. \tag{2.17b}$$

For some problems, it may be more convenient to have a characterization of the net
revenue functions that are consistent with aggregation. The following theorem, which is
proved in the appendix, provides conditions on the net revenue functions which are
equivalent to the conditions on Hamiltonian functions given in Theorem 1.

Theorem 2. The conditions of Theorem 1 hold if and only if the aggregate net revenue
function can be written as

$$A(P, k, i, s, q) = \max_{\begin{Bmatrix} i^k, i^s, i^0 \\ q^k, q^s, q^0 \end{Bmatrix}} \{A^k(P, k, i^k, q^k) + A^s(P, s, i^s, q^s)$$

$$+ A^0(P, i^0, q^0)/i^k + i^s + i^0 = i \text{ and } q^k + q^s + q^0 = q\} \tag{2.18}$$

and for $f = 1, \ldots, F$

$$A^f(P, K^f, i^f, S^f, q^f) = \max_{\substack{i^{fk}, i^{fs}, i^{f0} \\ q^{fk}, q^{fs}, q^{f0}}} \{\alpha^f A^k(P, K^f, i^{fk}, q^{fk}) +$$

$$+ \beta^f A^s(P, S^f, i^{fs}, q^{fs})$$

$$+ A^{0f}(P, i^{f0}, q^{f0})/i^{fk} + i^{fs} + i^{f0} = i \text{ and}$$

$$q^{fk} + q^{fs} + q^{f0} = q\} \tag{2.19}$$

where A^k is linearly homogeneous in (k, i^k, q^k) and A^s is linearly homogeneous in (s, i^s, q^s).

To satisfy the conditions for aggregation, the aggregate net revenue function and the firms' net revenue functions must be expressable as the net revenue one obtains by allocating investment and extraction to three independent net revenue functions, two of which are linearly homogeneous. One interpretation of this is that each firm has three planty, a capital-using plant, a resource-using plant and one which depends only on variable inputs and is firm specific. The firm then allocates any given amount of investment and extraction optimally across the three plants. Note that the capital and resource using plants are the same for all firms except for a multiplicative constant. These structures however are still quite general and allow for considerable interaction between the stocks. This is perhaps most easily seen by considering the special cases in which the firms' technologies and the economy's technology break down into nonjoint capital and resource sectors.

Case i: Suppose H^k is independent of γ, H^s is independent λ, and $\mathring{H}^f$ is zero. Then, for $f = 1, \ldots, F$

$$a^f(t) = \alpha^f \bar{A}^k(P, K^f, i^f) + \beta^f \bar{A}^s(P, S^f, q^f) \tag{2.20}$$

in which case

$$a(t) = \bar{A}^k(P, k, i) + \bar{A}^s(P, s, q) \tag{2.21}$$

where $\bar{A}^k$ and $\bar{A}^s$ are linearly homogeneous in their last two arguments.

Case ii: Suppose H^k is independent of λ and γ, H^s is independent of λ and $\mathring{H}^f$ is independent γ. Then, for $f = 1, \ldots, F$

$$a^f(t) = \mathring{A}^k(P) \alpha^f K^f + \tilde{A}^{fk}(P, i^f) + \beta^f \bar{A}^s(P, S^f, q^f) \tag{2.22}$$

in which case

$$a(t) = \mathring{A}^k(P) k + \tilde{A}^k(P, i) + \bar{A}^s(P, s, q) \tag{2.23}$$

where $\bar{A}^s$ is linearly homogeneous in the last two arguments.

Case iii: Suppose H^k is independent of γ, H^s is independent of λ and γ and $\mathring{H}^f$ is independent of λ. Then, for $f = 1, \ldots, F$

$$a^f(t) = \alpha^f \bar{A}^k(P, K^f, i^f) + \mathring{A}^s(P) \beta^f S^f + \tilde{A}^{fs}(P, q^f) \tag{2.24}$$

in which case

$$a(t) = \bar{A}^k(P, k, i) + \mathring{A}^s(P)s + \tilde{A}^s(P, q); \tag{2.25}$$

where $\bar{A}^k$ is linearly homogeneous in its last two arguments.

In all other cases, the capital-using plant and the resource-using plant are joint. The investment path and the extraction path are interrelated. Optimal investment and optimal extraction depend on both the capital stock and the resource stock and on the shadow values of both the capital and resource stock.

For a particular functional from of a net revenue function, it may be difficult to determine if it can be written as in (2.18). If a research wants to ascertain if a particular net revenue function is consistent with aggregation, it would be convenient to have a characterization that is more easily checked. The following theorem provides such a characterization. Let $|M|$ denote the determinant of the matrix M.

Theorem 3. The conditions of Theorem 1 are satisfied if and only if

$$|\nabla^2 A(P, k, i, s, q)| = 0 \tag{2.26}$$

and only if for $f = 1, \ldots, F$

$$|\nabla^2 A^f(P, K^f, i^f, S^f, q^f)| = 0 \tag{2.27}$$

where $\nabla^2 A$ and $\nabla^2 A^f$ are the Hessian matrices with respect to the last four arguments of A and A^f.

In the case where one is only interested in a problem with a single resource and no capital then these results can easily be specialized to solve that problem. For example a representation of an aggregate technology which is consistent with the aggregation of a single resource is

$$h(t) = \bar{H}^s(P, \gamma)s + \mathring{H}(P, \gamma) \tag{2.28}$$

where

$$s = \sum_f \beta_f^f S^f,$$

$$a(t) = A(P, s, q) = \max_{\{q^s, q^0\}} \{A^s(P, s, q^s) + \mathring{A}(P, q^0) \mid q^s + q^0 = q\} \tag{2.29}$$

and

$$|\nabla_{sq}^2 A(P, s, q)| = 0. \tag{2.30}$$

An application of this single stock case is pursued in the concluding remarks.

3. Aggregation with Firms Extracting from a Single Resource Deposit

In section 2, we have assumed that each firm extracts from its own resource deposit and that the extraction technologies of different firms are independent. In this section, we investigate the existence of an aggregate model when many firms are extracting from a single resource deposit. In this case, the extraction technologies of the firms are necessarily interdependent. We also alter the model of section 2 by treating capital as a freely variable input.

The net revenue function for firm f is denoted by

$$a^f(t) = A^f(P, S, q^f) \tag{3.1}$$

where S is the single resource stock. Although we continue to treat prices as parametric, it is no longer possible to ignore the interactions of firms. We assume that the firms engage in intertemporal Cournot-Nash behaviour yielding a unique intertemporal Cournot-Nash equilibrium. [For a discussion of this assumption, see *Lewis/Schmalensee*].

The wealth function of each firm f is defined by

$$W^f(\{P\}, S, \{\bar{q}^f\}) = \max_{\{q^f\}} \int_{0}^{\infty} a^f(t)\, dt \tag{3.2a}$$

subject to

$$\dot{S} = -\sum_{g=1}^{F} q^g \tag{3.2b}$$

and

$$q^f \geqslant 0, S \geqslant 0 \tag{3.2c}$$

where $\{\bar{q}^f\} = (q^1, \ldots, q^{f-1}, q^{f+1}, \ldots, q^F)$ is the time path of the vector of extraction rates of all firms $g \neq f$. Treating the extraction paths of all firms other than firm f as given, we obtain the following optimal extraction functions:

$$\hat{q}^f(t) = \hat{Q}^f(\{P\}, S, \{\bar{q}^f\}) \tag{3.3}$$

for $f = 1, \ldots, F$. The structure of this problem is different than the problem in section 2 since in this problem the optimal extraction path of one firm depends on the extraction paths of the other firms.

The aggregate optimization problem is characterized by a wealth function W defined by

$$W(\{P\}, S) = \max_{\{q\}} \int_{0}^{\infty} A(P, q, S)\, dt \tag{3.4a}$$

subject to

$$\dot{S} = -q \tag{3.4b}$$

and

$$q \geqslant 0, S \geqslant 0. \tag{3.4c}$$

The optimal extraction function in the aggregate problem is denoted by

$$\overset{*}{q} = Q(\{P\}, S). \tag{3.5}$$

The aggregation problem is to find conditions on the firm net revenue functions that are necessary and sufficient for there to exist an aggregate net revenue function A with image $A(P, q, S)$ where S is the resource stock and q is an aggregate extraction rate and and an aggregate wealth function W defined by (3.4) such that $W = \sum_{f=1}^{F} W^f$ for some admissible set of extraction paths.

We do not require, however, that $W = \sum_{f=1}^{F} W^f$ for arbitrary extraction paths for the firms. Rather, we ask that the aggregate problem produce the same wealth as the sum of the firm problems only for equilibrium configurations of extraction paths. We define an equilibrium extraction rate for firm f, $\overset{*}{q}^f$, as the extraction rate for a given stock and price path when all firms are in a Cournot-Nash equilibrium. The equilibrium extraction function for firm f, Q^f, is defined by

$$\overset{*}{q}^f = Q^f (\{P\}, S) = \hat{Q}^f (\{P\}, S, \{\overset{*}{q}^f\}) \tag{3.6}$$

for $f = 1, \ldots, F$.

Define the equilibrium wealth function for firm f, $\overset{*}{W}^f$, by

$$\overset{*}{W}^f (\{P\}, S) = W^f (\{P\}, S, \{\overset{*}{q}^f\}) \tag{3.7}$$

for $f = 1, \ldots, F$. The consistency requirement imposed on the aggregate model is that

$$W = \sum_{f=1}^{F} \overset{*}{W}^f. \tag{3.8}$$

An important characteristic of the equilibrium extraction and the equilibrium wealth of each firm is that they depend only on future price paths and the common pool. There are no firm specific variables influencing the equilibrium extraction or wealth. This fact enables us to specify a consistent aggregate problem for any set of firm technologies.

Since W has the same arguments as $\overset{*}{W}^f$ for $f = 1, \ldots, F$, one can define W by

$$W (\{P\}, S) = \sum_{f=1}^{F} \overset{*}{W}^f (\{P\}, S). \tag{3.9}$$

Similarly define the aggregate extraction function, Q, by

$$Q (\{P\}, S) = \sum_{f=1}^{F} Q^f (\{P\}, S). \tag{3.10}$$

Then, the equation

$$A (P, S, Q (\{P\}, S)) = \sum_{f=1}^{F} A^f (P, S, Q^f (\{P\}, S)) \tag{3.11}$$

determines the aggregate net revenue function, A, for all points (P, S, q) that would ever be observed. The function, A, can be defined arbitrarily at all other points except that regularity conditions should be preserved.

Therefore, without restricting the firm technologies at all, we have found an aggregate technology that can replicate the aggregate extraction of all firms from the common resource. This is a consequence of the fact that the extraction rates of all firms are determined by a common set of variables. Of course, the aggregate problem can not mirror extraction paths of the firms the are not equilibrium paths.

4. Conclusions

The lesson to be learning from the results of this paper is that assuming an aggregative model of resource extraction without checking the implied restrictions on the firm technologies is a dangerous procedure that should be avoided. One difficulty with using an aggregate model is that it may not be able to replicate the actual behaviour of industries or economies extracting from heterogeneous deposits with heterogeneous technologies. A second and equally serious difficulty is that if the restriction implied by aggregation assumptions are not checked, then models can be constructed that are internally inconsistent. Some models that assume the existence of aggregates are not consistent with any technologies for the firms. We conclude with an example.

Consider a model in which net revenues depend only on the extraction rate and do not depend on the resource stock. This model was initially used by *Hotelling* [1931] and has been used frequently in the modern literature on nonrenewable resources [see *Dasgupta/ Heal*, 1979, Chapter 6, for examples and references]. We can easily show that there are no firm technologies that are consistent with the existence of an aggregate net revenue function that depends only on the aggregate extraction rate.

Define the wealth function of firm f by

$$W^f (\{P\}, S^f) = \max_{\{q^f\}} \int_0^\infty A^f (P, q^f) \, dt \tag{4.1a}$$

subject to

$$- \dot{S}^f = q^f \tag{4.1b}$$

and

$$q^f \geqslant 0, S^f \geqslant 0. \tag{4.1c}$$

Define the aggregate wealth function by

$$W (\{P\}, s) = \max_{\{q\}} \int_0^\infty A (P, q) \, dt \tag{4.2a}$$

subject to

$$- \dot{s} = q \tag{4.2b}$$

and

$$q \geqslant 0, s \geqslant 0. \tag{4.2c}$$

where q is the aggregate extraction rate, A is the aggregate net revenue function, and

$$s = S (S^1, \ldots, S^F) \tag{4.3}$$

is the aggregate resource stock.

The aggregation problem is to find conditions on A^f for $f = 1, \ldots, F$ that insure the existence of aggregates, q, s, and A, such that

$$W = \sum_{f=1}^F W^f. \tag{4.4}$$

Using an argument identical to that in the proof of Theorem 1, it can be shown that a necessary condition for aggregation is that the shadow value of the resource is independent of the resource stock. Hence,

$$\overset{*}{\gamma} = \Gamma\left(\{P\}\right) \tag{4.5}$$

is the multiplier associated with the constraint (4.2b).

Necessary conditions for an optimal extraction path in the aggregate problem are

$$\frac{\partial A\left(P, q\right)}{\partial q} - \lambda = 0 \tag{4.6a}$$

and

$$\dot{\gamma} = 0. \tag{4.6b}$$

It is not possible, however, for (4.6b) to be satisfied for arbitrary price paths if $\overset{*}{\gamma}$ is independent of S. Therefore, there cannot be an aggregate technology, extraction rate, and resource stock in this problem for any technologies of the firms.

This result demonstrates that aggregative models of the extraction of a nonrenewable resource in which the net revenue function is independent of the resource stock are internally inconsistent. There are no firm technologies that can be consistently represented by such an aggregate model. Therefore, all results derived from such models must be considered unproven for industries or economies with different firms extracting from different resource deposits.

Appendix

In the proofs we use the following well-known relationships between wealth functions, Hamiltonian functions, multipliers, and net revenue functions:

$$\frac{\partial W\left(\{P\}, K, S\right)}{\partial t} = -H\left(P, K, S \frac{\partial W\left(\{P\}, K, S\right)}{\partial K}, \frac{\partial W\left(\{P\}, K, S\right)}{\partial S}\right), \tag{A.1}$$

$$\frac{\partial W\left(\{P\}, K, S\right)}{\partial K} = \Lambda\left(\{P\}, K, S\right) = \overset{*}{\lambda}, \tag{A.2}$$

$$\frac{\partial W\left(\{P\}, K, S\right)}{\partial S} = \Gamma\left(\{P\}, K, S\right) = \overset{*}{\gamma}, \tag{A.3}$$

$$-\dot{\lambda} = \frac{\partial H\left(P, K, S, \lambda, \gamma\right)}{\partial K}, \tag{A.4}$$

$$-\dot{\gamma} = \frac{\partial H\left(P, K, S, \lambda, \gamma\right)}{\partial S}, \tag{A.5}$$

and

$$h\left(t\right) = H\left(P, K, S, \lambda, \gamma\right) = \max_{i, q} \left\{A\left(P, i, K, q, S\right) \lambda i - \gamma q\right\} \tag{A.6}$$

where $\left[\partial W\left(\{P\}, K, S\right)\right]/\partial t$ is the partial derivative of wealth with respect to t as it affects $\{P\}$ for given (K, S).

The consistency requirement for aggregation is that

$$W(\{P\}, K(\langle K^f \rangle), S(\langle S^f \rangle)) = \sum_{f=1}^{F} W^f(\{P\}, K^f, S^f) \tag{A.7}$$

for all admissible $(\{P\}, \langle K^f \rangle, \langle S^f \rangle)$ where

$$\langle K^f \rangle = (K^1, \ldots, K^F) \text{ and } \langle S^f \rangle = (S^1, \ldots, S^F).$$

Proof of Theorem 1: Differentiating (A.7) with respect to K^f and S^f for $f = 1, \ldots, F$ and using (A.2) and (A.3) yields the following necessary conditions for consistent aggregation:

$$\bar{\Lambda}^f(\{P\}) = \alpha^f \Lambda(\{P\}), \tag{A.8a}$$

and

$$\bar{\Gamma}^f(\{P\}) = \beta^f \Gamma(\{P\}). \tag{A.8b}$$

Since λ^f and γ^f are independent of (K^f, S^f) for $f = 1, \ldots, F$, (A.4) and (A.5) imply

$$\frac{\partial^2 h^f(t)}{\partial K^{f^2}} = \frac{\partial^2 h^f(t)}{\partial S^{f^2}} = \frac{\partial^2 h^f(t)}{\partial S^f \partial K^f} = 0 \tag{A.9}$$

which imply

$$h^f(t) = \bar{H}^f(P, \lambda^f, \gamma^f) K^f + \tilde{H}^f(P, \lambda^f, \gamma^f) S^f + \hat{H}^f(P, \lambda^f, \gamma^f) \tag{A.10}$$

for $f = 1, \ldots, F$. An identical argument shows that

$$h(t) = \bar{H}(P, \lambda, \gamma) \{ \sum_{f=1}^{F} \alpha^f K^f \} + \tilde{H}(P, \lambda, \gamma) \{ \sum_{f=1}^{F} \beta^f S^f \} + \hat{H}(P, \lambda, \gamma). \tag{A.11}$$

Differentiating (A.7) with respect to time and using (A.1) yields

$$H(P, k, s, \overset{*}{\lambda}, \overset{*}{\gamma}) = \sum_{f=1}^{F} H^f(P, K^f, S^f, \overset{*}{\lambda}^f, \overset{*}{\gamma}^f). \tag{A.12}$$

Using (A.15) yields

$$\bar{H}(P, \lambda, \gamma) \{ \sum_{f=1}^{F} \alpha^f K^f \} + \tilde{H}(P, \lambda, \gamma) \{ \sum_{f=1}^{F} \beta^f S^f \} + \hat{H}(P, \lambda, \gamma) =$$

$$\sum_{f=1}^{F} \{ \bar{H}^f(P, \alpha^f \lambda, \beta^f \gamma) K^f + \tilde{H}^f(P, \alpha^f \lambda, \beta^f \gamma) S^f + \hat{H}^f(P, \alpha^f \lambda, \beta^f \gamma). \tag{A.13}$$

This implies that

$$\bar{H}^f(P, \alpha^f \lambda, \beta^f \gamma) = \alpha^f \bar{H}(P, \lambda, \gamma), \tag{A.14a}$$

$$\tilde{H}^f(P, \alpha^f \lambda, \beta^f \gamma) = \beta^f \tilde{H}(p, \lambda, \gamma), \tag{A.14b}$$

and

$$\sum_{f=1}^{F} \hat{H}^f(P, \alpha^f \lambda, \beta^f \gamma) = \hat{H}(P, \lambda, \gamma). \tag{A.14c}$$

This proves that (2.12) and (2.13) are necessary for consistent aggregation. Sufficiency is shown by direct calculations using (A.1), (A.2), and (A.3) with (A.8), (A.13), and (A.14).

Proof of Theorem 2: Define net revenue functions, A^k, A^s, and A^0 by

$$A^k (P, k, i^k, q^k) = \min_{\lambda, \gamma} \{H^k (P, \lambda, \gamma) k - \lambda i^k + \lambda q^k\}$$

$$A^s (P, s, i^s, q^s) = \min_{\lambda, \gamma} \{H^s (P, \lambda, \gamma) s - \lambda i^s + \lambda q^s\}$$

$$A^0 (P, i^s, q^s) = \min_{\lambda, \gamma} \{H^0 (P, \lambda, \gamma) - \lambda i^0 + \lambda q^0\}.$$

Theorem 2.23 in *Diewert* [1973] shows that A^k is linearly homogeneous in (k, i^k, q^k) and that A^s is linearly homogeneous in (s, i^s, q^s). The duality between the Hamiltonian H and the net revenue function A implies that

$$A (P, i, k, q, s) = \min_{\lambda, \gamma} \{H^k (P, \lambda, \gamma) k + H^s (P, \lambda, \gamma) s + H^0 (P, \lambda, \gamma) - \lambda i + \gamma q\}.$$

By introducing new variables $(i^k, i^s, i^0, q^k, q^s, q^0)$, we have

$$A (P, i, k, q, s) = \min_{\lambda, \gamma} \{ \max_{\substack{i^k, i^s, i^0 \\ q^k, q^s, q^0}} [H^k (P, \lambda, \gamma) k - \lambda i^k + \gamma q^k$$

$$+ H^s (P, \lambda, \gamma) s - \lambda i^s + \gamma q^s + H^0 (P, \lambda, \gamma) - \lambda i^0 + \gamma q^0]/i^k + i^s + i^0 = i,$$

and $q^k + q^s + q^0 = q\}$

or, reversing the order of optimization,

$$A (P, i, k, q, s) = \max_{\substack{i^k, i^s, i^0 \\ q^k, q^s, q^0}} \{\min_{\lambda, \gamma} [H^k (P, \lambda, \gamma) k - \lambda i^k + \gamma q^k]$$

$$+ \min_{\lambda, \gamma} [H^s (P, \lambda, \gamma) s - \lambda i^s + \gamma q^s] + \min_{\lambda, \gamma} [H^0 (P, \lambda, \gamma) - \lambda i^0 + \gamma q^0]/$$

$$i^k + i^s + i^0 = i \text{ and } q^k + q^s + q^0 = q\}.$$

Then, using the definitions of A^k, A^s, and A^0, we have

$$A (P, i, k, q, s) = \max_{\substack{i^k, i^s, i^0 \\ q^k, q^s, q^0}} \{A^k (P, k, i^k, q^k) + A^s (P, s, i^s, q^s) + A^0 (P, i^s, q^s)/$$

$$i^k + i^s + i^0 = i \text{ and } q^k + q^s + q^0 = q\}.$$

An analogous argument proves that

$$A^f (P, i^f, K^f, q^f, S^f) = \max_{\substack{i^k, i^s, i^0 \\ q^k, q^s, q^0}} \{\alpha^f A^k (P, K^f, i^k, q^k) + \beta^f A^s (P, S^f, i^s, q^s)$$

$$+ A^{f0} (P, i^0, q^0)/i^k + i^s + i^0 = i^f \text{ and } q^k + q^s + q^0 + q^f\}.$$

Proof of Theorem 3: It is sufficient to prove (2.26). Using the definition (2.10) and the first-order conditions yields the following equations which hold in the neighbourhood of the optimum:

$$\overset{*}{A}_i = \lambda, \, i = -H_\lambda, \, \overset{*}{A}_k = H_k,$$
$$\overset{*}{A}_q = \gamma, \, \overset{*}{q} = -H_\gamma, \, \overset{*}{A}_s = H_s,$$

where the * means the optimal solution has been substituted into the objective function. Totally differentiating these with respect to (λ, γ, k, s) allows us to write the Hessian of A in terms of the Hessian of H. Using the fact that

$$\begin{bmatrix} H_{kk} & H_{ks} \\ H_{sk} & H_{ss} \end{bmatrix} = \begin{bmatrix} 0 & 0 \\ 0 & 0 \end{bmatrix}$$

yields

$$\nabla^2 \overset{*}{A} = \begin{bmatrix} B & BC \\ C^T B & C^T BC \end{bmatrix}$$

where

$$B = \begin{bmatrix} H_{ii} & H_{iq} \\ H_{qi} & H_{qq} \end{bmatrix}^{-1},$$

and

$$C = \begin{bmatrix} H_{ik} & H_{is} \\ H_{qk} & H_{qs} \end{bmatrix}.$$

Multiplying the top block of rows in $\nabla^2 \overset{*}{A}$ by C^T and subtracting from the bottom block of rows produces a matrix with rows containing only zeroes. Hence, $\nabla^2 \overset{*}{A}$ is singular. ‖

References

Blackorby, C., and W. Schworm: Intertemporal Technologies and the Existence of an Aggregate Investment Function. Discussion Paper 80–18, Department of Economics, University of British Columbia, 1980.

Bliss, C.: Capital Theory and the Distribution of Income. Amsterdam–New York 1975.

Burt, O., and R. Cummings: Production and Investment in Natural Resource Industries. American Economic Review 60, 1970, 576–590.

Clark, C., F. Clarke and G. Munro: The Optimal Exploitation of Renewable Resource Stocks: Problems of Irreversible Investment. Econometrica 47, 1979, 25–48.

Dasgupta, P., and G. Heal: The Optimal Exploitation of Exhaustible Resources. Review of Economic Studies, Symposium, 1974, 1–28.

–: Economic Theory and Exhaustible Resources, Cambridge 1979.

Diewert, W.: Functional Forms for Profit and Transformation Functions. Journal of Economic Theory 5, 1973, 284–316.

—: Applications of Duality Theory. Frontiers of Quantitative Economics, II. Ed. by M. Intrilligator and D. Kendrick. Amsterdam 1974.

Gorman, W.: Measuring the Quantities of Fixed Factors. Value Capital, and Growth. Ed. by J. Wolfe. Edinburgh 1968.

Hotelling, H.: The Economics of Exhaustible Resources. Journal of Political Economy 39, 1931, 137–175.

Klein, L.: Macroeconomics and The Theory of Rational Behavior. Econometrica 14, 1946, 93–108.

Levhari, D., and *N. Liviatan*: Notes on Hotelling's Economics of Exhaustible Resources. Canadian Journal of Economics 10, 1977, 177–192.

Lewis, T., and *R. Schmalensee*: On Oligopolistic Markets For Nonrenewable Resources. Quarterly Journal of Economics, forthcoming, 1980.

Nataf, A.: Sur La Possibilité De Contribution De Certain Macromodèles. Econometrica 16, 1948, 232–244.

Puu, T.: On the Profitability of Exhausting Natural Resources. Journal of Environmental Economics and Management 4, 1977, 185–199.

Economic Theory of Natural Resources. ©Physica-Verlag, Würzburg–Wien, 1982.

Resource Extraction under Alternative Investment and Financing Opportunities

Klaus Hellwig and *Hartmut Kogelschatz*

1. Introduction

In the theory of exhaustible resources one usually assumes a perfect capital market which implies that financial restrictions do not exist since borrowing and lending can take place at a given market rate of interest.

This assumption underlies, for example, the well-known Hotelling rule [*Hotelling*], which 'is the fundamental principle of the economics of exhaustible resources' [*Solow*, p. 3]. It was derived by Hotelling as a condition of flow equilibrium in the market for an exhaustible resource where the owner maximizes the present value of profits. This rule can also be deduced as a condition of stock equilibrium in the asset market [cf. *Solow*, p. 2; *Dasgupta/Heal*, p. 155].

In this paper the decision problem of the owner of a mine is reconsidered under alternative production, investment, and financing opportunities where constraints are taken into account. In particular, we allow for imperfections in the capital market.

Whereas the introduction of constraints usually causes no difficulties, the absence of a perfect capital market gives rise to the question which rate of return one should choose in the objective function when maximizing the present value of profits. In the case of a finite planning horizon the additional problem arises which amount of the resource should rest after the planning period.

To overcome these difficulties we renounce the objective function and introduce the requirement of preserving present value of future income discounted by the marginal rates of return. This requirement can be regarded as a criterion for the preservation of economic viability which, in particular, meets the long run interest of the oil producing countries. In the classic approach with a perfect capital market the marginal rates of return are equal to the market rate of interest and present value maximization implies the present value of marginal profits from the resource to be constant [cf. *Dasgupta/Heal*, p. 160]. However, this does not necessarily mean that economic viability is preserved.

In the following we will first formally describe the above mentioned decision problem. We then state necessary and sufficient conditions for the existence and uniqueness of a solution. As an application, we finally regard a resource-owner who has an alternative investment opportunity and ask for the timing of production over a given planning period.

2. Formulation of the Problem

If a rate of return is prespecified, the decision problem can be formulated as follows:

$$e = A x + b \qquad \text{(budget equation)}, \tag{1}$$

where $e = (0, e_1, \ldots, e_T)$ with $e_t \geqslant 0$ $(t = 1, \ldots, T)$ is a $(T + 1)$ − column vector of income[1]). A is a $(T + 1) \times n$ matrix of net cash inflow coefficients[2]), x is a n-column vector of decisions concerning production, investment and financing opportunities and b is a $(T + 1)$ column vector of autonomous net cash inflows from all other decisions.

In addition, the activity levels are constrained by

$$x \in X = \{x \in \mathbf{R}^n : 0 \leqslant x_j \leqslant k_j \quad (j = 1, \ldots, n) \sum_{j \in J} x_j \leqslant K, \quad J \subseteq \{1, \ldots, n\}\}, \tag{2}$$

where k_j may be an upper bound given by the production capacity, by demand, investment opportunities or the terms of finance. K may be interpreted as total capacity which can be distributed among a given number of activities. For example, K may be the total stock of a resource, which is an upper bound for total production over the planning period T.

The decision problem is completed by an objective function

$$\sum_{t=0}^{T} e_t q^{-t} \tag{3}$$

where $q := 1 + r$ and r is the rate of return desired by the decision maker.

The aim is to find a decision x and a corresponding income e which maximizes the net present value of future income given by (3), subject to (1) and (2).

The optimization problem (1) to (3) causes some difficulties. Thus, it may be difficult to prespecify a rate of return, in particular, when there are several decision makers. In addition, the problem arises how to ensure sufficient income for the time after the planning horizon.

One way to handle these problems consists in imposing the additional requirement, that economic viability should be preserved, where economic viability is defined as the net present value of future income discounted by the (possibly time-dependent) marginal rates of return.

This requirement, in particular, meets the long run needs of the owners of exhaustible resources, if other sources of income are negligible, a situation typical for many oil-producing countries.

If there is a perfect capital market, this requirement causes no trouble. For this case a well-known separation theorem states that production decisions can be made independent from the time preferences for consumption [cf. *Fisher*].

The net present value of future income is then given by

$$V = \sum_{t=0}^{T} e_t (1 + r)^{-t}, \tag{4}$$

---

[1]) It is assumed that positive income becomes feasible one period after the date of decision.
[2]) a_{ij} denotes the net cash inflow in period i per unit of activity j.

where r is the market rate of interest. In order to preserve economic viability in all periods consumption must be equal to the periodic increase in V which is $r \cdot V$.

If the assumption of a perfect capital market is dropped, then e must be of the form

$$e = (0, \bar{r}_1 V, \ldots, \bar{r}_{T-1} V, (1 + \bar{r}_T) V), \text{ with } V = \sum_{t=1}^{T} e_t \prod_{\tau=1}^{t} (1 + \bar{r}_\tau)^{-1} \tag{5}$$

where $\bar{r}_\tau$ is the marginal rate of return in period τ [3]).

The decision maker then is confronted with the dilemma that the marginal rates of return are not known before the optimization problem is solved.

3. Existence and Uniqueness of a Viability Preserving Solution

One way to get out of this dilemma is to ask first for necessary conditions for preserving economic viability and then try to find a solution $(\bar{e}, \bar{x})$ of (1) and (2) which satisfies these conditions.

Necessary conditions are:

i) $\bar{e}, \bar{x}$ is feasible, i.e. satisfies (1) and (2).
ii) Income is discounted with the marginal rates of return $\bar{r}_t$ $(t = 1, \ldots, T)$ or, equivalently, $\bar{r}_t$ $(t = 1, \ldots, T)$ are the correct rates of return for the evaluation of the optimal decision $\bar{x}$, i.e.

$$\max_{x \in X} \sum_{j=1}^{n} K_j X_j = \sum_{j=1}^{n} K_j \bar{x}_j,$$

where $K_j := \bar{q} a^j$ with $\bar{q} = (\bar{q}_1, \ldots, \bar{q}_T), \bar{q}_t = \prod_{\tau=1}^{t} (1 + \bar{r}_\tau)^{-1}$ is the unit present value

of activity j and a^j denotes the j-th column vector of A.
iii) Economic viability is preserved: Equation (5) holds.

A solution $(\bar{e}, \bar{x}, \bar{q})$ which satisfies i) to iii) is called a viability preserving solution. Obviously, for every viability preserving solution $(\bar{e}, \bar{x}, \bar{q})$

$$V = \sum_{j=1}^{n} K_j \bar{x}_j + \hat{q} b + b_0, \text{ where } \hat{q} := (0, \bar{q}).$$

One might argue that as a fourth condition $\bar{e}$ should be efficient. However, this is already implied by conditions i) to iii) as the following statement shows:

Proposition 1:

a) If $(\bar{e}, \bar{x}, \bar{q})$ is a viability preserving solution, then $\bar{e}$ is efficient.
b) If $\bar{e}$ is efficient, then there exists a vector $\bar{x}$ such that $(\bar{e}, \bar{x})$ satisfies i) and ii).

Part a) follows from the fact that if $(\bar{e}, \bar{x}, \bar{q})$ is a viability preserving solution then $(\bar{e}, \bar{x})$ is optimal for max $\bar{q}e$ subject to (1) and (2) since the Kuhn-Tucker conditions are met. If,

---

[3]) The last component of e results form the requirement that V must be preserved at the end of the planning period. The marginal of return $\bar{r}_\tau$ is defined as the rate of return of the marginal realized project.

on the other hand, $\bar{e}$ is efficient, then there exist vectors $\bar{x}$, $\bar{q}$, such that $(\bar{e}, \bar{x})$ is an optimal solution of max $\bar{q}e$ subject to (1) and (2) with Lagrange multipliers $\bar{q}$.

In order to find a viability preserving solution it is therefore sufficient to concentrate on the set of efficient income vectors. This set can be obtained by maximizing income in any period subject to (1) by a parametric change of income in all other periods. Such a multiparametric linear program can be solved by existing computer programs [see *Gal/ Nedoma*, p. 406f.].

For the two period case the set of efficient income vectors can be represented by a piecewise linear concave function which is called the efficient line. The slope of the linear parts of the efficient line is determined by the marginal rates of return in period two.

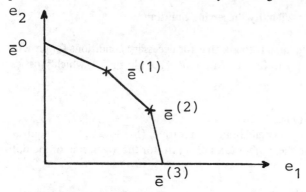

Efficient line for the two period case.

Let $\bar{e}^{(i)} = (\bar{e}_1^{(i)}, \bar{e}_2^{(i)})$, $(i = 0, \ldots, m)$, be the extreme points except for the origin of the set of feasible income vectors e and let $P(\hat{e}_1)$ be the parametric program

$$\max e_2 \text{ s.t. (1) and (2) for any fixed } e_1 = \hat{e}_1 \in [0, \bar{e}_1^m],$$

then the following proposition holds [see *Hellwig*]:

Proposition 2: If the following conditions are satisfied

α) $P(\hat{e}_1)$ is not degenerated for $\hat{e}_1 \in (\bar{e}_1^{(i-1)}, \bar{e}^{(i)})$, $(i = 1, \ldots, m)$,
β) every column of A has at most one change in sign,

then there is a unique viability preserving solution.

These conditions are not restrictive. A violation of condition α) can be remedied by a small change of the vector b in (1). Condition β) means that for every activity j the sequence of net cash inflows shows not nore then one change in sign, which usually is fulfilled.

If, as a special case, the capital market is perfect, then the marginal rates of return are equal to the market rate of interest r and $(\tilde{x}, \tilde{e}, \tilde{q})$, where $\tilde{x}$ solves iii) with $\tilde{q}_t = (1 + r)^{-t}$, $(t = 1, \ldots, T)$, and $\tilde{e} = A\tilde{x} + b$, is a viability preserving solution.

Concerning the T period case we consider a simple production problem from the economics of exhaustible resources. Let us regard a resource market which is characterized by a group of producers organized in a cartel setting the prices and another group, the competi- tive fringe, which takes the prices announced by the cartel as given [cf. *Gilbert*], *Dasgupta/*

Heal , p. 345; Ulph]. This type of a partially cartelized market seems to fit better than the familiar market structures of economic theory to some resource markets such as the oil market with the OPEC cartel. In the literature cited solution concepts as Nash or Stackelberg equilibria are discussed when present value maximization is the objective. Since these solutions show that usually cartel and fringe will not produce simultaneously, the question arises how to ensure a steady income for each producer. We just consider a single producer as a price-taker and assume that he intends to preserve economic viability.

Let s_t be the growth rate of marginal profit in period t resulting from the price and cost change in the same period, where $s_t \geqslant r_t$ and r_t is the interest rate for a short-term lending opportunity in period t. We further assume demand to be inelastic.

The resource owner wants to plan the timing of production in such a way that the resource with an initial stock K is maintained as a source of income in the sense of preserving economic viability.

The decision problem can be formulated as follows: Find a solution $(\bar{e}, \bar{x}, \bar{q})$ satisfying conditions i) to iii) for

$$A = m x_{10} - x_{20}$$

$$e_t = \prod_{\tau=1}^{t} (1 + s_\tau) m x_{1t} - x_{2t} + (1 + r_t) x_{2t\text{-}1} \qquad t = 1, \ldots, T-1$$

$$e_T = \prod_{\tau=1}^{T} (1 + s_\tau) m x_{1T} + (1 + r_T) x_{2T\text{-}1}$$

$$x_{1t} \leqslant k_{1t}, \ k_{1t} \geqslant x_{10} \qquad t = 0, \ldots, T$$

$$x_{2t} \leqslant k_{2t}$$

$$\sum_{t=0}^{T} x_{1t} \leqslant K$$

$$x_{1t}, x_{2t}, e_t \geqslant 0 \qquad \text{for all } t$$

where

x_{1t} quantitiy produced in period t
x_{2t} amount invested in period t at the interest rate r_t
A initial investment
K total stock of the resource
m marginal profit at $t = 0$.

It can be shown that for the viability preserving solution:

$$\bar{r}_t = s_t \qquad t = 1, \ldots, T$$

$$\bar{e}_t = s_t V \qquad t = 1, \ldots, T-1$$

$$\bar{e}_T = (1 + s_T) V$$

$$V = \sum_{t=1}^{T} \bar{e}_t \prod_{\tau=1}^{t} (1 + s_\tau)^{-1} = m \left(K - \frac{A}{m} \right) =: m\bar{K}$$

$$\bar{x}_{1t} = \bar{K} s_t \prod_{\tau=1}^{t} (1 + s_\tau)^{-1} \qquad t = 1, \ldots, T-1$$

$$\bar{x}_{1T} = \bar{K} \prod_{t=1}^{T-1} (1 + s_\tau)^{-1}$$

$$\bar{x}_{2t} = 0 \qquad t = 0, \ldots, T-1.$$

If marginal profits rise at a constant rate $s_t = s$, income is constant over time whereas production is diminishing at a constant rate $s/(1 + s)$ [4]). A constant real income would be obtained, if the cartel would choose the growth factor of the price to be $s_t =$

$$= \prod_{\tau=1}^{t} (1 + \gamma_\tau),$$ where γ_τ is the rate of inflation in period τ which is supposed also to hold

for the production costs.

We conclude with some possible extensions. Further investment and financing opportunities can be introduced. In the context of an exhausitible resource it may be of particular interest to invest in a backstop technology which is apt to substitute the resource output by a producible good, e.g., nuclear energy [cf. *Nordhaus*]. Demand restrictions can be taken into account either by price-independent bounds for each period or by a linear demand function which often is assumed in the literature on exhaustible resources; with a non-linear demand function the problem becomes more complicated. For the price policy of the cartel the interesting question arises whether there are future prices which equilibriate the total production sequence resulting from the viability preserving solutions of the cartel and the fringe with the demand sequence expected at the announced prices.

These extensions, however, complicate the derivation of a solution since it is necessary to solve a multiparametric linear program, in general. An explicit solution as in the simple model above can usually not be given.

References

Dasgupta, P.S., and *G.M. Heal*: Economic Theory and Exhaustible Resources. Cambridge 1979.

Fisher, I.: The Theory of Interest. New York 1930.

Gal, T., and *J. Nedoma*: Multiparametric Linear Programming. Management Science **18**, 1972, 406–422.

Gilbert, R.J.: Dominant Firm Pricing in a Market for an Exhaustible Resource. Bell Journal of Economics **9**, 1978, 385–395.

Hellwig, K.: Erfolgskapitalerhaltung bei unvollkommenem Kapitalmarkt. Zeitschrift für Betriebswirtschaftliche Forschung 1980.

Hotelling, H.: The Economics of Exhaustible Resources. Journal of Political Economy **39**, 1931, 137–175.

Nordhaus, W.D.: The Allocation of Energy Resources. Brookings Papers on Economic Activity **3**, 1973.

Siebert, H.: Erschöpfbare Ressourcen. Schriften des Vereins für Sozialpolitik Bd. 108, 1980.

Solow, R.M.: The Economics of Resources or The Resources of Economics. American Economic Review, Papers and Proceedings, Richard T. Ely Lecture, 1974, 1–14.

Ulph, A.M.: Modelling Partially Cartelized Markets for Exhaustible Resources. This Volume, 1981.

---

[4]) This solution is also obtained by the classic approach, if there is an isoelastic demand function $x_t = c p_t^{-1}$ with $c = s \bar{K} m$.

Economic Theory of Natural Resources. ©Physica-Verlag, Würzburg–Wien, 1982.

On the Development of a Substitute for an Exhaustible Natural Resource

Murray C. Kemp and *Ngo Van Long*

1. Introduction

The exhaustibility of stocks of natural resources causes societies to search for flow substitutes for those resources, and it causes them to invest in physical capital and to undertake research-and-development expenditures designed to improve the quality or reduce the production cost of the substitutes. What then are the socially optimal trajectories of resource-extraction, of output of the substitutes, and of investment in equipment and in research and development? And how do the socially optimal trajectories compare with those generated by various alternative market structures? In the present paper we examine these questions.

Assumptions must be made. In particular, it is assumed that there is just one natural resource and just one perfect flow substitute for it. The average cost of producing the substitute depends on the amount produced and also on the state of the arts. At any moment, the state of the arts is given, but it can be changed gradually by expenditure on research and development. On the other hand, the average cost of extracting the resource is constant, independent both of the rate of extraction and of the outstanding stock of the resource.

After calculating the socially optimal trajectory (in Section 2), we describe the trajectory associated with each of several alternative market situations. Thus (in Section 3) we treat the case of universal monopoly, in which the resource is owned by a single firm and the same firm has the exclusive legal right to develop and produce the substitute. Then (in Section 5) we visit the opposite pole and examine the case of universal competition, in which ownership of the resource is dispersed over many small firms and in which there is complete freedom of entry to the activity of developing and producing the substitute. As a preliminary to the analysis of Section 5, we examine (in Section 4) the mixed case in which ownership of the resource is dispersed but the right to develop and produce the substitute is legally restricted to a single firm.

Our work builds on that of *Vousden* [1977]. Vousden developed a model of social optimization slightly more general than ours, but he stopped short of comparing the socially optimal trajectory with the outcomes of alternative market structures. Our work also bears an affinity to that of *Dasgupta/Stiglitz* [1980a] and *Dagupta/Gilbert/Stiglitz* [1980]. Dasgupta and Stiglitz do compare the socially optimal trajectory with the outcomes when decisions and asset-holdings are decentralized in various market situations. However, whereas we suppose that expenditure on research and development generates reductions of cost continuously and without delay, Dasgupta and Stiglitz see the objective of such expenditure as the reduction of the period of waiting for an invention of given characteristics.

Unlike Vousden, but like Dasgupta and Stiglitz we ignore the possibility that there is uncertainty about the size of the resource-stock, about the returns to expenditure on research and development, and about future demand.

2. The Social Optimum

A single natural resource is available in known amount Q_0. It can be extracted at the constant average cost k, where k may be zero. The total cost of extraction at time t is therefore $kq(t)$, where q is the rate of extraction.

A perfect substitute for the resource can be produced at a total cost of $c(R, y)$, where y is the rate of output and R represents the state of the arts. Expenditure on research and development is $g(r)$, where $r \equiv \dot{R} \equiv dR/dt$.

Total revenue from the sale of the resource and its substitute is $\pi(q+y) \equiv \pi(x)$, so that average revenue is $p(x) \equiv \pi(x)/x$. Subject to the usual qualifications, the social surplus is

$$u(x) - c(R, y) - kq - g(r)$$

where

$$u(x) \equiv \int_0^x p(z)\, dz.$$

Evidently $u'(x) \equiv du(x)/dx = p(x)$.

It is supposed that all functions are continuous and that all second derivatives exist. Moreoever, it is assumed that

$c(R, y)$ is convex in (R, y)

$c_R \leqslant 0, c_{RR} \geqslant 0, c_y > 0, c_{yy} \geqslant 0, c_{yR} < 0$

$c(R, y)$ is bounded by $\underline{c}(y) > 0$ and $\bar{c}(y)$

$c_y(R, 0) < p(0)$

$g' > 0, g'' \geqslant 0$

$\pi(x)$ is strictly concave.

The social problem is to find

$$\max_{q,y,r} \int_0^\infty \exp(-\rho t)\,[u(q+y) - c(R, y) - kq - g(r)]\, dt \qquad (\mathrm{P}^S)$$

s.t. $\dot{Q} = -q, \quad Q(0) = Q_0 > 0, \quad \lim_{t \to \infty} Q(t) \geqslant 0$

$\dot{R} = r, \quad R(0) = R_0$

$q, y, r \geqslant 0.$

The Lagrangean is

$$L = u(q + y) - c(R, y) - kq - g(r) - \psi_1 q + \psi_2 r$$

where ψ_1 and ψ_2 are the costates associated with Q and R respectively. Among the first-order conditions we have

$$\partial L/\partial q = u' - k - \psi_1 \leqslant 0 \qquad (= 0 \text{ if } q > 0) \tag{1}$$

$$\partial L/\partial y = u' - c_y \leqslant 0 \qquad (= 0 \text{ if } y > 0) \tag{2}$$

$$\partial L/\partial r = -g' + \psi_2 \leqslant 0 \qquad (= 0 \text{ if } r > 0) \tag{3}$$

$$\dot{\psi}_1 = \rho \psi_1 \tag{4}$$

$$\dot{\psi}_2 = \rho \psi_2 + c_R. \tag{5}$$

Both ψ_1 and ψ_2 are non-negative. For let us define $V(Q(t), R(t))$ as

$$\max_{q,y,r} \int_0^\infty \exp(-\rho(z - t)) [u(q + y) - c(R, y) - kq - g(r)] \, dz$$

s.t. $\dot{Q} = -q, \quad Q(t) \geqslant 0, \quad \lim_{z \to \infty} Q(z) \geqslant 0$

$\dot{R} = r$

$q, y, r \geqslant 0.$

Then it is well known that $\partial V/\partial Q = \psi_1 \geqslant 0$ and that $\partial V/\partial R = \psi_2 \geqslant 0$.

Let x^s be defined by

$$u'(x^s) = p(x^s) = k$$

and R^s by

$$c_y(R^s, x^s) = k;$$

let $y^s(R)$ be defined by

$$c_y(R, y^s) = p(y^s)$$

and $p^s(R)$ by

$$p^s \equiv p(y^s);$$

and let R^{s*} be defined by

$$-c_R(R^{s*}, y^s(R^{s*}))/\rho = g'(0).$$

It will be shown that, if R^{s*} exists, it is unique (see the proof of Proposition 3 c)).

Proposition 1 (Social Optimum):

a) If $R_0 \geqslant R^s$ then the resource is of no value and it is optimal to set $q(t) = 0$ always.
b) If $R_0 < R^s$ then either (i) $x(t) \geqslant x^s$ always and $p(x)$ is non-increasing always or
  (ii) $x(0) < x^s$ and $p(x)$ rises until the resource-stock is exhausted and thereafter is non-increasing.
c) After exhaustion of the resource-stock, the optimal output of the substitute is $y^s(R)$,

if it exists. If y^s (R) does not exist, the optimal output is zero. If the optimal output is positive, it is an increasing function of R.

d) (i) It is optimal to invest in research (that is, r $(t) > 0$ for some t) if $| c_R$ $(R_0, y^s$ $(R_0))/\rho\,| > g'$ (0). (ii) No investment in research will take place after time t if and only if R $(t) \geqslant R^{s*}$. (iii) Investment in research and development can occur before production of the substitute begins, that is, it may be optimal to allow the product of research and development to lie dormant for a season.

Proof:

a) This part of the proposition is obvious. It is illustrated by Figures 1a) and 1b).

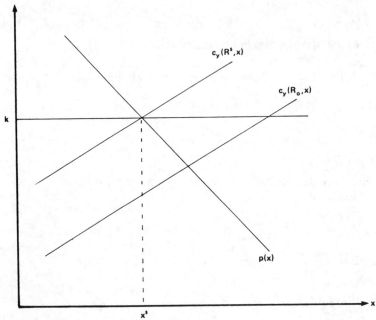

Fig. 1a): $c_{yy} > 0$

b) Either ψ_1 $(0) = 0$ so that, from (4), ψ_1 $(t) = 0$ always; or ψ_1 $(0) > 0$ so that ψ_1 $(t) > 0$ always. Suppose that ψ_1 $(0) = 0$. Then, from (1), x $(t) = x^s$ and p $(t) = k$ until R (t) reaches R^s; at that time, any remaining resource-stock can be abandoned. (If ψ_1 $(0) = 0$, it is suboptimal to exhaust the resource-stock before R (t) reaches R^s; for, if that did occur, price would jump up from k, implying that the path to exhaustion is suboptimal. Moreover, if ψ_1 $(0) = 0$, R (t) must reach R^s, at least asymptotically; for, otherwise, q $(t) \geqslant \epsilon > 0$, implying exhaustion in finite time and, in particular, exhaustion before R (t) reaches R^s.) If R (t) is asymptotic to R^s but never reaches R^s then the resource-stock is never exhausted and there must exist an unbounded interval of time during which extraction of the resource and production of the substitute proceed simultaneously. If R (t) rises beyond R^s then p (t) steadily falls and x (t) steadily rises as R (t) increases.

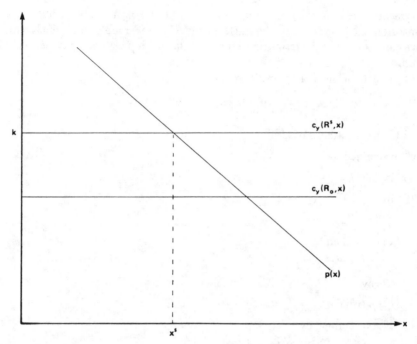

Fig. 1b): $c_{yy} = 0$

Suppose, alternatively, that $\psi_1 (0) > 0$. Since $\partial V/\partial Q = \psi_1 (t) > 0$, the resource-stock will never be abandoned before it is exhausted. If $q (t) > 0$ then, from (1), price must be rising: $p (t) = k + \psi_1 (0) \exp (\rho t)$. After exhaustion (which may or may not occur) price is non-increasing, falling if and only if R is increasing. If exhaustion does not occur, there must be an interval during which extraction and production of the substitute occur simultaneously; if exhaustion does occur, there may be such an interval.

c) This proposition is obvious.

d) (i) Suppose that the inequality is satisfied but $r (t) = 0$ always. Eventually either the resource-stock will be exhausted or the rate of extraction will be arbitrarily small. Then the marginal gain from an increase of knowledge is $c_R (R_0, y^s (R_0))/\rho$ while the cost of such an increment is $g' (0)$. Hence the trajectory $r (t) \equiv 0$ is suboptimal. (ii) This proposition follows from d) (i) by treating time t as the origin. (iii) From the strict concavity of π, p is a declining function of x. Hence the average utility cost of investment in research and development is an increasing function of the rate of investment. Any investment therefore should take place over an interval of time; in particular, this is true of investment before production of the substitute begins.   Q.E.D.

3. A Single Monopoly of the Resource and of its Substitute

We have described those trajectories which are optimal from the vantage point of society (viewed, for example, as a collection of individuals with identical preferences and endowments). We now swing to the opposite extreme and examine the policies which are optimal from the point of view of a single individual or subgroup of individuals with exclusive control both of the resource itself and of the development and production of its substitute.

The problem of the monopolist is to find

$$\max_{q,y,r} \int_0^\infty \exp(-\rho t)\,[\pi\,(q+y)-c\,(R,y)-kq-g\,(r)]\,dt \qquad (\mathrm{P}^m)$$

s.t. the constraints of (P^s).

Let x^m be defined by

$$\pi'\,(x^m)=k$$

and R^m by

$$c_y\,(R^m,x^m)=k;$$

let $y^m\,(R)$ be defined by

$$c_y\,(R,y^m)=\pi'\,(y^m)$$

and $p^m\,(R)$ by

$$p^m \equiv p\,(y^m);$$

and let $R^{m\,*}$ be defined by

$$-c_R\,(R^{m\,*},y^m\,(R^{m\,*}))/\rho=g'\,(0).$$

It will be shown that, if $R^{m\,*}$ exists, it is unique (see the proof of Proposition 3 c)).

Proposition 2 (Monopolist's Optimum):

a) If $R_0 \geqslant R^m$ then the resource is of no value and it is optimal to set $q\,(t)=0$ always.
b) If $R_0 < R^m$ then either (i) $x\,(t)\geqslant x^m$ always and $\pi'\,(x)$ is non-increasing always or
   (ii) $x\,(0)<x^m$ and $\pi'\,(x)$ rises until the resource-stock is exhausted and thereafter is non-increasing.
c) After exhaustion of the resource-stock, the optimal output of the substitute is $y^m\,(R)$, if it exists. If $y^m\,(R)$ does not exist, the optimal output is zero. If the optimal output is positive, it is an increasing function of R.
d) (i) It is optimal to invest in research (that is, $r\,(t)>0$ for some t) if $-c_R\,(R_0,y^m\,(R_0))/\rho>g'\,(0)$. (ii) No investment in research will take place after time t if and only if $R\,(t)\geqslant R^{m\,*}$. (iii) Investment in research and development can occur before production of the substitute begins; that is, it may be optimal to allow the product of research and development to lie dormant for a time.

Proof: The proof is similar to that of Proposition 1.

Proposition 3 (Comparison of Social Optimum and Monopolist Optimum):

a) $x^s > x^m$.
b) $R^s > R^m$ if $c_{yy}>0$, $R^s = R^m$ if $c_{yy}=0$.
c) $R^{s\,*} > R^{m\,*}$.

Proof: a) and b) are obvious.

c) Let us define

$$F^s(R) = -c_R(R, y^s(R))/\rho - g'(0)$$
$$F^m(R) = -c_R(R, y^m(R))/\rho - g'(0)$$

so that R^{s^*} is the solution of $F^s = 0$ and R^{m^*} is the solution of $F^m = 0$. Now

$$dF^m/dR = -(c_{RR} + c_{Ry}(dy^m/dR))/\rho.$$

But

$$dy^m/dR = c_{Ry}(\pi'' - c_{yy}).$$

Hence

$$\begin{aligned}
dF^m/dR &= -(c_{RR} + (c_{Ry})^2/(\pi'' - c_{yy}))/\rho \\
&\leqslant (\pi'' c_{RR} - (c_{Ry})^2))/(\rho(c_{yy} - \pi'')) \\
&< 0 \quad \text{[from the convexity of } c(R, y)\text{]}.
\end{aligned}$$

Similarly, $dF^s/dR < 0$. Moreover, $y^m(R) > y^s(R)$ and $c_{Ry} < 0$, implying that the curve $F^m(R)$ lies everywhere below the curve $F^s(R)$, as in Figure 2.　　　Q.E.D.

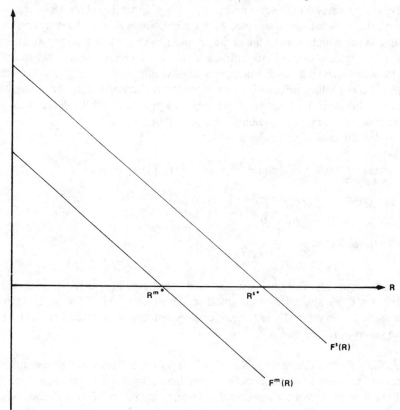

Fig. 2

Corollary: A resource-stock is socially valuable but worthless to a monopolist if $R^s > R_0 > R^m$. In that case, the monopolist over-conserves to the point of never using the resource. On the other hand, if $R^{s*} > R_0 > R^{m*}$, it is socially optimal to eventually invest in research and development but suboptimal for a monopolist to do so.

4. Dispersed Ownership of the Resource, Monopoly of the Substitute

In Section 3 we characterized the trajectories which emerge when both ownership of the resource and the right to develop and produce a substitute lie with a single firm or individual. We now review the analysis of that section on the revised assumption that ownership of the resource is dispersed (competitive) while the development and production of the substitute remain subject to monopoly.

The monopolist faces a large number of small price-taking resource-owners and therefore is in a position to play the role of Stackelberg leader. We suppose that at the outset the leader announces a path $\{p\,(t)\}$ of selling prices, that is, prices for the extracted resource or its substitute, and then, given the assumption of perfect foresight, sticks to it. We also suppose that the leader buys the entire stock of the (unextracted) resource at the outset, paying whatever in-the-ground price $p_0 - k$ is optimal for him. Of course the announced price path is then constrained by the requirement that over any interval of time beginning at the initial moment the in-the-ground price rise at an average rate not greater than ρ. It might seem that it would suit the leader to announce a zero in-the-ground price. However such an announcement, in a context of perfect foresight, would bind the leader to charge a selling price of k for ever. Evidently the leader must strive for the best compromise between the desire to keep the buying price low and the desire to minimize the transition to the monopoly-selling-price of Section 3.

Formally, the task of the leader is to find

$$\max_{q,y,r,p_0} \int_0^\infty \exp\left(-\rho t\right) \left[\pi\left(q+y\right)-kq-c\left(R,\,y\right)-g\left(r\right)\right] dt - p_0\,Q_0 \qquad \text{(Pm*)}$$

$$\text{s.t. } \dot{Q} = -q, \quad Q\left(0\right) = Q_0, \quad \lim_{t\to\infty} Q\left(t\right) \geqslant 0$$

$$\dot{R} = r, \quad R\left(0\right) = R_0$$

$$\dot{p}/(p-k) \leqslant \rho$$

$$q,\, y,\, r,\, p_0 \geqslant 0.$$

Until the matter is mentioned again, it will be supposed that, everywhere on the optimal path, $r = 0$. We also rule out the trivial case in which $p^m\left(R_0\right) \leqslant k$, so that the resource-stock has no value. There remain for consideration three cases, defined by the relative values of R_0, R^s and R^m.

Case 1 ($R_0 \geqslant R^s$): In this case $c_y\left(R_0,\,y^m\left(R_0\right)\right) \leqslant k$, as in Figure 3. The resource stock would be of no value to the monopolist of Section 3, for it is cheaper to produce the substitute than to extract the resource. However, in the hands of competitive owners the resource is a threat to the leader. Hence it is optimal for the leader to buy the entire unextracted resource stock at the present-value price $p_0 - k$, $p_0 \leqslant p^m$ (R_0), then permanently withdraw the stock from the market, producing only the less costly substitute commodity. Until p^m (R^0) is reached, the leader's optimal selling price rises from p_0 according to the formula

$$\dot{p}/(p - k) = \rho. \tag{6}$$

Thereafter, price is constant at the level p^m. Of course, if $p_0 = p^m$ then the leader's selling price is equal to p^m from the outset.

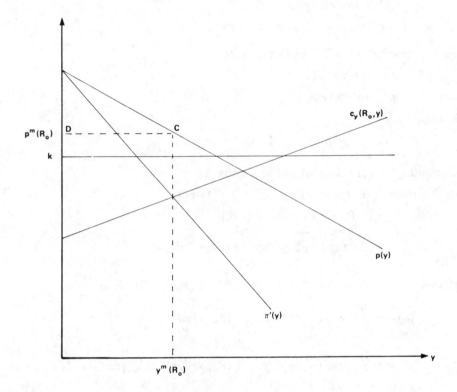

Fig. 3

It remains to determine the optimal p_0. If p_0 were set equal to p_m, the leader would receive the same amount, represented by the area ABCD of Figure 3, during each period. If p_0 were set below p^m then, by virtue of the constraint (6), profits would be lower during some initial interval; but the amount paid for the resource stock also would be less. The optimal p_0 equates marginal gain and loss. Setting $p_0 = p^m - \delta$, $\delta > 0$ the gain from setting p_0 below p^m is

$$G(\delta) \equiv \delta Q_0$$

so that

$$G'(\delta) = Q_0. \tag{7}$$

On the other hand, the loss of revenue while the leader's selling price rises to p^m is

$$L(\delta) \equiv \int_0^{T(\delta)} \exp(-pt)[(p^m y^m - py)$$
$$- (c(R_0, y^m) - c(R_0, y))]\, dt \qquad (8)$$

where

$$p(t) = (p_0 - k)\exp(\rho t) + k$$
$$= (p^m - \delta - k)\exp(\rho t) + k$$
$$y \quad = y(p) = y((p_0 - k)\exp(\rho t) + k) \qquad (9)$$

and T is the solution of $p^m = p(T)$, that is, of

$$p^m = (p_0 - k)\exp(\rho T) + k$$
$$= (p^m - \delta - k)\exp(\rho T) + k. \qquad (10)$$

Solving (10),

$$T(\delta) = (1/\rho)[\log(p^m - k) - \log(p^m - \delta - k)]. \qquad (11)$$

Substituting from (11) into (8), and differentiating,

$$L'(\delta) = T'(\delta)\exp(-\rho T)(p^m y^m - p(T)y(T))$$
$$- (c(R_0, h^m) - c(R_0, y(T)))]$$
$$- \int_0^{T(\delta)} \exp(-\rho T)[d(py - c(R_0, y))/d\delta]\, dt.$$

However, $p^m y^m = p(T)y(T)$ and $c(R_0, y^m) = c(R_0, y(T))$; hence

$$L'(\delta) = - \int_0^{T(\delta)} \exp(-\rho t)[d(py - c(R_0, y))/d\delta]\, dt$$

$$= - \int_0^{T(\delta)} \exp(-\rho t)[d(py - c(R_0, y))/dp][dp/d\delta]\, dt.$$

Moreover, $dp/d\delta = -\exp(\rho t)$; hence

$$L'(\delta) = - \int_0^{T(\delta)} [\pi'(y) - c_y(R_0, y)][dy/dp]\, dt.$$

For $p < p^m$, $\pi' > c_y$; and, of course, $dy/dp < 0$. Hence

$$L'(\delta) \geqslant 0 \quad (= 0, \text{ if } T = 0, \text{ that is, if } \delta = 0).$$

The choice of optimal δ, say δ^*, is illustrated by Figure 4. Clearly δ^* is positive, implying that the optimal p_0, say p_0^*, is less than p^m. Moreover, from (9), $(p_0 - k)\exp(\rho T) = = p^m - k$, implying that $p_0^* > k$. Thus

$$k < p_0^* < p^m.$$

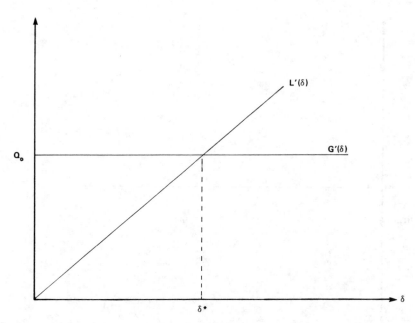

Fig. 4

Case 2 ($R_0 < R^m$): In this case, evidently, it is never optimal to retire the resource-stock, either in whole or in part. It is convenient to distinguish two subcases, according as a) $c_y (R_0, 0) > k$, as in Figure 5 a), or b) $c_y (R_0, 0) \leqslant k$, as in Figure 5 b).

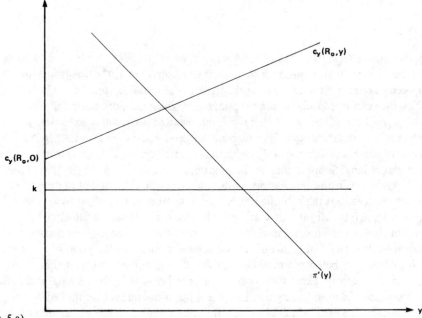

Fig. 5 a)

58

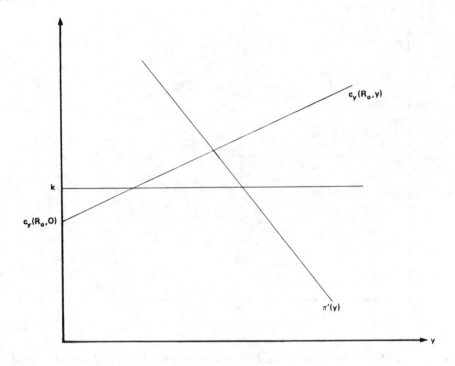

Fig. 5 b)

a) Suppose that $c_y(R_0, 0) > k$ so that, whatever the level of sales, it is less costly to extract the resource than to produce the substitute. As in Case 1, the leader may be supposed to purchase the entire resource-stock at the outset, at price $p_0 - k$. The stock is then extracted and sold at a net price $p - k$, which grows exponentially, beginning at $p_0 - k$, until $p = p^m(R_0)$. Before $p = p^m$, the resource-stock will be exhausted and production of the substitute begun. For suppose that, at the point of exhaustion, $p > p^m$. Then the cost of purchase is unnecessarily high and the period during which no profit is earned unnecessarily long. Suppose that, at the point of exhaustion, $p = p^m(R_0)$, as in Section 3. Again the cost of purchasing the resource stock and the period of no profit could be reduced; but these considerations are now more or less offset by the need (imposed by (6)) to sell for a time at a price less than p^m. It can be shown, by an argument similar to that developed for Case 1, that if at the point of exhaustion p is sufficiently close to p^m then the offset is incomplete, and if at the point of exhaustion p is sufficiently far below p^m the offset is more than complete, implying that, along the optimal trajectory, exhaustion occurs at a price below p^m. Thus the optimal policy consists of three phases. During the first phase, the entire market is supplied by the resource-stock at a price which obeys (6); that phase ends with the exhaustion of the stock. During the second phase, price continues to obey (6) but the entire market is supplied by the substitute. In the third phase, the price is constant at p^m. [1])

b) Suppose alternatively that $c_y (R_0, 0) \leqslant k$. Then it is optimal to always produce the substitute commodity. The first phase of the optimal policy a) is replaced by a phase during which the market is supplied partly from the resource-stock and partly by the substitute. Otherwise, the new policy has the same characteristics as the old.

Case 3 ($R^m \leqslant R_0 < R^s$): This case is illustrated by Figure 6. It might seem that the optimal policy must have the same characteristics as in Case 1:

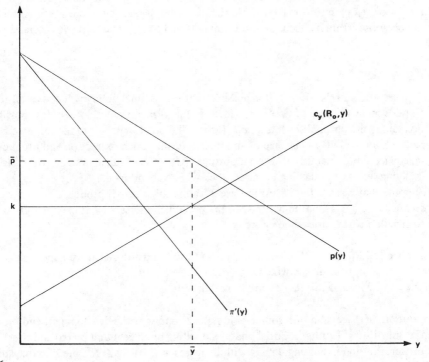

Fig. 6

Buy the resource-stock at the outset, at price $p_0 - k$, retire the entire stock, and let $p - k$ climb exponentially until $p = p^m$ (R_0). However reflection reveals that such a policy is not always optimal. Let us define $\bar{y}$ by

$$c_y (R_0, \bar{y}) = k$$

and $\bar{p}$ by

$$\bar{p} = p (\bar{y}).$$

---

[1]) In the course of their examination of the market structure of this section, *Dasgupta/Stiglitz* [1980], working with the special assumption of constant marginal cost, derived a three-stage policy similar to that just described.

Clearly, $\bar{p} > k$ because $R_0 < R^s$. Let us suppose that $\bar{p} > p_0$. Then, during an initial interval of time, the leader will wish to sell more than $\bar{y}$ and it is optimal to extract some of the resource. That first phase ends when $p = \bar{p}$. Thereafter the optimal policy is as in Case 1.

We have proceeded to this point on the strong assumption that $R_0 \geqslant R^{m*}$ so that, everywhere along the optimal trajectory, $r = 0$. Let us now drop that assumption. Again we consider three cases, the first of which is a generalization of Case 1, the second of Case 2 and the third of Case 3.

Case 1' ($R_0 \geqslant R^s$): In this general outline, the optimal policy of the leader is the same as in Case 1. The resource-stock is purchased by the leader at a present-value price $p_0 - k$, with $p_0 < p^m (R_0)$, but is then withheld. Until $p^m (R)$ is reached, the leader's optimal selling price rises from p_0 according to formula (6) and thereafter falls with increases in R.

Case 2' ($R_0 < R^m$):

a) Suppose that $c_y (R_0, 0) > k$. It is possible that the optimal policy will consist of three phases similar to those of Case 2 a). However things might be otherwise. It is possible that, along the optimal trajectory, $c_y (R, 0)$ will dip below k before the resource is exhausted, implying the existence of an interval during which extraction and production take place simultaneously. It is even possible that, before exhaustion, $c_y (R, y^m (R)) \leqslant k$, implying that any remaining resource-stock will be abandoned.

b) Suppose that $c_y (R_0, 0) < k$. As in Case 2 b), the substitute is produced from the outset. As in Case 2' a), but in contrast to the outcome in Case 2 b), it may be optimal to abandon part of the resource-stock.

Case 3' ($R^m \leqslant R_0 < R^s$): The outcome is as in Case 1' except that there may exist an initial interval of time during which the resource is extracted.

The conclusions of this section are summarized in

Proposition 4 (Dispersion of resource-holding, monopoly of the development and production of substitute): During an initial phase, the selling price is bound by (6) and rises; thereafter, it is non-increasing, falling with increases in R. If $R_0 \geqslant R^s$, the resource-stock will be abandoned in its entirety; if $R_0 < R^m$, the resource-stock has value to the leader and will be exploited, in whole or in part, during the initial price-phase; if $R^m \leqslant R_0 < R^s$, the resource-stock may or may not have value to the leader and therefore may or may not be extracted. While the resource-stock is being exploited, production of the substitute may take place simultaneously, and must do so if $c_y (R_0, 0) < k$.

5. Dispersed Ownership of the Resource, Freedom of Entry to the Development and Production of the Substitute

In Section 4 it was supposed that the development and production of a substitute for the resource is in the hands of a single, legally-protected firm. We now vary that assumption by supposing that the development and production of the substitute is open to any and every firm. We suppose further that inventions are protected by unlimited patent.

One can imagine that there takes place an initial meeting of all firms and individuals. At that meeting a complete set of contracts for present and future delivery are formed. The characteristics of an equilibrium price path will depend on the nature of the game played at the meeting. Since there is complete freedom of entry one feels justified in insisting that the price path is such that any firm which develops and produces the substitute will just break even. Beyond that, various possibilities present themselves. Here we follow as closely as possible the analysis of Section 4 and suppose that, although bound by the no-profit restriction, each firm seeks to play the role of Stackelberg leader. Detailed analysis is organized under the three subheadings of Section 4.

Case 1" ($R_0 \geqslant R^s$): We can imagine that each firm, seeking to secure the role of leader, bids for the resource-stock. Bidding stops when the price reaches that level, say $p_0^{**} - k$, at which the present value of the net cash flow is exactly offset by the cost of buying the resource-stock. Since all firms have the same information, all firms will have the same maximum bid. Which firm makes the purchase is of no importance; we can imagine that it is determined by a random device.

The price paid may be greater or less than p^m (R_0) $- k$, depending on the cost function c (R, y), on the size of the stock Q_0 and on the rate of interest. If $p_0^{**} > p^m$ (R_0) then the price path contains a jump at the initial moment. If $p_0^{**} < p^m$ (R_0) then the price path is as in Case 1': there is an interval during which p is bounded by (6) and which terminates when p (T) equals p^m (R (T)); thereafter, p (t) $= p^m$ (R (t)). The two possibilities are illustrated by Figures 7 a) and 7 b), respectively.

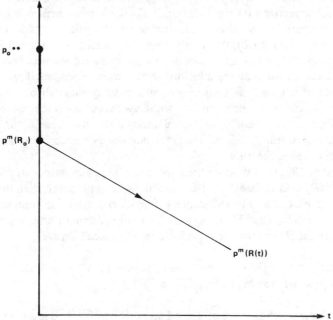

Fig. 7 a): $p_0^{**} > p^m$ (R_0)

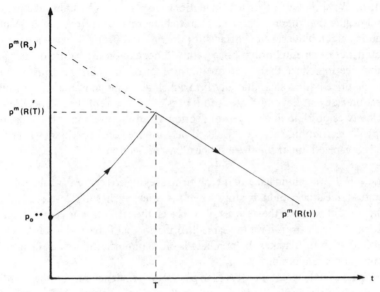

Fig. 7 b): $p_0^{**} < p^m (R_0)$

Case 2" ($R_0 < R^m$): Again we can imagine that at the initial point of time some particular firm purchases the entire resource-stock at the break-even price $p_0^{**} - k$.

a) Suppose that $c_y (R_0, 0) > k$. If $p_0^{**} > p^m (R_0)$ then, as in Case 1", there is an initial jump in price; thereafter $p (t) = p^m (R (t))$. If $p_0^{**} < p^m (R_0)$ then, as in Case 2' a), the equilibrium path has two phases: an initial phase with price bound by (6) and a later phase with price $p^m (R (t))$ not increasing. The initial phase may consist of two specialized subphases, as in Case 2 a), with only the extracted resource being sold in the first subphase and only the substitute in the second subphase. However that is not inevitable: as in Case 2' a), there may be an interval of simultaneous extraction and production, and it may be optimal to withdraw part of the resource-stock. Moreover, as in Case 1", there may be no interval during which the substitute is produced under conditions of rising price; in fact, at the point of exhaustion there may be a discontinuous drop in the price.

b) Suppose that $c_y (R_0, 0) \leqslant k$. Again there will be an initial discontinuous drop in price if $p_0^{**} > p^m (R_0)$. As in Case 2' b), the substitute will be produced from the outset, and the resource-stock may be abandoned before its exhaustion. In contrast to our conclusion concerning Case 2" a), there can be no discontinuous drop in price at any time after the initial moment, for the substitute is produced always.

Case 3" ($R^m \leqslant R_0 < R^s$): The outcome is the same as in Case 3' except that there will be an initial discontinuous drop in price if $p_0^{**} > p^m (R_0)$.

Proposition 5: If the purchase-price of the resource-stock $p_0^{**} - k$, is less than $p^m (R_0) - k$, that is, if p_0^{**} is less than $p^m (R_0)$, then the equilibrium price, production and extraction paths have the qualitative properties described in Section 4. If $p_0^{**} \geqslant p^m (R_0)$ there is no initial phase with increasing price; indeed, if $p_0^{**} > p^m (R_0)$ then the price path begins with an abrupt jump from p_0^{**} down to $p^m (R_0)$.

References

Dasgupta, P., and *J. Stiglitz*: Market Structure and Resource Depletion: A Contribution to the Theory of Intertemporal Monopolistic Competition. Unpublished typescript, 1980a.

Dasgupta, P., R. Gilbert, and *J. Stiglitz*: Invention and Innovation under Alternative Market Structures: The Case of Natural Resources. Unpublished typescript, 1980b.

Vousden, N.J.: Resource Scarcity and the Availability of Substitutes: A Theoretical Model. Frontiers of Quantitative Economics, Volume IIIB. Ed. by M.D. Intriligator. Amsterdam 1977, 507–532.

Economic Theory of Natural Resources. ©Physica-Verlag, Würzburg–Wien, 1982.

Extraction and Recycling of
Depletable Natural Resources[1])

Rüdiger Pethig

1. Introduction

There are various devices recommended to escape or relax the increasing scarcity constraint on depletable resources. Among them, recycling takes a prominent position since it promises to contribute to a solution of three resource problems: First, it economizes on the reserves of the recycled material under consideration; second, it may be less energy intensive than virgin material production (extraction) and third, it may, in addition, reduce environmental pollution generated by the discharge of unreused waste products.

The professional literature on these different aspects of recycling[2]) has been rapidly growing in recent years. But there is not yet an established "economic theory of recycling" that integrates the complex technological, economic and ecological interdependencies [see also *Hoel; Jaeger*]. Moreover, most contributions use extremely restrictive assumptions, particularly with respect to extraction and recycling technologies. Therefore we feel that there is still considerable need to achieve a better understanding of the technological and resource conserving aspects of recycling. This is the issue of the present paper.

In the analysis which follows, we consider a raw material that can not only be produced from "underground" reserves by an extraction technology but that can also be reclaimed from secondary material (scrap) by a recycling technology. The principle objective is to study the optimal allocation of extraction and recycling activities, both in a one-period setting and in the intertemporal context. In section 2 of this paper we introduce and discuss the extraction and recycling technologies. It is assumed that virgin material can be extracted from existing reserves by means of some productive factor (labour) at decreasing returns to scale. Moreover, for the intertemporal analysis of section 3 we apply the hypothesis that the productivity in the extraction activity depends inversely on the accumulative virgin material output of the past.

Recycling is considered to be the process of regaining material (homogeneous to the extracted material) from secondary material that is a waste product with positive material contents. Recycling of material requires, of course, the input of productive factors, i.e.

[1]) Helpful comments from two anonymous referees are gratefully acknowledged. The author is, of course, responsible for the remaining errors.
[2]) See, for example, *Fisher/Peterson* [1977], *Pearce/Walter* [1977], *Hoel* [1978], *Jaeger* [1980] and *Vogt* [1980], and in particular the recycling literature surveyed by Jaeger, and Fisher and Peterson.

labour in our model. We further assume that in some range of substitution recycling is possible at variable labour intensities and that the material reclaimed from one unit of secondary material increases (up to some limit) with increasing labour intensity.[3])

Under these assumptions we first investigate the non-trivial (static) optimizing problem of how to choose the activity levels of recycling and extraction if the material output is required to be maximal for given secondary material and for given total labour input. Various aspects of this issue of "efficient technology mix" are studied in section 2.

Section 3 focuses on the optimal intertemporal allocation between extraction and recycling. The analytical problem is to maximize the integral of discounted intertemporal material output flows subject to some technological and scarcity constraints. The two state variables are the stock of secondary material and an inefficiency parameter in the extraction process, that increases with extraction output over time. We could not find sufficient information in the local optimality conditions to completely characterize the optimal trajectory. In particular, little could be revealed about intervals (and their sequence) in which extraction and/or recycling takes place. A rather surprising result is that the optimal labour intensity in the recycling process is constant (non-increasing) when the stock of secondary material is positive (zero).

2. The Technology: Assumptions and Some Implications

2.1 Assumptions

We consider a world in which one and the same natural resource — called material — can be produced by two different technologies: the virgin material technology or extraction technology and the recycling technology.[4])

The extraction technology is described by a production function $E: D_e \to \mathbf{R}_+$, $D_e \subset \mathbf{R}_+^2$. Its image $e = E(a_e, \alpha)$ is interpreted as the material that can be extracted when the labour input is a_e and when α is the value of an efficiency parameter. E satisfies[5]):

Assumption E:

AEi: E is a twice differentiable concave function with domain

$$D_e := \{(a_e, \alpha) \in \mathbf{R}_+^2 \mid \alpha \in [0, \bar{\alpha}], \bar{\alpha} \in \mathbf{R}_{++}\},$$

and it is strictly concave on the interior of D_e.

AEii: $E(0, \alpha) = E(a_e; \bar{\alpha}) = 0$ and $E_a \geq 0, E_\alpha < 0$ and $E_{a\alpha} < 0$.

---

[3]) After the first version of the present paper was written, the author's attention was pointed to the analysis of *Kemp/Long* [1980]. In their paper, Kemp and Long study a model with essentially the same recycling technology which to our knowledge was first introduced by *Pethig* [1977]. Besides this similarity there are differences in assumptions and results that will be indicated below.

[4]) Some aspects of the subsequent model are based on *Pethig* [1977, 1979] and in particular on *Siebert* et al. [1980, chap. 12].

[5]) In this paper we apply the convention $f_x := (\partial f)/(\partial x)$, $f_{xy} := (\partial f)/(\partial x \partial y)$ etc., if there is a function f with arguments x and y. If the function f has only one independent variable, we write f', f'' etc. for its derivatives.

Diminishing marginal productivity of labour (strict concavity of E) is a highly plausible assumption for the extraction technology of a depletable resource.[6]) α is an efficiency term that is treated as a (parametrically changeable) constant as long as the analysis is atemporal. The rationale behind the parameter α is as follows: Extraction from given reserves is highly productive when the reserves are large but it becomes increasingly less productive the more material has been extracted before (i.e. in the past). Therefore increasing material production from reserves makes current extraction a less competitive technology as compared to recycling. In a first step this effect can be studied in a comparative-static analysis with exogenous changes in α. We shall see below that this procedure provides already some interesting insights for choosing an optimal production mix between extraction and recycling.

However, the proper rôle and significance of α will be developed not before the intertemporal setting of section 3, where α will be determined endogeneously and then represents the cumulative virgin material output of the past.

The recycling technology is formalized by a production function $R : D_r \rightarrow R_+$ such that $r = R (a_r, s)$ is interpreted as the amount of material that can be regained from processing s units of secondary material with the help of the labour input a_r. For the first part of the paper it is not necessary to specify the origin of secondary material.

Empirical observation often shows that both extracted and recycled material are inputs into the production of some (consumption) good and that in the course of production or consumption of this good secondary material is generated as a waste product (e.g. scrap). From an analytical point of view the relevant fact is that secondary material contains material and that it is technically feasible to reclaim (part of) this material with the help of labour. Since the material content of secondary material is limited it is clear that there must be an upper bound to the reclaiming ratio $R (a_r, s)/s$. It is also plausible that the recycling process may operate at varying labour intensities (a_r/s) such that — in some range — the reclaiming ration increases with increasing labour intensity. These considerations are formally stated in

Assumption R:

ARi: R is a twice differentiable concave and linear homogeneous function with domain

$$D_r := \{(a_r, s) \in R_+^2 \mid (a_r/s) \leqslant x_l \in R_{++}\}.$$

ARii: $R_s (a_r, s) = 0$, if $(a_r/s) = x_l$,

$R_a (a_r, s) = 0$, if $(a_r/s) \geqslant x_u > x_l$,

$R (0, s) = R (a_r, 0) = 0$.

In AR we defined the relevant range of substitution between a_r and s by some given lower and upper bounds (x_l and x_u) of the labour intensity. In the definition of D_r we excluded free disposal for secondary material[7]), whereas free disposal for labour is allowed for since

---

[6]) In the recycling literature (see footnote 2) the linear technology or fixed cost assumption is prevailing. See also *Kemp/Long* [1980].

[7]) This exclusion is a non-trivial assumption for the case that one considers secondary material as a waste product causing detrimental effects if discharged into the environment. For more details see also *Pethig* [1977, 1979].

it is "harmless" and analytically convenient. Observe also, that by the condition $R(a_r, 0) = 0$ for $a_r \geq 0$ in ARii we exclude the possibility of virgin material production by means of the recycling technology.

It is obvious that the linear homogeneity assumption as well as the assumptions on R_a and R_s are unnecessarily restrictive for several results to be deduced in the sequel. They allow, however, for some useful simplifications that illuminate the characteristics of recycling. In particular, ARi implies $\lambda r = R(\lambda a_r, \lambda s)$, $\lambda \in \mathbf{R}_+$, and hence $y = f(x)$, where $y := r/s$, $x := a_r/s$ and $f(x) := R(x, 1)/s$. It is easy to show that $f' = R_a$ which is positive for $x < x_u$ by ARii. Hence we conclude that the reclaiming ratio $y = f(x) = R(a_r, s)/s$ is a strictly monotone increasing function of the labour intensity x.

2.2 The Efficient Mix between Extraction and Recycling (Statics)

We recall that labour is a necessary input for both recycling and extraction in our model. Hence there exists the allocation problem as to which technology should be applied on which scale, if the maximum feasible amount of material is to be produced from given amounts s and $a \geq a_r + a_e$ of secondary material and labour, respectively. In order to answer this question we have to investigate the solution to the problem of maximizing $\hat{M}(a, s, \alpha, a_e) := R(a - a_e, s) + E(a_e, \alpha)$ for given $(a, s, \alpha) \in D_m := D_r \times [0, \bar{\alpha}]$ on the interval $[0, a - x_l s]$. Clearly, this interval is non-empty, compact and $\hat{M}$ is a strictly concave function in a_e on $[0, a - x_l s]$ by AR and AE. Hence there exists a unique solution

$$M(a, s, \alpha) := \max_{a_e \in [0, a - x_l s]} \hat{M}(a, s, \alpha, a_e). \tag{1}$$

Such a maximizer exists for every $(a, s, \alpha) \in D_m$, so that (1) defines the mixed material production function $M: D_m \to \mathbf{R}_+$, that combines and integrates the extraction and recycling technologies for efficient material production. Some properties of this function are summarized in Lemma 1.

Lemma 1: Let the assumptions AE and AR be given.

(i) M is a concave function.

(ii) $M_a = \begin{cases} E_a, & \text{if } E_a > R_a \\ R_a, & \text{if } E_a \leq R_a \end{cases}$

$M_s = \begin{cases} (R_a - E_a) x_l, & \text{if } E_a > R_a \\ R_s, & \text{if } E_a \leq R_a \end{cases}$

$M_\alpha = E_\alpha$

(iii) Let $a > 0$ and α be fixed, let $a_e(s)$ be the maximizer of problem (1) for $s \in [0, a/x_l]$, and denote

$x(s) := a_r(s)/s := [a - a_e(s)]/s$.

a) Then $x(s) < x_u$ for every $s \in (0, a/x_l)$.

b) Then there exists $\hat{s} \in (0, a/x_l)$ such that

$\dfrac{dx\,(s)}{ds} < 0$ for $s \in [0, \hat{s}]$, and

$x\,(s) = x_I$ for $s \in [\hat{s}, a/x_I]$,

if and only if $E_a\,(a, \alpha) < f'\,(x_I)$.

(iv) Suppose that s^* maximizes M on $[0, a/x_I]$ for given $a > 0$ and α.

a) Then $x\,(s^*) = x_I$.

b) If the solution satisfies $E_a \begin{Bmatrix} \leq \\ = \\ > \end{Bmatrix} R_a$, then

$a_e \begin{Bmatrix} = \\ \in \\ = \end{Bmatrix} \begin{matrix} 0 \\ [0, a] \\ a \end{matrix}$, and if the solution satisfies

$a_e \begin{Bmatrix} = \\ \in \\ = \end{Bmatrix} \begin{matrix} 0 \\ (0, a) \\ a \end{matrix}$, then $E_a \begin{Bmatrix} \leq \\ = \\ \geq \end{Bmatrix} R_a$.

(v) Let $a > 0$ and s be fixed, let $a_e\,(\alpha)$ be the maximizer of problem (1) for $\alpha \in [0, \bar{\alpha}]$, and define $x\,(\alpha) := [a - a_e\,(\alpha)]/s$. If $x\,(\alpha) > x_I$, then

$$\frac{\partial}{\partial \alpha} \left[\frac{R\,(a - a_e\,(\alpha), s)}{M\,(a, s, \alpha)} \right] > 0 \text{ and } \frac{dx\,(\alpha)}{d\alpha} > 0.$$

Proof: (i) We define $\Gamma_e := \{(e, a_e, s, \alpha) \in \mathbf{R}_+^4 \mid (a_e, \alpha) \in D_e, s = 0 \text{ and } e \leq E\,(a_e, \alpha)\}$ and $\Gamma_r := \{(r, a_r, s, \alpha) \in \mathbf{R}_+^4 \mid (a_r, s) \in D_r, \alpha = 0 \text{ and } r \leq R\,(a_r, s)\}$. From AR and AE we know that Γ_r and Γ_e are convex sets. Hence $\Gamma := \Gamma_e + \Gamma_r$ is convex. Since the "upper boundary" of this set Γ, i.e. $\Gamma_0 := \{(m, a, s, \alpha) \mid (m, a, s, \alpha) \in \Gamma \text{ and } (\bar{m}, a, s, \alpha) \notin \Gamma,$ if $\bar{m} > m\}$, is the graph of the function M, the concavity of the function M follows from the convexity of the set Γ.

(ii) The differential of $m = e + r = E\,(a_e, \alpha) + R\,(a - a_e, s)$ yields $dm = = (E_a - R_a)\,da_e + R_a\,da + R_s\,ds + E_\alpha\,d\alpha$. Therefore

$$M_a = \frac{dm}{da} = (E_a - R_a)\,\frac{da_e}{da} + R_a, \tag{2}$$

$$M_s = \frac{dm}{ds} = (E_a - R_a)\,\frac{da_e}{ds} + R_s \tag{3}$$

and

$$M_\alpha = \frac{dm}{d\alpha} = (E_a - R_a)\,\frac{da_e}{d\alpha} + E_\alpha. \tag{4}$$

Next we consider the maximization procedure as stated in (1). Under AR and AE, the Kuhn-Tucker conditions from the Lagrangean $L = R\,(a - a_e, s) + E\,(a_e, \alpha) + + \lambda\,(a - x_I s - a_e)$ are necessary and sufficient for a solution of (1). These conditions encompass:

$$E_a - R_a - \lambda \leq 0 \text{ and } a_e\,(E_a - R_a - \lambda) = 0, \tag{5}$$

$$a - x_I s - a_e \geq 0 \text{ and } \lambda\,(a - x_I s - a_e) = 0. \tag{6}$$

We now determine M_a, M_s and M_α with the help of (2) – (6). Lemma 1 (ii) follows trivially from (2) – (4) for $E_a = R_a$. Suppose now, that $E_a < R_a$. Since $\lambda \geqslant 0$, (5) yields $a_e = 0$ and hence $E_a (0, \alpha) < R_a (a, s)$. E_a and R_a are continuous functions, so that (very) small changes in a_e and a, α or s do not reverse the above inequality. Hence we have also $a_e = 0$ if (a, s, α) is replaced by $(a + da, s, \alpha)$, $(a, s + ds, \alpha)$ or by $(a, s, \alpha + d\alpha)$. Therefore $(da_e/dz) = 0$ for $z = a, s, \alpha$ in (2), (3), and (4), respectively, if $E_a < R_a$. Suppose next that $E_a > R_a$. Then $\lambda > 0$ by (5) and $a_e = a - x_l s$. By the argument above the inequality $E_a > R_a$ remains unchanged if small variations of a, s, α and a_e occur. But from $a_e = a - x_l s$ we obtain $(da_e/da) = 1$ for $ds = d\alpha = 0$, $(da_e/ds) = - x_l$ for $da = d\alpha = 0$, and $(da_e/d\alpha) = 0$ for $da = ds = 0$. We consider these results in the equations (2) – (4) and have thus completed the proof of lemma 1 (ii).

(iii) a) For all (a, s), such that $a/s < x_u$, lemma 1 (iii) a) is obvious. Therefore we consider (a, s) satisfying $a/s \geqslant x_u$. Suppose $x (s) = x_u$. Then $E_a > R_a$, since $R_a = f' (x_u) = = 0$ by ARii, but $E_a > 0$. From the proof of lemma 1 (ii) we recall that $E_a > R_a$ implies $a_e = a - x_l s$ and hence $a_r = x_l s$ or $a_r/s = x (s) = x_l$. This contradiction proves lemma 1 (ii) a).

b) Sufficiency: $E_a (a, \alpha) < f' (x_l)$ is compatible with $E_a (0, \alpha) \gtrless f' (x_l)$. Suppose $E_a (0, \alpha) \leqslant f' (x_l) = R_a (x_l s, s)$ for some arbitrary $s \in [0, a/x_l]$. Note that R_a is a strictly monotone decreasing and continuous function of a_r on $[x_l s, x_u s]$ satisfying $R_a (x_u s, s) = = 0$ and that E_a is continuous and non-increasing in a_e on $[0, a - x_l s]$. Hence there exists $\hat{a}_e \in (0, a - x_l s)$ such that

$$E_a (\hat{a}_e, \alpha) = R_a (a - \hat{a}_e, s). \tag{7}$$

Clearly, $\hat{a}_e$ is the maximizer for problem (1). If now a small change of s is considered, one obtains $(da_e)/(ds) = R_{as}/(R_{aa} + E_{aa}) > 0$ from the condition $E_a = R_a$ in view of AR and AE. Furthermore, using the definition of $x (s)$ one has $(dx)/(ds) = = - \{s (da_e/ds) + [a - a_e (s)]\}/s^2 < 0$. Since the above argument holds for every $s \in [0, a/x_l]$, the proof of lemma 1 (iii) a) for $E_a (0, \alpha) \leqslant f' (x_l)$ is completed by setting $\hat{s} = a/x_l$. Suppose now that $E_a (0, \alpha) > f' (x_l)$ and let $s = a/x_l$. Then $E_a (0, \alpha) = = E_a (a - x_l s, \alpha)$. In this case $E_a (a - x_l s, \alpha)$ can be continuously decreased by decreasing s. Hence there is $s' < a/x_l$ such that $a_e (s) = a - x_l s$ for every $s \in [a', a/x_l]$ and $a_e (s) < a - x_l s$ for $s < s'$. Therefore we put $s' = \hat{s}$. This completes the proof of the sufficiency part.

Necessity: Suppose, the statement of lemma 1 (iii) b) holds except that $E_a (a, \alpha) > > f' (x_l)$. Then $E_a (a - x_l s, \alpha) \geqslant R_a (x_l s, s) = f' (x_l)$ for every $s \in [0, a/x_l]$ where the inequality sign holds for $s \neq 0$. It follows that $E_a > R_a$ also holds for $s \in (0, a/x_l]$ if the maximizing problem (1) is solved. Thus one obtains $\lambda > 0$ and $a_e = a - x_l s$ from (5) and (6) and therefore $x (s) = x_l$ for every $s \in (0, a/x_l)$. This contradiction proves the necessity part.

(iv) a) Suppose $x (s^*) > x_l$. Then $(a - a_e, s^*) \in \text{int } D_r$ and $R_s > 0$ evaluated at $(a - a_e, s^*)$ by ARii. But due to $R_s > 0$ for every $s^{**} \in (s^*, a/x_l]$ we have $R (a - a_e, s^{**}) > R (a - a_e, s^*)$. This contradicts the presupposition that s maximizes M on $[0, a/x_l]$.

b) From lemma 1 (iv) a), $s = (a - a_e)/x_l$ is a necessary condition for a maximum. For analytical convenience it is therefore possible to replace the function R by $\hat{R}: R_+ \to R_+$ such that $\hat{R} (a - a_e) := R [a - a_e, (a - a_e)/x_l]$. Hence it suffices to look for a maximum of $E(a_e, \alpha) + \hat{R}(a - a_e)$ on $[0, a]$. Under AR and AE, necessary and sufficient for a solution of this problem are the Kuhn-Tucker conditions stemming from the Lagrangean $L = E(a_e, \alpha) + \hat{R}(a - e_e) + \beta(a - a_e)$. In particular, one obtains

$$E_a - \hat{R}_a - \beta \leqslant 0 \text{ and } a_e(E_a - \hat{R}_a - \beta) = 0, \tag{8}$$

$$a - a_e \geqslant 0 \text{ and } \beta(a - a_e) = 0. \tag{9}$$

We recall that $x(s^*) = x_l$ (lemma 1 (iv) a)) implies $R_s = 0$ by ARii and hence $\hat{R}_a = R_a + (R_s/x_l) = R_a$. The rest of the proof of lemma 1 (iv) b) is straightforward.

(v) It follows from lemma 1 (iii) b) that $x(\alpha) > x_l$ implies $E_a[a_e(\alpha), \alpha] = R_a[a - a_e(\alpha), s]$ in (5). Differentiation of this condition with respect to α yields $(da_e(\alpha))/(d\alpha) = E_a/(E_{aa} + R_{aa}) < 0$. Hence $\{\partial R[a - a_e(\alpha), s]\}/(\partial\alpha) > 0$, whereas $M_\alpha = E_\alpha[a_e(\alpha), \alpha] < 0$ by lemma 1 (ii). This proves the first part of lemma 1 (iv). The second part follows obviously from $(da_e(\alpha)/d\alpha) < 0$ and $(dx(\alpha)/d\alpha) = -(da_e(\alpha)/d\alpha) s$.

q.e.d.

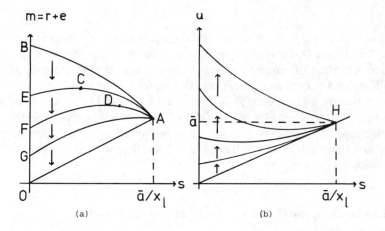

Fig. 1

Figures 1a) and 1b) illustrate some properties of function M, as exhibited by lemma 1. Fig. 1a) shows maximum material output m for constant $a = \bar{a}$, for variable s and under parametric changes of α. Assigning α_0 to the contour line BA in fig. 1a, α_1 to ECA and α_2 to FDA etc., one obtains $\alpha_0 < \alpha_1 < \alpha_2$ etc. Hence it is easy to see, that maximal material output for $\alpha = \alpha_0$ occurs at point B, i.e. by extraction only. Increasing α implies, however, that maximum material output is successively shifted toward recycling, as indicated by the points C, D and A in fig. 1. There is always $\hat{\alpha} \in [0, \bar{\alpha}]$ large enough such that recycling dominates extraction for all $\alpha > \hat{\alpha}$. Fig 1b) illustrates a class of material isoquants associated to the function M. All these isoquants represent the same material output $M(\bar{a}, \bar{a}/x_l, \alpha = 0)$ for different values of α, and they shift upward as α increases while keeping H in fig. 1b) as their rotating point.

A different way to illustrate the effects of an upward shifting of α is provided by fig. 2. If we attach the values $O_e O_r = a$, $O_r A = O_e B = f'(x_l)$, $E_a(a, \alpha_0) = C_0$, and $E_a(0, \alpha_0) = D_0$ in fig. 2, then it is clear from lemma 1 (iv) and from fig. 2 that $s^* = 0$

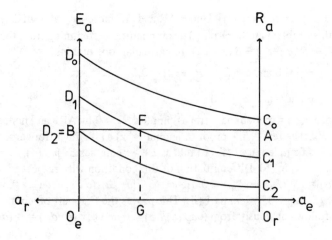

Fig. 2

maximizes M on $[0, a/x_l]$ for given $a > 0$ and $\alpha = \alpha_0$. In case of an exogenous increase $\alpha_1 - \alpha_0 > 0$ the line $D_0 C_0$ moves downward to some line $D_1 C_1$, because $E_{a\alpha} < 0$ is implied by AE. Since AB remains unchanged due to lemma 1(iv) a), the point of intersection F represents the maximum of M on $[0, a/x_l]$ for given $a > 0$ and α.

If we denote the maximizer by s^* (as in lemma 1 (iv)) then fig. 2 is linked to lemma 1 (iv) by $a_e (s^*) = O_e G$ and $s^* = (a - a_e (s^*))/x_l > 0$. It follows immediately that with further increases of α the intersection point F moves toward B in fig. 2. There is some $\alpha_2 > \alpha_1$ such that $C_2 D_2$ is the graph of $E_a (., \alpha_2)$, and lemma 1 (iv) implies $a_e (s^*) = 0$ and $s^* = a/x_l$ for every $\alpha \geq \alpha_2$.

3. Optimal Intertemporal Choice between Extraction and Recycling

3.1 The Problem and Some Principle Properties of Its Solution

In this section we wish to investigate the optimal time path of labour input flows and material output flows from extraction and recycling in the subsequent very simple model: We assume that in a continuous time framework the total instant labour supply at time (or moment) t is exogenously fixed at[8]) $a_t = a$ for all $t \geq 0$. The objective is to maximize the intergral of the discounted material flows from extraction and recycling subject to a number of constraints. In addition to the labour supply constraint and the technological constraints already introduced before we assume that the (in-)efficiency parameter α in the extraction technology increases at a rate determined by the flow of extracted material.

More specifically, we assume $\alpha_t = \int_0^t e_\tau d\tau$ which implies

$$\dot{\alpha} = e. \tag{10}$$

The next important step is to close the material cycle. We think of material as an essential input (intermediary good) for the production of some consumption good. It is known from material balance considerations that all material once used as input is contained in some waste products – called secondary material – that is generated in the course or at the end of consumption and production processes. Suppose for simplicity that secondary material arises instantaneously in the sense that all material being produced and used as input at some point of time is completely turned to secondary material in the same moment. Suppose further, that the secondary material is homogeneous, i.e. it has a fixed material content which we denote $b > 0$. Then the flow of secondary material stemming from a flow m of material is bm. By definition of b it must be true that $b R (a_r, s) - s \leqslant 0$, since one cannot regain more material from secondary material than is contained in the latter. The strict inequality sign is probably the empirically relevant assumption for most types of materials. Hence we introduce the assumption

$$b R (a_r, s) - s < 0. \tag{11}$$

We further assume that secondary material can be piled up for later use in the recycling activity. The stock of secondary material is denoted β and thus we have

$$\dot{\beta} = b (e + r) - s. \tag{12}$$

Note that $\dot{\beta}$ is unrestricted in sign as long as $\beta > 0$. But

$$\dot{\beta} \geqslant 0, \text{ if } \beta = 0. \tag{13}$$

In summary, we wish to investigate the properties of a solution to the problem of maximizing

$$\int_0^\infty e^{-\delta t} (r + e) \, dt \tag{14}$$

subject to (10) to (13) and subject to

$$r = R (a - a_e, s), \tag{15}$$

$$e = E (a_e, \alpha), \tag{16}$$

$$a - a_e \geqslant 0, \tag{17}$$

$$\alpha (0) = 0, \beta (0) \geqslant 0, \tag{18}$$

where $\delta \geqslant 0$ is a time independent discount rate.

An issue of major interest is the intertemporal profil of the labour intensity $x := a_r/s$ in the recycling activity on the optimal time path associated to this dynamic programming problem.

Lemma 2: Suppose there is a solution to maximizing (14) subject to (10) – (13) and (15) – (18). Then $\delta = 0$ implies $x = x_u$ for all t.

Proof: For an infinite time horizon and for $\delta = 0$ the problem of maximizing (14) subject to (10) – (13) and (15) – (18) is equivalent to the problem of determining the maximum material output from extraction and from repeated recycling without any labour supply constraint. Suppose that in the first time interval no recycling takes place but only extraction, and that extraction is continued until the existing reserves are completely exhausted. (10) and (18) imply that $\bar{\alpha}$ is the maximum amount of material that can be extracted from the reserves. Hence $B := b\bar{\alpha} + \beta(0)$ is the overall amount of secondary material available for recycling. Recycling with labour intensity x yields $f(x) B$ units of material, where $f(x) := R(x, 1)/s$ as derived in subsection 2.1.

When these $f(x) B$ units of material have been consumed, they generate, in turn, $bf(x) B$ units of secondary material etc. Thus the maximum overall amount $\hat{M}(x)$ of material is determined by the sum of the following geometric series:

$$\hat{M}(x) = B(1 + f(x)) + f(x) B [bf(x) + b^2 f(x)^2 + \ldots]$$

$$= B(1 + f(x)) + (\sum_{n=1}^{\infty} bf(x)^n) f(x) B$$

$$= B(1 + f(x)) + \frac{f(x) B}{1 - bf(x)}.$$

Since (11) and AR imply $1 - bf(x) > 0$ for all feasible x it is easy to see that $\hat{M}(x) > 0$ and $(d\hat{M}(x)/dx) > 0$ which proves lemma 2. q.e.d.

Lemma 2 tells us that if $x < x_u$ is optimal then this result is due ot $\delta > 0$, that is, the society's time preference (or "intertemporal impatience").

The next step is to investigate the properties of the intertemporal allocation problem in more detail. Associated to the problem of maximizing (14) subject to (10) – (13) and (15) – (18) is the Hamiltonian[9])

$$H = R(a - a_e, s) + E(a_e, \alpha) + pE(a_e, \alpha) + q[b(R(a - a_e, s) + E(a_e, \alpha)) - s](19)$$

and the Lagrangean

$$L = H + \lambda[b(R(a - a_e, s) + E(a_e, \alpha)) - s] + \lambda_a^1 (a - a_e). \tag{20}$$

Along the optimal trajectory the following conditions must be satisfied:

$$(1 + v) E_a - R_a - \lambda_a^1/z \leqslant 0, [= 0, \text{ if } a_e > 0], \tag{21}$$

$$q \geqslant zR_s - \lambda = \frac{R_s}{1 - bR_s} - \lambda, [= 0, \text{ if } s > 0], \tag{22}$$

$$\dot{p} = -(1 + v) E_\alpha, \tag{23}$$

$$\dot{q} = 0, \text{ except at junction times}, \tag{24}$$

where $z := 1 + b(q + \lambda)$ and $v := p/z$.

In addition, one obtains

$$(1 + v) E_a - R_a - \lambda_a^2 \geqslant 0, [= 0, \text{ if } a_r > 0], \tag{25}$$

---

[9]) For the solution to our control problem we refer to Guinn's theorem, as stated e.g. in *Long/ Vousden* [1977]. A similar application of this theorem can be found in *Kemp/Long* [1980]. We do not investigate here sufficiency conditions for the existence of a solution.

if $\lambda_a^1 \, (a - a_e)$ in (20) is substituted by $\lambda_a^2 \, (a - a_r)$ and if a_e is substituted by $a - a_r$ everywhere else in (20) and (19). It is obvious that this substitution does not change the problem at hand.

Furthermore,

$$\lambda_a^1 \geqslant 0, [= 0, \text{ if } a - a_e > 0],\tag{26}$$
$$\lambda_a^2 \geqslant 0, [= 0, \text{ if } a - a_r > 0],$$

and also[10])

$$\lambda \geqslant 0, [= 0, \text{ if } \beta > 0],$$
$$\dot\lambda \leqslant 0.\tag{27}$$

From (21), (25) and (26) it is obvious that

$$(1 + v) E_a \begin{Bmatrix} \geqslant \\ = \\ < \end{Bmatrix} R_a \Rightarrow a_r \begin{Bmatrix} \equiv 0 \\ \in \\ = a \end{Bmatrix} [0, a],\tag{28}$$

$$a_r \begin{Bmatrix} \equiv 0 \\ \in \\ = a \end{Bmatrix} (0, a) \Rightarrow (1 + v) E_a \begin{Bmatrix} \geqslant \\ = \\ < \end{Bmatrix} R_a.\tag{29}$$

3.2 Positive Stock of Secondary Material

In this section we study the optimal trajectory during a time interval in which $\beta > 0$ and hence $\lambda = 0$ by (27). For convenience we introduce the notation

$$T(\beta) := \{t \geqslant 0 \mid \beta(t) > 0\},$$
$$T(r) := \{t \in T(\beta) \mid r(t) > 0\}.$$

First we wish to give a sufficient condition for $e > 0$. For that purpose we consider the maximal values of R_a and E_a that are feasible at t, i.e.

$$R_a^0 := R_a(x_l s, s) \quad (\text{some } s > 0),$$
$$E_a^0(t) := E_a(0, \alpha_t).\tag{30}$$

Lemma 3: For $t \in T(\beta)$: $E_a^0(t) > R_a^0$ implies

(i) $e(t) > 0$ and
(ii) $v(t) \geqslant -1$.

Proof: (i) Suppose $a_e = 0$. Then $(1 + v) E_a \leqslant R_a$ by (28), where $E_a = E_a(0, \alpha_t) = E_a^0(t)$. Since $R_a \leqslant R_a^0$ and since $E_a^0(t) > R_a^0$ by assumption we have $E_a > R_a$. We further observe that if $a_e = 0$ is optimal at $t \in T(\beta)$, it is also optimal for every $t' > t$, $t' \in T(\beta)$. Consider the equation

$$\dot m = (E_a - R_a)\dot a_e + eE_\alpha + R_s \dot s\tag{31}$$

obtained from differentiation of $m = e + r$, and suppose that, in t, $\dot m^*$, $\dot a_e^*$ and $\dot s^*$ are the optimal values (given $\dot a_e^* = e^* = 0$). Using (31) it must then be true that $\dot m^* = R_s \dot s^* \geqslant$

---

[10]) These conditions stem from Guinn's theorem. See also (2) and (3) in *Kemp/Long* [1980].

$\geq (E_a - R_a)\dot{a}_e + R_s s^*$ for all $\dot{a}_e > 0$. But this inequality does not hold for $\dot{a}_e > 0$ since we showed $E_a > R_a$. This contradiction proves $a_e > 0$ and hence $e > 0$.

(ii) Suppose that $v < -1$. Then $(1 + v) E_a < R_a$ and $a_r = a$ by (28). But $e > 0$ by lemma 3 (i). Contradiction.

q.e.d.

If $\beta(0) > 0$, it is conceivable (and could not be excluded) that $e = 0$ for all t where $\beta(t) > 0$. But on the other hand it is evident that $\emptyset \neq T(r) \subset T(\beta)$, whenever $T(\beta)$ is non-empty. Moreover, it is also true that $x(t) = x(t')$, $x(t) \in [x_l, x_u]$, for every $t, t' \in T(r)$. In order to see this we observe that for $r > 0$ (22) holds as an equality and thus can be rewritten as $R_s = q/(1 + qb)$ for $\lambda = 0$. Since $\dot{q} = 0$ by (24) we obtain $R_s(t) = R_s(t')$ for all $t \in T(r)$ which implies $x(t) = x(t')$ by ARi.

This result may be considered to be rather unexpected since one might argue that de-creasing material in situ and a decreasing secondary material inventory when combined with constant labour supply flows should make it optimal to increase the labour intens-ity in recycling. *Kemp/Long* [1980] show in a similar model, after all, that $\dot{x} > 0$ at $r > 0$ holds for a profit maximizing firm. Given this contrast, one would also like to know more about the value of the constant $x \in [x_u, x_l]$ in the present model. But apparently x can take any value in this domain. From (21) we only learn that $x > x_l$ iff $q > 0$, but conditions for $q > 0$ could not be found.[11])

Consider $x = x_u$ as a polar case that occurs according to lemma 2, if $\delta = 0$. If, in addi-tion $r > 0$ and $e > 0$, by (29) we then have $(1 + v) E_a = R_a$. Furthermore, $x = x_u$ implies $R_a(x) = 0$ by ARi and hence $v = -1$. Also $\dot{p} = \dot{v} = 0$ from (23) and hence $v(t) = -1$ for every subsequent t in $T(\beta)$. In this case it is not clear how the optimal production mix between extraction and production develops in time.

Some information about the case $x < x_u$ is summarized in

Lemma 4: Suppose that $x(t) < x_u$ for $t \in T(r)$ on an optimal trajectory.

(i) $E_a^0(t) = R_a(x(t))$ implies $v(t) \leq 0$ and $e(t) = 0$

(ii) If $E_a^0(\bar{t}) > R_a^0$, then there is $t' > \bar{t}$ such that $v(t)$ is strictly increasing on $[\bar{t}, t']$. If t' satisfies $E_a^0(t') = R_a^0$, then $e(t') = 0$ and $v(t') = 0$, if $x(\bar{t}) = x_l$, and $v(t') < 0$ otherwise.

Proof: (i) $E_a^0 = R_a$ implies $E_a(a - a_r, \alpha) - R_a < 0$ for every $a_r \in [0, a]$.

a) Suppose $v \leq 0$ and $a_r < a$. Then $E_a < R_a$, $(1 + v) E_a < R_a$, and $a_r = a$ by (28), which contradicts our presupposition $a_r < a$. Hence lemma 3 (i) is shown, if "$v > 0$ and $a_r \leq a$" can be excluded.

b) Suppose now, that $v > 0$ and $a_r = a$, and let $(1 + v) E_a < R_a$. (28) shows, in fact, that $(1 + v) E_a < R_a$ implies $a_r = a$, but $v > 0$ and $(1 + v) E_a^0 < R_a^0$ also yield $E_a^0 < R_a^0$, which establishes a contradiction, since we presupposed $E_a^0 = R_a^0$. Therefore we next consider $v > 0$, $a_r = a$ and $(1 + v) E_a = R_a$. But from $v > 0$ we then have $E_a < R_a$ and compatibility with $E_a^0 = R_a^0$ requires $a_r \in [0, a)$. Contradiction. Let finally $(1 + v) E_a > R_a$. Then $a_r = 0$ by (28) and $E_a < R_a$, which again contradicts $a_r = a$.

The above arguments showed that contradictions can only be avoided, if

---

[11]) Since the auxiliary variable q measures the marginal contribution of the state variable β to the objective functional [see *Arrow*, 1968, p. 88] we conjecture that $q > 0$ for $\beta > 0$ and $q = 0$ for $\beta = 0$.

$[v > 0, a_r < a$ and $(1 + v) E_a \geqslant R_a]$, and that such a situation implies $E_a < R_a$. But from the total differential of (12),

$$d\dot{\beta} = (R_a - E_a) b da_r - (1 - bR_s) ds, \tag{32}$$

we observe that $da_r > 0$ and $ds = 0$ increase $e + r$ as well as $\dot{\beta}$ and decrease $\dot{\alpha}$, if $E_a < R_a$. Hence all feasible paths satisfying $r > 0$ and $a_r < a$ are suboptimal. This proves lemma 4 (i).

(ii) We first observe that lemma 3 applies for $t = \bar{t}$ under the presupposition of lemma 4 (ii). Suppose that $v(\bar{t}) = -1$. Since $R_a(x(\bar{t})) > R_a(x_u) = 0$, $v = -1$ yields $(1 + v) E_a = 0 < R_a$ and $e = 0$ by (28). But $e > 0$ by lemma 3 (i). Hence from this contradiction one obtains $v(\bar{t}) > -1$ and $\dot{p} = \dot{v} > 0$ by (23) and (24). Clearly, $E_a^0(t)$ diminishes during some time interval following $\bar{t}$ as long as $E_a^0(t) > R_a^0$ since this inequality implies $e(t) > 0$ by lemma 3 (i). We denote the supremum element in $T(\beta)$ by t_β and by t_1 the first point of time where $E_a^0(t_1) = R_a^0$ is satisfied on the optimal trajectory. Define $t' = \min [t_\beta, t_1]$. If $t' = t_1$ then lemma 4 (i) applies, and it remains to determine the sign of $v(t')$. Suppose first that $v(t') < 0$ when $x(\bar{t}) = x_l$. Then $R_a(x_l) = R_a^0$. Since $E_a(t') = E_a^0(t')$ (because $a_e(t') = 0$) one obtains $E_a(1 + v) < R_a$ at t'. By continuity of α and v there exists some $t_2 < t'$ such that for every $t \in [t_2, t')$ one has $E_a^0(t) > R_a^0$ but $E_a(1 + v) < R_a$. The last inequality requires $e = 0$ by (28) whereas $e > 0$ follows from $E_a^0(t) > x_l$. Then $R_a(x(\bar{t})) < R_a^0$ but $E_a(t') = E_a^0(t')$. Hence $E_a(1 + v) > R_a$ at t' which requires $r(t') = 0$ by (28). Contradiction.   q.e.d.

Lemma 4 provides only partial insight into the characteristics of the optimal trajectory. In the cases that are covered by this lemma $v(t)$ and hence $p(t)$ turned out to be non-positive. With negative p the allocation is biased toward recycling as compared to myopic (one period) material output maximization. Suppose, that it is intertemporally optimal, to start with extraction only. Then the optimal path requires a mix of extraction and recycling even though the instantaneous material output maximum would be attained if the extraction technology is used exclusively. Figure 2 illustates this case if for some t the line $C_0 D_0$ is supposed to be the graph of $E_a(a_e, \alpha_t)$, if $R_a := R_a[a - a_e, (a - a_e)/x] = = f'(x)$ is given by $O_e B = O_r A$ and if $|v| = C_0 C_1 = D_0 D_1$. Then the optimality condition $(1 + v) E_a = R_a$ is satisfied at point F in fig. 2 which implies $R_a[a - a_e^F, (a - a_e^F)/x] > > 0, a_e^F = O_e G$. At the same time we have $E_a(a, \alpha_t) > R_a$ which implies $s^* = 0$ and $a_e(s^*) = a$ in lemma 1 (iv).

In the case of lemma 4 (ii) it would be interesting to know whether the extraction activity is continuously reduced during this time period. Since $a_e \in (0, a)$ implies $(1 + v) E_a = R_a$ we may differentiate this equation with respect to time and obtain

$$\dot{a}_e = - \frac{(1 + v) [eE_{a\alpha} - E_a E_\alpha]}{R_{aa} + (1 + v) E_{aa}} \gtrless 0 \Leftrightarrow eE_a \gtrless E_a E_\alpha,$$

if AE, AR and $v \in (-1, 0]$ is considered. Hence $\dot{a}_e > 0$ cannot be ruled out.

3.3 Zero Stock of Secondary Material

We now suppose that $\beta(t) = 0$ at time t on the optimal time path. Then we know from (11), (12) and (13) that $e(t) > 0$ is a necessary condition for $m(t) > 0$. Hence extraction will take place (at $\beta = 0$) as long as $E_a > 0$ for some $a_e \in [0, a]$, that is (by AE) as long as $\alpha < \bar{\alpha}$. It is also clear that recycling will take place (at $\beta = 0$) as long as $e > 0$ since secondary material would be wasted otherwise. Suppose now that there is a non-degenerate time interval characterized by $\beta = 0$. Then $\dot{\beta} = 0$ and $\ddot{\beta} = 0$ or, equivalently,

$$b (E_a - R_a) \dot{a}_e - (1 - bR_s) \dot{s} = - ebE_\alpha > 0. \tag{33}$$

We consider $\dot{s} = - (s\dot{x} + \dot{a}_e)/x$ and $f(x)/x = R_a(x) + R_s(x)/x$ to obtain

$$\dot{a}_e = - \frac{exbE_\alpha + (1 - bR_s) s\dot{x}}{xbE_a + (1 - bf(x))} \tag{34}$$

and

$$\dot{s} = \frac{b [s (R_a - E_a) \dot{x} + eE_\alpha]}{xbE_a + (1 - bf(x))}. \tag{35}$$

Note that (11) and AR imply $(1 - bf(x)) > 0$ and $(1 - bR_s(x)) = (1 - b(f(x) - xf'(x)) \geq 0$ for every $x \in [x_l, x_u]$. Therefore $\dot{x} \leq 0$ is sufficient for $\dot{a}_e > 0$ in (34).

Lemma 5: $\dot{x} \leq 0$ if $\beta = 0$ and $\dot{\beta} = 0$.

Proof: Since $s > 0$, (22) holds as an equality. Therefore (24) requires that the derivative with respect to time of the righthand side of (22) is zero. We consider $R_s(x) := f(x) - xf'(x)$ and obtain

$$\dot{\lambda} = - zxf''(x) \dot{x} \tag{36}$$

or sign $\dot{\lambda} =$ sign $\dot{x}$. Thus $\dot{x} \leq 0$ by (27).   q.e.d.

$\dot{x} \leq 0$ from lemma 5 when combined with (32) rigorously confirms that $\dot{a}_e > 0$ and hence $r > 0$ and $e > 0$ if and only if $E_\alpha < 0$, i.e. as long as $\alpha < \bar{\alpha}$.

It is also interesting to know whether $\dot{x} < 0$ can be expected to be optimal. Even though a conclusive argument for that case could not be provided, we wish to indicate the basic allocative principle underlying the choice between $\dot{x} = 0$ and $\dot{x} < 0$. For that purpose consider a time path characterized by $x^* < x_u$ and $\dot{x}^* = 0$ associated with $\dot{a}_e^* > 0$ and $\dot{s}^* < 0$ from (34) and (35), respectively, from some point of time until $\alpha = \bar{\alpha}$. Then we know from AE that $\lim_{\alpha \to \bar{\alpha}} E_a = 0$ and hence $R_a - E_a > 0$ for

sufficiently large t'. If at $t \geq t'$ one deviates from that path by choosing $\dot{x}' < 0$, we obtain $\dot{s}' > \dot{s}^*$ by (35) and $\dot{a}_e' > \dot{a}_e^*$ by (34). Since $m = s/b$ by (12) in t it follows that $\dot{m}' - \dot{m}^* = (1/b)(\dot{s}' - \dot{s}^*) > 0$. Hence a decline in x provides a temporary increase in m relative to the time path with constant x. But this temporary increase is necessarily overcompensated by later decreases in material production, if the discount rate is disregarded. It can be argued, therefore, that if $\dot{x} < 0$ is optimal this is due to a positive discount rate in the objective functional (14) that puts higher weights to faster or earlier material provision and underrates later decreases in supply.

Suppose finally that there is a non-degenerate interval with $\beta = 0$ and that $p \leq 0$ throughout this interval. Then $x(t) = x_l$ for all t or $x(t)$ monotonically decreases toward

x_l in time. If, on the contrary, $x(t) > x_l$ were constant over time then $(1 + v) E_a < R_a$ with $E_a > 0$ could not be excluded for sufficiently large t and thus $e(t) = 0$ by (28). But then $m(t) = 0$ even though further extraction would yield additional output.

4. Summarizing Remarks

Recycling of depletable natural resources had long been recognized as an important device of resource conservation. It is treated in this paper as an alternative (and competitive) technology to virgin material production, i.e. to extraction of natural resources from reserves. Consequently, there are two sets of relevant questions: (1) Under which conditions should recycling take place in addition to or instead of extraction? (2) To which extend and with which "intensity" should the recycling activity be carried out? The analytical model that is constructed to answer these questions considers decreasing productivity of extraction as well as variable labour intensity in recycling.

For a better understanding of the interaction of recycling and extraction it is therefore convenient (and non-trivial) as a first step to study the characteristics of an efficient mix between extraction and recycling in a static framework. We show that both technologies can be integrated to form a "well-behaved" joint production function which defines a unique production mix for every point of its domain. There are several interesting results: If the inputs of labour and secondary material in the recycling process are fixed, then the labour intensity of recycling is below its maximum value and its moves toward its minimum, if the input of secondary material increases ceteris paribus. Moreover, if secondary material is not limited in supply, then recycling (extraction) does not take place at all if it is "dominated" by extraction (recycling) or — alternatively — there is no clear domination in which case both technologies are applied. Whenever recycling is active the respective labour intensity is minimal, i.e. a considerable amount of material is not reclaimed from secondary material. We investigate also the effects of (parametrically) decreasing labour productivity in extraction on the optimal production mix. In accordance with one's intuition, the production mix shifts towards recycling and the labour intensity of recycling increases until recycling dominates extraction.

As to the intertemporal interaction of extraction and recycling we were not able to achieve a complete characterization of the optimal trajectory of the corresponding control problem. The major positive results are that the labour intensity in recycling attains its maximum value at all points of time, if the discount rate is zero, and that the labour intensity is constant or non-increasing otherwise. In view of the results in the static analysis our conjecture is that labour intensity will be maximal along the optimal time path also for positive discount rates. Another important implication for optimal intertemporal allocation is due to the assumption that the productivity of the extraction process decreases with increasing accumulative past extraction output. On an optimal path this future burden of present (and past) extraction must be adequately reflected which leads to a bias toward recycling as compared to myopic static material output maximization.

80

References

Arrow, K.J.: Applications of Control Theory to Economic Growth. Mathematics of the Decision Sciences. Ed. by Dantzig and Veinott. Providence 1968, 85–119.

Fisher, A.C., and *F.M. Peterson*: The Exploitation of Extractive Resources: A Survey. Economic Journal 87, 1977, 681–721.

Hoel, M.: Resource Extraction and Recycling with Environmental Costs. Journal of Environmental Economics and Management 5, 1978, 220–235.

Jaeger, K.: Ansätze zu einer ökonomischen Theorie des Recyclings. Erschöpfbare Ressourcen. Ed. by H. Siebert. Berlin 1980, 149–182.

Kemp, M., and *N.V. Long*: The Firm As Resource-Farmer. Exhaustible Resources, Optimality and Trade. Ed. by M.C. Kemp and N.V. Long. Amsterdam 1980, 19–29.

Long, N.V., and *N.Vousden*: Optimal Control Theorems. Applications of Control Theory to Economic Analysis. Ed. by J.D. Pitchford and S.J. Turnowsky. Amsterdam 1977, 11–34.

Pearce, D.W., and *I. Walter* (eds.): Resource Conservation: Social and Economic Dimensions of Recycling. New York 1977.

Pethig, R.: Trade in Secondary Material: A Theoretical Approach. Resource Conservation: Social and Economic Dimensions of Recycling. Ed. by D.W. Pearce and I. Walter. New York 1977, 353–383.

–: Umweltökonomische Allokation mit Emissionssteuern. Tübingen 1979.

Siebert, H. et al.: Trade and Environment: A Theoretical Inquiry. Amsterdam 1980.

Vogt, W.: Zur intertemporal wohlfahrtsoptimalen Nutzung knapper natürlicher Resourcen. Tübingen, 1981.

Economic Theory of Natural Resources. ©Physica-Verlag, Würzburg–Wien, 1982.

A Note on Resource Use, Substitute Production, and Governmental Intervention

Florian Sauter-Servaes

Resource markets have traditionally been a wide field for governmental activities. Except for some notable contributions, for instance by *Burness* [1976], *Sweeney* [1977] and by *Dasgupta/Heal* [1979], the effects of such interventions on the intertemporal allocation of an exhaustible nonrenewable resource have not been examined in the literature. Furthermore, the analysis has been restricted to the pure theory of exhaustion, where there is no substitute for the resource.

In this paper an attempt will be made to analyse the question of how governmental interventions will influence the transition from an exhaustible nonrenewable resource to a substitute that can be produced by means of a backstop technology.

Three different kinds of governmental intervention will be taken into consideration: (1) The imposition of a sales tax on the resource, (2) subsidies for the substitute, and (3) the imposition of a minimum price for the resource. As reference case we will use the price and quantity paths in competitive equilibrium without governmental actions. So let us first review those briefly.

Consider an exhaustible resource whose finite stock is known and can be extracted at no cost. The size of this stock will be denoted with S, the rate of extraction of the resource at time t with x_t, and the price at which the resource is sold at time t with p_t. If the market rate of interest is $r > 0$, then the fundamental principle of the economics of exhaustible resources, the Hotelling Rule, tells us that in competitive equilibrium the price of the resource must rise at the market rate of interest, i.e.

$$\frac{\dot{p}_t}{p_t} = r. \tag{1}$$

Now we assume the existence of a so called backstop technology that allows the production of a perfect substitute for the exhaustible resource in unlimited quantities at constant unit costs $\bar{p}$. We further assume that the substitute is competitively supplied, i.e. nobody holds a patent for the backstop technology.

In this situation the Hotelling Rule still applies except for one modification. In competitive equilibrium the price of the resource must rise at the market rate of interest as long as the resource has not been exhausted; however, there is now a ceiling for the resource price. If it rises above $\bar{p}$ (the competitive price for the substitute), the substitute will take over the market and the resource cannot be sold any longer. Thus, in competitive equilibrium the resource stock must be exhausted just in that point of time T, when the resource price reaches the level $\bar{p}$. In order to insure this, the initial price of the resource p_0 must be set properly. The resulting price path for a competitive equilibrium is depicted in Figure 1. It is easy to see that the cumulated discounted profit derived from the resource stock amounts to $p_0 \cdot S$.

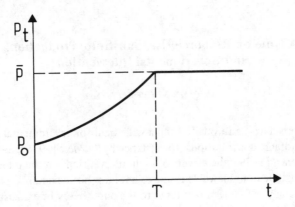

Fig. 1

All this is well known and has been stated in greater detail for instance by *Nordhaus* [1973] and *Dasgupta/Stiglitz* [1976].

The purpose of this paper is to demonstrate the effects of governmental interventions in the resource market. Taxation, price regulations, and subsidies are the most common governmental actions with respect to resource markets.

Let us first consider the effects of a sales tax on the resource. We assume that no direct governmental action is taken towards the substitute. If we denote the sales tax per unit of resource at time t with θ_t and remember that the resource extraction is cost-less, we see that the price of the resource splits into two parts, the so called scarcity rent π_t and the sales tax θ_t; that is

$$p'_t = \pi_t + \theta_t. \quad [1)$$

(2)

In our first case without taxation, price and scarcity rent were, of course, identical. Now the Hotelling Rule for a competitive equilibrium requires that the scarcity rent rise at the market rate of interest. Therefore in competitive equilibrium we have

$$\frac{\dot{p'_t}}{p'_t} = \frac{\dot{\pi}_t}{\pi_t} \cdot \frac{\pi_t}{\pi_t + \theta_t} + \frac{\dot{\theta}_t}{\theta_t} \cdot \frac{\theta_t}{\pi_t + \theta_t}$$

$$= r \cdot \frac{\pi_t}{\pi_t + \theta_t} + \frac{\dot{\theta}_t}{\theta_t} \cdot \frac{\theta_t}{\pi_t + \theta_t},$$

(3)

and we see that the price path in competitive equilibrium is not altered by taxation, if the sales tax θ_t increases at the rate r. For then (3) implies

$$\frac{\dot{p'_t}}{p'_t} = r \cdot \frac{\pi_t}{\pi_t + \theta_t} + r \cdot \frac{\theta_t}{\pi_t + \theta_t} = r,$$

(4)

---

[1]) p'_t denotes the resource price with taxation in contrast to the resource price without taxation, p_t.

which in turn makes it necessary that $p'_0 = p_0$ (otherwise the resource stock would not be exhausted just at the moment when p'_t reaches $\bar{p}$).

This type of taxation reduces the cumulated discounted profit derived from the resource stock by $\theta_0 \cdot S$ and leaves $\pi_0 \cdot S = p_0 \cdot S - \theta_0 \cdot S$ to the resource owners. This shows that the tax is paid by the resource suppliers and cannot be charged to the consumers. Therefore an exponentially rising sales tax (at the rate r) can be viewed as a tax on the profits of the resource owners.

If the sales tax is constant in time, i.e. $\theta_t = \theta$ for all t, (3) reduces to

$$\frac{\dot{p}'_t}{p'_t} = r \cdot \frac{\pi_t}{\pi_t + \theta} < r, \tag{5}$$

which implies that the price of the resource increases at a slower rate than it does without taxation. For a better characterization of the price path p'_t we shall rule out some conceivable paths.

Assume $p'_0 \leqslant p_0$. Because of (5) this implies $p'_t < p_t$ for all $0 < t \leqslant T$. Assuming a regular demand function for the resource, we get $x'_t > x_t$ for all $0 < t \leqslant T$, implying

$$\int_0^T x'_t \, dt > \int_0^T x_t \, dt = S,$$

which is impossible. So we can state:

$$p'_0 > p_0. \tag{6}$$

Using a similar argument it can be shown that $p'_t \geqslant p_t$ for all $t \leqslant T$ would lead to a contradiction. Now we have sufficient information about the competitive equilibrium price path under the assumption of a constant sales tax θ to compare its graph with the price path in case of no taxation. This is done in Figure 2.

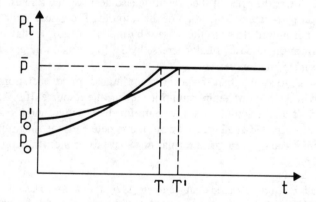

Fig. 2

Thus a constant sales tax implies that the resource price will initially be higher than without taxation for a certain length of time. Afterwards it will be lower until the resource is exhausted. The date of exhaustion is retarded by the constant sales tax (that

84

is $T' > T$); in this sense, the constant sales tax has a resource conserving effect.[2])

Furthermore we have $\pi_T = p'_T - \theta < p'_T < p_T = \bar{p}$ and therefore $\pi_0 < p_0$ because $\dot{\pi}_t/\pi_t = \dot{p}_t/p_t = r$. This implies that a constant sales tax decreases the cumulated discounted profit derived from the resource stock, so that at least part of the tax is not charged to the consumers.

At this point it should be noted that all these observations are independent of the size of the resource stock. The changes in resource extraction caused by governmental actions will always have the same characteristics no matter how large or small the resource stock is.[3])

As an alternative governmental intervention in the resource market, let us now analyse an indirect intervention that influences the resource extraction via subsidies of the substitute. We consider the simplest form of subsidy by supposing that it lowers the competitive price of the substitute from $\bar{p}$ to $\bar{\bar{p}} < \bar{p}$. It is easy to see (by means of indirect proof) that this subsidy changes the price path for the resource in competitive equilibrium as depicted in Figure 3.

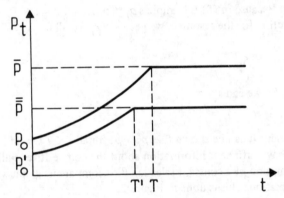

Fig. 3

Subsidies that lower the price of the substitute also decrease the resource price, which is equivalent to a higher rate of utilization of the resource. The date of exhaustion of the resource, T', is thus moved closer to the present by the subsidies. Cumulated discounted profits derived from the resource stock decrease by $S \cdot (p_0 - p'_0)$, whereas cumulated discounted consumers' rent increases.

Finally, we want to assume that the government imposes price regulations on the resource market in the form of a minimum price, $\underline{p}$, for the resource. If $\underline{p} \leqslant p_0$, there is, of course, no effect on the equilibrium price path for the resource, and if $\underline{p} \geqslant \bar{p}$, the resource will not be extracted at all, since it cannot compete with the substitute, which is assumed to be unaffected by the price regulation. So we can concentrate on the relevant case, $p_0 < \underline{p} < \bar{p}$.

---

[2]) Similar results have been obtained e.g. by *Burness* [1976] for the case, where there is no substitute for the resource. Yet the methods employed there yield no results, when we allow the existence of a backstop technology.

[3]) The validity of this statement as well as our entire analysis depends, of course, crucially on the assumption of constant extraction costs. But constant (or zero) extraction costs appear to be a good approximation in studying the transition from a cheap resource to a dear substitute.

As the government sets the minimum price $\underline{p}$, resource suppliers realize that the Hotelling equilibrium price path has become infeasible, because if the resource price increased at the market rate of interest, it would hit the substitute price, $\bar{p}$, before the resource stock had been depleted. Thus a resource deposit becomes a relatively unprofitable capital asset, and the resource owners try to sell it as fast as possible. This leads to an excess supply on the resource market, which keeps the resource price at its minimum level $\underline{p}$. [4]) There it remains until the resource stock has been reduced to a size $\underline{S}$ for which $\underline{p}$ is the initial price in intertemporal competitive equilibrium. From t_1 on, the resource price rises at the rate r. It reaches $\bar{p}$, just when the resource stock is exhausted. This price path is illustrated in Figure 4.

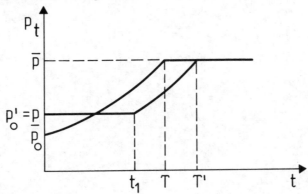

Fig. 4

In Figure 4 it can be seen that the imposition of a minimum price for the resource has effects similar to those implied by the imposition of a constant sales tax for the resource. Again the introduction of the substitute is retarded by the governmental action and the initial loss of consumers' rent caused by the higher price $\underline{p}$ is partly made up for by the lower price in the time interval (t_1, T').

References

Burness, H.S.: On the Taxation of Nonreplenishable Resources. Journal of Environmental Economics and Management **3**, 1976, 289–311.

Dasgupta, P., and *G.M. Heal*: Economic Theory and Exhaustible Resources. Cambridge 1979.

Dasgupta, P., and *J.E. Stiglitz*: Uncertainty and the Rate of Extraction under Alternative Institutional Arrangements. SEER Technical Report No. 8, Stanford University, 1976.

Hotelling, H.: The Economics of Exhaustible Resources. The Journal of Political Economy **39**, 1931, 137–175.

Nordhaus, W.D.: The Allocation of Energy Resources. Brookings Papers on Economic Activity **3**, 1973, 529–570.

Sauter-Servaes, F.: Der Übergang von einer erschöpfbaren Ressource zu einem synthetischen Substitut. Erschöpfbare Ressourcen. Ed. by H. Siebert, Berlin 1980.

Sweeney, J.L.: Economics of Depletable Resources: Market Forces and Intertemporal Bias. Review of Economic Studies **44**, 1977, 125–142.

---

[4]) We assume that the government successfully enforces the minimum price, without buying the excess supply.

Part II
Locational Aspects and Fishery

Economic Theory of Natural Resources. ©Physica-Verlag, Würzburg–Wien, 1982.

Locational Aspects of Resource Depletion

Martin J. Beckmann

1. Resource availability has a locational component which will be explored in this paper.

Economic history abounds with examples of regions and locations that at one time were rich sources of some mineral until the mines were depleted. In many cases depletion means that physically at some greater depths or in some lesser concentration the material is still available but at prevailing market prices set up by other sources of supply it is uneconomical to continue mining.

Such is the history of the famous Gold Rushes in California 1849, and in Alaska and Australia later that century. Only regions where wages are low enough such as South Africa and the Soviet Union continue to produce gold in significant quantities today.

It appears that many of the "Mittelgebirgs" location in Germany and Austria were at one point mining towns where copper, silber and lead were produced. All these mines have been exhausted but in many cases, unlike the gold mining camps that were abandoned, these places have continued their economic existence. The example of iron ore is illuminating here. Important sources were located at one time in the Siegerland and in the Bergische Land. While their economic importance has declined relatively, the activity levels of these regions have not fallen since the processing industries remained in spite of the disappearance of local sources. They now draw their raw material from elsewhere. The handicap of larger distances from sources of supply has been overcome by their proximity to product markets and by the preservation of traditions of technological know how.

What has happened over and over again is that the locations of active extraction have shifted for any particular resource, from places that were close to the general centers of economic activity — the world market — to locations more remote. Apparently this phenomenon will continue in the future.

In this paper we attempt to model this process of repeated relocation in a general way. Since problems of location have enough inherent richness and difficulty we must omit some features which are important enough in themselves but not essential to the relocation process as such. Among these is the aspect of uncertainty of future discoveries. We postulate that all sites are known, and that the costs of extraction, the feasible rates of extraction and the total amounts available at the various sites are also known. In fact at one point we shall assume that the field of a given ore extends continuously and without limit from a certain point on through a one-dimensional region. Such assumptions may seems strange, even heroic at first blush but the student of location theory must learn not to be timid. Each area of study has its own conventions to which the practicioner becomes used in due course, and a one-dimensional economy located on an unbounded line is one of the more esoteric conventions of location theory.

A second idea will be taken from Hotelling's famous analysis [*Hotelling*] of the economics of exhaustible resources. This is the idea of a utility function for resource consumption which makes it possible to adjust the economical rate of consumption to prevailing prices. A logarithmic utility function will serve for that purpose. Notice that in assigning utility to the resource itself we skip the intermediate processing activities that convert the natural resource, e.g. the natural ore into the final product that consumers demand. Also not treated explicitly is the possibility of partial or complete substitution by other inputs of the given resource material. All this is contained in the utility function which is a derived utility, derived from consumption and production to apply to the raw material, the ore itself.

2. Before introducing the specific model it is necessary to give a brief exposition of our principal locational tool, the continuous flow models of commodity, production, shipment and consumption . We consider the production and consumption activities to be dispersed continuously over two dimensional subsets of the Euclidean plane.

Let

$q(x_1, x_2)$ denote the area density of the consumption activity i.e. tons consumed per km^2 at location point (x_1, x_2)

$z(x_1, x_2)$ the density of production activity, i.e. tons produced per km^2 at location (x_1, x_2).

$\phi(x_1, x_2)$ the vector whose direction denotes that in which the commodity is shipped through point (x_1, x_2) and whose length denotes the quantity that passes through a unit cross section normal to the flow direction. This is measured in tons/km.

There is only one direction of movement of the commodity. This means that we assume that all uneconomical cross hauling has been eliminated by an effectively functioning spatial market in this commodity. The relationship between production, consumption, and shipment is now that of sources, sinks, and flow in a two dimenional continuous flow field. We can utilize the apparatus of mathematical physics developed for two dimensional flow of either heat or fluids to all of which the same law of conservation applies. The important fact for our purposes is that

excess supply = net outflow

$$z - q = \operatorname{div} \phi. \tag{1}$$

Here the div operator is defined by

$$\operatorname{div} \phi = \frac{\partial \phi_1}{\partial x_1} + \frac{\partial \phi_2}{\partial x_2}$$

where ϕ_i are the vector components of ϕ. This well known relationship (1) will not be discussed here. The reader is refered to e.g. *Courant/John* [1965].

If the region is selfcontained with regard to the commodity the boundary condition states that

$$\phi_n = 0 \qquad \text{on } \Gamma. \tag{2}$$

Here Γ denotes the boundary and n the direction of the normal to the boundary, pointing outward.

To determine the flow field additional relationships are necessary and these must be supplied by economic analysis — the physics of flow fields is of no further help.

If a competitive market exists, then there must be prices

$$p\,(x_1, x_2)$$

and these must govern the direction and extent of flow, as well as the intensities of production and consumption.

Now by a well-known argument from vector analysis

$$\text{grad } p$$

determines the direction of steepest increase of prices per unit distance. Here

$$\text{grad } p = \begin{pmatrix} \dfrac{\partial p}{\partial x_1} \\[2ex] \dfrac{\partial p}{\partial x_2} \end{pmatrix}$$

This is the direction in which shipments are most profitable. Compare the revenue $|\text{ grad } p\,|$ from a unit shipment in the gradient direction with its cost. Let this cost be independenent of the direction and given by

$$k = k\,(x_1, x_2).$$

Under conditions of competitive market equilibrium when all profits have been eliminated

$$|\text{ grad } p\,| = k.$$

Moreover flow must move in the most profitable direction

$$\text{grad } p = k\,\frac{\phi}{|\phi|}. \tag{3}$$

Here $\phi/|\phi|$ is the unit vector, indicating the direction of shipment.

In the theory of the Continuous Model of Transportation [*Beckmann*] it is shown that conditions (1), (2), and (3) suffice to determine the direction $\phi/|\phi|$ of the flow field uniquely. Moreover if

$$z\,(p) - q\,(p)$$

is a strictly monotone increasing function of p almost everywhere, then the prices $p\,(x_1, x_2)$ are also determined uniquely. What need not be unique is the quantity of flow $|\phi|$ as shown by examples from the discrete or ordinary transportation problem of linear programming. (The discrete model of transportation is contained in the continuous formulation as a special case.)

Sometimes the existence and mode of operations of a competitive market can be inferred from an underlying optimization problem, typically the maximizations of a consumers' and producers' surplus function. This is the path that we shall follow in the locational model of optimum resource extraction to be developed next.

3. At location (x_1, x_2) let there be a total $A(x_1, x_2)$ of the resource in the ground, but let the maximum feasible rate of extraction be $a(x_1, x_2)$. Thus if $z(x_1, x_2, t)$ is the rate of extraction at location (x_1, x_2) at time t one has two restrictions

$$z \leqq a \tag{4}$$

$$\int_0^t z(s) \, ds \leqq A. \tag{5}$$

With a planning horizon T one may restrict oneself to $t \leqq T$. The technology assumed is one of fixed coefficients. Thus the cost of extraction should depend only on location

$$c = c(x_1, x_2).$$

Presumably, the exhaustible resource will be converted at some point into consumable products which then generate utility. We may side-step this conversion and feed the resource directly into the utility functions

$$u = u(x_1, x_2, q)$$

where q is the rate of consumption (in the form of final products) of the exhaustible resource at location (x_1, x_2).

The cost of transportation will be treated as exogenous. With a flow ϕ at location (x_1, x_2) is associated a transportation cost

$$k(x_1, x_2) \, | \phi(x_1, x_2) |.$$

The welfare function to be optimized is thus a sum of utilities minus costs. Therefore utility must also be measured in money units.

$$W = \int_0^T \int_A \int u(x_1, x_2, q(x_1, x_2)) - k(x_1, x_2) \, | \phi(x_1, x_2) |$$

$$- c(x_1, x_2) z(x_1, x_2) \, dx_1 dx_2 \, dt.$$

In addition to the constraints on resource extraction we have the source-sink equation

$$\text{div } \phi(x_1, x_2) = z(x_1, x_2) - q(x_1, x_2).$$

Consider the Lagrangian

$$\int_0^T \int_A \int \{u - k \, |\phi| - cz\} + \lambda \, [z - q - \text{div } \phi]$$

$$+ \mu \, [a - z] + \nu(t) \, [A - \int_0^t z(s) \, ds] \, dx_1 dx_2 dt$$

$$= \int \int \int L \, dx_1 dx_2 \qquad \text{(say)}$$

where all variables except A and a depend on location (x_1, x_2) and on time t. For simplicity, we have not discounted future utilities and costs.

The efficiency conditions — the Kuhn-Tucker theorem extended to concave variational problems — as follows

$$q(x_1, x_2) \begin{Bmatrix} = \\ > \\ = \end{Bmatrix} 0 \Longleftrightarrow \frac{\partial u}{\partial q} \begin{Bmatrix} < \\ = \end{Bmatrix} \lambda(x_1, x_2, t). \tag{6}$$

Obviously λ is the price of the resource at location (x_1, x_2) and time t (if the resource is not shipped directly but after some transformation, then λ is the value of the resource content of this transformed good at location (x_1, x_2) and time t).

The condition states that consumption should not take place if marginal utility even at the zero level falls short of the resource price, and otherwise that marginal utility should be made equal to price. With Cobb-Douglas or logarithmic utility functions when marginal utility is infinite at zero consumption, some of the resource must be consumed everywhere and at all times.

Next

$$z \left\{ {\stackrel{=}{>}} \right\} 0 \Longleftrightarrow \lambda \left\{ {\stackrel{<}{=}} \right\} c + \mu + \int_t^T v(s)\, ds. \tag{7}$$

This conditions specifies where extraction should take place at a given time. It should not take place where the market price λ falls short of extraction cost c plus capacity rent μ plus exhaustion rents

$$\int_t^T v(s)\, ds.$$

Notice that

$$\mu \left\{ {\stackrel{=}{>}} \right\} 0 \Longleftrightarrow z \left\{ {\stackrel{<}{=}} \right\} a \tag{8}$$

and

$$v \left\{ {\stackrel{=}{>}} \right\} 0 \Longleftrightarrow \int_0^t z\, ds \left\{ {\stackrel{<}{=}} \right\} A. \tag{9}$$

Thus rent μ is incurred only when the location is worked to capacity a, and the rent v falls due only after exhaustion of the site. Finally,

$$k \frac{\phi}{|\phi|} = \text{grad } \lambda \qquad \text{where } \phi \neq 0$$

$$k \geqslant | \text{grad } \lambda | \qquad \text{where } \phi = 0. \tag{10}$$

Equation (10) states the familiar equilibrium condition for interlocal trade in a 2-dimensional spatial market.

4. This general model will now be illustrated in terms of a simple one-dimensional example. Let consumption be concentrated in a single location, placed at zero, and let resource be available in an interval extending from r_0 to the right to infinity (Fig. 1).

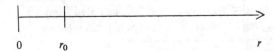

$\qquad$ 0 $\qquad$ r_0 $\qquad\qquad\qquad\qquad\qquad\qquad$ r

Fig. 1

Let

$$a(r) = a$$

$$A(r) = A$$

extraction cost $c(r) = c$

transportation cost $k(r) = k$ all be constant.

Assume the utility function to be logarithmic

$$u = \log q. \tag{11}$$

The welfare function is then

$$\int_0^T \int_0^\infty [\log q - k \mid \phi \mid - cz] \, dr \, dt.$$

Let $r_1(t)$ be the largest distance from which the resource is shipped to the consumption point initially. Then (7) implies

$$\lambda(r_1, t) = c$$

and (10) implies

$$\lambda(0, t) = kr_1 + c.$$

From (6)

$$c + kr_1 = \lambda(0, t) = \frac{\partial u}{\partial q} = \frac{1}{q}$$

so that

$$q = \frac{1}{c + kr_1}. \tag{12}$$

Since the marginal utility of consumption equals the marginal cost of production, the rate of consumption depends thus on the distance from which the resource must be brought, and as this distance increases with time, the rate of consumption necessarily falls.

Consider now production. At time zero the resource must be extracted in an interval (r_0, r_1) such that supply equals demand

$$q = \frac{1}{c + k r_1} = a \cdot (r_1 - r_0). \tag{13}$$

From this

$$r_1 = \frac{1}{2}\left[r_0 - \frac{c}{k}\right] + \sqrt{\frac{1}{4}\left[r_0 - \frac{c}{k}\right]^2 + \frac{1}{ak} + \frac{c}{k} r_0}. \tag{14}$$

The initial period during which resource extraction takes place in the interval (r_0, r_1) lasts $A/a = \alpha$ units of time. If $\alpha < T$ then after that, the operation shifts to an interval (r_1, r_2). Clearly each successive termination point r_{n+1} may be calculated from the previous one r_n in the same manner, for (12) and (13) must apply again yielding

$$r_{n+1} = \frac{1}{2}\left[r_n - \frac{c}{k}\right] + \sqrt{\frac{1}{4}\left[r_n - \frac{c}{k}\right]^2 + \frac{1}{ak} + \frac{c}{k} r_n}. \tag{15}$$

Although the setting of this problem is essentially continuous, the solution consists in a sequence of discrete shifts of operations.

This result cleary applies also in a 2-dimensional context. Thus the interval can be replaced by concentric rings surrounding a von Thünen city in succession as the mining operations are being shifted farther away. Each interval of operations has the same duration A/a. But the discrete nature of the selection of mining sites still applies and continues to apply even when the resource does not occur in all places beyond distance r_0 but only in selected areas, and also when consumption is not concentrated in one place but indispersed in a continuous manner. The details must be worked out in every concrete case, but the qualitative nature of the solution applies in general.

References

Beckmann, M.: A Continuous Model of Transportation. Econometrica **20**, 1952, 643–660.

Beckmann, M., and *T. Puu*: The Continuous Transportation Model. Research Report, International Institute for Applied Systems Analysis, Laxenburg, forthcoming.

Courant, R., and *F. John*: Introduction to Calculus and Analysis. 2 Volumes. New York–London–Sidney 1965.

Hotelling, H.: The Economics of Exhaustible Resources. Journal of Political Economy **39**, 1931, 137–175.

Economic Theory of Natural Resources. ©Physica-Verlag, Würzburg–Wien, 1982.

Concentration Profiles and the Production and Management of Marine Fisheries

Colin W. Clark

Besides the normal inputs — capital and labor — the production rate of a natural resource stock depends on the *size* of the resource stock:

$$Q = Q(K, L, X) \tag{1}$$

where Q is the rate of production (recovery) of the resource, K, L, and X are respectively capital, labor, and resource stock ("reserves"). In general, all four variables in this expression may be multidimensional.

The production of the resource also affects its abundance:

$$\frac{dX}{dt} = F(X) - Q(K, L, X), \tag{2}$$

where $F(X)$ denotes the natural rate of replenishment of the resource (so $F = 0$ for the case of an exhaustible resource stock). Here the variables X, K, L are functions of time; also the functions F, Q may be explicitly time dependent in general.

In practice, the resource stock X is usually not directly observable, or only partially so. We thus have a "black box" situation (Fig. 1), in which inputs and outputs can be measured, but the contents *and dynamic laws* of the black box can only be inferred. In contrast to most engineering applications, it is usually not possibly in resource production to carry out much "testing" of the system's response to different inputs, and thus only limited information about the resource system ever becomes known. On the other hand, a certain amount of observation (sampling, exploration) of the resource stock may be possible independently from the exploitation program; but this is usually quite expensive.

Fig. 1: Resource production

Concentration Profiles

The most commonly assumed production function in fisheries is:

$$C = qEX \tag{3}$$

where C denotes the harvest or catch rate (e.g. tons/day), E is an index of "fishing effort" (e.g. number of standardized vessels actively fishing on a given day), X is the fish stock biomass (tons) and q = constant is the "catchability coefficient" (/vessel day). Note that q = constant amounts to assuming that catch per unit effort (CPUE), C/E, is a direct index of stock abundance X. This assumption is commonly employed in fishery management, although fishery biologists are well aware of its potential biases [see *Gulland*, 1964a]. It is also the basis of many economic models of fishing.

For any resource stock, one would expect that the ratio of the recovery rate to exploitation "effort" should be at least roughly proportional to the *concentration* of the resource at the time and place of exploitation. Eq. (3) thus assumes that this concentration is itself directly proportional to the size of the remaining stock. Let us now investigate this latter hypothesis.

Solid state resource stocks

In order to discuss more general forms of Eq. (3), let us first consider the case of an exhaustible resource, such as a mineral. Let $f(\rho)\,d\rho$ denote the total amount (tons) of the pure mineral, in a given stock, existing at concentrations between ρ and $\rho + d\rho$ (where ρ is measured in percentage by weight). The "stock" under consideration is arbitrarily specified as to geographic location.

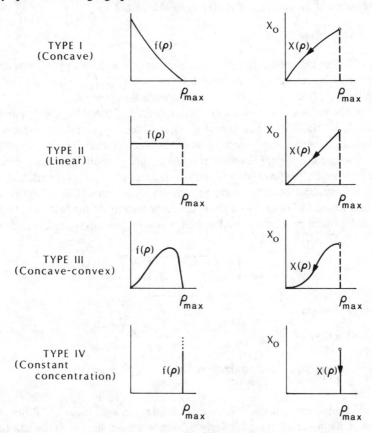

Fig. 2: Concentration profiles (left) and total reserve profiles (right)

Four general types of concentration profiles may be imagined: Fig. 2. In Type I, the amount of ore increases monotonically at progressively decreasing grades. For Type II, the amount available is the same at all concentrations, whereas for Type III there exists a particular concentration at which ore is most abundant. In the limiting case of Type IV, all ore occurs at one and the same concentration $\rho = \bar{\rho} = \rho_{max}$ and $f(\rho) = X_0 \delta(\rho - \bar{\rho})$ is a delta-function. (Other possibilities, such as multi-peaked curves $f(\rho)$, will be ignored here.)

The curves $X(\rho)$ on the right in Fig. 2 represent the total amount of mineral available in concentrations $\leqslant \rho$:

$$X(\rho) = \int_0^\rho f(\rho)\, d\rho. \tag{4}$$

In particular, $X_0 = X(\rho_{max})$ equals the total (initial) stock of the mineral.

To a first approximation, ores of high grade will be extracted prior to ores of lower grades. With this as an assumption, we see that as the ore stock is depleted, the marginal concentration ρ will decrease monotonically over time, as $X = X(\rho)$ is decreased. (For Type IV, ρ stays constant at $\bar{\rho}$ until the ore is exhausted.) If "mining effort" is defined to equal the rate at which mineral-containing ore is processed, then the "return per unit effort" will (by our assumption) be equal to the current marginal concentration $\rho(t)$. Thus the four curves $X = X(\rho)$ in Fig. 2 represent the relationship between stock abundance, X, and return per unit of mining effort, ρ. As the resource is depleted, the values of $X = X(t)$ and $\rho = \rho(t)$ trace out the corresponding curve (X, ρ).

Now what sort of bias would be introduced by assuming (as in Eq. 3) that $X \propto \rho$? For Type I concentration curves, the remaining stock X would be progressively *underestimated* by this procedure (ρ declines more rapidly than X), whereas for Type IV curves it would be *overestimated* (indeed, until the stock was exhausted, it would be "assumed" that it was not being depleted at all!). For Type III, X is first underestimated and later overestimated. Only for the apparently unlikely case of Type II concentration profiles is the assumption $X \propto \rho$ unbiased.

The assumption of Eq. (3) thus appears rather restrictive for resource stocks such as minerals; the bias can be remedied, even in a qualitative sense, only if some *a priori* idea of the concentration profile is available.

Diffusive exhaustible resource stocks

Next let us consider an exhaustible resource stock which, like a deposit of petroleum or natural gas, diffuses through its medium as it is exploited. First consider a single pool, with the property that the concentration always remains uniform throughout the pool. Then we have simply $\rho \sim X$, a Type II result.

More realistically, suppose there are n unconnected pools, with concentrations $\rho_i(t) = a_i X_i(t)$. Number the pools so that initially $\rho_1 \geqslant \rho_2 \geqslant \ldots \geqslant \rho_n$. Then the first pool will be exploited exclusively until $\rho_1(t) = \rho_2(0)$, after which pools 1 and 2 will be exploited simultaneously until $\rho_1(t) = \rho_2(t) = \rho_3(0)$, and so on. If $X = \sum_1^n X_i$ denotes the total reserves, it is easy to see that $X(\rho)$ is piecewise linear and concave, as in

Fig. 3, the slope of the k-th segment from the right being $\sum_{1}^{k} a_i^{-1}$. This case is of Type I.

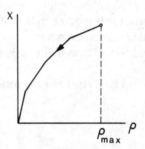

Fig. 3: Stock abundance vs. marginal concentration, for n unconnected diffusive pools

Next, suppose that the n pools are interconnected (as in a porous medium). To be explicit, let us suppose that the resource flows between the pools in such a manner as always to maintain the original concentration *ratios*, $\rho_i(t) \div \rho_1(t) = \text{const.}$ for each i. This case, it is easily seen, is exactly linear — Type II — with $X \sim \rho_1$ (only the first pool is exploited).

Thus the linear hypothesis of Eq. (3), which we found to be unrealistic for solid, mineral-type resource stocks, appears much more reasonable for interconnected diffusive resource pools, at least under the assumption to instantaneous equilibrating flow between pools.

More generally, let us consider the case of finite flow rates. For simplicity, take $n = 2$:

$$\left.\begin{aligned} \frac{dX_1}{dt} &= k\,(X_2 - mX_1) - Q_1 X_1 \\[2mm] \frac{dX_2}{dt} &= -k\,(X_2 - mX_1) - Q_2 X_2 \end{aligned}\right\} \tag{5}$$

where $k, m > 0$, and where the exploitation rates satisfy (bo be explicit):

$$Q_i \geqslant 0, \quad Q_1 + Q_2 = \bar{Q} = \text{const.} \tag{6}$$

For the unexploited system ($Q_i = 0$) we see that the line $X_2 = mX_1$ consists entirely of stable equilibria for Eqs. (5). As before, let $\rho_i = a_i X_i$ denote the concentrations of the two pools; assume that

$$\rho_1^0 = a_1 X_1(0) > \rho_2^0 = a_2 X_2(0). \tag{7}$$

The unexploited pools start in equilibrium, $X_2 = mX_1$, so that

$$\frac{a_1}{a_2} > m. \tag{8}$$

By assumption, only the higher concentration pool is extracted:

$$Q_2 = 0 \quad \text{if } \rho_2 < \rho_1 \tag{9}$$

and vice versa.

Hence at first $Q_1 = \bar{Q}$ and $Q_2 = 0$, and this holds as long as $\rho_1 > \rho_2$. Thereafter $\rho_1 \equiv \rho_2$ so that $a_1 X_1 \equiv a_2 X_2$. Substituting into Eq. (6), we arrive at the equation

$$Q_2 - Q_1 = -k\mu \left(1 + a_2/a_1\right) \tag{10}$$

where

$$\mu = \frac{a_1}{a_2} - m > 0. \tag{11}$$

Eg. (6) and (10) uniquely determine values of $Q_i = Q_i^*$, and there are two cases to consider, depending on the ratio of the flow-rate parameter k and the exploitation rate $\bar{Q}$.

Case 1: $k/\bar{Q} < \lambda = \mu^{-1} \left(1 + a_2/a_1\right)^{-1}$. This corresponds to a low rate of flow, or a high rate of extraction. In this case the solution Q^* to Eqs. (6) and (10) is feasible: $0 < Q_i^* < \bar{Q}$ ($i = 1,2$). The solution to the system (5) under conditions (6) – (9) thus consists, first, of a phase of exclusive extraction of the first pool:

$$\left.\begin{array}{l} dX_1/dt = k \left(X_2 - mX_1\right) - \bar{Q} \\[2mm] dX_2/dt = -k \left(X_2 - mX_1\right). \end{array}\right\} \tag{12}$$

When this trajectory reaches $\rho_1 = \rho_2$ (Fig. 4a)), Q switches to $Q_i = Q_i^*$ and the two pools are exhausted along the line $\rho_1 = \rho_2$. The corresponding *dynamic* relationship between total stock $X = X_1 + X_2$ and marginal concentration $\rho = \rho_1$ is shown by the top curve in Fig. 5b).

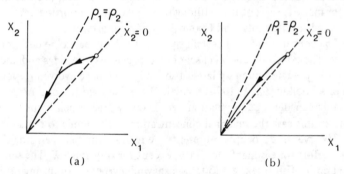

Fig. 4: Trajectories of Eqs. (5): (a) $k/\bar{Q} < \lambda$; (b) $k/\bar{Q} > \lambda$

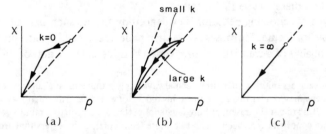

Fig. 5: Stock abundance vs. marginal concentration for two connected pools with finite diffusion rate k

Case 2: $k/\bar{Q} > \lambda$, This corresponds to high flow rate, or low exploitation rate. In this case Q^* is not feasible, and hence $Q_1 = \bar{Q}$ for all t. The trajectory of Eqs. (5) is shown in Fig. 4b), and the corresponding (X, ρ) curve in Fig. 5b).

Note that the two limiting cases $k = 0$ and $k = +\infty$ correspond to the case of unconnected pools (Fig. 3) and to the case of instantaneous adjustment, respectively.

To summarize these models (which can be extended to n pools), we see that the linear Type II curve is realistic for diffusive resources whose diffusion rates are large compared to the exhaustion rate, but that as this ratio $k/\bar{Q}$ decreases, the curve is transformed into a Type I concave curve.

Fishery resources

A fish population in the sea is obviously diffusive. But in contrast to the examples considered above, fish presumably swim around (diffuse) with some *purpose*. Thus the standard diffusion model of Eqs. (12) may not be appropriate for fish.[1])

However, if the purpose of diffusion is primarily to locate food concentrations, the concentration of fish in any given area should be related to the food abundance there. Thus the ratios of fish concentration in different parts of the sea could stay roughly constant over a fair range of total population sizes. If so, and if the fish move fairly rapidly to fill places vacated by harvested fish, our above argument shows that the linear Type II relationship between catch per unit effort ($\propto$ fish concentration) and stock should be a good first approximation. Note that the concentration of fish does not have to be or remain *uniform*, but only the concentration ratios have to remain fixed as the population is exploited. This is probably a reasonable assumption (at least in some time-averaged sense) for many species of fish, although I know of no supporting data — except for the fact that good fishing spots tend to remain good year after year.

However, the concentrations of certain species of fish appear to be determined by different rules. These include the small schooling species, like herrings and anchovies, which are heavily predated upon by larger fish, and which have evolved responsive behavior patterns of schooling [*Clark*, 1974; *Steele*]. These fish tend to concentrate in large schools, regardless of the total population size. Likewise, fishermen focus their efforts on these schools. In this case the marginal concentration of fish tends to remain constant, and a Type IV curve thus probably represents the relationship between stock size X and catch per unit effort to reasonable accuracy, except for very small X. The same applies to concentrations of fish stocks exploited on spawning grounds, or during migration. As will be discussed in the next section, this has serious implications for management of fisheries based on these "Type IV" species.

Another type of schooling behavior is evidenced by species such as tuna, which appear to form schools for feeding purposes rather than to decrease losses due to predation. Such schools are probably of a transient nature, with a considerable portion of the fish popu-

---

[1]) What about the assumption that fishermen always exploit the densest available concentrations? Various phenomena may render this assumption invalid — for example, fishermen may not always *know* where the fish are concentrated, although general patterns are probably rapidly learned. More important, if high concentrations occur in areas remote from ports, or in waters that are difficult to fish, such concentrations will not necessarily be preferred. See *Hilborn/Ledbetter* [1979], who discuss this question in relation to salmon purse-seine fleets.

lation not formed into schools at any given time. Several models of this aggregation phenomenon have been discussed by *Clark/Mangel* [1979]. These models fall into two categories, depending on whether the schooled portion of the population a) is proportional to the entire population X, or b) has a fixed upper size limit. These give rise to Type II and Type IV concentration profiles respectively. In practice an intermediate Type III relationship may be most realistic, but no direct data appears to be available which could be used to test these hypotheses.

Finally, certain species of fish undergo limited movements, and tend to remain "fished out" of areas where exploitation rates have been high. This may be the result of behavioral patterns, or may even be genetically determined — as is the case for salmon stocks. The concentration profile of such species will simply (at least over the short run) reflect the initial concentrations.

The foregoing possibilities are summarized in Table 1. [See *Gulland,* 1979 for further discussion]. While this characterization should obviously not be taken too literally, it does suggest that behavioral characteristics of fish species may significantly affect fishery production and management. This topic is further discussed below [see also *Steele*].

Behavior	Concentration profile
Foraging	Type II: linear
Schooling against predation, or for spawning, migration	Type IV: constant concentration
Schooling for feeding	Type II – Type IV
Sedentary	variable – Type I – IV

Tab. 1: Concentration profile types as a function of behavioral characteristics of fish species

Multi-species fisheries

Most, if not all, fishing fleets capture more than one species of fish. Fishermen are opportunistic, and tend to go not just where the fish are, but where the most valuable fish are most readily caught. As the relative abundance — or the market value — of different species changes, fishermen will tend to switch effort accordingly. Species which at one time are the "target", or most favored species, later occur as bicatches of fishing upon another "target" species. This opportunistic switching is very common and leads to severe difficulties in the estimation of stock abundance of individual species.

Consider, for example, two species, X and Y, and let X_i, Y_i $(i = 1, 2, \ldots, n)$ denote their abundance in n different areas. If effort E_i is applied to area i, assume the catch rates of the two species are

$$\left. \begin{array}{l} h_X^i = q_X^i \, X_i \, E_i \\[2mm] h_Y^i = q_Y^i \, Y_i \, E_i \end{array} \right\} \tag{13}$$

respectively. If p_X, p_Y denote the ex-vessel prices of the two species, then the rate of return from effort E_i is

$$\Pi_i = p_X \, h_X^i + p_Y \, h_Y^i$$

$$= (p_X \, q_X^i \, X_i + p_Y \, q_Y^i \, Y_i) \, E_i. \tag{14}$$

Thus return per unit effort in area i is given by

$$\gamma_i = \Pi_i / E_i = p_X \, q_X^i \, X_i + p_Y \, q_Y^i \, Y_i \tag{15}$$

and the opportunistic switching rule is that effort will be applied exclusively to that area (or those areas) with the largest γ_i.

In order to simplify the discussion, and to concentrate on the switching process, take $n = 2$ and ignore both diffusion and population growth. Thus for $i = 1,2$

$$\left. \begin{array}{l} dX_i/dt = -q_X^i \, X_i \, E_i \\[2mm] dY_i/dt = -q_Y^i \, Y_i \, E_i \end{array} \right\} \tag{16}$$

where $E_1 + E_2 = \bar{E}$. [2]) Initially suppose $\gamma_1 > \gamma_2$, so that $E_1 = \bar{E}$, $E_2 = 0$. At some time $t_1 > 0$ we will have $\gamma_1 = \gamma_2$ and some effort will switch to area 2. For $t < t_1$ and t close to t_1 we must have *either*

$$q_X^1 \, X_1 > q_X^2 \, X_2 \ \ or \ \ q_Y^1 \, Y_1 > q_Y^2 \, Y_2$$

but not both (although initially both could hold). If, for example, $\gamma_1 > \gamma_2$ and

$$q_X^1 \, X_1 > q_X^2 \, X_2 \ \ and \ \ q_Y^1 \, Y_1 < q_Y^2 \, Y_2 \tag{17}$$

we will refer to X as the *target* species, since effort is directed entirely towards the more productive area for species X, ignoring the fact that the other area is more productive for Y. At t_1, however, some effort is switched to area 2, and both species become "targets."

For $t > t_1$ both areas are exploited simultaneously, with $\gamma_1 \equiv \gamma_2$, i.e.

$$p_X \, q_X^1 \, X_1 + p_Y \, q_Y^1 \, Y_1 \equiv p_X \, q_X^2 \, X_2 + p_Y \, q_Y^2 \, Y_2.$$

Substituting into Eq. (16) and solving for E_1, E_2, we find that the effort distribution must satisfy:

$$E_1 = \frac{\alpha_2}{\alpha_1 + \alpha_2} \, \bar{E}, \ \ E_2 = \frac{\alpha_1}{\alpha_1 + \alpha_2} \, \bar{E}$$

where

$$\alpha_i = p_X \, (q_X^i)^2 \, X_i + p_Y \, (q_Y^i)^2 \, Y_i.$$

(When $p_Y = 0$ this reduces to $E_1 = q_2 \bar{E}/(q_1 + q_2)$, etc., which agrees with the single-resource (two pools) case discussed earlier.)

Now we are interested in the situation where management does not have information on the switching behavior, but merely uses catch and effort data to estimate stock abundance of the two species. Before the switch at t_0, catch per unit effort equals

$$q_X^1 \, X_1 = q_X^1 \, (X - X_2 \, (0))$$

for species X, and we have the same bias as before — see Fig. 5; the same applies for Y.

---

[2]) Eqs. (16) constitute a model of two unconnected pools of mixed diffusive exhaustible resource stocks.

But under the assumption of Eq. (18), for example, catch per unit effort of species X just *after* the switch will equal

$$\frac{q_X^1 X_1 E_1 + q_X^2 X_2 E_2}{E_1 + E_2} < q_X^1 X_1$$

i.e. there will be a sudden downwards *shift* in CPUE for species X. Similarly Y will show a sudden upwards jump in CPUE – see Fig. 6.

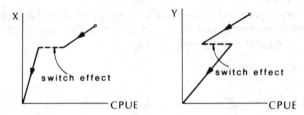

Fig. 6: Stock abundance vs. catch per unit effort for two-species resource

In qualitative terms, this model describes quite well what transpired in the Antarctic whaling industry in the early 1960's. Here there were two main species of baleen whales, blues and fins, the former being approximately twice the size (and value) of the latter. Originally, blue whales were most common at the more Southerly latitudes, and fin whales predominated further North. Whaling at first occurred almost exclusively in the South, with blue whales as the target. About 1961, however, the whaling fleets switched largely to the Northern fin whale stocks, taking blue whales only incidentally. Since they were unaware (at first) of this switch, scientists appointed by the International Whaling Commission [1964] severely underestimated the reamining stocks of Antarctic blue whales. Their original estimate of 200 blue whales was later revised to around 8,000, after switching had been allowed for.

Further results pertaining to the multi-species model, including inter-pool diffusion and population dynamics will appear elsewhere.

Fishery Production

For a single-species fishery, the above theroy gives rise to a harvest production function Q of the form

$$Q(E, X) = q\rho(X) E, \quad q = \text{const.} \tag{18}$$

where $\rho(X)$ is the marginal concentration, i.e. $\rho = \rho(X)$ is the inverse function to $X = X(\rho)$ in Fig. 2.

Let us now assume, for simplicity, infinite elasticity of demand for the product (i.e. fish of species X), and infinite elasticity of effort supply, at least over some specified range $0 \leqslant E \leqslant E_{\max}$. Then the net flow of economic rent to the fishing fleets is

$$\Pi(X, E) = pQ - cE$$
$$= (pq\rho(X) - c) E \tag{19}$$

or, expressed in terms of output Q,

$$\Pi = \left(p - \frac{c}{q\rho\,(X)} \right) Q. \tag{20}$$

The economic theory of the fishery is concerned with the relationship between competitive "open-access" exploitation and the socially optimal level of exploitation, and also with predicting the effects of alternative methods of regulation. Let us look into the role of concentration profiles in this body of theory.

Gordon's theory of the open-access fishery [Gordon] predicts that an equilibrium will be achieved in which economic rent is dissipated: $\Pi = 0$. By Eq. (19), the corresponding fish population biomass $X = X_\infty$ is then given by

$$\rho\,(X_\infty) = \frac{c}{pq} \tag{21}$$

(or else, if $pq\rho\,(X) < c$ for all feasible X, by $E = 0$ – in this case the concentration is nowhere high enough to support economic recovery). Since this is by definition an equilibrium, i.e. $\dot{X} = 0$, we have also

$$F\,(X) = Q\,(E,\,X) = q\rho\,(X)\,E \tag{22}$$

from which the equilibrium effort level E_∞ can also be obtained:

$$E_\infty = F\,(X_\infty)/q\rho\,(X_\infty). \tag{23}$$

Eqs. (21) and (23) characterize the "bionomic equilibrium" of the open-access (and unregulated) fishery.

In the standard (Schaefer) fishery model we have $\rho\,(X) = X$ and $F\,(X) = rX\,(1 - X/K)$, so that

$$X_\infty = \frac{c}{pq} \quad \text{and} \quad E_\infty = \frac{r}{q}\left(1 - \frac{X_\infty}{K} \right). \tag{24}$$

Thus both X_∞ and E_∞ are linear expressions in the cost/price ratio c/p. In the general case, Eq. (21), the relationship between X_∞ and the cost/price ratio c/p is (except for the scale factor $1/q$) the same as the relationship between stock size X and marginal concentration ρ (Fig. 2). The extreme cases, Type I and Type IV are shown again in Fig. 7.

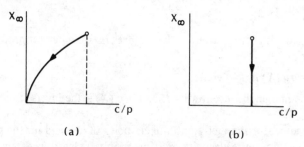

(a)   (b)

Fig. 7: Relationship between bionomic equilibrium population biomass X_∞ and cost/price ratio c/p, for (a) Type I and (b) Type IV concentration profiles

Assume, for example, that the cost/price ratio for fish X declines slowly over time. If X has a Type I (or Type II) concentration profile, the fishery will develop slowly and smoothly, following the curve in Fig. 7a. Catch per unit effort will fall slowly as the standing equilibrium biomass level is reduced (with the decline in CPUE more rapid than the decline in biomass, under Type I profiles). Actual catches $Q = F(X_\infty)$ will rise slowly to a peak (maximum sustainable yield) and then slowly decline – assuming that c/p continues to decrease. (The dynamics of adjustment will perturb this picture somewhat, depending on the rate of change of c/p and the response of the fishery.)

The development of a Type IV fishery follows a very different pattern. Once c/p reaches the critical level where the fishery becomes viable, development proceeds rapidly. The fish population biomass is reduced, in theory to the point of extinction,[3]) but catch per unit effort remains high and fishing remains profitable even at low population levels. A "perfect" Type IV profile is probably unrealistic; most fisheries become nonviable at some level of depletion short of actual biological extinction.

The expected characteristics of fisheries based on Type I (or II) vs. Type IV (or III) concentration profiles are summarized in Table 2.

Concentration Profile	Development	Catch per unit effort
Type I–II	Slow, smooth development phase; depletion gradual	Falls smoothly; tends to overestimate decline of stock
Type III–IV	Sudden development; depletion rapid	Remains high until stock is at a low level; underestimates stock decline

Tab. 2: Characteristics of unregulated open-access fisheries

Some examples

Among marine fisheries, the most extreme examples of depletion have involved whales and other marine mammals, sea turtles, and numerous stocks of pelagic schooling species (anchovies, herrings, etc.).

Antarctic right whales, which were once an abundant species, supported important industries from the 17th – 19th centuries. But by the 20th century this species had all but disappeared, with a few small populations remaining off the coasts of South Africa and Argentina. Right whales were easily captured by small boats in the bays and inlets where they bred. Moreover, these populations tended to be quite distinct, with very little mixing or transfer between adjacent areas. The resource can thus be classified as sedentary, non-diffusive, with concentration relatively constant. In other words, right whales probably had a Type IV concentration profile.

Two other species depleted by 19th century whalers were the Arctic bowhead and Pacific grey whales (the grey whale stocks have subsequently recovered, as a result of a 40-year moratorium on this species). Both these species migrated along narrow coastal zones, where they were easily exploited. (The western Pacific grey whales also congregated for breeding in a *single* bay in Mexico – Scammon's lagoon, named after the whaling captain who discovered and exploited this concentration.) Clearly these species also exhibited Type IV concentration profiles.

---

[3]) If the demand is not infinitely elastic, it is possible that development of the fishery will be smoothed out. In the long run, however, severe depletion can be expected to occur.

It is less clear what concentration profile applies to the main Antarctic whale species (blue, fin, and sei whales). These whales were hunted, in the 20th century primarily, throughout the 10 million square miles of the Antarctic Ocean, but the different species tended to favor different subareas. Also the whaling fleets are known to have regularly exploited the most productive areas, switching area and species as stocks were depleted. It seems likely that a fairly sharply peaked Type III concentration profile would be most appropriate for Antarctic whales (treated as a single economic resource), but this deserves more careful study.

Other marine mammals which probably possess Type IV concentration profiles include: fur seals (usually killed on their breeding grounds), sea otters, sea cows, etc. (coastal populations).

Sea turtles, most of the seven species of which are now very severely depleted world-wide, are also basically Type IV, since they are exploited either on the beaches where eggs are laid (the eggs are also taken), or in adjacent waters. In the same category are those species of sea bird whose populations were depleted by egg-collectors. (It is customary to refer to industries based on species such as whales, seals, and other marine species, as "fisheries," even though this term is hardly accurate. But perhaps the term should not be extended to the marine avifauna.)

Although extremely important commercially, the sperm whale does not seem to have been depleted to the same extent as other species. The concentration profile for this worldwide species, which is captured in both polar and tropical seas, is probably of Type I or II.

The next main class of depleted marine species is the clupeoids — herrings, sardines and anchoveta [see *Murphy*, who lists seven major clupeoid fisheries that have collapsed under heavy fishing]. These are small, schooling species of fish, subject to predation. In some cases, spawning concentrations are exploited. As noted above, such species would be ex-pected to possess Type IV concentration profiles.

Important fish species whose behavioral characteristics would indicate Type I − II concentration profiles include demersals (cod, flounders, soles, halibut) and also highly migratory, widespread species such as tunas. An example of this kind is given by *Gulland* [1964b], who discusses the English fisheries for plaice, cod, and sole during 1945 and 1946. Stocks of these fish had grown significantly because of reduced fishing during World War II. Gulland shows that CPUE for all three species fell markedly over the two-year period, but that the stocks themselves did not decline to the same degree. The dis-crepancy between CPUE and abundance is attributed to the distribution (i.e. concentra-tion) of fish and fishing — in other words, a Type I concentration profile.

Management Economics

Consider next the following optimization model [*Clark/Munro*, 1975];

$$\underset{0 \leqslant E(t) \leqslant E_{\max}}{\text{maximize}} \int_0^\infty e^{-\delta t} \, \Pi(t) \, dt \tag{25}$$

subject to

$$\frac{dX}{dt} = F(X) - q\rho(X)E(t) \tag{26}$$

where

$$\Pi(t) = \{pq\rho(X(t)) - c\}E(t). \tag{27}$$

For this model there exists an optimal equilibrium fish biomass $X = X^*$ given by

$$F'(X) + \frac{c'(X)F(X)}{p - c(X)} = \delta \tag{28}$$

where

$$c(X) = \frac{c}{q\rho(X)} \tag{29}$$

i.e. $c(X)$ equals the *unit harvest cost* at biomass level X. The optimal fishing policy is given by the "bang-bang" rule:

$$E(t) = \begin{cases} E_{\max} & \text{for } x(t) > X^* \\ E^* & \text{for } x(t) = X^* \\ 0 & \text{for } x(t) < X^* \end{cases} \tag{30}$$

where of course $E^* = F(X^*)/q\rho(X^*)$.

Eq. (28) is the standard marginal productivity rule $F'(X) = \delta$, modified by the addition of the term

$$\frac{c'(X)F(X)}{p - c(X)}$$

which *Clark/Munro* [1975] call the "marginal stock effect." The presence of this term implies that the optimal stock level X^* is affected by costs and prices, with $X^* > X_\delta$ where $F'(X_\delta) = \delta$.

Note, however, that for a Type IV concentration profile we have $c'(X) \equiv 0$, and the marginal stock effect vanishes. Under these circumstances the optimal biomass $X^* = X_\delta$ is independent of costs and prices. In fact for sufficiently large δ (viz $\delta > F'(0^+)$) we obtain $X^* = 0$ — extinction is the "optimal" policy. [See *Clark/Munro*, 1978 for further discussion on the optimality of extinction.] Except for this extreme case, however, we always have

$$X^* > X_\infty$$

i.e. the bionomic equilibrium is suboptimal.

Four general methods of fishery regulation are:

(i)   Total Allowable Catch limits (and similar policies);
(ii)   Vessel license limitation;
(iii) Taxes;
(iv) Allocated catch quotas.

These have been discussed in detail elsewhere [see *Clark*, 1980 and references therein]; here we discuss briefly the role of concentration profiles.

The traditional approach to fishery management used Total Allowable Catch quotas (TAC's) or similar methods such as seasonal closures, to prevent the depletion of stocks. Except for the fact that depletion is more difficult to detect for species with Type IV, rather than Type I or II concentration profiles, the problems of TAC-based management appear to be independent of concentration profile. As noted by *Clark* [1980] and others, this method almost automatically ensures overcapacity of fishing fleets, unless accompanied by other controls. Overcapacity might tend to be more severe for Type I than for Type IV concentration profiles, since CPUE increases with population size in the former case, but not the latter. In all cases, however, high catches (which are the *aim* of TAC management) will attract surplus vessel capacity.

Vessel (or fishermen) license programs now exist for many fisheries. The optimal number of licenses is determined by the minimum number of vessels needed to harvest the annual catch. Vessel license programs involve various forms of economic distortion (unless accompanied by other controls), however, resulting from competition between vessels for the total allowable catch. While the precise form of the distortion will be affected by, among other things, the concentration profile, the basic characteristics of license programs are not dependent on concentration profiles, and we will not discuss the subject further here.

Royalties, or taxes, on catch are in a formal sense economically equivalent to allocated vessel quotas [*Clark,* 1980]. The equivalence, however, involves dual variables (shadow prices), and we shall see that concentration profiles severely influence the *stability* of the two instruments.

A tax τ on catch affects net fleet revenue:

$$\Pi_\tau (X, E) = (p - \tau) Q - cE$$
$$= \{(p - \tau) q\rho (X) - c\} E. \tag{31}$$

The adjusted bionomic equilibrium (τ = constant), $X = X_\infty (\tau)$, is determined by

$$\rho (X_\infty (\tau)) = \frac{c}{(p - \tau) q} \tag{32}$$

or else $X_\infty (\tau) = K$ (natural population level) if the RHS $> \rho (K)$. The relationship between $X_\infty (\tau)$ and tax τ is shown, for Type I and Type IV concentration profiles in Fig. 8.

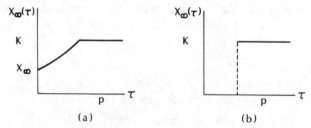

Fig. 8: Relationship between adjusted bionomic equilibrium $X_\infty (\tau)$ and catch tax τ, for (a) Type I and (b) Type IV concentration profiles

Under Type I (and II) profiles this relationship is smooth, but for Type IV there is a knife-edge discontinuity; large tax rates τ inhibit fishing entirely, but smaller rates have no effect. Of course this is the same phenomenon as the critical cost/price ratio discussed earlier. In practice, this knife-edge would probably be somewhat smoothed out by variations in vessel efficiency, etc.

In one sense the Type IV fishery might be considered highly controllable via the tax instrument, since small shifts in tax could in theory be used to open or close the fishery as desired. In practice, however, it is doubtful whether such shifting taxes would be politically feasible. In the U.S.A., for example [*Crutchfield*], tax changes require Congressional approval. Since taxes have never been used to regulate fish catches (to my knowledge), further discussion seems pointless.

Allocated, transferable vessel (or fisherman) quotas provide a direct approach to economic rationalization of common-property fisheries. Let Q now denote the total catch quota (e.g. in terms of tons per year); assume for simplicity that Q is divisible into arbitrarily small quota units which can be bought or sold, or retained and utilized to permit the harvest and sale of fish. If X represents the current fish biomass, the market clearing price m for quotas is given by

$$\frac{\partial \Pi (X, Q)}{\partial Q} = m$$

or:

$$m = m (X) = p - \frac{c}{q\rho (X)}. \tag{33}$$

(This supposes that the demand for quotas is fixed and exceeds the supply Q; see *Clark* [1980] for a much more detailed analysis.) Thus the demand price for quotas is an increasing function of stock abundance; for the Type IV profile, however, with $\rho (X) = \bar{\rho} = $ constant, we have $m (X) = $ constant for all $X > 0$ (Fig. 9). The stability of quota price relative to stock level is thus greatest for Type IV concentration profiles.

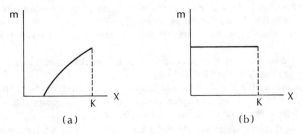

Fig. 9: Demand (and market clearing) price m for quota units, as a function of stock biomass X:
    (a) Type I, (b) Type IV

If, for example, Q is fixed at $F (X^*)$, the natural production rate corresponding to some predetermined stock level X^* (with $p > c/q\rho (X^*)$) and if $X_0 > X^*$, fish will be harvested at the rate Q, reducing $X (t)$ to an equilibrium at X^*. The quota price $m (t)$ will converge to the corresponding equilibrium $m^* = m (X^*)$, which also equals the optimizing catch tax τ^*, Eq. (26). The quota Q may also vary over time, for example during the recovery of a depleted stock. Our simple model has quota price dependent on X but independent of Q, but a more detailed analysis of vessel operations indicates a coupling between clearing price m and Q, with $\partial m/\partial Q < 0$ [*Clark*, 1980].

These simple considerations suggest that an allocated quota system should have a stabilizing economic influence on the fishery. In fact, quota prices are most stable for the otherwise unstable case of Type IV concentration profiles. Of course in all cases, quota prices shift directly in response to market prices for fish. Under a taxation program these shifts would have to be emulated by the taxing authority in order to prevent distortions.

In fact, if catch taxes *and* allocated quotas are used simultaneously, the quota price m would be determined by

$$m = p - \tau - \frac{c}{q\rho\,(X)}. \tag{34}$$

With τ fixed, price (or stock) fluctuations would be reflected in variations in m. Under these circumstances the tax is primarily of distributional significance, and the efficiency objective is achieved via the quota market.

The application of these concepts to multi-species fisheries will be taken up elsewhere.

References

Clark, C.W.: Possible effects of schooling on the dynamics of exploited fish populations. J. du Cons. Int. Expl. Mer **36**, 1974, 7–14.

—: Towards a predictive model for the economic regulation of commercial fisheries. Can. J. Fish. Aqua. Sci. **37**, 1980, 1111–1119.

Clark, C.W., and *M. Mangel*: Aggregation and fishery dynamics: a theoretical study of schooling and the purse-seine tuna fisheries. Fish. Bull. **77**, 1979, 317–337.

Clark, C.W., and *G.R. Munro*: The economics of fishing and modern capital theory: a simplified approach. J. Envir. Econ. Manag. **2**, 1975, 92–106.

—: Renewable resource management and extinction – a note. J. Envir. Econ. Manag. **5**, 1978, 198–205.

Crutchfield, J.A.: Economic and social implications of the main policy alternatives for controlling fishing effort. J. Fish. Res. Board Canada **36**, 1979, 742–752.

Gordon, H.S.: The economic theory of a common-property resource: the fishery. J. Polit. Econ. **62**, 1954, 124–142.

Gulland, J.A. (ed.): On the measurement of abundance of fish stocks. Conseil Perm. Intern. pour l'Explor. Mer, Rapp. et Proc.-Verbaux **155**, 1964a.

—: The reliability of the catch per unit effort as a measure of abundance of the North Sea trawl fisheries. Conseil Perm. Intern. pour l'Explor. Mer, Rapp. et Proc.-Verbaux **155**, 1964b, 98–102.

—: The stability of fish stocks. J. du Cons. Int. Explor. Mer **37**, 1979, 199–204.

Hilborn, R., and *M. Ledbetter*: Analysis of the B.C. salmon purse seine fleet: dynamics of movement. J. Fish. Res. Board Canada **36**, 1979, 384–391.

International Whaling Commission: 14th annual report: Special Committee of Three Scientists: Final Report. London 1964.

Murphy, G.I.: Clupeoids. Fish Population Dynamics. Ed. by J.A. Gulland. New York 1977, 283–308.

Steele, J.H.: Patterns in plankton. Oceanus **23** (2), 1980, 3–8.

Economic Theory of Natural Resources. ©Physica-Verlag, Würzburg–Wien, 1982.

Linear Filter Methods:
An Application to a Stock Production Model

Peter Haas and *Claus Hild*

In this paper, Pella and Tomlinson's generalization of the Schaefer model [Pella/Tomlinson], which allows for skewness of the stock production curve relating production with population size, is discussed. From the generalized stock production model the stock production curve can be determined for an exploited population using only the catch and effort history of the fishery.

Various methods are discussed for computing catch or effort predictions by means of a discrete econometric model based on a linearization of the mentioned stock production model. In addition to usual estimation methods filter methods are applied, based on the assumption of stochastic parameter evolution. A modification of the Kalman filter referred to as a "block filter" is developed.

The main purpose of this research is to derive an order of precedence of various prediction methods using several quality measures, rather than the computation of single prediction values.

1. Introduction

Stock production models represent an attempt by fisheries biologists to assess directly the relationship between the sustainable yield from a stock (or population) and the stock size. An analytic approach of this type is due to *Schaefer* [1954]. He developed a modified form of the logistic model to describe the growth of a fish resource and proposed a technique to estimate the logistic parameters under non-equilibrium exploitation conditions. The information required is the catch and effort history for the stock, together with an independent estimate of the catchability coefficient. In a subsequent paper *Schaefer* [1957] extended his method to estimate the catchability coefficient from the catch and effort history, also.

A generalization of the Schaefer model, described by *Pella/Tomlinson* [1969], permits positive or negative skewness of the stock production curve. A modified estimation technique based on the mere catch and effort information enables one to determine the magnitude and direction of skewness.

The following research, also based on this model, deals with the prediction of catch or effort data. Besides the usual methods assuming constant parameters, estimation methods are developed using a model with stochastic parameters.

2. Description of the Model

It is assumed that the stock or population under consideration has at each level x a certain potential for growth. If at time t the population has size $x(t)$, then it is assumed that the instantaneous rate of growth of the population at time t is

$$\dot{x}(t) = a \cdot x(t) - b \cdot x(t)^c \tag{2.1}$$

where $x(t)$ is the population size at time t (measured in terms of biomass), $\dot{x}(t)$ the natural growth of the stock and a, b, c are constant biological parameters with $a < 0$, $b < 0, c \in \,]0, 1[$ or $a > 0, b > 0, c > 1$.

Equation (2.1) describes the case of an increase without external interference. On the other hand, if individuals are removed from this population, the rate of growth will change. If a fishery is operating on the population at time t with an effort rate, say $e(t)$, the instantaneous catch rate is

$$h(t) = \dot{y}(t) = q \cdot e(t) \cdot x(t) \tag{2.2}$$

where $h(t)$ represents the catch rate and q is a technological parameter called the catchability coefficient.

The production function (2.2) contains a proportional relation between the ratio $h(t)/e(t)$ of catch and effort rate and the population size $x(t)$ which seems to be useful especially in the case of demersal fisheries [*Cushing; Holden/Raitt;* FAO e.g.].

In reality the rate of growth of the population given by (2.1) is reduced by the catch rate (2.2) leading to a modified growth rate

$$\dot{x}(t) = a \cdot x(t) - b \cdot x(t)^c - q \cdot e(t) \cdot x(t). \tag{2.3}$$

The importance of production models like (2.3) [cf. *Schnute*] stems from the possibility that one can derive econometric models for the estimation of all the parameters only by means of catch and effort histories. The estimates can be used to predict catches for any given effort strategy or efforts for given catch plans.

The approximation of the continuous deterministic model (2.3) by a discrete stochastic model are described in detail in *Pella/Tomlinson* [1969] or *Haas/Nuske* [1979]. In this paper we restrict ourselves to the result of the linearization approach:

$$u(t) = \frac{H(t)}{E(t)} \tag{2.4}$$

$$u(t+1) - u(t) = a \cdot u(t) - b \cdot q^{1-c} u(t)^c - q \cdot H(t) + z(t), \tag{2.5}$$

where $H(t)$ is the annual catch in year t, $E(t)$ the annual effort in year t and $u(t)$ the annual catch per unit of effort in t ($u(1)$ is assumed fix and known). The entry $z(t)$ is an additive white noise which represents all possible error sources; it is assumed that:

$$E(z(t)) = 0, \; E(z(s) z(t)) = \delta_{st} r(t). \; ^1) \tag{2.6}$$

Equation (2.5) can be used to develop a variety of estimation schemes for fixed c ^{2}). A series of estimation methods may be applied to the model parameters a, b, c, q. As for the missing information, the error variance is assumed to be constant $r(t) =: r$.

---

^{1}) δ_{st} is the Kronecker delta $\delta_{st} = 1$ if $t = s$ and $\delta_{st} = 0$ if $t \neq s$.

^{2}) This assumption seems not to be too strong as the quality of the predictions of the described methods is relatively insensitive to a changing c.

3. Parameter Estimation by Kalman Filter

If we let the parameter vector

$$\underline{d} := (d_1, d_2, d_3)' := (1 + a, -bq^{1-c}, -q)' \tag{3.1}$$

and the information vector

$$\underline{x}(t+1) := (x_1(t+1), x_2(t+1), x_3(t+1))' := (u(t), u(t)^c, H(t))', \tag{3.2}$$

then (2.5) can be written in the more familiar from

$$u(t+1) = \underline{x}'(t+1)\underline{d} + z(t+1). \tag{3.3}$$

This model is linear and hence usual regression methods are applicable to estimate the parameters d_1, d_2, d_3. Given these estimates and a fixed c, we can obtain the estimates $\hat{a}, \hat{b}, \hat{q}$. For any admissible value of parameter c, classical LS-method could be applied, assuming the parameter vector to be constant. Relaxing this assumption seems to be useful as in reality the structure of a fishery economy is not likely to be continuous for year and decades. Therefore in the following we will consider a model with variable parameters, such that

$$u(t+1) = \underline{x}'(t+1)\underline{d}(t+1) + z(t+1) \qquad t = 1, 2, \ldots, T. \tag{3.4}$$

To take gradual variations of the structure into account we will apply a kind of moving window regression [Belsley; Hild e.g.] instead of LS. Various window functions could be used to 'age' data so that only the most recent values are given any weight. By LSℓmethod we mean the application of LS to the u und H data of the past ℓ years. For the concrete research in mind we will have $4 \leqslant \ell \leqslant 15$, where we especially concentrate on $\ell = 6,8,$ 9,14 for the reason of comparability with several preliminary results.

Another method to estimate varying parameters is given by the filter algorithm. As this technique requires a parameter space representation of our estimation problem we have to complete the measurement equation (3.4) by a parameter equation:

$$\underline{d}(t+1) = \underline{d}(t) + \underline{v}(t) \qquad t = 1, 2, \ldots, T-1 \tag{3.5}$$

which is called random walk model.

In addition we have to make the following assumptions:

a) $\underline{d}(1)$ is a Gaussian random vector with known mean $\bar{d}(1)$ and known covariance $\bar{P}(1)$:

$$E(\underline{d}(1)) = \bar{d}(1) \quad E[(\underline{d}(1) - \bar{d}(1))(\underline{d}(1) - \bar{d}(1))'] = P(1); \tag{3.6}$$

b) $\underline{v}(t)$ is a Gaussian random vector with zero mean for all $t = 1, \ldots, T-1$ and independent in time (discrete white noise):

$$E(\underline{v}(t)) = 0 \quad E(\underline{v}(s)\underline{v}'(t)) = \delta_{st} Q(t); \tag{3.7}$$

c) $z(t)$ is a Gaussian random scalar with zero mean for all $t = 2, \ldots, T$ and independent in time (discrete white noise):

$$E(z(t)) = 0 \quad E(z(s)z(t)) = \delta_{st} r(t); \tag{3.8}$$

d) $\underline{d}(1)$, $\underline{v}(t)$ and $z(s)$ are mutually independent for all s and t.

It is desired to construct a "best" estimate of $\underline{d}\,(t)$, given past values of the measurement vector

$$U\,(t) = \{u\,(1), \ldots, u\,(t)\} = \left\{ \frac{H\,(1)}{E\,(1)}, \ldots, \frac{H\,(t)}{E\,(t)} \right\}. \tag{3.9}$$

The best estimate will be denoted by $\hat{\underline{d}}\,(t \mid t)$ and is defined as the conditional mean of $\underline{d}\,(t)$ given $U\,(t)$. The linearity of equations (3.4) and (3.5), together with the Gaussian assumptions on $\underline{d}\,(1)$, $\underline{v}\,(t)$, $r\,(t)$ implies that the probability density $p\,(\underline{d}\,(t) \mid U\,(t))$ is Gaussian and, hence, it is uniquely characterized by its conditional mean $\hat{\underline{d}}\,(t \mid t)$ and conditional covariance matrix $P\,(t \mid t)$.

The discrete Kalman filter (KF) [Kalman; Kalman/Bucy; Jazwinski; Sage/Melsa; Athans e.g.] yields a sequential algorithm which we will use to generate $\hat{\underline{d}}\,(t \mid t)$ and $P\,(t \mid t)$:

Initialization at $t = 1$:

$$\hat{\underline{d}}\,(1 \mid 1) = \bar{\underline{d}}\,(1), \qquad P\,(1 \mid 1) = P\,(1); \tag{3.10}$$

Prediction equation:

$$P\,(t \mid t - 1) = P\,(t - 1) + Q\,(t - 1) \quad {}^{3}); \tag{3.11}$$

Update equations:

$$\hat{\underline{d}}\,(t) = \hat{\underline{d}}\,(t - 1) + \underline{k}\,(t)\,[u\,(t) - \underline{x}'\,(t)\,\hat{\underline{d}}\,(t - 1)] \tag{3.12}$$

$$P\,(t) = P\,(t \mid t - 1) - \underline{k}\,(t)\,\underline{x}'\,(t)\,P\,(t \mid t - 1); \tag{3.13}$$

Filter gain calculation:

$$\underline{k}\,(t) = P\,(t \mid t - 1)\,\underline{x}\,(t)\,[\underline{x}'\,(t)\,P\,(t \mid t - 1)\,\underline{x}\,(t) + r\,(t)]^{-1}. \tag{3.14}$$

The finally computed vector $\hat{\underline{d}}\,(T)$ then is transformed into the requested estimates $\hat{a}\,(T)$, $\hat{b}\,(T)$ and $\hat{q}\,(T)$.

To apply this algorithm to our stock model (2.5) there must be available:

1. An initial guess for $\bar{\underline{d}}\,(1)$. If the sample size is sufficiently large the arbitrary assumption $\bar{\underline{d}}\,(1) = 0$ is satisfactory; on the other side this is the usual procedure if no information about $\underline{d}\,(1)$ is available. Variations of the initial value as for example LS-estimates did not yield better estimates and predictions in our empirical application.
2. An initial guess of the parameter variances and covariances represented by $P\,(1)$: As we have no information about the relations between the components of $\underline{d}\,(1)$ it seems reasonable to assume the matrix $P\,(1)$ to be diagonal. For simplification we assume $P\,(1) = \lambda \cdot I$. By simulation a suitable value of the variance λ of all the parameters can be determined [cf. Otter].
3. The mean and variance or covariance matrix of the white noises $z\,(t)$ and $\underline{v}\,(t)$ respectively must be known. Because of the lack of special information we assume that the variance $r\,(t)$ is constant, say $r := r\,(t)$. We have also to test a suitable value for r by systematic variation. By the application of OLS we can get an idea of the order of magnitude of r. In the same way we proceed in case of the covariance matrix $Q\,(t)$ which is assumed to be a constant diagonalmatrix, say $Q := Q\,(t)$.

---

^{3}) For simplification let us define $P\,(t) := P\,(t \mid t)$ and $\hat{\underline{d}}\,(t) := \hat{\underline{d}}\,(t \mid t)$.

4. The skewness parameter c is to be known. The fish resource production function is often assumed to have positive skewness; the range $]1, 2[$ should give suitable values for c [Schaefer/Beverton; Pella/Tomlinson].

By a systematic variation of the parameters λ, r, Var (v_1), Var (v_2), Var (v_3) and c we can obtain estimates of the parameters a (t), b (t), q (t). It is clear, that a sensitivity analysis of filter methods means extensive computations. We have to come to terms with the question whether this effort is justified by the improvement of the estimates and predictions.

4. Parameter Estimation by Block Filters

In this chapter two versions of a filter algorithm are derived which we will denote as block filter (BF ℓ) and as moving block filter (mBF ℓ). The fundamental idea of these modifications is to gather up ℓ successive measurement vectors in a matrix, referred to as an information block. In this way a lot of information is available for the actual estimation — by the information block — instead of that contained in a single measurement vector. So possibly myopic policies may be avoided, or in other words, prediction and planning errors resulting from the mere knowledge of the present situation are kept away from the analysis.

Using not only data of the present but also of past periods continual effects of specific ecologic or climatic events are taken into account. According to a possible equalization of the different evolutions of the parameters during ℓ periods the updating within the block filters is likely to be more moderate than by equation (3.12). So the application of block filters instead of KF is a similar effect to the representation of the parameter evolution by an ARIMA model of higher order instead of the random walk model [cf. Sarris].

In contrary to Fahrmeir's [1976] "natural" block structure assuming that the data arrive in groups, here the information block is constructed artificially; e.g. think of gathering vouchers to be exploited not until a certain number is at hand.

The formation and evaluation of an information block is possible by applying mBF ℓ, where each information block is constructed from the preceding by deleting the oldest measurement and adding the most recent. So each single measurement appears in different blocks. The block construction is derived from the following equation which is to be obtained from the parameter equation (3.5) by successive substitution:

$$\underline{d}\,(t) = \underline{d}\,(s) + \sum_{i=s}^{t-1} \underline{v}\,(i) \qquad s \leqslant t. \tag{4.1}$$

Using this equation the parameters of the periods s to t may be expressed by $\underline{d}$ (t). The coefficients of the $(t\text{-}\ell + 1)$-th information block consisting of the measurements of the periods $t - \ell + 1$ to t can be represented as

$$
\begin{pmatrix} \underline{d}\,(t-\ell+1) \\ \cdot \\ \cdot \\ \cdot \\ \underline{d}\,(t) \end{pmatrix} = \begin{pmatrix} \underline{d}\,(t) \\ \cdot \\ \cdot \\ \cdot \\ \underline{d}\,(t) \end{pmatrix} \begin{pmatrix} -I\;-I\;\cdots\;-I\;\,0 \\ 0\;-I\;\cdots\;-I\;\,0 \\ \cdot\quad\cdot\qquad\cdot\;\;\cdot \\ \cdot\qquad\;\cdot\qquad\cdot\;\;\cdot \\ \cdot\qquad\qquad\cdot\;\;\cdot \\ 0\qquad\qquad\;\;-I\;\,0 \\ 0\;\cdots\cdots\;0 \end{pmatrix} \begin{pmatrix} \underline{v}\,(t-\ell+1) \\ \cdot \\ \cdot \\ \cdot \\ \underline{v}\,(t) \end{pmatrix}
\tag{4.2}
$$

or more compactly

$$
\overline{\underline{d}}\,(t) = \underline{\iota} \otimes \underline{d}\,(t) + S\overline{\underline{v}}\,(t) \qquad t = 1, 2, \ldots, T - \ell + 1
\tag{4.3}
$$

where $\underline{\iota}$ is an ℓ-vector of ones, $\overline{\underline{d}}\,(t)$, S, $\overline{\underline{v}}\,(t)$ are defined, resp. The symbol $\otimes$ denotes the Kronecker product. Substituting equation (4.1) into the measurement equation (3.4) and collecting the outputs of the periods $t - \ell + 1$ to t in an information block, the parameter space of mBF ℓ can be represented as

$$
\overline{\underline{u}}\,(t) = X\,(t)\,\underline{d}\,(t) + \overline{\underline{w}}\,(t)
\tag{4.4}
$$

$$
t = 1, 2, \ldots, T - \ell + 1
$$

$$
\underline{d}\,(t) = \underline{d}\,(t-1) + \underline{v}\,(t-1)
\tag{4.5}
$$

where

$$
\overline{\underline{w}}\,(t) = D\,(t)\,S\overline{\underline{v}}\,(t) + \overline{\underline{z}}\,(t)
\tag{4.6}
$$

with $D\,(t) := \mathrm{diag}\,(\underline{x}'\,(t-\ell+1), \ldots, \underline{x}'\,(t))$, $\overline{\underline{u}}\,(t) := (u\,(t-\ell+1), \ldots, u\,(t))'$ is an ℓ-vector consisting of the measurements of the periods $t - \ell + 1$ to t, $X\,(t)$: $= (\underline{x}\,(t-\ell+1), \ldots, \underline{x}\,(t))'$ is an $(\ell \times n)$-information block for the estimation at time t, $\overline{\underline{z}}\,(t) = (z\,(t-\ell+1), \ldots, z\,(t))'$ is an ℓ-vector of measurement noise. All other variables are as defined in the KF-system (3.4), (3.5), and the assumptions a), b), c), d) are the same as above.

Consequently $\overline{\underline{v}}\,(t)$ and $\overline{\underline{z}}\,(t)$ are Gaussian random vectors with zero mean and known covariance matrices, say $\overline{\overline{Q}}\,(t-s)$ and $\overline{R}\,(t-s)$, resp., where $\overline{\overline{Q}}\,(t-s)$ and $\overline{R}\,(t-s)$ are easily derived from the covariance matrices of the terms $\underline{v}\,(t-\ell+1), \ldots, \underline{v}\,(t)$ and $z\,(t-\ell+1), \ldots, z\,(t)$. The Gaussian random vector $\overline{\underline{w}}\,(t)$ also has zero mean; but the construction of a moving block causes a colored noise, because the covariances between $\overline{\underline{w}}\,(t)$ and $\overline{\underline{w}}\,(s)$ are given by

$$
\Sigma\,(t-s) = \begin{cases} D\,(t)\,S\overline{\overline{Q}}\,(t-s)\,S'D'\,(s) + \overline{R}\,(t-s) & \text{for } |t-s| < \ell \\ 0 & \text{else.} \end{cases}
\tag{4.7}
$$

Another way to construct a filter working with blocks is due to *Fahrmeir* [1976]. For the application of this method, referred to here as a block filter (BF ℓ), the whole observation period is divided into disjunct parts, where each part is associated with a disjunct block of observations. Within each of these information blocks a homogeneous structure is assumed. If the disjunct subperiods are of the same length the parameter space of BF ℓ is:

$$\bar{u}(i) = X(i)\,\underline{d}(i) + \bar{z}(i) \tag{4.8}$$

$$i = 1, 2, \ldots, m; \; m = [T/\ell] + 1; \; \ell < T$$

$$\underline{d}(i) = \underline{d}(i-1) + \bar{v}(i-1) \tag{4.9}$$

where $\bar{u}(i) := (u((i-1)\,\ell + 1), \ldots, u(i\ell))'$ is an ℓ-dimensional output vector consisting of the measurements of the periods $(i-1)\,\ell + 1$ to $i\ell$, $X(i) :=$ $(\underline{x}((i-1)\,\ell + 1), \ldots, \underline{x}(i\ell))'$ is the $(\ell \times n)$ information block of the i-th subperiod, $\bar{z}(i) := (z((i-1)\,\ell + 1), \ldots, z(i\ell))'$ is an ℓ-dimensional vector and $\bar{v}(i)$ is an n-dimensional Gaussian vector (parameter noise) affecting the temporal development of the parameters between block i and $i + 1$ with zero mean and covariance $E(\bar{v}(i)\,\bar{v}'(j)) = \bar{Q}(i)\,\delta_{ij}$. The remaining variables are as defined in the system of KF; the assumptions a), b), c), d) continue to be valid. Therefore the Gaussian random vector $\underline{z}(i)$ has zero mean and a diagonal covariance matrix $\bar{R}(i)$ to be derived from the variances $r(t)$ of the measurement noise in the KF-system.

The comparison of the block filters and KF shows that the former computationally cause nothing but a change in the dimension of the KF-algorithm as it is represented in this paper, and therefore corresponds to the original form as state estimator. The application of block filters to the stock model (2.5) requires the same considerations and sensitivity analysis as for KF. The variation of parameter ℓ offers a further tool of tuning up the estimation and prediction. The finally computed vector is transformed into the required estimates.

The unbiasedness, minimal variance, and asymptotic behaviour of BF ℓ can be proved analogously to that of KF taking the construction of the blocks into account. Because of the special form of colored noise of $\bar{\bar{w}}(t)$ these results cannot be carried over to mBF ℓ.

5. Catch and Effort Predictions

Our interest is concentrated on the predictions of effort and catches by means of the estimation methods OLS, LS ℓ, KF, BF ℓ, and mBF ℓ applied to the econometric model (2.5). Starting from the exact knowledge of future catches we will compute predictions of the future efforts $E(t + 1), E(t + 2), \ldots, E(t + 5)$ e.g., or equivalently of the future H/E-ratios $u(t + 1), u(t + 2), \ldots, u(t + 5)$. A similar research may analogoulsy be carried out in case of effort planning. In the following the prediction of an unknown $u(t + i)$ which is computed at the end of year t using the data $u(1)$ to $u(t)$ is denoted as $\hat{u}_t(t + i)$.

For comparative purposes we will apply the prediction method of moving averages (MA ℓ), where ℓ is the number of the most recent u-data to be averaged. The predictions $\hat{u}_t(t + i), i = 1, 2, \ldots, 5$, obtained by MA ℓ are successively computed as

$$\hat{u}_t(t + 1) = 1/\ell \cdot (u(t) + u(t - 1) + \ldots + u(t - \ell + 1)) \tag{5.1a}$$

$$\hat{u}_t \, (t+2) = 1/\ell \cdot (\hat{u}_t \, (t+1) + u \, (t) + \ldots + u \, (t - \ell + 2)) \tag{5.1b}$$

$$\vdots$$

$$\hat{u}_t \, (t+5) = 1/\ell \cdot (\hat{u}_t \, (t+4) + \ldots + \hat{u}_t \, (t+1) + u \, (t) + \ldots + u \, (t - \ell + 5)). \tag{5.1e}$$

Multistage predictions are computed by including predicted u-values.

If the fishery has been in a steady state for a long time the u-values change gradually. In this case MA ℓ-methods are expected to give quite good predictions. These methods are evident and computationally simple.

Let $\hat{d}_1(t), \hat{d}_2(t), \hat{d}_3(t)$ be a synonym for the estimates resulting from the application of OLS, LS ℓ, KF, BF ℓ, and mBF ℓ. The predictions of u are given by

$$\hat{u}_t \, (t+1) = \hat{d}_1(t) \, u \, (t) - \hat{d}_2(t) \, u \, (t)^c - \hat{d}_3(t) \, H \, (t) \tag{5.2a}$$

$$\hat{u}_t \, (t+i+1) = \hat{d}_1(t) \, \hat{u}_t \, (t+i) - \hat{d}_2(t) \, \hat{u}_t \, (t+i)^c - \hat{d}_3(t) \, H \, (t+i)$$

$$i = 1, \ldots, 4. \tag{5.2b}$$

For comparative purposes we have to define some quality measures expressing the degree of confidence of the predictions obtained by the various prediction methods. We consider three measures for both onestage and multistage predictions:

MAPE = mean absolute prediction error: $\dfrac{1}{n} \sum\limits_t |\hat{u}_t \, (t+1) - u \, (t+1)|$

SPE = standard prediction error $= \sqrt{\dfrac{1}{n} \sum\limits_t (\hat{u}_t \, (t+1) - u \, (t+1))^2}$

TC = Theil's coefficient $= \sqrt{\dfrac{\sum (\hat{u}_t \, (t+1) - u \, (t+1))^2}{\sum (u \, (t+1) - u \, (t))^2}}$

MAPE (5) = mean absolute prediction error of five step ahead predictions

$$= \dfrac{1}{n} \sum\limits_t |\hat{u}_t \, (t+5) - u \, (t+5)|$$

SPE (3) = standard prediction error of three step ahead predictions

$$= \sqrt{\dfrac{1}{n} \sum\limits_t (\hat{u}_t \, (t+3) - u \, (t+3))^2}$$

MAWS = mean absolute weighted sum of prediction errors

$$= \dfrac{1}{n} \sum\limits_t \left(\left| \sum\limits_{i=1}^{5} \dfrac{6-i}{15} (\hat{u}_t \, (t+i) - u \, (t+i)) \right| \right).$$

The prediction methods described in this paper are applied to the catch and effort history of the yellowfin tuna fishery in the eastern Pacific Ocean [Schaefer, 1957]. The stock is measured in millions of pounds and the effort in thousands of boat days (standardized to bait vessels of 201 to 300 short tons capacity). The first application consists of predictions from $t = 10$ and the second from $t = 15$. The results of this empirical study are discussed in the following chapter, and the used data are summarized in table 1 of the appendix.

6. Evaluation of the Prediction Methods

Prediction by MAℓ

The application of MAℓ merely requires the determination of parameter ℓ. Searching for the best predictions we have to vary ℓ and to compare the computed measures of quality. One of the first results of our empirical application is the superiority of a prediction from $t = 15$ to that from $t = 10$ – a fact which is evidently caused by the nature of the u-data expressing violent fluctuations during the first two decades. A stabilization appears not until 1952, but from that date quite good results are obtained by MAℓ predictions especially with a small parameter ℓ.

All the methods MA1, MA2, . . . , MA10 and (in the case of $t = 15$) MA11, . . . , MA15 are applied and compared with regard to the quality of predictions. It turns out that an ℓ-value ($\ell \geqslant 6$) yields poorer measures of quality. "Optimal" onestage predictions are got by the application of MA5 and MA6, "optimal" multistage predictions by MA2 and MA4; as a compromise we propose the utilization of $\ell = 4$. The quality measures for MA1, MA4, MA6, and MA8 are summarized in the appendix.

Prediction by LSℓ

LSℓ prediction methods (OLS is equal to LSℓ with $\ell = T$) depend on two parameters to be varied:

– parameter of the model c
– parameter of the method ℓ.

Therefore we have to apply various LSℓ-methods and to observe the effects of the c-variations on the predictions. The superiority of predictions from $t = 15$ is verified especially in case of onestage predictions. For multistage predictions a general statement cannot be given; beyond that they are poorer than the MA-predictions especially for small ℓ. Therefore we do not attach any practical value to multistage LSℓ-predictions.

In order to determine an optimal parameter ℓ we came to the following results: For all arbitrary values of the parameter c in $[0.7, 2.9]$ an increasing ℓ generally improved the predictions. This improvement is especially marked in case of passing from $\ell = 4$ to $\ell = 9$. Larger ℓ-values first make the predictions worse and later on lead to an improvement. Altogether the OLS-method is superior to LSℓ for all quality measures and the above c-values. Our analysis shows that an improvement of the estimates cannot be reached by forgetting past data.

A sensitivity analysis of parameter c did not yield an unique optimum; depending on the quality measure and the beginning of the prediction period different trends could be distinguished. Summarizing, the quality of OLS-predictions seemed to be relatively insensitive to a variation of parameter c. To a certain degree c-values in $[1.4, 2.3]$ could be considered as optimally chosen.

With regard to the biological meaning of the skewness parameter c this empirically verified interval $[1.4, 2.3]$ can be reduced to $[1.4, 1.8]$, taking the positively skewed growth function of yellowfin tuna into account[4]) [cf. *Schaefer*, 1957; *Schaefer/Beverton*].

The comparison of the best $LS\ell$-predictions (i.e. OLS) and the best $MA\ell$-predictions demonstrates the slight superiority of MA4 and MA6 respectively; this implies that the more extensive computations of LS-methods do not pay.

Prediction by filter methods

KF-, $mBF\ell$- and $BF\ell$-predictions require the determination of six model parameters c, r, λ, Var (v_i) $(i = 1, 2, 3)$ and the procedural parameter ℓ. The independent variation of all these parameters is evidently associated with extensive computational experiments.

According to the analysis by LS-methods first several c-ℓ-combinations ($c \in [0.7, 2.9]$, $\ell \in \{1, \ldots, 9\}$) are to be determined, and then the other parameters are properly changed to study the effects on the prediction quality. The order of magnitude of r and λ has been determined as follows: As for the u-data a value between 0.1 and 1 seems to be realistic for the standard deviation $\sqrt{r}$ of the measurement noise z. Prior information concerning the parameter vector $\underline{d}$ do not exist. Because of the uncertainty corresponding to a prior estimate $\overline{\underline{d}}(1) = 0$ the λ-value is assigned to $\lambda = 100$.

Beyond these considerations the parameters λ and r are independently varied using the following rule: In the case of small variances of the components of the parameter noise $\underline{v}$ the effect of changing r and λ on the measures of quality only depends on the ratio $\theta := r/\lambda$ [5]).

The variation of θ within $[10^{-4}, 100]$ results in best onestage predictions for $\theta \in [10^{-3}, 1]$ and best multistage predictions for $\theta \in [1, 10]$. The experiment showed that for $\theta \geqslant 5$ the problem of wrong signs of parameter estimates arises, so $\theta \in [10^{-2}, 1]$ is proposed. Varying the diagonal elements of $Q = \text{diag}$ (Var (v_1), Var (v_2), Var (v_3)) the best predictions were computed by assuming an order of magnitude of $10^{-2}, 0, 10^{-13}$, resp.

For distinct values of c the quality measures of KF-predictions are summarized in table 2 and 3 of the appendix. A summary of all results indicates:

a) the superiority of predictions from $t = 15$ to that from $t = 10$;
b) although a best value of c does not exist, small values of c in $[0.7, 1.8]$ turn out to be quite good;
c) KF-predictions with $c \in [0.7, 1.8]$ are superior to OLS-predictions. Their quality is corresponding to that of the best MA-predictions, but does not exceed it in general.

Taking all these circumstances into consideration the computational effort of KF seems not to be justified.

A sensitivity analysis with $BF\ell$ and $mBF\ell$ concerning the parameter $\theta = r/\lambda$ does not yield new results, so the above r and λ are retained. Just the increase of the values of Var (v_1) and Var (v_3) from 0.01 to 0.1 and 10^{-13} to 10^{-6} resp., proved to be more favourable to the application of $BF\ell$ for onestage predictions.

One difficulty appears with the application of $BF\ell$: The problem of wrong signs,

---

[4]) *Pella/Tomlinson* [1969] suggested $c = 1.4$.
[5]) This rule is also demonstrated by a numerical example of *Otter* [1978, p. 50].

especially with small ℓ. The best BF ℓ-predictions are obtained for $\ell = 6$, the prediction quality of which however is poorer than that of the best mBF ℓ-predictions.

Varying the block size ℓ best mBF ℓ-predictions are obtained for $\ell \in \{4,5,6\}$. The statements a), b), and c) given in the case of KF-predictions are valid for mBF ℓ-predictions, too. Supplementary we point out the following facts:

d) mBF ℓ-predictions are superior to KF-predictions for $c \in [1.4, 1.8]$ and $\ell \in \{4, \ldots, 8\}$. This is valid especially in the case of onestage predictions. The quality measures of multistage predictions by mBF ℓ are superior to that of KF except for MAPE(5).

Comparison of methods

To finish this chapter we compare the quality of the best mBF ℓ-predictions with that of the best MA ℓ- and OLS-predictions, resp. Restricting the choice of parameter c to [1.4; 1.8], which has proved to be the best compromise for most of the methods applied in this research, the following statements can be given[6]):

By the application of the best mBF ℓ-methods onestage predictions (especially from $t = 15$) can be obtained which are superior to the best MA ℓ-values and essentially better than OLS-predictions. Best multistage filter predictions are computed by mBF4; generally the quality of these values is not superior to those of MA4. These results are partially summarized in table 2 and 3 of the appendix.

7. Conclusion

Our research is useful for the analyst as it gives an order of precedence of several prediction methods and may give hints for the management of natural resources, e.g. Naturally we must be aware of the errors possibly contained in the predictions caused by the derivation of the econometric model and the computational difficulties arising from the implementation of the various methods on a computer. Unfortunately only data for standardized bait vessels are available which may cause additional errors.

Using all quality measures defined in our empirical research mBF4 proved to be the best. The u-predictions computed by the results of this method generally were superior to the MA ℓ-predictions obtained without using an econometric model. The prediction methods basing on LS-estimates produced poorer predictions than the filter methods KF and mBF ℓ. On the other hand the application of filter methods requires extensive computations if there are no prior informations available of fishery. Past numerical researches of fish resources have generally assumed constant parameters. But our analysis showed that the predictions obtained by the assumption of stochastic parameters and the consequent application of filter methods is superior to those results.

Another advantage of the filter methods is their applicability even if there are less observations available than the number of coefficients in the econometric model, provided that there exists a sufficient prior information.

In contrast to MA ℓ, filter methods presume an underlying econometric model that gives a certain insight into the structure of the resource. Thus estimates of the parameters

---

[6]) Cp. results tabled in the appendix.

of this model by filter methods are appropriate to give quantitative statements concerning the influence of an already practiced or planned strategy on the development of the resource.

Appendix

year	effort	catch	catch per unit of effort
1934	5 879	60 913	10.361
1935	6 295	72 294	11.484
1936	6 771	78 353	11.571
1937	8 233	91 522	11.116
1938	6 830	78 288	11.463
1939	10 488	110 418	10.528
1940	10 801	114 590	10.609
1941	9 584	76 841	8.018
1942	5 961	41 965	7.040
1943	5 930	50 058	8.441
1944	6 475	64 869	10.019
1945	9 377	89 194	9.512
1946	13 958	129 701	9.292
1947	20 383	160 151	7.857
1948	24 781	206 993	8.353
1949	23 923	200 070	8.363
1950	31 856	224 810	7.057
1951	18 403	186 015	10.108
1952	34 834	195 277	5.606
1953	36 356	140 042	3.852
1954	26 228	140 033	5.339
1955	17 198	140 865	8.191
1956	27 205	177 026	6.507
1957	26 768	163 020	6.090
1958	31 135	148 450	4.768
1959	28 198	140 484	4.982
1960	35 841	244 331	6.817
1961	41 646	230 886	5.544
1962	42 248	174 063	4.120
1963	33 303	145 469	4.368
1964	42 090	203 882	4.844
1965	43 228	180 086	4.166
1966	40 393	182 294	4.513
1967	33 814	178 944	5.292

Tab. 1: Catch, effort, and catch per unit of effort for yellowfin tuna from the eastern Pacific Ocean during 1934 through 1967. The data were corrected for changes in efficiency of the fishing gear. The stock is measured in thousands of pounds and the effort in boat days [*Schaefer*, 1957, 1967; *Pella/Tomlinson*].

Method of Prediction	Quality of Predictions					
	multistage predictions			onestage predictions		
	SPE (3)	MAPE (5)	MAWS	MAPE	SPE	TC
MA1	1.6526	1.0889	.2403	1.0967	1.3310	1.0000
MA4	.9047	1.3688	.1317	.9343	1.1177	.8398
MA6	1.2688	1.4529	.1650	.9146	1.0438	.7842
MA8	1.3944	1.6565	.2163	1.1346	1.2755	.9583
OLS	1.8005	2.2076	.2360	.9073	1.0951	.8228
LS6	6.7048	6.3859	.5590	1.2848	2.1055	1.5819
LS8	4.9878	4.7578	.4529	1.1650	1.5979	1.2005
LS14	2.0104	2.2397	.2897	1.1310	1.3061	.9813
KF	1.2801	1.1597	.1818	.8536	1.0846	.8148
BF6	1.6822	1.9794	.1760	.8134	1.0706	.8043
mBF4	1.0873	1.2425	.1456	.8104	1.0048	.7549
mBF6	1.1600	1.3953	.1544	.8310	1.0133	.7613
mBF8	1.1418	1.2387	.1602	.8145	1.0040	.7543

Tab. 2: ($c = 1.4$; predictions from $t = 15$)

Method of Prediction	Quality of Predictions					
	multistage predictions			onestage predictions		
	SPE(3)	MAPE(5)	MAWS	MAPE	SPE	TC
MA1	1.6526	1.0889	.2404	1.0967	1.3310	1.0000
MA4	.9047	1.3688	.1317	.9343	1.1177	.8398
MA6	1.2688	1.4529	.1650	.9146	1.0438	.7842
MA8	1.3944	1.6565	.2163	1.1346	1.2755	.9583
OLS	1.8001	2.2582	.2361	.9210	1.1084	.8328
LS6	7.7293	6.6994	.6337	1.3873	2.2654	1.7021
LS8	5.1133	4.8513	.4709	1.1735	1.6405	1.2325
LS14	2.0563	2.3069	.2989	1.1497	1.3153	.9882
KF	1.3410	1.2029	.1897	.8785	1.1113	.8350
BF6	3.0931	2.9381	.3006	.9821	1.2413	.9326
mBF4	1.1370	1.2661	.1460	.7955	.9556	.7179
mBF6	1.1862	1.4064	.1501	.7777	.9751	.7326
mBF8	1.2195	1.4323	.1531	.7993	.9772	.7342

Tab. 3: ($c = 1.8$; predictions from $t = 15$)

References

Athans, M.: The Importance of Kalman Filtering Methods of Economic Systems. Annals of Economic and Social Measurement **3** (1), 1974, 49–64.

Belsley, D.A.: On the Determination of Systematic Parameter Variation in the Linear Regression Model. Annals of Economic and Social Measurement **2** (4), 1973, 487–494.

Cushing, D.H.: Fisheries Biology, A Study in Population Dynamics. Madison 1968.

Fahrmeir, L.: Recursive Parameter Estimation in Linear Statistical Models. Compstat 1976. Wien 1976, 139–145.

FAO: Monitoring of Fish Stock Abundance: The Use of Catch and Effort Data. FAO Fisheries Technical Paper 155. Rome 1976.

Haas, P., and *M. Nuske*: Anwendung der linearen Filtertheorie zur Parameterschätzung bei verallgemeinerten Schaeferschen Produktionsmodellen. Reprint Series 9, Inst. f. Statistik u. Mathematische Wirtschaftstheorie, Universität Karlsruhe, 1979.

Hild, C.: Schätzen von zufälligen bzw. stochastischen Koeffizienten durch Regression mit gleitenden Zeitabschnitten. Reprint Series 3/80, Inst. f. Statistik u. Mathematische Wirtschaftstheorie, Universität Karlsruhe, 1980.

Holden, M.J., and *D.F.S. Raitt*: Manual of Fisheries Science, Part 2 – Methods of Resource Investigation and Their Application. FAO Fisheries Technical Paper 115 (Revision 1). Rome 1974.

Jazwinski, A.H.: Stochastic Processes an Filtering Theory. New York 1970.

Kalman, R.E.: A New Approach to Linear Filtering and Predictions Problems. Trnas. ASME, Journal of Basic Engineering **82D**, 1960, 35–45.

Kalman, R.E., and *R.S. Bucy*: New Results in Linear Filtering and Prediction Theory. Trans. ASME, Journal of Basic Engineering 83D, 1961, 95–108.

Otter, P.W.: The Discrete Kalman Filter Applied to Linear Regression Models: Statistical Considerations and an Application. Statistica Neerlandica **32**, 1978, 41–56.

Pella, J.J., and *P.K. Tomlinson*: A Generalized Stock Production Model. Bulletin of the Inter-American Tropical Commission **13**, 1969, 421–496.

Sage, A.P., and *J.L. Melsa*: Estimation Theory with Applications to Communications and Control. New York 1971.

Sarris, A.H.: A Bayesian Approach to Estimation of Time-Varying Regression Coefficients. Annals of Economic and Social Measurement **2** (4), 1973, 501–523.

Schaefer, M.B.: Some Aspects of the Dynamics of Populations Important to the Management of the Commercial Marine Fisheries. Bulletin of the Inter-American Tropical Tuna Commission **1**, 1954, 25–56.

–: A Study of the Dynamics of Yellowfin Tuna in the Eastern Tropical Pacific Ocean, Bulletin of the Inter-American Tropical Tuna Commission **2**, 1957, 245–285.

–: Fishery Dynamics and Present Status of the Yellowfin Tuna Population of the Eastern Pacific Ocean. Bulletin of the Inter-American Tropical Tuna Commission **12**, 1967, 89–136.

Schaefer, M.B., and *R.J.H. Beverton*: Fishery Dynamics – Their Analysis and Interpretation. The Sea, Vol. 2. Ed. by M.N. Hill. New York 1963, 464–483.

Schnute, J.: Improved Estimates from the Schaefer Production Model: Theoretical Considerations. Journal of the Fisheries Research Board of Canada 34, 1977, 583–603.

Shimada, R.M., and *M.B. Schaefer*: A Study of Changes in Fishing Effort, Abundance, and Yield for Yellowfin and Skipjack Tuna in the Eastern Tropical Pacific Ocean, Bulletin of the Inter-American Tropical Tuna Commission **1**, 1956, 351–469.

A New Oil Search Technology and its Economic Relevance

Gerhard O. Müller

1. Introduction

The search for oil and gas is based on ground measurements carried out in order to identify geometrical configurations typical of oil and gas deposits within certain geological layers. Only after this search has been successful does investment in drilling (costing at least $ 2 million per km) become feasible. The measurements and their evaluation are rather complicated, since the relevant information is hidden in the amplitude of waves reflected by geological layers.

The classical *seismic method* uses mechanical waves created by explosions. The new *magnetotelluric method* (M.T.) uses natural electromagnetic radiation in the spectrum between 250 Hz and 300 kHz produced in the ionosphere by electrical particles coming from the sun. (It would be extremely expensive to create this spectrum artificially.)

2. A Comparison Between the Two Methods

a) *Transportation*: M.T. equipment can be transported by helicopter. Seismic equipment requires ground transportation, making it nesessary to build roads or in arctic areas to wait for the winter. Especially mountain, jungle and taiga environments offer many obstacles. (This fact definitely contributes to the yearly decrease of known oil reserves.)

b) *Efficiency*: M.T. (though generally less precise) works at most locations whereas seismic fails in many places (because mechanical waves do not penetrate or give enough information). M.T. also reaches much deeper (the deepest exploration drillings nowadays go down to 10 kilometers).

c) *Costs*: M.T. for one site costs approximately $ 50,000 (it is remarkable that 30% of this sum comprises computing cost). Seismic is many times more expensive, varying very much with the location.

d) *Environment*: Seismic does extensive damage, leaving holes in the ground and unsafe subsoil conditions.

e) *Availability*: M.T., which requires very advanced electronic and mathematical noise filtering techniques, fast computers and highly qualified experts, has only recently become efficient. Most companies do not have sufficient equipment and experience.

3. M.T. as an Identification Procedure

Let us assume n unknown geological layers $l_1, \ldots, l_n$ with thicknesses $h_1, \ldots, h_n$, $h_n = \infty$ and complex-valued electrical conductivities $\sigma_1, \ldots, \sigma_n$. Our goal is to determine these parameters. The first step is the indentification of n; this is done by general geological and geophysical analysis.

We now put all the parameters into a step function $\sigma: (-\infty, 0] \to C$ (C denoting the complex numbers) showing conductivity as a function of depth z. Let $x_\omega: (-\infty, 0] \to C$ be the amplitude of the magnetic component of the radiation with frequency $\omega/(2\pi)$ and $m_\omega := (dx_\omega)/(dz)/x_\omega$. Then according to the Maxwell equations (neglecting any small terms and taking $\tau = \sigma/(i\mu_0)$ as conductivity in the usual sense) we obtain

$$\frac{dx^2 x_\omega}{dz^2} = \omega \, \sigma \, (z) \, x_\omega \tag{1}$$

and (putting $z_0 = 0, z_\mu = - \sum_{\nu=1}^{\mu} h_\nu, \mu = 1, \ldots, n-1$) by the boundedness of x_ω (see also Lemma 1)

$$m_\omega \, (z_{n-1}) = \sqrt{\omega \, \sigma_n}. \tag{2}$$

From M.T. data we gain (by highly sophisticated noise filtering methods and Fast Fourier analysis) the numerical values

$$m_{\omega_\kappa} (0), \kappa = 1, \ldots, k, 2,5 \cdot 10^2 \leqslant \frac{\omega_\kappa}{2\pi} \leqslant 3 \cdot 10^5. \tag{3}$$

The differential equation (1) with the boundary values (2), (3) presents a typical so-called identification problem:
Identify σ from the measurements $m_{\omega_\kappa} (0), \kappa = 1, \ldots, k$.

Tychonoff [1965] showed that $\sigma (z)$ is uniquely determined by $m_\omega (0), 0 \leqslant \omega < \infty$ and *Weidelt* [1972] demonstrated that $\sigma (z)$ is already uniquely determined by the values of $m_\omega (0)$ if ω varies in an infinite bounded set.

It is interesting that (1) is equivalent to a Riccati equation for the variable m_ω:

Theorem 1: (1) is equivalent to

$$\frac{dm_\omega}{dz} = \omega \, \sigma - (m_\omega)^2. \tag{1'}$$

Proof: Substitute $m_\omega = \dfrac{dx_\omega}{dz} / x_\omega$.

4. Numerical Identification as a Combination of a Forward and a Backward Algorithm

The forward algorithm: Construct the values of $m_{\omega_\kappa} (0)$ as a function of $\sigma_1, \ldots, \sigma_n$, $h_1, \ldots, h_{n-1}$.

The backward algorithm: Identify the most likely parameters by making an optimal fit between the measurements and the constructed values of $m_{\omega_\nu} (0)$.

5. Forward Algorithms in the Analysis of M.T. Data

a) Interpretation of initial condition (2):

The solution of (1) for $z \leqslant z_{n-1}$ is (by the theory of linear differential equations)

$$x_\omega(z) = A\, e^{-\sqrt{\omega\sigma_n}(z - z_{n-1})} + B\, e^{\sqrt{\omega\sigma_n}(z - z_{n-1})}, \; Re\sqrt{\omega\sigma_n} > 0, (A, B) \neq (0,0).$$

Clearly x_ω is bounded if, and only if, $A = 0$.

Lemma 1: (2) $m_\omega(z_{n-1}) = \sqrt{\omega\sigma_n}$ if, and only if, x_ω is bounded. This is equivalent to $A = 0$ and in this case m_ω does not depend on the value of B.

Proof: $m_\omega(z_{n-1}) = \dfrac{x'_\omega}{x_\omega}(z_{n-1}) = \sqrt{\omega\sigma_n}\,\dfrac{B - A}{B + A} = \sqrt{\omega\sigma_n}$ if, and only if, $A = 0$, i.e.

$$\binom{x'_\omega}{x_\omega}(z_{n-1}) = B\binom{\sqrt{\omega\sigma_n}}{1}.$$

q.e.d.

Now let us assume that $\binom{x_\omega}{x'_\omega}(z_{n-1}) = \binom{1}{\sqrt{\omega\sigma_n}}$ and that $h_\nu, \sigma_\nu, \nu = 1, \ldots, n$ are given. We calculate $m_\omega(0), 0 \leqslant \omega < \infty$ (the so-called "frequency response").

b) The present author suggests the following algorithm:

Theorem 2: $m_\omega(0) = \dfrac{C}{D}, \binom{D}{C} = \Psi_1 \cdot \Psi_2 \ldots \Psi_{n-1}\binom{1}{\alpha_n}$

$$\Psi_\nu = 1| + \begin{pmatrix} 0 & \alpha_\nu^{-1} \\ \alpha_\nu & 0 \end{pmatrix} \tan h\, \alpha_\nu h_\nu, \alpha_\nu = \sqrt{\omega\sigma_\nu}, \quad \nu = 1, \ldots, n$$

$$\left(\text{note that } 1| := \begin{pmatrix} 1 & 0 \\ 0 & 1 \end{pmatrix}, \cosh x\,(\sinh x) = \frac{e^x \overset{+}{(-)} e^{-x}}{2}, \tan h\, x = \frac{\sinh x}{\cosh x}\right)$$

Proof: We use Lemma 2,3:

Lemma 2: (1) and $(1'')\binom{x_\omega}{x'_\omega}' = \begin{pmatrix} 0 & 1 \\ \omega\sigma & 0 \end{pmatrix}\binom{x_\omega}{x'_\omega}$ are equivalent. Moreover

$$\Phi_\nu(z) = \begin{pmatrix} x_1 & x_2 \\ x'_1 & x'_2 \end{pmatrix} = 1|\cosh\alpha_\nu(z - z_\nu) + \begin{pmatrix} 0 & \alpha_\nu^{-1} \\ \alpha_\nu & 0 \end{pmatrix}\sinh\alpha_\nu(z - z_\nu) \text{ on } [z_\nu, z_{\nu-1}]$$

satisfies $\Phi'_\nu(z) = \begin{pmatrix} 0 & 1 \\ \omega\sigma_\nu & 0 \end{pmatrix}\Phi_\nu(z), \Phi_\nu(z_\nu) = 1|$ and hence is a fundamental system of $(1'')$ on $[z_\nu, z_{\nu-1}], \nu = 1, \ldots, n - 1$.

Lemma 3: Let the elements $m_{\mu\nu}: [z_{n-1}, z_0] \to C, \mu, \nu = 1, \ldots, k$ of the quadratic matrix function M be integrable (but not necessarily continuous) and assume that Φ_ν, $\nu = 1, \ldots, n - 1$ are fundamental systems of $\vec{x}' = M\vec{x}$ on $[z_\nu, z_{\nu-1}]$ satisfying $\Phi_\nu(z_\nu) = 1|$. Then $\vec{x}(z_0) = \Phi_1(z_0)\Phi_2(z_1)\ldots\Phi_{n-1}(z_{n-2})\,\vec{x}(z_{n-1})$ for any solution $\vec{x}$.

Proof: Since $\Phi_\nu (z_\nu) = 1|$, and by definition of a fundamental system, we obtain

$$\vec{x} (z_{\nu-1}) = \Phi_\nu (z_{\nu-1}) \vec{x} (z_\nu)$$
q.e.d.

Proof of Theorem 2: Let $\beta := \left(\prod_{\nu=1}^{n-1} \cosh \alpha_\nu (z_{\nu-1} - z_\nu) \right)^{-1}$. Now $m_\omega (0) = \dfrac{\beta x'_\omega}{\beta x_\omega} (0)$ and

by Lemma 2,3

$$\begin{pmatrix} \beta x_\omega \\ \beta x'_m \end{pmatrix} = \beta \, \Phi_1 (z_0) \dots \Phi_{n-1} (z_{n-2}) \begin{pmatrix} 1 \\ \alpha_n \end{pmatrix} = \Psi_1 \dots \Psi_n \begin{pmatrix} 1 \\ \alpha_n \end{pmatrix}$$
q.e.d.

c) The improved version of Cagniard's algorithm by W. Müller:

This algorithm (used in exploration) is based on the following definitions:

$$Y = - \frac{\rho_1}{\sqrt{i \mu_0 \omega}} \, m_\omega (0), \, \rho_\nu = \frac{i \mu_0}{\sigma_\nu}, \, \eta_\nu = \left(\frac{i \mu_0 \omega}{\rho_\nu} \right)^{1/2}, \, \nu = 1, \dots, n.$$

Theorem 3 [Müller]:

$$Y = - \sqrt{\rho_1} \, \frac{E_1 - F_1}{E_1 + F_1}, \begin{pmatrix} E_1 \\ F_1 \end{pmatrix} = w_1 w_2 \dots w_{n-1} \begin{pmatrix} 0 \\ 1 \end{pmatrix}$$

$$w_\nu = \begin{pmatrix} e^{\eta_\nu h_\nu} & 0 \\ 0 & e^{-\eta_\nu h_\nu} \end{pmatrix} \begin{pmatrix} \sqrt{\rho_\nu} + \sqrt{\rho_{\nu+1}}, \sqrt{\rho_\nu} - \sqrt{\rho_{\nu+1}} \\ \sqrt{\rho_\nu} - \sqrt{\rho_{\nu+1}}, \sqrt{\rho_\nu} + \sqrt{\rho_{\nu+1}} \end{pmatrix}.$$

6. Acknowledgement

M.T. technology, recently also used in mineral exploration definitely has a future ahead. The author would like to thank the exploration companies he contacted in Toronto and Dr. Knödel, head of the M.T. research group at the Bundesanstalt für Rohstoffe und Geowissenschaften, for the many discussions on practical aspects of this new technology.

References

Müller, W.: Dissertation, Bundesanstalt für Rohstoffe und Geowissenschaften, 1978.

Tychonoff, A.N.: Mathematical Basis of the Theory of Electromagnetic soundings. USSR, Comput. Math. and Math. Phys. **5**, 1965, 207–211.

Weidelt, P.: The inverse Problem of Geomagnetic Induction. Zeitschrift für Geophysik **38**, 1972, 257–289.

Economic Theory of Natural Resources. ©Physica-Verlag, Würzburg–Wien, 1982.

Analysis of Marine Fishery Systems
Based on Commercial Catch and Effort Data

Manfred Nuske

The economic theory of fishery regulation is concerned with the description, forecasting, and control of basic production within fishery systems. Because of the complexity and the generally high degree of inherent unobservability of such systems, for management purposes detailed information would be desirable concerning the resource itself as well as the fleet of fishing boats operating on the resource. Often, however, the only data available to fishery economists are time series of total annual catches from the resource and corresponding values of some index of fishing effort. On a data base of this kind in many cases a preliminary assessment of the state and dynamics of a whole fishery, including estimates of the magnitude and productivity of the resource, is required by some national or international management agency. The purpose of this paper is to give a systematic overview of such catch-and-effort techniques. It is shown that in the fields of economics and engineering there already exists a large number of estimation and prediction methods which easily can be formulated in such a way that efficient catch-and-effort techniques for the analysis of marine fishery systems result.

Introduction

One of the major concerns of the theory of marine fishery regulation is the description and forecasting of the basic production processes on the water. A good understanding and appropriate modeling of the dynamic interaction between the fishery resource itself, the fleet of boats operating on the resource, and the catches resulting from fishing operations is of crucial importance in any attempt to control a fishery in an effective way.

Clearly enough, marine fisheries are highly complex systems with biological and ecological, technological, economic, and social aspects, driven by a multitude of different factors which, like for example changes in the natural environment of the resource or in the socio-economic environment of the fishermen, are difficult to observe and interpret, or even to predict. Management agencies concerned with the regulation of marine fisheries typically have to operate in a world of uncertainty and conflicting objectives where decisions usually have to be taken under severe financial, legal, and political restrictions.

So it is not surprising that some of the once largest commercial fisheries of the world, although controlled by national or international commissions, are in bad condition today. High technological standards of the fleets, worldwide rapidly increasing demand for fishery products, and the lack of sound management principles — perhaps in combination with unfavourable environmental conditions — have led to the collapse of, for example, the Peruvian anchoveta and the North Atlantic herring fisheries [*Idyll; Sætersdal; Holt*].

To understand, predict, or even control the behaviour of a commercial fishery in all relevant aspects clearly is an interdisciplinary task which requires a large amount of different kinds of information. In many cases, however, not much information is available, especially not on the unobservable biological and ecological conditions of the resource, and yet at least a preliminary assessment of the fundamental characteristics of the resource itself and of the dynamic interaction between the resource and the fleet of fishing boats is desired. Questions arising in such a context might concern the actual magnitude of the resource stock, its natural equilibrium size with no fishing at all, the maximum productivity of the resource, and the total fishing effort that could be used per year to catch for instance just the amount of maximum surplus production of the resource without further reducing the stock.

Among the first data that *are* available for stock assessment purposes, one usually has information on past catch and effort values, and one would want to start with an analysis of these fundamental fishery data to get at least a rough idea of the basic characteristics of the resource and of the influence that fishing operation might have on the stocks and on present and future catches. Even when there exists detailed knowledge about the biological and environmental aspects of the resource, for example about the stock-recruitment relationship and natural mortality of the stock, about its spawning or feeding migrations, or about the age and length composition of the catches, even in such cases catch and effort statistics, in addition, are carefully analyzed by fishery scientists because the ratio of catch and effort, the socalled cpue value (catch per unit of effort), often can be considered a reliable index of the actual density and overall magnitude of the stock. That is, if the cpue values show a downward trend, then in many cases it can be inferred that the abundance of the stock has been diminishing, too [FAO, 1976].

Besides for giving direct hints on probable changes in the stock size over time, catch and effort statistics can be used in various ways for a direct or indirect description of the basic production processes within a fishery. The purpose of this paper is a systematic discussion of such possibilities. In particular, an overview of a number of estimation and prediction procedures is given which allow for basic stock assessments and catch predictions with catch and effort statistics as the only data requirement.

To begin with, we look more closely at the production process within a fishery. We discuss several general possibilities of building models which could give an adequate description of production in one or another real-world fishery. Considering the usual amount of observable fluctuations in the production processes, we feel that random disturbances should be explicitly recognized and incorporated into the models. Also, because of the general scarcity of available data, in our view it seems more natural to describe the dynamics of the system by means of difference instead of differential equations. So we only consider production models which can be written as stochastic difference equations in catch, effort, and cpue values.

We first give an overview of those methods which presume a direct relationship between present, past, and future catch and effort values and thus allow for quick and easy prediction for example of future catch values. Regression techniques and time series methods belong to this group of direct catch-and-effort methods.

Although these *direct* prediction methods have some obvious advantages over more sophisticated catch-and-effort techniques, only few of their many possible versions have been proposed and occasionally applied in fishery sciences. The *"black box"* approach, so common in econometrics, is not very popular with fishery scientists. For the description of production within fishery systems models and methods are preferred which give explicit consideration to some fundamental biological and technological characteristics of the fishery. Methods have been developed which allow for the estimation of these fundamental characteristics on the basis of commercial catch and effort data only. The socalled Schaefer approach is the predominant method of this class of catch-and-effort techniques which, to contrast it with the more direct black box methods, could be named the class of *state oriented* or *indirect* catch-and-effort techniques.

Because of several obvious shortcomings of the traditional Schaefer method, and also of its modern versions, we suggest the use of more flexible identification procedures which have become available in recent years from different fields of systems engineering [see, e.g., *Jazwinski; Sage/Melsa; McGarty*]. As an example from this class of state oriented methods we use the Kalman filter to construct indirect catch-and-effort techniques for the description of production in marine fishery systems. These methods necessarily will be of a Bayesian character, that is, they allow for efficient utilization of all kinds of "soft" prior information which might be available in addition to the "hard" catch and effort data. On the other hand, a possible disadvantage of these methods lies in the fact that they also *need* some prior information. Without such information state oriented catch-and-effort techniques, after much computational work, can yield stock assessments and catch predictions only with a high level of uncertainty.

This paper is concerned only with methods for the observation and forecasting of production in fishery systems. No further questions concerning fishery regulation will be considered. Clearly enough, for control purposes historical catch and effort statistics would not be sufficient as a data base. For such a purpose one obviously would have to look at a fishery within its economic, social, and political environment, that is, one would have to think not only about the questions of what to fish, how to fish, when and where to fish, but also about the questions of why to fish, how much to fish now and how much to fish later, and how much to use of the necessary but scarce productive factors like manpower, boats, and fuel.

Fishery Systems and Production

To describe basic production processes within a fishery, a first approach would be to regard all productive factors like manpower and experience, boats, equipment and fishing gear, etc. as the inputs to and the resulting catches as the outputs from the process. One then could try to model the relationship between inputs and outputs in the usual way by means of a production function [*Eichhorn; Shephard; Johansen*].

To simplify such an approach, it is common practice in fishery sciences to condense all input goods and services into a scalar index called "effort" [FAO, 1976]. The physical dimension of such an index, usually calculated at a very high level of aggregation, might for instance be "total fishing time per year", measured in boat-days. Other definitions of "effort" are possible and for many types of fisheries also advisable [see, e.g., *Gulland*, 1969; *Rothschild; Holden/Raitt*]. The theoretical problems concerning the aggregation of different types of inputs in constructing fishing effort indices are discussed by *Huang/Lee* [1976].

The output from the production process, the catch from the resource under consideration, can be measured, for example, as "total live weight of annual catch" in pounds or numbers. Catch measurements, too, are not free from difficulties [see, e.g., FAO, 1973]. We do not discuss these difficulties here but think of both catch and effort data as being calculated in a meaningful way, recorded at equally spaced intervals of time. In practice, catch and effort data usually are provided with a monthly or a yearly sampling interval. Monthly fishery data, in general, exhibit significant seasonal patterns, and also contain relatively more „noise" than yearly data. Thus, for state estimation purposes the available data first have to be aggregated to yearly data. We only consider such aggregated data, although an analysis of monthly data could give valuable additional information within the framework of direct catch-and-effort techniques.

Based on the two time series of available catch and effort data, $c_1, c_2, \ldots, c_n$ and $e_1, e_2, \ldots, e_n$, where the indices $1, 2, \ldots, n$ correspond to n successive years, one would like to specify a production function Q which relates the effort input to the catch output. With regard to the uncertainty and ambiguity in the data collection procedure, and also to take care of the many important factors which, like weather conditions, experience of the skippers, or just luck in fishing at the right time in the right place, are unaccounted for by the effort data but nevertheless have great influence on the resulting catches, it seems natural to include a random term into the production model. That is, one first would think of a theoretic relationship between input and output values as given by a stochastic model of the general form

$$c_i = Q_i\,(e_i, \eta_i); \qquad\qquad i = 1, 2, \ldots \qquad\qquad (1)$$

where the quantities $\eta_1, \eta_2, \ldots$ are individual random variables from a stochastic sequence $\{\eta_i : i = 1, 2, \ldots\}$, the realizations of which cannot be observed directly.

By appropriately identifying and specifying a sequence of functions Q_i and a probability law for the disturbance process $\{\eta_i\}$,[1]) a general production model of form (1) clearly always can be fitted to any set of observed data pairs $(e_1, c_1), (e_2, c_2), \ldots, (e_n, c_n)$. Nevertheless, such an approach may be of little value concerning explanation and prediction purposes, because (1) does not explicitly reflect the influences which past effort and catch values might have on the current production situation.

For a comparison of different equilibrium situations, however, a useful description of the input-output relationship of the production process might be given by a model of type (1), even with a time-independent production function Q. Here we consider a fishery "in equilibrium" or "in a stationary phase" if it exhibits two properties of stationarity. The first property is that, during the time period under consideration, no structural changes occur in the fishery, e.g. concerning the environmental conditions of the resource or the technological characteristics of the fleet. The second requirement for a fishery being in equilibrium is that the effort inputs of successive years do not differ very much from each other.

The reason for the first requirement simply is that structural changes within the production process would change at least some parameters of the model. The reason for the

---

[1]) When there is no possible confusion, we omit the parameter space of a stochastic sequence. We also do not make a notational distinction between random variables and their realizations.

second requirement is that during fishing operations not simply excess fish is harvested, but the stock itself is reduced. A change in the effort level usually would result in a change in the catch level which, in return, would influence the stock size and by that the availability and natural productivity of the resource. A change in these fundamental resource characteristics normally would have influence on future catches. This complex feedback relationship between catch and stock size clearly would complicate the use of a model of type (1) for situations in which an already developed fishery shows a nonstationary behaviour with significant annual changes in the effort input.

For the case of an *equilibrium fishery* model (1) could be written, for example, as

$$c_i = Q(e_i) \exp(\eta_i) \tag{2}$$

where Q now is some concave function of the effort input only, defined up to a certain value e_{max}, and $\{\eta_i\}$ is a stationary zero-mean disturbance sequence, uncorrelated with the e sequence. A comparison of different equilibrium situations for a fishery now can be made by analyzing (2) for different possible effort sequences $\{e_i\}$, where each sequence is assumed to be nearly constant.

Deterministic versions of (2) have been studied in fishery sciences since long [*Graham; Schaefer*, 1954]. The shape of the effort-yield function Q, in general, is assumed parabola-like, with Q starting in the origin, increasing in a nearly proportional way as long as effort values are small enough to produce catches of which the influence on the stock size is negligible. With medium-size effort values usually a law of diminishing returns begins to work, the catch output will suffer decreasing increments if the effort input is increased. After reaching some maximum value, called the MSY level (maximum sustainable yield) of the fishery, with further increasing e values the Q values begin to decline. An equilibrium situation with such high effort values clearly could be termed a case of overfishing. In such a case a certain proportion of the total effort input is wasted and, in addition, even has the negative effect of reducing the level of available total catch. This general shape of the deterministic part of the production model (2) for equilibrium situations is well-established in fishery sciences [*Clark*]. The properties of the stochastic part $\{\eta_i\}$, however, have not yet received much attention.

There is a second situation for which a model of type (1) can be useful — the situation of an *undeveloped fishery*. Here we speak of an "undeveloped" fishery if the technology of the fleet does not change much through time and if the annual effort values e_i are relatively small, so that the resulting catches have no significant influence on the stock size. For such a situation a simple model of the form

$$c_i = qe_i \exp(\eta_i) \tag{3}$$

with q being a positive constant, might give an adequate description. Algebraically (3) looks like a special case of (2), but while (2) is meant only for equilibrium situations with all three sequences $\{e_i\}$, $\{\eta_i\}$, and $\{c_i\}$ being stationary, model (3) describes equilibrium as well as nonequilibrium situations as long as the series of the logarithms of the cpue values u_i can be considered an observation of a stationary stochastic process.

Model (3) also can be used for the description of *developing fisheries*, that is, for situations in which the effort series contains a significant positive trend while improving technology of the fleet offsets the effects of the law of diminishing returns — at least up to a certain effort level — in such a way that again the series of the transformed data $\ln (u_i)$ can be considered a realization of some stationary stochastic process.

For the description of an arbitrary, in particular a *developed nonstationary fishery*, a production model of type (2) or (3) is not suitable. Instead, a model has to be constructed which takes into account the dynamic aspects of the production process. In principle there are two possibilities to build such a model — the "black box" approach and the "state oriented" approach.

The *"black box"* or *"input-output"* approach would be to directly insert into the model all catch and effort values of the past which might have influence on present and future catches, e.g. as

$$c_i = Q\,(e_i; c_{i-1}, c_{i-2}, \ldots, c_{i-r}; \eta_i) \tag{4}$$

or as

$$c_i = Q\,(e_i, e_{i-1}, e_{i-2}, \ldots, e_{i-r}; \eta_i). \tag{5}$$

In both models r is some sufficiently large number, for example, if such information is available, taken as the average natural life-time of an individual animal of the resource. If not only effort and catch values but also some important features of the structure of the fishery are changing significantly through time, then at least some parameters of Q would be time-dependent and a subscript i should be added on Q.

The second possibility to model the dynamic aspects of the production process would be to explicitly consider all biological and technological characteristics of the system which might have significant influence on the catches. These characteristics could be collected into some vector y called the *state* of the fishery. Then, instead of (4) or (5), production within a nonstationary fishery could be modeled as

$$c_i = Q\,(y_i, e_i, \epsilon_i) \tag{6}$$

where the disturbances ϵ_i now represent a white noise sequence, that is, a sequence of independent and identically distributed random variables. In many applications the state y is just defined as the magnitude of the resource, measured, for example, as the "total biomass of the stock". If structural changes occur in the fishery, instead of taking Q to be time-varying, one could try to take care of such changes by augmenting the state vector y appropriately.

The difficulty with a state oriented production model (6) clearly is that not only the function Q and the probability law of the disturbances ϵ_i have to be identified and fully specified on the basis of the available catch and effort data, but that also the generally unobservable state of the fishery, y_i, has to be estimated for each year. On the other hand, if there is some extra information available concerning the fundamental characteristics of the fishery, then this information could be included into the state estimation procedure. The more direct approaches (4) and (5) do not offer this possibility.

Up to now we only considered effort as the quantity which characterizes the input to a fishery and catch as the corresponding output from the production system. From such a viewpoint the connection between these two quantities can either be modeled directly through a black box approach (models (4) or (5)) or indirectly with explicit consideration of the state of the fishery (model (6)). Mathematically the difference between these two approaches is only superficial — one clearly could define, for example, a vector $(e_{i-1}, e_{i-2}, \ldots, e_{i-r})$ as the "state" y_i. We nevertheless make a formal distinction between the two methods because in practice they are used for different purposes. While input-output methods are sufficient for catch predictions, state oriented catch-and-effort techniques might give more insight into the structure and dynamics of a fishery.

From a system theoretic standpoint a much more general view is possible and sometimes advisable. For example, one also could consider both catch and effort values as observable outputs from, and a number of ecological factors, specific control measures, informations and expectations, market signals, and other influences from the natural and socio-economic environment as the inputs to the fishery. Information on past catch and effort values, too, would be part of the total input to the system. It might well be the case that high catches of the past attract new fishermen to the system and thus influence current and future effort values. Models of this type, which consider dynamic interaction between the resource and the fleet of fishing boats to occur like in a predator-prey system, have been proposed occasionally [*Schaefer*, 1954; *Smith; Gatto/Rinaldi/Walters*] but, considering the common scarcity of information on general inputs and structural relationships, clearly are difficult to identify and to work with. For the sake of simplicity we confine ourselves to situations where unidirectional causality between effort and catch values can be assumed with effort as the determining and catch as the dependent variable. The models (1) until (6) clearly correspond to such a view of a fishery.

Catch and Effort Forecasts

Direct forecasts of catch and effort values can be obtained in a number of different ways by means of more or less sophisticated methods. Each method, however, is based on some particular information set which consists of a collection of "hard" data and a certain amount of "soft" information like intuitive knowledge from experience with similar situations, assumptions, theories, etc. We denote the total amount of information as available in year n by I_n. The hard data lying in the information set I_n are, for our purposes, the available catch and effort data up to year n. If the fishery is controlled through effort values, say, then also e_{n+1} would belong to I_n. The soft part of I_n might, for example, consist of some general information on the structural conditions of the fishery, whether it is in a stationary or in a nonstationary phase, etc. Also assumptions concerning the shape of the production function Q or the probability law of the disturbance sequence $\{\eta_i\}$ belong to I_n.

On the basis of a specific information set I_n one would like to forecast, for example, next year's total catch from the resource, that is, the value of the random variable c_{n+1}. A complete specification of the conditional distribution of c_{n+1} given I_n, perhaps through the conditional probability density $p(c_{n+1} | I_n)$, would perfectly solve the forecasting problem, but, of course, may be difficult to obtain. In many cases, however, a point prediction might suffice. A particularly useful point forecast of c_{n+1} is the conditional expectation $E[c_{n+1} | I_n]$, but other forecast values also may have their advantages. In general we denote a specific forecast based on the information set I_n as $\hat{c}_{n+1|n}$. Equivalently, a point forecast of next year's effort value e_{n+1} is denoted as $\hat{e}_{n+1|n}$.

Although we are mainly interested in methods which use catch *and* effort data for forecasting production within fishery systems, we also want to shortly consider the case where the hard part of the information set I_n is very small and consists only of a series of annual catch data. Clearly it is more appealing to relate catch values in a causal way to effort and state values, but because of the notorious difficulties with the definition and recording of the effort index, and because of the usual lack of information concerning the state and dynamics of the resource, it may be possible to extract sufficient information from the observed catch values themselves, without explicit use of any effort data. This may be a reasonable approach especially in cases where the fishery seems to be either in a stationary or in a developing stage. In both cases, according to (2) and (3) respectively, the general structure of the sequence $\{e_i\}$ would be reflected directly in the sequence $\{c_i\}$, so that an explicit consideration of effort data need not improve the catch predictions.

Also, in practice effort data often are calculated through catch data by comparing total catches with the catches of a specific standard vessel of which fishing time has been observed accurately [see, e.g., *Gulland*, 1969]. In such cases it might be inappropriate to regard fishing effort as an independent, catch determining variable, and one maybe better would remove such "artificial" effort data from the information set.

If the fishery is in a stationary phase with only small changes through time in fishing effort as well as in fishing methods and technology, this being an assumption which one would have to include into the information set I_n, then the theoretical catch sequence $\{c_i\}$ can be considered a stationary stochastic process. If the fishery is in an early developing stage where increasing demand for fish products increases prices and profits, and thus attracts new fishermen to the resource, it might be reasonable to assume a trend component for the catch generating process. In both cases, however, the basic properties of the theoretical catch sequence have to be first inferred from the information set I_n and then extrapolated to the future to produce the desired forecasts.

In the following we shortly mention several univariate time series forecasting procedures which, for some fisheries, could give predictions of future catch values with sufficient accuracy. Although this body of methods has a long history in economics, it has not yet attracted much interest in the literature of fishery regulation. This is regrettable because univariate time series methods, in general, are quick and easy to apply and may nevertheless produce catch forecasts which, in the cases of a stationary or a developing fishery, might be as good as any forecast obtained by much more sophisticated catch-and-effort techniques.

To describe the theoretical catch sequence $\{c_i\}$ resulting from a stationary fishery, a good model may be of the linear form

$$c_i = K + \sum_{j=1}^{r} \alpha_j \, c_{i-j} + \eta_i \tag{7}$$

where K and $\alpha_1, \alpha_2, \ldots, \alpha_r$ are some constants and $\{\eta_i\}$ is a stationary disturbance sequence. A convenient form for $\{\eta_i\}$ would be a white noise sequence or, more generally, a moving average model

$$\eta_i = \epsilon_i + \sum_{j=1}^{s} \beta_j \, \epsilon_{i-j} \tag{8}$$

where $\beta_1, \beta_2, \ldots, \beta_s$ are constants and $\{\epsilon_i\}$ is a zero-mean white noise process.

The simplest special case of (7) would be the random walk model

$$c_i = c_{i-1} + \epsilon_i. \tag{9}$$

Although this model would not result in a stationary theoretical catch sequence $\{c_i\}$, it nevertheless might be a good prediction model for stationary fisheries, at least in cases where only short time periods are considered and the estimated noise variance σ_ϵ^2 is not too large. The great advantage of the prediction model (9) obviously lies in the simplicity of the resulting point forecasts which, if defined as conditional expectations $E\,[c_{n+1}|I_n]$, plainly are

$$\hat{c}_{n+1|n} = c_n. \tag{10}$$

Forecasts of this kind could be termed "no change forecasts".

A very simple prediction formula also results from an autoregressive model of the type

$$c_i = \sum_{j=1}^{r} \alpha_j\, c_{i-j} + \epsilon_i \tag{11}$$

with the additional assumption that the "weights" α_j all are positive numbers of which the sum is just 1. A particular simple weighting scheme would be to set all parameters α_j equal to $1/r$, but it may be more reasonable to put more weight on the latest observations and less weight on the older catch data. The resulting forecasts

$$\hat{c}_{n+1|n} = \sum_{j=1}^{r} \alpha_j\, c_{n+1-j} \tag{12}$$

usually are termed "(weighted) moving average forecasts". The problem with a forecasting procedure of this type clearly lies in the choice of the values of r and $\alpha_1, \alpha_2, \ldots, \alpha_r$.

Another convenient prediction model for a stationary fishery could be the integrated moving average model

$$c_i = c_{i-1} + \epsilon_i - (1 - \beta)\, \epsilon_{i-1} \tag{13}$$

where β is a constant, $\beta \in (0, 1)$. It is easily shown [see, e.g., *Nelson*] that for this theoretical catch generating process the optimal point forecast $\hat{c}_{n+1|n}$, again defined as the conditional expectation $E\,[c_{n+1}|I_n]$, can be calculated recursively by the "updating" formula

$$\hat{c}_{n+1|n} = \hat{c}_{n|n-1} + \beta\,(c_n - \hat{c}_{n|n-1}). \tag{14}$$

As a "starting up" assumption one, for example, could set $\hat{c}_{2|1}$ equal to c_1. Forecasts obtained by (14) are termed "exponential smoothing forecasts". The constant β is called the "smoothing parameter". Numerical values for β can be chosen, for example, in such a way that by (14) the sum of squared prediction errors, for a number of recent years, is minimized.

A fourth special case of the linear prediction model (7) would be an autoregressive model of the type

$$c_i - c_{i-1} = \sum_{j=1}^{r} \alpha_j\,(c_{i-j} - c_{i-j-1}) + \epsilon_i \tag{15}$$

where the attention now is directed to changes $c_i - c_{i-1}$ rather than to the levels c_i themselves. There are several reasons for such an approach [see, e.g., *Granger/Newbold*]. An appropriate value for r and values for the corresponding parameters $\alpha_1, \alpha_2, \ldots, \alpha_r$ can be found, for example, by techniques referred to as "stepwise regression" [see, e.g., *Daniel/Wood*]. If the model (15) has been correctly specified, then the optimal catch prediction clearly is

$$\hat{c}_{n+1\,|n} = c_n + \sum_{j=1}^{r} \alpha_j \, (c_{n+1-j} - c_{n-j}). \tag{16}$$

These forecasts could be termed "autoregression forecasts of catch increments".

The most flexible approach to the description and prediction of a sequence of catches from a stationary fishery, however, would be the Box-Jenkins methodology [*Box/Jenkins*]. Following this path, one would slightly specialize the general linear model (7), (8) such that a stationary mixed autoregressive moving average process $\{c_i\}$ with mean μ_c would result, i.e. a model of the form

$$c_i - \mu_c = \sum_{j=1}^{r} \alpha_j \, (c_{i-j} - \mu_c) + \epsilon_i + \sum_{j=1}^{s} \beta_j \epsilon_{i-j}. \tag{17}$$

This model, now, can be fitted to the observed catch data by means of an iterative cycle of identification, estimation, and diagnostic checking. After a satisfactory specification of (17) has been achieved, the optimal forecast would be

$$\hat{c}_{n+1\,|n} = \mu_c \, (1 - \sum_{j=1}^{r} \alpha_j) + \sum_{j=1}^{r} \alpha_j \, c_{n+1-j} + \sum_{j=1}^{s} \beta_j \epsilon_{n+1-j} \tag{18}$$

where the quantities ϵ_{n+1-j} simply are the observed residuals from the fitted model (17). For the calculation of these quantities clearly some "starting up" assumption has to be made such as defining values $c_0, c_{-1}, \ldots, c_{1-r}$ all as being equal to μ_c, and values $\epsilon_0, \epsilon_{-1}, \ldots, \epsilon_{1-s}$ as being equal to 0. To avoid a cumbersome notation, in (18), as before, we assume that all model parameters have been correctly specified so that no notational difference has to be made between the observable residuals and the unobservable disturbance terms themselves.

The difficulty with the Box-Jenkins approach here is that the set of available catch data only in very few cases would be large enough to allow for the whole specification process. Even if there are, say, 50 data available, then the assumption of stationarity for such a long time period hardly ever would hold for a fishery. For this reason the extrapolation techniques mentioned earlier could well be reasonable alternatives. Also it might be possible to calculate several point predictions by different methods, assemble all of them into a "forecast portfolio", and then find that linear combination of individual forecasts which, in some sense, is optimal. Here the same ideas can be used as developed by Markowitz in the context of optimal diversification among risky securities [*Markowitz;* see also *Bates/Granger; Newbold/Granger*].

For the description of a developing fishery without any effort data, there are two main possibilities to take care of trends in the catch sequence. The first set of methods is concerned with the transformation and differencing of the original catch data until a new series is generated which can be assumed a realization of some stationary process. This new time series now is analyzed, and predictions of this series are translated back to catch predictions. The second possibility to take care of obvious trends in the catch data would be to directly introduce for example an additive trend term into the prediction model. This trend term could be identified as some appropriate time function and specified by a filtering or regression procedure on the available catch data.

While methods of the first type do not appear in the literature of fishery regulation, simple methods of the second type have been used, especially during the decade from 1965 until 1975, in the context of long-term forecasting of total annual world catches [see, e.g., *Schaefer*, 1965; *Chapman*; *Gulland*, 1971; *Paiva Pinto* et al.]. The reason for the use of simple trend models like, for example,

$$c_i = \alpha + \beta i + \epsilon_i \tag{19}$$

has been the obvious tendency of world catch data to center around a straight line in the time-catch plane for the years from 1950 until 1970 [see fig. S1. in *Gulland*, 1971]. Since 1971, however, a trend model of type (19) does not give a good description of world catches any more [see fig. 1 in *Hennemuth*]. Nevertheless, for individual fisheries in early growth periods linear trend models of form (19) still may be useful.

If the interest of a management agency is not only concentrated on future catches but also on future effort values, then all univariate time series procedures outlined for the forecasting of catch values can be used in an analogous way. The information set now would consist of a series of annual effort data $e_1, e_2, \ldots, e_n$, together with some general information on the effort-driving forces of the system. We do not want to discuss this subject any further but consider now the case where catch *and* effort data are available.

If catch and effort data are available and both time series exhibit a nonstationary behaviour, it often is the case that the cpue data u_i form a series which is much smoother than the original two series. A common situation is that the u data show a downward trend [see, e.g., table 1 in *Garrod*]. An obvious possibility for the calculation of catch predictions now would be to apply appropriate univariate time series methods on the u data, calculate forecasts $\hat{u}_{n+1|n}$, and then compute the corresponding catch predictions by means of

$$\hat{c}_{n+1|n} = e_{n+1}\,\hat{u}_{n+1|n}. \tag{20}$$

If the future effort value e_{n+1} is not completely controllable but also must be considered an uncertain quantity, then one could either give a set of conditional predictions (20) for different possible values of e_{n+1}, or one could try to predict e_{n+1} first and then use (20) with $\hat{e}_{n+1|n}$ instead of e_{n+1}.

The forecasting procedure (20) should be particularly useful for undeveloped or developing fisheries. For such cases model (3) suggests that the sequence $\{\ln(u_i)\}$ be stationary. Predictions of this series are readily transformed into predictions $\hat{u}_{n+1|n}$.

For an arbitrary fishery it might be possible to identify (6) as

$$c_i = q\,(y_i)\,e_i\,\exp(\eta_i) \tag{21}$$

where q now is a function of the state of the fishery. If the fishery can be assumed stationary, then the state y_i should not change much during the period under consideration, and (21) can be approximated by

$$c_i = q e_i \exp(\eta_i) \tag{22}$$

which is of the same form as (3). Consequently, the same prediction procedure can be applied as for undeveloped or developing fisheries.

If a developed fishery shows a significantly nonstationary behaviour, time series methods applied on the u data, in general, would not lead far. For such cases regression models may be more suitable, e.g. models of one of the following forms:

$$c_i = \sum_{j=0}^{r} \beta_j e_{i-j} + \eta_i \tag{23}$$

$$u_i = \alpha + \sum_{j=0}^{r} \beta_j e_{i-j} + \eta_i \tag{24}$$

$$u_i = \alpha + \sum_{j=0}^{r} \beta_j c_{i-j} + \eta_i. \tag{25}$$

An approach similar to (24) has been suggested by *Gulland* [1969, p. 120]. Because of the influence which effort and catch values of the past may have on current stock size and catch, the regression parameters $\beta_1, \beta_2, \ldots, \beta_r$ of model (23) should be negative, whereas β_0 clearly is positive. In (24) and (25) one would expect α to be positive and all β values to be negative. All three models can be fitted to a set of available catch and effort data, for example, by means of stepwise regression techniques. Also, to take into account prior information on the parameter values or to allow the parameters to be time-varying, Bayesian specification procedures might be appropriate [*Zellner;Athans*]. The corresponding prediction equations are constructed in an obvious manner.

Although for the different types of fisheries in their different stages a large number of efficient procedures obviously is available for direct catch predictions, these methods only occasionally are used for practical fishery regulation purposes. A more common approach in such a context is the Schaefer technique which we describe in the next section.

The Schaefer Approach

One of the earliest attempts to identify a parabolic production function Q of type (2) has been made by *Graham* [1935]. His approach was brought into a mathematically more transparent formulation and applied to several real-world fisheries by *Schaefer* [1954, 1957]. Schaefer extended the method to the case of nonequilibrium fisheries, and also developed an estimation procedure which allows for a complete specification of a production function of type (6) with catch and effort statistics as the only data requirement. The basic assumption of the now commonly called Schaefer approach is that the state of the fishery is sufficiently described by the stock size ("total biomass") x, of which the dynamics can be expressed by means of a deterministic differential equation as

$$\frac{dx(t)}{dt} = G(x(t), t) - c(t) \tag{26}$$

where G is the natural net growth rate of the resource and c is the rate of harvesting.

It is clear that neither x nor G can be observed directly and that c is a flow variable which cannot be recorded in continuous time. Also, at least for most cold water fisheries, one would have to assume G to be a periodic time function, which again would complicate a direct specification of (26). To avoid these difficulties, for our purposes a formulation in terms of a stochastic difference equation seems more appropriate, e.g. in the form

$$x_{i+1} - x_i = G(x_i, \epsilon_{1i}) - c_i \tag{27}$$

where x_i is the size of the resource at the beginning of year i, G is the total net growth (in biomass) of the resource during year i, and c_i is, as before, the total catch from the resource during year i. The sequence $\{\epsilon_{1i}\}$ is a white noise sequence.

The socalled Schaefer method now can be described as follows:
First, a growth function G and a production function Q of type (6),

$$c_i = Q(x_i, e_i, \epsilon_{2i}) \tag{28}$$

are postulated for the fishery and identified up to some unknown parameters. Then, from equation (28) each value x_i is expressed in terms of c_i, e_i, ϵ_{2i} and the unknown model parameters. These expressions are substituted for the x values in (27), thus giving an equation which only contains observable catch and effort quantities, unobservable model parameters, and a number of random variables. If one is lucky, the outcome of this procedure is a stochastic equation amenable to some regression technique by which the unknown model parameters can be estimated. From these estimates, finally, estimates of the current stock size and other quantities of interest are calculated.

To give an example of this method, we present a slightly simplified version of the original Schaefer approach. *Schaefer* [1954, 1957] transformed a differential equation of type (26) into a stochastic equation (27), the growth function G of which he identified as a stochastic modification of the logistic equation such as

$$G(x_i, \epsilon_{1i}) = \alpha x_i \left(1 - \frac{x_i}{\beta} + \epsilon_{1i} \right) \tag{29}$$

where α represents the intrinsic growth rate and β the average carrying capacity of the natural environment of the resource. For the production function Q Schaefer assumed a deterministic function which is proportional in effort as well as in stock size,

$$Q(x_i, e_i, \epsilon_{2i}) = q x_i e_i \tag{30}$$

where q is a technological parameter. Following the procedure outlined above, a regression model in terms of observable e and u values results:

$$\frac{u_{i+1}}{u_i} = (1 + \alpha) - \frac{\alpha}{\beta q} u_i - q e_i + \alpha \epsilon_{1i}. \tag{31}$$

After fitting this equation to the available cpue and effort data, the original model parameters α, β, and q can be estimated in an obvious way. From these estimates which for the moment we denote as $\hat{\alpha}$, $\hat{\beta}$, and $\hat{q}$, estimates of the series of past and current stock size values can be obtained by (28) and (30) as

$$\hat{x}_i = \frac{u_i}{\hat{q}}. \tag{32}$$

For management purposes it clearly would be interesting to compare these estimates with the estimated natural carrying capacity $\hat{\beta}$, as well as with an estimate of that stock size which, for an equilibrium fishery, would maximize the expected annual net growth of the resource.

It is clear that by (31) the state oriented production model (30) can be rewritten in an input-output formulation as

$$c_i = Q'(e_i, e_{i-1}, c_{i-1}, \epsilon_{1,i-1}) \tag{33}$$

which can be used for catch prediction purposes.

In a deterministic framework, that is, with omission of the disturbance terms in (27) and (28), one could define a maximum stock size x_{max}, a maximum sustainable annual catch c_{MSY}, and related equilibrium quantities by means of

$$x_{max} = \max\{x : G(x) = 0\} \tag{34}$$

$$c_{MSY} = \max\{G(x) : 0 \leqslant x \leqslant x_{max}\} \tag{35}$$

$$x_{MSY} = \max\{x : G(x) = c_{MSY}\} \tag{36}$$

$$e_{MSY} = \min\{e : Q(x_{MSY}, e) = c_{MSY}\} \tag{37}$$

so that the special model (29), (30) would yield

$$x_{max} = \beta, x_{MSY} = \frac{\beta}{2}, e_{MSY} = \frac{\alpha}{2q}, c_{MSY} = \frac{\alpha\beta}{4}. \tag{38}$$

In a stochastic setting the quantities x_{max} etc. have no well-defined meaning. Nevertheless, one could compute the terms $\hat{\beta}$, $\hat{\beta}/2$, $\hat{\alpha}/2\hat{q}$, and $\hat{\alpha}\hat{\beta}/4$ to get some rough idea of the current situation of the fishery.

It is obvious that the estimates obtained by the regression model (31) are by no means optimal. In our view, the main weaknesses of the standard procedure (31) are as follows:

First, the assumed constancy of the model parameters α and β in (29) for periods of several decades may be an inadequate simplification of real-world phenomena. It is well-known in fishery sciences that especially some pelagic fish resources show strong cyclical fluctuations which are due solely to natural causes [see, e.g., *Cushing; Gulland*, 1974].

A second shortcoming of the traditional Schaefer technique lies in the inconsistency of (28) and (30). To overcome this inconsistency, one clearly would have to either add an error term to the right side of (30) or allow q to be time-varying. It might be a reasonable approach to introduce instead of a constant q a stochastic sequence $\{q_i\}$, perhaps with some positive trend.

Third, it may be inappropriate to assume white noise characteristics for the random input in (29) and (31). In practical applications, the observed residuals of (31) might well suggest heteroscedasticity and serial dependence for the disturbance sequence. Also, the time lag structure of (31), in general, would produce biased least-squares estimates. Even if one neglects these econometric difficulties, an ad hoc calculation of the estimate $\hat{\beta}$ from the previously estimated regression coefficients may be suboptimal, and also the derived quantities $\hat{\alpha}/2\hat{q}$ and $\hat{\alpha}\hat{\beta}/4$ may be less meaningful than often is assumed. The reason for this lies in the simple fact that a product or a ratio of somehow optimal estimates need not be an optimal estimate of the corresponding product or ratio.

Attempts have been made to partly overcome some of the shortcomings of the traditional Schaefer approach. Modifications which allow for skewness in the growth function G are discussed by *Pella/Tomlinson* [1969] and *Fox* [1970]. More attention to estimation aspects has been paid by *Walters/Hilborn* [1976], *Schnute* [1977], *McGaw* [1980], and *Gatto/Rinaldi* [1980]. Interesting results from simulation studies are reported by *Hilborn* [1979]. Attempts to incorporate into the Schaefer procedure the effects of changes in the age structure of the resource have been made by *Walter* [1978] and *Deriso* [1980]. A method for the estimation of the time delays to be expected in bringing a fishery from one equilibrium level to another has been developed by *Fletcher* [1978].

Although these modern versions of the Schaefer method offer some possibilities for improved modeling and estimating of the vital characteristics of a fishery, a system theoretical approach with a clear distinction between a state model and a measurement model seems to be a much more flexible and also a more natural approach to the problem of estimating the unobservable and time-varying state of a fishery. Before we are going to outline several possibilities of how the Schaefer approach can be extended to an efficient filter algorithm, we shortly want to mention a method which is closely related to the Schaefer approach.

For an equilibrium fishery, from (27) until (30) it follows that

$$\alpha x_i \left(1 - \frac{x_i}{\beta} + \epsilon_{1i} \right) = q x_i e_i. \tag{39}$$

This equilibrium condition can be written as

$$u_i = \beta q - \frac{\beta q^2}{\alpha} e_i + \beta q \epsilon_{1i}. \tag{40}$$

So if there are data available for at least two equilibrium periods with different effort levels, the quantities βq and q/α can be estimated from (40). If, in addition, the catchability coefficient q is known, e.g. from tagging experiments [see, e.g., *Schaefer*, 1954; *Beverton/Holt*, 1957; *Ricker*; ICES; *Gulland*, 1969], then all model parameters and derived quantities (38) can be estimated.

If the fishery is not in an equilibrium stage but effort values are changing only slowly from year to year, then a technique frequently used in practice [cf., e.g., fig. 2.3.2 of *Grosslein/Brown/Hennemuth*, or page 120 of *Gulland*, 1969] is to relate the cpue values to averages of the fishing effort values of the previous years. This "equilibrium approximating" procedure clearly is a special case of the method described by (24).

Since it has been observed that a plot of equilibrium yield per unit of effort against effort not always approximates a straight line [*Ricker*; *Gulland*, 1961], alternatives to (40) are easily developed by, for example, introducing skewness into the growth function G. If, for instance, instead of the logistic-like equation (29), a Gompertz-like growth law is assumed such as

$$G(x_i, \epsilon_{1i}) = \alpha x_i \left(\ln \left(\frac{\beta}{x_i} \right) + \epsilon_{1i} \right) \tag{41}$$

then, together with (30), the following linear regression equation for equilibrium situations results:

$$\ln(u_i) = \ln(\beta q) - \frac{q}{\alpha} e_i + \epsilon_{1i}. \tag{42}$$

This equilibrium condition corresponds to the methods used by *Garrod* [1969] and *Fox* [1970].

State Estimation with Kalman Filtering Techniques

We are going to describe two possibilities of how Kalman filtering techniques [*Kalman*] can be used for state and parameter estimation purposes in connection with the Schaefer method. The first approach aims at the specification of regression models of type (31) with time-varying parameters. The second approach is to cast the estimation problem more directly into the system theoretical framework through the introduction of a phenomenological state of which the dynamics can be described by a nonlinear stochastic vector difference equation.

We start with a regression model similar to (31) but allow now for time-varying parameters:

$$u_{i+1} = (1 + \alpha_i) u_i - \frac{\alpha_i}{\beta_i q_i} u_i^2 - q_i c_i + \epsilon_{2i} \tag{43}$$

where $\{\epsilon_{2i}\}$ is a Gaussian zero-mean noise sequence of which the individual random variables are serially independent but may have different variances. The regression coefficients are collected into a three-dimensional parameter vector

$$d_i^T = \left(1 + \alpha_i, -\frac{\alpha_i}{\beta_i q_i}, -q_i \right) \tag{44}$$

(*T* denotes transposition). The dynamics of this parameter vector has to be identified and fully specified by prior knowledge about the fishery. A simple but nevertheless reasonable "parameter equation" might be a linear model of the form

$$d_{i+1} = A_i d_i + \epsilon_{1i} \tag{45}$$

where the A_i are 3–3 matrices and $\{\epsilon_{1i}\}$ is a three-dimensional Gaussian zero-mean noise sequence of serially independent random variables. The sequences $\{\epsilon_{1i}\}$ and $\{\epsilon_{2i}\}$ are assumed to be uncorrelated. If, as a starting up assumption, d_1 is defined as a constant or a Gaussian random vector, then the solution $\{d_i\}$ of (45) is a Gauss-Markov sequence.

The transition matrices A_i have to be specified. If no particular information is available on the evolution of the intrinsic growth rate α or of the carrying capacity β, then one could assume a simple random walk model for $\{1 + \alpha_i\}$, that is, the first row of A_i would consist of the values 1, 0, 0. If new boats with improved technology have been introduced to the fishery during year i, it might be possible to estimate the influence of this improvement directly by specifying the third row of A_i as 0, 0, δ_i, where δ_i could be taken, for example, as 1.1 or 1.2 according to prior information. The second row of A_i then could be specified as 0, $1/\delta_i$, 0.

The covariance matrices of the noise terms ϵ_{1i} and the variances of ϵ_{2i} also have to be specified according to prior knowledge and according to the structure of (45) and (43). In particular, a comparison of (31) and (43) suggests that the variance of ϵ_{2i} should be taken proportional to u_i^2.

Considering d_i as the "state" of the system, one could regard (45) as the "state equation" and (43) as a corresponding "observation equation". With the definition of an "information vector"

$$m_i^T = (u_i, u_i^2, c_i) \tag{46}$$

(43) can be written as

$$u_{i+1} = m_i^T d_i + \epsilon_{2i}. \tag{47}$$

If one believes that the equations (45) and (47) constitute a reasonable basis for an estimation procedure, then "best" estimates of the "states" d_i are calculated recursively by means of the Kalman filter. This sequential estimation algorithm yields the conditional expectations

$$\hat{d}_{i|i+1} = E[d_i | I_{i+1}] \tag{48}$$

and also, as a measure of estimation errors, a sequence of conditional covariance matrices

$$P_{i|i+1} = E[(d_i - \hat{d}_{i|i+1})(d_i - \hat{d}_{i|i+1})^T | I_{i+1}]. \tag{49}$$

In these formulae the information set I_{i+1} contains the "hard" data $c_1, c_2, \ldots, c_{i+1}$ and $e_1, e_2, \ldots, e_{i+1}$ or, equivalently, the values $m_1, m_2, \ldots, m_{i+1}$. The "soft" part of I_{i+1} consists of the assumption that (45) and (47) together with all specifications concerning the error terms and the initial conditions reflects reality sufficiently well. A summary of the filter algorithm is given in Table 1.

Parameter Model	$d_{i+1} = A_i d_i + \epsilon_{1i}; \epsilon_{1i} \sim N(0, R_i); A_i, R_i$ known
Measurement Model	$u_{i+1} = m_i^T d_i + \epsilon_{2i}; \epsilon_{2i} \sim N(0, s_i); m_i, s_i$ known
Initial Conditions	$\hat{d}_{0|1}$ guess for d_0 $P_{0|1}$ guess for $E[(d_0 - \hat{d}_{0|1})(d_0 - \hat{d}_{0|1})^T]$
Parameter Prediction	$\hat{d}_{i+1|i+1} = A_i \hat{d}_{i|i+1}$
Error Covariance Prediction	$P_{i+1|i+1} = A_i P_{i|i+1} A_i^T + R_i$
Filter Gain	$k_{i+1} = P_{i+1|i+1} m_{i+1} (m_{i+1}^T P_{i+1|i+1} m_{i+1} + s_{i+1})^{-1}$
Parameter Estimation	$\hat{d}_{i+1|i+2} = \hat{d}_{i+1|i+1} + k_{i+1}(u_{i+2} - m_{i+1}^T \hat{d}_{i+1|i+1})$
Error Covariance Matrix	$P_{i+1|i+2} = (I - k_{i+1} m_{i+1}^T) P_{i+1|i+1} (I - k_{i+1} m_{i+1}^T)^T + k_{i+1} s_{i+1} k_{i+1}^T$

Tab. 1: Kalman Filter for Model (45)/(47)

The main advantage of the filter algorithm outlined so far is the flexibility it adds to the traditional Schaefer approach and, in a similar way, to its modern variants and generalizations. It takes care of time-varying system characteristics and allows for an efficient utilization of all kinds of prior information concerning the resource or the fleet. Numerical experimentations with various modifications of the filter have been encouraging so far [*Haas/Nuske*; see also the paper of *Haas/Hild* in this volume], although without any specific "insider" information on the state and development of the fishery, which is not directly reflected in catch and effort data, the necessary computational effort can be quite large.

In the following, a second possibility for the use of filtering techniques in connection with the Schaefer approach is outlined.

The time-varying state y_i of the fishery now is described by a quadruple

$$y_i^T = (x_i, b_i, g_i, q_i) \tag{50}$$

of which x_i is the magnitude of the resource, b_i reflects the environmental carrying capacity ("x_{max}"), g_i is the hypothetical maximum equilibrium catch ("c_{MSY}"), and q_i represents, in the sense of equations (28) and (30), the technological standard of the fleet. These four quantities have been chosen to identify the state of the fishery because of their phenomenological character: They are not abstract parameters but correspond directly to real-world phenomena and thus are easily imagined and communicated and, for cross-checking purposes, can also be estimated by methods which are independent of the procedures outlined here.

The dynamics of the system is modeled by a four-dimensional nonlinear stochastic difference equation as

$$y_{i+1} = F(y_i, \delta_i, e_i) + \epsilon_{1i} \tag{51}$$

where δ and e represent influences which are exogenous to the system. As before, e_i stands for the total fishing effort of year i, and the values δ_i track systematic changes in the catchability coefficient q. If nothing is known about such changes, all δ_i can be taken as 1. The transition function F can be specified, for example, as

$$F(y_i, \delta_i, e_i) = \begin{bmatrix} x_i + 4 g_i \dfrac{x_i}{b_i} \left(1 - \dfrac{x_i}{b_i}\right) - q_i x_i e_i \\ b_i \\ g_i \\ \delta_i q_i \end{bmatrix} \tag{52}$$

which would be closely related to the Schaefer approach. In fact, with (52) the first row equation of (51) is a restatement of the simple model given by (27), (28), (29), (30), (38).

In addition to the state model (51), an observation model is given by the nonlinear scalar stochastic difference equation

$$c_i = Q(y_i, e_i) + \epsilon_{2i} \tag{53}$$

where c_i is the reported catch of year i and $Q(y_i, e_i)$ represents the theoretical value of the total catch. To guarantee for consistency with (52), Q is assumed to be of the form

$$Q(y_i, e_i) = q_i e_i x_i. \tag{54}$$

So the observation equation (53) explicitly includes measurement errors.

Equations (51) and (53) now form a nonlinear filtering problem which can be solved approximately with the socalled extended Kalman filter. The idea of this estimation procedure is first to linearize both the propagation function F as well as the observation function Q by a Taylor series expansion about some appropriate sequence of possible state vectors, and then to construct an optimal linear filter for the linearized model. If linearization is successively performed about the path of optimal linear estimates $\hat{y}_{i|i}$, one would expect the procedure to work well as long as previous estimates do not deviate too much from the corresponding actual state values. Another requirement for a good filter performance is a relatively large variance for the observation errors ϵ_{2i}, because then the modeling error from neglecting the nonlinearities of the system would be small compared to the overall noise in the model.

An outline of the approximately optimal filter algorithm is given in Table 2. Details on this algorithm can be found, for example, in the books of *Jazwinski* [1970], *Sage/Melsa* [1971], or *McGarty* [1974]. These authors also propose other approximation procedures and discuss the qualitative effects of such approximations.

System Model	$y_{i+1} = F(y_i, \delta_i, e_i) + \epsilon_{1i}; \epsilon_{1i} \sim N(0, R_i); F, \delta_i, R_i$ known
Measurement Model	$c_i = Q(y_i, e_i) + \epsilon_{2i}; \epsilon_{2i} \sim N(0, S_i); Q, S_i$ known
Initial Conditions	$\hat{y}_{0|0}$ guess for y_0
	$\hat{P}_{0|0}$ guess for $E[(y_0 - \hat{y}_{0|0})(y_0 - \hat{y}_{0|0})^T]$
State Prediction	$\hat{y}_{i+1|i} = F(\hat{y}_{i|i}, \delta_i, e_i)$
State Transition Linearization	$F_i = \left[\dfrac{\partial F(\hat{y}_{i|i}, \delta_i, e_i)}{\partial y_i} \right]$
Error Covariance Prediction	$\hat{P}_{i+1|i} = F_i \hat{P}_{i|i} F_i^T + R_i$
Measurement Linearization	$Q_{i+1} = \left[\dfrac{\partial Q(\hat{y}_{i+1|i}, e_{i+1})}{\partial y_{i+1}} \right]$
Filter Gain	$k_{i+1} = \hat{P}_{i+1|i} Q_{i+1}^T (Q_{i+1} \hat{P}_{i+1|i} Q_{i+1}^T + S_{i+1})^{-1}$
State Estimation	$\hat{y}_{i+1|i+1} = \hat{y}_{i+1|i} + k_{i+1}(c_{i+1} - Q(\hat{y}_{i+1|i}, e_{i+1}))$
Error Covariance Estimation	$\hat{P}_{i+1|i+1} = (I - k_{i+1} Q_{i+1}) \hat{P}_{i+1|i} (I - k_{i+1} Q_{i+1})^T + k_{i+1} S_{i+1} k_{i+1}^T$
Remark	$\hat{P}_{i+1|i}$ and $\hat{P}_{i+1|i+1}$ are approximations of the real error covariance matrices

Tab. 2: Extended Kalman Filter for Model (51)/(53)

Summary and Conclusion

An overview has been given on different estimation and prediction techniques which, in the context of fishery regulation, allow for basic stock assessments and catch forecasts with catch and effort statistics as the only data requirement. To simplify the discussion, a distinction has been made between "input-output methods" and "state oriented methods". Methods of the first group model the relationship between catch and effort values in a direct way by means of an explicit consideration of lagged variables, whereas methods of the second group concentrate on the state of a fishery and combine current catch and effort values via an appropriate state variable. Input-output methods can be used for catch prediction purposes, and state oriented methods for a deeper understanding of the fishery system.

In order to systematize and enlarge the portfolio of already available catch-and-effort techniques, we started with a general stochastic production model which we successively adapted to the special cases of "undeveloped", "developing", "developed stationary" and "developed nonstationary" fisheries. For each type of fishery we identified suitable production models in such a way that standard time-series methods, regression techniques, or filtering algorithms can be applied on historical catch and effort data to give the desired estimates and predictions.

Although our compilation of catch-and-effort techniques definitely is not complete, we hope that it has become clear that there is a variety of such methods already available. In particular we wanted to demonstrate that there are numerous alternatives to the traditional Schaefer approach, quick and easy ones as well as more sophisticated procedures. For a real-world application, we feel that it is a good idea to try several approaches, perhaps under different sets of prior assumptions, and to finally combine the results in some appropriate way.

References

Athans, M.: The Importance of Kalman Filtering Methods for Economic Systems. Annals of Economic and Social Measurement **3**, 1974, 49–64.

Bates, J.M., and *C.W.J. Granger*: The Combination of Forecasts. Operational Research Quarterly **20**, 1969, 451–468.

Beverton, R.J.H., and *S.J. Holt*: On the Dynamics of Exploited Fish Populations. UK Ministry of Agriculture, Fisheries and Food, London 1957.

Box, G.E.P., and *G.M. Jenkins*: Time Series Analysis, Forecasting and Control. San Francisco 1970.

Chapman, W.McL.: Some Problems and Programs in Fishery Oceanography. Fisheries Oceanography. Ed. by I. Hela and T. Laevastu. Farnham (Surrey) 1970.

Clark, C.W.: Mathematical Bioeconomics: The Optimal Management of Renewable Resources. New York 1976.

Cushing, D.H.: Fisheries Biology, A Study in Population Dynamics. Madison 1968.

Daniel, C., and *F.S. Wood*: Fitting Equations to Data. New York 1971.

Deriso, R.B.: Harvesting Strategies and Parameter Estimation for an Age-Structured Model. Canadian Journal of Fisheries and Aquatic Sciences **37**, 1980, 268–282.

Eichhorn, W.: Theorie der homogenen Produktionsfunktion. Berlin 1970.

FAO: "Nominal Catches" and "Landings": Definitions and Notes. FAO Fisheries Circular **428**, Rome 1973.

– : Monitoring of Fish Stock Abundance: The Use of Catch and Effort Data. FAO Fisheries Technical Paper **155**, Rome 1976.

Fletcher, R.I.: Time-Dependent Solutions and Efficient Parameters for Stock-Production Models. Fishery Bulletin **76**, 1978, 377–388.

Fox, W.W.: An Exponential Surplus-Yield Model for Optimizing Exploited Fish Populations. Transactions of the American Fisheries Society **99**, 1970, 80–88.

Garrod, D.J.: Empirical Assessments of Catch/Effort Relationships in North Atlantic Cod Stocks. Bulletin of the International Commission for the Northwest Atlantic Fisheries 6, 1969, 26–34.

Gatto, M., and *S. Rinaldi*: On the Determination of a Commercial Fishery Production Model. Ecological Modelling **8**, 1980, 165–172.

Gatto, M., S. Rinaldi and *C.J. Walters*: A Predator-Prey Model for Discrete-Time Commercial Fisheries. Applied Mathematical Modelling **1**, 1976, 67–76.

Graham, M.: Modern Theory of Exploiting a Fishery, and Application to North Sea Trawling. Journal du Conseil Permanent International pour l'Exploration de la Mer **10**, 1935, 264–274.

Granger, C.W.J., and *P. Newbold*: Forecasting Economic Time Series. New York 1977.

Grosslein, M.D., B.E. Brown and *R.C. Hennemuth*: Research, Assessment, and Management of a Marine Ecosystem in the Northwest Atlantic – A Case Study. Environmental Biomonitoring, Assessment, Prediction, and Management – Certain Case Studies and Related Quantitative Issues. Ed. by G.P. Patil and W.E. Waters. Fairland (Maryland) 1979, 289–357.

Gulland, J.A.: Fishing and the Stocks of Fish at Iceland. London 1961.

– : Manual of Methods for Fish Stock Assessment, Part 1. Fish Population Analysis. Rome 1969.

– : The Fish Resources of the Ocean. West Byfleet 1971.

– : Some Considerations of Management Problems in Relation to Pelagic Fisheries of the IPFC Area. Proceedings of the 15th Session (Wellington/New Zealand), Section III, of the Indo-Pacific Fisheries Council. Bangkok 1974, 19–26.

Haas, P., and *M. Nuske*: Anwendung von Filterverfahren zur Verbesserung von Aufwand- und Ertragprognosen für die Fischerei auf den Ostpazifischen Gelbflossenthunfisch. Diskussionsbeitrag 13/79 des Instituts für Statistik und Mathematische Wirtschaftstheorie, Karlsruhe 1979.

Hennemuth, R.C.: Man as Predator. Contemporary Quantitative Ecology and Related Ecometrics. Ed. by G.P. Patil and M. Rosenzweig. Fairland (Maryland) 1979, 507–532.

Hilborn, R.: Comparison of Fisheries Control Systems that Utilize Catch and Effort Data. Journal of the Fisheries Research Board of Canada **36**, 1979, 1477–1489.

Holden, M.J., and *D.F.S. Raitt*: Manual of Fisheries Science, Part 2 – Methods of Resource Investigation and Their Application. Rome 1974.

Holt, S.: Marine Fisheries. Ocean Yearbook 1. Ed. by E.M. Borgese and N. Ginsburg. Chicago 1978, 38–83.

Huang, D.S., and *C.W. Lee*: Toward a General Model of Fishery Production. Southern Economic Journal **43**, 1976, 846–854.

ICES: A Guide to Fish Marks. Journal du Conseil Permanent International pour l'Exploration de la Mer **30**, 1965, 89–160.

Idyll, C.P.: The Anchovy Crisis. Scientific American **228**, 1973, 22–29.

Jazwinski, A.H.: Stochastic Processes and Filtering Theory. New York 1970.

Johansen, L.: Production Functions. Amsterdam 1972.

Kalman, R.E.: A New Approach to Linear Filtering and Prediction Problems. Transactions of the ASME – Journal of Basic Engineering **82 D**, 1960, 35–45.

Markowitz, H.M.: Portfolio Selection. New York 1959.

McGarty, T.P.: Stochastic Systems and State Estimation. New York 1974.

McGaw, R.L.: Confidence Intervals for Optimal Effort Estimates from the Schaefer Production Model. Canadian Journal of Fisheries and Aquatic Sciences **37**, 1980, 288–289.

Nelson, C.R.: Applied Time Series Analysis for Managerial Forecasting. San Francisco 1973.

Newbold, P., and *C.W.J. Granger*: Experience with Forecasting Univariate Time Series and the Combination of Forecasts. Journal of the Royal Statistical Society **A 137**, 1974, 131–146.

152

Paiva Pinto, M., et al.: Prospects for the World Marine Fishery Production. Arquivo das Ciências do Mar **15**, 1975, 127–131.

Pella, J.J., and *P.K. Tomlinson*: A Generalized Stock Production Model. Bulletin of the Inter-American Tropical Tuna Commission **13**, 1969, 421–496.

Ricker, W.E.: Handbook of Computations for Biological Statistics of Fish Populations. Ottawa 1958.

Rothschild, B.J.: An Exposition on the Definition of Fishing Effort. Fishery Bulletin **70**, 1972, 671–679.

Sætersdal, G.: A Note on the State of Fishery Research in the North-East Atlantic. FAO Fisheries Report **171** (1), 1975, 77–85.

Sage, A.P., and *J.L. Melsa*: Estimation Theory with Application to Communications and Control. New York 1971.

Schaefer, M.B.: Some Aspects of the Dynamics of Populations Important to the Management of the Commercial Marine Fisheries. Bulletin of the Inter-American Tropical Tuna Commission **1**, 1954, 27–56.

– : A Study of the Dynamics of Yellowfin Tuna in the Eastern Tropical Pacific Ocean. Bulletin of the Inter-American Tropical Tuna Commission **2**, 1957, 245–285.

– : The Potential Harvest of the Sea. Transactions of the American Fisheries Society **94**, 1965, 123–128.

Schnute, J.: Improved Estimates from the Schaefer Production Model: Theoretical Considerations. Journal of the Fisheries Research Board of Canada **34**, 1977, 583–603.

Shephard, R.W.: Theory of Cost and Production Functions. Princeton 1970.

Smith, V.L.: On Models of Commercial Fishing. Journal of Political Economy 77, 1969, 181–198.

Walter, G.G.: A Surplus Yield Model Incorporating Recruitment and Applied to a Stock of Atlantic Mackerel (Scomber scombrus). Journal of the Fisheries Research Board of Canada **35**, 1978, 229–234.

Walters, C.J., and *R. Hilborn*: Adaptive Control of Fishing Systems. Journal of the Fisheries Research Board of Canada **33**, 1976, 145–159.

Zellner, A.: Introduction to Bayesian Inference in Econometrics. New York 1971.

Part III
Markets and Prices

Economic Theory of Natural Resources. ©Physica-Verlag, Würzburg–Wien, 1982.

Efficient Pricing of Natural Resources and Intertemporal Externalities

Wolfgang Eichhorn and *Klaus Spremann*

1. Introduction

This paper analyses the implications of intertemporal effects in production and demand on pricing rules, market structure, and validation of economic modelling in the context of natural resources. Intertemporal effects in demand find their rationale in externalities due to habit formation, saturation, and pollution effects. Such effects obviously play an essential role with the consumption of energy and natural resources by households and with their utilization as inputs in production. Intertemporal effects on production cost have different reasons. One of them is that less efficient layers must be tackled in the future as current output increases. In the fishing industry, current harvesting volume clearly has an impact on tomorrow's effort levels.

At first, the classic Hotelling rule for monetary stock equilibrium is extended to cover the case of externalities by introducing the concept of dynamic marginal cost which include a term for the future outcomes of current output decisions. Thereby we reduced the technical tool to the simplest apparatus which is appropriate to capture dynamics, namely to a model with two stages of time.

In the second part of the analysis we ask, whether the sole owner can delegate the execution of his pricing strategy to a private industry without exerting regulation, imposing taxes or paying direct subsidies. In some cases of intertemporal effects this can be achieved by an appropriate market structure between pure monopoly and complete competition, in others not: From the firms of a competitive industry, however, only decision making on a short-term basis can be expected. The absence of barriers to entry implies the risk of becoming displaced from the resource market. Therefore, under positive externalities like habit formation or technical progress, it is possible that a private industry fails to support intertemporal efficiency.

Thirdly, positive externalities give rise to the question, whether economic modelling for determining allocations of natural resources reaches its limits when intertemporal effects are present. Since under positive externalities there is a strong economic force to consume the biggest part of the cake of given size in the present in order to increase the economic value of the last crumb remaining for the future. From the point of view that consumption patterns should be more or less uniformly distributed over time, these outcomes have something paradoxical which finally will be clarified.

This material is organized in three parts. Chapter 2 focusses on modelling these intertemporal effects in tastes and technology (Section 2.1), presents the model (2.2) and our main theorem on efficiency (3.3), and discusses two intrinsic examples (2.4). In Chapter 3 we ask whether efficient pricing can be achieved by a private industry without exerting regulation, even if externalities are present. According to our result (Theorem 2), decentralized decision making becomes feasible if the externalities are compensated by an appropriate shift of the market structure. Chapter 4 concludes by taking a glance at a paradoxical aspect of resource allocation over time which turns out to be a consequence of the externalities. In order to keep the presentation clear, we formulate these outlined questions for only two point of time, $t = 1, 2$, although quite similar results can be deduced for more periods or for continuous time. This considerable reduction in the technical tools necessary to analyse the questions we aim at was motivated by a former control-theoretic approach which provided no additional understanding of the problems involved with intertemporal externalities.

2. Efficient Pricing

Most of the recent contributions to the economic theory of exhaustible resources turn out to be generalizations and extensions of the basic problem formulated and solved by Hotelling fifty years ago. In a discrete time formulation, and without focussing on the question whether the planning horizon is infinite or a fixed endtime is given beforehand, this problem can be stated as follows: Find and characterize a path $q = (q_t)_{t=1,2,...}$ of quantities $q_t \geq 0$ to be produced and consumed in periods $t = 1, 2, \ldots$ such that the sum of discounted utility values $V_t(q_t)$ derived from consumption is maximized subject to the constraint that cumulative quantities cannot exceed the total amount $Q > 0$ of the depletable resource. Hence

$$\text{maximize} \quad \sum_{t=1,2,...} \beta^{t-1} V_t(q_t)$$
$$\text{subject to} \quad \sum_{t=1,2,...} q_t \leq Q \text{ and } q_1, q_2, \ldots \geq 0, \tag{1}$$

where $\beta \in \,]0, 1[$ denotes the discount factor representing the exogeneously given time preference. Note that the utility in period t is assumed to depend on q_t alone. Neither the history $q_1, \ldots, q_{t-1}$ nor the future has an impact on single-period utility. The common use of the constrained resource provides the only intertemporal link.

Problems of the basic structure (1) are today widely used also in the design of organizational mechanisms for coordinating decentralized decision making. The well-known answer to these problems is, that for a quantity path q^* to be optimal, the present value of marginal utilities should be the same for all periods (in which the resource is used),

$$\beta^{t-1} V_t'(q_t^*) \equiv \lambda \quad \text{(all } t \text{ with } q_t^* > 0), \tag{2}$$

and must further have such a level $\lambda \geq 0$, that $\lambda \geq 0$ implies exhaustion $\Sigma q_t = Q$. To this application of the Kuhn-Tucker theorem we remark only that Slater's condition as constraint qualification is satisfied for $q_t \equiv 0$ and $Q > 0$.

Writing $\beta = 1/(1 + r)$, the condition (2) means that marginal utility must rise at the rate of interest $r > 0$. And in the case the values V_t are defined as revenues minus cost, it is the difference of marginal revenues and marginal cost that must be raised at the rate of interest by appropriate advances in prices. This Hotelling rule has found further interpretation in terms of momentary stock equilibrium, see *Weinstein/Zeckhauser* [1975]. The condition on the multiplier $\lambda \geqslant 0$ demands in this context, that the initial level of the price, from where it starts growing according to the Hotelling rule, must be sufficiently high to press demand down to zero not later than the resource becomes exhausted. And if even under the "marginal revenue equals marginal cost" condition, that is $\lambda = 0$, cumulative consumption never reaches the physical supply, the resource should not be called exhaustible.

2.1 Dynamics in Tastes and Technology

Rather than pursuing the various directions in which this basic model has been extended, our subsequent analysis is devoted to questions of *efficiency and market structure* within a deterministic framework. In contrast to previous work on this topic, see *Stiglitz* [1976] and *Sweeney* [1977], we focus on *intertemporal externalities* in demand and production cost. Besides these dynamics in tastes and technology, a growth process for the stock of the natural resource is introduced. Some of the conceptual elements which will be integrated into our model have been studied before. Here we focus on the rationale behind these dynamics, suggest simple but intrinsic examples, and provide biographical notes.

Effects of the total output in former periods on the current level of production cost have a long tradition in the literature on learning phenomena, where manufacturing processes are observed to be accompanied by cost reductions [*Hirsch*]. On the other hand, for most kinds of exhaustible resources, good reasons can be found which argue that current production cost increases with past output quantity. Consider the mining industry: as the total volume of extraction increases, deeper and poorer underground layers have to be tackled such that mining becomes more and more expensive. *Gordon* [1967] mentioned further concrete examples and introduced the concept of dynamic cost functions. Unlike *Cummings* [1969] and *Levhari/Liviatan* [1977], he did not come to results in closed form. *Cremer* [1979] studied the cost phenomenon, where increasing rates of exploitation lead to a short supply of permanent equipment such that its rental rate goes up. In the literature on natural resources, optimal harvesting and fishing, detailed models have been established to predict the impacts of current output decisions on effort levels needed in the future, see *Clark* [1976, 82]. Recent generalizations in the theory of the mining firm [*Kemp/Long*] also include effects, where current production cost depend on both the current quantity produced and an index which comprises the history of output levels. We conclude with a rather simple but still interesting example. Extraction of the total volume x is assumed to cause total cost $k(x)$, where $k: R_+ \rightarrow R_+$ is an arbitrary monotonically increasing function. If extraction falls on two periods of time and q_1, q_2 denote the respective quantities, one gets the cost functions c_1, c_2 defined by

$$c_1(q_1) := k(q_1)$$

$$c_2(q_1, q_2) := k(q_1 + q_2) - k(q_1).$$

(3)

158

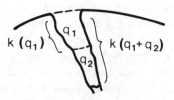

Fig. 1: Illustration of intertemporal effects in production cost (3)

Here, the cost c_2 in the second period is not only depending on q_2 since there is an influence of the output history represented by q_1. The marginal external effect of decisions in period $t = 1$ on production cost in period 2 is given by the difference of marginal extraction cost

$$\partial c_2 / \partial q_1 = k'(q_1 + q_2) - k'(q_1). \tag{4}$$

The idea of external effects in tastes and demand, where consumption decisions realized by individuals influence the preference orderings of others, dates back to *Veblen* [1898] and *Leibenstein* [1950]. These externalities are positive in case of habit formation, bandwagon effects or imitation-oriented consumer behavior. Further, the use of a resource will often go hand in hand with the development of a complementary infrastructure which, by its durability, implies positive impacts on future consumption levels and results in stabilizing demand patterns. Fishing leads to tinning factories; and once investments of this kind are realized there is the need for employment of capacities. The refining of oil is related via chemistry and car industry to the construction of highways. And each developed traffic network promotes future demand for gas. On the other hand, negative externalities of current consumption on future tastes and demand may occur likewise. Possible explanations for negative intertemporal externalities are pollution effects as well as saturation. While using a resource, man becomes acquainted with its properties. He learns about inadequate or even periculous characteristics which initially were not known to him. Observations of this kind would provide strong incentives to search for better alternatives and to develop substitutes. Current demand is thus declining. Technical tools for formalizing these dynamics of tastes and demand have been provided by *Gorman* [1967], *Peston* [1967], *Bass* [1969], *Pollak* [1970, p. 76], *Krelle* [1973], *Spremann* [1978]. The next step in the analysis was to build these dynamic demand functions into decision models of marketing management [*Spremann* 1975, p. 78] and resource allocation over time [*Cyert/deGroot*; *Manning*].

As an example for intertemporal effects in tastes we suggest in our two-period world the demand functions

$$q_1 = f_1(p_1) = p_1^{\eta_1}$$

$$q_2 = f_2(q_1, p_2) = (1 + \alpha q_1) p_2^{\eta_2}, \quad \alpha > -1/q_1, \tag{5}$$

with constant price elasticities $\eta_1, \eta_2 < -1$. For $\alpha = 0$, demand (5) is intertemporally uncoupled. In the case $\alpha \neq 0$, the demand functions describe a process of purchasing behavior which increases (if $\alpha > 0$) or declines (if $\alpha < 0$) with the sales volume realized in period $t = 1$. Thus the parameter α determines the kind of intertemporal externalities

$$\partial q_2 / \partial q_1 = \alpha p_2^{\eta_2}. \tag{6}$$

Note that instead of (5) the inverse demand relations

$$p_1 = h_1(q_1) = q_1^{1/\eta_1}$$

$$\tag{7}$$

$$p_2 = h_2(q_1, q_2) = [q_2 / (1 + \alpha q_1)]^{1/\eta_2}$$

could be taken for further analysis.

Natural resources are living in the sense that there might be biological or ecological growth as well as depreciation. Denote this process by $G: R_+ \to R_+$ such that the reserve $G(x)$ results at $t = 2$ from starting at $t = 1$ with a stock of size $x \geq 0$. The case $G(x) > x$ refers to predominant birth whereas $G(x) < x$ means that death outweights birth on the average. Of course, both cases could occur depending on the initial size x of the resource stock. Complete durability of the resource without any growth or decline is described by the identity $G(x) \equiv x$. The constraint, that consumption can never exceed what has been left, now takes the form

$$q_2 \leq G(Q - q_1), q_1 \leq Q. \tag{8}$$

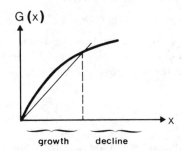

Fig. 2: Growth and decline depending on the initial size x of the resource stock.

2.2 The Model

Now the basic assumptions of our model will be stated. As indicated in the introductory part, the essential implications of intertemporal externalities will be explored within a model that spans two stages of time, $t = 1, 2$, interpretable as present and future. Consider two commodities, the *resource* and the rest of the goods represented by some numeraire which is called *capital*. There are further two agents in this simple economy. The resource can be produced exclusively by one of them, called *sole owner*, either for legal reasons or because of technological or geographic circumstances. The second agent represents *consumers*. The sole owner is initially endowed with the amount $Q > 0$ of the resource. For what follows, there is no need to specify capital endowments, which of course enter implicitly into the demand functions. In order to specify the preferences we determine contemporaneous and intertemporal rates of substitution between capital and the resource. So we make the subsequent assumptions:

160

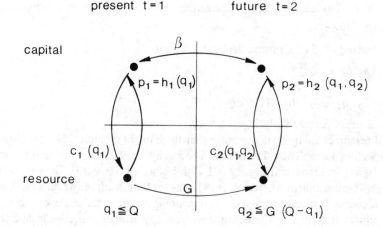

Fig. 3: The essential features of the model

(A1) For consumers, substitution between the resource and capital at $t = 1, 2$ is implicitly given by the inverse demand functions h_t,

$$p_1 = h_1 (q_1), \quad p_2 = h_2 (q_1, q_2) \tag{9}$$

which relate quantities (q_1, q_2) of the resource to prices (p_1, p_2). Remark that a specialization of (9) is presented in (7).

(A2) For the sole owner, the substitution between the resource and capital is described by production costs,

$$c_1 (q_1), \quad c_2 (q_1, q_2). \tag{10}$$

Note that (3) might serve as an illustrative example.

(A3) Production is possible as long as the resource is not exhausted. This feasibility condition is formalized by (8). Consequently, the growth function G describes the substitution of the resource between the two periods as far as the sole owner is concerned. For consumers, on the other hand, resource arbitrage between the times is assumed to be impossible, storage after production being too costly for consumers or impractical.

(A4) Capital at times $t = 1, 2$ can be exchanged. For both the sole owner and the consumers the rate of substitution is given by the discount factor $\beta \in [0, 1]$.

It is now our aim to find and characterize efficient terms of trade in this economy. Exchange is fully described by the quantities q_1, q_2 of the resource transferred from the producer to consumers and by the prices p_1, p_2 which determine the amounts of capital $p_1 q_1, p_2 q_2$ transfered from consumers to the sole owner in exchange. Terms of trade $(q_1, q_2; p_1, p_2)$ which do not satisfy (9) fail to be efficient. Thus we can restrict our attention to terms of trade $(q_1, q_2; h_1 (q_1), h_2 (q_1, q_2))$ which are characterized alone by the quantities (q_1, q_2). In order to find in the feasible set

$$\{(q_1, q_2) \mid q_1 \leq Q, q_2 \leq G (Q - q_1)\} \tag{8'}$$

those quantity paths, which are here just pairs (q_1, q_2), that can be recognized as efficient, we introduce utility functions (11), (12). These are derived in consistency with (A1), (A2),

(A3), (A4). For the sole owner, the present value of net revenues

$$R(q_1, q_2) = R_1(q_1) + \beta R_2(q_1, q_2)$$
$$= (p_1 q_1 - c_1(q_1)) + \beta(p_2 q_2 - c_2(q_1, q_2)) \tag{11}$$

gives indirect utility in money metric. The corresponding utility in money metric for the consumers is called welfare W and defined as the sum of revenues and surplus

$$W = R + S, \, S(q_1, q_2) = S_1(q_1) + \beta S_2(q_1, q_2) \tag{12}$$

where

$$S_1(q_1) = \int_0^{q_1} h_1(x)\,dx - p_1 q_1,$$
$$\tag{13}$$
$$S_2(q_1, q_2) = \int_0^{q_2} h_2(q_1, x)\,dx - p_2 q_2.$$

In (11) and (13), p_1 and p_2 stand for $h_1(q_1)$ and $h_2(q_1, q_2)$, respectively. For a detailed discussion of consumer's surplus see *Willig* [1976], *Chipman/Moore* [1980]. The sole owner tries to exchange quantities q_1, q_2 which maximize R whereas the consumers seek to realize a path (q_1, q_2) that maximizes W.

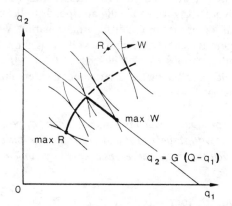

Fig. 4: Efficient quantity paths (q_1, q_2) with respect to R and W under the constraint (8)

In addition to R and W, consider a mediatorship with the task to maximize a convex combination of these criteria,

$$V_\omega := \omega R + (1 - \omega) W \overset{(12)}{=} R + (1 - \omega) S$$
$$V_\omega(q_1, q_2) = R_1(q_1) + (1 - \omega) S_1(q_1) \tag{14}$$
$$+ \beta(R_2(q_1, q_2) + (1 - \omega) S_2(q_1, q_2)),$$

where $\omega \in [0, 1]$. Clearly, $V_0 = W$ and $V_1 = R$ such that the weight ω makes think of a degree of monopoly. We have now two problems to solve. The first is one of vector maximization: find those of the feasible quantity paths which are efficient with respect to the two criteria R and W. The second problem is to optimize quantity paths with respect to the real-value criterion (14).

2.3 Efficient Pricing and Dynamic Marginal Cost

For both problems stated above we aim at explicit formulas like Hotelling's rule and the "marginal revenue equals marginal cost" condition. These rules, of course, are valid in their simple form only if externalities are absent. It is however possible to incorporate intertemporal externalities by a slight modification: marginal cost have to be replaced by what here is called dynamic marginal cost [*Spremann*, 1975, p. 80]. These dynamic marginal costs are defined as the sum of marginal values for the consumption and utilization of

(i)   inputs such as material assets and manpower,
(ii) opportunities which otherwise would remain for future periods,
(iii) immaterial abstract assets such as goodwill.

Whereas the first term denotes marginal cost of production in the usual sense, the second term is the opportunity cost multiplier. The third term reflects the intertemporal effects in tastes and technology. It might be referred to as marginal use-up of goodwill, denoted by $-mg$. Since this third term $-mg$ is subsumed under "cost" it will be positive ($mg < 0$) in the case one unit more of present quantity reduces future utility. And it will be negative, $mg > 0$, if an increase in current output promotes the following development. In a control-theoretic framework, marginal goodwill corresponds to the current value costate variable which is the solution of the adjoint differential equation. We finally remark that the following results require as technical assumptions differentiability and monotonicity of demand, cost, and growth functions, $h'_1 < 0, \partial h_2/\partial q_2 < 0, c'_1 > 0, \partial c_2/\partial q_2 > 0, G' > 0$. Different cases corresponding to the sign of intertemporal externalities $\partial h_2/\partial q_1$, $\partial c_2/\partial q_1$ are discussed below.

Theorem 1: Let (q_1, q_2) be a path (which is here just a pair) of positive quantities $q_t > 0$, $t = 1, 2$, which is efficient with respect to R and W for the feasible set (8'). Then there exists some $\omega \in [0, 1]$ such that marginal revenue equals dynamic marginal cost at all times,

$$p_t\left(1 + \frac{\omega}{\eta_t}\right) = dmc_t \qquad \text{for } t = 1, 2. \tag{15}$$

Thereby p_t denote prices (9), η_t are the elasticities of demand with respect to price, and the dynamic marginal cost are given by

$$dmc_1 = c'_1(q_1) + \lambda - mg_1,$$

$$mg_1 = \beta\left(\left(p_2 - \frac{\partial c_2}{\partial q_2}\right)\frac{\partial q_2}{\partial q_1} + (1 - \omega)\frac{\partial S_2}{\partial q_1} - \frac{\partial c_2}{\partial q_1}\right), \tag{16}$$

$$dmc_2 = \frac{\partial c_2(q_1, q_2)}{\partial q_2} + \frac{\lambda}{\beta G'(1 - q_1)}.$$

The partial derivative $\partial q_2/\partial q_1$ in (16) stands for $(\partial h_2/\partial q_1)/(\partial h_2/\partial q_2)$ in (9), and $\lambda \geq 0$ is the multiplier associated with (8). If (q_1, q_2) maximizes V_ω for some $\omega \in [0, 1]$ subject to feasibility (8), and if $q_1, q_2 > 0$, then the condition (15) holds together with (16) for the chosen weight ω.

Proof: First note $\partial R_t/\partial q_t = p_t(1 + 1/\eta_t) - \partial c_t/\partial q_t$ and $\partial W_t/\partial q_t = \partial(R_t + S_t)/\partial q_t = $ $= p_t - \partial c_t/\partial q_t$, hence $V_{\omega,t} = \omega R_t + (1-\omega) W_t$ yields $\partial V_{\omega,t}/\partial q_t = p_t(1 + \omega/\eta_t) - $ $- \partial c_t/\partial q_t$, $t = 1, 2$. The new term in (16) which makes the difference between c_1', λ, and dmc_1 is easily recognized as $\partial[\beta V_{\omega,2}]/\partial q_1$. The term $\lambda/\beta G'$ in dmc_2 is the opportunity value of having one more unit at time $t = 1$, namely λ, raised by the capital rate of interest $1/\beta = (1 + r)$ and by the biological rate of interest G'. For the application of the Kuhn-Tucker theorem note, that the constraint qualification is satisfied because of $Q > 0$. Consequently for a V_ω-optimal quantity path (q_1, q_2) there exists some multiplier $\lambda \geqslant 0$ such that (15), (16) hold. Now suppose that (q_1, q_2) is (R, W)-efficient and define, for $t = 1, 2$, $\omega_t \in \mathbf{R} \in R$ such that $p_t(1 + \omega_t/\eta_t) = dmc_t$ holds for dmc_t defined according to (16) with $\lambda := \partial R/\partial Q$. From $\omega_1, \omega_2 \in [0, 1]$ follows a contradiction to the assumption of (R, W)-efficiency. If $\omega_1 \neq \omega_2$, (q_1, q_2) does not satisfy even the weak local Slater efficiency as a local version of the weak Pareto principle, i.e. there exists a slight variation $(\epsilon\Delta q_1, \epsilon\Delta q_2)$ such that $(q_1 + \epsilon\Delta q_1, q_2 + \epsilon\Delta q_2)$ is feasible and, in comparison to (q_1, q_2), yields an increase of R or W without decrease in the other criteria. Q.E.D.

Remember the definitions (11), (13) of the utilities R_2 and W_2 at $t = 2$. Verify the essential characterization of marginal goodwill in (16) as

$$mg_1 = \beta \frac{\partial(\omega R_2 + (1-\omega)W_2)}{\partial q_1}. \tag{17}$$

Some further remarks on Theorem 1 should be made. Note that there is no marginal goodwill mg_2 subtracted from marginal cost $\partial c_2/\partial q_2$ and opportunity cost $\lambda/\beta G'$ in the definition of dmc_2. Clearly one has $mg_2 = 0$ since there are no effects of decision making at this stage $t = 2$ on any period following later. In a control-theoretic framework this corresponds to the boundary condition for the adjoint system with free trajectory. And since the value of extracting one more unit of the resource at $t = 1$ equals λ, the reserve dynamics G make G' units less available in period 2. Thus, the opportunity value of having one more unit at time $t = 2$, that is $\lambda/\beta G'$, results from raising λ by the marginal growth rate of capital, $1/\beta = (1 + r)$, and discounting by the marginal growth rate G' of the resource. *Consequently, without externalities in demand or production cost, that is $mg_1 = 0$, marginal revenue minus marginal cost should rise at the compound rate $(1 + r) G'$.*

Consider now the role of the parameter $\omega \in [0, 1]$ in the condition (15) for efficient terms of trade between the sole owner and the consumers. Here the convex combination (14) shows that ω reflects the relative power the two agents have. A further interpretation is given only for illustrative purposes: Imagine consumers distributed all over the world such that only a part of them belongs to the country which is identified as sole owner. One could reason, that $\omega = 0$ fits well in the case all consumers belong to the sole owner country. On the other hand, $\omega = 1$ must perhaps be accepted if the sole owner country is so small that the resource is completely exported. Consequently, a certain value of the power index ω could be called acceptable in terms of economic policy, if $1 - \omega$ corresponds to the relative size of the sole owner country.

2.4 Two Intrinsic Examples

In order to focus on marginal goodwill in Theorem 1, we suggest two examples which are specialized in such a way that the implications of intertemporal externalities become evident. The first example concerns a mining industry with cost function (3) but without externalities in demand. Secondly we examine an enterprise without externalities in production cost but which faces dynamic demand according to (5) or (7) resp. In order not to burden notation, the constraint (8) will be simplified to the classic case $q_1 + q_2 \leqslant Q$.

Corollary 1: Let (q_1, q_2) be a path of positive quantities $q_t > 0, t = 1, 2$, which is efficient with respect to R and W for the feasible set given through $q_1 + q_2 \leqslant Q$. Let further production cost be given by (3) and demand satisfying $\partial h_2 / \partial q_1 \equiv 0$. Then marginal revenue equals dynamic marginal cost at all times (15), whereby

$$dmc_1 = (1 - \beta) k'(q_1) + \beta k'(q_1 + q_2) + \lambda,$$
$$dmc_2 = k'(q_1 + q_2) + \lambda/\beta. \tag{18}$$

If $q_1, q_2 > 0$ maximize V_ω subject to $q_1 + q_2 \leqslant Q$, then (15) holds for this chosen $\omega \in [0, 1]$ and for dmc_t, $t = 1, 2$, given through (18).

Proof: The assumed absence of intertemporal externalities in demand, $\partial h_2 / \partial q_1 \equiv 0$, implies $- mg_1 = \beta \partial c_2 / \partial q_1 = \beta k'(q_1 + q_2) - \beta k'(q_1)$ by (4), which together with (3) and (16) lead to the assertion $dmc_1 = (1 - \beta) k'(q_1) + \beta k'(q_1 + q_2) + \lambda$.   Q.E.D.

For $\beta = 1$, that is a world with a rate of interest equal zero, Corollary 1 says: *The price in the present period has to be based on future marginal cost in order to avoid failure of efficiency*, since $\beta = 1$ and (18) imply

$$dmc_1 = dmc_2 = k'(q_1 + q_2) + \lambda. \tag{19}$$

Pindyck [1978] pointed out, that even in later stages of resource use there is no "fixed" reserve base remaining for further exhaustion. Reserves can be increased through exploration activities, higher effort levels and by opening up poorer and more expensive layers. These observations suggest $\lambda = 0$ but give a hint to considerable future marginal production cost. Corollary 1 shows that under such circumstances there is a need for market structures and appropriate economic policies that guarantee high initial prices: The final levels of actual marginal production cost must be anticipated rather than an opportunity cost term.

The situation $q_1 + q_2 < Q$, that is $\lambda = 0$, is also supposed for our second concern in this section, which is intertemporal externalities in demand.

Corollary 2: Assume $q_1, q_2 > 0, q_1 + q_2 < Q$ and that there are no $\bar{q}_1, \bar{q}_2 \geqslant 0$ $\bar{q}_1 + \bar{q}_2 \leqslant Q$ with $R(\bar{q}_1, \bar{q}_2) > R(q_1, q_2)$ and $S(\bar{q}_1, \bar{q}_2) \geqslant S(q_1, q_2)$ or $R(\bar{q}_1, \bar{q}_2) \geqslant R(q_1, q_2)$ and $S(\bar{q}_1, \bar{q}_2) > S(q_1, q_2)$. Let thereby demand be given by (7) and suppose absence of any externalities in technology, $\partial c_2 / \partial q_1 \equiv 0$. Then there is *some $\omega \in [0, 1]$ such that marginal revenue equals dynamic marginal cost for*

$$p_1 \left(1 + \frac{\omega}{\eta_1}\right) = c_1' - \alpha\beta\left(\frac{\omega}{|\eta_2|} + \frac{(1-\omega)}{|\eta_2 + 1|} p_2^{\eta_2+1}\right),$$

$$p_2 \left(1 + \frac{\omega}{\eta_2}\right) = c_2'.$$

(20)

If (q_1, q_2) is optimal with respect to V_ω, then (20) holds for the chosen $\omega \in [0, 1]$.

Proof: Note that $p_2 (1 + \omega/\eta_2) = c_2'$ can be written in the form $p_2 - c_2' = \omega p_2 / |\eta_2|$ such that $\beta (p_2 - c_2') \partial q_2 / \partial q_1 = \alpha\beta\omega p_2^{\eta_2+1} / |\eta_2|$ because of (6). Then, by integration of $S_2 = \int (1 + \alpha q_1) p^{\eta_2} dp$ from p_2 to ∞, it follows $S_2 = (1 + \alpha q_1) p_2^{\eta_2+1} / |\eta_2 + 1|$ and $\beta (1 - \omega) \partial S_2 / \partial q_1 = \alpha\beta (1 - \omega) p_2^{\eta_2+1} / |\eta_2 + 1|$. Both terms define marginal goodwill (16), since $\partial c_2 / \partial q_1 \equiv 0$ by assumption. $\qquad$ Q.E.D.

In the case the demand process (7) is ruled by a promotional effect of initial sales volume q_1 on the marketing potential at the following stage of time $t = 2$, that is for $\alpha > 0$, it follows that $dmc_1 < c_1'$. Consequently, taking into account intertemporal externalities of this kind leads to a reduction of p_1 in favor of augmented quantity q_1. Efficiency turns out to be related to penetration policies in the case of demand processes which reflect growth-promoting habit formation or imitator-oriented consumers' behavior. On the other hand, growth-inhibiting dynamic effects on demand, $\alpha < 0$, imply $dmc_1 > c_1'$ such that higher initial prices at lower initial quantities turn out to be efficient. Skimming policies must be adopted when saturation or pollution effects in the demand process are taken into account. These results concerning the efficiency of the two antagonistic policies, penetration and skimming, lead to some paradoxical conclusions in the context of natural resources and exhaustibility which will be addressed in Chapter 4 below.

3. Market Structure

It should have been recognized that hitherto we did avoid to speak of market structure and of organization in the resource industry. In Theorem 1 and its corollaries neither the case $\omega = 1$ had been identified with pure monopoly, nor has $\omega = 0$ been classified as perfect competition. The reason is that there is a need for distinguishing between the *problem of choice* and the *problem of organizational design* for the allocation mechanism. After having analyzed efficiency and optimal policies the sole owner can decide on, we now address the question whether the realization of the chosen policy can be delegated to a private industry without exerting regulation but rather by selecting an appropriate market structure. Thus we assume that the sole owner has some liberty in endowing such an industry with property rights and claims and that he could set up barriers to entry as well as allow for free access.

3.1 The ω-choice and the σ-industry

In order to describe these different possibilities for organizing the industry, we propose that the sole owner can pick one *structure* σ from a continuum $[0, 1]$ of possible industrial organizations. Thereby $\sigma = 0$ indicates perfect competition with free access and hence marginal cost pricing as resulting policy. The other feasible extreme market structure, $\sigma = 1$, indicates the pure monopoly and insurmountable barriers to entry. Values $\sigma \in]0, 1[$ of the organizational design parameter are assumed to belong to market structures which yield price and quantity output in between, namely such that

$$p \left(1 + \frac{\sigma}{\eta} \right) = c' \tag{21}$$

holds in static circumstances or in a sequence of time-indexed but uncoupled markets. Consider (21) as a definition of the market structure parameter $\sigma \in [0, 1]$.

Furthermore, some degree of dynamic competition between free access and complete barriers to entry is inherent to industrial organizations with parameter $\sigma \in]0, 1[$. Our next step aims at quantifying this aspect.

As a minimal requisite start with supposing the price and quantity policy chosen by the sole owner to be either V_ω-optimal or (R, W)-efficient. Characterize this sole owner's choice by $\omega \in [0, 1]$ according to Theorem 1. The problem is then to identify, if possible, such a market structure parameter $\sigma = \sigma (\omega)$ that the realization of the chosen ω-policy can be delegated to a σ-industry. This question has obviously the trivial answer $\sigma (\omega) = \omega$ for all $\omega \in [0, 1]$ within a static framework or for a sequence of completely unlinked stages of time. This simple case corresponds to $c'_t = dmc_t$, $t = 1, 2$, in our context. But when there are intertemporal effects (which the ω-policy takes into account by decision making based on dynamic marginal cost) the length of the planning horizon faced by the firms in the industry becomes essential. Thereby the pure monopoly, due to the barriers protecting the survival of the monopolistic firm, will envisage long term planning. This includes the creation and the subsequent utilization of goodwill. In this sense *barriers to entry are property rights on goodwill*. Within a competitive industry, $\sigma = 0$, goodwill is not protected against utilization by newcomers. Consequently there are no incentives to create goodwill. Encouraging entry of new firms is related to the risk of older ones to be displaced. Allowing free access to the industry not only implies marginal cost pricing but also leads to decisions based on spot conditions. We conclude by emphasizing *this relation between the industrial organization σ and the planning horizon envisaged by the firms* in the σ-industry. This relation is here modelled by discount factors depending on the market structure $\sigma \in [0, 1]$. For simplicity of notation we assume this dependency to be proportional such that *the firms in the σ-industry discount by $\sigma\beta$ what happens at stage* $t = 2$. The quantity and price policy resulting from a σ-industry will hence maximize

$$(\sigma R_1 + (1 - \sigma) W_1) + \sigma\beta (\sigma R_2 + (1 - \sigma) W_2) \tag{22}$$

instead of $V_\sigma = (\sigma R_1 + (1 - \sigma) W_1) + \beta (\sigma R_2 + (1 - \sigma) W_2)$.

3.2 Delegation, Barriers to Entry, and Property Rights on Goodwill

Theorem 2: Let the quantities q_1, q_2 be the ω-choice of the sole owner. Then the realization of this choice, as far as the first period $t = 1$ is concerned, can be delegated to a σ-industry, if $\sigma = \sigma(\omega) \in [0, 1]$, where $\sigma(\omega)$ is defined according to

$$\sigma(\omega) := \frac{\omega c_1 + (dmc_1 - c_1')(-\eta_1)}{c_1' + (dmc_1 - c_1')(1 - \omega - \eta_1)}. \tag{23}$$

Proof: Apply the optimality condition of Theorem 1 to (i) criterion (22) and to (ii) V_ω. It follows

(i) $p_1(1 + \sigma/\eta_1) = c_1' + \sigma(dmc_1 - c_1')$
(ii) $p_1(1 + \omega/\eta_1) = c_1' + (dmc_1 - c_1')$

such that equal first period prices lead to $[c_1' + \sigma(dmc_1 - c_1')](\eta_1 + \omega) = [c_1' + (dmc_1 - c_1')](\eta_1 + \sigma)$ from which (23) follows by rearranging. *Q.E.D.*

Corollary 3: According to the sign of the difference between marginal cost of production c_1' and dynamic marginal cost dmc_1 one has the need for either stronger monopolization or more competition,

$$dmc_1 = c_1' \text{ implies } \sigma(\omega) = \omega, \tag{24}$$

$$\sigma(1) = 1 \quad \text{independent of the relation between } dmc_1 \text{ and } c_1', \tag{25}$$

$$dmc_1 > c_1' \text{ implies } \sigma(\omega) > \omega \text{ for } \omega \in [0, 1[, \tag{26}$$

$$dmc_1 < c_1' \text{ implies } \sigma(\omega) < \omega \text{ for } \omega \in [0, 1[. \tag{27}$$

If $\sigma(\omega) < 0$, then subsidies become necessary in order to realize the ω-choice, even if the owner has organized a competitive industry.

To prove this corollary of Theorem 2, recognize (24) through (27) as easy consequences of (23). Yet some remarks are apt. Ad (24): When there is no impact of output decisions at $t = 1$ on stage 2, the length of the planning horizon implemented by firms in an industry is of no importance since there are no immaterial abstract capital assets such as goodwill. Ad (25): If the sole owner chooses to maximize the discounted sum of profits, $\omega = 1$, this will be achieved by a monopoly. Barriers to entry encourage goodwill management. Within such an $\sigma = 1$-industry, goodwill is a completely private good and the monopolistic firm has unlimited property rights on goodwill. Hence $\sigma(1) = 1$ holds independently of the kind of intertemporal externalities. Ad (26): In the case one more unit of output at $t = 1$ reduces the outcomes at period 2, intertemporal efficiency demands a lower quantity and hence a higher price in the first period than would result from decision making in an ω-industry based on discount factor $\omega\beta$. This case $dmc_1 > c_1'$ is prevailing under scarcity of the resource, $\lambda > 0$, increasing production cost in the sense of $\partial c_2/\partial q_1 > 0$, and when saturation and pollution yield a diminution of demand, $\partial q_2/\partial q_1 < 0$. Under similar conditions we except indeed a certain necessity for stronger monopolization $\sigma(\omega) > \omega$ in order to obtain a reserved output policy. Ad (27): An industry with not too strong barriers to entry, where the firms are forced to behave rather short-sighted, might be confronted with positive intertemporal externalities. These effects require lower initial prices and it must be the economic policy to facilitate entry, to encourage more competition and perhaps to pay subsidies. Goodwill is then a public good and there is no incentive for the single competitive firm to create goodwill.

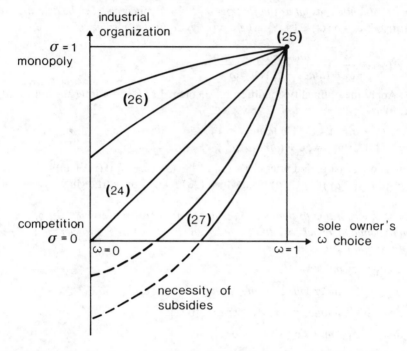

Fig. 5: Illustration of the mapping $\omega \to \sigma$ defined in (23) for nil (24), negative (26), and positive (27) intertemporal externalities. For instance, $\eta_1 = -2, c_1' = 1, dmc_1 = 2$ yields $\sigma(\omega) = (\omega + 2)/(4 - \omega)$. So, if the sole owner's choice is to maximize welfare $W = V_0, \omega = 0$, he has to organize an industry with $\sigma(0) = 1/2$ between competition and monopoly

3.3 Increasing Production Cost

We conclude with the example of production cost (3), which has been also the subject of Corollary 1 and (18). For this analysis, assume $\beta = 1$ for the discount factor and $\lambda = 0$ for the opportunity cost such that efficient output decisions in both periods should be based on the same future marginal production cost.

$$p_1 \left(1 + \frac{\omega}{\eta_1}\right) = k'(q_1 + q_2),$$

$$p_2 \left(1 + \frac{\omega}{\eta_2}\right) = k'(q_1 + q_2). \tag{28}$$

Without barriers to entry, of course, first period decisions were made according to the myopic first period marginal production cost $k'(q_1)$.

Corollary 4: The policy (28) will be relalized during the first period by an σ-industry, where

$$\sigma := \frac{\omega + K \cdot |\eta_1|}{1 + K \cdot (1 - \omega + |\eta_1|)}. \tag{29}$$

Thereby K denotes the relative growth of marginal production cost between the time stages $t = 1, 2$,

$$K := \frac{k'(q_1 + q_2) - k'(q_1)}{k'(q_1)}. \tag{30}$$

Proof: Note that $dmc_1 - c'_1$ in (23) is given here by $K \cdot k'(q_1)$.   Q.E.D.

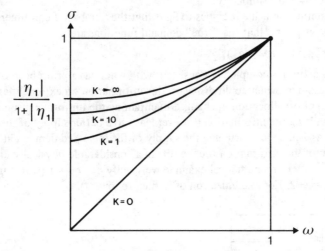

Fig. 6: Illustration of the mapping $\omega \rightarrow \sigma$ defined in (29) for various values of the cost growth ratio (30)

4. Efficiency Versus Equity

Our main thesis presented in the last chapter points out that economic modelling of intertemporal externalities results in a certain *bias of resource allocation towards uneven and physically unbalanced consumption patterns*. The approach presented in our paper was to internalize the intertemporal externalities through farsighted planning horizons such that the resource allocations over time clearly can be termed "intertemporally efficient" if not "optimal". But when farsighted decision making results in consumption patterns that appear to be unevenly distributed and physically unbalanced in comparison with short-sighted policies which abstain from intertemporal externalities, one might speak of a paradox. The question is whether the approach of internalization via goodwill management is paradoxical or the paradox consists in the myopia-based feeling according to which intertemporally efficient allocations seem less acceptable than nonefficient ones. Here we offer a paradigm that sheds light on the trade-off between intertemporal efficiency and equity.

4.1 Information on Intertemporalities

Let the resource being demanded by $n + m$ consumers who are distributed among the two periods $t = 1, 2$ in the way that the respective demand functions are

$$q_1 = np_1^\eta, \quad q_2 = (m + n)p_2^\eta. \tag{31}$$

Think of a growing population. Suppose the total amount of the resource as limited to $q_1 + q_2 \leqslant Q := 2n + m$ and assume equivalence between both periods in the sense of $\beta = 1$ for discounting. A feasible allocation that is notable for its equitable treatment of consumers over both generations is $q_1^0 = n$, $q_2^0 = n + m$. This allocation can be deduced from marginal cost pricing, for instance, if marginal cost is the same for both periods. Assume $c_1' = c_2' = 1$ for simplicity.

Now, a posteriori, imagine it comes to light that the number of consumers at stage $t = 2$ depends on q_1 and that the "true" demand functions are

$$q_1 = np_1^\eta, \quad q_2 = (m + q_1)p_2^\eta. \tag{32}$$

This new information is completely consistent with what has a priori been observed since $q_1^0 = n$. The resource owner could disregard this information on externalities in demand and leave the a priori allocation unchanged maintaining the uniform consumption pattern q_1^0, q_2^0. Internalizing the information however leads to a better supply of the n consumers at stage $t = 1$ as well as to shortening the supply of the increased demand at $t = 2$. The internalization of the information thus results in a considerable physically unbalanced allocation (q_1^*, q_2^*). For a numerical example we specify $n = m = 1$ (which implies $Q = 3$), and $\eta = -2$. For maximization of W then follows

	$t = 1$	$t = 2$
price p_t^0	1	1
quantity q_t^0	1	2
quantity per capita	100%	100%
price p_t^*	.73	1.58
quantity q_t^*	1.86	1.14
quantity per capita	186%	57%

by application of Corollary 2 with opportunity cost,

$$dmc_1 = c_1' - \alpha \left[\beta \left(\frac{\omega}{|\eta_2|} + \frac{(1 - \omega)}{|\eta_2 + 1|} \right) p_2 + \lambda \right] p_2^{\eta_2} + \lambda \tag{33}$$

for $\alpha = 1$, $\omega = 0$, $\eta = -2$, $c_1' = 1$, $\beta = 1$.

A more general analysis shows that this tendency to physically unbalanced consumption patterns turns out under negative intertemporal externalities, too. Internalization of information on effects of this kind leads to total quantities consumed $q_1^* + q_2^*$ which are lower than the total quantity consumed $q_1^0 + q_2^0$ under "myopic" criteria. The comparative static to prove this can easily be deduced from Theorem 1. Cost increases $\partial c_2/\partial q_1 > > 0$, saturation or pollution effects $\partial q_2/\partial q_1 < 0$ may prevail for a certain resource. But if these effects are explicitly taken into account, the level of total consumption will thus be reduced even more. And if for other resources, such as oil, habit formation goes hand in hand with consumption, intertemporally efficient policies are to make presents of the first barrels in order to promote subsequent demand and to apply skimming in later stages. Perhaps, the utilization of information on intertemporal externalities provides an explanation to the observation, that some resources seem to be exhaustible and others not.

4.2 A Paradigm

This conslusion takes up the paradigm

$$q_1 = p_1^{\eta}$$
$$q_2 = (1 + \alpha q_1) p_2^{\eta} \tag{34}$$

presented and analyzed in (5), Corollary 2, and Section 4.1. The pretended physical imbalance of intertemporal efficient allocations (q_1^*, q_2^*) resulting from goodwill management will be verified and compared with the uniform consumption pattern (q_1^0, q_2^0) in the "myopic" world without property rights on goodwill. The subsequent calculations are executed for different values of the market growth rate α, for $\eta = -2, c_1' = c_2' = 1$, and for the discount factor $\beta = 1$. The criterion chosen is welfare W. First have a look at the "short-sighted" allocation (q_1^0, q_2^0) resulting from marginal cost pricing without consideration of goodwill, well defined for $\alpha > -1$,

$$p_1^0 = c_1' = 1, q_1^0 = 1,$$
$$p_2^0 = c_2' = 1, q_2^0 = 1 + \alpha. \tag{35}$$

Remember that in (34) the factors 1 and $(1 + \alpha q_1)$ of the terms p_1^{η} and p_2^{η} respectively can be interpreted as "market size". Since $q_1^0/(\text{size of market 1}) = q_2^0/(\text{size of market 2}) = = (1 + \alpha)/(1 + \alpha q_1^0)$, the allocation (q_1^0, q_2^0) proofs to be a uniform supply of both markets. In what follows, we take this marginal cost pricing allocation (35) as a reference basis for the comparison with the "far-sighted" allocation (q_1^*, q_2^*)

$$p_1^* = dmc_1, \quad \text{see (33)},$$
$$p_2^* = c_2' + \lambda. \tag{36}$$

Thereby the constraint $q_1^* + q_2^* \leqslant Q := 2 + \alpha = q_1^0 + q_2^0$ is taken into account.

A first result concerns the overall level of supply in dependence of α.

α	$-.5$	$-.2$	$-.1$	0	$.1$	$.2$
$Q := q_1^0 + q_2^0$	1.50	1.80	1.90	2	2.10	2.20
$(q_1^* + q_2^*)/Q$	81%	86%	91%	100%	100%	100%
λ	0	0	0	0	0.05	.11

The next table shows supply levels SL_1, SL_2 under allocation (36), again in dependence of parameter α. The size of market at $t = 1$ is 1 as before whereas that of market 2 is $1 + \alpha q_1^*$, the sum being $2 + \alpha q_1^*$. Uniform distribution of the stock $Q = 2 + \alpha$ among both periods would therefore yield the quantity $1 \cdot [(2 + \alpha)/(2 + \alpha q_1^*)]$ for the market at $t = 1$ and $(1 + \alpha q_1^*)[(2 + \alpha)/(2 + \alpha q_1^*)]$ for $t = 2$. In order to define substantial indices we put the actual quantities q_1^*, q_2^* in relation to these entities,

$$SL_1 = q_1^*/[(2 + \alpha)/(2 + \alpha q_1^*)]$$
$$SL_2 = q_2^*/(1 + \alpha q_1^*)[(2 + \alpha)/(2 + \alpha q_1^*)].$$

(37)

Supply levels in % under allocation (36)											
α	−.5	−.2	−.1	0	.1	.2	.5	.8	1	1.5	2	3
SL_1	52	71	84	100	111	122	161	207	239	336	453	759
SL_2	119	103	101	100	91	82	65	55	51	47	42	38

Without property rights on goodwill, that is for the allocation (35), the supply levels are 100 % for both periods and all α.

These results stand for themselves. *In the case first period buyers have a positive influence ($\alpha > 0$) on the future development of the* market, they will be rewarded with a richer supply ($SL_1 > 100$ %) if goodwill management is possible. In the case first period buyers have a negative influence ($\alpha < 0$) on other consumers' demand, they will be punished by a poor supply ($SL_1 < 100$ %). What is to be learned from this? If these are interrelations between the strata of an economy it is the property rights on goodwill that give economic value to this influence.

References

Bass, F.M.: A New Product Growth Model for Consumer Durables. Management Science 15 (5), 1969, 215–227.

Chipman, J.S., and J.C. Moore: Compensating Variation, Consumer's Surplus, and Welfare. American Economic Review 70, 1980, 933–949.

Clark, C.W.: Mathematical Bioeconomics. New York 1976.

−: Concentration Profiles and the Production and Management of Marine Fisheries. This volume.

Cremer, J.: On Hotelling's Formula and the Use of Permanent Equipment in the Extraction of Natural Resources. International Economic Review 20, 1979, 317–324.

Cummings, R.G.: Some Extensions of the Economic Theory of Exhaustible Resources. Western Economic Journal 7, 1969, 201–210.

Cyert, R.M., and M. deGroot: Adaptive Utility Theory. Adaptive Economic Models. Ed. by R.H. Day and T.W. Groves. Amsterdam 1975.

Gordon, R.L.: A Reinterpretation of the Pure Theory of Exhaustion. Journal of Political Economy 75, 1967, 274–286.

Gorman, W.M.: Tastes, Habits and Choices. International Economic Review 8, 1967, 218–222.

Hirsch, W.Z.: Manufacturing Progress Functions. Review of Economics and Statistics 34, 1952, 143–155.

Hotelling, H.: The Economics of Exhaustible Resources. Journal of Political Economy 39, 1931, 137–175.

Kemp, M.C., and N.V. Long: Exhaustible Resources, Optimality, and Trade. Amsterdam 1980, 1–29.

Kotz, R., and K. Spremann: Das Aggregationsproblem der Logistischen Funktion. Zeitschrift für Operations Research 25, 1981, B9–B24.

Krelle, W.: Dynamics of the Utility Function. Carl Menger and the Austrian School of Economics. Ed. by J.R. Hicks and W. Weber. Oxford 1973.

Leibenstein, H.: Bandwagon, Snob, and Veblen Effects in the Theory of Consumers' Demand. Quarterly Journal of Economics 24, 1950, 183–207.

Levhari, D., and N. Liviatan: Notes on Hotelling's Economics of Exhaustible Resources. Canadian Journal of Economics 10, 1977, 177–192.

Manning, R.: Resource Use When Demand is Interdependent Over Time. Economic Record 54, 1978, 72–77.

Peston, M.H.: Changing Utility Functions. Essays in Mathematical Economics in Honor of Oskar Morgenstern. Ed. by M. Shubik. Princeton 1967.

Pindyck, R.S.: The Optimal Exploration and Production of Nonrenewable Resources. Journal of Political Economy 86, 1978, 841–861.

Pollak, R.A.: Habit Formation and Dynamic Demand Functions. Journal of Political Economy 78, 1970, 745–763.

–: Interdependent Preferences. American Economic Review 66, 1976, 309–320.

Spremann, K.: Optimale Preispolitik bei dynamischen deterministischen Absatzmodellen. Zeitschrift für Nationalökonomie 35, 1975, 63–76.

–: On Welfare Implications and Efficiency of Entrance Fee Pricing. Journal of Economics (Z. Nationalökonomie) 38, 1978, 231–252.

Stiglitz, J.E.: Monopoly and the Rate of Extraction of Exhaustible Resources. American Economic Review 66, 1976, 655–661.

Sweeney, J.L.: Economics of Depletable Resources: Market Forces and Intertemporal Bias. Review of Economic Studies 44, 1977, 125–142.

Veblen, T.: Why is Economics not an Evolutionary Science? Quarterly Journal of Economics 12, 1898, 373–397.

Weinstein, M., and R.J. Zeckhauser: The Optimal Consumption of Depletable Natural Resources. Quarterly Journal of Economics 89, 1975, 371–392.

Willig, R.D.: Consumer's Surplus Without Apology. American Economic Review 66, 1976, 589–597.

Economic Theory of Natural Resources. ©Physica-Verlag, Würzburg–Wien, 1982.

Trade Between Industrialized and Resource-Rich Countries: A Game-Theoretic Approach

Eckhard Höpfinger and *Hans-Paul Schwefel*

1. Introduction

During the past few years, it has become obvious that, whereas the consumption of some important resources has continually increased, their availability has lessened. Therefore one has to bear in mind the exhaustability of a number of significant resources. In all developed countries the research for substitutes has increased. However, even if substitutes are available, it is still necessary to determine the optimal rate of depletion of existing resources and the optimal timing of the transition to the substitutes. Much attention has recently been given in the literature to these problems of exhaustible but essential resources [e.g. *Dasgupta/Heal; Kemp/Long,* and literature cited there]. Most of the studies, however, formulate the problems in global terms as a centralized decision-making process. They do not consider that decisions may be dispersed among many countries and that the resource may be unevenly distributed over those countries. In fact, both reserves and production capacities for many exhaustible resources have an extremely uneven worldwide distribution. A number of interesting questions can be raised: How can resources be exchanged for consumption and investment goods? What are the optimal paths of substitution? Is there a preference for the concentration of production in one part of the world?

These questions have been treated in part in a special framework in the literature cited below. In the case of a game-theoretic approach the problem is usually modelled as a differential game with the NASH-equilibrium point as the solution concept.

We shall primarily be concerned with the substitution of fossil energy resources by non-fossil energy systems. The model given below, however, might also be used for other non-renewable resources. Two groups of countries exchange a fossil fuel, extracted from an exhaustible stock, for goods for either own consumption or indigenous investment. The economies of both groups are given as two-sector models, one sector being energy and the other representing the rest of the economy. These models are simpler than the one by *Reister/Edmonds* [1977] as fewer energy systems are considered and no price systems are introduced. The trade model here is based on the assumption that the two groups of countries differ in that

— one group has a small technological capacity but large fossil energy resources
— the other has a large technological capacity but few resources.

The size of the non-fossil energy system is assumed to be correlated to the level of technology. Both groups of countries strive to maximize their own long-term utility function which evaluates the consumption over time. The solution concept used for this two-person-non-zero-sum game is the NASH-bargaining solution.

2. Statement of the Model

Let F denote the group of countries with large fossil energy resources and N the group of countries which are highly industrialized and have an important non-fossil energy supply system. The energy sector of each group of countries ($i = F, N$) is characterized by two equations in each period of time $t = 1, 2 \ldots$

$$T_t^i = \delta T_{t-1}^i + I_{T,t}^i + \chi^i J_{T,t}$$

$$E_t^i = [\lambda (O_t^i)^\gamma + (1 - \lambda) (T_{t-1}^i)^\gamma]^{1/\gamma}$$

where

T_t^i = size of non-fossil energy system at period t

$I_{T,t}^i$ = investment into this energy system

$J_{T,t}$ = additional investment into this energy system by $i = F$ which is imported from $i = N$

$$\chi^i = \begin{cases} 0 \text{ if } i = N \\ 1 \text{ if } i = F \end{cases}$$

δ is an exogenously given aging factor which is close to one

E_t^i = energy available during period t

O_t^i = fossil fuel consumed

λ, γ are exogenously given parameters. Since fossil and non-fossil energy is assumed to be completely substitutable γ is only allowed to lie in the range $0 < \gamma < 1$ such that the production function of E_t^i is a CES-function.

It is assumed that the initial stock of fossil fuel G_0 is known to both groups of countries. Then the constraint

$$G_0 \geqslant \sum_{t=1}^{\infty} (O_t^F + O_t^N)$$

has to be satisfied. Furthermore, the initial values T_0^F and T_0^N are known to both groups. $O_t^i, I_{T,t}^i, J_{T,t}$ are regarded as decision variables whereas T_t^i and E_t^i are state variables.

The second sector of each group of countries, called the materials sector by analogy with *Reister/Edmonds* [1977], is characterized by the following two equations in each period of time

$$L_t^i = \epsilon L_{t-1}^i + I_{L,t}^i$$

$$M_t^i = \lambda_0 (L_{t-1}^i)^\beta (E_t^i)^{1-\beta}$$

where

L_t^i = amount of qualified labour force

$I_{L,t}^i$ = investment for education

M_t^i = amount of materials produced.

L_0^F and L_0^N are assumed to be known. ϵ, λ_0 and β are exogenously given parameters. $I_{L,t}^i$ are regarded as decision variables.

In this model we consider only utilities which are based on consumption c_t^i which is determined by

$$c_t^i = M_t^i - I_{L,t}^i - I_{T,t}^i + (\chi^i - 1) J_{T,t} + (2\chi^i - 1) J_{c,t}$$

where $J_{c,t}$ denotes those goods which are consumed by F and are produced by the group N. The decision variables $I_{L,t}^i$, $I_{T,t}^i$ $(i = F, N)$, $J_{T,t}$, $J_{c,t}$ are bounded by the condition $c_t^i \geqslant 0$ for each i and t.

In each period, the utility derived from the consumption of c_t^i is assumed to be given by an increasing and concave utility function u. Two examples will be considered

$$u_1(c) = c^\kappa \qquad \text{with } 0 < \kappa \leqslant 1$$
$$u_2(c) = \ln c.$$

The long-term objective of each group is assumed to be the maximization of its discounted integral utility

$$W^i = (1 - \rho) \sum_{t=1}^{\infty} \rho^{t-1} u(c_t^i) \qquad (i = F, N).$$

Let q^i denote the maximal pay-off to group i $(i = F, N)$ if group i optimizes over the set of all possible investment decisions and possible decisions on its consumption of fossil energy in the case of no trade, i.e. $O_t^N = 0$, $J_{T,t} = 0$ and $J_{c,t} = 0$ for each $t = 1, 2 \ldots$ As it turns out both groups can achieve a better pay-off than the status quo point (q^F, q^N) if trade is included. But what should the terms of trade be?

Since the market power of the resource owning states might be limited by the greater political power of the industrialized countries we have selected a rather fair solution concept, the NASH-bargaining solution. Given individual rationality, feasibility, Pareto optimality, independence of irrelevant alternatives, invariance with respect to utility transformations, symmetry and the feasible region being closed, bounded and convex, the NASH-bargaining solution is given as the unique feasible point (W^{F*}, W^{N*}) which makes $(W^F - q^F)(W^N - q^N)$ maximal. Since the verification of the required properties of the feasible set is cumbersome, we only look for a joint strategy σ^* that maximises $(W^F(\sigma) - q^F)(W^N(\sigma) - q^N)$ [c.p. *Owen*]. Later on we point to the possibility of using another solution concept.

3. Analytical Determination of the Status Quo Pay-Off q^N

Dropping the index $i = N$ the status quo pay-off q of the group of countries with negligible fossil resources is determined by

$$q = \max_{(I_{L,t}, I_{T,t})_{t=1,2,\ldots}} (1-\rho) \sum_{t=1}^{\infty} \rho^{t-1} u(c_t)$$

$$c_t = \lambda_0 L_{t-1}^{\beta} (1-\lambda)^{(1-\beta)/\gamma} T_{t-1}^{1-\beta} - I_{L,t} - I_{T,t}$$

$$T_t = \delta T_{t-1} + I_{T,t}$$

$$L_t = \epsilon L_{t-1} + I_{L,t}$$

$L_0, T_0, \rho, \lambda_0, \lambda, \beta, \gamma, \delta, \epsilon$ are given parameters.

Let $k_t := L_t + T_t$. Now we assume that only the sum $k_t > 0$ of L_t and T_t is given. As can be shown by a simple proof, the value of the Cobb-Douglas production function $L_t^{\beta} T_t^{1-\beta}$ is maximal for $L_t = \beta k_t$ and $T_t = (1-\beta) k_t$ among all L_t and T_t with sum k_t. Based on this we make the following assumptions in order to arrive at an easier solvable problem. Let

$$L_0 = \beta k_0, \quad T_0 = (1-\beta) k_0$$

for a given $k_0 > 0$. Let $\epsilon = \delta$ and let the investment $I_t = I_{L,t} + I_{T,t}$ be split constantly into $I_{L,t} = \beta I_t$, $I_{T,t} = (1-\beta) I_t$. Then $T_t = \delta T_{t-1} + (1-\beta) I_t$ and $L_t = \delta L_{t-1} + \beta I_t$. By a simple proof based on complete induction one gets

$$L_t = \beta k_t, \quad T_t = (1-\beta) k_t$$

where $k_t = \delta k_{t-1} + I_t$ for $t = 1,2\ldots$
Hence the problem can be formulated as follows

$$q = \max_{(I_t)_{t=1,2,\ldots}} (1-\rho) \sum_{t=1}^{\infty} \rho^{t-1} u(c_t)$$

$$c_t = \eta k_{t-1} - I_t$$

$$k_t = \delta k_{t-1} + I_t$$

where $\eta = \lambda_0 (1-\lambda)^{(1-\beta)/\gamma} \beta^{\beta} (1-\beta)^{1-\beta}$.

First let $u(c_t) = u_t^{\kappa}$ with $0 < \kappa \leqslant 1$ and assume a constant rate $\aleph = I_t/M_t$ of the total investments. The optimal pay-off q^+ is given by

$$q^+ = (1-\rho) \eta^{\kappa} k_0^{\kappa} \max_{0 \leqslant \aleph \leqslant 1} (1-\aleph)^{\kappa} \sum_{t=1}^{\infty} [\rho (\delta + \aleph \eta)^{\kappa}]^{t-1}.$$

The convergence of this series is given as soon as $\rho \, (\delta + \aleph\eta)^\kappa \leqslant 1$ for all $0 \leqslant \aleph \leqslant 1$ or $\rho \, (\delta + \eta)^\kappa \leqslant 1$. In this case

$$q^+ = (1 - \rho) \, \eta^\kappa \, k_0^\kappa \, \max_{0 \leqslant \aleph \leqslant 1} \frac{(1 - \aleph)^\kappa}{1 + [\rho \, (\delta + \aleph\eta)]^\kappa}.$$

The maximizing rate $\aleph^+$ can be found by putting the derivative of the right-hand function equal to zero.

Proposition 1: Let $u \, (c_t) = c_t^\kappa$ with $0 < \kappa \leqslant 1$ and assume a constant rate of investment $\aleph$. Let $\rho \, (\delta + \eta)^\kappa \leqslant 1$ hold. The maximizing $\aleph^+$ then is given by

$$\aleph^+ = \begin{cases} 0 \text{ if} & \kappa = 1 \\[4pt] 0 \text{ if } [\rho \, (\delta + \eta)]^{1/(1-\kappa)} < \delta \text{ and } \kappa < 1 \\[4pt] \dfrac{[\rho \, (\delta + \eta)]^{1/(1-\kappa)} - \delta}{\eta} \text{ if } [\rho \, (\delta + \eta)]^{1/(1-\kappa)} \geqslant \delta \text{ and } \kappa < 1. \end{cases}$$

Remark: Because $k_t = (\delta + \eta\aleph^+)^t \, k_0$ holds, growth is equivalent to $1 \leqslant \delta + \eta\aleph^+ = [\rho \, (\delta + \eta)]^{1/(1-\kappa)}$ or $1 \leqslant \rho \, (\delta + \eta)$ as $\delta < 1$.

In order to arrive at easier expressions however we have used another utility function u.

Proposition 2: Let $u \, (c_t) = \ln c_t$ and assume a constant rate $\aleph$ of investment, i.e. $I_t = \aleph M_t$. Then the optimal pay-off q^t is given by

$$q^t = \ln\eta + \ln k_0 + \ln (1 - \aleph^+) + \frac{\rho}{1 - \rho} \ln (\delta + \eta\aleph^+)$$

where

$$\aleph^+ = \max\left(0, \rho - (1 - \rho)\frac{\delta}{\eta}\right).$$

Growth is given if, and only if, $\rho \, (\delta + \eta) \geqslant 1$.

The proof is a simple analytical derivation where one has to bear in mind that $0 \leqslant \aleph \leqslant 1$ excluding negative investment rates. Since $k_t = (\delta + \eta\aleph^+)^t \, k_0$ growth is identical with $(\delta + \eta\aleph^+) \geqslant 1$.

By derivation $q^+ \leqslant q^N$ holds in the case of $\delta = \epsilon$ and $(1 - \beta) \, L_0 = \beta T_0$. However it seems that q^+ equals q^N even if we do not require $I_{L,t} = \beta I_t$, $I_{T,t} = (1 - \beta) I_t$ and that the rate of investment is constant. Since we only needed a correction term for the numerical calculations as indicated below the derivation of q^+ was sufficient and we made no effort to prove that $q^+ = q^N$.

4. Numerical Results

A series of examples were treated numerically. Since all of them showed the same qualitative behaviour, we shall present one example only and comment on its general importance.

Let
$$\epsilon = \delta = 0.95; \rho = 0.9; \lambda_0 = 2.1; \lambda = 0.66; \beta = 0.3; \gamma = 0.4;$$

$$L_0^N = 300; T_0^N = 700; L_0^F = 30; T_0^F = 70; G_0 = 500.$$

Since, for numerical reasons, only a finite number of periods can be treated, we replaced the pay-off function W^i with logarithmic utility function by

$$W_a^i = (1-\rho)\left\{ \sum_{t=1}^{\tau} \rho^{t-1} \ln c_t^i + \rho^{\tau} \left[\ln \eta + \ln k_{\tau}^i \right. \right.$$

$$\left. \left. + \ln\left(1 - \rho + (1-\rho)\frac{\delta}{\eta}\right) + \frac{\rho}{1-\rho} \ln\left(\rho\left(\delta + \eta\right)\right) \right] \right\}$$

where the pay-off from the periods $\tau + 1, \tau + 2, \ldots$ is replaced by the pay-off given in proposition 2. Thus no trade and no depletion of resources is taken into account after period τ. k_{τ}^i is defined by

$$k_{\tau}^i := \min\left(\frac{L_{\tau}^i}{\beta}, \frac{T_{\tau}^i}{1-\beta}\right).$$

In the example, $\tau = 30$ was chosen in order to avoid a too large computational effort.

The results are depicted by the following thirteen figures. In figures one and seven G_t denotes the remaining stock of fossil energy available in period t, i.e.

$$G_t = G_0 - \sum_{s=1}^{t-1} (O_s^N + O_s^F).$$

The first six figures describe the development of both groups of countries without cooperation by means of trade. As can be seen the economy of the countries in group F with important fossil energy resources overtakes after some time periods the economy of the countries in group N for the given set of parameters. Nevertheless, the maximal pay-offs $q^N = 4.66$ and $q^F = 4.87$ are not very different. This is the result of discounting the pay-offs over time. Thus the first periods have a greater importance.

The remaining seven figures relate to the development of both where trade is an essential ingredient. Comparing the figures one and seven it seems that the rate of depletion of the stock of fossil energy is the same whether the countries cooperate or not. Altogether the figures indicate that first the countries of group N receive a greater part of the depletable fossil energy stock, make large investments to increase their capacity for production. Hence N is able to pay back the lent fossil fuel by exporting consumption and investment goods. The final figure shows almost identical consumption for both groups which can be explained by the tendency of the NASH-bargaining solution to give both parties the same gain by trade, indeed the final values $W^{N*} = 5.26$, $W^{F*} = 5.34$ do not differ very much either. It should be noted that the time axis runs down from the top to the bottom and that it is translated by 1, i.e., number j relates to time period $j + 1$. The discontinuities between period 30 and period 31 are due to the approximation error generated by replacing the pay-offs of the later periods by the formula of section 3.

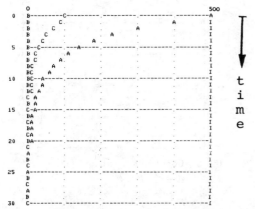

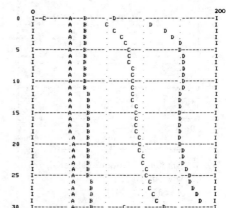

Fig. 1: Depletion and Consumption of Fossil
Energy without Trade
$$A = G_t, B = O_t^N = 0, C = O_t^F$$

Fig. 2: Investments without Trade
$$A = I_{T,t}^N, B = I_t^N = I_{T,t}^N + I_{L,t}^N$$
$$C = I_{T,t}^F, D = I_t^F = I_{T,t}^F + I_{L,t}^F$$

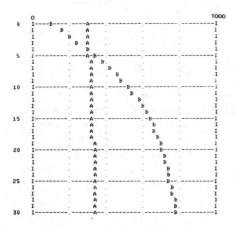

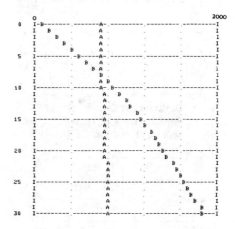

Fig. 3: Qualified Labour Force without Trade
$$A = L_t^N, B = L_t^F$$

Fig. 4: Non-Fossil Energy System without
Trade
$$A = T_t^N, B = T_t^F$$

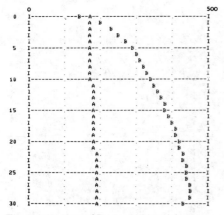

Fig. 5: Amount of Produced Materials without Trade
$$A = M_t^N, B = M_t^F$$

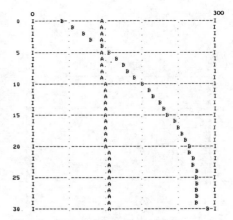

Fig. 6: Consumption without Trade
$$A = c_t^N, B = c_t^F$$

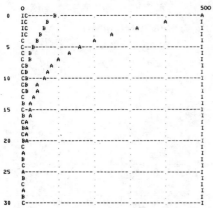

Fig. 7: Depletion and Consumption of Fossil Energy with Trade (Compare with Fig. 1, the non-Trade case)

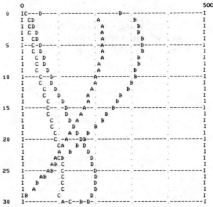

Fig. 8: Investments with Trade (Compare with Fig. 2)

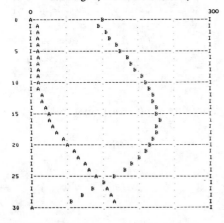

Fig. 9: Transfer of Goods from N to F
$$A = J_{T,t} \text{ investment goods}$$
$$B = J_{c,t} \text{ consumption goods}$$

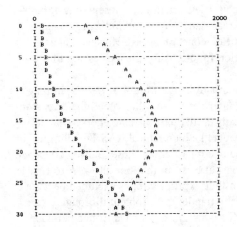

Fig. 10: Qualified Labour Force with Trade
$A = L_t^N$, $B = L_t^F$
(Compare with Fig. 3)

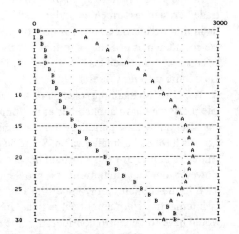

Fig. 11: Non-Fossil Energy System with Trade
$A = T_t^N$, $B = T_t^F$
(Compare with Fig. 4)

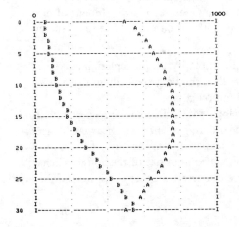

Fig. 12: Amount M_t^i of Produced Materials
with Trade
A for N, B for F
(Compare with Fig. 5)

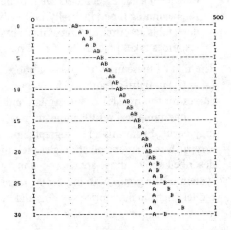

Fig. 13: Consumption c_t^i with Trade
A for N, B for F
(Compare with Fig. 6)

5. Conclusion

In this paper we have attempted to obtain some qualitative results of possible terms of trade between resource-rich and industrialized countries. The model presented is optimistic in that no inertia effects for investments are regarded, long-term binding agreements are considered as possible, and that a "fair" solution concept is used. However, inertia effects may quite well lead to different production functions for the parties and thus yield quite different results.

The NASH-bargaining solution lacks stability in a dynamic situation [*Haurie*] in that one party may have a much better position in a later period and then break the agreement, e.g. after a few time periods N has consumed a substantial part of fossil energy whereas exports have had a smaller value. Solution concepts like hierarchical NASH-equilibrium in strategies don't have this shortcoming and hence one might apply these solution concepts. However, one can circumvent this problem, in part at least, in that one allows F to engage itself in the economy of N under the assumption that expropriation is excluded because of internal or external political reasons. In order to handle this problem thoroughly one would have to take into consideration the benefits which F might have from a permanent engagement in N. This, however, is outside the scope of this study. It should be mentioned that short term NASH-bargaining solutions might also be considered.

The main results of the model are

— the depletion of the fossil energy resources seems to be the same whether there is trade or not,
— long term trade agreements seem to be most profitable for both parties such that in the beginning the industrially more advanced group receives a larger amount of the depletable resource and repayment by exports to the group with large fossil energy resources takes place in later time periods.

The first of these main results is supported by the similarity of the depletion curves $(A = G_t)$ in figures 1 and 7. The second main result is shown graphically in figure 9 by curves for the transfer of investment and consumption goods.

Other numerical results indicate that no development of the non-fossil energy system may occur. From this a lexicographic preference ordering of the strategies may be necessary such that among all strategies yielding maximal pay-offs of the pay-off functions described above, those are chosen which yield the maximum size of the non-fossil energy system of the group with important fossil energy resources. Further extensions of the model might include price systems and more parties.

References

Dasgupta, P.S., and *G.M. Heal*: Economic Theory and Exhaustible Resources. Cambridge 1979.
Haurie, A.: A Note on Nonzero-Sum Differential Games with Bargaining Solution. JOTA **18** (1), 1976, 31–39.
Kemp, M.C., and *N.V. Long* (eds.): Exhaustible Resources, Optimality and Trade. Amsterdam 1980.
Owen, G.: Game Theory. Philadelphia 1968.
Reister, D.B., and *J.A. Edmonds*: A General Equilibrium Two-Sector Energy Demand Model, Modeling Energy-Economy Interactions: Five Approaches, Resources for the Future. Ed. by Ch.J. Hitch. Washington, D.C. 1977.

Software Tools

As for the software used for the numerical calculations, i.e. a combined simulation and optimization package, we refer to

Drepper, F.: A Data-Model Interface for Modular Dynamic Simulation, Proceed. Winter Simulation Conference, Miami Beach, December 1978, 313–321.

Heckler, R., and H.P. Schwefel: Superimposing Direct Search Methods for Parameter Optimization onto Dynamic Simulation Models, Proceed. Winter Simulation Conference, Miami Beach, December 1978, 173–181.

Economic Theory of Natural Resources. ©Physica-Verlag, Würzburg–Wien, 1982.

Oligopolistic Supply on the World Cocoa Market

Hans Jürgen Jaksch

An oligopoly model is developed for application on the world cocoa market. The equilibrium points of the resulting supergame are characterized theoretically. Then, the actual behaviour of the five most important suppliers on this market is compared with the set of equilibrium points derived from the model. A tentative explanation is offered for the discrepancies between the theoretical and the empirical results. In addition, the likelihood of a stable agreement among the cocoa producing countries which does not involve the demanding countries is investigated. Reasons are provided why such an agreement probably is not stable over time.

1. Introduction

Price formation on commodity markets is sometimes erratic and appears to defy rational explanation, at least in the short run. Econometric models of these markets, mostly constructed with the intention to forecast commodity prices in the long run, in general fail to yield reliable forecasts and are therefore inapplicable in the short run. In recent years, it has become fashionable to regard the short run price prediction on a commodity market as impossible since, as it has been claimed, many spot and future markets are efficient in the sense that "prices fully reflect all available information" [*Praetz*]. Since I personally have difficulties to understand what is meant by this phrase, as well as by the statistical "tests" purporting to show that observed price changes are serially uncorrelated, I do not share this pessimistic attitude. Since some investigations clearly do not present an adequate picture of the institutional conditions on a market, it may be worthwhile to model markets more closely to reality. On the other hand, short run price forecasts may be difficult to obtain even with a more realistic model.

In this paper, a model is presented which should aid in the understanding of the suppliers' behaviour on the world cocoa market. Contrary to the existing long run models of this market [*Adams/Behrman; Behrman/Tinakorn-Ramangkura*] which link production directly to consumption, we regard the world market for cocoa as a chain of several interdependent, but separate markets: The world market where exporters and importers face each other, the market within each producing country where the producer sells his crop to the exporter, and the market in the consuming countries where the importer or manufacturer sells the processed product. If we want to study the short run quantity and price developments and explain them with a horizon varying between six and twentyfour months, then it is important to analyze the world market in the narrow sense. This market, in turn, clearly is not perfectly competitive: The supply is exercised or regulated strongly by governmental or semigovernmental agencies, and the demand, to some extent at least, is exercised by supranational or large national firms. Oligopolistic behaviour of some suppliers was already documented for the 1950's by *Behrman* [1968]; it became clearly apparent recently after the failure of the Geneva and London negotiations to renew the World Cocoa Agreement of 1975 which expired on March 31, 1980.

This paper concentrates on theory and the empirical application of this theory. Econometric estimations, especially of a short run demand function, are important for the applications presented here. However, these results are preliminary, and we therefore describe them only very shortly.

The basis of our analysis is a simple oligopoly model. The respective game possesses a unique equilibrium point. This game then is regarded as the constituent game of a stationary supergame [*Friedman,* 1971, 1977]. The set of equilibria of this game then is studied.

In the final section of this paper, we apply these results to the world cocoa market, using figures for the years 1974 to 1977. If one takes into account the present economic and social conditions in the supplying countries, some interesting results follow for the future development of this market.

2. The Theory

In this section, we describe a model of a sellers' oligopoly which reproduces the most important aspects of the world cocoa market. Because all actions on this market depend on time, and because we want to explain (and ultimately predict) the short run behaviour of the sellers on this market, we have selected the month as the reference period.

On the other hand, cocoa production and selling shows definite cycles over the crop year, beginning at October 1. The harvest extends into December, and sales of this harvest go on till the following August when the sellers' stocks in general have been depleted.

An exact monthly model would have to incorporate the fluctuation of these sales. However, as a first step it seemed advisable to start more simply and to assume that during each month of the crop year, more or less the same quantity is being sold. In this case, the model refers to a month, but the month is, at least for the time being, just one twelvth of a crop year. Thus, seasonal variations have been assumed not to exist here, and they will be introduced into the model at a later stage.

We consider a perfect market with n sellers numbered $1, 2, \ldots, n$. Seller i's sales curve: $i \in N = \{1, 2, \ldots, n\}$, is derived from the linear demand curve in this market:

$$p = a - bx \qquad (a > 0, b > 0). \tag{1}$$

Here, p denotes the price and x the (total) quantity which is demanded at this price. a and b are given parameters. For the application of the theoretical model they must be estimated econometrically.

By definition, x is the sum of the sales of each seller $i \in N$, denoted by $x_1, x_2, \ldots, x_n$:

$$x = \sum_{i=1}^{n} x_i.$$

Seller i derives his sales curve from the demand curve by considering the other sellers' sales $\bar{x}_1, \bar{x}_2, \ldots, \bar{x}_{i-1}, \bar{x}_{i+1}, \bar{x}_{i+2}, \ldots, \bar{x}_n$ as given:

$$f_i(x_i, \bar{x}_{)i(}) = -bx_i + a - b \sum_{\substack{j=1 \\ j \neq i}}^{n} \bar{x}_j \qquad (i = 1: n).$$

Here, $\bar{x}_{)i(} = (\bar{x}_1 \bar{x}_2 \ldots \bar{x}_{i-1} \bar{x}_{i+1} \bar{x}_{i+2} \ldots \bar{x}_n)$. Thus, $\bar{x}_{)i(}$ denotes the vector of the other sellers' sales which are not controlled by i and which i, for the time being, considers as given.

Seller i faces a cost function which relates total cost to the quantity sold. In the short run analysis where we consider the sales of a given crop, only costs which are related to these sales (e.g. transportation costs within the producing country) must be considered here. On the other hand, if a long run analysis is made, production cost must be included in the model and may indeed play a predominant role in the analysis. We assume that this cost, C_i, is a linear homogenous function of the quantity sold:

$$C_i = c_i x_i \qquad\qquad (c_i \geqslant 0, i = 1: n).$$

The c_i, $i \in N$, are given parameters. For brevity we define

$$a_i = a - c_i \qquad\qquad (i = 1: n).$$

We assume further that seller i has a given positive stock s_i of the commodity which his sales cannot exceed:

$$0 \leqslant x_i \leqslant s_i \qquad\qquad (i = 1: n). \tag{2}$$

s_i is a given positive number. $s_i = +\infty$ is not excluded from the model and may well be a reasonable assumption in a long run analysis when production cost will be the essential limit to supply.

Let us assume further that seller i wants to maximize the total net revenue from his sales. (That a cocoa selling country actually has this objective is a matter of fact.) Under this assumption, seller i maximizes

$$x_i f_i(x_i, \bar{x}_{)i(}) = -bx_i^2 + (a_i - b \sum_{\substack{j=1 \\ j \neq i}}^{n} \bar{x}_j) x_i$$

under the condition (2) where s_i is positive and given.

Note that, for $a_i \geqslant 0$, the term in the parantheses is non-positive, regardless of the precise value of $\bar{x}_{)i(} \geqslant 0$. Since $b > 0$, i maximizes his revenue if $x_i = 0$. We therefore assume

$$a_i > 0 \qquad\qquad (i = 1: n),$$

excluding all suppliers from our analysis if they cannot obtain a positive revenue from selling a positive quantity.

In order to simplify the notation we define

$$\bar{y}_i = b \sum_{\substack{j=1 \\ j \neq i}}^{n} \bar{x}_j \qquad\qquad (i = 1: n). \tag{3}$$

$\bar{y}_i$ denotes by how much the demand curve (1) is shifted in order to yield i's sales curve if i's competitors sell $\bar{x}_{)i(}$.

By standard analysis, we derive that $x_i = \bar{x}_i$ solves i's constrained maximum problem if, and only if

$$
\bar{x}_i = \begin{cases} \dfrac{a_i - \bar{y}_i}{2b} & \text{if } s_i \geqslant \dfrac{a_i - \bar{y}_i}{2b}, & a_i > \bar{y}_i \\[2ex] s_i & \text{if } s_i < \dfrac{a_i - \bar{y}_i}{2b}, & a_i > \bar{y}_i \\[2ex] 0 & \text{if } & a_i \leqslant \bar{y}_i. \end{cases} \tag{4}
$$

(4) denotes i's best reply to his competitors' given sales, $\bar{x}_{)i(}$. There exists exactly one best reply for each given $\bar{x}_{)i(}$.

Assume now that there exists a vector $\bar{x} = (\bar{x}_1 \; \bar{x}_2 \ldots \bar{x}_n)$ such that *every* $\bar{x}_i$ is a best reply. Then $\bar{x}$ constitutes an equilibrium point.

The literature on oligopoly models from *Cournot* is dominated by the investigation of equilibrium points. This interest follows from the simple observation that, if one would observe a sales vector on a market which is not an equilibrium point, it must be transitory since at least one seller would not reply best and hence may be expected to change his behaviour sooner or later. Thus, if exactly one equilibrium point exists for an oligopoly, one would expect to observe it in reality. (It is a different question if the constructed model really represents all important aspects of the oligopolistic market in question.)

Without further analysis, it is not clear that an equilibrium point in a certain market exists. However, for the simple oligopoly described above, the existence of exactly one equilibrium point has often been proved [*Selten; Friedman,* 1977].

Below, we therefore outline the procedure which we have used to compute an equilibrium point numerically. It is derived from a constructive proof of the existence of at most one equilibrium point.

Assume that $\bar{x} = (\bar{x}_1 \; \bar{x}_2 \ldots \bar{x}_n)$ is an equilibrium point. We now decompose N exhaustively into three subsets N_1, N_2, N_3 (with $N_r \cap N_s = \emptyset, r, s = 1,2,3$) implied by (3) and (4):

$$
\bar{x}_i + \sum_{j=1}^n \bar{x}_j = \frac{a_i}{b} \qquad (i \in N_1) \tag{5}
$$

$$
s_i \geqslant \bar{x}_i > 0 \qquad (i \in N_1) \tag{6}
$$

$$
\bar{x}_i + \sum_{j=1}^n \bar{x}_j < \frac{a_i}{b} \qquad (i \in N_2) \tag{7}
$$

$$
s_i = \bar{x}_i \qquad (i \in N_2) \tag{8}
$$

$$
\bar{x}_i + \sum_{j=1}^n \bar{x}_j \geqslant \frac{a_i}{b} \qquad (i \in N_3) \tag{9}
$$

$$
\bar{x}_i = 0 \qquad (i \in N_3). \tag{10}
$$

We define $n_1 = |N_1|$. From (5), (8) and (10) follows

$$\sum_{i=1}^{n} \bar{x}_i = \frac{1}{n_1 + 1}\left(\sum_{h \in N_1} \frac{a_h}{b} + \sum_{k \in N_2} s_k\right). \tag{11}$$

We now prove that N_1, N_2, N_3 are uniquely determined.
From (5) to (10) it follows directly that

$$\frac{a_l}{b} \leqslant \sum_{i=1}^{n} \bar{x}_i < \frac{a_g}{b} \qquad (l \in N_3, g \in N \setminus N_3) \tag{12}$$

$$\frac{a_h}{b} - s_h \leqslant \sum_{i=1}^{n} \bar{x}_i < \frac{a_k}{b} - s_k \quad (h \in N_1, k \in N_2). \tag{13}$$

After numbering the sellers such that

$$a_i - bs_i \leqslant a_{i+1} - bs_{i+1} \qquad (i = 1:(n-1)) \tag{14}$$

we determine a permutation Π of N, i.e.

$$N \underset{\Pi}{\to} \{j_1\, j_2 \ldots j_n\},$$

which orders the sellers according to their sales cost:

$$a_{j_i} \geqslant a_{j_{i+1}} \qquad (i = 1:(n-1)).$$

If there exists a subscript $i' \in \{1,2,\ldots,n-1\}$ such that

$$a_{j'} - bs_{j'} < a_{j_{i'}},\ a_{i'+1} - bs_{i'+1} \geqslant a_{j_{i'+1}}, \tag{15}$$

then it follows from (12) and (13) that

$$N_3 = \{j_{i'+1}, j_{i'+2}, \ldots, j_n\}$$

and

$$N_1 = \{i \in N \setminus N_3 \mid a_i - bs_i \leqslant a_{i'+1} - bs_{i'+1}\}$$

$$N_2 = \{i \in N \setminus N_3 \mid a_i - bs_i > a_{i'+1} - bs_{i'+1}\}.$$

If there does not exist a subscript i' such that (15) is valid, then (12) implies $N_3 = \emptyset$. (13) and (14) then imply the existence of an $m \in \{0,1,\ldots,n\}$ with the property

$$\frac{a_m}{b} - s_m \leqslant \frac{1}{n_1 + 1}\left(\sum_{e=1}^{m} \frac{a_e}{b} + \sum_{e=m+1}^{n} s_e\right) < \frac{a_{m+1}}{b} - s_{m+1}. \tag{16}$$

(In (16), the left hand inequality is invalid for $m = 0$, and the right hand inequality is invalid for $m = n$).
(16) implies

$$m\left(\frac{a_m}{b} - s_m\right) - \sum_{e=1}^{m-1}\left(\frac{a_e}{b} - s_e\right) \leqslant \sum_{j=1}^{n} s_j < (m+1)\left(\frac{a_{m+1}}{b} - s_{m+1}\right)$$
$$- \sum_{e=1}^{m}\left(\frac{a_e}{b} - s_e\right). \tag{17}$$

The function

$$F(z) = z\left(\frac{a_z}{b} - s_z\right) - \sum_{e=1}^{z-1}\left(\frac{a_e}{b} - s_e\right)$$

is monotonically non-decreasing for $z = 1,2,\ldots,n$. Since the sum $\sum_{j=1}^{n} s_j$ is a given
number, m is uniquely determined. Therefore N_1, N_2, N_3 are uniquely determined.
Because the system of linear equations (5) has a regular matrix of coefficients, there
exists at most one solution of (5) to (10).

Now assume that $\bar{x}$ is unknown and must be determined. This consideration implies
the following method of construction of $\bar{x}$ and therefore can be used to prove that there
exists at least one equilibrium point:

First, we number the sellers such that (14) is valid. Then, we determine a permutation
Π leading to (15). This leads to a unique decomposition of N into N_3 and $N \setminus N_3$ and
then of $N \setminus N_3$ into N_1 and N_2. Finally, we define $\bar{x}_h$, $h \in N_1$, by (5), $\bar{x}_k$, $k \in N_2$, by (8),
and $\bar{x}_l$, $l \in N_3$, by (10).

This construction of N_1, N_2, N_3 yields (12) and (13). This, in turn, implies the inequalities (6), (7) and (9). –

In the above model, we have assumed that all sellers make a decision referring to the
representative month in question. Nothing has been said about what happens after the
representative month has elapsed. The above theory clearly is valid if this month is
unique, i.e. if it is not a part of an infinite sequence of months for which a similar problem is defined. This uniqueness clearly is unrealistic, and it is probable that a more satisfying picture of reality is drawn if we assume that we deal with an infinite sequence of
months each of which is characterized in the same way, i.e. by the same set of parameters
a_i, b and s_i $(i \in N)$.

At first glance, the assumption of a sequence of months in which exactly the same
situation occurs for each seller does not seem to pose additional problems. However, the
fact that this situation is fundamentally different from the one analyzed above stems
from the fact that each seller now can make his behaviour during any one month but the
first dependent on the other sellers' actions in the previous months. Thus, in announcing
his strategy at the beginning of a certain period he may do so conditionally on the other
sellers' behaviour, and from the game theoretic point of view we now analyze a supergame
[*Luce/Raiffa; Friedman*, 1971, 1977]. Since we assume, for simplicity only, that the
environment which is characterized for each supplier by the parameters a_i, b and
s_i $(i \in N)$ remains static, we analyze a stationary supergame in the sense of *Friedman*. The
game which we have described above is the constituent game of the supergame.

In order to formalize this notion, we assume that at the beginning of an infinite sequence of months $t = 0,1,\ldots$, each seller announces his planned sales in month t,
$\bar{x}_i(t)$, $i \in N$. He may do so conditionally, i.e. announce that he will sell a certain quantity
$\bar{x}_i(t)$ provided that all other sellers actually follow a certain sales pattern in the years
$0, 1,\ldots,t-1$. Broadly speaking, this approach greatly enlargens the set of points which
qualify as equilibira in dependence of the seller's time perspective. Since collusion on the
world cocoa market is attempted without necessarily leading to a binding or enforcable
agreement among sellers, the theory of supergames seems to be the appropriate tool for
the analysis of the non-binding agreements among the sellers which we actually observe.
Needless to say, the investigation of a market in a stationary environment is only the first
step towards a more comprehensive theory in which the given conditions change over
time.

In the reformulation of the above theory, we now note that all variables depend on time. i's payoff $\pi_i(t)$ in period $t = 0, 1, \ldots$ equals his net revenue during that period:

$$\pi_i(t) = \quad \pi_i(x_i(t), \bar{x}_{)i(}(t))$$

$$= \quad x_i(t) f_i(x_i(t), \bar{x}_{)i(}(t))$$

$$= - bx_i^2(t) + (a_i - b \sum_{\substack{j=1 \\ j \neq i}}^{n} \bar{x}_j(t)) x_i(t) \qquad (i = 1: n). \qquad (18)$$

i's total payoff if the present value of the sum of these payoffs for a given discount factor d_i $(0 \leqslant d_i < 1)$, taking into account the restrictions wich limit i's supply. i therefore faces the problem

$$\max \sum_{t=0}^{+\infty} d_i^t \, \pi_i(x_i(t), \bar{x}_{)i(}(t)) \qquad (19)$$

under the restriction

$$0 \leqslant x_i(t) \leqslant s_i \qquad (t = 0, 1, \ldots). \qquad (20)$$

((19) has a finite value since $\pi_i(t)$ is bounded above.)

From seller i's maximum problem (18) to (20) we pass to a supergame by assuming that each seller $i = 1: n$ determines his $x_i(t)$ at the beginning of period t, taking into account $x_j(0), x_j(1), \ldots, x_j(t-1)$ for all $j = 1: n, j \neq i$. However, at the beginning of period 0 each seller i announces his sales strategy, i.e. the amounts $x_i(0), x_i(1), \ldots$ which he intends to sell at the beginning of each period, but $x_i(t)$ in general depends on $x_j(t-1), x_j(t-2), \ldots, x_j(0), j = 1: n, j \neq i$.

Note that the constituent game of this supergame is included in (18) to (20) if $d_i = 0$, $i = 1: n$, since $0^0 = 1$. In addition, the unique equilibrium of the constituent game, if repeated infinitely and announced unconditionally by all sellers, is an equilibrium of the supergame.

We concentrate our analysis now on two questions which refer to some important aspects of the world cocoa market.

First, assume that $\bar{x}$, the equilibrium point of the constituent game, is given. Assume further that over a period of time, $t = 0, 1, \ldots$ we observe a sequence of sales vectors $\hat{x}(t)$, denoted by $\{\hat{x}(t)\}$, with the property

$$\hat{x}(t) \geqslant \bar{x} \qquad (t = 0, 1, \ldots).$$

Does a discount vector $d = (d_1 \, d_2 \ldots d_n)$ exist such that $\{\hat{x}(t)\}$ is the equilibrium of a supergame (18) to (20)?

Second, assume that the suppliers restrict the supply below the one which is an equilibrium of the constituent game. We therefore have, for all sales vectors $\tilde{x}(t) = $
$= (\tilde{x}_1(t) \, \tilde{x}_2(t) \ldots \tilde{x}_n(t)), t = 0, 1, \ldots,$

$$\tilde{x}(t) \leqslant \bar{x}.$$

Does a discount vector $d = (d_1 \, d_2 \ldots d_n)$ exist such that $\{\tilde{x}(t)\}$ constitutes the equilibrium of a supergame?

The motivation for the first question is that on the world cocoa market we apparently observe some terms of a sequence $\{\hat{x}(t)\}$. Can it be understood as the equilibrium of a supergame?

The motivation for the second question is that the cocoa producing countries try to restrict their supply without a binding or enforcable agreement. Can they be successful if they restrict it below their equilibrium sales of the constituent game?

In order to answer these questions, we must develop the theory of stationary supergames a little further. We again follow the seminal work of Friedman.

Assume that two sales vectors $x'(t), x''(t)$ are given, and let seller i's payoff be

$$\pi_i(x''(t)) > \pi_i(x'(t)). \tag{21}$$

If, and only if, (21) is valid for all $i = 1: n$, we say that $x''(t)$ is superior to $x'(t)$.

Now assume that we consider two sales vectors $\bar{x}, \bar{\bar{x}}$, where $\bar{x}$ is the equilibrium point of the constituent game, and $\bar{\bar{x}}$ is superior to $\bar{x}$. Let player i's strategy be such that i chooses $\bar{\bar{x}}_i$ in all periods unless, in some previous period, at least one seller $j \in N$, $j \neq i$, deviates from $\bar{\bar{x}}_j$. Then, i chooses $\bar{x}_i$. Thus, i's strategy is

$$x_i(0) = \bar{\bar{x}}_i$$

$$x_i(t) = \begin{cases} \bar{\bar{x}}_i & \text{if } x_j(\tau) = \bar{\bar{x}}_j \quad \text{for all } \tau < t; j = 1: n, \\ & \hspace{6em} j \neq i \\ \bar{x}_i & \text{otherwise.} \end{cases} \tag{22}$$

Following Friedman, we now show that for d_i sufficiently large, but $d_i < 1$, (22) is a supergame equilibrium for (18) to (20).

Consider seller i. As long as all other sellers sell $\bar{\bar{x}}_j$, $j = 1: n, j \neq i$, i receives a payoff $\bar{\bar{\pi}}_i$ if he sells $\bar{\bar{x}}_i$. If he does not sell $\bar{\bar{x}}_i$ in a certain period τ, then $x_j(t) = \bar{x}_j$ for all $t > \tau$ and $j = 1: n$. This is true regardless of what amount i intends to sell in the months following τ, and therefore i's best reply is $\bar{x}_i$ for all $t > \tau$. Thus,

$$x_i(t) = \begin{cases} \bar{\bar{x}}_i & t = 0,1, \dots, \tau - 1 \\ \bar{x}_i & t = \tau + 1, \tau + 2, \dots, \end{cases}$$

and only $x_i(\tau)$ remains to be determined.

i's total payoff equals $(\bar{\bar{\pi}}_i = \pi_i(\bar{\bar{x}}), \bar{\pi}_i = \pi_i(\bar{x}))$

$$\sum_{t=0}^{\tau-1} d_i^t \, \bar{\bar{\pi}}_i + d_i \, \pi_i(\bar{\bar{x}}_1, \bar{\bar{x}}_2, \dots, \bar{\bar{x}}_{i-1}, x_i(\tau), \bar{\bar{x}}_{i+1}, \dots, \bar{\bar{x}}_n)$$

$$+ \sum_{t=\tau+1}^{+\infty} d_i^t \, \bar{\pi}_i. \tag{23}$$

If $x_i(\tau) \neq \bar{\bar{x}}_i(\tau)$, then $x_i(\tau)$ must be i's best reply to all other sellers' selling of $\bar{\bar{x}}_j(t), j = 1: n, j \neq i$, which in our model is uniquely determined by maximizing $\pi_i(x_i(\tau), \bar{\bar{x}}_{)i(})$ under the condition of (22). ($\bar{\bar{x}}_{)i(}$ is derived from $\bar{\bar{x}}$ by omitting $\bar{\bar{x}}$'s i-th element.) Assume that for period τ this yields a total payoff of $\tilde{\pi}_i$. Then (23) becomes

$$\sum_{t=0}^{\tau-1} d_i^t \, \bar{\bar{\pi}}_i + d_i^\tau \, \tilde{\pi}_i + \sum_{t=\tau+1}^{+\infty} d_i^t \, \bar{\pi}_i. \tag{24}$$

With (24) we compare i's payoff when he continues to sell $\bar{\bar{x}}_i$ in τ:

$$\sum_{t=0}^{+\infty} d_i^t \bar{\bar{\pi}}_i. \tag{25}$$

(25) exceeds (24) if, and only if,

$$\tilde{\pi}_i + \bar{\pi}_i \frac{d_i}{1-d_i} < \frac{\bar{\bar{\pi}}_i}{1-d_i}.$$

Solving this inequality with respect to d_i yields

$$d_i > \frac{\tilde{\pi}_i - \bar{\bar{\pi}}_i}{\tilde{\pi}_i - \bar{\pi}_i}$$

where

$$\tilde{\pi}_i \geqslant \bar{\bar{\pi}}_i > \bar{\pi}_i$$

and therefore

$$0 < \frac{\tilde{\pi}_i - \bar{\bar{\pi}}_i}{\tilde{\pi}_i - \bar{\pi}_i} \leqslant 1.$$

Thus, (22) is i's best reply if, and only if, d_i fulfils the inequalities

$$\frac{\tilde{\pi}_i - \bar{\bar{\pi}}_i}{\tilde{\pi}_i - \bar{\pi}_i} < d_i < 1. \tag{26}$$

If (26) is true for all $i = 1: n$, then, and only then, is (22) an equilibrium of the supergame. Note that (26) is only possible if $\tilde{\pi}_i > \bar{\pi}_i$. This is of importance in conncetion with our first question.

This derivation merits two remarks.

First, note that (26) is valid if, and only if $\tilde{\pi}_i > \bar{\bar{\pi}}_i$, which means that none of the best replies derived from (23) are equal to $\bar{\bar{x}}_i$, $i = 1: n$.

Second, the range of the admissible d_i depends on the differences $\tilde{\pi}_i - \bar{\pi}_i$, $\bar{\bar{\pi}}_i - \bar{\pi}_i$. Here, two cases are especially important:

If $\bar{\bar{\pi}}_i$ differs little from $\tilde{\pi}_i$, but $\bar{\pi}_i$ greatly from $\tilde{\pi}_i$ (and therefore greatly from $\bar{\bar{\pi}}_i$), then d_i can be relatively small and $\bar{\bar{x}}$ still an equilibrium of the supergame. On the other hand, if these differences are practically equal to each other, then d_i must be near to unity if $\bar{\bar{x}}$ were an equilibrium of the supergame.

Turning again to the two qeustions posed above, we assume first that $\hat{x} = (\hat{x}_1 \hat{x}_2 \ldots \hat{x}_n)$ is constant over time, and compare i's payoff $\hat{\pi}_i = \pi_i(\hat{x})$ with $\bar{\pi}_i$. Since in the equilibrium point of the constituent game the total supply on the market is at least as great as in the case of joint revenue maximization, at least one seller obtains a smaller revenue than in equilibrium. Let i be this seller. Then i's payoff is greater if already in the first period he sticks to his equilibrium sales, and he therefore has no reason to deviate from $\bar{x}_i$ to $\hat{x}_i$. Therefore, $\hat{x}_i$ cannot be an equilibrium of a supergame.

A similar argument would hold in the second case. However, here it is not necessarily so that the payoffs of all sellers increase if we lower their sales below their equilibrium sales. If this were the case, we could argue as in the proof that $\bar{\bar{x}}$ is an equilibrium of the supergame if d is sufficiently great. Or we could derive bounds for the d_i $(i = 1: n)$ from a hypothetical reduction of the equilibrium sales in the constituent game and then inquire if these are likely to be valid in practice. We have pursued this way in the following section.

3. The Results

We now turn to the application of the theory outlined above to the world cocoa market. Essentially, we try to answer two questions with the aid of the model:

1) Is the actual supply on the world cocoa market an equilibrium of a stationary supergame?
2) Can the attempts of the supplying countries to collude be successful if they do not involve the demanding countries?

In order to answer these questions, the parameters a, b, c_i and s_i $(i = 1: n)$ must be known. We therefore have estimated them econometrically or calculated them from the data. These estimates are preliminary, and we therefore describe them only briefly. An excellent previous study of the demand side of the world cocoa market is due to *Weymar* [1968]. We have followed it in some respects.

The data for estimating a short run demand function on the world cocoa market were the monthly indicator prices calculated under the World Cocoa Agreement of 1975 and published by UNCTAD 1976, and the quarterly raw cocoa grindings in the 13 most important industrial countries which were published by the firm Gill & Duffus. We had to resort to these grindings since quantities sold in the spot markets were not covered by any reliable statistics. Grinding is the first stage of raw cocoa processing, and we have covered about 85 per cent of these grindings in the developed market economies.

In order to overcome the incongruence of monthly price and quarterly quantity data, we have interpolated the quarterly quantity data and thus obtained a quantity series which is much smoother than the one that would result from monthly observations. Hence we expected heavy autocorrelation of the error terms, and this was confirmed by preliminary estimates. We have therefore used an estimation technique allowing for second degree autocorrelation of the error terms.

We have assumed that about four months elapse between the cocoa sales and the grindings. In addition, we have assumed a cubic lag pattern in order to capture the price effects on the quantity demanded.

This finally led to the following demand function:

$$NQRG = 66.7286 + 0.0627\,EWK - 0.0390\,WKPR_{-4} + 0.0181\,WKPR_{-5}$$
$$8.1557 \quad\ 2.3803 \qquad\quad 1.0620 \qquad\qquad 0.6282$$

$$+ 0.0163\,WKPR_{-6} + 0.0174\,WKPR_{-7}$$
$$0.7835 \qquad\qquad 0.9803$$

$$- 0.0563\,WKPR_{-8} - 0.0735\,WKPR_{-9}$$
$$2.6460 \qquad\qquad 3.0440$$

$$- 0.0416\,WKPR_{-10}$$
$$1.3110$$

$$R^2 = 0.8989, DW = 1.6389, \hat{\rho}_1 = 0.7400, \hat{\rho}_2 = 0.7173.$$
$$5.2539 \qquad 4.9367 \tag{27}$$

In (27) the symbols have the following meaning:

NQRG — interpolated quarterly grindings of raw cocoa in 13 developed market economies, in thousand metric tons

EWK — cocoa indicator price, three months future,

WKPR — cocoa indicator price, "spot Accra"
(all prices are in US $ cents per 1b.),
divided by the implicit price deflator of the OECD GNP
(which, in January 1976, = 1.0)

R^2 — coefficient of determination

DW — Durbin-Watson statistic

u_t — error term of the t-th equation ($u_t - \rho_1 u_{t-1} = \rho_2(u_{t-1} - \rho_1 u_{t-2}) + \epsilon_t$)

ϵ_t — error term, $E(\epsilon_t) = 0$, $E(\epsilon_s \epsilon_t) = 0$ for $s \neq t$ and $E(\epsilon_t^2) = \sigma^2$

$\hat{\rho}_i$ — estimates of the autocorrelation coefficients ($i = 1,2$).

The numbers under the estimated coefficients are t-values. Note that these t-values have less meaning than the ones which refer to the auxiliary variables with which the distributed lag pattern was estimated. They all exceed 2 and three of them exceed 2.5

In order to derive the parameters a and b in the demand curve (1), we transform (27) so that the distributed lag pattern disappears, eliminate the influence of the prices of futures and then solve for the resulting price variable. We do this on the basis of the following assumptions:

The prices $WKPR_{-t}$ ($t = 4,5, \ldots, 10$) can meaningfully be set equal to each other, thus forming a price index referring to month -8. In this month, decisions of purchases are made for the total grindings in the present month (month 0), and these decisions depend only on this index. These decisions are final in the sense that they cannot be altered in the meantime.

The variable EWK may be approximated by its mean over the sample period (i.e. 128.8342) and, multiplied by its coefficient, may be added to the estimated constant.

Under these assumptions we may add the price variables in (27) and change the constant by allowing for the impact of EWK. We obtain

$$x_t = 74.8065 - 0.1931 p_t. \tag{28}$$

The coefficients of (28) have been estimated from approximately 85 per cent of the raw cocoa grindings in the developed market economies. In addition, world imports exceed imports by the developed market economies by about 33 per cent [FAO, 1977b, 1978]. We therefore have taken the average dependent variable of (27) and applied this percentage after allowing for the assumed lag, and thus estimated a shift of (28) by 28.7504 outward. This yielded the demand curve

$$x_t = 103.5569 - 0.1931 p_t. \tag{29}$$

Solving for p_t we obtain

$$p_t = 536.2864 - 5.1787 x_t. \tag{30}$$

A crude estimation of the c_i $(i = 1: n)$ seemed to be sufficient since the sales cost are small if calculated in US \$. Since cocoa is a bush crop with a rather long gestation period [Bateman], the broad definition of sales cost in a short run model must comprise the cost of all activities from harvesting the fruit, extracting the cocoa beans, fermenting and drying, as well as the local transportation cost. However, the narrow definition of these cost probably would have to include only part of these costs since in general there are no adequate economic uses for the resources freed from these activities in the short run. In the first approach, we therefore have neglected the sales cost altogether. The assumption of a unifrom sales cost of say US \$ 0.05 per 1b. of raw cocoa would not have changed the result and, in addition, would have been in the broad margin of error which is un- avoidable in such an aggregate model. However, the inclusion of the cost variable in the theoretical analysis is justified by some questions which may be raised in connection with the empirical results discussed below.

We now turn to the estimation of the s_i $(i = 1: n)$. These numbers represent, in the evaluated model, the exportable surplus of the most important cocoa producers in the world. There are two important cocoa producing areas which must be considered here: The West African countries along the Gulf of Guinea, extending from Equatorial Guinea in the West to Cameroon in the East, and Northern Brazil. These West African countries produce and export cocoa in great quantities, at least in relation to their size, and only Benin, the former Dahomey, does not appear in the list of exporting countries at all. In relation to the total exports from this area, the exports of Sierra Leone and Liberia are negligible, and Equatorial Guinea and Togo produce only about 1 per cent each of the total world production. However, both qualify as important producers in the World Cocoa Agreement of 1975, and basic export quotas were assigned to them. Nevertheless, their exports are small in absolute terms, and we therefore concentrate on the remaining four West African producers and exporters, Ghana, Nigeria, the Ivory Coast and Cameroon. In addition, we consider Brazil as a big producer and exporter of cocoa. These five countries produce about 75 per cent of the total world production, and 85 per cent of the production of those countries which are considered as important producers in the World Cocoa Agreement of 1975. Only Brazil also consumes a sizable part of her produc- tion.

In the following calculations, we regard only these five countries as oligopolists, as- suming that all other producers sell their total exportable production on the world mar- ket for whatever price they receive. This means that the curve (29) is shifted inward by this amount, yielding the demand curve for the oligopolists' exports.

For each of the five oligopolists we have estimated the annual exportable surplus according to the following formula:

Exportable surplus = Carryover from the previous year
+ production in the current year
− internal consumption in the current year, including internal processing and losses due to inadequate storage.

The crop year lasts from October 1 to September 30, and we have identified a crop year with the calendar year of which it contains nine months in order to allow for lags between the harvesting, fermenting and drying of the cocoa beans and their exports.

From published statistics of the Food and Agricultural Organization of the United Nations [FAO, 1977a, 1977b, 1978], annual estimates of production, exports and imports of cocoa beans are available. These production statistics do not always correspond to the export statistics, and assuming that the export statistics are reliable, we have corrected four (of twenty) of the production figures (Ghana and Nigeria 1976, Ivory Coast and Cameroon 1977). As a basis for these corrections, we have chosen the relation of production to exports in the other years, the situation on the world market in the respective year, and the reported storage possibilities in these African countries.

After having thus estimated production, we turned to the calculation of the exportable surplus. All production figures were reduced by ten per cent to allow for waste in the time span between production and exports. Internal consumption was assumed to be considerable only in Brazil. We estimated it at 80 thousand metric tons annually. In the West African countries, we have assumed the internal consumption to be 10 thousand metric tons annually in Ghana and Nigeria, and about 5 thousand metric tons in the Ivory Coast and Cameroon. Admittedly, these estimates are crude, but our results which are presented below do not change appreciably if only these estimates are varied within reasonable bounds.

Finally, we had to estimate the carryovers. Since the West African countries apparently do not possess any sizable storage facilities which permit storage of cocoa beans for more than a year [see e.g. the remark in Republic of Ghana, 1977b, p. 55], we have assumed that these carryovers were nil in the African countries.

For Brazil, we must assume that some stocks were carried over from 1973 to 1974 since the difference between production and exports in 1974 is not sufficient to even cover internal consumption and the assumed losses of cocoa beans during the time span between production and exports. In addition, prices were comparatively high in 1974, and we have therefore assumed that no cocoa beans were stored in Brazil in the following years. This assumption is supported by the fact that the differences between the exportable surplusses calculated in this way and actual exports are negligible.

Finally, we have calculated from this data the equilibrium points for each representative (average) month of the years 1974 to 1977. In order to allow for the exports of all cocoa producing countries not considered in the oligopoly, we had to shift the demand curve (29) by the amount exported by the other countries [FAO, 1977b, 1978]. The method for calculating the equilibria has been described in section 2 above. This yielded the equilibrium sales presented in the Table below, together with the shift of the demand curve (29) and the value of m.

We now discuss some implications of our forecasts.

Equilibrium exports deviate markedly from actual exports only for Ghana, and this only in 1974 to 1976. In 1977, the equilibrium point of the constituent game almost was realized.

Thus, in the years 1974 to 1976 Ghana oversells strongly, and neither her reaction nor, as a matter of fact, that of her competitors is a best reply. The reduction of Ghana's production and exports in 1977 probably has caused the price increase on the world market observed in that year and was a move towards a best reply to the selling strategy of the other suppliers, but apparently it was or it would have been deplored by the Ghanaian government [Republic of Ghana, 1977a, 1977b]. The reason seems to be simply that

	1974	1975	1976	1977
Ghana				
amp	31.8	33.0	30.8	23.3
ams	27.8	28.9	26.9	20.2
ame	26.2	26.8	27.1	20.8
ames	16.2	19.1	19.3	20.2
Nigeria				
amp	17.8	18.3	20.3	18.3
ams	15.2	15.7	17.4	15.7
ame	16.4	18.2	18.6	16.7
ames	15.2	15.7	17.4	15.7
Ivory Coast				
amp	20.1	17.1	19.2	16.7
ams	17.7	15.0	16.8	14.6
ame	17.4	14.1	16.2	13.2
ames	16.2	15.0	16.8	14.6
Cameroon				
amp	9.8	8.0	6.8	5.8
ams	8.4	6.8	5.7	4.8
ame	7.4	6.0	5.7	4.8
ames	8.4	6.8	5.7	4.8
Brazil				
amp	16.7	24.2	20.9	19.0
ams	10.0	15.1	12.2	10.4
ame	10.8	14.1	10.7	9.1
ames	10.0	15.1	12.2	10.4
Shift	21.4	12.9	12.8	13.8
m	2	1	1	0

Source: FAO [1977a, 1977b, 1978] and own estimates

Tab. 1: Average monthly production, average monthly exportable surplus (s_i), average monthly exports, and average monthly equilibrium sales ($\bar{x}_i$) of five cocoa producing countries, in thousand metric tons

Ghana would like to sell a bumper crop at prices which perhaps would be paid for a cocoa bean if it was as rare as a diamond of equal size, which, of course is impossible since prices are related to quantities by the demand function.

This evaluation of the facts with the aid of the one-period model does not change appreciably if we introduce the supergame aspect which greatly widens the set of sales vectors qualifying for an equilibrium provided that the discount factor is sufficiently high. Because actually all sellers export at least their stationary equilibrium quantity, but Ghana strongly oversells it in three of four years, we have a situation to which the first question of our theory (p. 12 above) applies. It therefore follows that the observed sales in 1974 to 1976 cannot be regarded as the equilibria of a stationary supergame. The most likely explanation for Ghana's overselling therefore is that the parameters of the demand function are estimated differently by the Ghanaian government than we have done in this paper. Alternatively, the shift of factors of production to the production of other goods may be infeasible politically, and there may also be political obstacles against destroying some of the cocoa produced if there is no alternative internal use for it.

To be sure, there is one other factor which must be taken into account in order to settle this issue with a somewhat greater degree of finality: Under favourable cost conditions, the sales observed in 1974 to 1976 could have been equilibria, while 1977 was an accidental deviation from equilibrium. Let us see if this is a reasonable alternative.

With our model it is easy to measure the cost advantage which Ghana must have in the short run if this reasoning is correct, or to give an idea of the long run cost which leads to the equilibria observed historically. The latter is calculated by setting $s_i = +\infty$, $i = 1: n$, and calculating the c_i ($i = 1: n$) as a residual from the given numbers. The result is an estimated long run cost between US $ 0.42 to 0.69 per 1b. of exported cocoa for Nigeria, the Ivory Coast and Brazil, US $ 0.98 for Cameroon, and US $ −0.06 for Ghana. Whereas the first cost range seems plausible, the very high cost calculated for Cameroon probably is due to the fact that some capacity limitations have not been taken correctly into account even in the long run estimate. However, the small negative cost calculated for Ghana is of course completely unrealistic, and we conclude that also from this point of view Ghana's sales are greater than her best reply. This conclusion is confirmed by independent estimates of the relative long run cost of cocoa production which show that Ghana probably has an edge over some of her competitors, but probably a rather small one [Yeung].

Returning to the short run view, we now calculate in a similar fashion the advantage in sales cost which Ghana must have if the average exports in the years 1974 to 1976 were equilibrium sales of the constituent game. Calculated either for 1976 alone or from the average of the figures for 1974 to 1976, this yields a sales cost advantage for Ghana over the other countries of at least US $ 0.12 per lb. of cocoa exported. If we estimate total sales cost at perhaps ten to fifteen per cent of the price, this figure also seems to be too high, but perhaps less unrealistic then the long run cost figures calculated above. But it is quite possible that some of the differences between the equilibrium and the actual sales in 1974 to 1976 are explained by somewhat more favourable cost conditions in Ghana than in the other countries.

But the general conclusion remains that Ghana probably sells too much cocoa on the world market in the sense that smaller sales would lead to higher revenue for all sellers. However, it should be emphasized that our static model does not take into account a number of variables which may be important in reality, and the long run view may lean more heavily on production cost than we can do it in our short run model. Thus, a situation is imaginable where Ghana can retain her dominant role due to favourable cost conditions; on the other hand, quite the contrary development is possible and the Ivory Coast, which for some reasons not discussed in this paper seems to be Ghana's most serious competitor in the long run, may expand her sales to 17 or 18 thousand tons of cocoa, whilst Ghana's sales figures shrink to roughly the same number. Similar opportunity cost in both countries would further this development.

Finally, we turn to the possibility of collusion which is open to the sellers. The World Cocoa Agreement of 1975 established intervention prices at a level much below the actual prices during the period of validity of that agreement, and therefore no buffer stock of cocoa was formed. However, the levy on all cocoa sales during the past five years lead to the accumulation of a fund of approximately US $ 200 million, and this fund was to be divided among the cocoa producing countries in case the agreement was not extended beyond its expiration date of March 31, 1980. The temptation to slaughter this piggy bank may have been one of the reasons why the negotiations to extend this agreement have not been successful.

Another reason probably was the hope of the cocoa producing countries to arrive at an agreement to limit supply. As we have described above, such an agreement would have led to an equilibrium if Ghana alone would have reduced her sales by roughly 20 per cent in 1974 to 1976. However, it was the Ivory Coast that announced at the end of 1979 that sales would take place only at a minimum price of US $ 1.47 per lb, i.e. much above the market price in the second half or 1979 and above the intervention price (between US $ 1.10 and 1.20 per lb.) envisaged by the parties at the negotiations for a renewal of the World Cocoa Agreement.

It is clear that this high price could have been maintained only if the quantity sold would have been restricted, and it is highly questionable if the cocoa exporting countries could arrive at a binding and enforcable agreement on their own, i.e. without a participation of the demanding countries. According to my view, it is mandatory for the cocoa suppliers to get the demanding countries to agree formally to whatever agreement is negotiated. Only this leads to an agreement which is fulfilled by all sellers since no seller can take advantage of the fact that all other sellers fulfill the agreement to which set of strategies he selects his best reply. Seeing this from a game theoretic point of view, only this leads to a cooperative game and thus excludes the temptation for each seller to break the agreement. Even if there is no intervention price as in the World Cocoa Agreement of 1975, but only a pledge on the part of the demanding countries not to buy outside of the agreement, then this will safeguard the set of all suppliers against the violation of the agreement by any single supplier.

The theory of supergames as outlined in section 2 above provides an alternative to this interpretation. However, the existence of certain supergame equilibria which are not the equilibrium of the constituent game depends crucially on the discount factors $d_i (i = 1: n)$. If these were high enough, supergame equilibria yielding a higher payoff to each supplying country seem possible without enlisting the assistance of the developed countries.

In order to study this alternative, let us assume that all five principal suppliers of cocoa on the world market agree to limit their sales in 1978, 1979, 1980, . . . to 90 per cent of their average sales of 1974 to 1977. What is the lower bound of the discount vector which makes this agreement an equilibrium of a stationary supergame?

Our calculations show that Ghana must have a discount factor of at least 0.1861, whereas the Ivory Coast must have one of at least 0.7757. The respective value for Nigeria is 0.2832, for Cameroon 0.4449, and for Brazil 0.5383.

This result is interesting in several respects. First, according to my personal impression, the relatively low value of the necessary discount factor for Ghana may make a unilateral agreement interesting for her since the present social and economic problems in that country probably prohibits the planning with a horizon for more than perhaps three to four years. This implies that Ghana can enter the envisaged agreement only if her discount factor can be relatively low.

Second, the relatively high discount factor implied for the Ivory Coast is somewhat astonishing since this country seems to be a principal advocate for a unilateral agreement among the producing countries. On the other hand, the thriving economy of the Ivory

Coast may well be in a position to support the planning with a much longer horizon. In this case, all calculated lower bounds appear to reflect a realistic planning horizon for the five cocoa producing countries in question.

If, however, Ghana has a planning horizon for which even the relatively low bound of 0.1861 is too high, then a unilateral agreement among the producing countries does not seem to be feasible. That Ghana has a relatively short horizon is also borne out by the fact that Ghana would receive 60 million of the US $ 200 million mentioned above, and that the distribution of this fund would scarcely have been possible without Ghana's consent. In this case, Ghana bought an advantage in the very short run with perhaps sizable disadvantages in the longer run since the price range of US $ 1.10 to 1.20 per lb. of raw cocoa (which was the price range in the ultimate stage of the negotiations for a renewal of the World Cocoa Agreement) may well be much above the actual market price in a number of months to come.

Since Ghana is the most important supplier on the world cocoa market, it then is very questionable if an agreement not involving the demanding countries will be stable over an extended period of time. On the contrary, it then is very probable that the cocoa producing countries will soon realize that their situation is different from the situation of the oil producing countries in some important respects, and that they will try to reopen the negotiations for a new World Cocoa Agreement involving the developed countries.

References

Adams, F.G., and *J.R. Behrman*: Econometric Models of World Agricultural Commodity Markets: Cocoa, Coffee, Tea, Wool, Cotton, Sugar, Wheat, Rice. Cambridge, Mass. 1976.

Bateman, M.J.: Aggregate and Regional Supply Functions for Ghanaian Cocoa, 1946–1962. Journal of Farm Economics **47**, 1965, 384–401.

Behrman, J.R.: Monopolistic Cocoa Pricing. American Journal of Agricultural Economics **50**, 1968, 702–719.

Behrman, J.R., and *P. Tinakorn-Ramangkura*: Indexation of International Commodity Prices Through International Buffer Stock Operations. Journal of Policy Modeling **1**, 1979, 113–134.

Food and Agricultural Organization of the United Nations (FAO): Production Yearbook **30**, 1977a.

–: Trade Yearbook **30**, 1977b.

–: FAO Monthly Bulletin of Statistics **1**, 1978.

Friedman, J.W.: A Non-cooperative Equilibrium for Supergames. The Review of Economic Studies **38**, 1971, 1–12.

–: A Non-cooperative Equilibrium for Supergames: A Correction. The Review of Economic Studies **40**, 1973, 435.

–: Oligopoly and the Theory of Games. Amsterdam–New York–Oxford 1977.

Gill & Duffus: Cocoa Market Report No. 278, December 16, 1977, and various previous issues.

Luce, R.D., and *H. Raiffa*: Games and Decisions. New York–London–Sydney 1957.

Praetz, P. D.: Testing the Efficient Market Theory on the Sydney Wool Futures Exchange. Australian Economic Papers **14**, 1975, 240–249. Reprinted in B. A. Goss and B.S. Yamey, ed.: The Economics of Futures Trading. London–Basingstoke 1976, 205–216.

Republic of Ghana: Ghana 1977. An Official Handbook. Accra (1977a).

–: Five-Year Development Plan, 1975/76 – 1979/80, Part II. Accra 1977. (1977b).

Selten, R.: Preispolitik der Mehrproduktunternehmung in der statischen Theorie. Berlin–Heidelberg– New York 1970.

Weymar, F.H.: The Dynamics of the World Cocoa Market. Cambridge, Mass.–London 1968.

Yeung, P.: A Comparative Analysis of Cocoa Production in Selected Countries. Coffee, Tea, and Cocoa. Market Prospects and Development Lending. Ed. by S. Singh, et al. Baltimore–London 1977, 115–127.

Economic Theory of Natural Resources. © Physica-Verlag, Würzburg–Wien, 1982.

The Efficiency of Competitive Markets in a Context of Exhaustible Resources

Murray C. Kemp and *Ngo Van Long*[1])

1. Introduction

In recent years there has been an avalanche of theoretical analyses of economies based on exhaustible resources. For the most part, attention has been focused on the descriptive modelling of market economies. However, interwoven with ostensibly descriptive analysis there have been many obiter dicta concerning the efficiency of market outcomes; and, very recently, there have appeared several specialized studies of that subject. The picture emerging from the literature is extremely confusing. Some authors seem to take it for granted that, even in a competitive market economy, resources will be extracted in an inefficient fashion; others take it for granted that extraction will be efficient if only competition is perfect and there are enough futures markets (or, sometimes, if foresight is perfect). Nor have the more specialized studies achieved anything approaching a consensus, even under conditions of certainty. Thus *Weinstein/Zeckhauser* [1975] have argued that, under competitive conditions with perfect foresight, extraction is necessarily efficient; but *Heal* [1980] has denied it. Similarly, *Weinstein/Zeckhauser* [1975], *Heal* [1975] and *Hoel* [1978, 1980] have argued that if particular kinds of uncertainty are present and if firms are averse to risk then, under competitive conditions, the resource-stock will be extracted in an inefficient way; but *Kemp/Long* [1977a] have insisted that, given enough markets, competitive extraction is efficient.

In the present paper we report on the debate as it has unfolded to this point. In particular, we seek to appraise the arguments advanced by Heal, Hoel, Weinstein and Zeckhauser to the effect that the competitive outcome may be inefficient.

Throughout the paper it is taken for granted that the market outcome may be inefficient if any markets are infected by elements of monopoly, if there is a recognized risk of expropriation with inadequate compensation, if expectations of future spot prices are unreliable, if access to a resource-deposit is common to several firms, if technical production externalities intrude, if there is an inescapable moral hazard, or if the supplies of public goods (like information concerning the extent and location of resource-deposits and like public debt in a context of overlapping generations) are inadequate (because, for

---

[1]) We gratefully acknowledge the helpful comments of Micheal Hoel, Richard Manning, Hans-Werner Sinn and Leslie Young.

example, they are under private control).[2]) To allow us to focus on more controversial matters, all of these phenomena are assumed away at the outset. It also is recalled, from *Malinvaud* [1953], that in a developing economy with an infinite horizon saving may be excessive, even under conditions of perfect shortrun or myopic foresight. For an exhaustible resource is simply a special kind of capital good and excessive saving may take the form of incomplete exhaustion of the resource. Again to allow us to concentrate on contentious issues, this possibility is ignored throughout.[3])

Following *Kemp/Long* [1977a, 1978], it will be argued, in Sections 3 and 4, that if there are enough competitive markets then the market outcome is necessarily efficient but that if agents are sufficiently far-sighted and if resource-stocks are of unknown extent then markets cannot be competitive. These conclusions conflict with those of *Heal* [1980], on one hand, and of *Weinstein/Zeckhauser* [1975], *Heal* [1975] and *Hoel* [1978, 1980], on the other. We therefore begin with an examination of the arguments advanced by those authors. Heal's 1980 argument is discussed in Section 2, the arguments of *Weinstein/Zeckhauser* [1975], *Heal* [1975] and *Hoel* [1978, 1980] in Section 3.

---

[2]) There are special hairline cases in which extraction is efficient even when a monopolist controls the resource-stock (see *Weinstein/Zeckhauser* [1975] for the case of a non-renewable resource and *Kemp/Long* [1977c] for the case of renewable resource), and even when access to the resource-stock is in common [see *Kemp/Long*, 1977b].

[3]) For detailed analysis of the efficiency-implications of these phenomena in a context of exhaustible resources, the reader may refer to *Kemp/Long* [1977b] on common access, to *Long* [1975] on the risk of expropriation, to *Kay/Mirrless* [1975] on unreliable price expectations, and to *Sweeney* [1977] on monopoly. Numerical examples of "Malinvaud inefficiency" in a context of exhaustible resources have been provided by *Kemp/Long* [1979] and by *Mitra* [1980]. Kemp and Long have shown also that the inefficiency can be removed by the provision of public debt, properly timed and in sufficient quantity. In technical terms, the issue of debt forces the economy to behave in a manner consistent with the transversality conditions of the relevant optimal-control problem. In this connection, and in passing, we mention the interesting recent contribution of *Pazner/Razin* [1980]. Following *Samuelson* [1958], the authors develop a model with an infinite horizon but overlapping generations, each generation living for just two periods of time. However their model has several distinctive features. Each generation derives utility from the utility of the next generation and therefore has an incentive to raise children and make bequests to them. Moreover, on one interpretation of their model, there is a single commodity, a durable but exhaustible resource stock ("cake") which in each period must be divided between consumption and bequests. Thus in each period the old must choose both the rate of population growth and the division of the cake between consumption (the consumption of the young and of the old) and bequests. Pazner and Razin show that the outcome of the sequence of decisions by the old is Pareto-optimal. They contrast their finding with that of Samuelson, ascribing the disappearance of inefficiency to their assumption that population growth is a matter of choice. But in this they appear to be mistaken: given their other assumptions, inefficiency disappears even if population growth is exogenous. In fact the treatment of population growth by Pazner and Razin is unsatisfactory. For implicit in their model is the assumption that each child has only one parent. By means of this assumption the optimality-*destroying* public-goods nature of families (each family has two pairs of grandparents) is pushed out of sight. If each child had been allowed a full quota of parents, suboptimality (of an earlier-Samuelson type) would have reappeared. Thus, in summary, the modification of Samuelson's model to accommodate "overlapping" utility functions and resource-durability suffices to restore efficiency, but the further modification of the model to (properly) accommodate choice of population growth causes inefficiency to reappear.

2. Heal on the Possible Non-Convexity of the Attainable Set

Heal [1980] has argued that, even in the absence of all uncertainty and with markets of any degree of completeness, the competitive outcome may be inefficient.

"The fundamental theorem of welfare economics asserts that, under the appropriate assumptions, . . . a competitive equilibrium, if it exists, is Pareto efficient. In such a model, the vector of initial endowments, which will include the economy's endowment of exhaustible resources, is taken as exogenous and independent of all economic forces and activities. In fact this seems an unreasonable assumption, especially for endowments of resources. There is not a given endowment of oil, independent of market forces: rather, . . . the amount available depends on the price of oil. Geologists typically give figures for oil reserves, and reserves of most other minerals, as a function of price, describing in effect a supply curve for the resource . . . In such a case, the vector of initial endowments of the economy is best seen not as a given constant vector, say w, but as a price-dependent vector $w\,(p)$. In such a situation, the quantity of endowments becomes endogenous: a world with a high price of oil has larger economically relevant reserves than one with a low price.

Now, . . . if endowments are price-dependent, then a competitive equilibrium need no longer be efficient . . . [This] result depends on the fact that the set of allocations — consumption and production plans — which is in principle attainable by an economy, depends . . . on the initial endowment. So if the endowment changes with price, so does the attainable set. So for each price the economy has an attainable set which, under the usual assumptions, is convex. The overall attainable set for the economy is the *union* of the sets attainable at each price, and the union of convex sets need not be convex. . .

From this we see that the question "Will the competitive market allocate exhaustible resources efficiently?" may have a negative answer for reasons quite distinct from the normal causes of market failure." [*Heal*, 1980, 38–40]. See also *Chichilnisky/Heal* [1979]

Now in fact "the fundamental theorem of welfare economics" does not require for its validity that the attainable set of the economy be convex. Thus Heal's conclusion is a non sequitur.

Nor has Heal produced an example of competitive inefficiency. Heal's "supply curve for the resource" could be understood to relate extracted resource to the price of extracted resource. However, extracted resource is not a primary factor; it is the outcome of a productive process and is in parity with any other produced commodity. Heal's supply curve therefore must be understood as relating unextracted resource to the price of unextracted resource. (An example provided by Heal is consistent with this interpretation.)[4]) Now the amount of unextracted resource (of a particular quality, or in the aggregate) is a constant, independent of price. If then the supply of the resource depends on price that can be so only because the resource has alternative uses in the consumption plans of its owners (one thinks of private parkland and leisure). Thus one can imagine a linear transformation curve linking the amount offered to the factor market $w\,(p)$ to the amount withheld for private consumption, $\bar{w} - w\,(p)$. But the amount privately consumed appears neither in Heal's set of allocations nor in his utility functions. If it had done so, the stand-

---

[4]) For a detailed and critical examination of Heal's example, see *Breyer/Reiss* [1980].

ard arguments of Arrow and Debreu, or of Weinstein and Zeckhauser, would have sufficed to establish efficiency.

3. Hoel on the Possibility of Competitive Inefficiency in the Face of Uncertainty

Whereas Heal's 1980 case for competitive inefficiency was developed in the context of an uncertainty-free economy, his 1975 case, as well as those of Weinstein and Zeckhauser and of Hoel, rests squarely on the presence of a particular kind or source of uncertainty. We begin with Hoel's argument since it has been presented most explicitly and in greatest detail.

It is supposed by *Hoel* [1978] that after some known future date it will be possible to produce a resource-substitute but that the cost of producing the substitute is known now only in terms of an agreed-upon subjective probability distribution.

Hoel shows that if resource-extracting firms are risk-averse then they will over-extract at all points of time before the substitute becomes available.

However, Hoel's argument rests on the implicit assumption that the resource-extracting firms seek to maximize the present value of expected utility, where utility is a strictly concave function of the proceeds of sale of the resource, in terms of a third, numeraire commodity. No justification for such an assumption is provided. In fact, the assumption fits uncomfortably with two other of Hoel's assumptions: (i) that the community is sufficiently homogeneous to warrant the use of a cardinal social utility function and (ii) that the social utility function is concave in the combined consumption of the resource and its substitute but linear in the consumption of the numeraire. If (i) is justified by the common supposition that all individuals are alike, both in preferences and in asset-holdings, then one would expect that, in their capacity as shareholders, they would impose on the resource-extracting firms their own utility functions. But then the competitive outcome would be optimal, for each firm would be a small-scale replica of the economy as a whole.

Moreover it is assumed by *Hoel* that all commodity markets are spot. If instead he had introduced a complete set of contingent future markets, so that firms are led to seek maximum profits, then again he would have found that competitive equilibrium is socially optimal.

In his later work [1980, especially chap. 3], Hoel considered the implications for efficiency of uncertainty about the date of arrival of the new technology, with the cost of production of the substitute known in advance. Again he was able to show that if resource-extracting firms are risk-averse then they will over-extract before the substitute becomes available, and again the argument rests on inconsistent assumptions.

We turn briefly to the arguments for competitive inefficiency developed by *Weinstein/ Zeckhauser* [1975] and by *Heal* [1975]. Weinstein and Zeckhauser consider the possibility that the demand for an exhaustible resource is random while Heal introduces a kind of supply uncertainty distinct from that studied by Hoel. In each case it is shown that competitive extraction is inefficient (excessive) if the extracting firms are averse to risk. However, while the contexts of the Weinstein-Zeckhauser and Heal cases for competitive inefficiency are quite distinct from the context of Hoel's case, the three arguments are subject to the same objections. For in all three arguments one finds precisely the same set of mutually inconsistent assumptions concerning the utility functions of the extracting firms and of the eventual consumers.

We conclude that uncertainty of any of the kinds introduced by *Weinstein/Zeckhauser* [1975], *Heal* [1975] and *Hoel* [1978, 1980] is harmless in the sense that, by itself, it fails to destroy the efficiency of competitive outcomes.[5])

However that kind of uncertainty is of a special kind. In the world envisaged by Hoel et al., the probabilities attached to alternative states of the world are given by Nature independently of the activities of agents; that is, they are of a type admitted by Arrow and Debreu. It is not surprising therefore that uncertainty of the type studied by Hoel et al. is compatible with competitive efficiency.

It is possible that the probabilities attached to alternative states of the world depend on the planned actions of agents. For example, the capacity of an agent to deliver a commodity at a future date may be uncertain, with the degree of uncertainty depending on what the agent plans to do before the delivery date. In those circumstances, the probability which is attached to the state of the world in which the agent is unable to deliver on the due date is under the control, partial or complete, of the agent. Clearly the owner of a resource-deposit of unknown extent is such an agent. It follows that the Arrow-Debreu proof of competitive optimality is inapplicable when there is uncertainty concerning the extent of the deposit. The question of competitive optimality is re-opened.

Recently it has been shown by *Kemp/Long* [1977a] that if markets are sufficiently numerous and of the right kind then, even when the state-of-the-world probabilities depend on the choices of agents, the competitive outcome is optimal.[6]) We therefore seem to be justified in concluding that, whatever the source of uncertainty, the competitive outcome will be efficient if only there are enough markets.

4. The Implausibility of the Assumption of Competition

But is it plausible to assume that markets are competitive? Or is there an underlying incompatibility between the assumption of universal competition and the assumption that the economy is based on exhaustible resources? In this brief final section we oppose the drift of earlier parts of the paper by arguing that the answers to these questions should be, in order, No and Yes.

Suppose that the extent of the deposits of some exhaustible resource is unknown. Then, however numerous the extracting firms may be, provided only that they are sufficiently far-sighted, each firm will formulate its plan of extraction in the light of the possibility that, some day, it will be the only firm left with a positive stock of the resource and thus will enjoy monopolistic power. In other words, the required degree of foresight is incompatible with pure price-taking by the extracting firms.

---

[5]) The counter argument which has been directed to *Weinstein/Zeckhauser* [1975], *Heal* [1975] and *Hoel* [1978, 1980] can be reformulated and directed to the claim by *Batra/Russell* [1974] that, for a small trading country facing random world prices, free trade may be sub-optimal. See *Kemp/ Ohyama* [1978].

[6]) *Loury* [1978] has obtained a similar result. The proofs provided by Kemp, Long and Loury relate to a pure-exchange economy but can be extended to allow for production.

210

If competition must be abandoned so must the efficiency of competitive allocations. It is intuitively clear that a firm will extract less rapidly when it recognizes the possibility of eventual monopoly than when it fails to recognize the possibility. (For a formal proof, based on the assumption of perfectly foreseen spot prices, [7]) see *Kemp/Long* [1978].) Since the outcome is efficient when the possibility of eventual monopoly is ignored, the outcome will generally be inefficient when the possibility is recognized.

References

Batra, R.N., and *W.R. Russell:* Gains from trade under uncertainty. American Economic Review **64**, 1974, 1040–1048.
Breyer, F., and *W. Reiss:* Variable resource endowments and the convexity of the attainable consumption set. Economic Theory of Natural Resources. Ed. by W. Eichhorn et al. Würzburg–Wien 1982 (this volume).
Chichilnisky, G., and *G. Heal:* Welfare economics of competitive general equilibrium with variable endowments. Columbia University Working Paper, 1979.
Heal, G.: Economic aspects of natural resource depletion. The Economics of Natural Resource Depletion. Ed. by D.W. Pearce. London 1975, 118–139.
—: Intertemporal allocation and intergenerational equity. Erschöpfbare Ressourcen. Ed. by. H. Siebert, Berlin 1980, 37–73.
Hoel, M.: Resource extraction when a future substitute has an uncertain cost. Review of Economic Studies **45**, 1978, 637–644.
—: Extraction of an Exhaustible Resource under Uncertainty. Mathematical Systems in Economics. Ed. by W. Eichhorn and R. Henn, Vol. 51. Meisenheim am Glan 1980.
Kay, J.A., and *J.A. Mirrlees:* The desirability of natural resource depletion. The Economics of Natural Resource Depletion. Ed. by D.W. Pearce. London 1975, 140–176.
Kemp, M.C., and *N.V. Long:* Eating a cake of unknown size: pure competition versus social planning. Australian National University Working Paper, 1977a. Published as chapter 5 of Exhaustible Resources, Optimality and Trade. Ed. by. M.C. Kemp and N.V. Long. Amsterdam 1970.
—: Resource extraction under conditions of common access. University of New South Wales Working Paper, 1977b. Published as chapter 10 of Exhaustible Resources, Optimality and Trade. Ed. by M.C. Kemp and N.V. Long. Amsterdam 1980.
—: The management of a renewable resource: monopoly versus competition. University of New South Wales Working Paper, 1977c. Published as chapter 6 of Exhaustible Resources, Optimality and Trade. Ed. by M.C. Kemp and N.V. Long. Amsterdam 1980.
—: The optimal consumption of depletable natural resources: comment. Quarterly Journal of Economincs **92**, 1978, 345–353. Reprinted as chapter 4 of Exhaustible Resources, Optimality and Trade. Ed. by M.C. Kemp and N.V. Long. Amsterdam 1980.
—: The underexploitation of natural resources: A model with overlapping generations. Economic Record **55**, 1979, 214–221. Reprinted as chapter 9 of Exhaustible Resources, Optimality and Trade. Ed. by M.C. Kemp and N.V. Long. Amsterdam 1980.
Kemp, M.C., and *M. Ohyama:* The gain from free trade under conditions of uncertainty. Journal of International Economics **8**, 1978, 139–141.
Long, N.V.: Resource extraction under uncertainty about possible nationalization. Journal of Economic Theory **10**, 1975, 42–53.
Loury, G.C.: The optimal exploitation of an unknown reserve. Review of Economic Studies **45**, 1978, 621–636.
Malinvaud, E.: Capital accumulation and efficient allocation of resources. Econometrica **21**, 1953, 233–268.

---

[7]) A proof based on the alternative assumption of a complete set of conditional commodity markets can be constructed.

Mitra, T.: Efficient growth with exhaustible resources in an open neoclassical model. Econometrica, to appear, 1980.

Pazner, E.A., and A. Razin: Competitive efficiency in an overlapping-generation model with endogenous population. Journal of Public Economics **13**, 1980, 249–258.

Samuelson, P.A.: An exact consumption-loan model of interest with or without the social contrivance of money. Journal of Political Economy **66**, 1958, 467–482,

Sweeney, J.L.: Economics of depletable resources: Market forces and intertemporal bias. Review of Economic Studies **44**, 1977, 125–141.

Weinstein, M.C., and R.J. Zeckhauser: Optimal consumption of depletable natural resources. Quarterly Journal of Economics **89**, 1975, 371–392.

Economic Theory of Natural Resources. ©Physica-Verlag, Würzburg–Wien, 1982.

Speculation and Stability on Markets for Exhaustible Resources

Georg Pflug and *Georg Winckler*

1. Introduction

There are three equilibrium conditions in partial equilibrium models of exhaustible resources [See e.g. *Weinstein/Zeckhauser* and *Dasgupta/Heal*, ch. 6]:

A. *The momentary stock equilibrium* in the market for assets requires that the spot price of a unit stock rises with a rate equal to the rate of return of the numeraire asset (for simplicity we assume no costs of extraction). This equilibrium condition is often called the "Hotelling Rule".

B. Given the momentary stock equilibrium, the resource owners are indifferent between selling the resource and acquiring the numeraire asset or holding the resource in the ground as an investment. This indifference of suppliers in turn permits that the rate of extraction is determined by the flow demand. We refer to this equilibrium between the rate of extraction and the competitive demand at the current price as the *momentary flow equilibrium.*

C. The *intertemporal competitive equilibrium* requires a correct initial price of the exhaustible resource. This initial price has to be set at a level at which the resource price can start to grow according to the Hotelling Rule so that ultimately demand dwindles to zero precisely at the time when the resource is exhausted. If a complete set of forward markets is assumed the intertemporal competitive equilibrium condition would certainly be satisfied.

In this paper we analyse the stability of these equilibrium conditions in the standard model of the literature on exhaustible resources. We do so by starting with the assumption that there are no forward markets. Hence resource owners as well as speculators buy and sell according to their expectations about the forthcoming price trend of the exhaustible resource. This assumption seems plausible, since in reality the time horizon of the existing forward markets for exhaustible resources is negligible compared to the length of time during which these resources will still be available. Two stability questions now arise: Does the resource price still grow according to the Hotelling Rule (stability of the momentary stock equilibrium)? Will the demand be zero when the resource will be exhausted (stability of the intertemporal competitive equilibrium)?

In what follows we always take the existence of the momentary flow equilibrium (rate of extraction = flow demand at the current price) for granted. This existence is plausible for two reasons: (1) Speculative activities do not exhaust the exhaustible resource. For simplicity, we assume that speculators and resource owners behave alike (both are speculators) and that there are no extraction costs. Hence it does not matter whether the resource is in the hand of the resource owners or in the hand of the speculators. Consequently, the rate of extraction can be defined as the net sales of both groups together. So one can justify the assumption that the rate of extraction will equal the flow demand. (2) The flow demand must not necessarily coincide with the flow demand at the current price. There may be some sort of rationing. However, rationing the flow demand amounts to varying the stock of the exhaustible resource at the current price. As we analyse the stability of the momentary stock equilibrium and of the intertemporal competitive equilibrium due to unforeseen shocks in the amount of the initial stock (discovery of new or loss of old reserves) this case will be studied. Hence we do not bother about the stabilizing or destablizing effects of rationing and can safely assume the stability of the momentary flow equilibrium.

2. The Assumptions of the Model

The basic assumptions of the model are:

a) There is a given initial stock of the exhaustible resource, called S. Disequilibrium situations will be a consequence of an increase or decrease of S.

b) The flow demand "d" at each instant of time is a function of the momentary resource price "p". For simplicity, the shape of the demand function does not vary with time, i.e. $d(p(t), t) = d(p(t))$, and the price elasticity remains constant.

c) Extraction costs are nil.

d) There is a perfect market of a numeraire asset with a fixed rate of return "ρ".

e) The flow demand $d(p(t))$ is always satisfied at the current price and equals the extraction rate ("R"). Hence we assume a sequence of momentary flow equilibria. The rationale for this assumption has been explained in the introduction.

f) There are no forward markets for the exhaustible resource. However everyone knows the current stock $S(t)$ and the flow demand function $d(p(t))$.

There is a difficulty in modelling the behavior of the resource owners and speculators according to the portfolio choice literature. For simplicity, one likes to assume risk neutrality. However, in a partial equilibrium model where the assumption d) holds risk neutral individuals make a (0, 1) decision: They buy the resource if the expected spot price of the exhaustible resource increases faster than ρ; in the opposite case they try to sell the total stock of the exhaustible resource. A momentary stock equilibrium then could only exist in two variants: Either $S = R = d(p)$ if ρ is greater than the expected rate of change p (everything is sold). Consequently, p has to be settled low enough to make d equal to S. Or $d(p) = 0 = R$ if ρ is smaller than the expected rate of change of p. Both adjustment processes yield trivial results. Evidently, the intertemporal competitive equilibrium condition will not be met.

One could also assume non neutrality of the risk preferences or some sorts of wealth constraints. However, computational difficulties or ad-hockeries then quickly arise.

In order to avoid these difficulties we do not postulate momentary stock equilibria at each instant of time. So, buying or selling orders of the resource owners or speculators already influence the future price trends.

The literature on the "commodity boom" 1972–1975 suggests that there exist two different ways by which speculators form their price expectations.

- *Adaptive formation of price expectations*: Some speculators and resource owners use the current price trend as the basis of their expectations about the forthcoming price trend. We assume that this adaptive expectation about the future price trend ($d \log \bar{p}/dt$) is formed by an exponential smoothing of the logarithm of p. Hence

  g) $d \log \bar{p}/dt = \alpha (\log p\,(t) - \log \bar{p}\,(t)) + \rho$

  with $\alpha > 0$. The term ρ is added to permit the existence of a momentary stock equilibrium if $p\,(t) = \bar{p}\,(t)$. Speculators try to increase their stock of the exhaustible resource if $d \log \bar{p}/dt$ is greater than ρ and vice versa. This form of "adaptive" speculation can be encountered on many markets and is not typical for the market of an exhaustible resource.

- *Rational formation of price expectations*: During the last commodity boom 1972–75 there were other speculators who based their portfolio decisions concerning the exhaustible resource on the expected exhaustibility of the resource.[1]

The assumption is plausible that these "rational" speculators use the following decision model: They compare the current price $p\,(t)$ with the price $p^*\,(t)$ being the intertemporally efficient initial price at t. If $p^*\,(t)$ is greater (smaller) than $p\,(t)$ they buy (sell) the exhaustible resource because they expect that the future price trend of the exhaustible resource will exceed (fall short of) the equilibrium trend ρ due to market reevaluations. Hence the assumption holds

h) $d \log \bar{\bar{p}}\,(t)/dt = \beta (\log p^*\,(t) - \log p\,((t) + \rho$

  with $\beta > 0$ and $p^*\,(t)$ determined by $S\,(t) = \int\limits_{t}^{\infty} d\,(p^*\,(t) \cdot \exp\,(\rho\,(s - t)))\,ds$.

Finally we assume that the speculative activities influence the current price trend in an additive way ($\mu \geqslant 0, \nu \geqslant 0$):

i) $d \log p/dt = \rho + \mu\,(d \log \bar{p}/dt - \rho) + \nu\,(d \log \bar{\bar{p}}/dt - \rho)$.

In the final part of this paper, the reaction coefficients μ, ν are interpreted as parameters of a learning process.

   Note that the following statement holds (to shorten the notations we write: $l = \log p$, $\bar{l} = \log \bar{p}$, $l^* = \log p^*$, $e = l - \bar{l}$, $f = l - l^*$, $\dot{x}$ for the derivative of any x): $\dot{f}$ is only dependent on e and f (and not on l) iff the price elasticity is constant. The sufficiency of the second half of this statement can easily be proved by a straightforward calculation.

---

[1]) See *Cooper/Lawrence* [1975, p. 703]: "At the level of general public discourse, considerable attention had been given to 'The Limits of Growth', which strongly underlined . . . the finiteness of the earth's resources and drew public attention to their possible exhaustion within a foreseeable future." Solow already presumed similar portfolio considerations: ". . . producers do have some notion that the resource they own has a value anchored somewhere in the future, a value determined by . . . demand considerations . . ." [*Solow*, p. 6].

As to the necessity remark that $\dot{f} = -[d\,(l)]/[g\,(l-f)]$ where $g\,(z) = \int\limits_0^\infty d'(z + \rho u)\,du$. But whenever $\dot{f} = h\,(f)$ (say), then

$$h\,(f) \cdot g\,(l-f) = -d\,(l).$$

This functional equation implies in turn that $d\,(l)$ is of the form $\gamma \cdot \exp\,(-l\delta)$.

3. The Model

According to assumption b), the demand function is specified

$$d\,(l) = d\,(\log p) = \gamma \cdot p^{-\delta} = \gamma \cdot \exp\,(-l\delta). \tag{1}$$

Without any loss of generality, we may assume — by simply rescaling the demand — that $\gamma = 1$.

Given this demand function we obtain a $1-1$ mapping between actual prices and optimal equilibrium stock S^* as follows:

$$S^*\,(l) = \int\limits_0^\infty d\,(l + \rho \cdot u)\,du. \tag{2}$$

Inserting the special form of d given by (1) into (2) yields

$$S^*\,(l) = \frac{\exp\,(-l\delta)}{\rho \cdot \delta}.$$

The inverse function — which maps the actual stock onto the optimal (logarithmic) price — is given by

$$L^*\,(S) = \frac{-\log\,(S \cdot \rho \cdot \delta)}{\delta}.$$

Let S be the actual stock at time t and $l^* = \log p^* = L^*\,(S)$ the pertaining optimal logarithmic price. Since

$$l^* = l - f = L^*\,(S^*\,(l-f))$$

we get

$$\dot{l}^* = \frac{dL^*\,(S)}{dS} \cdot (-d\,(l)).$$

Using the special form of L^* and S^*, we find that

$$\dot{l}^* = \rho \exp\,(-\delta f). \tag{3}$$

The "adaptive" speculators form their price expectation according to assumption g)

$$\dot{\bar{l}} = \alpha\,(l - \bar{l}) + \rho. \tag{4}$$

Finally the influence of speculative activities on the price path is given by the equation (see assumption (i))

$$\dot{l} = \rho + \mu\,(\dot{\bar{l}} - \rho) + \nu\beta\,(l^* - l). \tag{5}$$

Since only the product $\nu\beta$ is of importance for the further analysis we rescale β to 1.

Rewriting the equations (3), (4) and (5) we get the following system of first order differential equations

$$\dot{l}(t) = \rho + \alpha\mu\, e\,(t) - \nu f\,(t)$$
$$\dot{e}(t) = a\,(\mu - 1)\, e\,(t) - \nu f\,(t) \tag{6}$$
$$\dot{f}(t) = \alpha\mu\, e\,(t) - \nu f\,(t) + \rho\,(1 - \exp\,(-\,\delta f\,(t)))$$

together with the initial conditions

$$l\,(0) = l_0$$
$$e\,(0) = e_0$$
$$f\,(0) = f_0.$$

The next section is devoted to the analysis of the qualitative behavior of the dynamical system induced by (6). Remember that — due to the constant price elasticity of the demand function — $\dot{e}, \dot{f}$ and $\dot{l}$ only depend on e and f. Hence we can omit the first equation in (6).

4. The Dynamics of the Model without Learning

a) Case $\mu = 0, \nu = 0$

This case is of no practical interest, since the speculation does not influence the price path. Nevertheless this is a situation where an explicit solution is easily available

$$l = l_0 + \rho \cdot t$$
$$e = e_0$$
$$f = -\frac{1}{\rho}\log\left(\frac{K \cdot \exp\,(-\,\rho\delta t)}{K \cdot \exp\,(-\,\rho\delta t) - 1}\right)$$

where

$$K = \frac{\exp\,(-\,\delta f_0)}{\exp\,(-\,\delta f_0) - 1}.$$

If $f_0 > 0$ then $f\,(t) \to \infty$ as $t \to \infty$ and when $f_0 < 0$ then $f\,(t) \to -\infty$ even in a finite interval of time.

b) Case $\mu > 0, \nu = 0$

In this case the solution is

$$l\,(t) = l_0 + \rho t + \frac{\alpha\mu}{\alpha\,(\mu - 1)} \cdot e_0\,(\exp\,(\alpha\,(\mu - 1)\,t) - 1)$$

and therefore stable (stability of the momentary stock equilibrium) if and only if $\mu < 1$. Note that there is a global instability of the intertemporal competitive equilibrium ($|f| \to \infty$ unless $e_0 = f_0 = 0$).

c) Case $\mu = 0$, $\nu > 0$

The pertaining differential equation for f is

$$\dot{f} = -\nu f + \rho (1 - \exp(-\delta f)). \tag{7}$$

The qualitative behavior of this equation depends on the sign of $\delta \rho - \nu$.

ca) $\nu > \rho \delta$

Let f^* be the nonzero solution of

$$\nu f^* = \rho (1 - \exp(-\delta f^*)).$$

Then $f \equiv 0$ is asymptotically stable for (7), the domain of attraction being (f^*, ∞). The second critical value f^* is unstable.

cb) $\nu \leqslant \rho \delta$

In that case, the critical value $f \equiv 0$ is unstable.

d) Case $\mu > 0$, $\nu > 0$

For the study of the stability of the zero solution, we consider the Jacobian (at zero) of the system (6):

$$A = \begin{pmatrix} \alpha (\mu - 1) & -\nu \\ \alpha \mu & -\nu + \delta \rho \end{pmatrix}.$$

Theorem 1. The zero solution is asymptotically stable if and only if

$$\nu > \rho \delta + \max (\alpha (\mu - 1), -\delta \rho \mu). \tag{8}$$

Proof: It is a well known result that the zero solution of a first order differential equation is asymptotically stable if the real parts of the eigenvalues of the Jacobian at zero are negative. In our case this is equivalent to (8).

Remark. Following statements hold about the set of admissible parameters in inequality (8)

(i)   If $\mu = 0$ the stability condition is $\nu > \rho \delta$.
(ii) If $0 < \mu < (1 + (\delta \rho)/\alpha)^{-1}$ the set of admissible ν increases with increasing μ.
(iii) If $(1 + (\delta \rho)/\alpha)^{-1} \leqslant \mu$ the set of admissible ν decreases with increasing μ.
(iv) If $0 < \mu < 1$ the set of admissible ν increases with increasing ρ and δ.
(v)   If $\mu = 1$ the stability condition simply is $\nu > 0$.
(vi) If $1 \leqslant \mu$ the set of admissible ν decreases with increasing ρ and δ.

We now study the qualitative behavior of the domain of attraction. First of all we remark that in case of asymptotic stability the origin is a node if $(\alpha (\mu - 1) - \rho \delta + \nu)^2 > 4 \alpha \mu \nu$, otherwise a focus. This follows from well known theorems on linear systems. Now two different cases must be distinguished.

da) $0 < \mu < 1$

There are two critical points, namely the origin and the point (e^*, f^*) where

$$\frac{\nu}{\mu - 1} f^* = \rho \exp(-\rho f^*) \ f^* < 0 \ \text{ and } \ e^* = \frac{\nu}{\alpha(\mu - 1)} f^*.$$

An inspection of the Jacobian demonstrates that the latter is a saddle point. The domain of attraction is an open, possibly unbounded, star shaped set. A typical phase portrait is shown in figure 1.

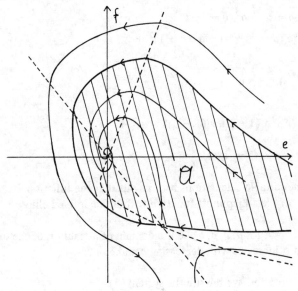

Fig. 1

db) $1 \leqslant \mu$

In this case there is no critical point apart from the origin. If the origin is a focus, there is a closed orbit being the boundary of the domain of attraction. A typical phase portrait is shown in figure 2.

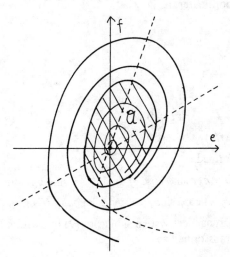

Fig. 2

For the estimation of the size of the domain of attraction the following theorem is useful.

Theorem 2. The domain of attraction contains the ellipse

$$\{Ae^2 + 2Bef + Cf^2 \leqslant y*^2 (C - B^2/A)\} \text{ where}$$

$$A = \alpha (\delta\rho (\mu - 1) + \nu) + (\rho\delta - \nu)^2 + \alpha^2 \mu^2$$

$$B = -\nu (\rho\delta - \nu) + \alpha^2 (\mu - 1) \mu$$

$$C = \alpha (\delta\rho (\mu - 1) + \nu) + \alpha^2 (\mu - 1)^2 + \nu^2$$

and

$$\rho (1 - e^{-y*\delta}) = \gamma \cdot y*$$

with

$$\gamma = \begin{cases} \min (\nu + \alpha (1 - \mu), \nu/(1 - \mu)) & \mu < 1 \\ \max (\nu + \alpha (1 - \mu), 0) & \mu \geqslant 1. \end{cases}$$

Proof. After some suitable calculations it turns out that the function $\Phi (e, f) = Ae^2 + 2Bef + Cf^2$ is a Ljapunoff-function within the defined ellipse.

Theorem 3. Let $A = A (\alpha, \mu, \nu, \rho, \delta)$ be the domain of attraction of the origin of the system (6). Then A increases with decreasing ρ and δ.

Proof. For easier notation, we rewrite the system (6)

$$\dot{e} = ae + bf$$

$$\dot{f} = ce + df + g (f) \tag{9}$$

where $g (f) = \rho (1 - \exp (- \delta f))$.

Introducing polar coordinates, namely

$$e = r \cos \phi$$

$$f = r \sin \phi$$

$$r = \sqrt{e^2 + f^2}$$

$$\phi = \begin{cases} \arctan (f/e) & \text{if } e > 0 \\ \dfrac{\pi}{2} \cdot \text{sgn} (f) & \text{if } e = 0 \\ \pi + \arctan (f/e) & \text{if } e < 0 \end{cases}$$

the system (6) is transformed to

$$\dot{r} = a r \cos^2 \phi + (b + c) r \sin\phi \cos\phi + dr \sin^2 \phi + \sin\phi g (r \sin\phi)$$

$$\dot{\phi} = c \cos^2 \phi + (d - a) \cos\phi \sin\phi - b \sin^2 \phi + \cos\phi g (r \sin\phi). \tag{10}$$

Consider now a second dynamical system similar to (9) but with $h (f)$ instead of $g (f)$. This system is also transformed to

$$\dot{R} = a\,R\,\cos^2\Phi + (b + c)\,R\,\sin\Phi\,\cos\Phi + d\,R\,\sin^2\Phi + \sin\Phi\,h\,(R\,\sin\Phi)$$
$$\dot{\Phi} = c\,\cos^2\Phi + (d - a)\,\cos\Phi\,\sin\Phi - b\,\sin^2\Phi + \cos\Phi\,h\,(R\,\sin\phi). \qquad (11)$$

We show that: If g and h are monotonic increasing, $g\,(0) = h\,(0) = 0$ and $|g\,(x)| \geqslant |h\,(x)|$ for all $x \in R$ then the set $\{r < R,\ \phi = \Phi\}$ is non attainable from outside. This is clear, since for $\phi = \Phi$ $\dot{r} - \dot{R} \geqslant 0$. Hence the domain of attraction of (10) is contained in the domain of attraction of (11).

Since for $h\,(f) = \rho_1\,(1 - \exp\,(-\delta_1 f))$ with $\rho_1 \leqslant \rho$ and $\delta_1 \leqslant \delta$ the above condition is fulfilled the assertion of the theorem follows.

Remark. If we increase μ or decrease ν, the area of the domain of attraction increases and hence the "probability of attraction." But no isotone inclusion relation holds as it can be seen by an argument similar to the one above.

5. Some Comments on a Learning Concept

Learning means a positive feedback between the success of speculation and the intensity responsible the change in the type of speculation. In our model the success of speculation can be measured by the difference between actual prices and adaptive responsible rational price expectations.

It seems plausible to specify this dependence by

$$\dot{\mu} = g\,(e, f)$$
$$\dot{\nu} = h\,(e, f).$$

The question is: Has learning a stabilizing effect or not? If we utilize the notion of "stabilizing effect" in the sense of *Fuchs* [1979] this means the following:

Let $A\,(\alpha, \rho, \delta, g, h)$ be the set of all $\{\mu_0, \nu_0, e_0, f_0\}$ such that the system

$$\dot{e} = \alpha\,(\mu - 1)\,e - \nu f$$
$$\dot{f} = \alpha\mu e - \nu f + \rho\,(1 - \exp\,(-\delta f))$$
$$\dot{\mu} = g\,(e, f)$$
$$\dot{\nu} = h\,(e, f)$$

with initial condition

$$e\,(0) = e_0;\, f\,(0) = f_0;\, \mu\,(0) = \mu_0;\, \nu\,(0) = \nu_0$$

converges to zero.

A pair of learning functions (g, h) is stabilizing in the sense of Fuchs, if $A\,(\alpha, \rho, \delta, g, h) \supseteq A\,(\alpha, \rho, \delta, 0, 0)$.

(More precisely according to Fuchs this inclusion must hold locally in a neighborhood of the origin). It is clear that only few learning functions satisfy this restrictive definition. Nevertheless there exist some stabilizing functions, which are intuitively plausible. Setting e.g.

$$\dot{\mu} = -c_1 e^2 + c_2 f^2$$
$$\dot{\nu} = c_1 e^2 - c^2 f^2 \tag{12}$$

(this specification ensures that $\dot{\mu} + \dot{\nu} = 0$ and hence the constancy of the overall intensity of speculation; furthermore $\dot{\mu}$ and $\dot{\nu}$ do not depend on the sign of the deviations e, f) this function is stabilizing in the sense of Fuchs (because it is quadratic). However one is interested not so much in the local as in the global properties of the domain of attraction. Only few remarks are possible:

Whenever the process is in the set $|e| > \sqrt{c_2/c_1} |f|$ there is a positive effect on the stability. Otherwise the effect on the stability is negative. Since we cannot exclude solutions spiraling around the origin, the outcoming effect seems unpredictable. In any case a detailed study of the global effect of learning behavior is apparently indispensable for further work.

6. Conclusion

We conclude that the speculation which takes into account the exhaustion of the exhaustible resource has strong stabilizing tendencies for the momentary stock equilibrium and the intertemporal competitive equilibrium. However, global results are difficult to obtain.

References

Cooper, R.N., and *R.Z. Lawrence*: The 1972–75 Commodity Boom. Brooking's Papers on Economic Activity 3, 1975, 671–723.
Dasgupta, P.S., and *G.M. Heal*: Economic Theory and Exhaustible Resources. Cambridge 1979.
Fuchs, G.: Is Error Learning Behavior Stabilizing? Journal of Economic Theory 20, 1979, 300–317.
Hahn, W.: Stability of Motion. Grundlehren der Math. Wissenschaften, Vol. 138. New York 1967.
Solow, R.: The Economics of Resources and the Resources of Economics. American Economic Review, Papers and Proceedings 64, 1974, 1–14.
Weinstein, M.C., and *R.J. Zeckhauser*: The Optimal Consumption of Depletable Natural Resources. Quarterly Journal of Economics 89, 1975, 371–392.

Economic Theory of Natural Resources. © Physica-Verlag, Würzburg–Wien, 1982.

Variable Resource Endowments and the Convexity of the Attainable Consumption Set[1])

Winfried Reiss and *Friedrich Breyer*

1. The Notion of Price-Dependent Resource Stocks

In the classic articles on the theory of exhaustible resources [e.g. *Hotelling; Dasgupta/ Heal; Solow*] it is in general assumed that the stock of the raw material under consideration is some exogenously fixed real number. Recently, however, it has occured to some writers that this picture is an oversimplification of the real world in which the endowment of an economy with natural resources may be dependent upon several other variables. Potential determinants of the resource quantity are, on the one hand, investment in explorative activities and, on the other hand, technical progress in resource extraction processes, which allows a known deposit to be exploited to a greater extent.

Apart from these technical factors, most attempts to define the "reserves" of a certain natural resource give some role to economic considerations. Due to the widely-adopted convention to include in the calculation of "known reserves" only those deposits that can be *profitably* exploited, the extraction costs as well as the selling price of the resource implicitly become determinants of its available quantity. So even when technological conditions are held constant, the resource quantity is no longer fixed, but depends on relative prices.

These considerations have led *Heal* [1980] — or, in a more explicit manner, *Chichilnisky/Heal* [1979] — to describe the resource endowment of an economy not as a fixed vector but as a vector-valued function of the price vector. Thus the endowment with one particular resource resembles very closely the normal supply function.

In *Breyer/Reiss* [1981] we discussed some difficulties involved in this concept of a "reserve supply function". We argued that the dependence of extractable reserves of a resource on prices merely reflects technological relationships: The supply of reserves of a resource i increases with an increase in its own price p_i and with a decrease of some other price p_j where good j is used as an input in the extraction of resource i. So an increase in the price ratio p_i/p_j clearly makes it more profitable to exploit some deposits of the reserve that would not have been touched otherwise because of their deepness in the ground or their low concentration[2]).

---

[1]) The authors are grateful to Malte Faber, Roy Gardner, Murray Kemp, Ngo Van Long, Gerhard Maier, Peter Saunders and Gunter Stephan for valuable comments and to Ailsa Gruber for a considerable stylistic improvement of the paper.

[2]) A slightly different explanation of the price-dependence is proposed by *Kemp/Long* [1981].

Now if those amounts of a resource that can be profitably extracted and are not re-used — directly or indirectly — as inputs in extraction activities are designated "net output", then the net outputs of all resources are obviously related to each other as in a transformation function. We proposed in the paper quoted above to derive this quantity relationship directly from the resource extraction functions thereby avoiding the potentially misleading detour via the price system.

In this paper we deal with a special problem brought about by the concept of price-dependent endowments. It has been claimed by *Heal* [1980, p. 38] that this price-dependence may give rise to a new type of market failure:

> ". . . the set of allocations — consumption and production plans — which is in priciple attainable by the economy depends — clearly — on the initial endowment. So if the endowment changes with price, so does the attainable set. So for each price [vector] the economy has an attainable set, which, under the usual assumptions, is convex. The overall attainable set for the economy is the *union* of the sets attainable at each price [vector], and the union of convex sets need not be convex."

A nonconvex set of feasible consumption bundles would, of course, mean that not every Pareto-optimal state corresponds to a market equilibrium.

We want to investigate in this paper if the nonconvexity claimed by Heal is still valid if the price-dependence is traced back to its underlying technological relationships as outlined above. Therefore, in Section 2 we study a general model with an arbitrary finite number of extractable resources. Since the question of convexity is independent of the intertemporal aspects of resource allocation, we choose a comparative-static model structure, i.e. we compress the whole time span into one single period. Correspondingly we presuppose a given technical knowledge and assume that within the period considered no exploration of new resource deposits takes place. In doing this we eliminate two of the three reasons for the variability of resource endowments mentioned above in order to concentrate entirely on the third reason, the price-dependence.

In Section 3 we analyze the two-resource example of *Heal* [1980] and *Chichilnisky/Heal* [1979] as a special case of our model in that we replace Heal's resource supply functions by their underlying extraction functions. We shall show that the non-convexity of the attainable consumption set disappears once the idea of exogenous prices is dropped and quantity relationships are directly considered.

2. A Price-Independent Description of Resource Endowments

We introduce our static model by a list of assumptions and definitions and then prove the convexity of the set of feasible consumption goods.

Our first two assumptions deal with the kinds of goods and with producibility.

Assumption 1 (primary factors)
We have k nonproducible primary factors, indexed by $h = 1, \ldots, k$, to which labour,

land etc. belong. The amounts or primary factors are bounded from above, i.e. no more than r_h $(r_h < \infty)$ is available of factor h. [3])

Contrary to extractable resources in situ the extracted resources do not belong to this group of goods since extraction is regarded as production. Extracted goods therefore belong to the group dealt with in the following assumption.

Assumption 2 (producible goods)
We have m producible goods, indexed by $i = 1, \ldots, m$. Production is described by the production function

$$z_i = f_i(x_{i1}, \ldots, x_{ik}, y_{i1}, \ldots, y_{im}) \tag{2.1a}$$

where $z_i \in R_+$ denotes the produced gross amount of good i, $x_{ih} \in R_+$ is the input of primary factor h and $y_{ij} \in R_+$ the input of produced good j necessary to produce z_i.
To simplify our notation, we combine inputs, outputs and the resource endowments into vectors and matrices in the following way.

First we define

$$x_i = (x_{i1}, \ldots, x_{ik}) \in R_+^k$$

$$y_i = (y_{i1}, \ldots, y_{im}) \in R_+^m$$

$$r = (r_1, \ldots, r_k) \in R_+^k$$

and

$$x = \begin{pmatrix} x_1 \\ \vdots \\ x_m \end{pmatrix} \in R_+^{m \cdot k}, \quad y = \begin{pmatrix} y_1 \\ \vdots \\ y_m \end{pmatrix} \in R_+^{m \cdot m}, \quad z = \begin{pmatrix} z_1 \\ \vdots \\ z_m \end{pmatrix} \in R_+^m.$$

If f is given by its components f_i

$$f = \begin{pmatrix} f_1 \\ \vdots \\ f_m \end{pmatrix},$$

we can rewrite (2.1a) as

$$z = f(x, y). \tag{2.1b}$$

Due to Assumption 1 we have

$$\sum_{i=1}^{m} x_{ih} \leqslant r_h \quad h = 1, \ldots, k. \tag{2.2a}$$

---

[3]) Primary factors which are (for practical use) available in infinite amounts, are not itemized in our model, since they cannot contribute to the limitation of the attainable consumption set.

So we can write

$$x^T u \leqslant r, \tag{2.2b}$$

where u denotes the $(m \times 1)$ unit vector and x^T is the transpose of x.

We now introduce two assumptions which deal with production.

Assumption 3 (concave production functions)

The production functions are concave, i.e. for $0 \leqslant \alpha \leqslant 1$ and each i we have

$$f_i \left(\alpha \left(\bar{x}_i, \bar{y}_i \right) + (1 - \alpha) \left(\bar{\bar{x}}_i, \bar{\bar{y}}_i \right) \right) \geqslant \alpha f_i \left(\bar{x}_i, \bar{y}_i \right) + (1 - \alpha) f_i \left(\bar{\bar{x}}_i, \bar{\bar{y}}_i \right). \tag{2.3}$$

Assumption 4 (production without input)

$$f_i \left(0, 0 \right) \geqslant 0.$$

According to Assumption 4 we allow for the possibility of positive output without inputs. This could occur if some resources were available without any use of extraction inputs. We do not want to discuss the possibility, the importance or even feasibility of this in reality but only want to point out the following:

a) it includes the case $f_i \left(0, 0 \right) = 0$ and is therefore a generalization and
b) it gives us the possibility of handling the model of *Heal* [1980].

The produced goods are partly used as inputs. These amounts are given by $y^T u$. The remainder, the net-output,

$$f \left(x, y \right) - y^T u$$

is available for consumption. Production is only feasible if no component in this expression is negative. These reflections lead to

Definition 1 (feasible consumption good bundle)

The vector $c \in R_+^m$ is called a feasible consumption good bundle if matrices

$$x \in R_+^{k \cdot m}, \quad y \in R_+^{m \cdot m}$$

exist so that

$$x^T u \leqslant r \tag{2.4}$$

and

$$0 \leqslant c \leqslant f \left(x, y \right) - y^T u. \tag{2.5}$$

The set of all feasible consumption good bundles is denoted by C.

Implicitly this definition includes the assumption of "free disposal", since in (2.5) the second inequality sign is tolerated. It is therefore possible that less than the whole net output is consumed.

Moreover it is admissible that not every producible good is desired as a consumption good. The selection is eventually found by a welfare function. If a good is not desired, this is expressed by

$$\frac{\partial W}{\partial c_i} = 0 \qquad \text{for all } c \in C.$$

We can now state our central proposition, which is neither surprising nor even new but which we will nevertheless establish since the proof is brief.

Proposition 1: Under Assumptions 1 to 4 the set of all feasible consumption good bundles C

a) contains the zero vector
b) is convex.

Proof:

a) follows directly from Assumption 4 and the definition of feasible consumption good bundles.
b) Let us assume that $\bar{c}$ and $\bar{\bar{c}}$ are feasible. Then, according to Definition 1 matrices $\bar{x}, \bar{\bar{x}}, \bar{y}, \bar{\bar{y}}$ exist so that

$$\bar{x}, \bar{\bar{x}} \, R_+^{k \cdot m}, \bar{y}, \bar{\bar{y}} \, R_+^{m \cdot m} \tag{2.6}$$

$$\bar{x}^T u \leqslant r \tag{2.7}$$

$$\bar{\bar{x}}^T u \leqslant r \tag{2.8}$$

$$0 \leqslant \bar{c} \leqslant f(\bar{x}, \bar{y}) - \bar{y}^T u \tag{2.9}$$

$$0 \leqslant \bar{\bar{c}} \leqslant f(\bar{\bar{x}}, \bar{\bar{y}}) - \bar{\bar{y}}^T u. \tag{2.10}$$

From (2.7) and (2.8) we get for $0 \leqslant \alpha \leqslant 1$

$$\alpha \bar{x}^T u + (1 - \alpha) \bar{\bar{x}}^T u \leqslant \alpha r + (1 - \alpha) r = r, \tag{2.11}$$

hence

$$(\alpha \bar{x} + (1 - \alpha) \bar{\bar{x}})^T u \leqslant r. \tag{2.12}$$

Because of (2.6) we have

$$(\alpha \bar{x} + (1 - \alpha) \bar{\bar{x}}) \in R_+^{k \cdot m}. \tag{2.13}$$

From (2.9) and (2.10) we derive

$$0 \leqslant \alpha \bar{c} \leqslant \alpha f(\bar{x}, \bar{y}) - \alpha \bar{y}^T u \tag{2.14}$$

$$0 \leqslant (1 - \alpha) \bar{\bar{c}} \leqslant (1 - \alpha) f(\bar{\bar{x}}, \bar{\bar{y}}) - (1 - \alpha) \bar{\bar{y}}^T u. \tag{2.15}$$

Adding (2.14) and (2.15) and using the concavity of f we obtain

$$0 \leqslant \alpha \bar{c} + (1 - \alpha) \bar{\bar{c}} \leqslant \alpha f(\bar{x}, \bar{y}) + (1 - \alpha) f(\bar{\bar{x}}, \bar{\bar{y}}) - (\alpha \bar{y} + (1 - \alpha) \bar{\bar{y}})^T u$$

$$\leqslant f(\alpha (\bar{x}, \bar{y}) + (1 - \alpha) (\bar{\bar{x}}, \bar{\bar{y}})) - (\alpha \bar{y} + (1 - \alpha) \bar{\bar{y}})^T u$$

$$= f(\alpha \bar{x} + (1 - \alpha) \bar{\bar{x}}, \alpha \bar{y} + (1 - \alpha) \bar{\bar{y}}) - (\alpha \bar{y} + (1 - \alpha) \bar{\bar{y}})^T u. \tag{2.16}$$

Because of (2.6) we have

$$\alpha \bar{y} + (1 - \alpha) \bar{\bar{y}} \in R_+^{m \cdot m}. \tag{2.17}$$

228

From (2.12), (2.13), (2.16) and (2.17) we conclude the convexity of the set of feasible consumption good bundles.

The vector c is, according to our assumptions, not necessarily bounded. If for example in a one-good economy the function f is given by

$$z_1 = 2y_1$$

we have

$$c_1 := z_1 - y_1 = z_1 - \frac{1}{2}z_1 = \frac{z_1}{2}.$$

By increasing the gross output z_1 we can make the consumable net output arbitrarily high. Such a property is, economically, somewhat inconvenient, particularly in a model which deals with the problem of resource limitations. In treating Heal's model with the instruments developed here, we will show that in his example the set C is bounded.

3. The Two-Resource-Example of Heal

The example proposed by *Heal* [1980, p. 38f.] to demonstrate the nonconvexity of the economy deals with two producible goods, energy and metal, as well as two extractable resources, oil and ore. Their amounts are denoted by E, M, Q and R. [4]) According to the terminology introduced in section 2 above these are all produced goods, therefore matrix x has zero columns since k is equal to zero.

Arranging the amounts in alphabetic order we get the vector and matrix

$$z = \begin{pmatrix} E \\ M \\ Q \\ R \end{pmatrix}; \qquad y = \begin{pmatrix} E_E & M_E & Q_E & R_E \\ E_M & M_M & Q_M & R_M \\ E_Q & M_Q & Q_Q & R_Q \\ E_R & M_R & Q_R & R_R \end{pmatrix}$$

and the vector c as $c^T = (E_c, M_c, Q_c, R_c)$. However only the first two goods, energy and metal, are consumed. This results from the fact that Heal uses the following welfare function [*Chichilnsky/Heal*, p. 42]:[5])

$$W(E_c, M_c, Q_c, R_c) = \gamma E_c + \delta M_c \quad (\gamma, \delta > 0). \tag{3.1}$$

The production functions for energy and metal are also specified by Heal in the following manner

$$E = f_1(E_E, M_E, Q_E, R_E) = \min\left(\frac{Q_E}{a_2}, \frac{R_E}{b_2}\right) \tag{3.2}$$

$$M = f_2(E_M, M_M, Q_M, R_M) = \min\left(\frac{Q_M}{a_1}, \frac{R_M}{b_1}\right). \tag{3.3}$$

---

[4]) Instead of Heal's O we use Q to avoid confusion with the number zero.

[5]) Chichilnsky/Heal implicitly assume that energy and metal are not used as inputs and therefore have $E_c = E$ and $M_c = M$. We will discuss the problematic nature of this assumption in the final section.

For the two resources, however, the following supply functions are used by Heal:

$$Q = \alpha \frac{p_Q}{p_E} + \bar{Q} \tag{3.4}$$

$$R = \beta \left(\frac{p_R}{p_E} \right)^2 + \bar{R} \tag{3.5}$$

with p_E, p_Q, p_R the prices of energy, oil and ore and α, β positive constants.

He then refers to a finding by *Chichilnisky/Heal* [1979, 40–47] who, starting out from the functions (3.2) to (3.5), construct a consumption possibility frontier, i.e. a locus of consumable (E, M)-pairs at varying price vectors. To do this they use the standard assumptions of profit maximization, competitive equilibrium and efficient production with full employment of all factors of production. Simple algebraic manipulations then enable them to express both E and M as functions of the price of energy, p_E. Substituting one into the other yields the desired consumption possibility frontier in form of a function $E = E (M)$. Inspection of the second derivative of this function reveals that $d^2 E/dM^2$ is always positive so that the area under this curve, the consumption possibility set, mut be nonconvex.

As outlined in Section 1 we want to show that the non-convexity vanishes as soon as the model is reduced to plain quantity relations. To do this we first investigate the quantity relations concealed behind the dependence of the values Q and R on the relative prices. We assume that (3.4) and (3.5) are the supply functions of profit-maximizing firms under perfect competition and ask on what extraction functions this behaviour is based.

Let us first examine the extraction of oil. In general terms the produced amount Q is a function of all inputs used:[6]

$$Q = f_3 (E_Q, M_Q, Q_Q, R_Q). \tag{3.6}$$

Since the prices of metal and ore do not appear in the supply function (3.4), we can safely conclude that these materials are not used for the extraction of oil. We can also ignore Q_Q by regarding Q as the *net* amount of oil gained in the oildrilling activity. Furthermore, since an amount $\bar{Q}$ is supplied independently of relative prices it can be inferred that this quantity is "produced" (or better: available) without inputs.[7] Therefore, (3.6) reduces to

$$Q = g (E_Q) + \bar{Q}. \tag{3.7}$$

Since the supply function in a static model is equal to the upward sloping part of the marginal cost function, we derive total and marginal costs of extracting Q units of oil as

$$K (Q) = p_E E_Q = p_E g^{-1} (Q - \bar{Q}) \tag{3.8}$$

$$K' (Q) = p_E \cdot \frac{d}{dQ} g^{-1} (Q - \bar{Q}). \tag{3.9}$$

---

[6] Oil in the ground is not specified as an input factor since it can be regarded as practically inexhaustibly available. See our remarks on Assumption 1.

[7] Remember that due to Assumption 4 a production of positive amounts (here: $\bar{Q}$) without inputs is admissible in our model.

Equating marginal cost to price of oil and using (3.4) we obtain[8])

$$\frac{d}{dQ} g^{-1} (Q-\bar{Q}) = \frac{P_Q}{P_E} = \frac{Q-\bar{Q}}{\alpha}. \tag{3.10}$$

By integrating the left-hand side and the right-hand side of (3.10) with respect to Q and using (3.8) we obtain

$$E_Q = g^{-1} (Q-\bar{Q}) = \frac{1}{2\alpha} (Q-\bar{Q})^2. \tag{3.11}$$

Solving (3.11) for Q gives us the specific form of the extraction function for oil which must underlie the supply function (3.4),

$$Q = f_3 (E_Q, M_Q, Q_Q, R_Q) = (2\alpha)^{1/2} E_Q^{1/2} + \bar{Q}. \tag{3.12}$$

Analogously we derive the extraction function of ore

$$R = f_4 (E_R, M_R, Q_R, R_R) = \left(\frac{9}{4}\beta\right)^{1/3} \cdot E_R^{2/3} + \bar{R}. \tag{3.13}$$

Both extraction functions exhibit the usual concavity properties. From (3.2), (3.3), (3.12), (3.13) and (2.5) we obtain the following system of 10 inequalities with the variables $E, E_Q, E_R, E_c, M, M_c, Q, Q_E, Q_M, R, R_E, R_M$, which must all be nonnegative.

$$E_Q + E_R + E_c = E \tag{3.14a}$$

$$M_c = M \tag{3.14b}$$

$$Q_E + Q_M \le Q \tag{3.14c}$$

$$R_E + R_M \le R \tag{3.14d}$$

$$E \le Q_E/a_2 \tag{3.14e}$$

$$E \le R_E/b_2 \tag{3.14f}$$

$$M \le Q_M/a_1 \tag{3.14g}$$

$$M \le R_M/b_1 \tag{3.14h}$$

$$Q \le (2\alpha)^{1/2} \cdot E_Q^{1/2} + \bar{Q} \tag{3.14i}$$

$$R \le \left(\frac{9}{4}\beta\right)^{1/3} \cdot E_R^{2/3} + \bar{R}. \tag{3.14j}$$

This set of inequalities implies directly that the set of all feasible (E_c, M_c)-bundles, C, is closed and bounded, as proved in the Appendix below. Moreover, the above example fulfils all the assumptions of our Proposition 1. We can, therefore, conclude that C is convex in this case. Consequently there is no reason for possible market failure.

---

[8]) The right-hand side of (3.10) makes sure that marginal costs are, in fact, an increasing function of Q as required for using our procedure.

4. Conclusions

In this section we want to discuss briefly what may be the real reason for the difference between Heal's and our result on the convexity of the attainable consumption set. For this purpose we take a closer look at Heal's resource supply functions (3.4) and (3.5). *Chichilnisky/Heal* [1979, p. 3] give the following three reasons for the dependence of resource endowments on relative prices:

1. factor migration,
2. relationships between the economy being modelled and the rest of the world,
3. the relationship between the present and the past of the economy.

Since we chose a timeless model for our discussion, only the first two of these reasons are relevant for us. Both refer to the allocation of factors of production to different countries. To be more specific, Heal's resource supply function (3.4) can, for example, be explained by the following reasoning: The quantity $\bar{Q}$ of the resource oil is already stored in the considered country X, therefore causing no extraction expenditures. The remainder has to be imported from another country, Y. The supplier in country Y extracts oil with the extraction function $Q = (2\alpha)^{1/2} \cdot E_Q^{1/2}$. He himself imports the required energy inputs E_Q (e.g. in the form of electrical current) at prices which prevail in country X and acts thereby as a price-taker. One can thus think of Y as a small country and X as a large one in which world market prices are determined.

Whereas country Y exports goods to country X, it does not get any goods in return since according to *Chilchilnisky/Heal* [1979] the total quantities of metal and energy produced in country X, namely E and M, are also consumed in X. In particular, nothing is subtracted from E, which might serve as input in the exploitation of oil and ore (like E_Q and E_R in our equation (3.14a)). Obviously, country Y has to import its energy inputs from a third country, Z, in which the same world market prices rule.

Since country X exports nothing but, on the other hand, obtains imports of oil and ore from foreign countries, which vary in response to changing prices, its balance of payments cannot, cet. par., be balanced in each situation. Therefore, foreign trade appears to be in systematic imbalance in Heal's model, and it is not surprising that under these circumstances the danger of market failure exists.

We tried to fill the gap in Heal's model by taking a global economic view. In our equation (3.14a) we took account of the fact that all inputs used in resource extraction activities detract from the consumable amount of energy. At the same time we eliminated the price-dependence and traced it back to the underlying quantity relationships. We established that the integration in a static equilibrium model of those resources which have to be extracted and are, therefore, available in variable quantities, does not by itself lead to a violation of convexity requirements and to market failure.

Appendix

Here we provide the proof that the set of feasible consumption bundles in our version of Heal's example is closed and bounded. For this purpose we string together the relations

(3.14b) to (3.14j) into the following two chains of inequalities and equalities.

$$a_2E + a_1M_c = a_2E + a_1M \leqslant Q_E + Q_M \leqslant Q \leqslant (2\alpha E_Q)^{1/2} + \bar{Q} \tag{A1}$$

$$b_2E + b_1M_c = b_2E + b_1M \leqslant R_E + R_M \leqslant R \leqslant \left(\frac{9}{4}\beta\right)^{1/3} E_R^{2/3} + \bar{R}. \tag{A2}$$

With efficient production, in (A1) the equality sign prevails except if E_Q is equal to zero. For if E_Q were greater than zero and one of the inequalities were strictly valid then E_Q could be decreased until either E_Q vanishes or the equality sign is valid. By this procedure M_c would not change, but E_c would be increased. These, and similar reflections for (A2) lead to

$$E_Q = \begin{cases} 0 & \text{if } K_1 < 0 \\ \frac{1}{2}\alpha^{-1}K_1^2 & \text{if } K_1 \geqslant 0 \end{cases} \tag{A3}$$

$$E_R = \begin{cases} 0 & \text{if } K_2 < 0 \\ \frac{2}{3}\beta^{-1/2}K_2^{3/2} & \text{if } K_2 \geqslant 0 \end{cases} \tag{A4}$$

where

$$K_1 \equiv a_2E + a_1M_c - \bar{Q}$$

and

$$K_2 \equiv b_2E + b_1M_c - \bar{R}.$$

Due to (A3), (A4) and (3.14a) the system (3.14) can be reduced to the following function with the three variables E_c, M_c and E

$$E_c = \begin{cases} E & \text{if } K_1, K_2 < 0 & \text{(A5a)} \\ E - \frac{1}{2}\alpha^{-1}K_1^2 & \text{if } K_1 \geqslant 0, K_2 < 0 & \text{(A5b)} \\ E - \frac{2}{3}\beta^{-1/2}K_2^{3/2} & \text{if } K_1 < 0, K_2 \geqslant 0 & \text{(A5c)} \\ E - \frac{1}{2}\alpha^{-1}K_1^2 - \frac{2}{3}\beta^{-1/2}K_2^{3/2} & \text{if } K_1, K_2 \geqslant 0. & \text{(A5d)} \end{cases}$$

We are interested in the properties of the set of feasible consumption bundles, i.e., the set of all admissible (E_c, M_c)-combinations. For this we show that the set is bounded as long as $\bar{R}$ and $\bar{Q}$ are finite.

From (3.14) we get

$$M_c = M \leqslant Q_M/a_1 \leqslant Q/a_1 \leqslant \frac{E_Q^{1/2} + \bar{Q}}{a_1} \leqslant \frac{E^{1/2} + \bar{Q}}{a_1} \tag{A6}$$

and

$$E_c \leqslant E.$$

It follows from this that M_c and E_c (and all their combinations) are bounded unless the production of E is unbounded, the impossibility of which we can see by examining (A5a) to (A5d): If E is made large enough none of these four equations can be satisfied.

To demonstrate this we take E to be

$$E > \max \left\{ \bar{R}/b_2, \bar{Q}/a_2, \frac{2\alpha}{a_2^2} + \frac{2\bar{Q}}{a_2} \right\} .$$

Hence $b_2 E > \bar{R}$ and $a_2 E > \bar{Q}$ and we are within the area described by (A5a).

Since

$$E > \frac{2\alpha}{a_2^2} + \frac{2\bar{Q}}{a_2}$$

we get

$$\frac{1}{2\alpha} (a_2^2 E - 2a_2 \bar{Q}) > 1$$

and hence

$$\frac{1}{2\alpha} (a_2 E - \bar{Q})^2 = E \frac{1}{2\alpha} (a_2^2 E - 2a_2 \bar{Q}) + \frac{\bar{Q}^2}{2\alpha} > E + \frac{\bar{Q}^2}{2\alpha} > E.$$

M_c being positive, we can conclude that $(1/2\alpha) K_1^2/2\alpha > E$.

As $K_2^{3/2}$ and E_c are positive, the equation (A5d) (and thus (A5a, b, c)) does not hold for sufficiently large E. The production of E and hence that of E_c and M_c is bounded.

From the system (3.14) it follows directly that the set of feasible consumption bundles is closed.

References

Breyer, F., and *W. Reiss*: Probleme des Konzepts preisabhängiger Ressourcenausstattungen. Zeitschrift für Wirtschafts- und Sozialwissenschaften **101**, 1981, 83–98.

Chichilnisky, G., and *G. Heal*: Welfare Economics of Competitive General Equilibrium with Variable Endowments. Unpublished manuscript, Columbia University, Nov. 1979.

Dasgupta, P., and *G. Heal*: The Optimal Depletion of Exhaustible Resources. Review of Economic Studies, 1974 (Symposium), 3–28.

Heal, G.: Intertemporal Allocation and Intergenerational Equity. Erschöpfbare Ressourcen. Ed. by H. Siebert. Schriften des Vereins für Socialpolitik, N.F. Vol. 108, Berlin–München 1980.

Hotelling, H.: The Economics of Exhaustible Resources. Journal of Political Economy **39**, 1931, 137–175.

Kemp, M., and *N.V. Long*: The Efficiency of Competitive Markets in a Context of Exhaustible Resources. Economic Theory of Natural Resources. Ed. by W. Eichhorn et al. 1982 (this volume).

Solow, R.M.: Intergenerational Equity and Exhaustible Resources. Review of Economic Studies, 1974 (Symposium), 26–46.

The Extraction Rate of an Exhaustible Resource in an Oligopolistic Market

Martin Schäfer

1. Introduction

Most papers analyzing optimal price or extraction paths of a nonrenewable resource are related to competitive or monopolistic markets. In comparison of the extraction paths of these two market-forms the monopolist takes a more conservationist policy [see e.g. *Stiglitz*], i.e. the total amount of the resource will be depleted slower than in a competitive market. The reason why seems to be intuitively clear: In competitive markets each supplier, who wants to increase his market share by decreasing his price will cause the others to decrease their prices too, if the resource is treated as a homogeneous good. Yet decreasing prices will possibly retard or stop the development of substitutes or technical progress in production. Hence an even faster depletion of the resource stock will take place.

First our model of resource depletion is formulated as a differential game. Secondly an algorithm of *Le Van* [1980] for localizing Nash equilibria is shown to be applicable to this model. Thirdly it is shown by an example that the general applicability of this algorithm can be strengthened to a feasible computational approach.

2. The Model

In this section we will formulate the problem how to extract and/or sell an exhaustible asset by oligopolists in an optimal fashion.

The following assumptions are adopted:

(I)   The resource is continuously depletable.
(II) Only the extraction rate is controllable.
(III) There is a fixed and finite resource stock (of possibly unknown amount).
(IV) The price is determined by a demand function so that the demand is always equal to the sum of the outputs of all oligopolists.

The market is described by a nonzero-sum differential game, which is governed by the state equation

$$\frac{dx}{dt} = f(t, x) + \sum_{i=1}^{N} B_i(t) u_i(t) \qquad t \in [0, T]$$

$$x(0) = x_0 = Q_0 \tag{1}$$

where

    $f: [0, T] \times \mathbf{R}^m \to \mathbf{R}^m$ is continuous,

    $x: [0, T] \to \mathbf{R}^m$ is continuously differentiable,

the $(m, 1)$-matrices $B_i(t)$ are all continuous and the controls

    $u_i: [0, T] \to \mathbf{R}$ are continuously differentiable,

$u_i(t) \in U_i \subseteq \mathbf{R}$ for all $i = 1, 2, \ldots, N$, $t \in [0, T]$ and Q_0 is the total amount of the resource at time 0.

The payoffs are the vector-valued functions

$$J(u_1, \ldots, u_N) = g(x(T)) + \int_0^T h(t, x)\, dt + \int_0^T s(t, u)\, dt \tag{2}$$

with functions g, h and s described below.

Theorem: Given the following assumptions (i) – (vi); then there exists an open-loop Nash equilibrium point of the above differential game.

(i) $f(t, x)$ is continuous in (t, x), satisfies a global Lipschitz condition in t, and is uniformly bounded in x.

(ii)   The control spaces U_i are all compact and convex.

(iii) $g(x(T)) = (g_1(x(T)), \ldots, g_N(x(T)))$ is concave.

(iv) $h(t, x) = h_1(t, x), \ldots, h_N(t, x))$ is continuous with respect to (t, x) and concave with respect to x.

(v) $s(t, u) = (s_1(t, u_1), \ldots, s_N(t, u_N))$ is continuous in (t, u) and concave in u.

(vi) The Hessian matrix $([\partial^2 s_i(t, u_i)]/[\partial u_i^2])$ exists and is continuous for all $i = 1, 2, \ldots, N$.

This is a weaker version of a theorem proved by *Scalzo* [1974].

Restriction (i) is obviously related to assumption (I). Its interpretation is as follows: The state equation (1) describes the change of the total amount Q_t at time $t \in [0, T]$ of the resource stock, dependent on the control functions $u_i(t)$, which are the extraction rates of the oligopolists. In addition to (i) function $f(t, x)$ can be assumed to be strictly increasing and concave with time. I.e. the initially known amount of the resource will steadily increase by exploration.

Strict concavity of $f(t, x)$ ensures the exhaustibility of the real total amount of the resource, i.e. even by exploration there will be a finite stock of the resource.

The Lipschitzian condition is obviously very mild; we only have to take the difference $L := |Q_T - Q_0|$ between the total amount Q_T known at time T and the initially known amount Q_0 as the Lipschitz constant.

The payoffs J_i of the oligopolists ($i = 1, 2, \ldots, N$) depend on the final stock $x(T) = (x_1(T), \ldots, x_N(T))$ where $x_i(t)$ is the part of the total amount Q_T at time T owned by oligopolist $i \in \{1, 2, \ldots, N\}$. If this part of the stock will be wholly exploited, one can set $g_i(x(T)) = 0$. For all other cases $g_i(x(T)) > 0$ can be interpreted as the expected profit of oligopolist i to be earned by setting $x_i(T)$.

Concavity of the functions $g(x)$, $h(t, x)$ and $s(t, u)$ makes it possible to take extraction costs into consideration. These costs will increase with decreasing amounts of the resource, as those deposits of the resource which are relatively easy to find and to explore are depleted first, and we suppose that increase of prices will be slower or even equal as increase of costs. This additional assumption can be dropped, when taking technical progress into consideration.

Assumption (vi) on the Hessian is a regularity condition convenient for optimization, and means that the change of the outputs will be "smooth". For a long-run analysis (vi) may be no strong restriction. By the same reasoning compactness and convexity of the control spaces (ii) are introduced, i.e. U_i are the closed one-dimensional intervals

$$[0, Q_t^i] \text{ with } \lim_{t \to \infty} Q_t^i = 0 \qquad \text{for all } i = 1, 2, \ldots, N;$$

the $Q_t^i = x_i(t)$ are, according to (1), the amounts of the resource belonging to oligopolist $i \in \{1, 2, \ldots, N\}$ at time $t \in [0, T]$.

3. Localisation of the Equilibrium Points

For introductory analysis we restrict ourselves to the case of a two-person game (duopoly) and use in order to compute the Nash equilibrium points an algorithm of Le Van [1980]:For this reason we have to take stronger assumptions with respect to the control functions u_i, which are continuously differentiable. Le Van used the compactness of bounded closed subsets of finite dimensional real spaces and so we choose pieces of polynomials with degree up to $n \in N$, concave on $[0, T]$ as control functions.

The set S of those polynomials is a subset of function space $P_n[a, b]$ of all polynomials with maximal degree n and with the sup-norm induced from $C[a, b]$. Further S is compact since each sequence out of $P_n[a, b]$ contains a convergent subsequence in S. This is a trivial consequence of Weierstraß Approximation Theorem. By Bolzano-Weierstraß it follows that S is closed and bounded since $P_n[a, b]$ is of finite dimension.

With the well-known definition of a Nash equilibrium point (u_1, u_2)

$$J_1(\bar{u}_1, \bar{u}_2) \geqslant J_1(u_1, \bar{u}_2) \qquad \text{for all } u_1 \in U_1$$

$$J_2(\bar{u}_1, \bar{u}_2) \geqslant J_2(\bar{u}_1, u_2) \qquad \text{for all } u_2 \in U_2$$

(3)

and defining

$$\phi_{(u_1, u_2)}(y, z) := J_1(y, u_2) + J_2(u_1, z) \tag{4}$$

we can rewrite (3)

$$\phi_{(\bar{u}_1, \bar{u}_2)}(\bar{u}_1, \bar{u}_2) = \max_{u_1, u_2} \phi_{(\bar{u}_1, \bar{u}_2)}(u_1, u_2). \tag{5}$$

Now we define

$$\psi_U(V) := \phi_U(V + U), \tag{6}$$

where $U = (u_1, u_2) \in \mathbf{R}^2$ and $V = (y, z) \in \mathbf{R}^2$. Then $\bar{U} = (u_1, u_2)$ is a Nash equilibrium point if and only if

$$\psi_{\bar{U}}(0) = \max_V \psi_{\bar{U}}(V). \tag{7}$$

To outline the algorithm of Le Van we have to give the following

Definition: Suppose D is an open bounded subset of $\mathbf{R}^n$, ∂D the boundary of $\bar{D}$, $\Phi \in C^1 (D)$ and $p \in \mathbf{R}^n$ with $p \in \Phi (\partial \bar{D})$; then the integer

$$\deg (p, \, \Phi, \, D) := \sum_{\Phi(x)=p} \text{sign} \det J_\Phi (x) \tag{8}$$

is called the topological degree of Φ with respect to p and D; $J_\Phi (x)$ is the Jacobian matrix of Φ.

The integer $\deg (p, \, \Phi, \, D)$ is finite, because the set $\Phi^{-1} (p)$ is discrete and possesses no limit in D by Implicit Function Theorem and because D is compact [*Schwartz*].

The algorithm now runs as follows:

Starting with an open bounded subset $M_0 \subset \mathbf{R}^2$, we compute the topological degree $\deg (\psi_V)$ of ψ with respect to $V = (y, z)$ and $V \in \partial M_0$, the boundary of M_0. If it is different from zero, we subdivide M_0 into M_{0i} and compute again $\deg (\psi_V)$ with $V \in \partial M_{0i}$ for all i until we find a subdivided M_{0n} with diameter as small as one likes and $\deg (\psi_V) \neq 0$, $V \in \partial M_{0n}$. Then Nash equilibria are lying in those regions M_{0n}.

4. Example

To show the working of the algorithm consider a simple example:

$$f (t, x) = Q_0 = \text{const. (no exploration)}$$

$u_i : [0, T] \rightarrow \mathbf{R}$ continuous for $i = 1,2$

$$B_i (t) = \begin{pmatrix} -1 & 0 \\ 0 & -1 \end{pmatrix} \qquad i = 1,2$$

$g (x (T)) = c_T = \text{const.}$

$h_i (t, x) = x_i (t) - x_{3-i} (t) \qquad i = 1,2$

$s_i (t, u_i) = u_i (t) \qquad i = 1,2.$

Then we have the state equation

$$\frac{dx}{dt} = Q_0 - u (t). \tag{1'}$$

The payoffs are

$$J_1 (u_1, u_2) = c_T^1 + \int_0^T (x_1 (t) - x_2 (t)) \, dt + \int_0^T u_1 (t) \, dt$$

$$J_2 (u_1, u_2) = c_T^2 + \int_0^T (x_2 (t) - x_1 (t)) \, dt + \int_0^T u_2 (t) \, dt. \tag{2'}$$

With the notation mentioned above we get

$$\phi_{(u_1,u_2)}(y, z) = C + \int_0^T (x_1 - x_2 + x_2 - x_1) \, dt + \int_0^T (u_1 + u_2 + y + z) \, dt =$$

$$= C + \int_0^T ((u_1 + y) + (u_2 + z)) \, dt. \tag{4'}$$

Hence

$$\psi_U(0) = \phi_{(u_1,u_2)}(u_1 + 0, u_2 + 0) = C + \int_0^T u_1(t) \, dt + \int_0^T u_2(t) \, dt. \tag{6'}$$

Now we have to determine regions G^i with deg $(\psi_U, 0, G^i) \neq 0$. The G^i correspond to the M_{0i} above. Following Le Van's algorithm Nash equilibria lie inside the regions G^i and they are precisely the zeros of $\psi_U(0)$.

In our simple case we are able to compute this zeros explicitly:
With

$$\psi_U(0) = C + \int_0^T u_1(t) \, dt + \int_0^T u_2(t) \, dt = 0$$

we have

$$\int_0^T u_1(t) \, dt = C - \int_0^T u_2(t) \, dt.$$

Using the state equation $(1')$ we recognize

$$x_2(t) = q_2 T - \int_0^T u_2(t) \, dt$$

and hence

$$\int_0^T u_1(t) \, dt = \tilde{C} + x_2(t).$$

Now, using again the state equation $(1')$, we finally have

$$\frac{d}{dt} \int_0^t u_1(s) \, ds = u_1(t) = q_2 - u_2(t) \qquad t \in [0, T]. \tag{7'}$$

5. Concluding Remarks

From $(7')$ one can see that the extraction rate of, say, player 1 is just the difference between the amount of the resource belonging to player 2 and the extraction rate of player 2. I.e. the faster the one of the oligopolists will deplete his part of the total amount of the resource the slower the other one will do so at any instant of time.

Obviously this is the only result which makes sense by the given assumptions. Since it is realized by using the above algorithm, this could be a feasible computational approach for determining optimal price or extraction paths, also when taking into account the extraction costs, technical progress, or demand functions which make more sense.

240

References

Friedman, A.: Differential Games. New York 1971.

Hoel, M.: Resource Extraction Under Some Alternative Market Structures. Meisenheim am Glan 1978.

Le Van, C.: Topological Degree of a Family of Convex Functions and Localization of Nash Equilibrium Points. J. Opt. Theory Appl. **30** (1), 1980, 33–44.

Scalzo, R.C.: Existence of Equilibrium Points in N-Person Differential Games. Differential Games and Control Theory. Ed. by Roxin, Liu, Sternberger. New York 1974, 125–140.

Schwartz, J.T.: Nonlinear Functional Analysis. New York 1969.

Stiglitz, J.E.: Monopoly and the Rate of Extraction of Exhaustible Resources. Amer. Econ. Rev. **66** (4), 1976, 655–661.

Economic Theory of Natural Resources. ©Physica-Verlag, Würzburg–Wien, 1982.

Information and Payoffs in Auction Games

Urs Schweizer and *Thomas von Ungern-Sternberg*[1])

This paper develops a simple model of auctions where bidders are uncertain about the true value of the object they bid for. Auctions are considered as noncooperative games. Special attention is paid to the question how the payoffs of players change with the quality of the information available to them. This allows one to get some idea about the incentives which lead potential bidders to invest in exploratory activity.

1. Introduction

A wide variety of goods is sold by *sealed bid auctions*. These are organized in the following way: Each interested party submits a sealed bid. The object is awarded to the highest bidder at a price equal to the value of his bid. A particularly important example of objects being sold by such auctions are the rights to extract crude oil from a given tract of land.

A few empirical facts about such auctions give some idea of the structure of the problem:

Firstly, the sums involved are quite important. *Hughart* [1975] reports, that the Department of the Interior estimated the price of a 'typical' tract in the Gulf of Mexico in 1972 at 10 million dollars. Prices must have risen even further since then.

Secondly, the degree of uncertainty about the value of a tract must be considerable. Even companies having essentially the same exploration results arrive at substantially different bids for the same tract. The ratio of the highest to the lowest bid for a given tract often exceeds 10:1, and even ratios of 100:1 have been observed [see *Capen/Clapp/Campbell*]. In the period 1954–1970, 1602 tracts were leased on the Outer Continental Shelf. By mid–1971, 680 of these leases had been allowed to expire without extraction [see *Hughart*].

Thirdly, large sums are spent on exploration. For each tract he won, a typical bidder on the Outer Continental Shelf did exploratory geophysical work on five tracts at a total cost of $ 800.000 [see *Hughart*]. The results of this exploration are the data, on which the bidder bases his offer. They are, of course, carefully hidden from other competitors.

These facts indicate, that one would like a model of the leasing process to have the following characteristics:

– The uncertainty about the value a tract has for the ultimate buyer must be explicitly taken into account.

---

[1]) The authors want to thank Martin Hellwig for helpful discussions.

- The interactions resulting from the bidding strategies of the participants should be examined.
- One would like to obtain some understanding of the interactions between the bidding process on one hand, and exploratory activity on the other.

Wilson [1977], *Case* [1979] and *Milgrom* [1979] among others, give useful insights into some of these problems. This paper differs from previous work mainly in the fact, that it tries to explicitly examine how the bidders' expected profits are affected by the quality of the information available to them. It turns out, that aggregate expected profits fall, as the quality of information increases. Thus it is mainly the seller who gains, when all the participants try to obtain more precise information about the true value of a tract. Nevertheless, any single bidder can increase his expected profit by obtaining an informational advantage over his competitors.

These results are derived under quite restrictive assumptions. Though care must be exercised in applying them to more general situations, we believe, that the following analysis does give some feeling for the type of results one may expect in more realistic situations.

2. The Model

Consider a tract on, say, the Outer Continental Shelf. The amount of petroleum it contains is unknown to the bidders at the time they place their offers. The best they can do is to use geographical survey results and other prior information (such as the yield on adjacent tracts) to form an estimate on which they base their bid.

We shall model this situation as follows: Denote by V the true but unknown value of the tract. Each bidder i, $i = 1, \ldots, N$ obtains a noisy signal about this true value. On the basis of this signal he forms an estimate E_i. This estimate is a random variable. We shall assume that the E_i's are *unbiased estimates of V*, whose distribution depends only on the true value of V, and they can be written as a product $E_i = \epsilon_i V$, where ϵ_i is a random variable independent of V. The ϵ_i's of the players are *independently distributed*. Thus for any real number t, the probability that $E_i \leq Vt$ is a function only of t, and does not depend on other bidders' estimates. This formalisation of the problem is very similar to that of *Capen/Clapp/Campbell* [1971].

What can we learn from this model about the structure of the problem? Assume for the moment, that there is only one bidder. When he places a bid equal to his estimate of the true value of the tract, his expected profit will be zero. This follows from the assumption, that his estimate is unbiased.

Will this result continue to hold, when there is more than one bidder? If several bidders form independent estimates of the true value of the tract, and each places a bid equal to his estimate, can the winner still expect to just break even? The answer is no. The highest bid is placed by the bidder with the highest estimate, and he is likely to having overestimated the true value. When several players place bids equal to their estimate of the true value of the tract, they all have to expect negative profits. This phenomenon has been aptly named the "winner's curse" [see *Case*]. A rational bidder has to be aware of this phenomenon. He will react by submitting only bids which lie below his estimate of the true value.

Auctions can be regarded as games of which the bidders are the players. The expected profit of these players is their pay-off, and their strategy is the choice of a function, which relates the amount of money offered to their estimate of the true value of the tract.

In the following, we examine a simple specification of the auction game. First, it is assumed that the estimates E_i of all players are uniformly distributed around the true value V, i.e. that the ϵ_i's are uniformly distributed around one. V is assumed positive. Denote by $[1 - A_i, 1 + A_i]$ the interval over which ϵ_i is uniformly distributed. We shall say that the quality of player i's information has improved, when A_i falls. Only values of A_i such that $0 \leqslant A_i \leqslant 1$ are considered. Put differently, only positive estimates are formed. The cumulative frequency distributions $F_i(t)$ of the ϵ_i's are given by

$$
F_i(t) = \begin{cases} 0 & \text{for } t \leqslant 1 - A_i \\[2mm] \dfrac{t + A_i - 1}{2A_i} & \text{for } (1 - A_i) \leqslant t \leqslant (1 + A_i) \\[2mm] 1 & \text{for } (1 + A_i) \leqslant t. \end{cases}
$$

Secondly, we assume that the players' choice is confined to a simple set of bidding strategies. Each player i places a bid equal to some *constant* fraction λ_i of his *estimate* E_i. The strategy set is thus reduced to the one dimensional set of real numbers between zero and 1 [compare *Case*].

For given values $\lambda_1, \ldots, \lambda_N$ of the players' strategy variables, player i's expected profit is given by

$$
\Pi_i = V \int (1 - s) \prod_{j \neq i} F_j \left(\frac{s}{\lambda_j} \right) F_i' \left(\frac{s}{\lambda_i} \right) \frac{ds}{\lambda_i}. \tag{1}
$$

(For the derivation of this equation see *Case* [1979, p. 80ff.].)

One can easily see from (1), that while the pay-offs of the game depend on the unknown value V, the optimal strategies do not. The scope of this paper is limited to the derivation and analysis of the properties of *non-cooperative* solutions of the game. A Nash equilibrium is defined as a situation in which no player can increase his expected profit by changing his λ_i, given that the other players keep their λ_j, $j \neq i$, constant. We consider, first, the case where all players' information is of the same quality and then the case, where two players with asymmetric information participate in the game.

2.1 The Symmetric Case

We begin with the situation, where all players have equally good information, i.e. $A_1 = \ldots = A_N = A$. A symmetric Nash equilibrium can be shown to exist, where all players choose to bid the same fraction λ^* of their estimate. Rather tedious computations lead to the following equation:

$$
\lambda^* = (N + 1) \, \frac{N + (N - 2) A}{(N^2 - N + 2) A^2 + 2 (N^2 - 1) A + N (N + 1)}. \tag{2}
$$

Moreover, it can be shown that

$$\lambda^* (1 + A) < 1 \tag{3}$$

and that the expected profit $\Pi_i^* = \Pi^*$ of each player is given by

$$\Pi^* = V (1 + A) \frac{1 - \lambda^* (1 + A)}{2 A}. \tag{4}$$

This equilibrium has the following interesting features:

First, it follows from (3) and (4) that $\Pi^* > 0$. Even in the absence of collusion, the expected profit of each player is positive.

Second, remember that $V (1 + A)$ is the maximum estimate a player derives for a tract of value V, i.e. $E_i \leqslant V (1 + A)$. It then follows from (3) that $\lambda^* E_i < V$ for each player i. Even though players do not cooperate, no bidder will ever place an offer exceeding the true value of the tract. This result crucially depends on the assumption, that the distribution of the estimators does not have a long tail end. For other stochastic environments it may well be the case, that players make losses with positive probability.

These first two results can be made plausible by a simple intuitive explanation: By choosing a value of $\lambda_i \leqslant 1/(1 + A_i)$, each player can ensure that he never has to pay more than the true value. For any reasonable bidding strategy of his opponents, he knows he will win, if they all grossly underestimate the true value of the tract. They will do so with positive probability. This establishes, that each player's expected profit must always be positive. The optimum value of λ_i is determined by the following trade-off:

As λ_i rises, the chance of winning the tract increases. On the other hand, the profits made in those situations, where he would have won even with a lower value of λ_i, fall. Third, it follows from (2) and (4), that

$$\lim_{N \to \infty} \lambda^* = \frac{1}{(1 + A)} \quad \text{and} \quad \lim_{N \to \infty} N \Pi^* = 0.$$

This is a result similar to the ones *Wilson* [1977] and *Milgrom* [1979] prove for more general auction games. As the number of participants in an auction increases, the value of the highest offer converges to the true value of the tract, and aggregate expected profits of all players tend to zero. The crucial assumption leading to this result is the independence of the players' estimates. As the number of players increases, the probability of some of them overestimating the true value of a tract by a factor close to $(1 + A)$ rises. The players who form this overestimate will be the winners of the auction. Competition among them forces them to choose values of λ close to $1/(1 + A)$.

Fourth, for any given number of bidders, a decrease in A leads to an increase in λ^* and to a decrease in expected profits Π^*. More precisely, it follows from (2) and (4) that $\lim_{A \to 0} \lambda^* = 1$ and $\lim_{A \to 0} \Pi^* = 0$. An *increase* in the quality of the information available to all players (a decrease in A) leads to a *higher* fraction of the estimates being bid, and a lower level of expected profits. In the limit, when information becomes perfect, profits will be zero, a result similar to that in *Vickrey* [1961].

This last result raises the following question: If expected profits decrease, as the quality of information improves, why do bidders typically spend so much on exploration to reduce the degree of uncertainty? The answer, of course, is simple: While the expected profits of all players fall when the quality of the information available to each of them improves, nevertheless, any single player can hope to increase his expected profit by obtaining an informational advantage over his competitors.

This can be illustrated as follows: Imagine that the quality of information of players $2, \ldots, N$ remains unchanged at A, and that they bid the same fraction λ^* of their estimate. Player 1, can, if the quality of his information increases from A to $(A - \Delta A)$, choose to bid a fraction $(\lambda + \Delta\lambda)$ of his estimate, such that $(\lambda^* + \Delta\lambda)(A - \Delta A) = \lambda^*A$.

Rather lengthy computations show that, by doing so, his profit will increase by

$$\Delta\Pi = V \frac{1 - \lambda^*(1 + A)}{2A^2} \Delta A. \tag{5}$$

The choice to fix the new λ_1 at $(\lambda^* + \Delta\lambda)$ is *not*, of course, an optimal strategy, but if profits can be increased by pursuing a suboptimal strategy, they will rise even more, when the optimal strategy is chosen. Thus we have established, that, when the other players' strategies are held fixed, each player can increase his expected profit, when better information becomes available to him.

In a more general model, where both, the λ's and the A's, are choice variables under the control of the players, we may expect the following type of situation: Each player has an incentive to improve the quality of his information beyond that of his competitors. He will do so, even if there are costs associated with acquiring this additional information. All he requires is that the expected benefits derived from the informational advantage exceed the costs. When all players participate in this race for better information, their aggregate profits fall for two reasons: First, they have all spent resources on exploration, and, second, as a result of this additional information, competition among the players will force them to choose higher values of λ. The pay-off, when winning the tract, falls accordingly.

One is familiar with this type of situation from the R+D literature. The fact, that there is a huge prize to be won for being the first to invent a cost reducing technology does not imply, that those investing in R+D can expect to make high profits. The race to be first may lead to situations, where all firms choose cost − intensive research strategies. Expected profits are reduced accordingly. In the case of the auction game, there is an additional twist to this story. The players spend resources in their efforts to procure themselves an informational advantage. It is the seller, who reaps the fruit of these efforts in the form of the higher price he receives.

2.2 Informational Asymmetry

In order to examine in more detail, how an informational advantage affects pay-offs and bidding strategies, we attempted to explicitly calculate Nash equilibria for auction games, where different players have different qualities of information. Unfortunately, these calculations turned out to become quite complex, so we limited ourselves to the case, where there are only two bidders. For notational convenience we introduce $A = A_1$, $B = A_2, \lambda = \lambda_1, \mu = \lambda_2, \Pi = \Pi_1$ and $\rho = \Pi_2$. To fix ideas, we assume that

$$A > B. \tag{6}$$

The first player is always the one, whose information is of lesser quality. The Nash equilibrium (λ^*, μ^*) which, of course, is no longer symmetric, can be shown to exist. Rather lengthy calculations lead to the following system of equations

$$\lambda = \sqrt{\frac{2\mu}{(1+A)^2} \left[1 - \mu \frac{B^2+3}{6}\right]} \tag{7}$$

$$\mu = \frac{3}{2(3+B^2)} \left[(1-A)\lambda + 1\right]. \tag{8}$$

Equation (7) gives player 1's optimal choice of λ, given that player 2 has chosen μ. Similarly, equation (8) gives player 2's optimal choice of μ, given that player 1 has chosen λ. These reaction functions are valid only if

$$\lambda(1-A) \leq \mu(1-B) < \mu(1+B) \leq \lambda(1+A). \tag{9}$$

The Nash equilibrium is given as the simultaneous solution of equations (7) and (8). Note that condition (9) will always hold at equilibrium.

Turning now to the profit functions, it can be shown that, as long as (9) holds, the first players' optimal strategy will lead to

$$\Pi = V(1+A) \frac{1 - \lambda(1+A)}{2A}. \tag{10}$$

Equation (10) gives the first player's pay-off, provided he has adjusted his λ such that $\partial \Pi / \partial \lambda = 0$. Similarly for player 2, when μ is chosen such that $\partial \rho / \partial \mu = 0$, then

$$\rho = \frac{V}{2A} \left(A - 1 + \frac{B^2+3}{3} \frac{\mu^2}{\lambda}\right). \tag{11}$$

Equations (7)–(11) give a full description of the Nash equilibrium in the two bidder case with different quality of information. Unfortunately, the analytical handeling of these equations proves rather complicated.

Looking at equations (7) and (8) one notes that each player's strategy depends on the quality of the other player's information. Each player is thus interested not only in the results of the other player's exploration. Even information about the precision of the results is of value.

Substituting the uniform probability distributions into (1) reveals that, if λ is an optimal reply to μ, we must have $\lambda(1+A) < 1$. Similarly, if μ is an optimal reply to λ, then $\mu(1+B) < 1$. Again, no player will ever place a bid exceeding the true value of the tract.

A further result can be derived from the reaction functions (7) and (8). Denote the right hand sides of (7) and (8) by $L(A, B, \mu)$ and $M(A, B, \lambda)$, respectively. The signs of the partial derivatives of these functions are given by

$$\frac{\partial L}{\partial A} < 0, \quad \frac{\partial L}{\partial B} < 0, \quad \frac{\partial L}{\partial \mu} > 0$$

and

$$\frac{\partial M}{\partial A} < 0, \quad \frac{\partial M}{\partial B} < 0, \quad \frac{\partial M}{\partial \lambda} > 0.$$

Moreover, one can easily check that

$$\frac{\partial L}{\partial \mu} \frac{\partial M}{\partial \lambda} < 1.$$

The equilibrium values of λ and μ are given by the system

$$\lambda^* = L\,(A, B, \mu^*) \quad \text{and} \quad \mu^* = M\,(A, B, \lambda^*).$$

Differentiation of this system and making use of the signs of the partial derivatives, leads to the following comparative statics result:

$$d\lambda^* = (-)\,dA + (-)\,dB$$

and   (12)

$$d\mu^* = (-)\,dA + (-)\,dB.$$

In other words, no matter who receives better information, both players will, in the new equilibrium, bid higher fractions of their estimates. Unfortunately, this result does not by itself allow us to say anything about changes in expected profits. Indeed, while increases in λ and μ would suggest, that expected profits fall, a reduction in A or B implies, that one of the players will no longer overestimate the true value of a tract by as much as he did before. To see what effect changes in the quality of information have on the equilibrium level of expected profits, we have to resort to a numerical example.

In Table 1, the equilibrium values of λ^* and of expected profits Π^* of player 1 are listed for different combinations of qualities of information A and B. Since the game is antisymmetric, the corresponding values for player 2 can be inferred from Table 1 as well. More precisely, the second player's expected profit, when the qualities of player 1's and player 2's information are given by A and B respectively, is equal to the first player's expected profit for the case, where the qualities of player 1's and player 2's information are given by B and A.

Table 1 confirms a number of results that were previously derived:
- Relation (9) does indeed hold at equilibrium.
- One observes that $\lambda^*\,(1 + A) < 1$ and $\mu^*\,(1 + B) < 1$.
- The comparative statics results (12) are correct. Both, λ^* and μ^*, fall as A or B rises.
- In the symmetric case $A = B$, expected profits decrease with an increase in the quality of information.

Some further results can be read off:
- Starting off from a symmetric situation, $A = B$, any decrease in A, i.e. an improvement in the quality of the first player's information, leads to an increase of his expected profit, even when all the adjustment processes have taken place. Equilibrium adjustment does not reverse the sign given by equation (5).
- Similarly, a decrease in B, i.e. an improvement in the quality of the other player's information, leads to a decrease of the first player's expected profits. This result can be easily derived from equation (10).

The only really surprising result can be read off, as we move from the diagonal to the right in Table 1. Such a move corresponds to a reduction in the quality of the first player's information. For values $B \leqslant 0.7$ such a move will lead to an *increase* of player 1's expected profit. In other words, a *decrease* in the quality of one player's information, can,

B \ A		0	.1	.2	.3	.4	.5	.6	.7	.8	.9	1
0	λ^*	1.00	.905	.821	.747	.682	.626	.577	.534	.496	.463	.433
	Π^*	0	47	89	125	156	183	205	224	241	255	268
.1	λ^*	.907	.904	.820	.746	.681	.625	.576	.533	.495	.462	.432
	Π^*	95	66	99	133	162	187	209	228	245	259	271
.2	λ^*	.828	.825	.815	.742	.678	.622	.573	.530	.493	.460	.430
	Π^*	179	167	130	155	180	202	222	240	255	268	279
.3	λ^*	.761	.758	.750	.735	.672	.616	.568	.526	.489	.456	.427
	Π^*	254	247	226	191	209	226	243	258	271	283	293
.4	λ^*	.705	.702	.694	.681	.664	.609	.561	.520	.483	.451	.422
	Π^*	319	315	301	278	248	259	272	283	294	304	312
.5	λ^*	.657	.654	.647	.635	.619	.600	.553	.512	.476	.444	.416
	Π^*	377	374	364	348	326	300	307	315	322	329	336
.6	λ^*	.615	.613	.606	.596	.581	.564	.543	.503	.468	.437	.409
	Π^*	427	425	418	406	390	370	348	351	355	359	363
.7	λ^*	.580	.578	.572	.562	.549	.532	.514	.493	.459	.428	.401
	Π^*	472	470	464	455	443	428	411	391	391	393	394
.8	λ^*	.550	.548	.542	.533	.521	.505	.488	.469	.449	.419	.393
	Π^*	511	510	505	498	489	477	463	448	431	429	428
.9	λ^*	.523	.521	.516	.508	.496	.482	.466	.448	.429	.410	.384
	Π^*	546	545	542	536	528	519	567	495	481	467	463
1	λ^*	.500	.498	.493	.485	.475	.462	.446	.430	.412	.394	.375
	Π^*	577	575	574	569	563	555	546	535	524	512	500

Tab. 1: Equilibrium values of player 1 for different informational structures. $V = 2000$ has been assumed as the true value of the object being auctioned.

after the adjustment of the strategy variables to their new equilibrium, lead to an *increase* in this player's expected profit.

At first glance, this result may seem counterintuitive. Remember, however, the result of section 2.1, which establishes, that aggregate expected profits of the bidders rise, as their uncertainty increases. When only one player's uncertainty increases, the corresponding increase in aggregate profits may be distributed in two ways: Either one player loses and the other gains. This occurs for values of $B > 0.7$. Or both players stand to win by the increase in aggregate profits. This is the case for values of $B \leqslant 0.7$.

If the quality of the information available to each player is endogenously determined, player 2 may now adopt the following strategy. If he is first to explore the tract, he may invest enough into obtaining precise information about its yield, that player 1 realises, he can only reduce his expected profits, were he also to invest in exploratory activity. Player 2 will make large expected profits, while player 1, with little information, places a low bid, which has a low probability of winning. Player 2 can effectively preempt player 1. This is a phenomenon one is well acquainted with from the R+D literature.

3. Conclusion

This paper develops a simple model of sealed-bid auctions, where buyers are uncertain about the true value of the object they are bidding for. The chosen form of the stochastic environment enables us to derive explicit solutions for the auction game. Special attention is paid to the question, how the pay-offs of the players change as functions of the information available. While all the results are shown to be strictly valid only under the assumptions of our simple model, we believe, that at least some of them can be generalised to more complicated and more realistic set-ups.

We briefly touched upon the question of why so much money is spent on exploration, which has the effect of reducing the uncertainty about the object's true value. While our results do shed some light on the structure of the problem, a more formal study of this aspect of the problem seems to be indicated.

The whole analysis is framed in terms of auctions for the rights to extract mineral deposits. Similar structures will emerge for other auctions, such as those for the right to fulfill a construction contract.

References

Capen, E.C., R.V. Clapp, and *W.M. Campbell*: Competitive Bidding in High-Risk Situations. Journal of Petroleum Economics, 1971, 641–653.

Case, J.H.: Economics and the Competitive Process. New York 1979.

Hughart, D.: Informational Asymmetry, Bidding Strategies, and the Marketing of Offshore Petroleum Leases. Journal of Political Economy 83 (5), 1975, 969–986.

Milgrom, P.R.: A Convergence Theorem for Competitive Bidding with Differential Information. Econometrica 47 (3), 1979, 679–688.

Vickrey, W.: Counter Speculations, Auctions and Competitive Sealed Tenders. Journal of Finance 16, 1961, 8–37.

Wilson, R.: A Bidding Model of Perfect Competition. The Review of Economic Studies 44 (3), 1977, 511–518.

Economic Theory of Natural Resources. ©Physica-Verlag, Würzburg–Wien, 1982.

Coordination of Optimal Exploitation Policies
for Natural Resources

Siegfried Trautmann

The purpose of this paper is two-fold: (1) a brief review of different coordination concepts in a unifying framework and (2) derivation of coordination methods for time-continuously formulated problems of natural resource management.

Coordination problems in the context of natural resource management arise, if the exploitation decisions in an economic system are decentralized among several decision-makers which agree to co-ordinate their decisions such that an overall goal beside the local ones is maximized. This may hold for sectors (fishery, forestry) of a macroeconomy and for decentrally organized firms where the property rights to natural resources rest with the state and the firm respectively.

This paper examines the coordinability of exploitation policies by means of transfer prices (like, e.g., royalties) and allocated quotas. Moreover, it is shown that coordination usually requires the announcement of transfer prices which depend on the extent of the resource transfer.

1. Introduction

In the economic literature modern control theory is more and more being applied for solving problems of natural resource management. A simple kind of such a management problem is, for instance, the optimal extraction of a *single* resource which is owned by a *single* decision maker. The essence of such an optimization problem is a differential equation of the form

$$\frac{dx}{dt} = f(x) - u(t) \tag{1.1}$$

where

$x(t)$ is the size of the resource stock at time t
$f(x)$ is the rate of natural growth
$u(t)$ is the rate of extraction.

This differential equation (1.1) describes the controlled stock evolution and reduces to

$$\frac{dx}{dt} = -u(t) \tag{1.1'}$$

if the considered resource is a *nonrenewable* (exhaustible) one, which growth rate is identical to zero. Now, the typical problem is to optimize some objective functional subject to (1.1) or (1.1') and the additional extraction rate restriction

$$u^{min} \leqslant u(t) \leqslant u^{max}. \tag{1.2}$$

A very popular and simple objective is the maximization of the total discounted extraction as described by the following expression

$$G(u) = \int_0^\infty e^{-kt} u(t) \, dt \qquad (1.3)$$

where k is a suitable chosen discount factor.

The solution of this optimal control problem can be very easily obtained by means of the *maximum principle* of *Pontrjagin* and is shown in Figure 1

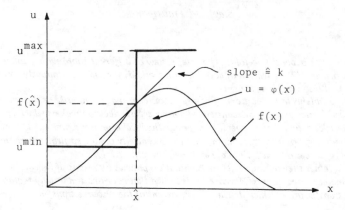

Fig. 1: Optimal extraction policy of a discounted renewable resource

As one can see, there is an optimal (equilibrium) resource stock level $\hat{x}$ which is essentially determined by the discount factor k. The thick line in Figure 1 corresponds to a *bang-bang* control policy, namely if

$x < \hat{x}$ the minimum extraction rate u^{min} is applied, while if
$x > \hat{x}$ the resource is exploited at the maximum rate u^{max}.

The optimal extraction policy $\hat{u} = \varphi(x)$ is therefore a combination of *bang-bang* and *singular* ($\hat{u} = f(\hat{x})$ if $x = \hat{x}$) controls.

Problems of this kind have been extended and modified in many different ways [see *Clark*, 1976; *Dasgupta/Heal*; *Kemp/Long*]. In the case of renewable resources a rather complex extension of the basic *production-exploitation-model* (1.1) is obtained, if age structured ecosystems and/or biological and economic interactions between several exploited populations are considered [see *Clark*, 1976, 256–335].

Most problems, however, have been formulated in *global* terms, with no allowance for the possibility that the exploitation decisions for natural resources are decentralized among *several* decision-makers in an economic system. Such a more realistic situation in which the objective functions of the decision-makers may be mutually conflicting, has for example recently been analysed by *Clark* [1980, 117–132] in the context of fisheries economics and by *Chiarella* [1980, 219–246] in the context of trade between resource-poor and resource-rich economies. In both papers the problem is formulated as a *noncooperative differential game* which solution satisfies the *Nash-Cournot* equilibrium conditions.

Now, in this paper we will concentrate on economic systems, in which all decision-makers exploiting and processing a certain natural resource agree to *coordinate* their decisions, such that a *global* objective functional beside the *local* ones is maximized. Thereby the coordination is achieved by means of a supremal coordinating agency which task consists in announcing royalties and/or allocated quotas for the natural resources to be exploited. Such a planning scheme corresponds to a large firm with full property rights to certain natural resources which planning and decision process is decentralized among several decision-centers. Its application is also imaginable to sectors (like fishery, forestry) of a competitive macro-economy, where the property rights to natural resources rest with the state. In this case the state, as a supremal coordinating agency, is probably interested in influencing the exploitation and processing decisions of independent firms such that a global goal, like the national income of the corresponding sector, is maximized.

In the next section we briefly review different coordination concepts in a unifying framework as developed in *Trautmann* [1981]. In section 3 we examine the coordinability of exploitation policies by means of transfer prices and allocated quotas.

2. Fundamental Coordination Concepts

We start our presentation with a very general formalization of the centralized decision problem of the underlying economic system, called *overall problem* which is partitioned into so-called *infimal subproblems* of the independent decision-makers. Subsequently the notion *coordinability* is introduced and several *coordination principles* and *coordination modes* are discussed.

The centralized decision problem of the economic system under consideration which is denoted by $\mathcal{D}$, may be written as follows:

$$\mathcal{D}: \left. \begin{array}{l} G(y) \to \text{Max} \\ P(y) = 0 \\ y \in \bar{Y} \subset Y \end{array} \right\} \tag{2.1}$$

where $P: Y \to \Lambda$ is an operator describing the consequences of the decisions within the economic system; and $G: Y \to \mathbf{R}$ an objective functional valuating the decisions over an finite planning horizon. Y and Λ are real and normed vector spaces, $\bar{Y}$ is a subset of Y, which elements $y \in \bar{Y}$ represent all possible (or weak-feasible, but not feasible!) decisions within the system. The chosen formulation of the problem includes thereby both time-discretely and time-continuously formulated models. If, for instance, the overall problem is time-discrete and linear, then we have

$$Y = \mathbf{R}^{n+m}, \bar{Y} = \mathbf{R}_+^{n+m}, G(y) = c^T x, P(y) = Ay - b$$

where $y = \binom{x}{u}$ is the vector of decision and slack variables, $c \in \mathbf{R}^n$, $b \in \mathbf{R}^m$ vectors and A a matrix of suitable dimension.

For such a planning problem, characterized by the 5-tupel $(Y, \bar{Y}, \Lambda, G, P)$, we use the notions defined in the following

Definition 2.1: The activity level $y^0 \in Y$ for the planning problem $(Y, \bar{Y}, \Lambda, G, P)$ is called

possible
(weak feasible)   : $\Leftrightarrow y^0 \in \bar{Y}$
feasible   : $\Leftrightarrow y^0 \in \bar{Y} \wedge P(y^0) = 0$
optimal   : $\Leftrightarrow y^0$ is feasible $\wedge\ G(y^0) \geqslant G(y)$ for all feasible y

sub-optimal
(local optimal)   : $\Leftrightarrow$ There exists a neighbourhood $U(y^0)$ of y^0, such that y^0 is optimal for the problem $(Y, \bar{Y} \cap U(y^0), \Lambda, G, P)$

optimal solution : $\Leftrightarrow y^0$ is optimal
sub-solution   : $\Leftrightarrow y^0$ is sub-optimal
epsilon-solution : $\Leftrightarrow y^0$ is feasible and there exists a $\epsilon > 0$ with
                      $G(y^0) + \epsilon \geqslant \sup\{G(y) \mid P(y) = 0 \wedge y \in \bar{Y}\}$

pseudo-solution   : $\Leftrightarrow y^0$ is optimal for a problem where $P(y^0) = 0$ is weakened to
                      $\|P(y^0)\| \leqslant \delta, \delta > 0$. Thereby $\|\cdot\|$ denotes the norm defined in the space Y.

For small and convex planning problems a decision-maker tries, of course, to find the optimal solutions whereas it may be reasonable to *accept* sub-solutions, epsilon-solutions and pseudo-solutions, if the problems are complex with respect to the extent and the mathematical structure. The latter holds especially in the case of mixed-integer and other nonconvex planning problems. Therefore we denote every $y \in \hat{Y}$, which is acceptable in the above sense, as a solution of the overall problem $\mathcal{D}$. $\hat{Y}$ is called the set of *acceptable solutions* of problem $\mathcal{D}$.

However, to continue with the coordination approach, suppose the decisions in the underlying economic system are decentralized among $(N + 1)$ decision-sectors $i = 0, \ldots, N$ and the supremal coordinating agency C. The planning problem of each decision-sector i $(i = 0, \ldots, N)$ is denoted by $\mathcal{D}_i(\gamma_i)$ and can be stated in correspondence to the global problem (2.1) as

$$\mathcal{D}_i(\gamma_i) : \quad G_i(z_i, \gamma_i) \to \text{Max} \tag{2.2}$$

$$P_i(z_i) = 0$$

$$z_i \in \bar{Z}_i(\gamma_i) \subset Z_i = Y_i \times V_i$$

where the space Y_i is a subspace of $Y = Y_C \times Y_0 \times \ldots \times Y_N$. The elements y_i of the space Y_i represent the activity levels concerning decision-sector i in the centralized problem (2.1), while V_i is the space of *coupling variables* v_i representing the extent of *interactions* between decision-sector i and the other sectors. The influence of the supremal coordinating agency C on the infimal decision-sector i and its optimal solution $\hat{z}_i \in \hat{Z}_i(\gamma_i)$ is described by the so-called *prospective index* γ_i $(i = 0, \ldots, N)$.

The infimal decision problem $\mathcal{D}_i(\gamma_i)$ can be parameterized by the announced prospective index γ_i $(i = 0, \ldots, N)$ according to the formulation (2.2) in essentially two ways: one way, referred to as the *goal coordination* mode, consists of modifying the objective functional of $\mathcal{D}_i$ (γ_i). In this case the prospective index γ_i is a *transfer price system*, denoted by π_i, and (2.2) can be specialized to

$$\mathcal{D}_i(\pi_i): \quad G_i(z_i, \pi_i) \to \text{Max} \tag{2.3}$$

$$P_i(z_i) = 0$$

$$z_i \in \bar{Z}_i \subset Z_i = Y_i \times V_i.$$

Such a coordination mode is also called *dual coordination*, because the transfer price system π_i can be identified with dual solution values or is at least influenced by such values.

The other way involves changing the model of $\mathcal{D}_i$ (γ_i) by fixing the extent of interactions v_i.[1]) Such a mode is therefore called *model coordination* (or *primal coordination*). It includes the budgeting and rationing mechanisms, which are prevailing in many economic systems and (2.2) can be replaced by the formulation

$$\mathcal{D}_i(v_i): \quad G_i(z_i) \to \text{Max} \tag{2.4}$$

$$P_i(z_i) = 0$$

$$z_i \in \bar{Z}_i(v_i) = \bar{Y}_i \times \{v_i\}$$

where

$$Z_i = Y_i \times V_i, \qquad Y = Y_C \times Y_0 \times \ldots \times Y_N, \bar{Y}_i \subset Y_i$$

$$v_i = K_i(y) \in V_i, v = (v_C, v_0, \ldots, v_N) = K(y)$$

$$K_i(y): Y_C \times Y_0 \times \ldots \times Y_{i-1} \times Y_{i+1} \times \ldots \times Y_N \to V_i.$$

If both coordination modes are combined, called *mixed coordination* throughout the paper, then the prospective index γ_i includes π_i and v_i ($\gamma_i = (\pi_i, v_i)$) and the corresponding planning problem reads

$$\mathcal{D}_i(\pi_i, v_i): \quad G_i(z_i, \pi_i) \to \text{Max} \tag{2.5}$$

$$P_i(z_i) = 0$$

$$z_i \in \bar{Z}_i(v_i) = \bar{Y}_i \times \{v_i\}.$$

The decision problem of the supremal coordinating agency, on the other hand, can be stated as

$\mathcal{D}_C$: Find for each infimal planning problem $\mathcal{D}_i$ a prospective index γ_i and for the own (possibly existing) decision-sector an optimal policy $\hat{z}_C \in \hat{Z}_C$, which meet

---

[1]) For the sake of a clear presentation we don't consider the modification of the operator P_i itself, as it is done in a method proposed in *Trautmann* [1981, 115–120].

the following conditions:

I) $\hat{Z}_i(\gamma_i) \neq \emptyset$ for $i = 0, \ldots, N$

II) $pr_Y(\hat{z}) = \hat{y} \in \hat{Y}$ for each

$$\hat{z} \in \hat{Z}_C \times \hat{Z}_0(\gamma_0) \times \hat{Z}_1(\gamma_1) \times \ldots \times \hat{Z}_N(\gamma_N).$$

Stated both conditions in words, the parameter $\gamma = (\gamma_0, \ldots, \gamma_N)$ and the optimal policy $\hat{z}_C$ must be such that, in the first place, each infimal subproblem has a solution; and, in the second place, that the optimal policies $\hat{z}_C, \hat{z}_0, \hat{z}_1, \ldots, \hat{z}_N$ determined by decentralized decision-making are at least acceptable for a single decision-maker. In order to compare a centralized solution $\hat{y}$ with a decentralized solution $\hat{z} = (\hat{z}_C, \hat{z}_0, \hat{z}_1, \ldots, \hat{z}_N)$ we have only to eliminate the coupling variables $\hat{v}_C, \hat{v}_0, \hat{v}_1, \ldots, \hat{v}_N$ in the latter solution. Formally this is done by means of the projection mapping $pr_Y : Z \to Y$, which projects the elements of the space Z into the space Y.

Now, we are able to introduce the notion of *coordinability* of the two-level planning system $(\mathcal{D}_C, \widetilde{\mathcal{D}}(\gamma))$, where $\widetilde{\mathcal{D}}(\gamma)$ denotes the composition of the infimal planning problems: $\widetilde{\mathcal{D}}(\gamma) = (\mathcal{D}_0(\gamma_0), \mathcal{D}_1(\gamma), \ldots, \mathcal{D}_N(\gamma_N))$.

Definition 2.2: A two-level planning system $(\mathcal{D}_C, \widetilde{\mathcal{D}}(\gamma))$ is called *coordinable* with respect to the overall problem $\mathcal{D}$, if there *exists* a prospective index $\gamma = (\gamma_0, \gamma_1, \ldots, \gamma_N)$ which is *determinable* by solving a suitable coordination problem $\mathcal{D}_C$, meeting the conditions

I) $\hat{Z}_i(\gamma_i) \neq \emptyset$ for $i = 0, \ldots, N$

II) $pr_Y(\hat{z}) = \hat{y} \in \hat{Y}$ for each
$$\hat{z} \in \hat{Z}_C \times \hat{Z}_0(\gamma_0) \times \hat{Z}_1(\gamma_1) \times \ldots \times \hat{Z}_N(\gamma_N).$$

As distinguished from the coordinability concepts developed by *Mesarovic/Macko/ Takahara* [1970] and *Jennergren* [1974], the above concept provides a ground on which all known coordination methods could be displayed. This holds true especially for a coordination method introduced in *Trautmann* [1981, 58–65] where the coordinating agency beside the coordination task has to determine the policy $\hat{z}_C$ of a certain decision sector, in order to guarantee the coordinability of the planning problems.

If the supremal coordinating agency C has no responsibility for a certain decision sector $(Y_C = Z_C = \emptyset)$, then the corresponding decision problem $\mathcal{D}_C$ is reduced to the pure coordination task of finding a prospective index $\hat{\gamma} = (\hat{\gamma}_0, \hat{\gamma}_1, \ldots, \hat{\gamma}_N)$ meeting both conditions. Such a prospective index $\hat{\gamma}$, if it exists, is called *optimal*, and its determination usually requires a multiple information exchange between the coordinating agency and the infimal decision-centers $i = 0, \ldots, N$, where a nonoptimal γ_i ($i \in \{0, \ldots, N\}$) is adjusted on the basis of the *feedback information* ω_i of the corresponding decision-center.

The design of γ_i and the corresponding ω_i ($i = 0, \ldots, N$) depends on the *coordination principle* chosen by the coordinating agency. There are *three* important coordination principles, which are sketched out in the following.

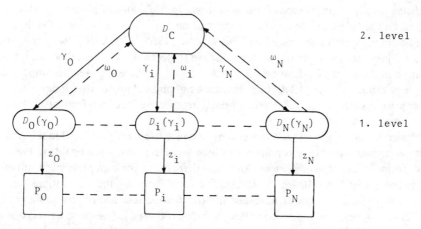

Fig. 2: Two-level planning system $(\mathcal{D}_C, \widetilde{\mathcal{D}})$

The so-called *balance principle* corresponds to the coordination by transfer prices, where the resource transfer between decision-sectors is interpreted as a unrestricted decision variable. In this case γ_i is the announced transfer price system and ω_i the resulting resource transfer which is optimal for decision-center $i = 0, \ldots, N$.

Just the opposite information exchange occurs, if the so-called *quota principle* is applied. γ_i is therefore a fixed resource transfer and ω_i the shadow price system which is associated with the transferred resources.

Both principles are pure in the sense that they are based either on the goal coordination or on the model coordination mode, while the so-called *prediction principle*[2]) is based on both. The prospective index for decision-center i $(i = 0, \ldots, N)$ contents a transfer price system and a fixed resource transfer. As opposed to the *quota principle*, however, γ_i fixes only the transfer of such resources which are controlled by decision-center i. In accordance with that ω_i describes the optimal transfer of such resources which are not controlled by decision-center i $(i = 0, \ldots, N)$.

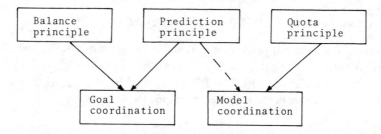

Fig. 3: Coordination principles and their underlying coordination modes

---

[2]) The notions balance principle and prediction principle are due to *Mesarovic/Macko/Takahara* [1970, 98–101]. A third principle introduced by them, called estimation principle, is not considered here.

Existing coordination methods for *time-discrete* formulations of planning problems are based on the *balance* or the *quota principle* or on both. So, for instance, the decentralized planning systems designed by *Kornai/Liptak* [1965], *Ten Kate* [1972] or *Jennergren* [1973] rest on the quota or balance principle respectively. On the other hand, a coordination in the sense of definition 2.2 which is based on the celebrated decomposition principle of *Dantzig/Wolfe* [1960] implies, that a nonoptimal prospective index γ is a transfer price system, in contrast to the optimal prospective index $\hat{\gamma}$ which has to be a fixed resource transfer.

However, in the following section we want to concentrate on coordination methods for *time-continuous* problem formulations which seem to be more reasonable in the context of *natural resource management*. Although there exists for *each principle* a suitable coordination method [see *Mesarovic/Macko/Takahara; Pearson*], the assumptions for economic applications are too rigid. Especially the method founded on the quota principle suffers from a certain disadvantage [see *Pearson*, 160–164]. Therefore we relax in the following the traditional assumptions and propose two coordination methods based on the balance and prediction principle.

3. Coordination of Time-Continuous Planning Problems

In this section we are concerned with the coordination of two-level planning systems as described in section 2, but with the additional assumption that the underlying problems are formulated in the space $L_2 [0, T]$ of real-valued square-integrable functions where T denotes the finite planning horizon. Accordingly, the global objective functional of the economic system under consideration is expressed as a integral plus a term valuating the final state, and the global model is formulated as a integrated differential equation system or *integral equation system* restricted by some additional constraints:

$$\mathcal{D}: \ G(x, u) = \int_0^T g(x(t), u(t), t) \, dt + g_T(x(T), T) \rightarrow \text{Max} \tag{3.1}$$

$$P(x, u)(t) = x(t) - x_a - \int_0^t f(x(\tau), u(\tau), \tau) \, d\tau = 0 \quad \text{for all } t \in [0, T] \tag{3.2}$$

$$(x, u) = y \in \bar{Y} = \{X \times U \mid R(x(t), u(t), t) \geq 0\}. \tag{3.3}$$

Precisely, G and P are the mappings $G : Y \rightarrow \mathbf{R}$ and $P : Y \rightarrow \Lambda$ respectively, where $Y = X \times U$, $X = L_2^n [0, T]$ is the space of state variables $x : [0, T] \rightarrow \mathbf{R}^n$, $U = L_2^m [0, T]$ is the space of control variables $u : [0, T] \rightarrow \mathbf{R}^m$ and $\Lambda = L_2^n [0, T]$ is an auxiliary space. Each element of the above function spaces is equipped with the norm

$$\| c \| := \sqrt{\langle c, c \rangle} = (\int_0^T (c(t))^2 \, dt)^{1/2}, \ c \in L_2 [0, T] \tag{3.4}$$

induced by the inner product $\langle c, c \rangle$. The control and state constraints are expressed by the mapping $R : \mathbf{R}^n \times \mathbf{R}^m \times [0, T] \rightarrow \mathbf{R}^r$.

Now we assume that the supremal coordinating agency C has, at least formally, no responsibility for a certain decision-sector ($Y_C = Z_C = \emptyset$) apart from the coordination task. In accordance with that decentralized decision-making among ($N + 1$) infimal decision-centers requires the partition of the state space X and the control space U in ($N + 1$) subspaces X_i ($X = X_0 \times X_1 \times \ldots \times X_N$) and U_i ($U = U_0 \times U_1 \times \ldots \times U_N$) respectively. The assumed separability of the global objective function

$$G(y) = G(x, u) = \sum_{i=0}^{N} G_i(x_i, u_i) \tag{3.5}$$

and the introduction of the spaces $V_i = L_2^{n_i}[0, T]$ of coupling variables $v_i : [0, T] \to \mathbf{R}^{n_i}$ ($i = 0, \ldots, N$, $V = V_0 \times V_1 \times \ldots \times V_N$) permits us to replace the mappings $G : X \times U \to \mathbf{R}$, $P : X \times U \to \Lambda$ and the overall problem (3.1)–(3.3) respectively by ($N + 1$) mappings $G_i : X_i \times U_i \to \mathbf{R}$, ($N + 1$) mappings $P_i : X_i \times U_i \times V_i \to \Lambda_i$ and ($N + 1$) infimal decision problems $\mathcal{D}_i$ ($i = 0, \ldots, N$) of the following type:

$$\mathcal{D}_i : G_i(x_i, u_i) = \int_0^T g_i(x_i(t), u_i(t), t)\, dt + g_{Ti}(x_i(T), T) \to \text{Max} \tag{3.6}$$

$$P_i(x_i, u_i, v_i)(t) = x_i(t) - x_{ia} - \int_0^t (f_i(x_i(\tau), u_i(\tau), \tau) + v_i(\tau))\, d\tau = 0 \tag{3.7}$$

$$\text{for all } t \in [0, T]$$

$$(x_i, u_i, v_i) = z_i \in \bar{Z}_i = \{X_i \times U_i \times V_i \mid R_i(x_i(t), u_i(t), v_i(t), t) \geqslant 0\} \tag{3.8}$$

$$X_i = L_2^{n_i}[0, T],\ U_i = L_2^{m_i}[0, T],\ V_i = L_2^{n_i}[0, T]$$

where the coupling variables v_i have to be determined such that the interactions between all other decision-sectors $j \in \{0, 1, \ldots, N\}\setminus\{i\}$, expressed by the *coupling operator* K_i applied to (x, u), are considered:

$$v_i = K_i(x, u) = \sum_{j=0}^{N} K_{ij}(x_j, u_j) \tag{3.9}$$

where

$$K_i : \underset{j \neq i}{\overset{N}{\times}} X_j \times \underset{j \neq i}{\overset{N}{\times}} U_j \to V_i$$

$$K_{ii}(x_i, u_i) = 0.$$

Within our scope the components of x_i describe levels of natural resource stocks, and in addition possibly levels of different capital stocks, processing and storage capacities, goodwill stocks and sales volumes, which are all *controlled* by decision-sector i ($i = 0, \ldots, N$). Now, the components of the coupling variable $-v_i$ represent the amount of natural and other resources *supplied* by sector i to all other sectors in the considered economic system, while $-K_{ij}(x_i, u_j)$ expresses the corresponding *demand* of sector j ($j \in \{0, \ldots, N\}\setminus\{i\}$).

Although for real management problems the dimension of v_i is lower than the dimension of x_i, we choose for the sake of simplicity the following uniform dimensions:

$$x^T(t) = (x_0^T(t), \ldots, x_N^T(t)), x_i(t) \in \mathbf{R}^{n_i}, \sum_{i=0}^{N} n_i = n \qquad (3.10)$$

$$u^T(t) = (u_0^T(t), \ldots, u_N^T(t)), u_i(t) \in \mathbf{R}^{m_i}, \sum_{i=0}^{N} m_i = m$$

$$v^T(t) = (v_0^T(t), \ldots, v_N^T(t)), v_i(t) \in \mathbf{R}^{n_i}, \sum_{i=0}^{N} n_i = n$$

3.1 Coordination by Means of Transfer Prices

According to the balance principle we envisage now the coordination process to take place just prior to initial time, with a coordinating agency C announcing time paths of transfer prices $\pi: [0, T] \to \mathbf{R}^n$, each decision-sector solving its own planning problem given those price time paths and hence determining dynamic supply and demand. Therefore the objective functional (3.6) of decision-sector i ($i = 0, \ldots, N$) is supplemented in the following way:

$$G_i(z_i, \pi) = G_i(x_i, u_i) - \int_0^T \pi_i^T(t) v_i(t) \, dt + \sum_{j=0}^{N} \int_0^T \pi_j^T(t) K_{ji}(x_i(t), u_i(t)) \, dt. \quad (3.11)$$

By assuming $\pi_i \in \Pi_i = L_2^{n_i}[0, T]$ ($i = 0, \ldots, N$) where

$$\pi^T = (\pi_0^T, \pi_1^T, \ldots, \pi_N^T) \in \Pi = L_2^n[0, T],$$

we can utilize the inner product notation and rewrite (3.11) as

$$G_i(z_i, \pi) = G_i(x_i, u_i) - \langle \pi_i, v_i \rangle + \sum_{j=0}^{N} \langle \pi_j, K_{ji}(x_i, u_i) \rangle. \qquad (3.12)$$

The term $-\langle \pi_i, v_i \rangle$ valuates the transfer of resources which are controlled by decision-sector i ($i = 0, \ldots, N$), whereas $\sum_{j=0}^{N} \langle \pi_j, K_{ji}(x_i, u_i) \rangle$ valuates the transfer of resources which are controlled by other decision-sectors.

Now, the coordinating agency continues to announce time paths of transfer prices until dynamic supply and demand are such that markets within the economic system clear at every instant of time:

$$\hat{v}_i(\pi) = K_i(\hat{x}(\pi), \hat{u}(\pi)) = \sum_{j=0}^{N} K_{ij}(\hat{x}_j(\pi), \hat{u}_j(\pi)) \quad \text{for all } i = 0, \ldots, N \qquad (3.13)$$

or equivalently

$$\hat{v}(\pi) = K(\hat{x}(\pi), \hat{u}(\pi)) \qquad (3.14)$$

where

$$\hat{v}^T(\pi) = (\hat{v}_0^T(\pi), \ldots, \hat{v}_N^T(\pi)) \text{ and}$$

$$K^T(\hat{x}(\pi), \hat{u}(\pi)) = (K_0^T(\hat{x}(\pi), \hat{u}(\pi)), \ldots, K_N^T(\hat{x}(\pi), \hat{u}(\pi))).$$

The exploitation of natural resources, for instance, will then take place along transfer price time paths $\hat{\pi}$ meeting condition (3.14). In the following we examine the conditions which guarantee the coordinability by the balance principle. First of all, a well-defined adjustment procedure for nonoptimal transfer price systems $\pi \in \Pi$ (violating condition (3.14)), requires that the following crucial assumption is satisfied:

A1: The resource transfers $\hat{v}_i(\pi)$, $K_{ji}(\hat{x}_i(\pi), \hat{u}_i(\pi))$, $j = 0, \dots, N$, which are optimal for decision-sector i $(i = 0, \dots, N)$, are *uniquely determined* for each transfer price system $\pi \in \Pi$.

In order to meet this basic requirement, traditionally *strict concavity* (in the context of minimization problems strict convexity) of the objective functional (3.6) with respect to (u_i, v_i) is assumed [see e.g., *Pearson*, p. 114]. However, the valuation of the resource transfer v_i in (3.6) would imply, according to relation (3.5), the valuation of v_i in the overall problem (3.1)–(3.3) which is devoid of any economic content.

Alternatively we can assume *strict concavity* of the objective functional (3.6) with respect to (x_i, u_i). Clearly, then the uniqueness of $K_{ji}(\hat{x}_i(\pi), \hat{u}_i(\pi))$, $j = 0, \dots, N$, results form the uniqueness of $(\hat{x}_i, \hat{u}_i)$ whereas $\hat{v}_i(\pi)$ is the unique solution of the integral equation system

$$P_i(\hat{x}_i, \hat{u}_i, v_i)(t) = \hat{x}_i(t) - x_{ia} - \int_0^t (f_i(\hat{x}_i(\tau), \hat{u}_i(\tau), \tau) + v_i(\tau)) \, d\tau = 0 \qquad (3.15)$$

$$\text{for all } t \in [0, T].$$

But for real management problems the assumption of *strict concavity* of the objective functional with respect to *all* control and state variables will be hardly fulfilled, because a management policy is often valued only on the basis of a few, e.g. financial, variables. Fortunately the requirement A1 will also be met, if the transfer prices *increase* and *decrease*, respectively, strict monotone with the *extent* to which the resources are transferred, and the objective functional $G_i(x_i, u_i)$ is at least concave with respect to (x_i, u_i). We propose therefore the following sector-specific transfer price system π_i for the decision-sector i $(i = 0, \dots, N)$:

$$\pi_i^T = (\pi_{i0}^T, \dots, \pi_{iN}^T), \pi_{ij}(t) \in \mathbf{R}^{n_j}, t \in [0, T], j = 0, \dots, N \qquad (3.16)$$

where

$$\pi_{ij} = \begin{cases} p_j + kv_j, & \text{if } i = j \\ p_j - kK_{ji}(x_i, u_i), & \text{if } i \neq j \end{cases}, \quad k \in \mathbf{R}^1_{++}$$

where $p^T = (p_0^T, \dots, p_N^T)$, $(p : [0, T] \to \mathbf{R}^n)$, called *basic transfer price system*, can be identified with the usual *constant transfer price system* π. The terms

$$kv_i, \quad -kK_{ji}(x_i, u_i) \quad (v_i > 0, K_{ji}(x_i, u_i) < 0, j = 0, \dots, N)$$

and

$$kv_i, \quad -kK_{ji}(x_i, u_i) \quad (v_i < 0, K_{ji}(x_i, u_i) > 0, j = 0, \dots, N)$$

correspond to *increasing marginal costs* for demanded resources and *decreasing marginal returns* for supplied resources respectively.

If a transfer price system of the type (3.16) is announced to decision-sector i $(i = 0, \ldots, N)$ and the coupling operators $K_{ji}(x_i, u_i), j = 0, \ldots, N$, are assumed to be linear[3]), then the following theorem ensures the requirement A1.

Theorem 1: Let $K_{ji} : Y_i \to V_j$ $(i, j = 0, \ldots, N)$ be a linear coupling operator, $k \in \mathbf{R}_{++}^1$ a positive constant and

$$\mathcal{D}_i(\pi_i): \ G_i(z_i, \pi_i) = G_i(x_i, u_i) - \langle p_i + kv_i, v_i \rangle \tag{3.17}$$

$$+ \sum_{j=0}^{N} \langle p_j - kK_{ji}(x_i, u_i), K_{ji}(x_i, u_i) \rangle \to \text{Max}$$

$$P_i(x_i, u_i, v_i) = 0$$

$$(x_i, u_i, v_i) = z_i \in \bar{Z}_i$$

the convex planning problem of decision-sector i $(i = 0, \ldots, N)$. If there are two optimal solutions (x_i^1, u_i^1, v_i^1) and (x_i^2, u_i^2, v_i^2), then $v_i^1 = v_i^2$ and $K_{ji}(x_i^1, u_i^1) = K_{ji}(x_i^2, u_i^2)$ $(j = 0, \ldots, N)$.

Proof: Clearly, the first assertion $v_i^1 = v_i^2$ follows from the strict concavity of $G_i(z_i, \pi_i)$ with respect to v_i.

To prove the second assertion, we assume without loss of generality, the functional $G_i(x_i, u_i)$ to be linear. By defining $z^T := (x_i^T, u_i^T)$, $\langle c, z \rangle := G_i(x_i, u_i)$, $A^T := (K_{0i}^T, \ldots, K_{Ni}^T), d^T := (p_0^T, \ldots, p_N^T)$, we get

$$\langle c, z^1 \rangle + \langle d - kAz^1, Az^1 \rangle = \langle c, z^2 \rangle + \langle d - kAz^2, Az^2 \rangle \tag{3.18}$$

where $z^1 \neq z^2$ are optimal solutions of (3.17). Because of the concavity of $G_i(z_i, \pi_i)$

$$\Theta (\langle c, z^1 \rangle + \langle d - kAz^1, Az^1 \rangle) + (1 - \Theta)(\langle c, z^2 \rangle + \langle d - kAz^2, Az^2 \rangle) \tag{3.19}$$

$$\leqslant \langle c, \Theta z^1 + (1 - \Theta) z^2 \rangle + \langle d - kA(\Theta z^1 + (1 - \Theta) z^2), A(\Theta z^1 + (1 - \Theta) z^2) \rangle$$

$$0 \leqslant \Theta \leqslant 1.$$

Since, however, both solutions are optimal with respect to (3.17), the inequality (3.19) has to fulfilled as a strict equation. The linear terms cancel each other out, and we get

$$\Theta k \langle Az^1, Az^1 \rangle + (1 - \Theta) k \langle Az^2, Az^2 \rangle \tag{3.20}$$

$$= k \langle A(\Theta z^1 + (1 - \Theta) z^2), A(\Theta z^1 + (1 - \Theta) z^2) \rangle.$$

If we divide (3.20) by k and partition the inner product on the right hand side we obtain

$$\Theta \langle Az^1, Az^1 \rangle + (1 - \Theta) \langle Az^2, Az^2 \rangle \tag{3.21}$$

$$= \Theta^2 \langle Az^1, Az^1 \rangle + \Theta(1 - \Theta) \langle Az^2, Az^1 \rangle$$

$$+ \Theta(1 - \Theta) \langle Az^1, Az^2 \rangle + (1 - \Theta)^2 \langle Az^2, Az^2 \rangle$$

---

[3]) Such an assumption seems not to be too rigid at this place, because of the statement of theorem 3. Accordingly, coordinability by the balance principle can only be guaranteed for linear coupling operators.

which can be written in the form

$$\Theta (1 - \Theta) \langle Az^2 - Az^1, Az^2 - Az^1 \rangle = 0. \tag{3.22}$$

This relation holds, if and only if $Az^1 = Az^2$. Making use of the above definitions we can conclude the second assertion $K_{ji} (x_i^1, u_i^1) = K_{ji} (x_i^2, u_i^2)$ $(j = 0, \dots, N)$. $\square$

Now we are able to formulate conditions which establish the coordinability by means of both types of transfer price systems.

Theorem 2:[4]) The planning problem $\mathcal{D}_i (\pi)$, $i = 0, \dots, N$, are coordinable by means of constant transfer price systems π, if and only if there exists a $\pi \in \Pi$ meeting the assumption A1 and

$$\sup_{\substack{P(y)=0 \\ y \in \overline{Y}}} G (y) = \sup_{\substack{P(z)=0 \\ z \in \overline{Z}}} \sum_{i=0}^{N} G_i (z_i, \pi) \tag{3.23}$$

where $P (z) = 0$ is a global model composed of the $(N + 1)$ models $P_i (z_i) = P_i (x_i, u_i, v_i)$ of the corresponding decision-sectors.

Proof: By summation of the objective functionals (3.11) we obtain

$$\sum_{i=0}^{N} G_i (z_i, \pi) = G (y) - \sum_{i=0}^{N} \langle \pi_i, v_i \rangle + \sum_{i=0}^{N} \sum_{j=0}^{N} \langle \pi_j, K_{ji} (x_i, u_i) \rangle \tag{3.24}$$

$$= G (y) - \sum_{i=0}^{N} \langle \pi_i, v_i \rangle + \sum_{j=0}^{N} \langle \pi_j, K_j (x, u) \rangle$$

$$= G (y) - \sum_{i=0}^{N} \langle \pi_i, v_i - K_i (x, u) \rangle.$$

Since coordinated optimal policies $(\hat{x}_i, \hat{u}_i, \hat{v}_i)$, $i = 0, \dots, N$, imply $\hat{v}_i = K_i (\hat{x}, \hat{u})$, the relationship (3.23) is necessary for the coordination by π. According to the required uniqueness of the resource transfer for a given $\pi \in \Pi$, (3.23) is also a sufficient condition. $\square$

By identifying the space of constant transfer price systems π with the dual space V^* of V, the following theorem supplies *sufficient* conditions ensuring requirement (3.23).

Theorem 3: Let $P (y) = 0$, $(P : Y \rightarrow \Lambda, Y = X \times U)$ be a linear overall planning model, $\overline{Y}$ a convex subset of Y, $G : Y \rightarrow \mathbf{R}$ a concave objective functional, where

$$\sup \{G (y) \mid y \in \overline{Y}, P (y) = c\}$$

exists for each c in the neighbourhood of the null element $(c \in U (0 \cap \Lambda))$.
Then there exists a constant transfer price system π such that

$$\sup_{\substack{P(y)=0 \\ y \in Y}} G (y) = \inf_{\pi \in V^*} \{ \sup_{\substack{P(z)=0 \\ z=(y,v) \in Z}} \{G (y) + \langle \pi, K (x, u) - v \rangle \}\}. \tag{3.25}$$

---

[4]) This theorem corresponds to proposition 5.22. in *Mesarovic/Macko/Takahara* [1970, p. 152].

Proof: As proved by, e.g., *Isii* [1964] the optimal objective functional values of the primal and dual overall problem are equal

$$\sup_{\substack{P(y)=0 \\ y\in\bar{Y}}} G(y) = \inf_{\lambda\in\Lambda^*} \{\sup_{y\in\bar{Y}} \{G(y) + \langle\lambda, P(y)\rangle\}\} \tag{3.26}$$

where Λ^* is the dual space of Λ.

That is, there exists no duality-gap. Because of the equivalence

$$\mathcal{D}: \; G(y) \to \text{Max} \qquad\qquad \mathcal{D}': \; G(y) \to \text{Max} \tag{3.27}$$

$$P(y) = 0 \qquad\Longleftrightarrow\qquad P(z) = 0$$

$$y \in \bar{Y} \qquad\qquad\qquad v = K(x, u)$$

$$z = (y, v) \in \bar{Z}$$

the ride hand side of (3.26) can be replaced by

$$\inf_{\lambda\in\Lambda^*,\pi\in V^*} \{\sup_{z\in\bar{Z}} \{G(y) + \langle\lambda, P(z)\rangle + \langle\pi, K(x, u) - v\rangle\}\} \tag{3.28}$$

or equivalently

$$\inf_{\pi\in V^*} \{\sup_{\substack{P(z)=0 \\ z=(y,v)\in\bar{Z}}} \{G(y) + \langle\pi, K(x, u) - v\rangle\}\} \tag{3.29}$$

This proves the asserted property. $\qquad\qquad\qquad\qquad\qquad\qquad\qquad\qquad\square$

It should be emphasized that relation (3.26) may also be met in the case of a nonconvex planning problem $\mathcal{D}$, i.e. for a *nonconvex* objective functional $G(y)$ and/or a *nonlinear* planning model $P(y) = 0$. However, weakened conditions for the *nonexistence* of a *duality-gap*, which are necessary and sufficient, are difficult to verify [see, e.g., *Ekeland/ Temam*, p. 51]. Hence, coordinability by the balance principle is in fact restricted to convex planning problems $\mathcal{D}_i$ implying *linear* planning models $P_i(z_i) = 0, i = 0, \ldots, N$. Nevertheless nonlinear models can also be admitted if those are approximated by linearized models. A suitable coordination method where the approximation is improved during the coordination process, is proposed in *Trautmann* [1981, 115–120].

Although theorem 2 and theorem 3 are formulated in the context of the *constant* transfer price system π, those apply with slight modifications also to the sector-specific *nonconstant* transfer price system (3.16) where the basis transfer price system p is identified with π. So we have instead of theorem 2

Theorem 4: The planning problems $\mathcal{D}_i(\pi_i), i = 0, \ldots, N$, are coordinable by means of sector-specific transfer price systems π_i of type (3.16), if and only if there exists for each sector a $\pi_i \in \Pi_i$ such that

$$\sup_{\substack{P(y)=0 \\ y\in\bar{Y}}} G(y) = \sup_{\substack{P(z)=0 \\ z\in\bar{Z}}} \sum_{i=0}^{N} (G_i(z_i, \pi_i) + \langle kv_i, v_i\rangle \tag{3.30}$$

$$+ \sum_{j=0}^{N} \langle kK_{ji}(x_i, u_i), K_{ji}(x_i, u_i)\rangle)$$

and if a epsilon-solution

$$\hat{y}_\epsilon = pr_Y\,(\hat{z}_0, \ldots, \hat{z}_N) \quad \text{where} \quad G\,(\hat{y}) - G\,(\hat{y}_\epsilon) \leqslant \epsilon \tag{3.31}$$

is accepted for the overall problem $\mathcal{D}$.

Proof: By summing up the infimal objective functionals we obtain instead of (3.24) the relationship

$$\sum_{i=0}^{N} G_i\,(z_i, \pi_i) = G\,(y) - \sum_{i=0}^{N} (\langle p_i, v_i - K_i\,(x, u)\rangle + \langle kv_i, v_i\rangle \tag{3.32}$$

$$+ \sum_{j=0}^{N} \langle kK_{ji}\,(x_i, u_i), K_{ji}\,(x_i, u_i)\rangle).$$

Hence, for coordinated optimal policies $(\hat{v}_i = K_i\,(\hat{x}_i, \hat{u}_i), i = 0, \ldots, N)$ the composition of infimal objective functionals differ from the overall objective functional. Therefore the optimal policies resulting from centralized and decentralized decision-making may not coincide. But there exists for each $\epsilon > 0$ a positive constant $k > 0$ such that

$$G\,(\hat{y}) - G\,(\hat{y}_\epsilon) \leqslant \epsilon \tag{3.33}$$

where $\hat{y}_\epsilon = pr_Y\,(\hat{z}_0, \ldots, \hat{z}_N), \hat{z}_i \in \hat{Z}_i\,(\pi_i), i = 0, \ldots, N$. $\qquad\square$

It should be remarked that for overall problems $\mathcal{D}$ formulated as *linear programs* (in finite dimensions), there exists always a small $k > 0$ such that each decentralized optimal solution is even an *optimal* centralized one

$$pr_Y\,(\hat{Z}\,(\hat{\pi})) \subseteq \hat{Y} \tag{3.34}$$

where $\hat{Y}$ is the set of *optimal* solutions for $\mathcal{D}$ [see *Jennergren*, 1973, p. 971]. This applies also for *linear autonomous control problems*, because of the connection between those and *generalized linear programs* [see, e.g., *Hadley/Kemp*, 301–304]. Sufficient conditions for the existence of a basis transfer price system p meeting relationship (3.30) are again supplied by theorem 3.

For the adjustment of a nonoptimal π^5) or p, the coordinating agency uses only feedback information concerning *excess demand* or *excess supply* in the resource markets of the considered economic system. This feedback information is formally the *Fréchet* derivative [defined in, e.g., *Luenberger*, p. 175]

$$(DG^d)_p = \hat{v}\,(p) - K\,(\hat{x}\,(p), \hat{u}\,(p)) \tag{3.35}$$

of the *dual* objective functional

$$G^d\,(p) = G\,(\hat{x}\,(p), \hat{u}\,(p), \hat{v}\,(p), p), \quad p \in V^*. \tag{3.36}$$

The coordination task can therefore be identified with the minimization of the functional

---

^{5}) In the following we denote also a constant transfer price π with p.

^{6}) Available "first order" methods are: 1. Gradient methods (steepest ascent), 2. Conjugate gradient methods, 3. Variable metric methods.

(3.36) by means of a suitable "first order" method.[6]) If, for instance, the *steepest descent method* is used then after the s-th policy revision p^s is adjusted in the following way:

$$p^{s+1} = p^s + \alpha \, [v^s - K \, (x^s, u^s)], \quad \alpha \in R^1_{++}. \tag{3.37}$$

Provided that G^d (p) fulfills certain regularity conditions [investigated in *Pearson*, 144–148 and *Trautmann*, 112–114], this adjustment procedure ensures at least a pseudo-solution for the whole economic system.

3.2 Coordination by Means of Transfer Prices and Allocated Quotas

As distinguished from the coordination method described in the preceding section, the coordinating agency announces now transfer price systems and transfer quotas for such resources which are controlled by the corresponding decision-center. After the s-th revision of the prospective index $\gamma_i = (\pi_i, v_i)$ the planning problem of decision-sector i $(i = 0, \ldots, N)$ reads now:

$$D_i \, (\pi_i^s, v_i^s) : G_i \, (\gamma_i, v_i^s, \pi_i^s) = G_i \, (x_i, u_i) - \langle \pi_{ii}^s, v_i^s \rangle + \sum_{j=0}^{N} \langle \pi_{ij}^s, K_{ji} \, (x_i, u_i) \rangle \rightarrow \text{Max} \tag{3.38}$$

$$x_i \, (t) = x_{ia} + \int_0^t (f_i \, (x_i \, (\tau), u_i \, (\tau), \tau) + v_i \, (\tau)) \, d\tau \tag{3.39}$$

$$R_i \, (x_i, u_i, v_i^s, t) \geq 0. \tag{3.40}$$

For *convex* planning problems (3.38)–(3.40) the adjustment of the prospective index $\gamma_i^s = (\pi_i^s, v_i^s)$ can be made analogous to (3.37). At this the adjustment

$$v_i^{s+1} = v_i^s + \beta \, [q_i^s - \pi_{ii}^s], \quad \beta \in R^1_{++} \tag{3.41}$$

depends on the gradient of the *Hamiltonian* function with respect to v_i

$$\frac{\partial H_i}{\partial v_i} = q_i^s - \pi_{ii}^s \tag{3.42}$$

where q_i^s includes the *costate* variables corresponding to transferred resources which stocks are controlled by decision-sector i $(i = 0, \ldots, N)$. Clearly, coordination of optimal policies $\hat{z}_0, \ldots, \hat{z}_N$ is achieved, if the resource markets in the considered economic system are in equilibrium

$$v_i^s = K_i \, (x^s, u^s), \qquad i = 0, \ldots, N \tag{3.43}$$

and for each sector $i = 0, \ldots, N$ the *shadow price system* of his controlled and transferred resources q_i^s equals to the corresponding transfer price system

$$\pi_{ii}^s = q_i^s. \tag{3.44}$$

This approach can also be extended to nonconvex problems, i.e. especially nonlinear models, but the coordination task is formally no more a trivial one. For the adjustment of the constant or basis transfer price system p the coordinating agency has to solve the *adjoined linear differential equation system* of the overall problem $\mathcal{D}$ whereas v_i is adjusted by simple inserting [see *Cohen*]. Although this coordination procedure works very well, its convergence has not proven yet.

4. Concluding Remarks

As mentioned in section 2, the coordination by means of the quota principle in the context of time-continuously formulated planning problems suffers from a certain disadvantage. That is, the coordination procedure works only, if all possible allocations of resource quotas are feasible for the planning problem of decision-sector i $(i = 0, \ldots, N)$. This results from the fact, that in the coordination problem of the supremal coordinating agency only current feedback informations are used, unlike to coordination methods for time-discrete problems, in order to adjust the allocation of resource quotas. Therefore repeated allocation of infeasible resource quotas cannot be avoided by a multiple information exchange. Hence, we can state the principal conclusion of this paper: Coordination of time-continuous problems of natural resource management usually has to be based on the balance and prediction principle where the essential ingredient is a sector-specific transfer price system which depends on the extent of the resource transfer.

References

Chiarella, C.: Trade between resource-poor and resource-rich economies as a differential game. Exhaustible Resources, Optimality and Trade. Ed. by M.C. Kemp and N.V. Long. Amsterdam–New York–Oxford 1980, 219–246.

Clark, C.W.: Mathematical Bioeconomics: The Optimal Management of Renewable Resources. New York 1976.

– : Restricted Access to Common-Property Fishery Resources: A Game-Theoretic Analysis. Dynamic Optimization and Mathematical Economics. Ed. by P.T. Liu. New York–London 1980, 117–132.

Cohen, G.: On an Algorithm of Decentralized Optimal Control. Journal of Mathematical Analysis and Application 59, 1977, 242–259.

Dantzig, G.B., and *P. Wolfe*: Decomposition Principle for Linear Programs. Operations Research 8, 1960, 101–111.

Dasgupta, P.S., and *G.M. Heal*: Economic Theory and Exhaustible Resources. Oxford 1979.

Ekeland, I., and *R. Temam*: Convex Analysis and Variational Problems. Amsterdam–Oxford–New York 1976.

Hadley, G., and *M.C. Kemp*: Variational Methods in Economics. Amsterdam–London–New York 1972.

Isii, K.: Inequalities of the Types of Chebychev and Cramér-Rao and Mathematical Programming. Annals of the Institute of Statistical Mathematics 16, 1964, 277–293.

Jennergren, L.P.: A Price Schedules Decomposition Algorithm for Linear Programming Problems. Econometrica 41, 1973, 965–980.

– : On the Concept of Coordinability in Hierarchical Systems Theory. International Journal of Systems Science 5, 1974, 493–497.

Kemp, M.C., and *N.V. Long* (Eds.): Exhaustible Resources, Optimality, and Trade. Amsterdam–New York–Oxford 1980.

Kornai, I., and *T. Liptak*: Two-Level-Planning. Econometrica **33**, 1965, 141–169.

Luenberger, D.G.: Optimization by Vector Space Methods. New York–London 1969.

Mesarovic, M.D., D. Macko and *Y. Takahara*: Theory of Hierarchical Multilevel Systems. New York 1970.

Neumann, K.: Operations Research Verfahren, Band II. München–Wien 1977.

Pearson, J.: Dynamic Decomposition Techniques. Optimisation Methods for Large Scale Systems. Ed. by D.A. Wismer, 1971, 121–190.

Ten Kate, A.: Decomposition of Linear Programs by Direct Distribution. Econometrica **40**, 1972, 883–898.

Trautmann, S.: Koordination dynamischer Planungssysteme. Wiesbaden 1981.

Economic Theory of Natural Resources. ©Physica-Verlag, Würzburg–Wien, 1982.

Modeling Partially Cartelised Markets for Exhaustible Resources

Alistair M. Ulph

1. Introduction

The theory of exhaustible resources exploited in either perfectly competitive or fully monopolised markets is now well-understood [for example, *Dasgupta/Heal* chs. 6 and 11]. However, neither of these models can be applied to some important real world markets for exhaustible resources, such as bauxite, copper, tin, and above all, crude oil. These are better characterised as consisting of one group of producers who form a cartel and set the price for the resource and a second group of price-takers forming a competitive fringe.

A number of studies of partially cartelised markets for exhaustible resources have now been produced, both at the empirical level [see *Hammoudeh* and *Gateley* 1979 for surveys of work related to crude oil], and the theoretical level [*Salant*, 1976; *Gilbert; Lewis/ Schmalensee*, 1978, 1979; *Marshalla; Ulph/Folie*, 1978, 1980a, 1980b; *Newbery; Kemp/ Long*]. There are a number of building blocks common to all these models — a specification of demand for the resource, cost functions and reserves for the various producers, and discount rates for the producers, and the studies vary widely in the assumptions made about these aspects. However, perhaps the most important component of such models is the solution concept employed. The two most widely employed solutions are what I will call open-loop Nash and Stackelberg solutions, which will be defined shortly. The major purpose of this paper is to argue that which solution concept one believes is reasonable will depend on the other assumptions of the model, and that for plausible assumptions neither of the two concepts mentioned above are reasonable.

The term open-loop strategy in this context means the following. The cartel announces a set of prices at all future dates for the exhaustible resource. The competitive fringe takes these prices as given and selects a path of production that maximises the present value of its profits. In order for the fringe to take the cartel's announced prices as given, it has to have confidence that these prices will actually prevail, so that the institutional framework required for this concept is either a set of complete future markets in which trading takes place now and then the markets are closed, or, equivalently, a set of costlessly enforceable long term contracts. By a Nash equilibrium I mean that the cartel takes the output path of the fringe as *given* when it determines its profit-maximising price path, while in a Stackelberg equilibrium the cartel recognises that the fringes' output path will be a function of the price path set by the cartel and takes this reaction function of the fringe into consideration when choosing its optimal price path.

In the next section of this paper I will determine the open-loop Nash and Stackelberg equilibria for a class of fairly simple models, and show how the equilibria are related. It is fairly obvious why the open-loop strategy is not very appealing — the institutional framework it requires is unlikely to exist. Instead the world is better characterised by a sequence of spot markets. In this case each group has to base its current decision on what it *expects* the other group will do in the future, and the *rational expectation* is that at each moment of time each group will act in a way that will maximise the present value of profits from *that moment* onwards. In other words in a *rational expectations* equilibrium the strategies of the cartel and the fringe must satisfy the principle of optimality.

In section 3 it will be shown that the open-loop Nash strategies will yield rational expectations equilibria, but that open-loop Stackelberg strategies need not be, and for important practical cases *will* not be, dynamically consistent. The appropriate solution concept then involves rational expectations (or feedback) Stackelberg strategies. Unfortunately such strategies are hard to compute, although *Maskin/Newbery* [1978] do so for a simple case in the related context of a cartel of *consumers* of an exhaustible resource. It might be conjectured that the feedback Stackelberg equilibrium is in fact the open-loop Nash equilibrium. However, while it is possible to generate examples in which this will be the case, it will be shown that in general the Nash equilibrium does not satisfy the necessary conditions for a feedback Stackelberg equilibrium.

The fact that the open-loop Stackelberg strategy is dynamically inconsistent means the cartel would have an incentive to cheat by deviating from its announced strategy. This form of cheating is fundamental as it is inherent in the structure of the problem. However, other forms of cheating have been considered, principally by *Lewis/Schmalensee* [1978, 1979]. They show that when the cartel and fringe have identical costs, then for a wide class of demand conditions it will not pay the cartel in a Nash equilibrium to deceive the fringe by falsely declaring the level of its reserves, if it is possible for the fringe to monitor the cartel's production. The latter condition is crucial for its means that the cartel's production plans have to be consistent with its falsely announced reserves figure, and the costs of validating its lies outweigh any benefits. Where this possibility of checking production does not arise, then falsely declaring reserves may be profitable. In section 4 it will be shown that once the assumption on costs is dropped, the condition on monitoring may no longer be required, for the simple reason that now there are equilibria where only the fringe produces initially, so no validation costs are incurred by the cartel.

The important conclusion to be drawn from the above analysis is that one cannot establish a priori the superiority of one solution concept over another — it will depend on the model to which it is applied. In this sense, then the solution concept should be *endogenous* to the model. The solution concepts studied so far still impose a considerable amount of a priori structure on firms behaviour — designating that some producers belong to a price-taking fringe and others to a cartel. A further extension would allow all aspects of firm behaviour to be determined endogenously, as occurs in the work on conjectural equilibria. However this is a topic for further research.

2. Open-Loop Nash and Stackelberg Equilibria

In this section I will present the open-loop Nash and Stackelberg equilibria for a particular class of models. I assume there are two groups of producers — a cartel group and a fringe group. Within each group the producers are identical and it will be assumed that the cartel acts as a cohesive group. With these assumptions, the cartel and the fringe can be treated as if each was a single producer. The reserves of the cartel and fringe at time t will be denoted by $\xi(t)$ and $\eta(t)$ respectively, while their production rates will be $x(t)$ and $y(t)$ respectively. $\xi(0)$ and $\eta(0)$ are given. Each group has costs of production which are independent of both current and cumulative production levels, and c will denote per unit production costs for the cartel, k for the fringe. For the present it will be assumed that both groups have the same rate of discount, δ, so that perfect capital markets are being assumed.

Finally, while costs of production may vary between the two producer groups, they produce a homogenous product for which the demand at time t is given by:

$$P(t) = \bar{P} - a(x(t) + y(t))$$

where $\bar{P}$ is the price at which demand drops to zero. The assumption of a linear demand schedule is clearly special, but none of the qualitative results would be affected if one assumed any static demand function for which the elasticity (in absolute value) decreased as output rose and the existence of a backstop technology which will be supplied perfectly elastically when the price of the resource reaches $\bar{P}$. The use of the linear form allows more precise results to be derived.

While the model is rather simple, there is one respect in which it is more general than a number of other studies and that is in allowing costs of the cartel and fringe to differ. By contrast, in the work of *Salant* [1976], *Lewis/Schmalensee* [1978, 1979], *Marshalla* [1980] it is assumed that all producers face identical costs of production. This assumption is more restrictive than the authors appear to realise and precludes many of the interesting results to be found in this area [*Ulph/Folie*, 1980a].

The set of open-loop strategies for the fringe is the set of all possible production paths that do not violate the fringe's initial resource endowment. Let FO denote this set of strategies where:

$$FO = \{y(t): \forall t \geqslant 0 \ y(t) \geqslant 0, \dot{\eta}(t) = -y(t), \eta(t) \geqslant 0; \eta(0) \text{ given}\}.$$

For the cartel the set of open-loop strategies is the set of all possible price paths it can set. Denoting this set by CO, this gives:

$$CO = \{P(t): \forall t \geqslant 0 \ 0 \leqslant P(t) \leqslant \bar{P}\}.$$

In both the Nash and Stackelberg equilibria, the fringe is a follower, and for any price path $P(t) \in CO$ will select a production profile $y(t) \in FO$ so as to maximise present value of profits. As is well-known, the profit maximising path of output must satisfy the condition that if $y(\bar{t}) > 0$, then for all $t \geqslant 0$

$$(P(t) - k) e^{-\delta t} \leqslant (P(\bar{t}) - k) e^{-\delta \bar{t}}; y(t) \geqslant 0 \tag{1}$$

where the inequalities in (1) hold with complementary slackness.

I now describe the equilibria for the Nash and Stackelberg models. Since these are presented elsewhere in more detail [*Ulph/Folie*, 1980a, 1980b], I need only sketch the results.

Nash Equilibrium

The cartel takes as given the output path of the fringe and sets prices so as to maximise

272

profits subject to the constraint that the output it would be required to produce each period to clear the market is non negative, and cumulative output does not exceed initial reserves. Thus in each period the cartel has an excess demand curve as shown in Fig. 1. *DD* is the market demand from which fringe output y (t) is subtracted to yield excess demand $D'D'$.

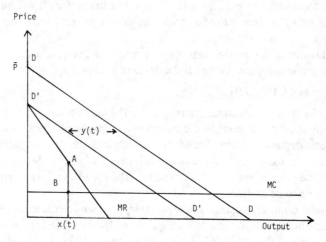

Fig. 1: Nash Equilibrium – Single Period

The cartel now acts like a monopolist faced by these excess demand curves and will allocate production so that the present value of marginal profits (marginal revenue less marginal cost – distance AB in Fig. 1) is constant in all time periods it produces. For the model of this paper marginal revenue is m $(t) = P$ $(t) - ax$ (t), so if at time $\hat{t}$, x $(\hat{t}) > 0$, then the cartels' production decisions must satisfy, for all $t \geqslant 0$

$$[P(t) - ax(t) - c] e^{-\delta t} \leqslant [P(\hat{t}) - ax(\hat{t}) - c] e^{-\delta \hat{t}}; x(t) \geqslant 0 \qquad (2)$$

where the inequalities in (2) hold with complementary slackness.

A Nash equilibrium is a price path and an output path for the fringe such that the output path is the fringe's profit maximising response to the price path while the price path is the cartel's profit maximising response to the fringes' output path. The equilibrium will consist, in general, of three phases: one in which the fringe only produces, and prices are given by the competitive rule (1); one in which the cartel alone produces, in which case the cartels' marginal revenue follows (2) and the price path is the one a pure monopolist would set; and one in which there is simultaneous production in which case both (1) and (2) must be satisfied. In the latter case, the price follows the competitive path, and the cartel sets its output so that:

$$x (t) = \frac{1}{a} [P (t) - m (t)]$$

and hence

$$y (t) = \frac{1}{a} [\bar{P} - 2P (t) + m (t)].$$

(3)

There are a number of cases that can occur and these are presented in Appendix A together with the set of appropriate necessary and sufficient conditions. For the present purposes it suffices to consider two extreme cases, depicted in Fig. 2a) and 2b). I employ the useful expository device of *Newbery* [1980] of showing time running backwards from the final exhaustion date. I will call the situation depicted in Fig. 2a) Case I, and it occurs when the cartel has a substantial cost advantage over the fringe, specifically

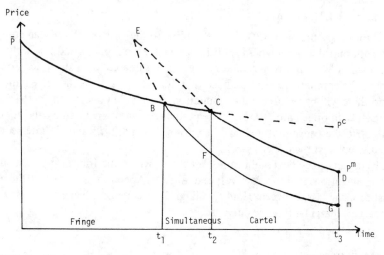

Fig. 2a): Nash Equilibrium for Case I

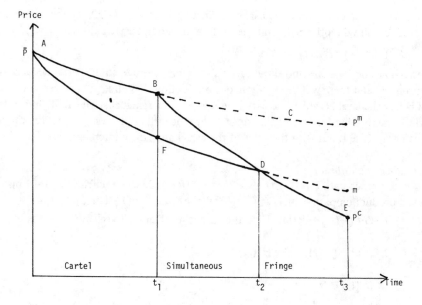

Fig. 2b): Nash Equilibrium for Case II

$k > (1/2)\,(\bar{P} + c)$, and the cartel also has a substantial level of reserves, in a sense defined precisely in Appendix A. In this case, the last phase to occur will be one in which the high cost fringe depletes by itself. So between 0 and t_1, $x\,(t) = 0$, $y\,(t) > 0$, and price follows the *competitive* price path $P^c\,(t) = k + (\bar{P} - k)\,e^{-\delta t}$. At t_1 the cartel starts to produce, and so its marginal revenue at t_1 will be just the competitive price. From then its marginal revenue will be given by

$$m\,(t) = c + (P\,(t_1) - c)\,e^{-\delta\,(t - t_1)} \quad t \geq t_1,$$

and this is shown by the path BFG. Corresponding to the path $m\,(t)$, one can compute the price path that the cartel would set if it was a pure monopolist, and this is the path $P^m\,(t)$, shown as ECD. Between t_1 and t_2 the cartel is unable to set this price, for it is undercut by the competitive price path, so that between t_1 and t_2, the price path will be BC and there will be simultaneous production. Finally, beyond t_2, the cartel produces by itself with price path CD. The time periods t_1 and t_2 are fixed by the conditions that along ABC the fringe must exhaust its resources and at $t_2 P^c$ and p^m intersect. t_3 is then fixed to exhaust the cartel's stock.

Fig. 2b) depicts the Nash equilibrium for Case II, where the fringe has a cost advantage, $k < c$, and also significant reserves, as defined in Appendix A. Now it is the cartel that must produce last, between 0 and t_1. Marginal revenue at exhaustion is just $\bar{P}$, so that the cartel's marginal revenue curve is:

$$m\,(t) = c + (\bar{P} - c)\,e^{-\delta t}, \text{ shown as } AFD.$$

The monopoly price path is again $P^m\,(t)$, which is

$$P^m\,(t) = (1/2)\,\{(\bar{P} + c) + (\bar{P} - c)\,e^{-\delta t}\}, \text{ shown as } ABC.$$

So between 0 and t_1 only the cartel produces and price is AB. At t_1 the fringe starts to produce, and the price path will then follow the competitive path BDE given by

$$P^c\,(t) = k + (P^m\,(t_1) - k)\,e^{-\delta\,(t - t_1)} \quad t \geq t_1.$$

Between t_1 and t_2 this is above the cartel's marginal revenue, so the cartel will also wish to produce, and there will be simultaneous production. Beyond t_2, however, price will fall below the level at which the cartel can cover its marginal cost plus rent, and so the cartel ceases production leaving the fringe to produce till t_3. Times t_1, t_2 and t_3 are determined as in Case I, but with the roles of the cartel and fringe interchanged.

Stackelberg Equilibria

For any price path $P\,(t) \in CO$, let $y^*\,(t) \equiv f\,(P\,(t))$ denote the fringe's profit maximizing production path, which will satisfy the inequalities (1). Let $x\,(P\,(t)) = = (1/a)\,[\bar{P} - af\,(P\,(t)) - P\,(t)]$. Then the cartels' problem is to select $P\,(t)$ so as to

$$\max_{P\,(t)\,\in\,CO} \int_0^\infty [P\,(t) - c]\,x\,(P\,(t))\,e^{-\delta t}\,dt$$

s.t. $x\,(P\,(t)) \geq 0$

$$\int_0^\infty x\,(P\,(t))\,dt \leq \xi\,(0).$$

The comparison with the Nash equilibrium can be seen from Fig. 3, illustrating the position for a single period.

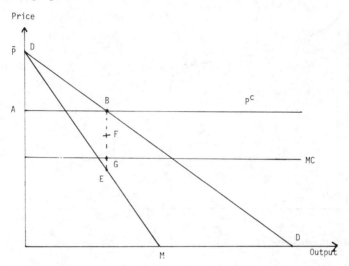

Fig. 3: Stackelberg Model

DD is the demand curve, *DM* the corresponding marginal revenue. The cartel would like to price like a monopolist, setting marginal revenue equal to marginal cost plus an exhaustion rent. It is constrained however by the need to allow the fringe to deplete its resources, and this is represented by the competitive price P^c. As is familiar, this introduces a kinked marginal revenue curve, *ABEM*, and it is clear that there can be three situations. The competitive price may prove ineffective as a constraint, so the cartel sets the monopoly price. The cartel may be constrained by the competitive price, but this is above marginal cost plus exhaustion rent. This is the situation shown in Fig. 3 where marginal costs are *MC* and exhaustion rent is *FG*. In this situation the cartel will set the competitive price but produce all the output the market needs. Finally the competitive price can be so binding that it does not allow the cartel to cover its marginal costs plus exhaustion rent, and only the fringe will produce. A crucial difference between the Nash and Stackelberg models, then, is that there can be no simultaneous production in a Stackelberg equilibrium. The full range of possible equilibria are given in Appendix A, but for the present it suffices to consider the two extreme cases used for the Nash equilibrium. These are shown in Fig. 4a) and b). While these look very similar to Figs. 2a) and b) there are crucial differences.

In Case I (Fig. 4a)), the fringe again produces last, but now it will produce by itself until its resources are completely exhausted, at t_1. Again marginal revenue for the cartel at this point will be the competitive price, and $m(t)$ will again be given by

$$m(t) = c + (P^c(t_1) - c) e^{-\delta(t-t_1)}, \quad t \geq t_1.$$

Between t_1 and t_2, the cartel is constrained to set price at the fringe's limit price $P^c(t)$, but the cartel is the *sole* producer at this stage. Beyond t_2, the fringe's price constraint

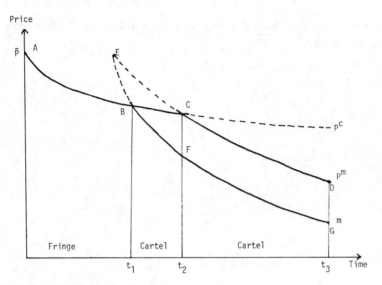

Fig. 4a): Stackelberg Equilibrium for Case I

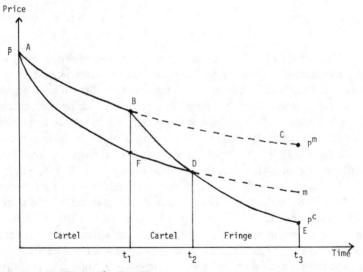

Fig. 4b): Stackelberg Equilibrium for Case II

ceases to bind, and the cartel is free to act as a pure monopolist. In other words, with a sufficient cost advantage the cartel can start off acting like a monopolist. Now t_1 is fixed by the exhaustion of the fringe's reserves, t_2 by the intersection of $P^c(t)$ and $P^m(t)$ and t_3 by the exhaustion of the cartel's reserves.

The story for Fig. 4b) should now be obvious. With no cost advantage, the cartel can only act like a monopolist in the final phase of production, and there will be an intermediate phase when the cartel is constrained to set the competitive price while producing enough to clear the market.

Comparison of Nash and Stackelberg Equilibria

It is now straightforward to compare the Nash and Stackelberg equilibria for Cases I and II, and this is done in Figs. 5a) and b) which superimpose Figs. 2a) and 4a) and 2b) and 4b) respectively. For Case I, (Fig. 5a)), the Nash price path is $ABCDG$, while the Stackelberg path is $ABCDEF$. The rationale for the relationship between these paths is simple. In the Nash equilibrium, the cartel starts producing at t_1^N while the fringe still has resources left, while in the Stackelberg equilibrium the cartel does not commence until the fringe is exhausted, at t_1^S, so clearly $t_1^S > t_1^N$. It is straightforward to show that $(t_2^S - t_1^S)$ must be greater than $(t_2^N - t_1^N)$, so clearly $t_2^S > t_2^N$. Finally up to t_3^N, the prices for the Stackelberg model have been at least as high as for the Nash model, so when all resources are exhausted in the Nash model at t_3^N, there will still be resources left in the Stackelberg model, and hence $t_3^S > t_3^N$.

For Case II (Fig. 5b)), the Stackelberg price path is $ABCD$, that for Nash $ABEFG$. The rationale now is that along ABC, the cartel exhausts its resources, while along $ABEF$ all of the cartel's and some of the fringe's resource are used. So $t_1^N > t_1^S$ and $t_2^N > t_2^S$. Again prices for the Nash model are at least as high as for the Stackelberg model, so $t_3^N > t_3^S$.

One important feature emerges immediately from these diagrams. In both cases, the cartel devotes *less* resources to the pure monopoly phase in the Stackelberg equilibrium than in the Nash equilibrium. This is seen directly from Fig. 5b) where the pure mono-poly phase lasts till t_1^S in the Stackelberg equilibrium and until t_1^N in the Nash equili-brium. For Fig. 5a), it is seen that the phase during which the cartel is constrained by the competitive price is $(t_1^S - t_2^S)$ while for the Nash it is $(t_1^N - t_2^N)$. The former occurs later, lasts longer and has only the cartel producing (while in the latter both the cartel and fringe produce). For all these reasons, the cartel must deplete more of its resources at competitive prices in the Stackelberg model than in the Nash, and hence devotes less of its resources to the monopoly phase in Stackelberg than Nash equilibrium.

As a consequence, when the price paths are drawn with time running forward, as in Figs. 5c) and 5d), it can be seen that these reductions of resources devoted to the pure monopoly phase in the Stackelberg equilibrium lead to higher prices during that phase. The cartel is thus acting more like a monopolist in the Stackelberg model by trying to restrict its output and raise the price. An interesting consequence of this is that compe-titive price path is *lower* in the Stackelberg equilibrium than in the Nash equilibrium, so the fringe is worse off in a Stackelberg equilibrium than in a Nash equilibrium. This result is similar to that for the static model [*Ulph/Folie*, 1980c] where the fringe is better off in a Nash than a Stackelberg equilibrium. In the static case, however, this is because the cartel excessively restricts its output in the Nash equilibrium.

It is not possible to say what happens to consumer welfare in the two equilibria, since prices will be higher at one stage and lower at another. If it is assumed that with reason-able discount rates consumer welfare will be affected largely by what happens in the early periods, then it can be seen that when the cartel is in a strong position (Case I) then comparing the Stackelberg to Nash Equilibrium the cartel is better off while the fringe and consumers lose. However, when the cartel is in a weak position (Case II), the cartel *and* the consumers are better off in a Stackelberg equilibrium, and only the fringe loses.

One final point should be emphasised. The comparison between Nash and Stackelberg equilibria has only been carried out for the extreme cases I and II. It is less easy to make

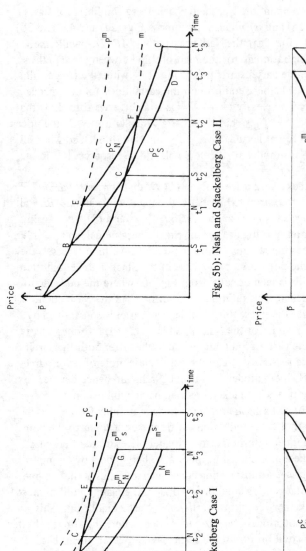

Fig. 5a): Nash and Stackelberg Case I

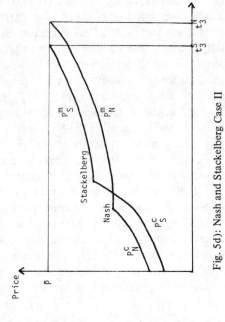

Fig. 5b): Nash and Stackelberg Case II

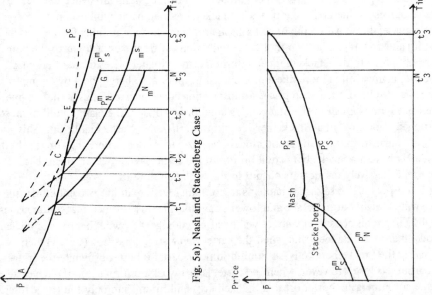

Fig. 5c): Nash and Stackelberg Case I

Fig. 5d): Nash and Stackelberg Case II

comparisons for the intermediate case where $c \leqslant k \leqslant (1/2) (\bar{P} + c)$ since, as shown in Appendix A, it is much harder to characterise the Stackelberg solution for this case. One interesting case can be reported, however, for it is shown in *Ulph/Folie* [1980a] that when $k = c$ the Nash and Stackelberg equilibria are identical. Similar results have been found by *Gilbert* [1978] and *Lewis/Schmalensee* [1979]. This equivalence clearly makes the case of identical costs of production rather special.

3. Dynamic Inconsistency and Rational Expectations Equilibria

In the previous section I outlined the equilibria that would result from the cartel and fringe using open-loop Nash and Stackelberg strategies. In assessing whether either of these strategies is reasonable, one can ask whether Nash or Stackelberg models should be used, and also whether open-loop strategies should be used. On the former question, there is little to add to the usual statements that Nash equilibria are 'secure' [*Starr/Ho*] in the sense that no player can achieve a better result by deviating from his Nash strategy so long as other players continue to play their Nash strategies. However, in the context of the markets analysed in this paper, it seems more plausible to assume that the cartel understands the way in which the fringe will react to its price and will seek to exploit that knowledge by playing Stackelberg strategies. Indeed, it has been shown elsewhere [*Ulph/Folie,* 1978] that the cartel can be worse off playing the Nash strategy than if markets had been perfectly competitive.

Turning to the desirability of open-loop strategies, it was noted in the introduction that in order for these to be reasonable one needs to assume that the institutional framework is one of either perfect future markets with no recontracting or equivalently one of binding contracts. If these are absent, then the only reason to suppose that players will not deviate from their announced open-loop strategies is if these obey the *principle of optimality*. That is if players start off playing their open-loop strategies then at each moment of time the optimal strategy from that point onwards is to continue to play their open-loop strategy. If strategies obey the principle of optimality I will say they are dynamically consistent.

Two general points can be made at the outset. First, the strategy of a follower must always be dynamically consistent; since it takes as given the strategy of other players, it is left solving a standard dynamic optimisation problem and this will be dynamically consistent [*Cruz*]. In this context, as long as the cartel continues to set the original price path, there is no incentive for the fringe to deviate from its original production path. As an extreme example, in a world of perfect competition no dynamic inconsistency would be expected.

Second, it follows from the above point that Nash equilibria are always dynamically consistent, since all players are followers in a Nash equilibrium [*Zarrop; Cruz*]. In the context of this paper, the cartel is acting like a monopolist with a given set of excess demand functions. Provided the fringe's output path is unchanged, the set of excess demand functions remains unchanged, and the cartel will have no incentive to deviate from its announced policy, just as a pure monopolist would have no incentive to change policy.

So problems of dynamic inconsistency can only affect the cartel's open-loop Stackel-

280

berg strategy. To see that such problems can arise in the models presented in this paper, consider the Case II Stackelberg equilibrium, reproduced in Fig. 6 with time running forward. The price path is $ABCD$ with the fringe alone producing till t_1 and the cartel alone producing thereafter.

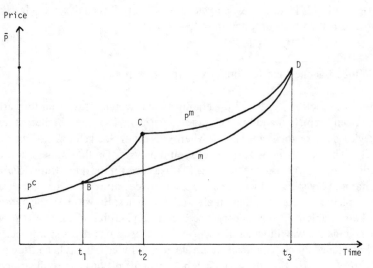

Fig. 6: Stackelberg Equilibrium Case II

However once t_1 is reached in real time, the fringe's resources are exhausted and are no longer a constraint on the cartel, and the cartel will immediately raise price to the full monopoly level.

However, it should be emphasised that open-loop Stackelberg equilibria *need* not be dynamically inconsistent. For example, in the Case I equilibrium, the fringe does not deplete until the cartel has exhausted its resources, so no problem of dynamic inconsistency can occur. Dynamic inconsistency must occur however, when $k < c$.

A rather different kind of dynamic inconsistency also occurs when $c < k < (1/2) (\bar{P} + c)$, i.e. the cartel has a cost advantage over the fringe, but not as substantial a cost advantage as occurs in a Case I solution. In this case the cartel has a continuous incentive to *cut* the price, *Ulph* [1980]. The same kind of inconsistency as for Case II can also occur for these cost conditions, however, if the cartel faces a lower discount rate than the fringe [*Newbery*]. Again this characterises the crude oil market, where a familiar complaint of the "Low Absorbing" OPEC countries is their inability to earn a reasonable rate of return on their overseas assets. If δ denotes the discount rate for the cartel, and ρ the discount rate for the fringe, then Newbery has shown that a sufficient condition for dynamic inconsistency to occur is

$$\frac{\rho}{\delta} > \frac{\bar{P} - c}{\bar{P} + c - 2k} > 1.$$

Plausible figures for the crude oil market would certainly satisfy this condition. Since multiple discount rates make the equilibrium paths more complex, for the rest of this paper attention is restricted to the original case of equal discount rates.

That Stackelberg open-loop strategies may be dynamically inconsistent has been noted by *Maskin/Newbery* [1978], *Kemp/Long* [1980], *Ulph/Folie* [1980a] and *Newbery* [1980], in the context of exhaustible resources. The problem is not peculiar to this application, of course, and can arise in any non-zero sum dynamic game [*Simaan/Cruz; Cruz; Gardner/Cruz; Zarrop*][1]).

When open-loop Stackelberg models are dynamically inconsistent, another solution concept is required. In differential games literature this is referred to as a 'feedback' Stackelberg strategy, and is simply a Stackelberg strategy which is constrained to satisfy the principle of optimality. In economic terms, one thinks of a sequence of spot markets for the resource in which the cartel sets the spot price and the fringe sets its current output. The optimal decision depends not just on the spot market but also on what each group expects will happen in the future. The *rational expectation* is that at each moment of time each group will act so as to maximise the present value of its profits from that moment onwards. An equilibrium set of 'feedback' strategies will be referred to then as a *rational expectations equilibrium, Maskin/Newbery* [1978], *Newbery* [1980].

Unfortunately the calculation of such feedback strategies is extremely complex, except for simple examples such as the two period model solved by *Maskin/Newbery* [1978]. It might be conjectured that the rational expectations equilibrium is simply the Nash equilibrium. An argument for this would be that the rational expectations equilibrium must satisfy two conditions: the fringe must not exhaust before reaching the unconstrained monopoly price trajectory if it is to remove the risk of a price jump, and the monopolist must have no power to deviate from the price path before it reaches the unconstrained monopoly path. This is unexceptionable and the Nash equilibrium certainly satisfies the first condition. However the argument for the second condition is simply a restatement of the Nash concept — if the fringe supplies its output according to the Nash equilibrium and convinces the cartel it will supply this amount no matter what the cartel does, then the cartel's optimal response is also to play the Nash strategy.

But this is not a rational expectations equilibrium, it is just a restatement of the rationale for Nash equilibrium. For there is no way that the fringe can signal to the cartel it's plan to keep its output in each period fixed at the Nash level. To see this, consider time as discrete and suppose at time $\bar{t}$ reserves are $\xi(\bar{t})$ and $\eta(\bar{t})$ respectively. The Nash strategy requires the fringe to produce $\bar{y}(\bar{t})$, the cartel $\bar{x}(\bar{t})$. But suppose the cartel plays $x^*(\bar{t}) \neq \bar{x}(\bar{t})$. Then at $\bar{t}+1$ reserves are $\xi(\bar{t}+1) = \xi(\bar{t}) - x^*(\bar{t})$, $\eta(\bar{t}+1) = \eta(\bar{t}) - \bar{y}(\bar{t})$. The original Nash strategy is no longer consistent with these reserves. If it was correct for the fringe to play the Nash strategy at $\bar{t}$, it should be correct for it to do so now, but because of the change in the reserves, the Nash strategy will

---

[1]) In the text the problem of dynamic inconsistency is discussed with reference to open-loop strategies. Another solution concept found in differential games is that of closed-loop strategies, where the players announce *decision functions* which indicate what move each player will make at each point of time *depending* on the state of the game at that point in time. In the context of this paper, the state variables would be the reserves of the cartel and fringe, so the price set by the cartel and the output set by the fringe in each period would depend on the level of reserves of both groups. One might think of this as a set of future and contingent markets where the state of the world on which markets are contingent are reserve levels. Clearly such markets are less likely to exist than the future markets required for open-loop strategies, and without them the problem of dynamic inconsistency will reappear.

change, and hence the output of the fringe at $\bar{t} + 1$ will differ from that which it would have announced at $\bar{t}$ to be produced in $\bar{t} + 1$. The absence of binding contracts affects the fringe's ability to make the cartel believe its future output plans just as much as it destroys the fringe's belief in any price path the cartel may announce.

One study which attempts to compute a RESE is that of *Kemp/Long* [1980]. They consider the case where $k = c$, but allow a more general demand specification than simply linear. They argue that the RESE for this case consists of a competitive phase in which *only* the fringe produces followed by a pure monopoly phase in which only the cartel produces. Two points should be noted about this. First, Kemp and Long argue that the cartel must always be better off in this equilibrium than in a competitive market. This is simply false. If one considers the case where $P = 100 - (x + y)$, $\delta = .1$, $\xi(0) = 1000$, $\eta(0) = 4000$, then it is readily shown that per unit profit for the cartel in competitive equilibrium is .248, while per unit profit in the Kemp and Long equilibrium is .244. Of course, this need not be worrying, for as already noted it may well be the case that the cartel can sometimes be worse off in a RESE than in competitive equilibrium. My second point is that I find the argument of Kemp and Long for their equilibrium unconvincing. What they argue is that any solution which had the cartel producing in the competitive phase is untenable because the cartel would simply arrange for the fringe to do all its production first and then when the fringe's resources were exhausted raise the price immediately to the monopoly price. But this just shows that the *open-loop* Stackelberg solution (which has the cartel producing in the competitive phase) is dynamically inconsistent. The Kemp and Long solution is *one* method of convincing the fringe the cartel will not cheat, but it need not be the only one, nor need it be the profit maximising one. A policy in which the cartel depleted some of its resources simultaneously with the fringe, so that the fringe did not deplete its resources before the monopoly phase, could also protect the fringe against the cartel cheating and yield higher profits to the cartel than the Kemp and Long solution.

In the rest of this section I will suggest how to formulate a rational expectations Stackelberg equilibrium (RESE) and show that in general it will not be an open-loop Nash equilibrium. However it is possible to construct simple examples in which the RESE is the same as the Nash equilibrium (Appendix B).

Let $\pi^c(\xi, \eta)$ and $\pi^f(\xi, \eta)$ denote the maximum profits that can be made by the cartel and fringe respectively when the reserves of the cartel and fringe are ξ and η respectively and when both the cartel and the fringe play their optimal feedback Stackelberg strategies. Then if $x\Delta t$, $y\Delta t$ denote the amounts produced by the cartel and fringe in period Δt when following their optimal feedback strategies, then, by definition:

$$\pi^c(\xi, \eta) \equiv (P - c)x\Delta t + e^{-\delta\Delta t}\pi^c(\xi - x\Delta t, \eta - y\Delta t)$$
$$\pi^f(\xi, \eta) \equiv (P - k)y\Delta t + e^{-\delta\Delta t}\pi^f(\xi - x\Delta t, \eta - y\Delta t).$$

Taking a Taylor expansion of the last terms, dividing by Δt and letting $\Delta t \to 0$, yields the basic recursive equations:

$$\delta\pi^c(\xi, \eta) = (P - c)x - \pi^c_\xi x - \pi^c_\eta y$$
$$\delta\pi^f(\xi, \eta) = (P - k)y - \pi^f_\xi x - \pi^f_\eta y.$$

I now want to determine the optimal values for x and y, and will assume that π_ξ^c, π_η^c, π_ξ^f, π_η^f, can be treated as parameters, which I shall denote by α, β, γ, ω, respectively. So x and y are determined as solutions to a Stackelberg problem in which the cartel sets the price for the current period and the fringe decides how much of the demand available at that price it should meet from its own production. I will be concerned only with the case where $\xi > 0$, $\eta > 0$. Let $d\,(P)$ denote the demand function,

$$d\,(P) = \frac{1}{a}\,(\bar{P} - P).$$

The fringe's problem then is to

$$\text{Max}_{y}\ (P - k)\,y - \gamma\,(d\,(P) - y) - \omega\,y$$

s.t. $0 \leqslant y \leqslant d\,(P)$.

Introducing Lagrange multipliers λ and μ, the first order conditions for the fringe are

$$\left.\begin{array}{l} P = k + \omega - \gamma - \lambda + \mu \\[4pt] \lambda \geqslant 0\ y \geqslant 0 \\[4pt] \mu \geqslant 0\ y \leqslant d\,(P) \end{array}\right\} \tag{4}$$

where the inequalities in (4) hold with complementary slackness. (4) implicitly defines the fringe *reaction function*.

The cartel's problem can then be characterised as

$$\underset{x \geqslant 0\ y \geqslant 0}{\text{Max}}\ [\bar{P} - a\,(x + y) - c]\,x - \alpha x - \beta y$$

s.t. $\bar{P} - a\,(x + y) = k + \omega - \gamma - \lambda + \mu$

$$\lambda y = 0, \qquad \mu x = 0.$$

Introducing Lagrange multipliers ν_1, ν_2, ν_3, the first order conditions for the cartel are

$$\left.\begin{array}{ll} \bar{P} - ay - c - 2ax - \alpha + \nu_1\,a + \nu_3\,\mu \leqslant 0\ x \geqslant 0 & \\[4pt] -ax - \beta + \nu_1\,a + \nu_2\,\lambda \leqslant 0 & y \geqslant 0 \\[4pt] \bar{P} - a\,(x + y) = (k + \omega - \gamma) - \lambda + \mu & \\[4pt] -\nu_1 + \nu_2\,y \leqslant 0\ \lambda \geqslant 0 & \\[4pt] \nu_1 + \nu_3\,x \leqslant 0 \qquad \mu \geqslant 0 & \\[4pt] x \geqslant 0 \qquad\qquad \mu \geqslant 0 & \\[4pt] y \geqslant 0 \qquad\qquad \lambda \geqslant 0. & \end{array}\right\} \tag{5}$$

The particular case in which I am interested is where $x > 0$, $y > 0$. Then from (5) it can be seen that $\lambda = \mu = 0$ and by subtracting the second inequality from the first one obtains a necessary condition

$$P = \bar{P} - a\,(x + y) = k + \omega - \gamma = c + \gamma - \beta$$

or

$$P = k + \pi_\eta^f - \pi_\xi^f = c + \pi_\xi^c - \pi_\eta^c. \tag{6}$$

This condition has a natural interpretation saying that if both groups are to produce then price must equal the *full marginal cost* of production, where the full marginal cost equals the current marginal cost of production plus the loss of profits caused by depleting its own reserves by one unit plus the loss of profits caused by *increasing* the reserves of the other group by one unit (since to maintain the optimal price an increased unit of output by one group must be matched by a loss of a unit of output from the other).

Consider now a Nash equilibrium for the case where $k < c$ and simultaneous production is taking place. Then the profit functions π^c and π^f are defined implicitly as follows. Let t_1 denote the length of the competitive phase, t_2 the time of final exhaustion, and let $u = \delta t_1$, $v = \delta t_2$. Then u and v are given by

$$u + e^{-u} = \frac{a\delta\eta}{\bar{P} + c - 2k} + 1$$

$$v + e^{-v} = \frac{2\,a\delta\xi + a\delta\eta}{\bar{P} - c} + 1.$$

π^c and π^f are then

$$\pi^c = \frac{1}{4a\delta}\,\{4u\,(k-c)\,(\bar{P}+c-2k)\,e^{-u} + 4\,(k-c)^2$$

$$+ 2e^{-u}\,(\bar{P}-c)\,(\bar{P}+c-2k) - (\bar{P}+c-2k)^2\,e^{-2u}$$

$$+ (\bar{P}-c)^2\,e^{-2v} - 2\,(\bar{P}-c)^2\,e^{-v}\}$$

$$\pi^f = \frac{\bar{P}+c-2k}{2a\,\delta}\,\{(\bar{P}-c)\,ue^{-v} + u\,(\bar{P}+c-2k)\,e^{-u}$$

$$- (\bar{P}-c)\,(e^{-v} - e^{-v}e^{-u}) - (\bar{P}+c-2k)\,(e^{-u} - e^{-2u})\}.$$

Suppose now that $\xi = 1000$, $\eta = 200$, $\bar{P} = 100$, $a = 1$, $c = 20$, $k = 0$, $\delta = .1$. Then it can be shown that $k + \pi^f_\eta - \pi^f_\xi = .7001$ while $c + \pi^c_\xi - \pi^c_\eta = 38.35$.

So the Nash equilibrium does not satisfy the necessary conditions for a RESE. However, it is less easy to say what the RESE will be, and this remains a topic for further work.

If the RESE was indeed the Nash equilibrium, then an immediate consequence would be that the absense of binding contracts must make the cartel worse off. An example by *Newbery* [1980] which corresponds roughly to the parameters for the crude oil market suggests the losses could be substantial – 30% of the open-loop Stackelberg profits. Consumers also lose, as was noted earlier, while the gains to the fringe are small relative to the cartel losses.

Indeed, to the extent that in some Nash equilibria the cartel is worse off than in a competitive equilibrium, as noted above, this would be an example of disadvantageous monopoly power. It is of some interest, then to compute the RESE so that one can check whether these results would apply for the correct RESE. I suspect they are unlikely to generalise. That is, there may well be RESE where the cartel is *better* off than if it signed binding contracts. There are certainly examples of dynamic games where the leader is better off playing feedback Stackelberg strategies than open-loop Stackelberg strategies, [*Simaan/Cruz*].

To conclude this section, then there are some cases where the open-loop Stackelberg strategy is reasonable, but when it is dynamically inconsistent, as it is likely to be for plausible models, than a more appropriate strategy concept is the rational expectations Stackelberg strategy. However these are very difficult to compute.

It should be emphasised, perhaps, that the proof that Nash equilibria are not RESE in no way conflicts with the previous statements that Nash equilibria are dynamically consistent. The latter is only the case as long as the cartel acts like a *Nash* player. The necessary conditions derived in this section are for a cartel acting as a Stackelberg leader.

4. Other Forms of Cartel Deception

In this section I shall make a brief comment about another form of cheating by the cartel — that of lying about the level of reserves it possesses. *Lewis/Schmalensee* [1978] consider the case where the cartel and fringe have identical costs of production and show that, for a wide class of demand conditions, it will not pay the cartel, in a Nash equilibrium, to lie about its reserves. A crucial assumption for this result is that it is possible for the fringe to monitor cartel production, for now the cartel has to choose a production path that is consistent with its falsely announced reserves (at least up to such a time as it choses to reveal the truth). The costs of doing this outweigh any benefits. Indeed, for the case of the linear demand curve studied here, there are *no* benefits, for the only way the cartel could benefit is by inducing the fringe to alter its production pattern. However, *Salant* [1976] showed that for the case considered here the fringe production profile is *independent* of the cartel's reserves. Higher cartel reserves will certainly lower the price during the competitive phase, but the increased demand is met entirely from increased cartel production.

The point I wish to make is that this result depends quite strongly on the assumption of equal costs. To see this consider the Nash equilibrium for Case II, shown in Fig. 7.

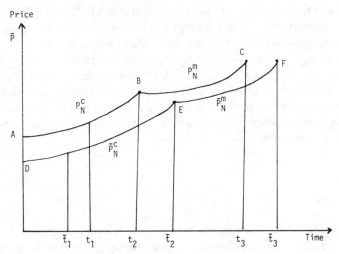

Fig. 7

The price path is ABC, with the fringe producing by itself till t_1, simultaneous production to t_2, and the cartel alone producing till t_3. The price path corresponding to a higher level of cartel reserves is shown as DEF. By considering Fig. 2b) it can be readily seen that the period in which the fringe alone produces must now be shorter. However, the important point is that since the price is lower along DE than along AB the fringe must have depleted more of its reserves by $\bar{t}_1$ along DEF than it did along ABC. Moreover, *only* the fringe has changed its production plans along DEF before $\bar{t}_1$. Thus *if* the cartel can persuade the fringe that its reserves are higher than they are, and can induce it to deplete along a path DE, it *must* pay the cartel to do so, at least up to time $\bar{t}_1$.

The reason why this result differs from *Lewis/Schmalensee* [1978] is obviously that since the cartel does not have to produce, no validation costs are incurred, and there must be *some* response by the fringe. The difficulty of course is how the cartel is to make the fringe believe its lies about the extent of the cartel's reserves. It should also be noted that the scope for cheating is somewhat limited. The larger the reserves announced by the cartel, the smaller is $\bar{t}_1$, and eventually $\bar{t}_1$ becomes zero, requiring the cartel to start production immediately at levels consistent with its falsified reserves.

5. Conclusions

It has been shown in this paper that the solution concepts used so far to study partially cartelised markets for exhaustible resources may be unsatisfactory. Nash strategies make naive behavioural assumptions while for some parameter values the Stackelberg open-loop strategy will be dynamically inconsistent. When the latter occurs, a more appropriate solution concept is the RESE, but this is very difficult to compute. However, it was argued that the RESE is not, in general, the Nash equilibrium, so the absence of future markets or binding contracts does not provide a rationale for the rather common use of Nash strategies.

The purpose of the paper has not been to suggest that RESE is inherently superior to the other solution concepts. Rather the moral to be drawn is that which solution concept is reasonable will depend on other parameters of the model being studied. In this sense, the solution concept should be *endogenous* to the model. Since the essence of various solution concepts is the view each player takes of other player's likely response, this suggests that further work should try to link research in this area with work on conjectural equilibria. An example of this approach is the work by *Ulph* [1979] on *locally rational conjectures* in the theory of oligopoly and it is hoped to apply this approach to exhaustible resource markets.

Acknowledgements

I am grateful to David Newbery and David Ulph for helpful discussions on the issues discussed in this paper. Neither of them is responsible for any errors I have committed in the paper.

I. $k > 1/2\,(\bar{P} + c)$

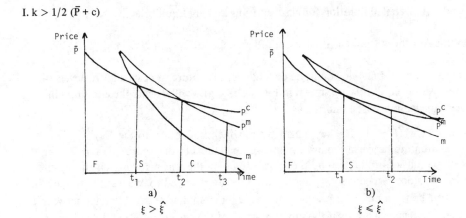

a)
$\xi > \hat{\xi}$

b)
$\xi \leqslant \hat{\xi}$

II. $k \leqslant c \leqslant 1/2\,(\bar{P} + c)$

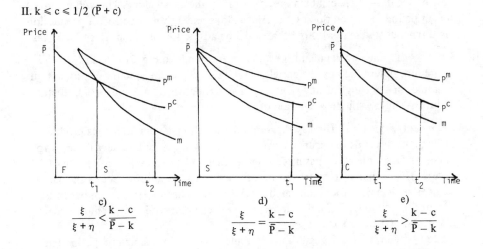

c)
$\dfrac{\xi}{\xi + \eta} < \dfrac{k - c}{\bar{P} - k}$

d)
$\dfrac{\xi}{\xi + \eta} = \dfrac{k - c}{\bar{P} - k}$

e)
$\dfrac{\xi}{\xi + \eta} > \dfrac{k - c}{\bar{P} - k}$

III. $k < c$

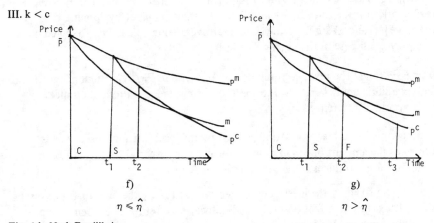

f)
$\eta \leqslant \hat{\eta}$

g)
$\eta > \hat{\eta}$

Fig. A1: Nash Equilibria

Appendix A: Detailed Solution for Nash and Stackelberg Equilibria

In this Appendix I present briefly the full set of solutions for Nash and Stackelberg equilibria.

Nash. The range of possible equilibria depends on the nature of costs and the levels of reserves. All the equilibria are shown in Fig. A1a) – g). I will discuss the equilibria in terms of the various cost conditions.

I. $k > (1/2)(\bar{P} + c)$ The key diagram is a) which is identical to Fig. 2a). The relationship between the price paths was explained in the text. F, S, and C refer to periods of production by the fringe alone, by the fringe and cartel, and by the cartel alone respectively. t_1 and t_2 are fixed by the need to exhaust the fringe stock. Let $\hat{\xi}$ be the amount of production that will be required from the cartel between t_1 and t_2. Then a) occurs if the initial reserves of the cartel are $\xi > \hat{\xi}$. If $\xi \leqslant \hat{\xi}$ then case b) occurs – there can be no production by the cartel alone. This will mean a longer period of production by the fringe alone and a shorter period of production simultaneously than in a). Note that $\hat{\xi}$ will be a function of η, the fringe's reserves.

III. $k < c$ Again the key diagram is g) which corresponds to Fig. 2b). As in I, t_1 and t_2 are now determined by the cartel's reserves. Let $\hat{\eta}$ be the amount of production required for the fringe during t_1 and t_2. Then g) occurs iff $\eta > \hat{\eta}$. If $\eta \leqslant \hat{\eta}$, then f) occurs. As in I, $\hat{\eta}$ will be a function of ξ.

II. $k \leqslant c \leqslant (1/2)(\bar{P} + c)$ The key diagram is d) which yields simultaneous production throughout. For this to occur, the ratio of reserves has to be precisely that shown under d). When the cartel has more reserves than indicated by the ratio, case e) occurs. This is similar to f), except that P^c and m can never intersect. If the cartel's reserves are less than those indicated by the ratio, c) occurs. This is similiar to b) except that P^m and P^c cannot intersect. As special cases, if $k = c$, e) must occur; if $k = (1/2)(\bar{P} + c)$ c) must occur.

While I have presented 7 possible cases, there are only 5 possible production paths, since b) and c) are equivalent, and e) and f) are equivalent. There are only three possible price profile since b), c) and d) are the same (competitive pricing through-out) and e), f) and g) are the same – competitive pricing comes first followed by monopoly pricing (with time going forwards).

Stackelberg Equilibria. The possible equilibria are outlined in Fig. A2. Much of the details of the Nash equilibria apply here, but the absense of simultaneous production makes a number of important differences.

I. t_1 is the same in both a) and b) and is fixed by the level of fringe reserves. $\bar{\xi}$ is defined as the amount of production by the cartel between t_1 and t_2 in Fig. A2a) when the cartel produces *alone* for that period.

III. t_1 and t_2 are fixed by the level of cartel reserves and t_3 by the level of fringe reserves. The fringe has no effect on the cartel's allocation of output between the competitive and monopoly phase.

I. $k > 1/2\,(\bar{P} + c)$

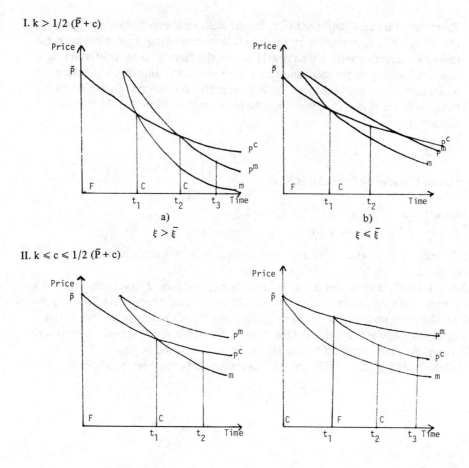

a)

$\xi > \bar{\xi}$

b)

$\xi \leqslant \bar{\xi}$

II. $k \leqslant c \leqslant 1/2\,(\bar{P} + c)$

III. $k < c$

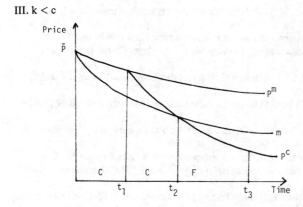

Fig. A2: Stackelberg Equilibria

II.   There can be no case equivalent to e) for the Nash equilibrium. d) is like b) except that P^c and P^m do not intersect. In e) there is the interesting case where the cartel splits its production into two phases. However, the diagram cannot determine how the cartel decides on the split, and this needs to be found directly by checking which allocation yields the cartel the highest profit. It is the inability to tie down this case that makes comparison with the Nash model difficult for the intermediate cost range.

Appendix B: Esample where RESE is Nash

There are two periods, $t = 1, 2.$ $\xi = 2, \eta = 2,$

$$P = (1.1)^{t-1} [10 - 2 (x + y)], \rho = .1, k = 0, c = 5.5.$$

Both the fringe and cartel are constrained to produce only in discrete units, $x\,(t) = 0, 1, 2,$ $y\,(t) = 0, 1, 2.$

Then it is readily shown that the open-loop Nash equilibrium is to set price (6,6) with both groups producing one unit in each period. The open-loop Stackelberg also has price (6,6) but the cartel makes more profit by producing only in the second period. This is dynamically inconsistent for once the fringe has exhausted in the first period the cartel's best strategy is to sell only 1 unit of output in the second period at price of 8.

It is readily seen that the RESE for this example must be the Nash equilibrium.

References

Cruz, J.B.: Survey of Nash and Stackelberg Equilibrium Strategies in Dynamic Games. Annals of Economic and Social Measurement **4**, 1975, 339–344.

Dasgupta, P., and *G. Heal*: Economic Theory and Exhaustible Resources. Nisbet Welwyn 1979.

Gardner, B.F., and *J.B. Cruz*: Feedback Stackelberg Strategy for a Two-player Game. IEEE Trans AC-**22** (2), 1977, 270–271.

Gately, D.: The Prospect for OPEC Five Years After 1973/4. European Economic Review **12**, 1979, 369–379.

Gilbert, R.J.: Dominant Firm Pricing in a Market for an Exhaustible Resource. Bell Journal of Economics 9, 1978, 385–395.

Hammoudeh, S.: The Future Price Behaviour of OPEC and Saudi Arabia; a survey of optimisation models. Energy Economics 1, 1979, 156–166.

Kemp, M.C., and *N.V. Long*: International Monopoly – Monopsony Power Over Exhaustible Resources. Essay 18 in Exhaustible Resources, Optimality and Trade. Ed. by M.C. Kemp and N.V. Long. Amsterdam 1980.

Lewis, T.R., and *R. Schmalensee*: Cartel and Oligopoly Pricing of Nonreplenishable Natural Resources. Dynamic Optimisation and Application to Economics. Ed. by P.T. Liu. New York 1978.

–: Cartel Deception in Nonrenewable Resource Markets. Cambridge, Mass., mimeo, 1979.

Marshalla, R.S.: The Theory of Nonrenewable Resources under Partially Cartelised Market Structures. Decision Focus Incorporated Report, 1980.

Maskin, E., and *D. Newbery:* Rational Expectations with Market Power – the Parado of the disadvantageous Tariff on Oil. Warwick Economic Research Paper, No. 129, 1978.

Newbery, D.: Oil Prices, Cartels and a Solution to Dynamic Inconsistency. Cambridge, mimeo, 1980.

Salant, S.W.: Exhaustible Resources and Industrial Structure: a Nash-Cournot Approach to the World Oil Market. Journal of Political Economy **84**, 1976, 1079–1094.

Salant, S.W., et al.: Imperfect Competition in the International Energy Market: A Computerised Nash-Cournot Model. ICF Inc., 1979.

Simaan, M., and *J.B. Cruz:* Additional Aspects of the Stackelberg Strategy in Nonzero-sum Games. Journal of Optimisation Theory and Applications **11**, 1973, 613–626.

Starr, M., and *Y.C. Ho:* Further Properties of nonzero-sum Differential Games. Journal of Optimisation Theory and Applications **3**, 1969, 207–219.

Ulph, A.M.: Stackelberg Models of Partially Cartelised Markets for Exhaustible Resources. Southampton, mimeo, 1980.

Ulph, A.M., and *G.M. Folie:* Gains and Losses to Producers from Cartelisation of an Exhaustible Resource. C.R.E.S. Working Paper R/WP 26, A.N.U., Canberra 1978.

–: Dominant Firm Models of Resource Depletion. Paper presented to A.U.T.E. Conference, Durham 1980a.

–: Exhaustible Resources and Cartels – An Intertemporal Nash Cournot Model. Canadian Journal of Economics **13**, 1980b, 645–658.

–: Economic Implications of Stackelberg and Nash-Cournot Equilibria. Zeitschrift für Nationalökonomie, 1980c.

Ulph, D.T.: Locally Rational Conjectures and the Theory of Oligopoly. University College, London, mimeo, 1979.

Zarrop, M.B.: A Dynamic Game Framework for Economic Policy Evaluation. PREM Discussion Paper No. 27, Department of Computing and Control, Imperial College, London 1978.

Part IV
Production and Growth

Economic Theory of Natural Resources. ©Physica-Verlag, Würzburg–Wien, 1982.

On the Possibility of Economic Growth
with Exhaustible Resources

Wolfgang Buchholz

1.

Whether the exhaustibility of natural resources puts an end to economic growth is controversial. Whereas pessimists even predict the economic doom most economists [e.g. *Beckerman; Houthakker*] consider the situation as much less dramatic. In their opinion the limits to growth can be overcome by substituting renewable inputs — especially reproducible capital — for exhaustible resources.

In the meantime this not at all new conception [e.g. *Scott; Hayek*] was also introduced into the framework of the theory of economic growth. But primarily one was looking for conditions under which a constant positive level of consumption — a positive "sustainable yield" — could forever be maintained with exhaustible resources. Results concerning the feasibility of growth with exhaustible resources were only obtained as by-products of an optimality analysis in the Cobb-Douglas case [e.g. *Dasgupta/Heal*, 1974; 1979, 292–308]. In this special situation it could be inferred that an unlimited growth with exhaustible resources is possible if and only if a positive sustainable yield exists. My first aim is to generalize this result and to prove it directly only by means of production theory. In a second step I shall investigate how the maximum speed of growth is reduced by the exhaustibility of natural resources.

2.

Let $F(x, y)$ be a production function depending on the stock x of reproducible capital and on the input y of a natural resource. F is supposed to have the usual properties (i.e. strictly increasing, and at least twice differentiable in both variables with $F_{11} < 0$, $F_{22} < 0$) and to be homogeneous of degree one. If an initial stock x_0 of the reproducible capital is given we shall consider paths $(x_t, y_t, c_t)_{t \geqslant 0}$ for which the identity

$$F(x_t, y_t) = c_t + \dot{x}_t \text{ is valid for all } t \text{ and which observe the resource restriction } \int_0^\infty y_t \, dt < \infty.$$

I.e. in every period the whole production has to be divided between consumption c_t and investment $\dot{x}_t$, and the whole process is allowed to use up not more than a finite quantity of the natural resource.

In the beginning *Solow* [1974] first of all tried to describe the class of production functions for which there are paths $(x_t, y_t, c_t)_{t \geqslant 0}$ with $c_t \geqslant c_0 > 0$ for a certain c_0 and all $t \geqslant 0$. In the special case of Cobb-Douglas production functions $F(x, y) =$

$= x^a y^b$ $(a, b \geqslant 0, a + b \leqslant 1)$ it could be shown that positive sustainable yields exist with a finite quantity of the natural resource if and only if we have $a > b$, i.e. the elasticity of production of reproducible capital is greater than that of the natural resource. This result can be generalized to all linear homogeneous production functions: If the real-valued function $g(\cdot)$ is defined by $F(x, g(x)) = 1$ for all x in the maximum interval $]d_1, d_2[$ for which this definition applies, then a positive level of consumption can be maintained if and only if $(*) \int_d^{d_2} g(x) \, dx < \infty$ is satisfied for one (and therefore for all) $d > d_1$.

The condition $(*)$ can be interpreted as a requirement concerning the degree of substitutability between the natural resource and reproducible capital. For example $(*)$ is fulfilled in any case if $d_2 < \infty$, i.e. $g(\cdot)$ meets the abscissa. In this special case we must have $F(x, 0) > 0$ for all $x > 0$, and so the natural resource must be "inessential" for production in the sense of *Dasgupta/Heal* [1979, p. 198].

Furthermore, it is not difficult to grasp the economic meaning of $(*)$: If an initial stock of reproducible capital is given we assume that in every period t the constant quantity q is produced and the constant share sq ($s \in {]}0,1{[}$) is invested. Then the consumption level is time-invariant, too, and always equal to $(1 - s) q$. If such a simple accumulation program is followed the stock of reproducible capital available at t is equal to $x_0 + sqt$. Then, we obviously need $y_t = q \, g(x_t/q)$ to produce the planned quantity q, as we have $F(x_t, q \, g(x_t/q)) = q \, F(x_t/q, g(x_t/q)) = q$. On this linear accumulation program we totally need the resource quantity $\int_0^\infty y_t \, dt = \int_0^\infty q \, g((x_0 + sqt)/q) \, dt$ which obviously is finite if and only if the condition $(*)$ is fulfilled. Consequently a positive sustainable yield can be realized with a finite quantity of the natural resource only if this is possible with a program for which the produced quantity and the savings rate remain permanently constant. Now we can prove the following basic result:

Theorem 1: Let F be a linear homogeneous production function and let an initial stock x_0 of reproducible capital be given. If with F a positive level of consumption can permanently be maintained with a finite stock of the natural resource then — in spite of the exhaustibility of the natural resource — an unlimited growth of consumption is also possible.

Proof: As a pattern of the unbounded consumption path in question we define a function $h(\cdot)$ in the following manner. Let $(z_n)_{n \in N}$ with $z_0 := 0$ be a sequence of positive real numbers for which $(z_{n+1} - z_n)_{n \in N}$ is strictly increasing and for which we have
$$\int_{z_n}^\infty g(x) \, dx < 2^{-n} \text{ for all } n \in N.$$
Such a sequence $(z_n)_{n \in N}$ can be constructed for all production functions for which $(*)$ is fulfilled and $g(\cdot)$ does not meet the abscissa. (For $d_2 < \infty$ the assertion of the theorem is valid in any case.) Using this $(z_n)_{n \in N}$ we get the function $h(\cdot)$ graphically by connecting all neighbouring points of the form (z_n, n) with straight lines.

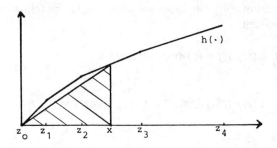

Fig.

(Thus $h(\cdot)$ is defined by

$$h(x) = \frac{1}{z_{n+1} - z_n} x + \frac{n z_{n+1} - (n+1) z_n}{z_{n+1} - z_n} \quad \text{for all } x \in [z_n, z_{n+1}]).$$

The function $h(\cdot)$ has the following important properties:

1. $\lim_{x \to \infty} h(x) = \infty$

2. $\int_d^\infty h(x) g(x) dx < \infty$ for one (and therefore for all) $d > 0$.

   For $d := z_1$ we get

$$\int_d^\infty h(x) g(x) dx = \sum_{n=1}^\infty \int_{z_n}^{z_{n+1}} h(x) g(x) dx$$

$$\leq \sum_{n=1}^\infty (n+1) \int_{z_n}^\infty g(x) dx$$

$$\leq \sum_{n=1}^\infty (n+1) 2^{-n} < \infty$$

3. $\int_0^x h(z) dz \geq 1/2 \, h(x) x$ for all $x > 0$. This inequality is valid because $(z_{n+1} - z_n)_{n \in \mathbb{N}}$
   is strictly increasing and thus $h(\cdot)$ is concave. Looking at the picture above we see that
   the integral of $h(\cdot)$ between zero and every $x > 0$ can never be smaller than the area
   of the hatched triangle which is exactly $1/2 \, h(x) x$. Mathematically the inequality
   follows from $h(z) > z \, h(x)$ for all $x > 0$ and all $z \in \,]0, x[$.

Now we define a path $(x_t, y_t, c_t)_{t \geq 0}$ by $c_t := h(t)$ and $\dot{x}_t := h(t)$ for all $t > 0$. Then we

have $x_t = x_0 + \int_0^t h(v) \, dv$ for all $t > 0$. From the definition of $g(\cdot)$ we get

$y_t = 2h(t) g(x_t/2h(t))$ for all $t > 0$. With (*) the total amount $\int_0^\infty y_t \, dt$ of resource in-

puts must therefore be finite as — because of the monotonicity and convexity of $g(\cdot)$ and the last two properties of $h\,(\cdot)$ listed above — we can make the following estimates for every $d > 0$ small enough:

$$\int_0^\infty y_t\,dt \leqslant 2 \int_d^\infty h\,(t)\,g\,((\int_0^t h\,(v)\,dv)/2h\,(t))\,dt$$

$$\leqslant 2 \int_d^\infty h\,(t)\,g\,(t/4)\,dt \leqslant 32 \int_d^\infty h\,(t)\,g\,(t)\,dt < \infty. \qquad\qquad \text{QED}$$

3.

Although unbounded growth of consumption is not necessarily prohibited by the exhaustibility of the natural resource the speed of growth may be considerably reduced. So exponential growth with a constant growth rate $w > 0$ is only possible if we have $F\,(x, 0) > 0$ for one (and therefore for all) $x > 0$, i.e. the natural resource is dispensable for production. (If the total production q_t grew with a constant rate $w > 0$ and the whole q_t were always reinvested, we should totally use up the quantity $\int_0^\infty q_0 e^{wt} g\,((x_0 + q_0 \int_0^t e^{wv}\,dv)/q_0\,e^{wt})\,dt$ of the natural resource, which is approximately equal to $\int_0^\infty q_0\,e^{wt}\,g\,(q_0/w)\,dt$ and thus infinite.)

In the Cobb-Douglas case we can easily calculate the maximum speed of growth which is still possible if production depends on an exhaustible natural resource. In another way *Mitra* [1980] proved similar results:

Theorem 2: Let F be a linear homogeneous Cobb-Douglas production function for which there are positive sustainable yields; i.e. $F\,(x, y) = x^a\,y^b$ with $a, b \in]0,1[$, $a + b = 1$ and $a > b$. If we define $p^* = a/b - 1$ we have: For every $p < p^*$ and every given initial stock x_0 of reproducible capital there is a program $(x_t, y_t, c_t)_{t \geqslant 0}$ with $\int_0^\infty y_t\,dt < \infty$ and $\lim_{t \to \infty} c_t/t^p > 0$; so we may say that $(c_t)_{t \geqslant 0}$ can grow at least as fast as $(t^p)_{t \geqslant 0}$. But for all programs $(x_t, y_t, c_t)_{t \geqslant 0}$ with $\int_0^\infty y_t\,dt < \infty$ it must always be $\lim_{t \to \infty} \inf c_t/t^{p^*} = 0$, i.e. there is no consumption path $(c_t)_{t \geqslant 0}$ wich grows as fast as $(t^{p^*})_{t \geqslant 0}$.

Proof:

a) For a given $p < p^*$ we set $\dot{x}_t := t^p$ and $c_t := t^p$ for all $t \geqslant 0$. Then we have $x_t = x_0 + t^{p+1}/(p + 1)$ for all t's and so we need a resource input of

$$y_t = (2t^p)^{1/b} \cdot \left(x_0 + \frac{t^{p+1}}{p + 1} \right)^{-a/b}$$

$$\leqslant (2t^p)^{1/b} \cdot \left(\frac{t^{p+1}}{p + 1} \right)^{-a/b}$$

to produce $q_t := \dot{x}_t + c_t = 2t^p$ in t. The total input of the natural resource is therefore

$$\int_0^\infty y_t \, dt \leqslant (2(p+1)^a)^{1/b} \int_0^\infty t^{(p-(p+1)a)/b} \, dt.$$

But this integral is finite, as $p < a/b - 1$ implies $(p - (p+1)a)/b < -1$.

b) *Solow* [1974, p. 43] has shown that for every path $(x_t, y_t, c_t)_{t \geqslant 0}$ with $\int_0^\infty y_t \, dt < \infty$

there are constants $A > 0$ and $T > 0$ such that $x_t < A \, t^{a/b}$ for all $t > T$. If total production $(q_t)_{t \geqslant 0}$ grew as fast as $(t^{p^*})_{t \geqslant 0}$, i.e. there were a $B > 0$ with $q_t > B \, t^{p^*}$ for all $t > T$, we could derive the following inequality for all $t > T$:

$$y_t = q_t^{1/b} \cdot x_t^{-a/b} \geqslant B^{1/b} \, t^{((a/b)-1)1/b} \cdot A^{-a/b} \, t^{-(a/b)^2}$$

$$= A^{-a/b} \, B^{1/b} \, t^{(a-b-a^2)/b^2}.$$

Then the integral $\int_0^\infty y_t \, dt$ would diverge as

$$(a - b - a^2)/b^2 = -(a^2 - 2a + 1)/b^2 = -(1-a)^2/b^2 = -1 \qquad \text{QED}$$

Especially we can conclude that linear growth is only possible if $a/b - 1 > 1$, i.e. $a > 2/3$. With $a \leqslant 2/3$ the absolute increments in consumption must decrease in the long run.

4.

"If a permanently sustainable consumption level is possible it may seem plausible, that unbounded consumption is possible as well." Here, this supposition of *Dasgupta/ Heal* [1979, p. 205] could be confirmed constructively for a very general class of production functions. The statement that there is no real frontier between unbounded growth and the stationary state seems to be fairly universal: If an economy offers no possibility for unlimited economic growth, then a steady state cannot be sustained forever, too. – But even if unlimited growth of consumption is still possible with an exhaustible natural resource the growth *rates* must inevitably tend to zero.

References

Beckerman, W.: In Defence of Economic Growth. London 1974.

Dasgupta, P., and *G. Heal*: The Optimal Depletion of Exhaustible Resources. Review of Economic Studies, Symposium on the Economics of Exhaustible Resources, 1974, 3–28.

–: Economic Theory and Exhaustible Resources. Cambridge 1979.

Hayek, F.A.: The Constitution of Liberty. London 1960.

Houthakker, H.S.: The Economics of Nonrenewable Resources. Beihefte zur Konjunkturpolitik **23** (Die Versorgung der Weltwirtschaft mit Rohstoffen), 1976, 115–124.

Mitra, T.: On Optimal Depletion of Exhaustible Resources: Existence and Characterization Results. Econometrica **48**, 1980, 1431–1450.

Scott, A.: Natural Resources: The Economics of Conservation. Toronto 1955.

Solow, R.: Intergenerational Equity and Exhaustible Resources. Review of Economic Studies, Symposium on the Economics of Exhaustible Resources, 1974, 29–46.

Economic Theory of Natural Resources. © Physica-Verlag, Würzburg–Wien, 1982.

The Comparative Dynamics of Efficient Programs of Capital Accumulation and Resource Depletion[1])

W. Erwin Diewert and *Tracy R. Lewis*

1. Introduction

Dorfman/Samuelson/Solow [1958, Chap. 12] partially characterize efficient paths of capital accumulation (or resource depletion) using the first order necessary conditions for a finite horizon intertemporal profit maximization problem, where the maximization is constrained by a sequence of one period production function constraints (which describe how current period stocks of capital and current inputs are transformed into current outputs and next period stocks of capital). However, surprisingly little has been done on the comparative statics (or dynamics) of such efficient programs of capital accumulation; i.e., little has been done in determining how the optimal stocks and flows react to changes in initial stocks or to changes in (expected) prices and interest rates.[2]) The purpose of the present paper is to add to the existing stock of comparative dynamics knowledge.

We follow the standard comparative statics methodology due to *Samuelson* [1947]; that is, we assume that we have an initial (interior) equilibrium that is characterized by the usual first order necessary conditions and that the (strong) second order sufficient conditions for a maximum are satisfied. We then attempt to use this information in order to determine how the endogenous variables in our model of producer behavior respond to changes in exogenous variables such as initial stocks, expected future prices, and interest rates.

[1]) This work was supported by the Department of Energy Contract No. DE-AS03-76SF00326 at the Institute for Mathematical Studies in the Social Sciences, Stanford University and Social Sciences and Humanities Research Council of Canada. The first author thanks the National Bureau of Economic Research–Palo Alto, and the second author thanks the Bureau of Economics at the Federal Trade Commission for office space. Both authors thank C. Blackorby, W.A. Brock and W. Eichhorn for their valuable comments.

[2]) Perhaps the most comprehensive results in the infinite horizon case have been obtained by *Araujo/Scheinkman* [1977, 1979]. In the finite horizon case, the most comprehensive results are perhaps still found in *Hicks* [1946]. However, Hicks' results are limited for two reasons: (i) he assumes that all capital or resource stocks have market prices, and (ii) he does not make use of the *Malinvaud* [1953] and *Dorfman/Samuelson/Solow* [1958] one period technology sets, which the latter authors use in order to *construct* the Hicksian multiperiod production function. Finally, various comparative dynamics results are available in the natural resources literature [e.g., *Dasgupta/Heal*], but these results are obtained usually by assuming very specific production functions (e.g., Cobb-Douglas) and by assuming expected future prices to be constant in each period. However, some fairly general comparative dynamic results have been obtained by *Sweeney* [1977], *Epstein* [1978], Hartwick [1978] and *Dasgupta/Heal/Stiglitz* [1980] in a continuous time framework.

In section 2 we outline our model of intertemporal producer behavior. In section 3 we study how the endogenous stock and flow variables in our model respond to changes in resource stock taxes, while sections 4, 5 and 6 study the response of endogenous variables to changes in initial stocks, prices and interest rates respectively. Section 7 offers some concluding remarks, and section 8 is an appendix which indicates some properties of the (maximized) value function under various hypotheses on the one period technology.

2. The Basic Model and Preliminary Results

Denote the one period technology set of a firm by $S \equiv \{(x, s^0, s^1)\}$, where $x \equiv (x_1, x_2, \ldots, x_M)^T$ is an M dimensional vector of current period outputs (good m is an input if $x_m < 0$), $s^0 \equiv (s_1^0, \ldots, s_N^0)^T \geqslant 0_N$ [3]) is a nonnegative vector of beginning of the period stocks available to the firm, and $s^1 \equiv (s_1^1, \ldots, s_N^1)^T \geqslant 0_N$ denotes a nonnegative vector of end of the period stocks (which are available to the firm at the start of the next period).

The "stock" variables s^0 and s^1 are to be distinguished from the "flow" variable x on the following basis: well defined market prices $p \equiv (p_1, \ldots, p_M)^T \geqslant 0_M$ exist for the flow variable vector x, but no market prices exist for the stock variables. There are at least four possible economic interpretations that can be placed on the stock variables: the stocks could be: (i) inventories and goods in process, (ii) bolted-down pieces of capital equipment (as opposed to uninstalled pieces of capital equipment which appear as purchased inputs in the x vector), (iii) stocks of various grades of "tree" (or other renewable natural resources) on a plot of land that is owned or leased by the firm, or (iv) stocks of various grades of "ore" (or other nonrenewable natural resources) on a plot of land owned by the firm.

The technology set represents the set of "tradeoffs" that the producer can make: given an initial stock vector s^0, the producer can produce more current net output x (or use less current input) at the cost of running down its internal stocks (i.e., less s^1 will be available at the start of next period). This is basically the *Malinvaud* [1953] model of producer behavior.

For given beginning and end of period stock vectors s^0 and s^1, it makes sense for the producer to maximize profits. Thus for $p \gg 0_M$, $s^0 \geqslant 0_N$ and $s^1 \geqslant 0_N$, define the one period variable profit function[4] π as

$$\pi (p, s^0, s^1) \equiv \begin{cases} \sup_x \{p \cdot x : (x, s^0, s^1) \in S\} & \text{if there exists an } x \\ & \text{such that } (x, s^0, s^1) \in S, \\ -\infty & \text{otherwise.} \end{cases} \tag{1}$$

---

[3]) x^T denotes the transpose of the (column) vector x, $x^T y$ or $x \cdot y$ denotes the inner product of the vectors x and y, 0_N denotes an N-dimensional vector of zeros, $x \geqslant 0_M$ means each component of x is nonnegative, $x \gg 0_M$ means each component of x is positive and $x > 0_M$ means $x \geqslant 0_M$ but $x \neq 0_M$.

[4]) This is *Diewert's* [1973, 1974] term. The concept is due to *Samuelson* [1953–54, p. 20], who uses the term "gross national product function." *Gorman* [1968] uses the term "gross profit function," while *McFadden* [1978] and *Lau* [1976] use the term "restricted profit function." See these references for proofs of the properties of π.

Irrespective of the properties of S it can be shown that $\pi(p, s^0, s^1)$ is a convex and (positively) linearly homogeneous function in p. Moreover, if π is differentiable at (p, s^0, s^1) with respect to the components of p, then by a result due originally to *Hotelling* [1932, p. 594], we have

$$x(p, s^0, s^1) = \nabla_p \pi(p, s^0, s^1) \tag{2}$$

where $x(p, s^0, s^1)$ is the profit maximizing net output vector that is the solution to the profit maximization problem defined in the right hand side of (1) and $\nabla_p \pi(p, s^0, s^1) \equiv$ $\equiv [\partial\pi/\partial p_1, \ldots, \partial\pi/\partial p_M]^T$ denotes the column vector of partial derivatives of π with respect to the components of p.

Throughout the paper we assume that S is a nonempty, closed set, an empirically harmless assumption. At times we shall place additional restrictions on S such as:

S satisfies free disposal in the stock variables,[5]) $\tag{3}$

S is a convex set,[6]) and $\tag{4}$

S is a cone.[7]) $\tag{5}$

If S satisfies (3), (4) and (5), then it can be shown that π satisfies (6), (7) and (8) below respectively:

$\pi(p, s^0, s^1)$ is nondecreasing in the components of s^0 and nonincreasing
in the components of s^1, $\tag{6}$

$\pi(p, s^0, s^1)$ is a concave function[8]) in (s^0, s^1) in (s^0, s^1) for fixed p, and $\tag{7}$

$\pi(p, s^0, s^1)$ is a (positively) linearly homogeneous function[9]) in (s^0, s^1)
for fixed p. $\tag{8}$

Before proceeding to the firm's intertemporal profit maximization problem, we consider a few special cases for the one period technology.

Perhaps the simplest case to consider is that of a mining firm that can exploit an ore body at constant marginal cost. Let $s^0 > 0$ denote the initial stock of ore (a positive scalar). Then s^1 denotes the amount of ore left after mining one period ($0 \leqslant s^1 \leqslant s^0$), $p_1 > 0$ denotes the price of one unit of mined ore sold on the market and $p_2 > 0$ denotes the price of the amount of variable input required to mine one unit of ore. If $p_2 < p_1$, then the variable profit function that corresponds to this one period technology is

$$\pi(p_1, p_2, s^0, s^1) \equiv \begin{cases} (p_1 - p_2)(s^0 - s^1) & \text{for } s^0 - s^1 \geqslant 0, s^1 \geqslant 0 \\ \\ -\infty & \text{elsewhere.} \end{cases}$$

---

[5]) This means: if $(x, y^1, z^1) \in S, y^2 \geqslant y^1 \geqslant 0_M, z^1 \geqslant z^2 \geqslant 0_M$, then $(x, y^2, z^2) \in S$.

[6]) This means: if $(x^1, y^1, z^1) \in S, (x^2, y^2, z^2) \in S, 0 \leqslant \lambda \leqslant 1$, then $(\lambda x^1 + (1-\lambda) x^2,$ $\lambda y^1 + (1-\lambda) y^2, \lambda z^1 + (1-\lambda) z^2) \in S$.

[7]) This means: if $\lambda \geqslant 0, (x, y, z) \in S$, then $(\lambda x, \lambda y, \lambda z) \in S$.

[8]) This means: for $0 \leqslant \lambda \leqslant 1, \pi(p, \lambda s^{0*} + (1-\lambda) s^{0**}, \lambda s^{1*} + (1-\lambda) s^{1**}) \geqslant \lambda \pi(p, s^{0*}, s^{1*}) +$ $+ (1-\lambda) \pi(p, s^{0**}, s^{1**})$.

[9]) This means: for $\lambda \geqslant 0, \pi(p, \lambda s^0, \lambda s^1) = \lambda \pi(p, s^0, s^1)$.

304

Note that the above π is convex and linearly homogeneous in $p \equiv (p_1, p_2)$. π also satisfies (6), (7) and (8). In Figure 1, some level curves of π as functions of s^0 and s^1 are graphed with the price of output set equal to 2 and the price of variable input set equal to 1; i.e., the curves $\pi (2, 1, s^0, s^1) = k$ are graphed with $k = 0, 1, 2, 3$. Note that the isoprofit curves are straight lines, that $\pi (p_1, p_2, s^0, s^1) = -\infty$ if $s^0 < s^1$, so that profit decreases as we increase s^1 holding s^0 fixed. The latter property will hold for most technologies; the amount of variable profit will decrease for a fixed initial stock s^0 as we increase the amount of stock held over for the next period s^1 until a maximal amount of s^1 is reached beyond which it is impossible to carry over an additional amount of stock to the next period (variable profits are $-\infty$ in this region). Finally, note that π exhibits property (8) so that the corresponding one period technology set S exhibits constant returns to scale. Thus any positive isoprofit curve can be generated by radially inflating (or deflating) the unit isoprofit curve. For example, the point $(s^0, s^1) = (4, 2)$ on the $k = 2$ isoprofit curve is obtained by multiplying the point $(2, 1)$ on the unit isoprofit line by 2 (see the dashed line in Figure 1).

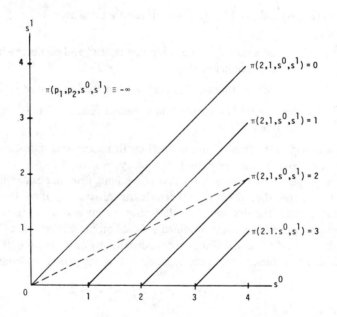

Fig. 1

In the above example, the firm could exploit its entire initial ore body s^0 at constant marginal cost. For example, if $s^0 = 4$, then the firm could mine one unit of ore and make variable profit 1 ($\pi (2, 1, 4, 3) = 1$), or it could mine 2 units of ore and make profit 2 ($\pi (2, 1, 4, 2) = 2$), etc. In many real life examples, ore can be mined only at increasing marginal cost. For example, consider the family of isoprofit curves graphed in Figure 2.

In Figure 2 as in Figure 1, each positive isoprofit curve is a radial blowup of the unit isoprofit curve; that is, the variable profit function π which corresponds to Figure 2 also satisfies property (8) above. Moreover, the variable profit functions that correspond to

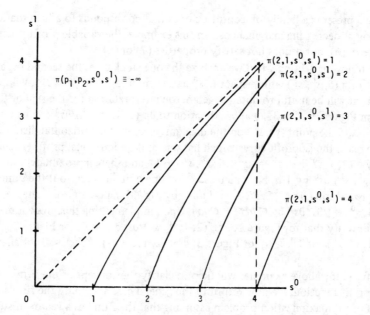

Fig. 2

Figures 1 and 2 both satisfy properties (6) and (7) as well. To show that the technology that is associated with Figure 2 exhibits increasing marginal cost, suppose that the firm's initial stock of ore is $s^0 = 4$. Then the firm could mine 1/6 of a unit of ore and make profit 1 (π (2, 1, 4, 3 5/6) = 1), it could mine 1/2 of a unit of ore and make profit 2 (π (2, 1, 4, 3 1/2) = 2), it could mine 1 1/2 units of ore and make profit 3 (π (2, 1, 4, 2 1/2) = 3), or it could mine all 4 units of ore and make profit 4.

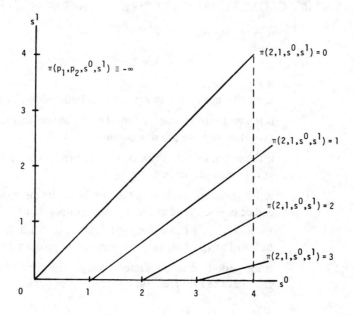

Fig. 3

Figure 3 presents a family of isoprofit curves that corresponds to a firm that can mine its orebody at decreasing marginal cost. In this example, the variable profit function satisfies property (6), but it does not satisfy properties (7) or (8).

In the following section when we analyze the one stock case, the second order partial derivative of $\pi\,(p, s^0, s^1)$ with respect to s^0 and s^1, $\partial^2\pi\,(p, s^0, s^1)/\partial s^0\,\partial s^1$, will play a key role. Thus, it will be useful to obtain a geometric interpretation for the sign of this derivative. From Figures 1, 2 or 3, an approximation to $\partial\pi\,(2, 1, s^0, s^1)/\partial s^0$ can be obtained as follows: locate the point (s^0, s^1) on the diagram, measure the horizontal distance d required to reach the isoprofit curve which has one unit of additional profit (i.e., d is determined by $\pi\,(2, 1, s^0 + d, s^1) = \pi\,(2, 1, s^0, s^1) + 1)$, and then approximate $\partial\pi\,(2, 1, s^0, s^1)/\partial s^0$ by $1/d$. Now increase s^1 by one unit and carry out the same procedure, approximating $\partial\pi\,(2, 1, s^0, s^1 + 1)/\partial s^0$ by $1/d^*$. Finally, approximate $\partial^2\pi\,(2, 1, s^0, s^1)/\partial s^0\,\partial s^1$ by $(1/d^*) - (1/d)$. Upon implementing this procedure, the reader will verify that for Figure 1, $\partial^2\pi\,(2, 1, s^0, s^1)/\partial s^0\,\partial s^1 = 0$; for Figure 2, $\partial^2\pi\,(2, 1, s^0, s^1)/\partial s^0\,\partial s^1 > 0$; for Figure 3, $\partial^2\pi\,(2, 1, s^0, s^1)\,\partial s^0\,\partial s^1 < 0$ for all $s^1 > 0$, $s^0 > s^1$.

Hopefully, the above examples will help to clarify the concept of the firm's one period variable profit function. We now return to the general case and study the firm's intertemporal profit maximization problem assuming that the firm has a vector of stocks s^0 at its disposal at the beginning of period 1.

We assume that the firm has a T period horizon (where $T \geqslant 2$) and that its intertemporal profit maximization problem can be written in terms of the one period variable profit function π as follows:

$$\max_{s^1 \geqslant 0_N, \,\ldots,\, s^T \geqslant 0_N} \{\pi\,(p^1, s^0, s^1) + \delta_1\,[\pi\,(p^2, s^1, s^2) - \tau^1 \cdot s^1]$$

$$+ \delta_1\delta_2\,[\pi\,(p^3, s^2, s^3) - \tau^2 \cdot s^2] + \ldots + \delta_1\delta_2 \ldots \delta_{T\text{-}1}\,[\pi\,(p^T, s^{T\text{-}1}, s^T)$$

$$- \tau^{T\text{-}1} \cdot s^{T\text{-}1}] + \delta_1\delta_2 \ldots \delta_T\,[q \cdot s^T - \tau^T \cdot s^T]$$

$$\equiv V\,(\tau^1, \tau^2, \ldots, \tau^T, s^0, p^1, p^2, \ldots, p^T, q, \delta_1, \delta_2, \ldots, \delta_T)\} \qquad (9)$$

where

π	is the one period variable profit function defined by (1)
$p^t \geqslant 0_M$	is the vector of (variable) output and input prices that is expected to prevail during period t, $t = 1, 2, \ldots, T$
$s^0 \geqslant 0_N$	is the vector of initial stocks that the firm has at its disposal at the beginning of period 1
$s^t \geqslant 0_N$	is the vector of stocks that the firm has at its disposal at the end of period t (and at the beginning of period $t + 1$) for $t = 1, 2, \ldots, T$ (note that $s \equiv (s^1, s^2, \ldots, s^T)$ is the vector of decision variables in the maximization problem (9))
$\delta_t \equiv 1/(1 + r_t) > 0$	is the period t discount factor; i.e., r_t is the period t interest rate that the firm faces for $t = 1, 2, \ldots, T$

$\tau^t \equiv [\tau_1^t, \tau_2^t, \ldots, \tau_N^t]^T$ is a vector of stock tax (or subsidy) rates that the firm must pay on its holdings of stocks at the end of period t but the taxes are actually paid in period $t+1$

$q \geqslant 0_N$ is the vector of scrap value prices that is expected to prevail during period $T+1$ for the components of the firm's final period stock vector s^T, and

V is the firm's *value function*, which is defined to be the maximized (with respect to s) discounted stream of profits that firm can earn over the T period horizon.

Note that V depends on five sets of variables: (i) the NT-dimensional vector of stock tax rates $\tau \equiv (\tau^1, \tau^2, \ldots, \tau^T)$, (ii) the N-dimensional vector of initial stocks s^0, (iii) the MT vector of expected variable input and output prices $p \equiv (p^1, p^2, \ldots, p^T)$, (iv) the N-dimensional vector of scrap value prices for the final period stocks q, and (v) the T-dimensional vector of discount factors $\delta \equiv (\delta_1, \delta_2, \ldots, \delta_T)$. Define the $NT + N + MT + N + T$ vector of exogenous variables as $z \equiv (\tau, s^0, p, q, \delta)$ and the NT vector of endogenous variables as $s \equiv (s^1, s^2, \ldots, s^T)$. Then the value function can be written as $V(z)$ and the solution to (9) as $s(z)$.

It should be noted that in many applications the tax variables τ^t will be identically zero; i.e., $\tau^t = 0_N$ for all t. We have introduced these variables for two reasons: (i) in many natural resource applications of our model, governments may be interested in imposing such resource stock taxes or subsidies in order to encourage depletion or conservation, and (ii) developing the comparative statics properties of our model with respect to these tax variables helps us to interpret the comparative statics properties with respect to other variables.

We now follow the standard *Hicks* [1946] *Samuelson* [1947] approach for obtaining comparative statics results. We assume that the solution $s* \equiv (s^{1*}, \ldots, s^{T*})$ to (9) is unique and that

$$s^{t*} \gg 0_N \qquad \text{for } t = 1, 2, \ldots, T \qquad (10)$$

so that we have an interior solution. We assume that $s*$ satisfies the first order conditions for the unconstrained maximization problem (9):

$$\nabla_{s^1} \pi(p^1, s^0, s^{1*}) + \delta_1 \nabla_{s^1} \pi(p^2, s^{1*}, s^{2*}) = \delta_1 \tau^1$$

$$\delta_1 \nabla_{s^2} \pi(p^2, s^{1*}, s^{2*}) + \delta_1 \delta_2 \nabla_{s^2} \pi(p^3, s^{2*}, s^{3*}) = \delta_1 \delta_2 \tau^2$$

$$\vdots$$

$$\delta_1 \cdots \delta_{T-2} \nabla_{s^{T-1}} \pi(p^{T-1}, s^{T-2*}, s^{T-1*}) + \delta_1 \cdots \delta_{T-1} \nabla_{s^{T-1}} \pi(p^T, s^{T-1*}, s^{T*})$$
$$= \delta_1 \delta_2 \cdots \delta_{T-1} \tau^{T-1}$$

$$\delta_1 \cdots \delta_{T-1} \nabla_{s^T} \pi(p^T, s^{T-1*}, s^{T*}) + \delta_1 \cdots \delta_{T-1} \delta_T q = \delta_1 \cdots \delta_{T-1} \delta_T \tau^T. \qquad (11)$$

We further assume that the one period variable profit function is such that

$\pi(p^t, s^{t-1}, s^*)$ is twice continuously differentiable in a neighborhood around

(p^t, s^{t-1*}, s^{t*}) for $t = 1, 2, \ldots, T$. $\qquad\qquad$ (12)

Finally, we assume that the second order sufficient conditions for an unconstrained interior maximum hold; i.e., we assume that the NT by NT matrix (call it A) of second order partial derivatives of the objective function in (9) with respect to the components of s evaluated at s^* is negative definite. (The matrix A can also be obtained by differentiating the first order conditions (11) with respect to the components of s.)

Our last assumption implies that A^{-1} exists. Hence, we may apply the Implicit Function Theorem and conclude that a unique solution to (9), $s(z)$, exists in a neighborhood of the vector of exogenous variables $z^* \equiv (\tau, s^0, p, q, \delta)$ with $s(z^*) = s^* \equiv$
$\equiv (s^{1*}, s^{2*}, \ldots, s^{T*})$.

Using our differentiability assumption (12) and Hotelling's Lemma (2), the optimal period t variable output and input vector is

$$x^{t*} \equiv \nabla_p \pi(p^t, s^{t-1*}, s^{t*}), \qquad\qquad t = 1, 2, \ldots, T.$$

We can define the period t net supply functions in a neighborhood of $z^* \equiv (\tau, s^0, p, q, \delta)$ by

$$x^t(z) \equiv \nabla_p \pi(p^t, s^{t-1}(z), s^t(z)), \qquad\qquad t = 1, 2, \ldots, T \qquad (13)$$

where $s(z) \equiv (s^1(z), s^2(z), \ldots, s^T(z))$ is the NT-dimensional vector of optimal stock functions.

We can also define a vector of competitive imputed values or shadow prices for the initial stock vector s^0 by differentiating the value function with respect to the components of s^0, i.e., define the initial shadow price vector w^* as $w^* \equiv \nabla_{s^0} V(z^*)$ and for z close to z^*, define

$$w(z) \equiv \nabla_{s^0} V(z) \qquad\qquad\qquad (14)$$

$$= \nabla_{s^0} \pi(p^1, s^0, s^1(z)) \qquad\qquad (15)$$

where (15) follows by differentiating the value function with respect to s^0 and then using the first order conditions (11) (except that the s^{t*} are replaced by $s^t(z)$ in (11)). (Note that in (15), $\nabla_{s^0} \pi(p^0, s^0, s^1(z))$ means differentiate π with respect to its second set of arguments only.) Note that if the free disposal assumption (3) is satisfied, using (6) yields $w(z) \geqslant 0_N$.

Now we can state precisely the aim of the present paper: we want to determine how the endogenous variables $V(z)$ (the value function), $s(z)$ (the NT-dimensional vector of optimal stocks), $x(z) \equiv [x^1(z), x^2(z), \ldots, x^T(z)]$ (the MT vector of optimal variable in inputs and outputs) and $w(z)$ (the N-dimensional vector of imputed prices for the components of the initial stock vector s^0) change as the exogenous variables $z \equiv (\tau, s^0, p, q, \delta)$ change in a neighborhood of the initial equilibrium. In the following section we consider variations in the stock tax variables.

3. The Comparative Statics of Changes in Stock Taxes

Let us first write the matrix A that is obtained by differentiating equations (11) with respect to the components of s in terms of T^2 N by N blocks, A_{rt}, r, $t = 1, 2, \ldots, T$. Assuming that $T \geqslant 2$ and defining $\delta_0 \equiv 1$, it can be verified that

$$A_{tt} \equiv \delta_0 \delta_1 \delta_2 \ldots \delta_{t-1} \nabla^2_{s^t s^t} \pi (p^t, s^{t-1*}, s^{t*}) + \delta_1 \delta_2 \ldots \delta_t \nabla^2_{s^t s^t} \pi (p^{t+1}, s^{t*}, s^{t+1*})$$

$$\text{for } t = 1, 2, \ldots, T-1 \qquad (16)$$

$$A_{TT} \equiv \delta_1 \delta_2 \ldots \delta_{T-1} \nabla^2_{s^T s^T} \pi (p^T, s^{T-1*}, s^{T*}), \qquad (17)$$

$$A_{t,t+1} \equiv \delta_1 \delta_2 \ldots \delta_t \nabla^2_{s^t s^{t+1}} \pi (p^{t+1}, s^{t*}, s^{t+1*}), \quad \text{for } t = 1, 2, \ldots, T-1 \qquad (18)$$

$$= [A_{t+1,t}]^T, \text{ the transpose of } A_{t+1,t}, \text{ and}$$

$$A_{r,t} \equiv 0_{N \times N} \qquad\qquad\qquad \text{if } |r - t| > 1. \qquad (19)$$

Thus A is a block tridiagonal matrix. It is also negative definite and symmetric by our assumptions. Thus A^{-1} exists and A^{-1} is also negative definite and symmetric.

Define the NT by NT diagonal matrix D where the t-th N by N block is the diagonal matrix $\delta_1 \delta_2 \ldots \delta_t I_N$ where I_N is the N by N identity matrix. Then differentiating the first order conditions (11) with respect to the components of s and τ yields the following expression for the NT by NT matrix of partial derivatives of the optimal stocks with respect to the components of τ, $\nabla_\tau s (z^*)$, evaluated at the initial equilibrium $z^* \equiv (\tau, s^0, p, q, \delta)$:

$$\nabla_\tau s (z^*) = A^{-1} D \equiv S_{\tau\tau} D \qquad (20)$$

where we have defined the symmetric, negative definite stock tax "substitution" matrix $S_{\tau\tau} \equiv A^{-1}$. Negative definiteness of A^{-1} implies that the diagonal elements of A^{-1} are negative and since the elements of the diagonal matrix D are positive, we have

$$\partial s^t_n (z^*) / \partial \tau^t_n < 0 \qquad \text{for } n = 1, 2, \ldots, N \text{ and } t = 1, 2, \ldots, T. \qquad (21)$$

Symmetry of A^{-1} implies that $D \nabla_\tau s (z^*) = DA^{-1}D = D^T S_{\tau\tau} D$ is symmetric so that

$$\delta_1 \delta_2 \ldots \delta_t \partial s^t_n / \partial \tau^r_i = \delta_1 \delta_2 \ldots \delta_r \partial s^r_i / \partial \tau^t_n, \quad r, t = 1, \ldots, T; i, n = 1, \ldots, N. \qquad (22)$$

In the case of only one stock variable (i.e., $N = 1$), we can deduce a great deal more about the "off diagonal" responses of optimal stocks to changes in stock taxes, $\partial s^t_n (z^*) / \partial \tau^r_i$, as we shall see at the end of this section

We now study how the value function $V (z) \equiv \sum_{t=1}^{T} \delta_0 \delta_1 \delta_2 \ldots \delta_{t-1} [\pi(p^t, s^{t-1}(z),$

$s^t (z)) - \tau^{t-1} \cdot s^{t-1} (z)] + \delta_1 \delta_2 \ldots \delta_T [q \cdot s^T (z) - \tau^T \cdot s^T (z)]$ changes as the components of τ change.[10]) Differentiating V with respect to τ at the initial equilibrium yields, using the first order conditions (11):

---

[10]) Define $\tau^0 \equiv 0_N$ and $\delta_0 \equiv 1$ when necessary.

$$\nabla_\tau V(z^*) = -Ds^* \leqslant 0_{NT}. \tag{23}$$

Thus $\partial V(z^*)/\partial \tau_n^t = -\delta_1 \delta_2 \ldots \delta_t s_n^{t^*} < 0$ for $n = 1, 2, \ldots, T$; i.e., as stock taxes increase, discounted optimal profit decreases.

In order to work out how the MT-dimensional vector of optimal variable quantities $x(z)$ changes as the components of the NT-dimensional vector of stock tax rates τ change, it is useful to define the following NT by MT dimensional intensity[11]) matrix Γ:

$$\Gamma \equiv \begin{bmatrix} \nabla_{s^1 p}^2 \pi^1, & \nabla_{s^1 p}^2 \pi^2, & 0_{N \times M}, & \cdots, & 0_{N \times M}, & 0_{N \times M}, & 0_{N \times M} \\ 0_{N \times M}, & \nabla_{s^2 p}^2 \pi^2, & \nabla_{s^2 p}^2 \pi^3, & \cdots, & 0_{N \times M}, & 0_{N \times M}, & 0_{N \times M} \\ \vdots & \vdots & \vdots & & \vdots & \vdots & \vdots \\ \vdots & \vdots & \vdots & & \vdots & \vdots & \vdots \\ 0_{N \times M}, & 0_{N \times M}, & 0_{N \times M}, & \cdots, & 0_{N \times M}, & \nabla_{s^{T-1} p}^2 \pi^{T-1}, & \nabla_{s^{T-1} p}^2 \pi^T \\ 0_{N \times M}, & 0_{N \times M}, & 0_{N \times M}, & \cdots, & 0_{N \times M}, & 0_{N \times M}, & \nabla_{s^T p}^2 \pi^T \end{bmatrix} \tag{24}$$

where

$$\pi^t \equiv \pi(p^t, s^{t-1*}, s^{t*}) \text{ and } \nabla_{s^t p}^2 \pi^t \text{ means } \nabla_{s^t p}^2 \pi^t \text{ for } t = 1, 2, \ldots, T.$$

Using Hotelling's Lemma (2) and the linear homogeneity of $\pi(p^t, s^{t-1*}, s^{t*})$ in p^t yields the identities (using Euler's Theorem on homogeneous functions) for $t = 1, 2, \ldots, T$:

$$\pi(p^t, s^{t-1*}, s^{t*}) = p^t \cdot \nabla_p \pi(p^t, s^{t-1*}, s^{t*}) = p^t \cdot x^t(z^*), \tag{25}$$

$$\nabla_{pp}^2 \pi(p^t, s^{t-1*}, s^{t*}) p^t = 0_M, \tag{26}$$

$$\nabla_{s^{t-1} p}^2 \pi(p^t, s^{t-1*}, s^{t*}) p^t = \nabla_{s^{t-1}} \pi(p^t, s^{t-1*}, s^{t*}) \geqslant 0_N \tag{27}$$

and

$$\nabla_{s^t p}^2 \pi(p^t, s^{t-1*}, s^{t*}) p^t = \nabla_{s^t} \pi(p^t, s^{t-1*}, s^{t*}) \leqslant 0_N \tag{28}$$

where the inequalities in (27) and (28) follow from assumption (6). Define the MT by MT block diagonal matrix D^* where the t-th M by M block is $\delta_0 \delta_1 \delta_2 \ldots \delta_{t-1} I_M$, $t = 1, 2, \ldots, T$ with $\delta_0 \equiv 1$. Using (24), (27), (28) and the definition of D^*, we find that the first order conditions (11) can be rewritten as:

$$\Gamma D^* p + \delta_1 \delta_2 \ldots \delta_T [0_{M(T-1)}^T, q^T]^T = D\tau. \tag{29}$$

The above identities will be useful later.

Using Hotelling's Lemma (2) and definition (24), we obtain the following general formula for the response of the MT dimensional vector of net outputs $x(z^*)$ to changes in the components of the NT dimensional vector of stock tax rates τ:

---

[11]) *Diewert* [1974, p. 145] defines a normalization of a second order partial derivative of a variable profit function with respect to a price and a quantity as an elasticity of intensity.

$$\nabla_\tau x \, (z^*) = \Gamma^T \nabla_\tau s \, (z^*)$$

$$= \Gamma^T S_{\tau\tau} D \qquad\qquad \text{using (20).} \tag{30}$$

In general, we cannot deduce much about the signs of the entries in the MT by NT matrix $\nabla_\tau x \, (z^*)$.[12] The problem is that the components of the intensity matrix Γ can be of either sign. Even in the simplest case where there is only one variable good ($M = 1$) and one stock ($N = 1$), using (27) and (28) it can be seen that the elements along the main diagonal of Γ are nonpositive, while the off diagonal elements are nonnegative. However, there is one set of interesting general restrictions on the elements of $\nabla_\tau x \, (z^*)$ that we can deduce: premultiply both sides of (30) by $p^T D^{*T} = p \cdot D^*$, use (29) and deduce that

$$p \cdot D^* \nabla_\tau x \, (z^*) + \delta_1 \ldots \delta_T q \cdot \nabla_\tau s^T \, (z^*) = \tau \cdot D^T S_{\tau\tau} D \tag{31}$$

or

$$\sum_{t=1}^{T} \delta_1 \delta_2 \ldots \delta_{t-1} p^t \cdot \nabla_\tau x^t \, (z^*) + \delta_1 \ldots \delta_T q \cdot \nabla_\tau s^T \, (z^*) =$$

$$= \tau \cdot DS_{\tau\tau} D = 0_{NT}^T \qquad \text{if } \tau = 0_{NT}. \tag{32}$$

In the above equations, one can regard the final period stock vector s^T as an output vector since it can be sold at the market price vector $\delta_1 \ldots \delta_T q$. Thus the left hand sides of (31) or (32) represent the response of the discounted value of net production to changes in stock tax rates. On the right hand sides, we have the negative definite symmetric matrix $DS_{\tau\tau} D$ premultiplied by the transpose of the stock tax rate vector τ.

Now postmultiply both sides of (32) by τ and obtain (if $\tau \neq 0_{NT}$),

$$\sum_{t=1}^{T} \delta_1 \delta_2 \ldots \delta_{t-1} p^t \cdot \nabla_\tau x^t \, (z^*) \tau + \delta_1 \ldots \delta_T q \cdot \nabla_\tau s^T \, (z^*) \tau =$$

$$= \tau \cdot DS_{\tau\tau} D\tau < 0 \tag{33}$$

where the last inequality follows from the negative definiteness of $S_{\tau\tau}$. Thus (32) and (33) place some restrictions on the responses of net outputs to changes in stock taxes.

We conclude this section by considering the one stock case; i.e., $N = 1$. In this case, A is a T by T tridiagonal matrix. Let $A \, (i_1, i_2, \ldots, i_L)$ denote the determinant of the submatrix of A that consists of rows and columns $i_1, i_2, \ldots, i_L$. Thus $A \, (1, 2, 3, \ldots, T) \equiv |A|$. Since A is negative definite, the determinant of any submatrix of A which lies on the main diagonal is negative. Using the cofactor formula for the inverse of a matrix and making use of the triangularity of A, it can be verified that:

---

[12]) Note that $\nabla_\tau x \, (z^*) \, D^{-1} \Gamma = \Gamma^T S\Gamma$, a negative semidefinite symmetric matrix.

$$A_{11}^{-1} = A\,(2, 3, \ldots, T)/|A| < 0 \tag{34}$$

$$A_{12}^{-1} = (-1)\,a_{12}\,A\,(3, 4, \ldots, T)/|A|$$

$$\vdots$$

$$A_{1T}^{-1} = (-1)^{T-1} a_{12} a_{23} \cdots a_{T-1,T}/|A|$$

$$\vdots$$

$$A_{tt}^{-1} = A\,(1, 2, \ldots, t-1, t+1, \ldots, T)/|A| < 0, \quad t = 1, 2, \ldots, T \text{ and for } t > r,$$

$$A_{rt}^{-1} = (-1)^{r+t} A\,(1, 2, \ldots, r-1)\,a_{r,r+1}\,a_{r+1,r+2} \cdots a_{t-1,t}\,A\,(t+1, t+2, \ldots, T)/|A|$$

where

$$a_{t,t+1} \equiv \delta_1 \ldots \delta_t \partial^2 \pi\,(p^{t+1}, s^{t*}, s^{t+1*})/\partial s^t \partial s^{t+1}$$

for $t = 1, 2, \ldots, t-1$ and $A\,(1, 2, \ldots, r-1) \equiv 1$ when $r = 1$ and
$A\,(t+1, t+2, \ldots, T) \equiv 1$ when $t = T$. Inspection of the formulae in (34) tells us that
A_{tt}^{-1} is negative for all t and the sign of $A_{rt}^{-1} = A_{tr}^{-1}$ for $r \neq t$ is given by minus the sign of
$a_{r,r+1}\,a_{r+1,r+2} \cdots a_{t-1,t}$. Thus $A^{-1} \equiv S_{\tau\tau}$ is *completely* signed in the one stock case.

When $N = 1$, we say that s^t and s^{t+1} are *substitutes* (complements[13]) in the production of aggregate output during period $t + 1$ if $a_{t,t+1} \equiv \delta_1 \ldots \delta_1 \partial^2 \pi\,(p^{t+1}, s^{t*},$
$s^{t+1*})/\partial s^t \partial s^{t+1} \geqslant 0\ (< 0)$. We say that s^t and s^{t+1} are *strong substitutes* if $a_{t,t+1} > 0$.
From (34), we deduce that all elements of A^{-1} are nonpositive when the stocks are substitutes in all periods and all elements of A^{-1} are negative when the stocks are strong substitutes (which is necessarily the case when the one period technology set S is convex and exhibits constant returns to scale). For geometric interpretations of substitutability and complementarity, recall that in Figure 1, $a_{01} = 0$; in Figure 2, $a_{01} > 0$; in Figure 3,
$a_{01} < 0$.

Thus when $N = 1$ and the stocks are strong substitutes, using (20) we deduce that
$\nabla_\tau s\,(z^*)$ is a T by T matrix consisting of negative elements. Thus, *if any stock tax increases, each optimal stock will decrease.* Under these conditions we can also deduce that
$$\sum_{t=1}^{T} \delta_1 \delta_2 \ldots \delta_{t-1}\,p^t \cdot \nabla_\tau x^t\,(z^*)$$
consists of positive elements if $\tau = 0_T$ and $q > 0$, and
negative elements if $\tau > 0_T$ and $q = 0$ (see (31)).

---

[13]) "Usually" s^t and s^{t+1} will be substitutes. More precisely, if the one period technology set S
satisfies property (7) (concavity in stocks), then $\partial^2 \pi\,(p^{t+1}, s^{t*}, s^{t+1*})/\partial s^t \partial s^t \leqslant 0$. If S also satisfies
property (8) (constant returns in stocks), by Euler's Theorem on homogeneous functions
$s^{t*} \partial^2 \pi\,(p^{t+1}, s^{t*}, s^{t+1*})/\partial s^t \partial s^t + s^{t+1*} \partial^2 \pi\,(p^{t+1*}, s^{t*}, s^{t+1*})/\partial s^t \partial s^{t+1} = 0$, and thus
$\partial^2 \pi\,(p^{t+1}, s^{t*}, s^{t+1*})/\partial s^t \partial s^{t+1} \geqslant 0$. The "substitutes" or "complements" terminology follows that of
Diewert [1974, 144–145].

4. The Comparative Statics of Changes in Initial Stocks

We now consider how the optimal NT-dimensional stock vector s $(\tau, s^0, p, q, \delta)$ changes as the components of the N-dimensional initial stock vector s^0 change. Differentiating the first order conditions (11) with respect to s and s^0 yields the following expression for the NT by N matrix of partial derivatives $\nabla_{s^0} s$ (z^*):

$$\nabla_{s^0} s \ (z^*) = -A^{-1} \left[\begin{array}{c} \nabla^2_{s^1 s^0} \pi \ (p^1, s^0, s^1 *) \\ \\ 0_{(T-1)N \times N} \end{array} \right] \tag{35}$$

where the NT by NT negative definite symmetric matrix A is defined by (16)–(19).

Recall that we defined the tax substitution matrix $S_{\tau\tau} \equiv A^{-1}$ in the previous section. Denote the t-th N by N block in the first block of columns of $S_{\tau\tau}$ by $S_{\tau_t \tau_1}$. Then from (35), the N by N matrix of partial derivatives of the period t optimal stock vector s^t (z^*) with respect to the components of the initial stock vector s^0 is

$$\nabla_{s^0} s^t \ (z^*) = - [S_{\tau_t \tau_1}] [\nabla^2_{s^1 s^0} \pi \ (p^1, s^0, s^1 *)], \quad t = 1, 2, \ldots, T,$$

$$= - (\delta_1 \delta_2 \ldots \delta_t)^{-1} \nabla_{\tau^1} s^t \ (z^*) \nabla^2_{s^1 s^0} \pi \ (p^1, s^0, s^1 *) \tag{36}$$

where the last equality follows using (20). Thus the partial derivatives of s^t with respect to s^0 are linearly related to the partials of s^t with respect to the components of the period 1 tax variables τ^1.

Let us call the period 0 and period 1 stock vectors *independent* if $\nabla_{s^1 s^0} \pi \ (p^1, s^0, s^1 *) = 0_{N \times N}$. In the case of independent period 1 stock vectors, from (35) we see that $\nabla_{s^0} s \ (z^*) = 0_{NT \times N}$, an intuitively obvious result.

In general, it appears that we cannot deduce too much about the signs of the partial derivatives in the matrices $\nabla_{s^0} s^t \ (z^*)$. However, if we premultiply both sides of (36) when $t = 1$ by the N by N matrix of second order partial derivatives $\nabla^2_{s^0 s^1} \pi \ (p^1, s^0, s^1 *)$, then we obtain

$$\nabla^2_{s^0 s^1} \pi \ (p^1, s^0, s^1 *) \nabla_{s^0} s^1 \ (z^*) = - \nabla_{s^0 s^1} \pi \ (p^1, s^0, s^1 *) S_{\tau^1 \tau^1} \nabla^2_{s^1 s^0} \pi \ (p^1, s^0, s^1 *)$$

$$= \text{a positive semidefinite symmetric } N \text{ by } N \text{ matrix.} \tag{37}$$

Thus, loosely speaking, positive signs should predominate in the matrix on the right hand side of (37).

In the one stock case (i.e., $N = 1$), we can deduce a great deal more. Defining $a_{01} \equiv \partial^2 \pi \ (p^1, s^0, s^1 *) / \partial s^0 \partial s^1 = \partial^2 \pi \ (p^1, s^0, s^1 *) / \partial s^1 \partial s^0$, using (34) and (35), we deduce that

$$\partial s^1 (z^*) / \partial s^0 = -A (2, 3, \ldots, T) a_{01} / |A|$$
$$\partial s^2 (z^*) / \partial s^0 = (-1)^2 a_{01} a_{12} A (3, 4, \ldots, T) / |A|$$
$$\partial s^3 (z^*) / \partial s^0 = (-1)^3 a_{01} a_{12} a_{23} A (4, 5, \ldots, T) / |A|$$

$$\vdots$$

$$\partial s^T (z^*) / \partial s^0 = (-1)^T a_{01} a_{12} \ldots a_{T-1,T} / |A|. \qquad (38)$$

Thus the sign of $\partial s^1 / \partial s^0$ is given by the sign of a_{01}, the sign of $\partial s^2 / \partial s^0$ by $a_{01} a_{12}$, the sign of $\partial s^3 / \partial s^0$ by $a_{01} a_{12} a_{23}, \ldots$, and the sign of $\partial s^T / \partial s^0$ by $a_{01} a_{12} \ldots a_{T-1,T}$. Thus in the one stock case the direction of change of the optimal stocks s^t to an increase in the initial stock s^0 is completely determined by the sign pattern of the $a_{t,t+1} \equiv \delta_1 \ldots \delta_t \partial^2 \pi (p^{t+1}, s^{t*}, s^{t+1*}) / \partial s^t \partial s^{t+1}$ coefficients (i.e., by the substitutability pattern of the stocks over time with respect to the production of net output during each period). In particular, in the (strong) substitutes case where all of the $a_{t,t+1} \geq 0 (> 0)$, we deduce that

$$\partial s^t (z^*) / \partial s^0 \geq 0 (> 0) \qquad \text{for } t = 1, 2, \ldots, T. \qquad (39)$$

We turn now to the partial derivatives of the value function $V (z^*)$ with respect to the components of the initial stock vector s^0. From (14) and (15), we have

$$\nabla_{s^0} V (z^*) = \nabla_{s^0} \pi (p^0, s^0, s^{1*}) \equiv w (z^*)$$

$$\geq 0_N \qquad \text{if (3) and (6) are satisfied.}$$

Partially differentiating again with respect to s^0, we obtain the following expression for the N by N matrix of partial derivatives of the shadow prices of the initial stocks with respect to the components of the initial stock vector s^0:

$$\nabla_{s^0} w (z^*) = \nabla_{s^0 s^0}^2 \pi (p^1, s^0, s^{1*}) + \nabla_{s^0 s^1}^2 \pi (p^1, s^0, s^{1*}) \, \nabla_{s^0} s^1 (z^*)$$

$$= \nabla_{s^0 s^0}^2 \pi (p^1, s^0, s^{1*}) - \nabla_{s^0 s^1}^2 \pi (p^1, s^0, s^{1*}) S_{T^1 T^1} \nabla_{s^1 s^0}^2 \pi (p^1, s^0, s^{1*})$$

$$= [\nabla_{s^0} w (z^*)]^T, \qquad \text{a symmetric matrix,} \qquad (40)$$

where the second equality follows from the first using (36) with $t = 1$. The n-th component of (40) may be rewritten as

$$\frac{\partial w_n (z^*)}{s_n^0} = \frac{\partial^2 \pi (p^1, s^0, s^{1*})}{\partial s_n^0 \partial s_n^0} - e_n^T \nabla_{s^0 s^1}^2 \pi (p^1, s^0, s^{1*}) S_{T^1 T^1} \nabla_{s^1 s^0}^2 \pi (p^1, s^0, s^{1*}) e_n \quad (41)$$

where e_n is a unit vector of dimension N with a one in component n. Since $S_{T^1 T^1}$ is a negative definite matrix, it can be seen that the second matrix on the right hand side of (41) is a positive semidefinite symmetric matrix (recall (37)) and hence the second term on the right hand side of (41) is nonnegative (positive if $\nabla_{s^1 s^0}^2 \pi (p^1, s^0, s^{1*}) e_n = = \partial [\nabla_{s^1} \pi (p^1, s^0, s^{1*})] / \partial s_n^0 \neq 0_N$). This second term gives the change in the shadow price $w_n (z^*) \equiv \partial \pi (p^1, s^0, s^1 (z^*)) / \partial s_n^0$ to the change in $s^1 (\tau, s^0, p, q, \delta)$ induced by a marginal increase in s_n^0. The first term on the right hand side of (41) gives the "atemporal" response in the n-th shadow price $w_n (z^*) \equiv \partial \pi (p^1, s^0, s^{1*}) / \partial s_n^0$ to an increase in s_n^0, holding $s^1 (z)$ fixed at s^{1*}. The term on the left hand side of (41) is the "general equilibrium" response in the n-th shadow price due to an increase in the n-th initial stock s_n^0. Thus (41) says that the general equilibrium response is equal to the atemporal response plus a nonnegative term that is due to the changes in the optimal stock vector $s (z)$ induced by the change in s_n^0. This last term can be called the "intertemporal" response.

If we assume that the one period technology set S is convex, then we have property (7), i.e., that $\pi (p^1, s^0, s^1)$ is a concave function in (s^0, s^0). This implies that the first matrix on the right hand side of (40), $\nabla^2_{s^0 s^0} \pi (p^1, s^0, s^{1*})$, is negative semidefinite in addition to being symmetric. From the Appendix, we can also deduce that the value function $V (\tau, s^0, p, q, \delta)$ is concave in s^0. Hence the general equilibrium response matrix on the left hand side of (40), $\nabla_s w (z^*)$, is also a symmetric *negative* semidefinite matrix

that is equal to the *negative* semidefinite atemporal response matrix plus the intertemporal response matrix, a *positive* semidefinite symmetric matrix. Thus when S is convex, in addition to (41), we obtain the following inequalities:

$$0 \geqslant \partial w_n (z^*) / \partial s_n^0 \geqslant \partial^2 \pi (p^1, s^0, s^{1*}) / \partial s_n^0 \partial s_n^0 \quad \text{for } n = 1, 2, \ldots, N \tag{42}$$

and the inequalities in (42) are strict if $\nabla^2_{s^1 s^0} \pi (p^1, s^0, s^{1*}) e_n \neq 0_N$. Hence *the general equilibrium decline in the n-th shadow price is not as great as the atemporal decline due to an increase in the n-th initial stock.* This result appears to be a discrete time counterpart to a continuous time Le Chatelier Principle first obtained by *Epstein* [1978; p. 107].

We now look at the response of the period t net output vector

$x^t (z) = \nabla_p \pi (p^t, s^{t-1} (x), s^t (x))$ to changes in the initial stock vector s^0. We find that the M by N matrix of partial derivatives of x^t with respect to the components of s^0 is

$$\nabla_{s^0} x^t (z^*) = \nabla^2_{p s^{t-1}} \pi (p^t, s^{t-1*}, s^{t*}) \nabla_{s^0} s^{t-1} (z^*) +$$

$$+ \nabla^2_{p s^t} \pi (p^t, s^{t-1*}, s^{t*}) \nabla_{s^0} s^t (z^*)$$

$$= - \nabla^2_{p s^{t-1}} \pi (p^t, s^{t-1*}, s^{t*}) S_{\tau^{t-1} \tau^1} \nabla^2_{s^1 s^0} \pi (p^1, s^0, s^{1*})$$

$$- \nabla^2_{p s^t} \pi (p^t, s^{t-1*}, s^{t*}) S_{\tau^t \tau^1} \nabla^2_{s^1 s^0} \pi (p^1, s^0, s^{1*}) \tag{43}$$

where we have used (36). The matrices $\nabla^2_{p s^{t-1}} \pi$ and $\nabla^2_{p s^t} \pi$ which appear in (43) are "intensity matrices; they indicate how the period t net output vector $x^{t*} \equiv \nabla_p \pi (p^t, s^{t-1*}, s^{t*})$ responds to changes in s^{t-1} and s^t respectively (holding s^t and s^{t-1} fixed respectively). Note that $\nabla_{s^0} x^t (z^*)$ also depends on the stock substitution matrix, $\nabla^2_{s^1 s^0} \pi (p^1, s^0, s^{1*})$, and on the tax substitution matrices, $S_{\tau^{t-1} \tau^1}$ and $S_{\tau^t \tau^1}$. In general, not much can be said about the signs of the elements of the matrices in (43). However, making use of the linear homogeneity of π in prices so that

$$p^t \cdot \nabla_p \pi (p^t, s^{t-1*}, s^{t*}) = p^t \cdot x^{t*} = \pi (p^t, s^{t-1*}, s^{t*}), \text{ we can deduce that}$$

$$\sum_{t=1}^{T} \delta_1 \ldots \delta_{t-1} p^t \cdot \nabla_{s_0} x^t (z^*) + \delta_1 \ldots \delta_T q \cdot \nabla_{s_0} s^T (z^*) - \sum_{t=1}^{T} \delta_1 \ldots \delta_t \tau^t \cdot \nabla_{s_0} s^t(z^*)$$

$$= \nabla_{s_0} V (z^*)$$

$$\geqslant 0_N \tag{44}$$

where the last equalities follow if π satisfies (6) (i.e., if S satisfies the free disposal property (3)). If π satisfies (6) and the tax variables are all zero (i.e., $\tau^t = 0_N$ for $t = 1, 2, \ldots, T$), then the inequalities in (44) indicate that the value of discounted net output does not decrease if any initial stock component increases marginally.

5. The Comparative Statics of Changes in Prices

Recall the definition of the diagonal matrix of discount rates, D^*, defined above (29). Now differentiate the first order conditions (11) with respect to the components of s and p. We find that the matrix of partial derivatives of s with respect to the components of p, evaluated at the initial equilibrium, is

$$\nabla_p s (z^*) = -A^{-1} \Gamma D^* = -S_{\tau\tau} \Gamma D^* = -\nabla_\tau s (z^*) D^{-1} \Gamma D^* \tag{45}$$

where D^* is defined below (19) and the last equality follows from (20). Thus the response matrix $\nabla_p s (z^*)$ decomposes into the product of the stock tax substitution matrix $S_{\tau\tau}$, the intensity matrix Γ and the discount matrix D^* (with a minus sign in front). Unfortunately, not much can be said in general about the signs of the elements in $\nabla_p s (z^*)$, because not much can be said about the signs of the elements in Γ. However, from (45), $D^* \Gamma \nabla_p s (z^*) = -D^* \Gamma^T S_{\tau\tau} \Gamma D^*$, a positive semidefinite matrix. Also if $\tau = 0_{NT}$, then (29) and (45) imply that

$$\nabla_p s (z^*) p = S_{\tau\tau} [D_{M(T-1)}^T, \delta_1 \delta_2 \ldots \delta_T q^T]^T$$

$$\leqslant 0_{NT} \qquad \text{if } S_{\tau\tau} \leqslant 0_{NT \times NT}. \tag{46}$$

Of course, in the one stock substitutes case, $S_{\tau\tau} \leqslant 0_{T \times T}$.

Recall that $x^t (z) \equiv \nabla_p \pi (p^t, s^{t-1} (z), s^t (z))$. Define the atemporal MT by MT net output substitution matrix $\bar{S}_{pp}$ as the following block diagonal matrix:

$$\bar{S}_{pp} \equiv \begin{bmatrix} \nabla_{pp}^2 \pi (p^1, s^0, s^{1*}), & 0_{M \times M}, & \cdots, & 0_{M \times M} \\ 0_{M \times M}, & \nabla_{pp}^2 \pi (p^2, s^{1*}, s^{2*}), & \cdots, & 0_{M \times M} \\ 0_{M \times M}, & 0_{M \times M}, & \cdots, & \nabla_{pp}^2 \pi (p^T, s^{T-1*}, s^{T*}) \end{bmatrix} \tag{47}$$

Note that $\bar{S}_{pp}$ and $D^*\bar{S}_{pp}$ are both symmetric, positive semidefinite (static) substitution matrices. Upon differentiating the identies $x^t (z) = \nabla_p \pi (p^t, s^{t-1} (z), s^t (z))$, $t = 1, 2, \ldots, T$ with respect to p, using (24) and (45), we find that

$$\nabla_p x (z^*) = \bar{S}_{pp} + \Gamma^T \nabla_p s (z^*) = \bar{S}_{pp} - \Gamma^T S_{\tau\tau} \Gamma D^*. \tag{48}$$

Now premultiply both sides of (48) by the diagonal matrix D^*:

$$D^* \nabla_p x (z^*) = D^* \bar{S}_{pp} - (\Gamma D^*)^T S_{\tau\tau} (\Gamma D^*)$$

$$= \text{atemporal substitution matrix} + \text{intertemporal substitution matrix}$$

$$= [D^* \nabla_p x (z^*)]^T. \tag{49}$$

Note that the first matrix on the right hand side of (49) gives the response of the discounted net supply vector $D^* x (z^*)$ to changes in net output prices p *holding all stocks fixed* at the initial optimal level before any changes in p occur. The second matrix, $- (\Gamma D^*)^T S_{\tau\tau} (\Gamma D^*)$, gives the response of the discounted net supply vector $D^* X (z^*)$ to changes in p due to the *intertemporal shifting of the optimal stock variables* induced by the changes in prices. Since $S_{\tau\tau}$ is negative definite, it can be seen that this intertemporal substitution matrix is positive semidefinite and hence augments the static substitution effect given by the atemporal substitution matrix $D\bar{S}_{pp}$. Hence even when there is no short-run substitutability in the one period technology when stocks are fixed (i.e., $\bar{S}_{pp} = 0_{MT \times MT}$), there generally will be net output substitutability due to price induced intertemporal shifts in optimal resource stocks.

By now the reader will have realized that our decomposition (49) of the total substitution matrix into atemporal and intertemporal effects is simply a special case of *Samuelson's* [1947, 36–39] *Le Chatelier Principle.*[14])

We now consider the response of $x (z)$ and $s (z)$ to changes in the components of the scrap value vector q. Fortunately, little additional work is required to do this because it can be seen from the last equation in (11) that the response of the endogenous variables to marginal changes in q is precisely equal to minus the response to changes in τ^T, the vector of resource stock tax rates in period T. Thus, in particular, from (20),

$$\nabla_q s (z^*) = -S_{\tau\tau} D [0_{N \times (T-1)N}, I_N]^T. \tag{50}$$

We are particularly interested in the final period stock vector $s^T (z^*)$. From (50), we have

$$\delta_1 \ldots \delta_T \nabla_q s^T (z^*) = - [0_{N \times (T-1)N}, I_N] D^T S_{\tau\tau} D [0_{N \times (T-1)N}, I_N]^T. \tag{51}$$

Note that the right hand side of (51) is a symmetric, positive definite matrix so that $\partial s_i^T (z^*)/\partial q_j = \partial s_j^T (z^*)/\partial q_i$ for $i, j = 1, \ldots, N$ and $\partial s_i^T (z^*)/\partial q_i > 0$ for $i = 1, 2, \ldots, N$.

---

[14]) Our decomposition also illustrates *Hicks'* [1946, p. 206] observation that long-run elasticities of substitution tend to be greater than short-run elasticities. For simple proofs of the Le Chatelier Principle, see *Eichhorn/Oettli* [1972, p. 241] or *Diewert* [1974, 146–150].

318

Postmultiplying both sides of (50) by $\delta_1\delta_2 \ldots \delta_T q$ yields if $\tau = 0_{NT}$

$$\delta_1 \ldots \delta_T \nabla_q s\,(z^*)\,q = -\nabla_p s\,(z^*)\,p \qquad \text{using (46)}$$

$$\geq 0_{NT} \qquad \text{if } S_{\tau\tau} \leq 0_{NT\times NT}. \tag{52}$$

It is also easy to calculate $\nabla_q x\,(z^*)$:

$$\nabla_q x\,(z^*) = \Gamma^T \nabla_q s\,(z^*) = -\Gamma^T S_{\tau\tau} D\,[0_{N\times(T-1)N},\, I_N]^T \tag{53}$$

where we have used (50). We also calculate the response of final period stocks to changes in p:

$$\delta_1 \ldots \delta_T \nabla_p s^T\,(z^*) = [0_{N\times(T-1)N},\, T_N]\,D\,\nabla_p s\,(z^*), \text{ and using (45)}$$

$$= -[0_{N\times(t-1)N},\, I_N]\,D^T S_{\tau\tau}\Gamma D^*$$

$$= [D^*\nabla_q x\,(z^*)]^T \tag{54}$$

where $\nabla_q x\,(z^*)$ is defined in (53). Note that there are NMT symmetry restrictions in (54).

If $\tau = 0_{NT}$, then using the first order conditions (29), the restrictions (26) which imply $\bar{S}_{pp}\,p = 0_{MT}$, (48), (51), (53), and (54), it can be shown that

$$\begin{bmatrix} D^*\nabla_p x\,(z^*), & D^*\nabla_q x\,(z^*) \\ \delta_1\ldots\delta_T\nabla_p s^T(z^*), & \delta_1\ldots\delta_T\nabla_q s^T(z^*) \end{bmatrix} \begin{bmatrix} p \\ q \end{bmatrix} = \begin{bmatrix} 0_{NT} \\ 0_N \end{bmatrix} \tag{55}$$

which places $NT + N$ additional restrictions on the derivatives of x and s^T with respect to the components of p and q.[15]

It is relatively easy to calculate the response of the value function $V\,(z)$ to changes in p and q: differentiation of (9) with respect to the components of p and q yields the following equalities (using (13) and the first order conditions (11)):

$$\nabla_p V\,(z^*) = Dx\,(z^*); \qquad \nabla_q V\,(z^*) = \delta_1 \ldots \delta_T s^{T*} \geq 0_N. \tag{56}$$

Thus if $x_n^{t*} > 0\ (<0)$ so that the n-th good is produced (used as an input) during period t, then an increase in the corresponding price p_n^t leads to an increase (decrease) in discounted profits. This is the usual *Samuelson* [1947] envelope theorem result.

We conclude this section by noting some formulae for the partial derivatives of the shadow price vector w defined by (14) with respect to the components of p and q:

$$\nabla_p w\,(z^*) = \nabla^2_{s^0 s^1}\pi\,(p^1, s^0, s^{1*})\,\nabla_p s^1\,(z^*) + [\nabla^2_{s^0 p^1}\pi\,(p^1, s^0, s^{1*}),\, 0_{N\times M(T-1)}]$$

$$= -\nabla^2_{s^0 s^1}\pi\,(p^1, s^0, s^{1*})\,[I_N, 0_{N\times N(T-1)}]\,S_{\tau\tau}\Gamma D^* + [\nabla^2_{s^0 p^1}\pi^1,\, 0_{N\times M(T-1)}]$$

using (45), and

$$\tag{57}$$

[15]) We can also show that the matrix in (55) is symmetric and positive semidefinite (we have already established the symmetry part).

$$\nabla_q w\,(z^*) = \nabla^2_{s^0 s^1} \pi\,(p^1,\,s^0,\,s^1\,{}^*)\,\nabla_q s^1\,(z^*)$$

$$= -\nabla^2_{s^0 s^1} \pi\,(p^1,\,s^0,\,s^1\,{}^*)\,[I_N,\,0_{N\times N(T\text{-}1)}]\,S_{\tau\tau}D\,[0_{N\times N(T\text{-}1)},\,I_N]^T \qquad (58)$$

where the last equality follows using (50). In the one stock substitutes case, it is easy to verify that each element of $\nabla_q w\,(z^*)$ is nonnegative. Finally, if $\tau = 0_{NT}$, using (15), (27) for $t = 1$, (29), (57) and (58), it can be shown that

$$w\,(z^*) = \nabla_p w\,(z^*)\,p + \nabla_q w\,(z^*)\,q. \qquad (59)$$

6. The Comparative Statics of Changes in Interest Rates

Recall that we defined the discount factors $\delta_t \equiv 1/(1 + r_t)$ where r_t was the period t interest rate. Thus an increase in δ_t corresponds to a decrease in r_t.

In order to work out how the NT-dimensional vector of optimal stocks $s\,(z)$ changes as the components of the T-dimensional vector of discount factors $\delta \equiv [\delta_1, \delta_2, \ldots, \delta_T]^T$ change, it is useful to define the following NT by T matrix W:

$$W \equiv - \begin{bmatrix} \delta_1^{-1}\nabla_{s^1}\pi\,(p^1,\,s^0,\,s^1\,{}^*), & 0_N, & \cdots, 0_N \\[2mm] 0_N, & \delta_2^{-1}\nabla_{s^2}\pi\,(p^2,\,s^1\,{}^*,\,s^2\,{}^*), & \cdots, 0_N \\[2mm] \vdots & \vdots & \vdots \\[2mm] 0_N, & 0_N, & \cdots, \delta_T^{-1}\nabla_{s^T}\pi\,(p^T,\,s^{T\text{-}1}\,{}^*,\,s^T\,{}^*) \end{bmatrix} \qquad (60)$$

If the free disposal assumption (3) is satisfied, then the vectors $\nabla_{s^t}\pi\,(p^t,\,s^{y\text{-}1}\,{}^*,\,s^t\,{}^*) \leqslant 0_N$ for each t and thus W is a nonnegative matrix. Note that $-w^t \equiv \nabla_{s^t}\pi\,(p^t,\,s^{t\text{-}1}\,{}^*,\,s^t\,{}^*)$ indicates how period t variable profits $\pi\,(p^t,\,s^{t\text{-}1}\,{}^*,\,s^t\,{}^*)$ change as we add marginal units to next period's starting stock vector $s^t\,{}^*$.

Differentiate the first order conditions (11) with respect to the components of s and δ. Using (11), we find that

$$\nabla_\delta s\,(z^*) = -A^{-1}W = -S_{\tau\tau}W. \qquad (61)$$

Thus if we have free disposal, only one stock $(N = 1)$, and all stocks are substitutes $(a_{ij} \geqslant 0)$, then $-S_{\tau\tau}$ is a nonnegative matrix as is W, and hence the elements of $\nabla_\delta s\,(z^*)$ are all nonnegative. Thus *in the one stock free disposal substitutes case a decrease in any interest rate will generally cause the components of the optimal stock vector s to increase* (at least not decrease). Hence if the optimal stocks are growing over time, a decrease in an interest rate will generally accelerate the growth rates, and if the optimal stocks are declining over time (as they will be in the typical natural resource application of our model), then a decrease in an interest rate will generally decrease (at least not increase) the depletion rates.

Since $x^t(z) \equiv \nabla_p \pi(p^t, x^{t-1}(z), s^t(z))$ for $t = 1, 2, \ldots, T$, we can readily calculate the MT by T matrix of partial derivatives of $x(z)$ with respect to the components of δ:

$$\nabla_\delta x(z^*) = \Gamma^T \nabla_\delta s(z^*)$$

$$= -\Gamma^T S_{TT} W \qquad \text{using (61).} \tag{62}$$

In order to determine how the value function $V(z)$ changes as the discount factors δ_t change, we need to introduce some additional notation. Define V^t to be the discounted optimal profit starting at period $t \geq 2$; i.e.,

$$V^t \equiv \sum_{t=t}^{T} \delta_1 \delta_2 \ldots \delta_{r-1} [\pi(p^r, s^{r-1*}, s^{r*}) - \tau^{r-1} \cdot s^{r-1*}]$$

$$+ \delta_1 \delta_2 \ldots \delta_T [q \cdot s^{T*} - \tau^T \cdot s^{T*}], \qquad t = 2, 3, \ldots, T. \tag{63}$$

Differentiating (9) and using (11) and the definition of V^t yields

$$\partial V(z^*)/\partial \delta_t = \delta_t^{-1} V^{t+1} \qquad \text{for } t = 1, 2, \ldots, T-1 \tag{64}$$

and

$$\partial V(z^*)/\partial \delta_T = \delta_1 \delta_2 \ldots \delta_{T-1} [q \cdot s^{T*} - \tau^T \cdot s^{T*}]. \tag{65}$$

Normally the partial present values V^t will be positive or at least nonnegative, for if $V^t < 0$ for some t, then the owner of the firm will simply discontinue producing at period t.

Finally, we note that

$$\nabla_\delta w(z^*) = \nabla^2_{s^0 s^1} \pi(p^1, s^0, s^1 *) \nabla_\delta s^1(z^*)$$

$$= -\nabla^2_{s^0 s^1} \pi(p^1, s^0, s^1 *) [I_N, 0_{N \times N(T-1)}] S_{TT} W \tag{66}$$

where we have used (61). As usual, in the free disposal, one stock substitutes case, the elements of $\nabla_\delta w(z^*)$ are nonnegative.

7. Conclusion

We have laboriously developed the comparative dynamics properties of a fairly general (but finite horizon) intertemporal production model. Perhaps our most interesting general results are the atemporal and intertemporal decompositions found in (40) and (49). In fact, (49) defines an intertemporal Le Chatelier effect.

Perhaps our most interesting more specific result is found in our treatment of the one stock case (recall our formula for the elements of A^{-1}, (34)). In the case of one stock, we were able to deduce a large number of interesting comparative dynamics results; e.g., see (38), (39), (58) and (61).

It is worth emphasizing that all of our results have been obtained for an *arbitrary pattern* of future expected prices and interest rates using very general assumptions on the one period technology. This is in sharp contrast to much of the natural resources literature.

We also note that our assumption that $s^{t*} \gg 0_N$ for $t = 1, 2, \ldots, T$ can be relaxed. If the n-th component of the period t optimal stock vector s_r^t (z^*) is zero initially and remains at zero for small variations in the vector of exogenous variables z around the initial point z^*, then $\nabla_z s_n^t (z^*) = 0$, and the equation corresponding to the variable s_n^t can be dropped from the first order conditions (11). The remaining formulae have to be reworked, omitting equations that correspond to s_n^t.

We conclude by noting that all of our results go through unchanged if we allow the one period technology set S to depend on time: simply replace $\pi (p^t, s^{t-1}, s^t)$ by $\pi^t (p^t, s^{t-1}, s^t)$.

8. Appendix: General Properties of the Value Function

Recall (9), the definition of the value function:

$$V (\tau^1, \ldots, \tau^T, s^0, p^1, \ldots, p^T, q, \delta_1, \ldots, \delta_T) = V (\tau, s^0, p, q, \delta)$$

$$\equiv \max_{s^1 > 0_N, \ldots, s^T > 0_N} \sum_{t=1}^{T} \delta_0 \delta_1 \ldots \delta_{t-1} \pi (p^t, s^{t-1}, s^t)$$

$$- \sum_{t=1}^{T} \delta_1 \ldots \delta_t \tau^t \cdot s^t + \delta_1 \ldots \delta_t q \cdot s^T$$

where $\delta_0 \equiv 1$ and the other variables are defined below (9).

Lemma 1: $V (\tau, s^0, p, q, \delta)$ is a convex function of τ, p, q.

Proof: Let $s^* \equiv (s^{1*}, s^{2*}, \ldots, s^{T*})$ be a solution to (9) when the producer faces prices p^*, q^* and tax rates τ^*. Let s^{**} be a solution for $p^{**}, q^{**}, \tau^{**}$ and let $0 \leq \lambda \leq 1$. Then

$$V (\lambda \tau^* + (1 - \lambda) \tau^{**}, s^0, \lambda p^* + (1 - \lambda) p^{**}, \lambda q^* + (1 - \lambda) q^{**}, \delta)$$

$$\equiv \max_{s^1, \ldots, s^T} \{ \sum_{t=1}^{T} \delta_0 \ldots \delta_{t-1} \pi (\lambda p^{t*} + (1 - \lambda) p^{t**}, s^{t-1}, s^t)$$

$$- \sum_{t=1}^{T} \delta_1 \ldots \delta_T (\lambda \tau^{t*} + (1 - \lambda) \tau^{t**}) \cdot s^t + \delta_1 \ldots \delta_t (\lambda q^* + (1 - \lambda) q^{**}) \cdot s^T \}$$

$$\leq \max_{s^1, \ldots, s^T} \{ \lambda [\sum_{t=1}^{T} \delta_0 \ldots \delta_{t-1} \pi (p^{t*}, s^{t-1}, s^t) - \sum_{t=1}^{T} \delta_1 \ldots \delta_t \tau^{t*} \cdot s^t$$

$$+ \delta_1 \ldots \delta_T q^* \cdot s^T] + (1 - \lambda) [\sum_{t=1}^{T} \delta_0 \ldots \delta_{t-1} \pi (p^{t**}, s^{t-1}, s^t)$$

$$- \sum_{t=1}^{T} \delta_1 \ldots \delta_t \tau^{t**} \cdot s^t + \delta_1 \ldots \delta_T q^{**} \cdot s^T]\}$$

since π is a convex function in prices

$$\leq \lambda V (\tau^*, s^0, p^*, q^*, \delta) + (1 - \lambda) V (\tau^{**}, s^0, p^{**}, q^{**}, \delta). \qquad \text{Q.E.D.}$$

If V is differentiable with respect to the components of τ, then by using duality theory, it can be shown that $\nabla_\tau V (\tau^*, s^0, p^*, q^*, \delta) = - Ds^*$ (we have shown this above under the assumption that A^{-1} exists – recall (23)). If V is twice continuously differentiable with respect to τ, then $\nabla^2_{\tau\tau} V (\tau^*, s^0, p^*, q^*, \delta) = - D\nabla_\tau s (\tau^*, s^0, p^*, q^*, \delta)$ is a positive semidefinite symmetric matrix (recall (20)).

Lemma 2: $V (\tau, s^0, p, q, \delta)$ is positively linearly homogeneous in (τ, p, q).

Proof: Follows readily using the linear homogeneity of y in prices. Q.E.D.

Lemma 3: $V (\tau, s^0, p, q, \delta)$ is nondecreasing in the components of the scrap value price vector q.

Proof: Let $q^{**} > q^*$. For some $s^{1*} \geqslant 0_N, \ldots, s^{T*} \geqslant 0_N$, we have

$$V (\tau, s^{0*}, p, q^*, \delta) = \sum_{t=1}^T \delta_0 \ldots \delta_{t-1} \pi (p^t, s^{t-1*}, s^{t*}) -$$

$$- \sum_{t=1}^T \delta_1 \ldots \delta_t \tau^t \cdot s^{t*} + \delta_1 \ldots \delta_T q^* \cdot s^{T*}$$

$$\leqslant \sum_{t=1}^T \delta_0 \ldots \delta_{t-1} \pi (p^t, s^{t-1*}, s^{t*}) -$$

$$- \sum_{t=1}^T \delta_1 \ldots \delta_t \tau^t \cdot s^{t*} + \delta_1 \ldots \delta_T q^{**} \cdot s^{T*}$$

since $\delta_1 > 0, \ldots, \delta_T > 0, s^{T*} \geqslant 0_N$ and $q^{**} > q^*$

$$\leqslant V (\tau, s^{0*}, p, q^{**}, \delta).$$ Q.E.D.

Lemma 4: $V (\tau, s^0, p, q, \delta)$ is nonincreasing in the components of the stock tax vector τ.

Proof: Follows in the same manner as the proof of Lemma 3. Q.E.D.

Lemma 5: $V (\tau, s^0, p, q, \delta_1, \delta_2, \ldots, \delta_T)$ is convex in δ_t for each t.

Proof: $V (\tau^1, \tau^2, \ldots, \tau^T, s^0, p^1, p^2, \ldots, p^T, q, \delta_1, \delta_2, \ldots, \delta_T)$

$$= V (\delta_1 \tau^1, \delta_1 \delta_2 \tau^2, \ldots, \delta_1 \ldots \delta_T \tau^T, s^0, p^1, \delta_1 p^2, \ldots, \delta_1 \ldots \delta_{T-1} p^T,$$

$$\delta_1 \delta_2 \ldots \delta_T q, 1, 1, \ldots, 1)$$

using definition (9) and the linear homogeneity of π in prices

$$= \text{a convex function of } \delta_t \text{ for } t = 1, 2, \ldots, T \text{ using Lemma 1.}$$ Q.E.D.

Lemma 6: If the one period technology set S satisfies free disposal in the stock variables so that the variable profit function π satisfies (6), then the value function $V (\tau, s^0, p, q, \delta)$ is nondecreasing in the components of the initial stock vector s^0.

Proof: Let $s^{1*}, \ldots, s^{T*}$ be a solution to (9) corresponding to the vector of exogenous variables $(\tau, s^{0*}, p, q, \delta)$ and let $s^{0*} < s^{0**}$. Then

$$V(\tau, s^{0*}, p, q, \delta) = \sum_{t=1}^{T} \delta_0 \ldots \delta_{t-1} \pi(p^t, s^{t-1*}, s^{t*})$$

$$- \sum_{t=1}^{T} \delta_1 \ldots \delta_t \tau^t \cdot s^{t*} + \delta_1 \ldots \delta_T q \cdot s^{T*}$$

$$\leqslant \pi(p^1, s^{0**}, s^{1*}) + \sum_{t=2}^{T} \delta_1 \ldots \delta_{t-1} \pi(p^t, s^{t-1*}, s^{t*})$$

$$- \sum_{t=1}^{T} \delta_1 \ldots \delta_t \tau^t \cdot s^{t*} + \delta_1 \ldots \delta_T q \cdot s^{T*} \quad \text{using } s^{0*} < s^{0**} \text{ and (6)}$$

$$\leqslant V(\tau, s^{0**}, p, q, \delta). \qquad \text{Q.E.D.}$$

Lemma 7: If S is a convex set so that π satisfies (7), then $V(\tau, s^0, p, q, \delta)$ is concave function of the initial stock vector s^0.

Proof: Let $s^{1*}, \ldots, s^{T*}$ be a solution to (9) corresponding to $(\tau, s^{0*}, p, q, \delta)$, let $s^{1**}, \ldots, s^{T**}$ be a solution (9) corresponding to $(\tau, s^{0**}, p, q, \delta)$ and let $0 \leqslant \lambda \leqslant 1$. Then

$$V(\tau, \lambda s^{0*} + (1-\lambda) s^{0**}, p, q, \delta) \equiv \max_{s^1, \ldots, s^T} \{\pi(p^1, \lambda s^{0*} + (1-\lambda) s^{0**}, s^1)$$

$$+ \sum_{t=2}^{T} \delta_1 \ldots \delta_{t-1} \pi(p^t, s^{t-1}, s^t) - \sum_{t=1}^{T} \delta_1 \ldots \delta_t \tau^t \cdot s^t + \delta_1 \ldots \delta_T q \cdot s^T \}$$

$$\geqslant \sum_{t=1}^{T} \delta_0 \delta_1 \ldots \delta_{t-1} \pi(p^t, \lambda s^{t-1*} + (1-\lambda) s^{t-1**}, \lambda s^{t*} + (1-\lambda) s^{t**})$$

$$- \sum_{t=1}^{T} \delta_1 \ldots \delta_t \tau^t \cdot [\lambda s^{t*} + (1-\lambda) s^{t**}] + \delta_1 \ldots \delta_T q \cdot [\lambda s^{T*} + (1-\lambda) s^{T**}] \}$$

since $s^t \equiv \lambda s^{t*} + (1-\lambda) s^{t**}$ is feasible for the maximization problem

$$\geqslant \lambda V(\tau, s^{0*}, p, q, \delta) + (1-\lambda) V(\tau, s^{0**}, p, q, \delta)$$

using the concavity of π in its stock variables. $\qquad$ Q.E.D.

Lemma 8: If the one period technology set S is subject to constant returns to scale so that the variable profit function π satisfies (8), then $V(\tau, s^0, p, q, \delta)$ is a positively linearly homogeneous function of the initial stock vector s^0.

Proof: Let $\lambda > 0$. Then

$$V(\tau, \lambda s^0, p, q, \delta) \equiv \max_{s^1, \ldots, s^T} \{\pi(p^1, \lambda s^0, s^1) + \sum_{t=2}^{T} \delta_1 \ldots \delta_{t-1} \pi(p^t, s^{t-1}, s^t)$$

$$- \sum_{t=1}^{T} \delta_1 \ldots \delta_t \tau^t \cdot s^t + \delta_1 \ldots \delta_T q \cdot s^T\}$$

$$= \max_{\lambda s^1, \ldots, \lambda s^T} \{\sum_{t=1}^{T} \delta_0 \delta_1 \ldots \delta_{t-1} \pi(p^t, \lambda s^{t-1}, \lambda s^t)$$

$$- \sum_{t=1}^{T} \delta_1 \ldots \delta_t \tau^t \cdot \lambda s^t + \delta_1 \ldots \delta_T q \cdot \lambda s^T\}$$

replacing the variables s^t by λs^t

$$= \lambda V(\tau, s^0, p, q, \delta)$$

since $\lambda > 0$ and $\pi(p^t, \lambda s^{t-1}, \lambda s^t) = \lambda \pi(p^t, s^{t-1}, s^t)$.   Q.E.D.

References

Araujo, A., and *J.A. Scheinkman*: Smoothness, Comparative Dynamics, and the Turnpike Property. Econometrica 45, 1977, 601–620.
− : Notes on Comparative Dynamics. General Equilibrium, Growth and Trade: Essays in Honor of Lionel McKenzie. Ed. by J.R. Green and J.A. Scheinkman. New York 1979, 217–226.
Dasgupta, P.S., and *G.M. Heal*: Economic Theory and Exhaustible Resources. Cambridge, England 1979.
Dasgupta, P., G.M. Heal and *J. Stiglitz*: The Taxation of Exhaustible Resources. Public Policy and the Tax System. Ed. by G.A. Hughes and G.M. Heal. London 1980, 150–172.
Diewert, W.E.: Functional Forms for Profit and Transformation Functions. Journal of Economic Theory 6, 1973, 284–316.
− : Applications of Duality Theory. Frontiers of Quantitative Economics, Vol. II. Ed. by M.D. Intriligator and D.A. Kendrick. Amsterdam 1974, 106–171.
Dorfman, R., P.A. Samuelson and *R.M. Solow*: Linear Programming And Economic Analysis. New York 1958.
Eichhorn, W., and *W. Oettli*: Parameterabhängige Optimierung und die Geometrie des Prinzips von Le Châtelier-Samuelson. Zeitschrift für Operations Research 16, 1972, 233–244.
Epstein, L.G.: The Le Chatelier Principle in Optimal Control Problems. Journal of Economic Theory 19, 1978, 103–122.
Gorman, W.M.: Measuring the Quantities of Fixed Factors. Value, Capital and Growth: Papers in Honour of Sir John Hicks. Ed. by J.N. Wolfe. Chicago 1968, 141–172.

Hartwick, J.M.: Exploitation of Many Deposits of an Exhaustible Resource. Econometrica **46**, 1978, 201–217.

Hicks, J.R.: Value and Capital (2nd ed.) Oxford 1946.

Hotelling, H.: Edgeworth's Taxation Paradox and the Nature of Demand and Supply Functions. Journal of Political Economy **40**, 1932, 577–616.

Lau, L.J.: A Characterization of the Normalized Restricted Profit Function. Journal of Economic Theory **12**, 1976, 131–164.

Malinvaud, E.: Capital Accumulation and the Efficient Allocation of Resources. Econometrica **21**, 1953, 233–268.

McFadden, D.: Cost, Revenue and Profit Functions. Production Economics: A Dual Approach to Theory and Applications, Vol. 1. Ed. by M. Fuss and D. McFadden. Amsterdam 1978, 3–109.

Samuelson, P.A.: Foundations of Economic Analysis. Cambridge, Mass. 1947.

– : Prices of Factors and Goods in General Equilibrium. Review of Economic Studies **21**, 1953–54, 1–20.

Sweeney, J.L.: Economics of Depletable Resources: Market Forces and Intertemporal Bias. The Review of Economic Studies **44**, 1977, 125–141.

Economic Theory of Natural Resources. ©Physica-Verlag, Würzburg–Wien, 1982.

Learning by Burning

Alan Ingham

This paper presents a model of optimal natural resource depletion with endogeneous technical progress. The form of technical progress chosen is that of learning by doing in the use of the natural resource. The model is outlined and necessary conditions for optimality are obtained and interpreted. The principal object of the analysis is to discuss the appropriate Hotelling rule for this economy. The reason for concentrating on this rule is that explicit analysis of the optimal solution will require detailed specifications of the functions in the model whereas the Hotelling rule merely relates the derivatives of these functions. The Hotelling rule for this economy differs from the usual one [see for example *Ingham/Simmons*] of equilibrium in asset markets. Decentralisation of the optimal plan requires firms in the economy to have access to a full set of future markets.

The model is one of a one good economy which produces a flow of output equal to $Y(t)$ at time t, of which an amount $C(t)$ may be consumed by a population $L(t)$. The remaining output is installed as productive capital. Production takes place using capital, labour and an exhaustive natural resource. As time goes on the available technology changes. Historical evidence suggests [see for example *Ingham; Landes; Mathias*] that major changes in technology took place with respect to the use of the natural resource and the process was a gradual one of changes taking place due to experience of using the resource. This is in contrast to the view of technical change taken by *Kamien/Schwartz* [1978] amongst others who view technical change as being a discrete change, the adoption of a backstop technology, and also the view of *Takayama* [1980] and others who use technical progress as of the factor augmenting type. (Takayama also discusses exploration of reserves which is a problem, not discussed here, where the level and location of reserves is known, or at most its discovery costs are subsumed in the production relationship.) As technical progress takes place in the engineering technique, rather than in organizational efficiency, then it must be embodied in the capital installed at each instant of time. The technical knowhow, in particular the natural resource using characteristics, will determine the nature of capital produced and installed and only limited, if any, changes in operation can be made. This is the standard ex ante – ex post distinction. Ex ante a wide variety of substitution possibilities exist in fixing the degree of capital, labour, and resource intensities. Ex post substitution possibilities no longer exist and the only change that can be made is one of capacity utilization. Following the standard notation the technological structure can be formulated in the following way.

Consider the capital installed at time v the quantity of which is $I(v)$. This produces at time t an output equal to $Y(v, t)$ using an amount $X(v, t)$ of the natural resource, and $L(v, t)$ of labour. $Y(v, v)$ is the planned full capacity output at the time of installation and the intended amounts of resource and labour input are $X(v, v)$ and $L(v, v)$ respectively. These quantities are related by an ex ante production function which reflects the substitution possibilities prior to capital installation and the current state of technology. Technology changes as the resource is used and technical and scientific knowledge about its characteristics obtained. So that if $Z(v)$ is the amount of resource used up to time v, $Z(v)$ will be an argument of the ex ante production function F i.e.:

$$Y(v, v) = F(I(v), L(v, v), X(v, v), Z(v)). \tag{1}$$

This relationship gives the quantities of labour and resources which can be used with an amount of capital $I(v)$, to produce output $Y(v, v)$ when the state of technical knowledge is given by the amount of resources used $Z(v)$.

   Once the capital is installed the output-labour and output-resource ratios are fixed and the output obtainable from the capital can only be varied by changing the utilization rate. An ex post production function is therefore given by the two equations

$$\left. \begin{array}{c} \dfrac{Y(v, t)}{L(v, t)} = \dfrac{Y(v, v)}{L(v, v)} \\[2ex] \dfrac{Y(v, t)}{X(v, t)} = \dfrac{Y(v, v)}{X(v, v)} \end{array} \right\}$$

if $X(v, t) \neq 0$ and $L(v, t) \neq 0$. In order to cover the case of zero resource or labour use, re-write the above as:

$$Y(v, t) = \frac{Y(v, v) L(v, t)}{L(v, v)} = \frac{Y(v, v) X(v, t)}{X(v, v)}. \tag{2}$$

   Total output is obtained by summing the output from all vintages. No capital is assumed to exist of vintage earlier than 0, although a given amount of capital equipment will be installed at that ime. So if total output at time t is $Y(t)$ then:

$$Y(t) = \int_0^t Y(v, t)\, dv \tag{3}$$

and if total natural resource use at time t is $X(t)$ then

$$X(t) = \int_0^t X(v, t)\, dv \tag{4}$$

and if all the population is employable then

$$L(t) \geqslant \int_0^t L(v, t)\, dv. \tag{5}$$

   Whether this constraint will be an equality or inequality one will depend on the economic structure of the model. In a control model with perfect foresight and complete information then all productive resources will be used and if one feasible plan does not fully utilize all labour at a certain time then there will exist another plan also feasible (feasible to be fully defined later) which makes use of ex ante substitution possibilities to fully utilize labour in that period and generate a Pareto improvement in increasing consumption at each time. However, in a market model in which such perfect knowledge is not available then the full employment of labour may require the employment of vintages which will require the use of natural resource now leading to a reduction in consumption possibilities in the future. The value of potential future output from leaving the resource unused may offset the loss of value from having idle resources (both labour and capital) at the present. Both these proposition will be considered later.

The constraint on the natural resource is imposed by firstly defining $Z(t)$, the amount of resources used up to the present to be

$$Z(t) = \int_0^t X(s)\, ds$$

alternatively

$$\dot{Z}(t) = X(t) \tag{6}$$

together with the constraints

$$Z(0) = 0, Z(t) \leqslant \bar{Z} \quad \text{for all } t. \tag{7}$$

A feasible production path can now be defined. The path $(Y(t))_0^T$ is feasible if constraints (1) – (7) are satisfied and

$$Y(t) \geqslant I(t) \geqslant 0 \quad \text{for all } t \in [0, T]. \tag{8}$$

For a planning model we will be interested in feasible consumption paths and this is defined by adding a national income identity

$$Y(t) = C(t) + I(t). \tag{9}$$

$(C(t))_0^T$ is feasible if (1) – (9) are satisfied.

Complexity is reduced by invoking an argument relating to returns to scale. In this production technology, equation (2) imposes constant returns at the ex post level to each vintage. An additional assumption of constant returns at the ex ante level with a particular technical progress relation is introduced, into the function given by equation (1).

$$Y(v, v) = F(I(v), L(v, v), Z(v)).$$

Returns to scale will be in the use of labour, capital and resources. However, we have a fourth argument, the total stock of resource used giving the level of technical knowledge. A proportionate increase in all variables, because of technical advance would be expected to lead to a more than proportionate increase in output, this is the usual result of *Arrow* [1962] concerning Learning by Doing models. If we restrict the learning by doing to the productivity of the resource then a separability structure can be imposed on the ex ante production function:

$$Y(v, v) = F(I(v), L(v, v), R(X(v, v), Z(v))).$$

$R(X(v, v) Z(v))$ is the quantity of resource used in some efficiency units. For example, if $X(v, v)$ is some physical quantity of resource used then $R(X(v, v), Z(v))$ would be the amount of energy extracted from that quantity, where the extractable energy/physical quantity relationship is given by the total amount used in the past. As I, L, R correspond to basic inputs in a plant then it is not unreasonable to think of constant returns to these inputs, and not with respect to I, L, X, Z. F is assumed to be homogeneous of degree one in I, L, R so

$$\frac{Y(v, v)}{L(v, v)} = F\left(\frac{I(v)}{L(v, v)}, 1, \frac{R(X(v, v), Z(v))}{L(v, v)}\right)$$

$$= f\left(\frac{I(v)}{L(v, v)}, \frac{R(X(v, v), Z(v))}{L(v, v)}\right).$$

Now define per capita variables

$$k(v) = \frac{I(v)}{L(v, v)} \quad x(v) = \frac{X(v, v)}{L(v, v)},$$

then the above ex ante production function can be written as

$$f(k(v), r(x(v), L(v, v), Z(v)))$$

where

$$r(x(v), L(v, v), Z(v)) = \frac{R(x(v)L(v, v), Z(v))}{L(v, v)}.$$

It will be assumed that f is concave in k and r. An optimal plan can be investigated for this model. To avoid problems of existence a very narrow objective will be chosen. Existence problems in previous resource models come from two sources. Firstly, from the degree of substitution between capital and resource and secondly the problem of spreading a finite quantity arbitrarily thinly over an infinite time period. A vintage model will increase the severity of the first problem as the possibility of ex post substitution will be ruled out, but the possibility of learning by doing may solve the second. For example, consider the Function

$$R(X(t), Z(t)) = \emptyset(a X(t) + Z(t)) \text{ and the path } X(t) = \frac{1}{a}\bar{Z} e^{-t/a}. \text{ This}$$

is feasible as $Z(t) = \int_0^t \frac{1}{a}\bar{Z} e^{-t/a} dt = \bar{Z}(1 - e^{-t/a})$ and

$$R(X(t), Z(t)) = \emptyset(\bar{Z}) = \text{constant along this path.}$$

The objective function will be $\int_0^T e^{-\rho t} U(C(t)) dt$, where ρ, T are such that an optimum exists.

The consequent control problem is

$$\text{maximize} \int_0^T e^{-\rho t} U(C(t)) dt$$

$$\text{subject to } Z = \int_0^t x(v) L(v, t) dt \tag{10}$$

$$C(t) + k(t) L(t, t) = \int_0^t f(k(v), r(v)) L(v, t) dv \tag{11}$$

$$r(v) = r(x(v), L(v, v), Z(v)) \tag{12}$$

$$L(t) \leqslant \int_0^t L(v, t) dv \tag{13}$$

$$0 \leqslant Z(t) \leqslant \bar{Z} \quad \text{for all } t, \quad 0 \leqslant t \leqslant T. \tag{14}$$

This problem can be solved using the Pontryagin maximum principle with an isoperimetric constraint imposed, see *Hadley/Kemp* [1974, 176–183].

Define $H = e^{-\rho t} U(C(t)) + \pi \int_0^t x(v) L(v, t) dv$ then necessary conditions for a maximum are that $C(t), k(h), x(h), L(h, t)$ for $0 \leqslant h \leqslant t$ maximize H subject to (11) – (14), that π satisfies the differential equation $\dot{\pi} = -H_Z^*$ where H^* is the maximum value of H in the above set of conditions, and finally that complementary slackness conditions hold with respect to the initial and terminal values of the state variable, Z. So we obtain the equation.

$$\dot{\pi} = -(e^{-\rho t} U'(C^*)) \frac{\partial C^*}{\partial Z} + \pi \int_0^t \left(x^*(v) \frac{\partial L^*}{\partial Z} + L^* \frac{\partial x^*}{\partial Z} \right) dv. \tag{15}$$

Alternatively the optimization problem can be formulated as follows.

$$\text{maximize } \int_0^T e^{-\rho t} U(C(t)) dt$$

$$\text{subject to } Z(t) = \int_0^t \int_0^h x(v) L(v, h) dv \, dh$$

$$C(t) + k(t) L(t, t) = \int_0^t f(k(v), r(v)) L(v, t) dv$$

$$r(v) = r(x(v), L(v, v), Z(v))$$

$$L(t) \leqslant \int_0^t L(v, t) dv$$

$$0 \leqslant Z(t) \leqslant \bar{Z}$$

and solving using a Lagrangean isoperimetric approach leads to conditions easier to interpret at a later stage.

Let

$$L = \int_0^T e^{-\rho t} U(C(t)) dt + \int_0^T \pi(t) \left(\int_0^t \int_0^h x(v) L(v, h) dv \, dh - Z(t) \right) dt$$

$$+ \int_0^T (\theta(t) \left(\int_0^t f(k(v), r(v)) L(v, t) dv - C(t) - k(t) L(t, t) \right)$$

$$+ \lambda(t) (L(t) - \int_0^t L(v, t) dv)) dt.$$

The necessary conditions with respect to variations in $k(v) x(v), L(v, t), C(t)$ are: –

$$0 = e^{-\rho t} U'(C(t)) - \theta(t) \tag{16}$$

$$0 = \int_h^T \theta(t) f_k(k(h), r(h)) L(h, t) dt - \theta(h) f(h) L(h, h) \tag{17}$$

$$0 = \int_h^T \pi(t) L(h, t) dt + \int_h^T \theta(t) f_r(k(h), r(h)) r_x(h) L(h, t) dt \tag{18}$$

$$0 = -\pi(h) + \int_h^T \theta(t) f_r(k(h), r(h)) r_z(h) L(h, t) dt \tag{19}$$

$$0 = \pi(h) x(h) + \int_h^T [\theta(t)(f_r(k(h), r(h)) r_L(h) L(h, t)$$

$$+ f(k(h), r(h)) L(h, t)) - \lambda(t) L(h, t)] dt - \theta(h) L(h, h) k(h). \tag{20}$$

These derivatives are calculated using the method of variation described by *Bliss* [1968]. These conditions can be interpreted as follows. (16) can be interpreted as an equation determining $\theta(t)$ which is the present price of output at time t. Using this equation (17) becomes a condition on the returns to capital. Evaluated at social prices the net return to installing an extra unit of capital at any moment of time, keeping labour and resource use constant, should equal zero. Equation (18) will be a condition on resource use. If $q(t)$ is the price of the resource at time t then the cost of resource used on vintage h at time t is

$$q(t) X(h, t) = q(t) \frac{X(h, t)}{L(h, t)} L(h, t) = q(t) L(h, t) x(h)$$

thus $q(t) L(h, t)$ is the price of the resource used per man. If $-\pi(t)$ is the price of resource then $-\pi(t) L(h, t)$ is the price of resource per man appropriate to vintage h and condition (18) says that the value of increasing output by using an extra unit of resource at time t on vintage h should equal the cost of doing so. Equation (20) becomes an equation giving $\lambda(t)$ for which the net value of output from reallocating labour between vintages and changing the productive coefficients should equal zero. These conditions seem very like the standard conclusions from any natural resource model, see (1) for example, with the added vintage complication. The main difference comes from (20). If no learning by doing were present then the Hotelling condition relating $\dot{\pi}$ to π and the marginal product of the resource (that the proportional rate of change of the marginal product of resource should equal the marginal product of capital) would be obtained. This is seen from the fact that the corresponding condition to (15) would be
$\dot{\pi} = -(e^{-\rho t} U'(C(t)))(\partial C^*)/(\partial Z)$ and we can use the results that $e^{-\rho t} U'(C(t)) = \theta(t) =$ marginal product of capital from the conditions equivalent to (16) and $\partial C^*/\partial Z$ will be the marginal product of resource, π. The second part of (15) is π multiplied by the marginal effect of past resource use on the optimal level of labour and resource use across vintages, as the total amount of resource used, i.e. the level of technical knowledge, varies.

A competitive firm[1] in this world will behave in the following way. Its output is determined by those vintages operated, which will be those that cover their variable costs as if $q(t)$ is the price of resource, $w(t)$ is the wage rate, $i(t)$ the rate of interest and $p(t)$ is the price of output then $L(v, t) > 0$ if $p(t) f(k(v), r(v)) > (w(t) + x(v) q(t))$. $L(v, t) = 0$ if $p(t) f(k(v), r(v)) < (w(t) + (x(v) q(t))$. The output of the resource owning industry will be that it will supply any amount of resource if $(\dot{q}(t))/(q(t)) = i(t)$, no resource if

---

[1]) Which is myopic.

$(\dot{q}\,(t))/(q\,(t)) < i\,(t)$, and the whole stock if $(\dot{q}\,(t))/(q\,(t)) > i\,(t)$. The supply of labour and capital is given at a moment of time by the exogenous population and past investment decisions.

At time h profits, discounted back to time zero, on capital equipment installed at time h will be

$$A = \int_h^T \left(p\,(t)\,f\,(k\,(h), r\,(h)) - w\,(t) - q\,(t)\,x\,(h)\right) L\,(t, h)\,e^{-D(t)}\,dt$$

$$- p\,(h)\,k\,(h)\,L\,(h, h) \tag{21}$$

where $D\,(t)$ is the discount factor $\int_0^t d\,(s)\,ds$.

Consider variations in A with respect to the decisions made about capital installation at time h, $k\,(h)$, $x\,(h)$.

$$\frac{\partial A}{\partial k\,(h)} = \frac{\partial f}{\partial k}\,(h) \int_h^T p\,(t)\,L\,(t, h)\,e^{-D(t)}\,dt - p\,(h)\,L\,(h, h)\,e^{-D(h)} \tag{22}$$

$$\frac{\partial A}{\partial x\,(h)} = \frac{\partial f}{\partial x}\,(h) \int_h^T p\,(t)\,L\,(t, h)\,e^{-D(t)}\,dt = \int_h^T q\,(t)\,L\,(t, h)\,e^{-D(t)}\,dt \tag{23}$$

where

$$\frac{\partial f}{\partial x}\,(h) = \frac{\partial f}{\partial r}\,(h) \cdot \frac{\partial r}{\partial r}\,(h)\,.$$

The allocation of labour to vintages in this model will be as usual that only machines generating positive quasi rents will be employed and labour will be allocated to the higher quasi rent vintages, rather than the lower ones. In equilibrium the wage rate and the machines used will be determined so that the quasi rent on the marginal vintage is zero.

Comparing conditions we obtain usual decentralisation results if

$$p\,(t)\,e^{-D(t)} = \theta\,(t)$$

$$q\,(t)\,e^{-D(t)} = -\pi\,(t)$$

so that a decentralised economy will follow the correct path if the current prices are chosen. However, it is clear that a much more complicated result than the Hotelling condition $(\dot{q}/p)/(q/p) = r$ will be obtained, as in this world $(\dot{q}/p)/(q/p) = (\dot{\pi}/\theta)/(\pi/\theta)$, π and θ being linked by equations (18) and (19).

This paper has not answered important questions such as the uniqueness of solution to necessary conditions, existence problems for infinite horizon models, and sufficiency, These problems will relate to the convexity or otherwise of the intertemporal production possibility set, which will be difficult to establish with a vintage production structure. The conclusion of this paper is that in this model, which has some claims to economic and historical plausibility, a naive Hotelling rule is not satisfied. This rule is found in almost all models dealing with problems of natural resources. We call the version used here naive as it is based on myopic behaviour by agents who do not anticipate the learning effects of using the natural resource. If the price of the resource reflected its marginal productivity both directly as an input and indirectly via the learning mechanism then a Hotelling rule could be derived. So one has the choice of either re-writing the Hotelling rule in a more sophisticated way or imposing an extra intertemporal condition. Whatever choice is used caution against regarding this rule as an optimal condition without careful discussion of the resource price and the markets determing it should be made.

References

Arrow, K.: The Economic Implications of Learning by Doing. Review of Economic Studies **29**, 1962, 155–173.

Bliss, C.: On Putty-Clay. Review of Economic Studies **35**, 1968, 105–132.

Hadley, G., and M. Kemp: Variational Methods in Economics. Amsterdam 1974.

Ingham, A.: Some historical notes on natural resource models. University of Southampton, (mimeo) 1981.

Ingham, A., and P. Simmons: Natural Resources and Growing Population. Review of Economic Studies **42**, 1975, 191–206.

Kamien, M., and N. Schwartz: Optimal Exhaustible Resource Depletion with Endogenous Technical Change. Review of Economic Studies **45**, 1978, 179–196.

Landes, D.: The Unbound Prometheus. Cambridge 1970.

Mathias, P.: Who Unbound Prometheus? Science and Technical Change, 1600–1800. Science in Society, 1600–1900. Ed. by P. Mathias. Cambridge 1970.

Takayama, A.: Optimal Technical Progress with Exhaustible Resources. Exhaustible Resources, Optimality and Trade. Ed. by M. Kemp and N.V. Long. Amsterdam 1980.

Economic Theory of Natural Resources. ©Physica-Verlag, Würzburg–Wien, 1982.

Unemployment Equilibria in a Small Resource Importing Economy with a Vintage Production Structure

Alan Ingham, Daniel Weiserbs and *F. Melese*[1])

1. Introduction

This model is designed to look at unemployment deriving from the essential role of resources in production. In most neoclassical resource depletion models, such as those discussed by *Dasgupta/Heal* [1979] for example, a smooth concave neoclassical production function is used to represent technology. Unemployment clearly cannot occur in these models, as the economy is on the boundary of the production possibility set at all times and so fully employs all its factors. Thus macro-economic effects are not present in these models, and so they cannot answer questions asked by politicians, and others, as to the effect of resource price increases and quotas, on employment in the economy. The question of rationing has been asked by *Malinvaud* [1980], and it is in the spirit of his analysis that we proceed.

The paper proceeds by examining a particular structure for production, which moves away from the smooth production function of other papers and which generates macro-economic phenomena. In another paper, one of the authors [*Ingham*] has argued for a vintage model of production. These arguments are not repeated here. That paper was addressed to justifying a more detailed representation of technology than is normally used and examining the implications for the control of a resource using economy.

In the model considered here, constraints on the availability of the resource will restrict the number of vintages in operation which will in turn limit the employed labour force to a level below that of full employment. These constraints may come about either from a physical rationing of the resource or an increase in its price (the profitability requirement then causes closure of some vintages). As we do not wish to explicitly model the causes of these restrictions, we consider the case where the economy imports a resource. We do not model the decision making process of the oil exporting country, but rather examine the implications of various policies they may adopt. Of course, our prime motivation is to model problems facing industrialized western countries importing oil from OPEC.

In *Ingham* [1982], two distinct types of productive decisions were involved. The putty-clay structure requires decisions to be taken about the nature of new capital to be installed, and, once this capital is in place, the intensity at which it should be operated is also decided. As we are concerned with this latter type of decision we will consider a

---

[1]) We are grateful to the referees for helpful comments.

clay-clay vintage structure, and, to simplify matters, avoid the nature of new investment decisions. However the capital, labour, and resource requirements per unit of output will change, because of technical progress. Technical progress is of the input saving type for labour and the resource, and also includes learning by doing in resource use. The economy evolves through time and it is the macro-economic aspects of this evolution we wish to consider. In this model the evolution is represented in a discrete rather than a continuous way as was done in *Ingham* [1982]. This has the usual advantages and disadvantages. As a sequel to this paper will have numerical simulations, we consider a discrete model ab initio.

In section 2, the model is fully specified. Appropriate concepts of equilibrium for the model and the possibility of Walrasian equilibrium in particular are then discussed. If the economy is in a non Walrasian equilibrium then unemployment will exist and controls of the economy to mitigate the effects of unemployment are considered. A central planner, concerned with both consumption per head and the unemployment rate, is introduced. The optimal path for the economy, and the equilibrium regimes in which it may lie are analysed, and some comparative statics conclude our study.

2. Structure of the Model

2.1 The Goods Market

We consider a clay-clay vintage model[2]) in which an economy combines labour services, capital services and a non-renewable natural resource to produce a single manufactured output, Q_t. The previous period's output (Q_{t-1}) is either consumed (C_t), invested (k_t) or used for export (X_t) in the current period. The output serves as numeraire of the system. Denoting effective demand by Y_t, we have

$$Y_t = C_t + k_t + X_t \leqslant Q_{t-1} \, . \tag{1}$$

If M_t is the quantity of the resource imported at a price p_t, and X_t is the amount of output exported in return, then the external debt evolves according to

$$B_t = (1 + r_{t-1}) B_{t-1} + p_t M_t - X_t \, , \tag{2a}$$

where r_t is the rate of interest on foreign debt. For simplicity we shall assume equilibrium in the balance of trade at every period t;

$$p_t M_t = X_t, \quad (\text{or } B_t = 0 \text{ for all } t). \tag{2b}$$

(Alternatively we could consider a country having deficits and surpluses, only constrained to be in balance at some terminal period T: $B_T = 0$.)

We further assume that no stockpiling of the resource may occur within the country.

2.2 Production

Each machine produces a constant amount of output v per period. An investment of k_θ machines at time θ yields an output at time t of $q_{t, \theta}$.

$$q_{t, \theta} = vk_\theta \, . \tag{3}$$

---

[2]) This structure of production is fully discussed in *Solow* et al. [1966].

Denoting s_t as the oldest vintage operating in period t, total output in the current period will be

$$Q_t = \sum_{\theta=s_t}^{t} q_{t,\theta} = v \sum_{\theta=s_t}^{t} k_\theta. \tag{4}$$

Due to technical progress, decreasing quantities of labour and the resources are required to operate successive vintages.

2.3 The Labour Market

The number of workers required to operate a machine of vintage θ is

$$l_\theta = (1 + \mu)^{-\theta} l_0. \tag{5}$$

where l_0 is the amount of labour required to operate one machine of the oldest vintage utilized at the beginning of the plan. This obviously corresponds to Harrod-neutral technical progress. Thus at time t the total amount of labour employed on all existing vintages in the economy is given by

$$L_t = l_0 \sum_{\theta=s_t}^{t} (1 + \mu)^{-\theta} k_\theta. \tag{6}$$

If the labour force grows at a constant rate, λ, unemployment in period t may be written

$$N_t - L_t = (1 + \lambda)^t N_0 - L_t \geq 0. \tag{7}$$

The unemployment rate, u_t, is thus

$$u_t = 1 - L_t/N_t. \tag{8}$$

If insufficient labour were available, some machines would have to be scrapped. Due to technical progress, the oldest vintages would be eliminated first.

2.4 The Resource Market

The resource requirement for a machine of vintage s at time t, $m_{t,s}$, is defined as

$$m_{t,s} = m_0 (1 + v)^{-s} (1 + \delta)^{s-t}. \tag{9}$$

The parameters v and δ correspond respectively to resource-saving technical progress (analogous to Harrod neutral technical progress) and to learning by doing.[3] Total demand for the resource will be

$$M_t = m_0 \sum_{\theta=s_t}^{t} (1 + v)^{-\theta} (1 + \delta)^{\theta-t} k_\theta. \tag{10}$$

Again, if demand for the resource, M_t, exceeds supply, X_t/p_t the oldest vintages will be scrapped.

The nonrenewable resource producing country acts as a monopolist maximizing its discounted future stream profits (subject to an exhaustibility constraint). The resulting optimal extraction plan defines the available supply in each period. The price of the re-

---

[3] See *Wan* [1971] for discussion of these points.

source is set on the world market over which our small country has no influence. Our economy is assumed to receive a constant share of the world market at the exogenously determined price p_t. Although the development of a joint two-country model is an interesting possibility it is beyond the scope of the present study.

3. Equilibrium

3.1 Typology of Equilibria

a) When Walrasian Equilibrium prevails, demand equals supply on the good, resource and labour markets and the oldest machine just covers its costs[4]):

$$Y_t = Q_{t-1};$$
$$M_t = X_t/p_t;$$
$$L_t = N_t;$$
$$v = w_t \, l_0 \, (1+\mu)^{-s} \, t + p_t \, m_0 \, (1+\delta)^{s \cdot t \cdot t} \, (1+v)^{-s_t},$$

where w is the wage rate.

b) If there is insufficient demand in both the goods market and the factor markets, *keynesian unemployment* will prevail:

$$Y_t < Q_{t-1}$$
$$M_t \leqslant X_t/p_t$$
$$L_t < N_t$$
$$v > w_t \, (1+\mu)^{-s} \, t + p_t \, m_0 \, (1+\delta)^{s \cdot t \cdot t} \, (1+v)^{-s_t}.$$

c) If, s_t, required to guarantee full employment of the labour force, is such that

$$v < w_t \, l_{s_t} + p_t \, m_{t, s_t}$$

then the costs of production are too high for all existing machines to be kept in operations and *classical unemployment* results.

d) If $M_t > X_t/p_t$ (and/or $L_t > N_t$), production is rationed through the factor market(s) and a sort of *"repressed inflation equilibrium"* à la Malinvaud will result (in the sense that there is excess demand on the input market).

3.2 Walrasian Equilibrium

We first consider Walrasian equilibrium under the Cambridge assumption that the economy's savings ratio is equal to the share of profit in the value added (or, equivalently, that all wages are consumed and all profits invested). Then by substituting for C_t, X_t and Q_{t-1} in the goods market, L_t and N_t in the labour market, and since (by

---

[4]) This places a restriction on the technical progress parameters, in particular the condition $w > \delta$ introduced infra is sufficient.

assumption) demand for the resource is satisfied at price p_t, we obtain the following system of equations:

$$w_t l_0 \sum_{\theta=s_t}^{t} (1+\mu)^{-\theta} k_\theta + k_t + p_t m_0 \sum_{\theta=s_t}^{t} (1+\delta)^{\theta-t} (1+\nu)^{-\theta} k_\theta$$

$$= \nu \sum_{\theta=s_{t-1}}^{t-1} k_\theta; \qquad (11a)$$

$$l_0 \sum_{\theta=s_t}^{t} (1+\mu)^{-\theta} k_\theta = (1+\lambda)^t N_0; \qquad (11b)$$

$$\nu = w_t l_0 (1+\mu)^{-s_t} + p_t m_0 (1+\delta)^{s_t-t} (1+\nu)^{-s_t}. \qquad (11c)$$

We thus have three sets of equations to be solved for w_t, k_t and s_t (where feasibility requires that $w_t > 0$, $k_t \geq 0$ and $s_t \leq t$). Hence the evolution of the system is completely specified.

No control of the economy is possible in such a Walrasian equilibrium. In essence, the economy chooses that path which ensures full employment. Of course existence and uniqueness of a solution to system (11a – c) is not guaranteed. However for suitable initial conditions and technical progress parameters a solution will exist, while in the case of multiple equilibria some choice may be effected.[5]

Even so, if, for example a governmental body has strong preferences concerning consumption per head then it must be prepared to forego Walrasian equilibrium properties for the economy. However, it may turn out that the optimal path corresponds to intertemporal Walrasian equilibrium, which is the usual decentralization result.

3.3 A Diagrammatic Representation of Equilibrium

While it is difficult to explicitly solve the system of equations (11) for the endogenous variables k_t, s_t, w_t, it is possible to produce a diagrammatic representation by considering the surface generated by each of the equations in turn. The intersection of the surfaces will be the Walrasian equilibrium, while the other equilibrium regimes will be surfaces in the (k_t, s_t, w_t) space determined by these equations. The surfaces are calculated by solving each of the equations for one of the endogenous variables in terms of the others and then calculating the appropriate derivatives and signing them. It turns out that to produce an unambiguous sketch the parametric restriction that the rate of resource saving technical progress is higher than the rate of learning by doing, or $(1 + \nu)/(1 + \delta) > 1$ has to be imposed. Each equilibrium condition is now considered in turn.

(11a) Equilibrium in the goods market implies

$$w_t l_0 \sum_{\theta=s_t}^{t} (1+\mu)^{-\theta} k_\theta + k_t + p_t m_0 \sum_{\theta=s_t}^{t} (1+\delta)^{\theta-t} (1+\nu)^{-\theta} k_\theta = \nu \sum_{\theta=s_{t-1}}^{t-1} k_\theta,$$

---

[5]) Discussion is contained in the next section.

340

given our assumption on the balance of trade (2b). Solving for w_t we obtain

$$w_t = \frac{v \sum\limits_{\theta=s_{t-1}}^{t-1} k_\theta - k_t - p_t m_0 \sum\limits_{\theta=s_t}^{t} (1+\delta)^{\theta-t} (1+v)^{-\theta} k_\theta}{l_0 \sum\limits_{\theta=s_t}^{t} (1+\mu)^{-\theta} k_\theta}.$$

It can be shown that

$$\frac{\partial w_t}{\partial k_t} < 0, \frac{\partial w_t}{\partial s_t} > 0, \frac{\partial^2 w_t}{\partial k_t \partial s_t} > 0, \frac{\partial^2 w_t}{\partial k_t^2} > 0.$$

Alternatively one could solve for k_t:

$$k_t = \frac{v \sum\limits_{\theta=s_{t-1}}^{t-1} k_\theta - w_t l_0 \sum\limits_{\theta=s_t}^{t-1} (1+\mu)^{-\theta} k_\theta - p_t m_0 \sum\limits_{\theta=s_t}^{t-1} (1+\delta)^{\theta-t} (1+v)^{-\theta} k_\theta}{1 + w_t l_0 (1+\mu)^{-t} + p_t m_0 (1+v)^{-t}},$$

and so $(\partial k_t)/(\partial s_t) > 0$ and $(\partial^2 k_t)/(\partial s_t^2) > 0$.
    This information generates the sketch below.

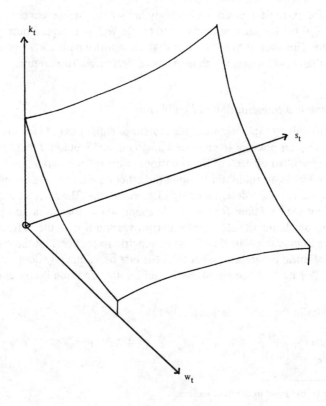

Fig. 1

(11b) Equilibrium in the labour market

$$l_0 \sum_{\theta=s_t}^{t} (1+\mu)^{-\theta} k_\theta = (1+\lambda)^t N_0,$$

this can be solved for k_t

$$k_t = (1+\lambda)^t (1+\mu)^t \frac{N_0}{l_0} - (1+\mu)^t \sum_{\theta=s_t}^{t-1} (1+\mu)^{-\theta} k_\theta,$$

so that $(dk_t)/(ds_t) = (1+\mu)^t (1+\mu)^{-s_t} k_{s_t} > 0$ while the second derivative $(d^2 k_t)/(ds_t^2)$ will depend on the historical path of investment, and hence the k_t, s_t relationship for equilibrium in the labour market may be concave, convex or neither.

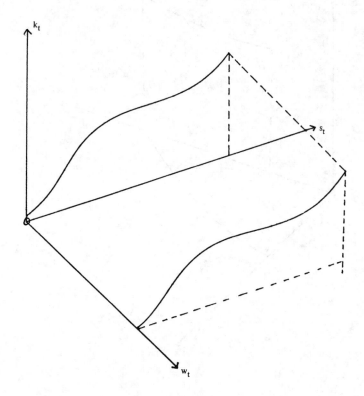

Fig. 2

(11c) Equilibrium in the capital market.

In equilibrium the marginal machine just covers its cost, so that the surplus on the oldest machine in operation is zero.

$$v = w_t l_0 (1+\mu)^{-s_t} + p_t m_0 (1+\delta)^{s_t-t} (1+v)^{-s_t}.$$

Solving for w_t we obtain:

$$w_t = \frac{v}{l_0} (1+\mu)^{s_t} - p_t\, m_0\, \frac{(1+\delta)^{s_t - t}\,(1+\mu)^{s_t}}{(1+v)^{s_t}},$$

$$\frac{dw_t}{ds_t} > 0 \text{ if } \frac{(1+\delta)}{(1+v)} < 1,$$

and

$$\frac{d^2 w_t}{ds_t^2} > 0.$$

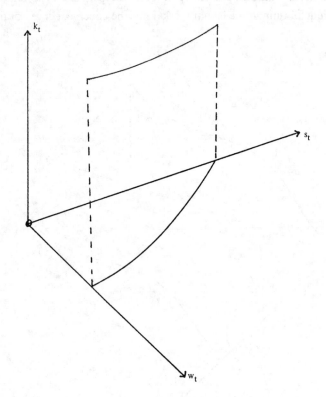

Fig. 3

The surfaces for (11a) and (11c) are unambiguous and can be put together as in fig. 4. The simultaneous solution is a path AB. Intersections of this path with the surface in fig. 2 will be the Walrasian equilibria for the economy. For a concave or convex relationship as the solution of (11b) are, at best unique equilibrium will result, existence depending on the parameters (which include the prices in the model). However, for an historical path of investment which is not monotonic, clearly multiple equilibria may emerge.

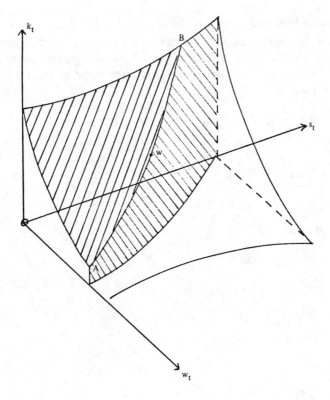

Fig. 4

4. A Planned Economy

4.1 Planner's Objective Function

Among all feasible paths satisfying the constraints, the planner will choose the one which maximizes his objective function

$$J = \sum_{t=1}^{T} (1 + \gamma)^{1-t} \, u \, [\alpha(c_t), \beta(-u_t)], \tag{12}$$

where c_t is consumption per capita.

If $\beta = 0$, we have the standard social welfare function of consumption per capita. But the planner may also take into consideration the rate of unemployment. Thus the higher the value of β/α, the larger the weight given to the distribution of income i.e. the greater the planner's sensitivity to social tensions. The discount factor may be justified by considering impatience and re-election pressures and is most convenient when $T \to \infty$.

A machine of vintage s at time t will be maintained in operation if it is profitable, i.e.:

$$v \geqslant w_t \, l_s + p_t \, m_{t,s}, \tag{13a}$$

or

$$v \geqslant w_t \, l_0 \, (1 + \mu)^{-s} + p_t \, m_0 \, (1 + \delta)^{s-t} \, (1 + \nu)^{-s}. \tag{13b}$$

4.2 Controlling the Economy

Once the full employment constraint is relaxed the prevailing unemployment regime may be identified through the other constraints. All possible regimes may be presented in a general Kuhn-Tucker formulation [as in *Intrilligator*, p. 49 for example].

Consider the problem:

$$\max_{(w_t, k_t, s_t)} \quad J = \sum_{t=1}^{T} (1+\gamma)^{1-t} u(c_t, -u_t) \quad (T \in [1, \infty]),$$

subject to

$$C_t + k_t + p_t M_t - Q_{t-1} \leqslant 0,$$

$$-u_t \leqslant 0,$$

$$p_t M_t - X_t \leqslant 0,$$

$$w_t l_{s_t} + p_t m_{t,s_t} - v \leqslant 0;$$

and

$$c_t = w_t L_t / N_t \quad (= C_t / N_t),$$

$$-u_t = L_t / N_t - 1;$$

where

$$L_t = \sum_{\theta = s_t}^{t} l_\theta k_\theta = l_0 \sum_{\theta = s_t}^{t} (1+\mu)^{-\theta} k_\theta,$$

$$N_t = (1+\lambda)^t N_0,$$

$$M_t = \sum_{\theta = s_t}^{t} m_{t,\theta} k_0 = m_0 \sum_{\theta = s_t}^{t} (1+\delta)^{\theta - t} (1+v)^{-\theta} k_\theta,$$

$$Q_{t-1} = v \sum_{\theta = s_{t-1}}^{t-1} k_\theta;$$

so that

$$c_t = w_t \frac{l_0}{N_0} (1+\lambda)^{-t} \sum_{\theta = s_t}^{t} (1+\mu)^{-\theta} k_\theta,$$

$$-u_t = \frac{l_0}{N_0} (1+\lambda)^{-t} \sum_{\theta = s_t}^{t} (1+\mu)^{-\theta} k_\theta - 1.$$

Define

$$H = \sum_{t=1}^{T} \left\{ (1+\gamma)^{1-t} u(c_t, -u_t) \right.$$

$$+ \eta_t \left[c_t - w_t \frac{l_0}{N_0} (1 + \lambda)^{-t} \sum_{\theta = s_t}^{t} (1 + \mu)^{-\theta} k_\theta \right]$$

$$+ \psi_t [v \sum_{\theta = s_{t-1}}^{t-1} k_\theta - C_t - k_t - p_t m_0 \sum_{\theta = s_t}^{t} (1 + \delta)^{\theta - t} (1 + v)^{-\theta} k_\theta]$$

$$+ \phi_t \left[u_t + \frac{l_0}{N_0} (1 + \lambda)^{-t} \sum_{\theta = s_t}^{t} (1 + \mu)^{-\theta} k_\theta - 1 \right]$$

$$+ \sigma_t u_t$$

$$+ \zeta_t [X_t - m_0 \sum_{\theta = s_t}^{t} (1 + v)^{-\theta} (1 + \delta)^{\theta - t} k_\theta]$$

$$+ \pi_t [v - w_t l_0 (1 + \mu)^{-s_t} - p_t m_0 (1 + \delta)^{s_t - t} (1 + v)^{-s_t}] \Big\}.$$

The necessary conditions, including the complementary slackness conditions, are in obvious notation

$$0 \geqslant \frac{\partial H}{\partial y_i}, y_i \frac{\partial H}{\partial y_i} = 0 \quad y_i \geqslant 0$$

$$b_j - g_j (y) \geqslant 0 \quad \xi_j (b_j - g_j (y)) = 0 \quad \xi_j \geqslant 0.$$

where the constraints are $g (y) \leqslant b$ and the multipliers are ξ.

Hence necessary conditions are

$$\frac{\partial H}{\partial c_t} = 0, \tag{14a}$$

$$\left. \begin{array}{l} \frac{\partial H}{\partial u_t} = 0 \\ \\ \sigma_t = 0 \end{array} \right\} u_t > 0 \text{ or } \left. \begin{array}{l} \frac{\partial H}{\partial u_t} < 0 \\ \\ \sigma_t > 0 \end{array} \right\} u_t = 0, \tag{14b}$$

$$\frac{\partial H}{\partial w_t} = 0, \tag{14c}$$

$$\frac{\partial H}{\partial k_t} = 0, \tag{14d}$$

$$\frac{\partial H}{\partial s_t} = 0, s_t > 0 \text{ or } \frac{\partial H}{\partial s_t} < 0, \ s_t = 0 \text{ (no machines are scrapped)} \tag{14c}$$

$$\text{or } \frac{\partial H}{\partial s_t} > 0 \ s_t = t \text{ (non existant machines cannot be scrapped)},$$

$$\left.\begin{array}{l} Y_t - Q_{t-1} < 0 \\[1em] \psi_t = 0 \end{array}\right\} \quad \text{or} \quad \left\{\begin{array}{l} Y_t - Q_{t-1} = 0 \\[1em] \psi_t > 0 \end{array}\right. \tag{14f}$$

together with the feasability conditions $c_t > 0$, $w_t > 0$ and $k_t \geqslant 0$; and where (denoting τ_t as the lifetime of a machine installed in period t)

$$\frac{\partial H}{\partial c_t} = (1+\gamma)^{1-t} \frac{\partial u}{\partial c_t} + \eta_t - \psi_t (1+\lambda)^t N_0 \tag{15a}$$

$$\frac{\partial H}{\partial u_t} = -\left\{ (1+\gamma)^{1-t} \frac{\partial u}{\partial u_t} - \phi_t - \sigma_t \right\} \tag{15b}$$

$$\frac{\partial H}{\partial w_t} = -\left\{ \eta_t (1+\lambda)^{-t} \sum_{\theta = s_t}^{t} (1+\mu)^{-\theta} k_\theta + \pi_t (1+\mu)^{-s_t} k_0 \right\} \tag{15c}$$

$$\frac{\partial H}{\partial k_t} = -\left\{ (1+\mu)^{-t} \sum_{\theta=t}^{t+\tau_t} \eta_\theta \frac{l_0}{N_0} (1+\lambda)^{-\theta} w_\theta + \psi_t - v \sum_{\theta=t+1}^{b+\tau_{t+1}} \psi_\theta \right.$$

$$+ \frac{l_0}{N_0} (1+\mu)^{-t} \sum_{\theta=t}^{t+\tau_t} (1+\lambda)^{-\theta} \phi_\theta + (1+v)^{-t} m_0 \sum_{\theta=t}^{t+\tau_t} \psi_\theta P_\theta (1+\delta)^{t-\theta}$$

$$\left. + m_0 (1+v)^{-t} \sum_{\theta=t}^{t+\tau_t} \xi_\theta (1+\delta)^{t-\theta} \right\} \tag{15d}$$

$$\frac{\partial H}{\partial s_t} = -\left\{ \eta_t \frac{l_0}{N_0} w_t (1+\mu)^{-s_t} k_{s_t} (1+\lambda)^{-t} \right\} + \psi_{t+1} \, v \, k_{s_t}$$

$$- \psi_t P_t m_0 (1+\delta)^{s_t-t} (1+v)^{-s_t} k_{s_t} + \phi_t (1+\mu)^{-s_t} (1+\lambda)^{-t} \frac{l_0}{N_0} k_{s_t}$$

$$- \xi_t m_0 (1+v)^{-s_t} (1+\delta)^{s_t-t} k_{s_t}$$

$$- \pi_t [w_t l_0 (1+\mu)^{-s_t} \log(1+\mu) + p_t m_0 (1+\delta)^{s_t-t} (1+v)^{-s_t} \log(1+v)]. \tag{15e}$$

4.3 Interpretation

These conditions are highly non-linear and will not be easy to solve for an explicit solution even for special functional forms. However the interpretation that we require can be obtained. We wish to know what the path of the economy will be when it is optimally controlled. This path is characterised, not by an explicit solution, but by the type of macro-economic equilibrium that the economy is in at a particular moment. The four possible equilibrium positions, Walrasian equilibrium, Classical unemployment equilibrium, Keynesian unemployment equilibrium, and Repressed inflation equilibrium are each characterised by whether weak inequality constraints on the economy hold with equality or as a strict inequality. For example, in Walrasian equilibrium all the constraints must hold with equality, so that when controlling the economy in a Walrasian equilibrium regime[6]) these constraints will be binding and consequently the appropriate Kuhn-Tucker multipliers will be positive. The other equilibrium regimes will give rise to various constraints holding with equality or strict inequality. The overall picture is given in the following table.

Kuhn-Tucker Multipliers and Equilibrium Regimes

		"Repressed inflation"	Keynesian	Classical	Walrasian
ψ		$= 0$	$= 0$	> 0	> 0
σ		$= 0$	$= 0$	$= 0$	> 0
ς		> 0	$\geqslant 0$	$\geqslant 0$	$\geqslant 0$
π		$= 0$	$= 0$	> 0	> 0
Goods market		$D \geqslant S$	$D < S$	$D \geqslant S$	$D = S$
	labor	$D \leqslant S$	$D < S$	$D < S$	$D = S$
Input markets					
	resource	$D > S$	$D < S$	$D < S$	$D \leqslant S$

with D = demand, S = supply.

As classical unemployment is the case where $\psi > 0$ $\sigma = 0$ $\varsigma \geqslant 0$ $\pi > 0$, while Keynesian unemployment has the restrictions $\psi = 0$ $\sigma = 0$ $\varsigma \geqslant 0$ $\pi = 0$, then it is possible for there to be a period $[\pi_1, \pi_2]$ during which $\sigma_t = 0$ for $t \in [T_1, T_2]$ while $(\psi_{T_1} > 0, \pi_{T_1} > 0)$ and $(\psi_{T_2} = 0, \pi_{T_2} = 0)$ so that the economy moves from Classical to Keynesian unemployment equilibrium without going through the point of Walrasian equilibrium. Furthermore solution of the equations does not automatically require $\sigma > 0$ so that optimal policies based on welfare being derived from both consumption and unemployment levels can result in strictly positive unemployment levels.

5. Conclusion

Detailed analysis of the equilibrium regimes is difficult. One reason for this is the fact that we have three inputs, capital, labour and a resource, whereas previous theoretical papers have only considered two. However a consumption/unemployment trade-off clearly emerges. This is the main conclusion, that external control of an essential input whether by quota, or by price setting, will cause non Walrasian equilibria to occur, and an optimal policy may not return the economy to Walrasian equilibrium. Whilst we have called this input over which the economy has no control, 'resource', it should be noted that no properties relating to depletion of a finite stock have been mentioned. The only requirements are its essential nature and externality to the economy. Some extensions of the model have been considered and we conclude with comments on these.

The relative price of the resource has been taken as given. For full employment Walrasian equilibrium (3.2), there are four conditions and four variables to be solved for k_t, p_t, s_t, w_t (where p_t will be determined to bring about equilibrium in the resource

---

[6]) That is when the optimal conditions suggest that all constraints should bind. Comments of section 3.2 apply to the possibility of control of an economy which is always in Walrasian equilibrium.

market). In particular, it will prevent excess demand on the resource market. However such excess demand may exist if there is separation of decisions and lack of communication between a small manufacturing country and a monopolistic resource producer supplying many countries. If this is the case and the resource price is fixed then disequilibrium is almost certain and one of the unemployment regimes will result. If the resource price is too low, then 'repressed inflation' as defined will occur. Spillovers into the labour market will exist for it will not be possible to fully employ labour. Vintages required to keep these workers employed will be scrapped as the resources to keep them in operation cannot be obtained. The effect of p_t on the equilibrium regime can be seen from its effect on the Kuhn Tucker multipliers as they are interpreted in section 4.2. To find the effect of a change in p_t, we must solve the full dynamic paths. However, as we are interested in the magnitudes of the multipliers (in particular whether they are zero or not) some analysis can be done. Without specifying the values of the parameters, it is not possible to make any prediction about what the values of multipliers will be. Whether the economy moves, for example, from Keynesian to Classical unemployment or vice versa will depend on the parameters of the economy.

An alternative to the indirect method of looking at the structure of the economy by examining which constraints bind in the planning exercise, is to simplify the model in various ways. One set of simplifications is to consider objectives of either maximising the discounted utility of consumption per head alone or ensuring full empolyment in each time period. As can be imagined from the previous analysis, the two sets of conditions are quite different, thus confirming the previous conclusion that full employment comes at a cost of discounted utility of consumption. Although in both cases the simultaneous equations are no easier to solve, iterative approximations can be found. For the full employment policy path this is done in the following way.

In the models considered, the scrapping rule, equation (12a), required the *current* solution for the wage rate in order to decide which machines should be retained and which scrapped.

An industry manager would find it inconvenient to base his investment and scrapping plans on one solution of current wage bargaining. Of course simultaneity should occur. The manager would realise that a particular scrapping/investment plan will influence what unions ask for, and unions are aware that the expectation of what wage level will eventually be decided, will affect the decision on scrapping/investment. This may occur as a long run phenomenon, a gradual adjustment to simultaneous determination, or as an iterative within period process to determine the simultaneous solution by a quasi-tatonnement method. To start, we assume the scrapping decision is based on the previous time period's wage level, where time may be real corresponding to long run adjustment or virtual corresponding to the quasi-tatonnement solution process. This is sufficient to determine a recursive process as follows

$$s_t = \frac{\log\left[(w_{t-1}\,l_0)/(v - p_t\,m_t)\right]}{\log(1 + \mu)}$$

providing that

$$\frac{w_{t-1}\,l_0}{v - p_t\,m_t} > 1.$$

This gives the scrapping rule as a function of last period's wage rate. The condition $\dfrac{w_{t-1}\, l_0}{v - p_t\, m_t} > 1$ is required to ensure a positive solution for s_t. Its interpretation, that using the current resource price and the previous wage rate period 0 machines are unprofitable, should not be of concern for lag t.

Once s_t is known, k_t can be calculated from the following rule

$$k_t = \frac{(1+\lambda)^t N_0 - l_0 \displaystyle\sum_{\theta = s_t}^{t-1} (1+\mu)^{-\theta}\, k_\theta}{l_0\,(1+\mu)^{-t}}.$$

Now that the date of the oldest machine and the level of current investment are known we can determine the level of output (which is necessary information for next period) and the affordable wage rate. Since

$$Q_{t-1} = v \sum_{\theta = s_{t-1}}^{t-1} k_\theta,$$

$$w_t = \frac{Q_{t-1} - k_t - p_t\, m_t \displaystyle\sum_{\theta = s_t}^{t} k_\theta}{(1+\lambda)^t N_0}.$$

Thus we have calculated values for this period and provided all the information needed for the solution of next period's problem. All that must be provided now are initial conditions. The quasi-tatonnement procedure can be calculated as follows.

$$s_t^{(i)} = \frac{\log\left[(w_t^{(i-1)}\, l_0)/(v - p_t\, m_t)\right]}{\log(1+\mu)};$$

$$k_t^{(i)} = \frac{(1+\lambda)^t N_0 - l_0 \displaystyle\sum_{\theta = s_t}^{t-1}{}_{(i)} (1+\mu)^{-\theta}\, k_\theta}{l_0\,(1+\mu)^{-t}};$$

$$w_t^{(i)} = \frac{Q_{t-1} - k_t - p_t\, m_t \displaystyle\sum_{\theta = s_t}^{t}{}_{(i)} k_\theta^{(i)}}{(1+\lambda)^t N_0};$$

$$w_t^{(0)} = w_{t-1}.$$

The contrasting policy is that of maximising the discounted sum of consumption per head which, because of the savings function assumption, is equal to the discounted wage bill. The scrapping rule now determines the wage rate as a function of the price of the resource. The wage rate decreases at the rate at which the resource price increases, but increases at the rate of labour productivity. Using the national income identity generates an investment equation. The maximum consumption per head path can be obtained based on initial conditions for the investment path. The main difference between the two sets of conditions is that for the present case the wage rate is determined by the national income identity, not the scrapping rule, and so is no longer determined by the marginal machine. Simulations for the economy may be based on these two procedures [*Weiserbs/Kervyn/Ingham*].

References

Dasgupta, P., and *G. Heal*: Economic Theory and Exhaustible Resources. Welwyn 1979.

Ingham, A.: Learning by Burning. Economic Theory of Natural Resources. Ed. by W. Eichhorn et al. Würzburg–Wien 1982 (this volume).

Intrilligator, M.: Mathematical Optimization and Economic Theory. Englewood Cliffs 1971.

Malinvaud, E.: Profitability and Investment. Cambridge 1980.

Solow, R., et al.: Neoclassical Growth with Fixed Factor Properties. Review of Economic Studies **33**, 1966, 79–116.

Wan, H.: Economic Growth. New York 1971.

Weiserbs, D., A. Kervyn and *A. Ingham*: Employment Policy for Balanced Growth Under an Input Constraint. I.S.E. Working Paper no 8107.

Economic Theory of Natural Resources. ©Physica-Verlag, Würzburg–Wien, 1982.

A Growth Model for the World Economy
Some Consequences for the Case of Exhaustible Resources

Wilhelm Krelle

1. Introduction

The paper deals with the following problem: what will be the economic consequences of a monopoly of certain countries on depletable resources? Will these countries finally get the total GNP on earth with the exception of a subsistance level consumption for the rest of the world? (This was the solution which Ricardo suggested to the similar problem of the monopoly of the British landlords on the arable land in Great Britain). These problems will be analysed on the base of a multi-commodity-, multi-country-model of international trade and capital flows. Only the long-term equilibrium relations will be considered. Assuming flexible exchange rates and free movements of commodities and capital, it will be shown that in those cases where the international economic system is capable of an equilibrium growth (or decline) at all, the asymptotic effect of ownership of depletable resources is equivalent to the right of taxing all other nations who do not own these resources. Thus the consequence will be a change in income and property distribution in favor of the countries owning the depletable resources. But this change will asymptotically reach an upper limit such that the "poor" nations will stay in line with the "rich" ones. Moreover, it will be shown that there is a tendency to reach a common real rate of growth per head of the population. Thus standards of life and degrees of industrialization will stay different. There is no tendency for an equal consumption per head in different countries. The asymptotic validity of the purchasing power parity theory of the exchange rate is proven.

Though the system is basically simple, it will best be understood when it is developed on the base of a prototype model of a closed economy. This is the topic of the next section. Here the basic assumptions on the production and demand functions are stated. In the following section a world economy consisting of different interrelated national economies will be considered. At the end we introduce the case of depletable resources. This will be done in such a way that the system remains almost unchanged. Thus this section will be rather short. The consequences to be drawn from the system with respect to the redistribution of economic activity on earth due to depletable resources are derived in the last section. Unfortunately, only some propositions could be stated and made plausible by hinting at the relevant equations of the system.

Since the system we are going to analyse is highly interdependent, we solve it in the spirit of the Gauss-Seidel procedure: keeping one set of variables constant, we solve the system for another set and vice versa. There is no proof that this procedure converges.

Usually it does. To put it in another way: we assume the existence of a solution of the total system and solve it partially around the solution point. Therefore, from the mathematical point of view, the article offers only partial solutions of the system.

2. The General Approach for the Closed Economy in Equilibrium Growth

2.1 The Real Side of the Economy

2.1.1 The Basic Model

Consider an economy with n productions $x_1, \ldots, x_n$ and homogeneous labor (commodity 0). The *production functions* are:

$$x_i = f_i(v_{0i}, v_{1i}, \ldots, v_{mi}, v_{m+1,i}, \ldots, v_{ni}), \quad i = 1, \ldots, n, \tag{1a}$$

f_i homogeneous of degree one. v_{0i} is the amount of labor employed in production of commodity i in efficiency units, i.e.

$$v_{0i} = L_i \cdot \pi, \tag{1b}$$

where L_i is the amount of labor used in production i and π is a productivity index, identical in all productions (we assume Harrod neutral technical progress), $v_{1i}, \ldots, v_{mi}$ are the current inputs, $v_{m+1,i}, \ldots, v_{ni}$ are the capital stocks. The user cost of the factors $v_{0i}, \ldots, v_{ni}$ are $p_0, \ldots, p_n$, the market prices are $\tilde{p}_0, \ldots, \tilde{p}_n$, where

$$p_j = \begin{cases} \tilde{p}_j / \pi & \text{for } j = 0 \text{ and } \tilde{p}_0 =: l, \\ \tilde{p}_j & \text{for } j = 1, \ldots, m \\ \tilde{p}_j (r + d_j) & \text{for } j = m+1, \ldots, n. \end{cases} \tag{1c}$$

l is the wage rate, r is the gross profit rate, d_j is the rate of depreciation for commodity j. Cost minimizing yields the *factor demand functions*

$$v_{ji} = Fji\left(\frac{p_0}{p_1}, \ldots, \frac{p_n}{p_1}\right) \cdot x_i, \quad \begin{array}{l} j = 0, \ldots, n \\ i = 1, \ldots, n. \end{array} \tag{2}$$

Take the market price $\tilde{p}_1$ of commodity 1 as deflator. Denote total real production by $\tilde{Y}$, real GDP by Y, real secondary deliveries by V, replacement by D and real capital by K, where

$$Y = \sum_{i=1}^n \frac{\tilde{p}_i}{\tilde{p}_1} \cdot x_i, \quad \tilde{Y} = \sum_{i=1}^n \frac{\tilde{p}_i}{\tilde{p}_1}\left(x_i - \sum_{j=1}^n v_{ij}\rho_i\right), \quad \rho_i := \begin{cases} 1 & \text{for } i = 1, \ldots, m \\ \\ d_i & \text{for } i = m+1, \ldots, n. \end{cases} \tag{3}$$

$$V = \sum_{i=1}^m \sum_{j=1}^n \frac{\tilde{p}_i}{\tilde{p}_1} \cdot v_{ij}, \quad D = \sum_{i=m+1}^n \sum_{j=1}^n \frac{\tilde{p}_i}{\tilde{p}_1} v_{ij} d_i, \quad K = \sum_{i=m+1}^n \sum_{j=1}^n \frac{\tilde{p}_i}{\tilde{p}_1} \cdot v_{ij}.$$

Let s be the savings ratio. It may depend on the bond rate r_B:

$$s = s(r_B). \tag{4a}$$

Thus real consumption C and real net investment I is given by

$$C = (1-s)\,\tilde{Y}, \quad I = s\tilde{Y}. \tag{4b}$$

The demand C_i for consumption good i and I_i for investment good i follows from utility maximizing of households and (in case of equilibrium growth) from the factor demand functions derived by cost minimization of firms. Thus *consumption and investment demand* functions may be written as

$$C_i = G_i\left(\frac{\tilde{p}_2}{\tilde{p}_1}, \ldots, \frac{\tilde{p}_n}{\tilde{p}_1}\right) \cdot C, \quad i = 1, \ldots, n,$$

$$I_i = w_K \cdot \sum_{j=1}^{n} v_{ij} = H_i\left(\frac{p_0}{p_1}, \ldots, \frac{p_n}{p_1}, \frac{\tilde{p}_{m+1}}{\tilde{p}_1}, \ldots, \frac{\tilde{p}_n}{\tilde{p}_1} \frac{x_2}{x_1}, \ldots, \frac{x_n}{x_1}\right) \cdot I,$$

$$i = m + 1, \ldots, n, \tag{4c}$$

where $\sum_{i=1}^{n} G_i(\cdot) \cdot \tilde{p}_i = \tilde{p}_1$ and $w_K := (s\tilde{Y})/K$ the rate of growth of real capital and

$$H_i := \frac{\sum_{j=1}^{n} F_{ij} x_j / x_1}{\sum_{i=m+1}^{n} \sum_{j=1}^{n} F_{ij} (\tilde{p}_i / \tilde{p}_1) \cdot x_j / x_1} \quad \text{such that } \sum_{i=1}^{n} H_i(\cdot) \cdot \tilde{p}_i = \tilde{p}_1. \text{ The demand } V_i \text{ of}$$

commodity i as a secondary input and D_i as reinvestment follows from (2) and (3):

$$V_i = H_{iV}(\cdot) \cdot Y, i = 1, \ldots, m, D_i = d_i H_i(\cdot) \cdot K, i = m + 1, \ldots, n, \text{ where}$$

$$H_{iV} := \frac{\sum_{j=1}^{n} F_{ij} x_j / x_1}{\sum_{j=1}^{n} (\tilde{p}_j / \tilde{p}_1) \cdot x_j / x_1}. \tag{4d}$$

From (4b) and (4c) we get the relations

$$\dot{K} = I \text{ and } K = \frac{I}{w_K}. \tag{4e}$$

Total production of commodity i is

$$x_i = \sum_{j=1}^{n} v_{ij} \rho_i + C_i + I_i, \quad i = 1, \ldots, n. \tag{5}$$

2.1.2 Determination of Price and Production Ratios and of the Gross Profit Rate

First, we determine the *production ratios*.

Substituting v_{ij}, C_i and I_i from (2) and (4c) into (5) and using (4b) and (3) yields the homogeneous system

$$x = Mx, \tag{6a}$$

where $x := (x_1, \ldots, x_n)'$ and M is the coordinated $n \times n$ matrix. The components of M are functions of F_{ij}, G_i, H_i, s, r, d_j, and $\tilde{p}_i / \tilde{p}_1$ which need not be reproduced here. Only H_i is a function of the production ratios x_j / x_1, too. Thus, in fact, (6a) is a nonlinear system of $(n-1)$ equations in the $n-1$ unknown production ratios x_i/x_1. The solution yields the production ratios as functions β of the savings ratio and of the price ratios:

$$\frac{x_i}{x_1} = \beta_i\left(s, \frac{p_0}{p_1}, \ldots, \frac{\tilde{p}_n}{\tilde{p}_1}\right), \quad i = 1, \ldots, n, \beta_1 = 1. \tag{6b}$$

The *price ratios* are determined by the supply conditions. We assume perfect competition on the commodity markets. Thus market prices equal marginal cost. The yields

$$p_i = \sum_{j=0}^{m} \tilde{p}_j \cdot F_{ji} + \sum_{j=m+1}^{n} \tilde{p}_j (d_j + r) F_{ji}, \quad i = 1, \ldots, n, \tag{7a}$$

or

$$\tilde{p} = N\tilde{\tilde{p}}, \tag{7b}$$

where $\tilde{p} := (\tilde{p}_1, \ldots, \tilde{p}_n), \tilde{\tilde{p}} := (\tilde{p}_0, \tilde{p}_1, \ldots, \tilde{p}_n)$ and N is the coordinated $n \times (n+1)$ matrix. The components of N are F_{ji}, r and d_j. Since the F_{ji} are functions of $\tilde{p}_i/\tilde{p}_1$, $i = 0, 2, \ldots, n$, the system (7b) boils down to a nonlinear inhomogeneous system of n equations in the n unknown price ratios $\tilde{p}_0/\tilde{p}_1, \tilde{p}_2/\tilde{p}_1, \ldots, \tilde{p}_n/p_1$. The solution gives these price ratios as functions γ_i of the gross profit rate, given the depriation rates d_j;

$$\frac{\tilde{p}_i}{\tilde{p}_1} = \gamma_i(r), \quad i = 0, 2, \ldots, n, \tag{7c}$$

where γ_i is the marginal rate of substitution between commodity i and 1.

The *gross profit rate* r is determined by equalizing total revenue and total cost plus profits:

$$\sum_{i=1}^{n} \tilde{p}_i x_i = \sum_{i=1}^{n} \sum_{j=0}^{n} F_{ji}(\ldots, r, \ldots) \cdot p_j x_j. \tag{8a}$$

After dividing through by $\tilde{p}_1 x_1$, the solution yields r as a function α of all price ratios and all production ratios, given the depreciation rates:

$$r = \alpha\left(\frac{\tilde{p}_0}{\tilde{p}_1}, \ldots, \frac{\tilde{p}_n}{\tilde{p}_1}, \frac{x_2}{x_1}, \ldots, \frac{x_n}{x_1}\right). \tag{8b}$$

As stated in the beginning of this section we assume that the gross profit rate is equal in all productions.

2.1.3 The Absolute Level of Production

In a homogeneous system as ours the absolute levels stay undetermined unless there is an exogenous boundary. As a rule, the labor supply $\bar{L}$ is taken as limiting factor. This determines the absolute level of production (indicated by x_1) by equating labor supply and demand:

$$\bar{L} = \frac{1}{\pi} \sum_{i=1}^{n} F_{0i} \beta_i x_1, \tag{9a}$$

and thus from (3):

$$Y = \sum_{i=1}^{n} \gamma_i x_i = x_1 \sum_{i=1}^{n} \beta_i \gamma_i. \tag{9b}$$

2.1.4 Some Simplifying Assumptions

2.1.4.1 Aggregator Functions for Secondary Deliveries and for Capital

We now introduce some simplifying assumptions. Assume that there are aggregator functions v_i and k_i such that the production functions (1a) are separable and may be written as

$$x_i = F_i (v_{0i}, v_i (v_{1i}, \ldots, v_{mi}), k_i (v_{m+1,i}, \ldots, v_{ni})), \quad i = 1, \ldots, n, \tag{10a}$$

where the aggregator functions are homogeneous of degree one and have the form

$$V_i := v_i (v_{1i}, \ldots, v_{mi}) = \sum_{j=1}^{m} v_{ji} \frac{\tilde{p}_j}{\tilde{p}_1}$$

$$K_i := k_i (v_{m+1,i}, \ldots, v_{ni}) = \sum_{j=m+1}^{n} v_{ji} \cdot \frac{\tilde{p}_j}{\tilde{p}_1}, \quad \text{cf. (3).} \tag{10b}$$

These are expressions for K_i and V_i which follow from cost minimization in the neighborhood of an equilibrium and may be accepted as a reasonable approximation. (10a) may be written as

$$x_i = F_i (L_i \pi, V_i, K_i), \quad i = 1, \ldots, n. \tag{10c}$$

Furthermore, we assume that all depreciation rates are equal: $d_i = d$.

The notation of the factor prices of L_i', V_i, K_i may be changed to

$$l = \tilde{p}_0, q = \tilde{p}_1, z = \tilde{p}_1 (r + d), \tag{10d}$$

respectively. The relations $(1) - (9)$ are preserved.

2.1.4.2 Aggregation of Production Functions

We now turn to the aggregation of the production functions[1]. Take the production functions (1a) and the demand functions (2). Rewrite the demand functions as

$$V_{ji} = \frac{p_i}{p_j} \tilde{F}_{ji} \left(\frac{p_0}{p_1}, \ldots, \frac{p_n}{p_1} \right) \cdot x_i \tag{11a}$$

or

$$v_{ji} = \frac{p_i}{p_j} g_{ji} (p_0, \ldots, p_n) \cdot x_i, g_{ji} \text{ homogeneous of degree zero.} \tag{11b}$$

Thus

$$v_{ji} \cdot \frac{p_j}{T_i} = g_{ji} \left(\frac{p_0}{T_i}, \ldots, \frac{p_n}{T_i} \right), T_i := p_i x_i, \quad \begin{array}{l} j = 0, \ldots, n \\ i = 1, \ldots, n. \end{array} \tag{11c}$$

---

[1] For the proofs of the statements in this section see: *Krelle/Pallaschke* [1981].

This system may be solved for the prices:

$$p_j = h_{ji} (v_{0i}, \ldots, v_{ni}) \cdot T_i \tag{11d}$$

or

$$\mu_{ji} := \frac{p_j v_{ji}}{T_i} = v_{ji} \cdot h_{ji} (v_{0i}, \ldots, v_{ni}) =: \varphi_{ji} (v_{0i}, \ldots, v_{ni}). \tag{11e}$$

In case that $p_i x_i = \sum_{j=0}^{n} p_j v_{ji}$, the term μ_{ji} is the cost share of factor j at production i.

Now expand φ_{ji} and stop with the linear terms. This turns (11e) into

$$\mu_{ji} = \bar{a}_{j0i} + \sum_{k=0}^{n} a_{jki} v_{Ki}. \tag{11f}$$

Summing up over all productions i yields

$$M_j = \bar{\alpha}_{j0} + \sum_{k=0}^{n} \alpha_{jk} \bar{V}_k, \tag{11g}$$

where

$$M_j := \frac{p_j V_j}{T}, \bar{V}_j = \sum_{i=1}^{n} v_{ji}, T = \sum_{i=1}^{n} T_i$$

and the $\bar{\alpha}_{j0}$ and α_{jk} are constant if the factor distribution over the different productions stay constant. Since distributions do not change in equilibrium growth we shall assume this.

If the $\bar{\alpha}_{j0}$ and α_{jk} are constant and fulfill certain integrability conditions,[2]) the total factor demand could have been derived from the aggregate production function[3])

$$Y = \phi (\bar{V}_0, \ldots, \bar{V}_n). \tag{12a}$$

In our case we get

$$Y = F (L\pi, V, K). \tag{12b}$$

---

[2]) They are: (1) $\sum_{j=0}^{m} \bar{\alpha}_{j0} = 1$; (2) for all $j = 0, \ldots, n$ there exist scalars c_j such that

$$\frac{\alpha_{jj}}{\sum_{\substack{k=0 \\ j \neq k}}^{n} \bar{\alpha}_{k0}} = -\frac{\alpha_{lj}}{\alpha_{l0}} = c_j, l \neq j.$$

[3]) If the integrability conditions are fulfilled, the aggregate production function ϕ is $\phi = \psi (G (\bar{V}_0, \ldots, \bar{V}_n))$ where ψ is an arbitrary monotonous function and

$$G (\cdot) = \prod_{k=0}^{n} (\bar{V}_k)^{-\bar{\alpha}_{k0}} - \sum_{j=0}^{n} c_j \left[\prod_{\substack{k=0 \\ k \neq j}}^{n} \left(\frac{\bar{V}_k}{\bar{V}_j} \right)^{-\bar{\alpha}_{k0}} \right],$$

see *Krelle/Pallaschke* [1980].

Econometric estimations have shown [see *Krelle/Pallaschke*] that the integrability conditions may be forced upon an aggregate demand system without much harm and sometimes without any harm at all (judging from forecasting errors).

Thus we assume that aggregator functions of the kind (10a, b) exist and that the production functions may be aggregated to the production function (12b) of a representative firm.

Now the factor demand functions (2) may be rewritten as

$$L = \frac{1}{\pi} \cdot F_L\left(\frac{l/\pi}{q}, \frac{z}{q}\right) \cdot Y, \; K = F_K\left(\frac{l/\pi}{q}, \frac{z}{q}\right) \cdot Y, \; V = F_V\left(\frac{l/\pi}{q}, \frac{z}{q}\right) \cdot Y. \qquad (12c)$$

2.1.5 Equilibrium Growth Rates

In equilibrium the rates of growth w_Y, $w_{\tilde{Y}}$, w_K, w_V of Y, $\tilde{Y}$, K, V, respectively, are constant and equal to the sum of the growth rate w_L of labor and the rate w_π of technical progress:

$$w_Y = w_{\tilde{Y}} = w_K = w_V = w_L + w_\pi, \qquad (12d)$$

where $\tilde{Y} = Y(1 - F_V - dF_K)$.

2.2 The Monetary Side of the Economy

We now come to the *monetary side* and to the *allocation of wealth*. We use the portfolio approach. Total nominal assets W_{nom} consist of money M and the value Kp of real capital. The latter is embodied in bonds B or shares S. The ratio β of total capital wealth is kept in bonds. Bonds are defined as assets yielding one unit of money per year. The distribution of total wealth among the three types of assets depends on their expected yields and their variances (or risks). This relationship is reproduced by function f_B, f_S, f_M. The notation for the rate of interest on bonds is r_B. Thus we have

$$W_{\text{nom}} = M + Kp \qquad (13a)$$

$$\beta \cdot Kp =: \frac{B}{r_B} = f_B(\cdot) \cdot W_{\text{nom}} \qquad (13b)$$

$$(1 - \beta) Kp = f_S(\cdot) \cdot W_{\text{nom}} \qquad (13c)$$

$$M = f_M(\cdot) W_{\text{nom}} \qquad (13d)$$

and

$$f_B + f_S + f_M = 1, \; 0 < f_B, f_S, f_M, \beta < 1. \qquad (13e)$$

The arguments of the functions f_B, f_S, f_M are the expected yields of money, bonds and shares:

$$f_j(\cdot) = f_j(-w_p, r_B - w_{rB} - w_p, r), \quad j \in \{B, S, M\}, \qquad (13f)$$

where w_p is the rate of inflation and w_{rB} the rate of change of the bond rate.

In equilibrium growth r_B and w_p are constant and therefore f_B, f_S and f_M too. Thus we get from (13a – d) for the growth rates of M, K and W_{nom} in equilibrium:

$$w_M = w_{W_{\text{nom}}} = w_B = w_K + w_p = w_Y + w_p. \tag{13g}$$

Moreover, from (13a − e):

$$M = \frac{f_M}{1 - f_M} Kp \tag{13h}$$

and

$$\beta = \frac{f_B}{f_S + f_B}. \tag{13i}$$

Considering the second equation in (12c), equation (13h) is equivalent to *Fisher's equation*:

$$p \cdot Y = v \cdot M, \tag{13k}$$

where the velocity of money

$$v := \frac{1 - f_M}{f_M} \cdot \frac{1}{F_K}$$

is a function of the factor price ratios, of the bond rate and of the rate of inflation.

The supply of money and bonds are exogenous and grow exponentially by the same rate:

$$M = M_0 e^{w_M t}, \quad B_t = B_0 e^{w_B t}, \quad w_B = w_M > 0. \tag{14a}$$

Moreover, from (4c) and (12d) we get for the growth path of real capital:

$$K_t = \frac{s}{w_Y} (1 - F_V - dF_K) \cdot Y_0 e^{w_Y t}. \tag{14b}$$

The system (13a − k) determines the rate of inflation w_p in equilibrium:

$$w_p = w_M - w_Y, \quad w_B = w_M = w_K + w_p \tag{15a}$$

and simultaneously the price level p_0 and the bond rate r_B:

$$p_0 = \frac{1 - f_M(r_B)}{f_M(r_B)} \cdot \frac{M_0}{K_0}, \tag{15b}$$

where $f_M(r_B) := f_M(-w_p, r_B - w_p, r_B)$, $w_{rB} = 0$, and

$$r_B = \frac{B_0}{M_0 + K_0 \cdot p_0} \cdot \frac{1}{f_B(r_B)}, \tag{15c}$$

where $f_B(r_B)$ is defined similarly as $f_M(r_B)$.

(13c) is linearly dependent on the other equations in (13a − d) because of (13e).

The solutions (15b) and (15c) give the price level and the rate of interest as functions φ of the asset ratios:

$$p_0 = \varphi_p\left(\frac{K_0}{M_0}, \frac{B_0}{M_0}\right), \quad r_B = \varphi_r\left(\frac{K_0}{M_0}, \frac{B_0}{M_0}\right). \tag{15d}$$

Since the savings ratio s depends on the bond rate r_B (because investment depends on the rate of interest) and since the bond rate in turn depends on real capital there is an interdependence between the monetary and the real side of the economy.

Wealth formation follows the equation:

$$\dot{W}_{nom,t} = \dot{M} + K\dot{p} + p\dot{K} = w_p \, W_{nom,t} + h \cdot e^{w M t}, \quad h := w_Y \, M_0 + p_0 \, I_0. \tag{16a}$$

The solution of this differential equation is

$$W_{nom,t} = W_{nom,0} \cdot e^{w p t} + \frac{h}{w_M} \cdot e^{w M t}. \tag{16b}$$

Since $w_M = w_Y + w_p$, the second term dominates the first one; thus, asymptotically

$$W_{nom,t} = \frac{h}{w_M} \cdot e^{w M t}. \tag{16c}$$

Nominal wealth grows by the rate of money supply. Real wealth $W := W_{nom}/p$ grows by the rate w_Y of production and of capital.

2.3 Concluding Remarks

This outline of a multi-sector model which allows the use of an aggregated production function for the economy as a whole should prove the consistency of the general approach in the following section. All assumptions as to the separability and the integrability conditions are retained. We shall not mention that any more. For simplicity we shall use a slightly changed and more general notation.

3. A Growth Model of World Trade and Capital Flows

3.1 The Real Side of the Economies

3.1.1 The Basic Model

The aggregate *production function* in each country j, $j = 1, \ldots, J$, may be written in the same way as in the one country case:

$$Y^j = y^j \, (L^j \, \pi^j, \, K^j, \, V^j) \tag{17a}$$

and

$$Y^j = \sum_{i=1}^{n} a_i^j \, x_i^j, \tag{17b}$$

where x_i^j is the production of commodity i in country j. The index functions for capital and secondary inputs have as arguments the commodities produced in all countries:

$$K^j = k^j \, (x_{1K}^j, \ldots, x_{nK}^j), \quad V^j = v^j \, (x_{1V}^j, \ldots, x_{nV}^j), \quad j = 1, \ldots, J, \tag{17c}$$

where

$$x_{\nu K}^j = (x_{\nu K}^{1j}, \ldots, x_{\nu K}^{Jj}) \text{ and } x_{\nu V}^j \text{ accordingly, } \nu = 1, \ldots, n.$$

$x_{\nu K}^{\mu j}$ is the quantity of capital goods of kind ν produced in country μ and installed in country j. The commodity ν produced in a different country is supposed to be a different product.

As in (10b), the indices are weighted averages of factors of productions where the weights are price ratios.

Let e^j be the exchange rate of the currency of country j with respect to an arbitrary base country, say country 1. We assume perfect arbitrage such that

$$\frac{e^j}{e^k} = \frac{e^j}{e^l} \cdot \frac{e^l}{e^k}, \quad j, k, l \in \{1, \ldots, J\},$$

and perfect competition on the commodity markets. Thus the market price ratios equal the marginal rate of substitution:

$$\frac{\tilde{p}_i^j}{\tilde{p}_k^j} = \frac{\tilde{a}_i^j}{\tilde{a}_k^j}, i, h \in \{1, \ldots, n\}, \quad j = 1, \ldots, J, \quad \text{cf. (6b).} \tag{18a}$$

The price level p^j in a country j is defined by $Y^j p^j = \sum_i x_i^j \tilde{p}_i^j$, thus, because of (18a) and (17b) and since the production ratios stay constant in equilibrium:

$$p^j = c^j \cdot \tilde{p}_1^j, c^j = \sum_{i=1}^{n} \frac{\tilde{a}_i^j}{\tilde{a}_1^j} \cdot \frac{x_i^j}{x_1^j} \bigg/ \sum_{i=1}^{n} a_i^j \frac{x_i^j}{x_1^j}. \tag{18b}$$

We shall prove later that asymptotically the relative purchasing power parity theory (PPPT) of the exchange rate is valid:

$$\frac{p^k}{p^j} = c^{kj} \cdot \frac{e^k}{e^j}, \tag{19}$$

where c^{kj} is a positive constant ($c^{kj} = 1$ in case of the absolute PPPT).

The *factor demand* x_i^{kj} of commodity i produced in country k and used in country j is as in (2):

$$x_i^{kj} = F_i^{kj} \left(\frac{p_0^2}{p_1^1} \cdot \frac{e^1}{e^2}, \ldots, \frac{p_n^J}{p_1^1} \cdot \frac{e^1}{e^J}, \frac{\tilde{p}_{m+1}^1}{\tilde{p}_1^1} \cdot \frac{e^1}{e^1}, \ldots, \frac{\tilde{p}_n^J}{\tilde{p}_1^1} \cdot \frac{e^1}{e^J} \right) \cdot Y^j, \tag{20a}$$

$$i = 1, \ldots, n, \quad j = 1, \ldots, J,$$

where x_i^{kj} is the stock of the specific capital good, if $i = m + 1, \ldots, n$, and is the flow of secondary inputs, if $i = 1, \ldots, m$.

Thus real GDP $\tilde{Y}^k$ in country k is defined by

$$\tilde{Y}^k = Y^k - \sum_{j=1}^{J} \sum_{i=1}^{n} x_i^{kj} \rho_i^k \cdot \frac{\tilde{p}_i^k}{\tilde{p}_i^j} \cdot \frac{e^j}{e^k}. \tag{20b}$$

The *commodity demand* $x_{iC}^{kj}, X_{iI}^{kj}, x_{iV}^{kj}, x_{iD}^{kj}$ of consumption, net investment, secondary input and replacement demand of country j from country k for commodity i is in case that the production ratios stay constant, cf. (4c, d):

$$x_{iC}^{kj} = F_{iC}^{kj}\left(\frac{\tilde{p}_1^2}{\tilde{p}_1^1} \cdot \frac{e^1}{e^2}, \ldots, \frac{\tilde{p}_n^J}{\tilde{p}_1^1} \cdot \frac{e^1}{e^J}\right) \cdot C^j,$$

$$x_{il}^{kj} = F_{il}^{kj}\left(\frac{p_0^2}{p_1^1} \cdot \frac{e^1}{e^2}, \ldots, \frac{p_n^J}{p_1^1} \cdot \frac{e^1}{e^J}, \frac{\tilde{p}_{m+1}^1}{\tilde{p}_1^1} \cdot \frac{e^1}{e^1}, \ldots, \frac{\tilde{p}_n^J}{\tilde{p}_1^1} \cdot \frac{e^1}{e^J}\right) \cdot I^j, \left.\begin{array}{l} j, k = 1, \ldots, J, \\ i = 1, \ldots, n \end{array}\right.$$

$$\text{(20c)}$$

$$x_{iV}^{kj} = F_{iV}^{kj}\left(\frac{p_0^2}{p_1^1} \cdot \frac{e^1}{e^2}, \ldots, \frac{\tilde{p}_n^J}{\tilde{p}_1^1} \cdot \frac{e^1}{e^J}\right) \cdot Y^j,$$

$$x_{iD}^{kj} = d_i \cdot F_{il}^{kj}\left(\frac{p_0^2}{p_1^1} \cdot \frac{e^1}{e^2}, \ldots, \frac{\tilde{p}_n^J}{\tilde{p}_1^1} \cdot \frac{e^1}{e^J}\right) \cdot K^j, \quad \begin{array}{l} j, k = 1, \ldots, J, \\ i = m + 1, \ldots, n. \end{array}$$

Labor demand in country j is (cf. (2)):

$$x_0^j = F_0^j\left(\frac{p_0^2}{p_1^1} \cdot \frac{e^1}{e^2}, \ldots, \frac{\tilde{p}^J}{\tilde{p}_1^1} \cdot \frac{e^1}{e^J}\right) \cdot Y^j. \tag{20d}$$

The *capital stock* x_{iK}^{kj} of commodity i produced in country k and invested in country j is

$$x_{iK}^{kJ} = F_{il}^{kj}(\cdot) \cdot K^j. \tag{20e}$$

If the PPPT is valid, the arguments of the functions $F_{i\rho}^{kj}$, $\rho \in \{C, I, V, D\}$, become constants in equilibrium growth:

$$\frac{\tilde{p}_\nu^\mu}{\tilde{p}_1^1} \cdot \frac{e^1}{e^\mu} = \frac{\tilde{p}_\nu^\mu}{\tilde{p}^\mu} \cdot \frac{p^1}{\tilde{p}_1^1} \cdot \frac{p^\mu}{p^1} \cdot \frac{e^1}{e^\mu} = \frac{c^1 \cdot \tilde{a}_\nu^\mu}{c^\mu \cdot \tilde{a}_1^\mu} \cdot c^{\mu 1}. \tag{21}$$

In this case the price level p_k^j of capital in country j and the price level p_V^j of secondary inputs are proportional to the general price level p^j. The *price level* p_K^j of capital K^j is defined by

$$K^j p_k^j = \sum_{i=m+1}^{n} \sum_{k=1}^{J} x_{iK}^{kj} \cdot \tilde{p}_i^k \cdot \frac{e^j}{e^k} = \sum_{i=m+1}^{n} \sum_{k=1}^{J} F_{il}^{kj}(\cdot) \cdot \tilde{p}_i^k \cdot \frac{e^j}{e^k} \cdot K^j. \tag{21a}$$

If the PPPT is valid we get for p_K^j in equilibrium growth, considering (18a), (18b) and (19):

$$p_K^j = g_K^j \cdot p^j, \text{ where } g_K^j := \sum_{i=m+1}^{n} \sum_{k=1}^{J} F_{il}^{kj}(\cdot) \cdot \frac{c^{kj}}{c^k} \cdot \frac{\tilde{a}_i^k}{\tilde{a}_1^k}. \tag{21b}$$

An equivalent relation holds for the price level of secondary inputs:

$$p_V^j = g_V^j \cdot p^j. \tag{21c}$$

The GDP components and the consumption and investment functions are similarly defined as in (3) and (4). Total production of commodity i in country k is, cf. (5):

$$x_i^k = \sum_{j=1}^{n} (x_i^{kj} \rho_i^k + x_{iC}^{kj} + x_{il}^{kj}). \tag{21d}$$

3.1.2 Determination of the Production and Price Ratios and of the Gross Profit Rates

We determine the *production ratios* similarly as in (6a, b) by substituting x_i^{kj} from (20a) and x_{iC}^{kj} and x_{il}^{kj} from (20c) into (21d) and considering (20b). This yields

$$x_i^k = \sum_{j=1}^{n} \left[F_i^{kj} \rho_i^k + \left(F_{iC}^{kj} (1 - s^j) + F_{il}^{kj} s^j \right) \left(1 - \sum_{l=1}^{J} F_i^{lj} \rho_i^l \frac{\tilde{p}_i^l}{\tilde{p}_1^l} \cdot \frac{e^j}{e^l} \right) \right] Y^j,$$

$$k = 1, \ldots, J$$
$$i = 1, \ldots, n. \tag{22a}$$

Since $Y^j = \sum_{i=1}^{n} a_i^j x_i^j$, the system (22a) may be written as

$$\hat{x} = \hat{M} \cdot \hat{x}, \tag{22b}$$

where $\hat{x} := (x_1^1, \ldots, x_n^1, \ldots, x_1^J, \ldots, x_n^J)$ and $\hat{M}$ is the coordinated $n \cdot J \times nJ$ matrix. (22b) determines all production ratios as function $\hat{\beta}_i^k$ of the savings ratios and the price ratios in terms of currency 1:

$$\frac{x_i^k}{x_1^1} = \hat{\beta}_i^k \left(s^1, \ldots, s^J, \frac{p_0^2 e^1}{p_1^1 e^2}, \ldots, \frac{\tilde{p}_n^J}{\tilde{p}_1^1} \cdot \frac{e^1}{e^J} \right), \quad \hat{\beta}_1^1 = 1. \tag{22c}$$

The *price ratios* follow from the supply conditions: prices equal marginal cost. Similarly to (7a) we get

$$\tilde{p}_i^k = \left[F_0^k \tilde{p}_0^k + \sum_{j=1}^{J} \sum_{l=1}^{n} F_i^{jk} \rho_e^j \cdot \tilde{p}_e^j \cdot \frac{e^k}{e^j} \right] \frac{\partial Y^k}{\partial x_i^k} \quad \begin{matrix} i = 1, \ldots, n \\ k = 1, \ldots, J, \end{matrix} \tag{23a}$$

where

$$\frac{\partial Y^k}{\partial x_i^k} = a_i^k,$$

or

$$\hat{p} = \hat{N} \cdot \hat{\hat{p}}, \tag{23b}$$

$\hat{p} := (\tilde{p}_1^1, \ldots, \tilde{p}_n^1, \ldots, \tilde{p}_1^J, \ldots, \tilde{p}_n^J)$, $\hat{\hat{p}} := (\tilde{p}_0^1, \ldots, \tilde{p}_n^1, \ldots, \tilde{p}_0^J, \ldots, \tilde{p}_n^J)$ and $\hat{N}$ the coordinated $Jn \times J (n + 1)$ matrix. The solution gives the price ratios of all productions in all countries as function $\hat{\gamma}_i^k$ of the profit r^j and the exchange rate ratios e^j/e_k^1, given the depreciation rates:

$$\frac{\tilde{p}_i^k}{\tilde{p}_1^1} = \hat{\gamma}_i^k \left(r^1, \ldots, r^J, \frac{e^2}{e^1}, \ldots, \frac{e^J}{e^1} \right), \quad \begin{matrix} i = 0, 2, \ldots, n \\ k = 1, \ldots, J \end{matrix}$$

$$\text{and} \quad \hat{\gamma}_1^1 = 1. \tag{23c}$$

The *gross profit rates* are similarly determined as in the one-country case (see (8a)) by the system

$$\sum_{i=1}^{n} \tilde{p}_i^k x_i^k = \left[F_0^k (\ldots, r, \ldots) + \sum_{i=1}^{n} \sum_{j=1}^{J} F_i^{jk} (\ldots, r^k, \ldots) \cdot \tilde{p}_i^j \cdot \frac{e^k}{e^j} \right] Y^k, \quad (24a)$$

$$k = 1, \ldots, J,$$

where $Y^k = \sum_{i=1}^{n} a_i^k x_i^k$. After dividing through by $\tilde{p}_1^1 x_1^1$, each equation provides a solution r^k as function $\hat{\alpha}^k$ of the price, production and exchange rate ratios:

$$r^k = \hat{\alpha}^k \left(\frac{\tilde{p}_0^2}{\tilde{p}_1^1} \cdot \frac{e^1}{e^2}, \ldots, \frac{\tilde{p}_n^J}{\tilde{p}_1^1} \frac{e^1}{e^J}, \frac{x_2^1}{x_1^1}, \ldots, \frac{x_N^J}{x_1^1} \right), \quad k = 1, \ldots, J. \quad (24b)$$

3.2 The Monetary Side of the Economies

3.2.1 The Basic Model

Let M^{kj}, B^{kj}, S^{kj} be the amount of money, bonds and shares, respectively, issued by country k (in currency of country k) and hold by country j. The bond price in country k is $1/r_B^k$, shares will be discounted by the same rate. Bonds and shares are defined such that B^{kj} and S^{kj} are the interest and dividend payments, respectively. Thus (cf. (21a) and (1c)):

$$K^k \cdot p_K^k r^k = \sum_{j=1}^{J} (B^{kj} + S^{kj}), \quad k = 1, \ldots, J. \quad (25a)$$

The portfolio equations are, similarly as in (13):

$$W_{\text{nom}}^j = \sum_{k=1}^{J} \left(M^{kj} + \frac{B^{kj}}{r_B^k} + \frac{S^{kj}}{r_S^k} \right) \frac{e^j}{e^k}, \quad j = 1, \ldots, J \quad (25b)$$

$$\frac{B^{kj}}{r_B^k} \cdot \frac{e^j}{e^k} = f_B^{kj} (\cdot) \cdot W_{\text{nom}}^j \quad (25c)$$

$$\frac{S^{kj}}{r_B^k} \cdot \frac{e^j}{e^k} = f_S^{kj} (\cdot) \cdot W_{\text{nom}}^j \quad (25d)$$

$$M^{kj} \cdot \frac{e^j}{e^k} = f_M^{kj} (\cdot) \cdot W_{\text{nom}}^j, \quad j, k = 1, \ldots, J \quad (25e)$$

$$\sum_{k=1}^{J} (f_B^{kj} + f_S^{kj} + f_M^{kj}) = 1, \quad (25f)$$

$$\sum_{k=1}^{J} B^{jk} = B^j, \quad \sum_{k=1}^{J} S^{jk} = S^j, \quad \sum_{k=1}^{J} M^{jk} = M^j, \quad j = 1, \ldots, J \quad (25g)$$

The total amounts B^j, M^j and K^j are given in this context. S^j depends on B^j because of (25a).

The arguments of the portfolio assignment functions f^{kj} are

$$f_\rho^{kj}(\cdot) := f_\rho^{kj}(\underbrace{w_e^{j1} - w_p^j, \ldots, w_e^{jJ} - w_p^j,}_{\substack{\text{profitability of holding} \\ \text{money}}}$$

$$\underbrace{r_B^1 - w_{rB}^1 + w_e^{j1} - w_p^j, \ldots, r_B^J - w_{rB}^J + w_e^{jJ} - w_p^j,}_{\text{profitability of holding bonds}}$$

$$\underbrace{r_B^1 - w_{rB}^1 + w_p^1 + w_e^{j1} - w_p^j, \ldots, r_B^J - w_{rB}^J + w_p^J + w_e^{jJ} - w_p^j),}_{\text{profitability of holdings shares}} \qquad (25\text{h})$$

where: $w_e^{j\mu} := \dfrac{\dot{e}^j}{e^j} - \dfrac{\dot{e}^m}{e^m}, \dot{e} := \dfrac{de}{dt}, \quad \rho \in \{B, S, M\}.$

3.2.2 Equilibrium Growth Rates

3.2.2.1 If the exchange rates are fixed, it follows from the system $(25a - g)$ that in equilibrium growth all nominal growth rates in all countries are equal[4]):

$$w_K^k + w_p^k = w_B^{kj} = w_S^{kj} = w_B^k = w_S^k = w_M^{kj} = w_M^k = w_{W\text{nom}}^j$$

for $k, j = 1, \ldots, J$. $\qquad (26\text{a})$

Here w_z^{kj} means the growth rate of the variable z^{kj}. Thus equilibrium growth is only possible if the money supply of all countries grows by the same rate. As we shall see below, the real growth rates of all countries are asymptotically equal; thus $w_K^k = w_K = w_Y$ for all countries k. Therefore the rates of inflation w_p^k will asymptotically be equal in all countries.

3.2.2.2 If the PPPT holds if follows from the same system, that all equations in (26a) remain valid with the exception of the last one. It has to be replaced by

$$w_M^k = w_{W\text{nom}}^j + w_p^k - w_p^j. \qquad (26\text{b})$$

Thus all *real* growth rates must be equal, that is to say: the rates of inflation w_p^k of all countries may be different.

3.2.3 The Portfolio Composition

Substitute the expression for W_{nom}^j from (25b) and the relation

---

[4]) p_K^k grows with the same rate as p^k, since $p_K^k = g_K^k \cdot p^k$ and $g_K^k = $ const. in equilibrium, see (21b).

$$f_M^{Jj} = 1 - \sum_{k=1}^{J} (f_B^{kj} + f_S^{kj}) - \sum_{k=1}^{J-1} f_M^{kj} \tag{27}$$

into the equations (25c – e). Divide the equations with the upper index k, by p^j.

Now the system (25c – e) may be written as

$$\frac{B^{kj}}{p^j} \cdot \frac{1}{r_B^k} \cdot \frac{e^j}{e^k} = f_B^{kj} \cdot \sum_{l=1}^{J} \left(M^{lj} + B^{lj} \cdot \frac{1}{r_B^l} + S^{lj} \cdot \frac{1}{r_B^l} \right) \frac{1}{p^j} \cdot \frac{e^j}{e^l} \tag{28a}$$

$$\frac{S^{kj}}{p^j} \cdot \frac{1}{r_B^k} \cdot \frac{e^j}{e^k} = f_S^{kj} \cdot \sum_{l=1}^{J} \left(M^{lj} + \cdots + S^{lj} \cdot \frac{1}{r_B^l} \right) \frac{1}{p^j} \frac{e^j}{e^l} \tag{28b}$$

$$\frac{M^{kj}}{p^j} \cdot \frac{e^j}{e^k} = f_M^{kj} \cdot \sum_{l=1}^{J} \left(M^{lj} + \cdots + S^{lj} \frac{1}{r_B^l} \right) \frac{1}{p^j} \cdot \frac{e^j}{e^l}, \quad k, j = 1, \ldots, J. \tag{28c}$$

3.2.3.1 If the exchange rates are fixed the system (28a – c) disintegrates into J independent linear homogeneous subsystems in the variables

$$z^j := \left(\frac{B^{1j}}{p^j}, \ldots, \frac{B^{Jj}}{p^j}, \frac{S^{1j}}{p^j}, \ldots, \frac{S^{Jj}}{s^j}, \frac{M^{1j}}{p^j}, \ldots, \frac{M^{Jj}}{p^j} \right)', j = 1, \ldots, J. \text{ Each system may be}$$

written as

$$z^j = F^j \cdot z^j, \tag{29a}$$

where F^j is the coordinated matrix the components of which are the interest rates and the exchange rates. Divide each equation in system j by M^{1j}/p^j, cancel the coordinated row and column and solve the remaining inhomogeneous linear system of the $3J - 1$ unknowns $\hat{z}^j := (B^{1j}/M^{1j}, \ldots, M^{Jj}/M^{1j})$. The solution gives the ratios between the *nominal* assets of each country j as a function δ of the interest rates and the exchange rates;

$$\frac{B^{kj}}{M^{1j}} = \delta_B^{kj} \left(r_B^1, \ldots, r_B^J, \frac{e^2}{e^1}, \ldots, \frac{e^J}{e^1} \right)$$

$$\frac{S^{kj}}{M^{1j}} = \delta_S^{kj} (\cdot), \quad \frac{M^{kj}}{M^{1j}} = \delta_M^{kj} (\cdot), \quad k, j = 1, \ldots, J, \delta_M^{1j} = 1. \tag{29b}$$

3.2.3.2 If the PPPT is valid, the system disintegrates into other J independent linear homogeneous subsystems in the variables

$$\varsigma^j := \left(\frac{B^{1j}}{p^1}, \ldots, \frac{B^{Jj}}{p^J}, \frac{S^{1j}}{p^1}, \ldots, \frac{S^{Jj}}{p^J}, \frac{M^{1j}}{p^1}, \ldots, \frac{M^{Jj}}{p^J} \right) \text{ such that:}$$

$$\varsigma^j = G^j \cdot \varsigma^j, \quad j = 1, \ldots, J. \tag{30a}$$

After dividing each equation in the system through by M^{1j}/p^1 and after cancelling one row and column, the system may be solved for the ratios between the *real* assets of each country j as a function ϵ of the interest rate:

$$\frac{B^{kj}/p^k}{M^{1j}/p^1} = \epsilon_B^{kj}(r_B^1, \ldots, r_B^J)$$

$$\frac{S^{kj}/p^k}{M^{1j}/p^1} = \epsilon_S^{kj}(\cdot), \quad \frac{M^{kj}/p^k}{M^{1j}/p^1} = \epsilon_M^{kj}(\cdot), \quad k, j = 1, \ldots, J, \quad \epsilon_M^{1j} = 1. \tag{30b}$$

3.2.4 Determination of the Price levels and of the Interest Rates

We now consider the three sets of equations in (25g).

3.2.4.1 If the exchange rates are fixed, these equations become (considering (29b) and (25a) and (21b), where $S^j = K^j g_K^j \cdot p^j r^j - B^j$ is substituted into the second equation in (25g)):

$$\sum_{k=1}^J \delta_B^{jk} \cdot M^{1k} = B^j \tag{31a}$$

$$\sum_{k=1}^J \delta_S^{jk} \cdot M^{1k} = K^j g_K^j \cdot p^j r^j - B^j \tag{31b}$$

$$\sum_{k=1}^J \delta_M^{jk} M^{1k} = M^j, \quad j = 1, \ldots, J. \tag{31c}$$

(31c) determines the J unknowns $M^{11}, \ldots, M^{1J}$ as functions η_M of the interest rates, exchange rates and the amounts of money in circulation (which is taken as exogenous):

$$M^{1j} = \eta_M^j \left(r_B^1, \ldots, r_B^J, \frac{e^2}{e^1}, \ldots, \frac{e^J}{e^1}, M^1, \ldots, M^J \right), \quad j = 1, \ldots, J. \tag{32a}$$

This will be substituted into (31b). Thus (31b) becomes a system of J equations for the J unknown price levels $p^1, \ldots, p^J$, as function η_S of the real capital $K^1, \ldots, K^J$, the gross profit rates $r^1, \ldots, r^J$, the amount of bonds $B^1, \ldots, B^J$ in circulation and the arguments of η_M^j:

$$p^j = \eta_S^j(r_B, M, B, K, r, e), \quad j = 1, \ldots, J, \tag{32b}$$

where $r_B := (r_B^1, \ldots, r_B^J)$ and M, B, K, r, e are similarly defined.

Now substitute M^{1j} from (32a) into (31a). This yields a system of J equations for the J unknown interest rates $r_B^1, \ldots, r_B^J$ as functions η_B of the exchange rates $e^2/e^1, \ldots, e^J/e^1$ and the amounts of money $M^1, \ldots, M^J$ and bonds $B^1, \ldots, B^J$ in circulation:

$$r_B^j = \eta_B^j(e, M, B), \quad j = 1, \ldots, J. \tag{32c}$$

Thus, given the money and bonds issued in all countries, the real capital (or real production which is related to it), the profit rates and the exchange rates for all countries, the rates of interest, the price levels and the asset compositions of all countries are determined.

3.2.4.2 If the PPPT applies, the same is true, but the way by which these variables are determined differs.

Instead of (31a − c) we get the system

$$\sum_{k=1}^{J} e_B^{jk} \cdot M^{1k} \cdot \frac{p^j}{p^1} = B^j \tag{33a}$$

$$\sum_{k=1}^{J} e_S^{jk} \cdot M^{1k} \cdot \frac{p^j}{p^1} = K^j g_K^j \cdot p^j r^j - B^j \tag{33b}$$

$$\sum_{k=1}^{J} e_M^{jk} \cdot M^{1k} \cdot \frac{p^j}{p^1} = M^j \tag{33c}$$

(33c) may be written as $E\,m = \bar{m}$, where

$$E := (e_M^{jk}),\ m = (M^{11}, \dots, M^{1J})'\ \text{and}\ \bar{m} := \left(M^1 \cdot \frac{p^1}{p^1}, \dots, M^J \cdot \frac{p^1}{p^J} \right)'.$$

Thus $m = E^{-1}\bar{m}$, or

$$M^{1j} = \sum_{k=1}^{J} e_M^{jk} M^k \cdot \frac{p^1}{p^k}\ \text{or}\ M^{1j} =: \delta_M^j\,(r_B, M, p),\ \ j = 1, \dots, J, \tag{34a}$$

where e_M^{jk} is the (jk)-th component E^{-1}, δ_M^j is a function and $r_B = (r_B^1, \dots, r_B^J)$, M, p accordingly.

Substituting M^{1j} from (34a) into (31b) yields after some manipulation:

$$M^1 a^{j1} \cdot \frac{1}{p^1} + \cdots + M^J a^{jJ}\,\frac{1}{p^J} = K^j g_K^j \cdot r^j - B^j \cdot \frac{1}{p^j},\ \ j = 1, \dots, J, \tag{*}$$

where $a^{jk} := e_S^{j1} e_M^{1k} + \cdots + e_S^{jJ} \cdot e_M^{Jk}$.

This is a system of J equations in the J unknown reciprocal price levels $1/p^1, \dots, 1/p^J$ which may be written as $(B + A)\,(1/p) = \kappa$, where

$$B = \begin{pmatrix} B^1 & & \\ & \cdot & \\ & & \cdot \\ & & & B^J \end{pmatrix},\ A = \begin{pmatrix} a^{11} & \cdots & a^{1J} \\ \cdot & & \\ \cdot & & \\ a^{J1} & \cdots & a^{JJ} \end{pmatrix} \begin{pmatrix} M^1 & & \\ & \cdot & \\ & & \cdot \\ & & & M^J \end{pmatrix},\ 1/p = \begin{pmatrix} 1/p^1 \\ \cdot \\ \cdot \\ 1/p^J \end{pmatrix},\ \kappa = \begin{pmatrix} K^1 g_K^1 r^1 \\ \cdot \\ \cdot \\ K^J g_K^J r^J \end{pmatrix}.$$

The solution may be written as

$$\frac{1}{p} = (B + A)^{-1}\kappa\ \text{or}\ 1/p^j = b^{j1}K^1 g_K^1 r^1 + \cdots + b^{jJ}K^J g_K^J \cdot r^J =:$$

$$=: \delta_S^j\,(r_B, M, B, K, r),\ \ j = 1, \dots, J, \tag{34b}$$

where b^{jk} is the (jk)-th component of $(B + A)^{-1}$.

Thus we see that the price level in country j also depends on all money and bonds issued in other countries, in general. As we shall show later, all K^j grow asymptotically by the same rate $w_K = w_Y$. Thus it follows from (*) that $w_M^j - w_p^j = w_Y$ for all $j = 1, \dots, J$. That means: each country may expand its money supply at an arbitrary rate w_M^j. It will induce a rate of inflation $w_p^j = w_M^j - w_Y$ independent of the rates of inflation of all other countries though the absolute price levels taken at time zero are related by the system (34b).

The system (*) may also be solved for the real money values $M^1/p^1, \ldots, M^J/p^J$ as functions of the real capital gains $K^j \cdot g_K^j \cdot r^j$ mins the real bond payments B^j/p^j.

After the price levels p^j and the variables M^{1j} have been determined, the system (33a) yields the bond rates r_B, since the e_B^{jk} are functions of r_B:

$$r_B^j = \delta_B^j (M, B, K, r), \quad j = 1, \ldots, J. \tag{34c}$$

Thus all monetary variables are simultaneously determined from the portfolio system, given the exogenous supply of money and bonds and the real capital and the profit rates in all countries and given the exchange rates or assuming the validity of the PPPT.

3.3 Asymptotically Equal Growth Rates

We shall now dynamize the real system by assuming that consumption and investment does not only depend on income of the same period (as the consumption and investment (4b)) but on past income as well[5]). In addition, we consider an exogenous growth term w_C^j and w_I^j for real consumption and real investment, respectively, which follows from technical progress and from population growth. Thus we assume the following consumption and investment functions for country j:

$$C_t^j = (1 - s^j)\,[\bar{b}_0^j\,(1 + w_C^j)^t + \sum_{\tau=0}^T b^j \cdot \tilde{Y}_{t-\tau}^j]$$

$$I_t^j = s^j\,[\bar{c}_0^j\,(1 + w_I^j)^t + \sum_{\tau=0}^T c^j\,\tilde{Y}_{t-\tau}^j], \quad j = 1, \ldots, J. \tag{35}$$

Thus we get from (17b), (20) and (22):

$$Y_t^j = \sum_{k=1}^J \sum_{i=1}^n a_i^j\,[F_{iV}^{jk}\,Y_T^K + F_{iD}^{jk}\,K_t^k + F_{iC}^{jk}\,(1 - s^k) \cdot [\bar{b}_0^k\,(1 + w_C^k)^t + \sum_{\tau=0}^T b_\tau^k\,\tilde{Y}_{t-\tau}^k] +$$

$$+ F_{iI}^{jk}\,s^k\,(\bar{c}_0^k\,(1 + w_I^k)^t + \sum_{\tau=0}^T c^k\,Y_{t-\tau}^k)]$$

$$K_t^j = K_{t-1}^j + s^j\,(\bar{c}_0^j\,(1 + w_I^j)^t + \sum_{\tau=0}^T c^j\,\tilde{Y}_{t-\tau}^j),$$

where

$$\tilde{Y}_t^k = Y_t^k - \sum_{l=1}^J \sum_{i=1}^n a_i^k\,[F_{iV}^{kl}\,Y_t^l + F_{iD}^{kl}\,K_t^l], \quad j, k = 1, \ldots, J,$$

or in matrix notation

$$y_t = \sum_{\tau=0}^T A_\tau y_{t-\tau} + \bar{y}_t, \tag{36a}$$

---

[5]) We now switch to difference equations.

where

$$y_t := (Y_t^1, \ldots, Y_t^J, K_t^1, \ldots, K_t^j)',$$

$$\bar{y}_t := (\sum_{k=1}^{J} [g_C^{1k} (1+w_C^k)^t + g_I^{1k} (1+w_I^k)^t], \ldots, \sum_{k=1}^{J} [g_C^{Jk} (1+w_C^k)^t + g_I^{Jk} (1+w_I^k)^t],$$

$$g_K^1 (1+w_I^1)^t, \ldots, g_K^J (1+w_I^J)^t)', \ g_C^{jk} := \sum_{i=1}^{n} a_i^j F_{iC}^{jk} (1-s^k) \cdot \bar{b}_0^k,$$

$$g_I^{jk} := \sum_{i=1}^{n} a_i^j F_{iI}^{jk} s^k \bar{c}_0^k, \ g_K^j := s^j \bar{c}_0^j$$

and A_τ are the coordinated $2J \times 2J$ matrices.

In equilibrium growth the factor price ratios and interest rates are constant. If the PPPT applies all elements of the matrices A_τ are constant as well.

The following theorem may be proved

Theorem 1: If the PPPT applies and if the world economy is connected there will be asymptotically equal equilibrium growth rates of real production, real income and real wealth in all countries.

Proof: Consider (36a). For $t \to \infty$ only the largest growth rates matter. Thus $\bar{y}_t$ may be substituted by $\tilde{y}_t := (g_y^1 (1+w_Y)^t, \ldots, g_Y^J (1+w_Y)^t, g_K^1 (1+w_I)^t, \ldots, g_K^J (1+w_I^J)^t)$, where $w_Y = \max (w_C^1, \ldots, w_C^J, w_I^1, \ldots, w_I^J)$ and g_y^j is the coordinated g_C^{jk} or g_I^{jk}.

The system may be rewritten as a first order difference equation system:

$$z_t = A z_{t-1} + \tilde{z}_t \tag{36b}$$

where

$$z_t = (y_t, y_{t-1}, \ldots, y_{t-T}) \text{ and } A := \begin{pmatrix} A_0 & \cdots & A_T \\ \hline I & & \\ & \ddots & \\ & & I \mid 0 \end{pmatrix}$$

and

$$\tilde{z}_t := (\tilde{y}_t, 0, \ldots, 0).$$

Let $\bar{w}$ be the largest growth rate in $\tilde{z}$. In case that A does not desintegrate to independent submatrices (i.e.: if the world economy is connected) and in case of different roots λ_j the solution of (30a) becomes

$$z_t = \sum_j \alpha_j \lambda_j^t + \bar{z} (1+\bar{w})^t, \tag{37}$$

where the vectors α_j depend on the characteristic vector and the initial conditions and $\bar{z} (1+\bar{w})^t$ is the solution of the inhomogeneous system. Thus for $t \to \infty$:

$$z_t \rightarrow \begin{cases} \alpha_{\max} \cdot \lambda_{\max}^t & \text{if } \lambda_{\max} := \max\left(\mid \lambda_1 \mid, \ldots, \mid \lambda_N \mid\right) > (1 + \bar{w}) \\ \bar{z}\,(1 + \bar{w})^t & \text{if } \lambda_{\max} < (1 + \bar{w}). \end{cases} \tag{37a}$$

This terminates the proof.

Thus there is a tendency to equalize the real growth rates of all economies on earth and therefore also the growth rates of real wealth, cf. (25a) and (30b). This does not mean that production per head will become equal. The rates of growth of the population may be different in different countries and the productivity level as well. But because of the asymptotically linear trade and income relations between the countries growth or decline spreads between them. At the end there will be one growth rate, either endogeneously determined by the demand system or exogenously determined by technical progress and population growth, whatever is larger.

3.4 Will there be Full Employment in All Countries?

The world system as it stands now does not guarantee full employment in all countries. In the one country case the appropriate real wage rate may generate full employment and the appropriate growth rate $w_y = w_\pi + w_L$ of demand will keep it for ever. If demand and world production grows by the common rate w determined by (37a) but the growth rates w_π^j of technical progress and the growth rates w_N^j of population N in country j differ and $w \neq w_\pi^j + w_N^j$ there will be underemployment or overemployment in some or all countries. Thus equilibrium growth on the world level requires that, given the rates of technical progress w_π^j of all countries, the population growth adapts to the employment and income conditions:

$$w_N^j = w - w_\pi^j. \tag{38}$$

This will be accomplished by international labor movements and, in case that they are prohibited, by adaption of the birth and death rates. The real wage level determines the level of employment in each country.

3.5 The Market for Foreign Currencies. Determination of the Exchange Rates

Exports $\tilde{E}^j$, imports $\tilde{M}^j$, capital inflow $\tilde{S}^j$ (= supply of foreign currency) and capital outflow $\tilde{D}^j$ (= demand of foreign currency) follow immediately from the system:

$$\tilde{E}^j = \sum_{k \neq j} \sum_i x_i^{jk}\, \tilde{p}_i^j \cdot \frac{e^1}{e^j} \tag{39a}$$

$$\tilde{M}^j = \sum_{k \neq j} \sum_i x_i^{kj}\, \tilde{p}^k \cdot \frac{e^1}{e^k}, \text{ where } x_i^{kj} := x_{iV}^{kj} + x_{iD}^{kj} + x_{iC}^{kj} + x_{il}^{kj} \tag{39b}$$

$$\tilde{S}^j = \sum_{k \neq j} \left[(B^{kj} + S^{kj}) \cdot \frac{e^1}{e^k} + \Delta M^{jk} \cdot \frac{e^1}{e^j} + \left(\frac{\Delta B^{jk}}{r_B^j} + \frac{\Delta S^{jk}}{r_S^j} \right) \cdot \frac{e^1}{e^j} \right] \tag{39c}$$

$$\tilde{D}^j = \sum_{k \neq j} \left[(B^{jk} + S^{jk}) \cdot \frac{e^1}{e^j} + \Delta M^{kj} \cdot \frac{e^1}{e^k} + \left(\frac{\Delta B^{kj}}{r_B^k} + \frac{\Delta S^{kj}}{r_S^k} \right) \cdot \frac{e^1}{e^k} \right]. \tag{39d}$$

All values are given in terms of currency 1. There might be an exogenous demand or supply F^j from the Central Bank. Now all exchange rates are determined simultaneously by the system

$$\tilde{E}^j - \tilde{M}^j + \tilde{S}^j - \tilde{D}^j + F^j = 0, \quad j = 1, \ldots, J. \tag{40a}$$

In the long run the capital flows must balance and $F^j = 0$. Thus we get

$$\tilde{E}^j - \tilde{M}^j = \tilde{D}^j - \tilde{S}^j = 0, \quad j = 1, \ldots, J. \tag{40b}$$

One equation may be canceled due to Walras' law; this corresponds to the fact that $e^1 := 1$.

3.6 The Asymptotic Validity of the PPP Theory

Now we may state the following

Theorem 2: If all real growth rates have converged to a common growth rate w and if there are no interventions of the Central Banks on the foreign exchange market ($F^j = 0$) the PPPT is valid in equilibrium growth:

$$\frac{e^j}{e^k} = c^{kj} \cdot \frac{p^j}{p^k}, \quad \text{cf. (19).} \tag{41}$$

Proof: Assume that all real growth rates have converged to the common rate w and that all interest rates are constant. In this case we get for the inflow of foreign capital for $e^1 := 1$:

$$\tilde{S}^j_t = \sum_k \tilde{b}^{jk} \frac{p^k_t}{e^k_t} (1 + w)^t \tag{42a}$$

where $\tilde{b}^{jk} := (B_0^{kj} + S_0^{kj}) \dfrac{1}{p_0^k}$ for $k \neq j$

$$\tilde{b}^{jj} := \sum_{k \neq 0} \left(M_0^{jk} + \frac{B_0^{jk}}{r^j_B} + \frac{S_0^{jk}}{r^j_B} \right) \left(1 - \frac{1}{(1 + w^j_p)(1 + w)} \right) \cdot \frac{1}{p_0^j},$$

cf. (39c) and (25b − e), and for the outflow of capital

$$\tilde{D}^j_t = \sum_k \tilde{c}^{jk} \cdot \frac{p^k_t}{c^k_t} (1 + w)^t, \quad j = 1, \ldots, J \tag{42b}$$

where the $\tilde{c}^{jk}$ are similarly defined as the $\tilde{b}^{jk}$.

Substitute these equations into the second equations of (40b), divide all equations by $(1 + w)^t$, delete the first equation and rewrite the system in matrix notation to get:

$$B_0 \cdot \frac{p}{e} = B_1 \cdot \frac{p^1}{e^1}, \quad \text{where } \frac{p}{e} := \left(\frac{p^2}{e^2}, \ldots, \frac{p^m}{e^m} \right), \frac{p^1}{e^1} := \underbrace{\left(\frac{p^1}{e^1}, \ldots, \frac{p^1}{e^1} \right)}_{m - 1 \text{ components,}}, \tag{43a}$$

B_0, B_1 are $(J-1) \times (J-1)$ matrices.

If B_0 has full rank, the solution of (43a) is:

$$\frac{p}{e} = B_0^{-1} B_1 \frac{p^1}{e^1} \text{ or } \frac{p^j}{e^j} = c^j \cdot \frac{p^1}{e^1}, \quad j = 2, \ldots, J, \, e^j > 0,$$

$$e^1 := 1. \tag{43b}$$

This terminates the proof. (43b) is the relative PPP theory.

4. Exhaustible Resources

4.1 General Approach[6])

We retain the approach of section 3 with the following modification. Some of the re-sources might be exhaustible. There are two types of exhaustible resources. The first type needs more factors of production per unit of extraction if the stock becomes smaller. Exhaustible resources of the second type may be exploited at constant marginal cost up to the last unit (think of a crude oil "lake" underground). Let commodity m in country k be an exhaustible resource. If the first case applies a_m^k in equation (17b) rises con-tinuously when the stock of the depletable resource becomes smaller (or in other words: the factor intensity of the extraction of commodity m rises). A reasonable assumption is that a_m^k rises by a rate which is equal to the ratio of the total stock x_0 at time zero to the amount c_0 which is extracted at time zero and that this rate x_0/c_0 stays constant. Thus we assume:

$$a(t) = c \cdot e^{(x_0/c_0)t}, \quad c > 0, \; a(t) := a_m^k(t) \tag{44a}$$

and

$$w_a = \frac{\dot{a}}{a} = \frac{x_0}{c_0} = \text{const.} \tag{44b}$$

In this case the resource will never be totally exhausted if the demand declines by this rate:

$$x_0 = c_0 \int_0^\infty e^{-w_a t} \, dt. \tag{44c}$$

The price p_m^k of the exhaustible commodity m rises faster than the general rate of infla-tion in country k, namely by the same rate as a_m^k:

$$\frac{p_m^k(t)}{p^k(t)} = \frac{p_{m0}^k}{p_0^k} e^{w_a t}. \tag{44d}$$

Since an exhaustible resource is only used as a secondary input in this model, the demand for it follows from (20c): $x_{iV}^{kj} = F_{iV}^{kj}(\cdot) \cdot Y^j$. In the long run the price elasticity of demand for any commodity with a steadily rising price must be unity otherwise the demand for it would eat up the demands for all other items or would disappear. Thus we assume the functions F_{iV}^{kj} to be of the following form:

---

[6]) In this section we use continuous time.

a) for the exhaustible commodity m produced in country k (with a rate of decline $-\bar{w}^k_{am}$ of demand per unit of output):

$$x^{kj}_{mV}(t) = e^{-\bar{w}^k_{am} \cdot t} \cdot F^{kj}_{mV0}\left(\frac{p^2_{10}}{p^1_{10}} \cdot \frac{e^1_0}{e^2_0}, \ldots, \frac{\tilde{p}^J_{n0}}{\tilde{p}^1_0} \cdot \frac{e^1_0}{e^n_0}\right) \cdot Y^j_t, \tag{45a}$$

b) for all other commodities i:

$$x^{kj}_{iV}(t) = F^{kj}_{iV0}(\cdot)\left[1 + a^{kj}_{im}\frac{F^{kj}_{mV0}}{F^{kj}_{iV0}}(1 - e^{-\bar{w}^k_{am}t})\right]Y^j_t, \quad i = 1, \ldots, n, \, i \neq m. \tag{45b}$$

The lower index zero indicates time zero. a^{kj}_{im} is positive and constant for substitutive products and negative for complementary products.

a^{kj}_{im} is the marginal rate of substitution between commodities i and m:

$$\dot{x}^{kj}_{iV}/\dot{x}^{kj}_{mV} = -a^{kj}_{im} \quad \text{for } Y^j_t = \text{const.}$$

Thus the basic assumption of this section is the constancy of the marginal rate of substitution between the exhaustible and the reproducible goods. The F^{kj}_{lV0} are constant in equilibrium, $l = 1, \ldots, n$. Therefore in equilibrium the rate of decline w^{-k}_{am} of the demand for the exhaustible resource is indeed equal to the additional rate of growth of its price. The total rate of decline of demand for the exhaustible resource is:

$$w^k_{am} = -w + \bar{w}^k_{am} > 0, \tag{45c}$$

where $\bar{w}^k_{am} = w_a$ in (44c).

Since $c_0 = \sum_j F^{kj}_{mV} \cdot Y^j_0$ the rate $\bar{w}^k_{am}$ should be such that

$$x_0 = c_0 \cdot \bar{w}^k_{am}, \text{ as in (44b)}. \tag{45d}$$

This determines w^k_{am} and puts a limit to w, see (45c). The rate of price increase of the exhaustible resource m in country k is:

$$w^k_{pm} = w^k_p + \bar{w}^k_{am}. \tag{45e}$$

Fig. 1 illustrates this case for two factors of production, where factor 1 is reproducible and factor 2 is exhaustible. For simplicity it is assumed that total production and the price level of factor 1 are constant. The demand x_{2V} for the exhaustible resource declines asymptotically to zero. The demand x_{1V} for the substitutive product rises asymptotically to an upper limit. Thus asymptotically an equilibrium growth is possible.

In the *second case* of an exhaustible resource the marginal cost does not rise ($a^k_m = $ = const. in equation (17b)). But now we assume that the owners of the resource are able to determine the price p^k_m of their product. If they wish to maximize their total profit over the life time of the resource they will follow the Hotelling rule and charge a price which exceeds the general price level by the rate of interest. Let this excess rate be z. Thus (44d) has to be replaced by

$$\frac{p^k_m(t)}{p^k(t)} = \frac{p^k_{m0}}{p^k_0}e^{zt}. \tag{46a}$$

374

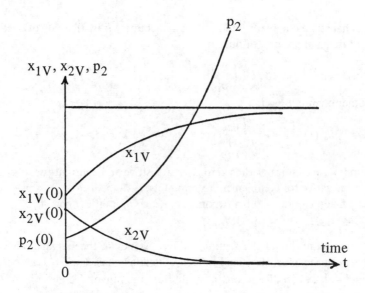

Fig. 1

Equations (45a and b) stay the same, only $\bar{w}^k_{am}$ has to be substituted by z. Fig. 1 remains valid.

In both cases the formulae determining the rates of inflation stay asymptotically unchanged. The same is true for the other equations in the foregoing sections with the following exceptions. Though the value of production of the exhaustible resource in any country k holds a constant relation to the value of production of all other commodities in that country, the use of factors of production goes to zero in the second case; it keeps a constant relation to other productions in the first case. Total production of the exhaustible resource goes to zero in any case. All this follows from the fact that (1) $w_{pm} + w_{xm} = w_p + w_x$, since $w_{pm} = w_p + \bar{w}_{am}$, $w_{xm} = w - \bar{w}_{am}$ and (2) in case 1: $w_{am} + w_{xm} = w$, since $w_{am} = w + \bar{w}_{am}$, and $w_{xm} = w - \bar{w}_{am}$ whereas in case 2: (3) $(w_{am} + w_{xm}) \to 0$ since $w_{am} = 0$ and $w_{xm} \to 0$.

Thus in case 2 the exhaustible resource is asymptotically negligible as far as production is concerned. We may disregard it in so far.

4.2 The Consequences of an Uneven Distribution of Exhaustible Resources

We first consider *case 1* where the marginal cost of extraction of the scarce resource rises and the resource is sold at marginal cost.

1) Since $Yp = Cp_C + Ip_I + Vp_V$ on the world level and p_V rises if a commodity becomes scarce it is clear that the main consequence of exhaustible resources consist of a fall of real world GDP, given real world production: $Y^{GDP} := Cp_C/p + Ip_I/p$ declines. Real production Y has to be devoted to a larger extent to the production of substitutive products, or to put it otherwise: a larger part of total production must be used for secondary inputs. It might be that the fall of GDP is so large that GDP per head is not

sufficient to sustain the former level of population. A decline of world population would follow — but not an extinction of mankind as Meadows report "Limits to Growth" suggests. From the lower level the growth process may start again.

2) The countries which own the exhaustible resources do not have a comparative advantage from it as far as production is concerned. Their factors of production allocated to the extraction of the scarce resource grow by the general rate of expansion of the world. This follows from (17) and (45a and b).

3) The countries which produce the substitutive products for the exhaustible goods are favored. The absolute level of demand for these products rises (see (45b)). Thus there is a reallocation of production on the world scale in favor of these countries.

4) Those countries which neither own exhaustible resources nor are able to produce substitutes and those who produce products which are complementary to the exhaustible goods suffer. The demand for their products falls to a lower level.

Thus we get a redistribution of economic activity on earth in favor of those countries who produce goods which are substitutes for the exhaustible resources and a total decline of world GDP. But this decline stops at a lower level, and from this level on the growth process may be continued.

In case 2 the situation is different.

1) Countries which own the exhaustible resources extract money from all other countries which use the resource. In other words: country k is in the position to tax these countries; it receives income without offering the services of factors of production in return. If country k sells the exhaustible resource m to country j, it gets income from it by the

amount $T_m^{kj} := x_{mV}^{kj} \cdot p_m^k = x_{mV0}^{kj} \cdot p_{m0}^k e^{(w+w_p^k)t}$ since $p_m^k = p_{m0}^k e^{(w_p^k + w_{pm}^k)t}$ and

$x_{mV}^{kj} = x_{mV0}^{kj} e^{(w-w_{pm}^k)t}$ in equilibrium and $w_{pm}^k > w$. Thus $x_{mV}^{kj} \to 0$ for $t \to \infty$, and country k gets that constant part of its GDP "for nothing".

2) Country k has no advantage with respect to real production from the "tax right" derived from the exhaustible resource if its investment function and its portfolio functions are the same as those of other countries. In that case only the ownership rights, i.e. the wealth structures change on the world level. Or, to put it otherwise: if the country does not offer a comparatively advantageous location for industry it will not have an advantage in production. But total investment or total consumption may change if the saving rates are different in the different countries. People in the ownership countries may "eat up their rent" (in that case the total level of investment on the world scale will decline) or they may invest a larger percentage of their income than the "taxed" countries do, e.g. because of a more unequal income distribution. In that case total investment will rise.

3) Since, in general, not all of the "tax income" will be used for consumption, real wealth of the country will rise. The country acquires ownership rights, bonds or money from other countries.

4) In equilibrium, the rate of growth of real wealth of a country k which owns an exhaustible resource is equal to the common real world economic growth rate. Only the level of real wealth of country k has risen after it took advantage of its monopoly

power. Thus country k will never get hold of all assets of the world as long as other countries save as well.

5) As to the redistribution of economic productive activity on earth, the same rules apply as in case 1 with the exception, that the economic activity in the resource owning country k is smaller if there is no basic change in investment incentives, see 2) above.

The details of the effects of exhaustible resources on the world economic activities may be derived from the model section 3. Only some very broad general statements could be made in this context.

In conclusion one may say that the ownership of scarce resources in this case 2 is not necessarily a blessing for the country. Of course, it grants money and ownership power but it does not guarantee a rise of real production in the country. Production may even decline when the resource gets more and more exhausted and when the country is not able to offer other locations of production comparable to other parts of the world.

Reference

Krelle, W., and *D. Pallaschke*: A General Demand System. Zeitschr. f. Nat. Ök. 41, 1981, 223–252.

Economic Theory of Natural Resources. ©Physica-Verlag, Würzburg–Wien, 1982.

Energy, Environment and Industrial Growth

Reiner Kümmel

A system of equations is developed from neoclassical growth theory which incorporates energy as a factor of production. Instrumental capital is defined in terms of work performance and information processing. The technical causality governing the interaction between capital, labor and energy in industrial production makes the gross national product Q a state function of the economic system, similar to thermodynamic state functions like the entropy. As a consequence Q must be a unique function of the production factors within a creativity-defined growth interval, and partial differential equations for the elasticities of production can be derived from the integrability conditions for the equation of growth. With their solutions the equation of growth is integrated. The production function thus obtained reproduces the development of the GNP of the Federal Republic of Germany in the years from 1970 to 1978 in good agreement with reality.

The pyhsical limits to growth are taken into account by recycling and pollution functions, where pollution is defined as the increase of entropy in the space of the economic system. Simple estimates are given, when, because of the Second Law of Thermodynamics, the "heat barrier", the ultimate limit to terrestrial industrial growth, might be reached, and investment costs are indicated for innovations which will allow to extend or even surmount the energetical and environmental limits to growth.

1. The Equation of Growth

In 1974 H.C. Binswanger and E. Ledergeber pointed out that the decisive mistake of traditional economics is the disregard of energy as a factor of production [*Binswanger/Ledergerber*]. Therefore it seems to be worthwhile to look into the question, how economic theory looks like, if one incorporates energy as production factor in it on an equal footing with capital and labor. Such an attempt has been made recently [*Kümmel, 1980*], and it is the purpose of this paper, to point out the main line of reasoning and some results of a theory that tries to take into account the productive and environmental effects of industrial energy use. For the details the reader is referred to *Kümmel* [1980].

We observe that each process which occurs in the realm of reality accessible to our senses and measuring instruments is based on the interaction of energy with matter. When considering the process of industrial production we see, that matter is transformed into products and services are rendered by the action of energy, where the flow of energy is controlled and directed by information processing and work performing agents. These agents are instrumental capital and human labor. Thus, capital, labor, and energy are the fundamental factors of industrial production.

In 1977 it was proposed [*Kümmel, 1977*] to relate the increment dQ of industrial production Q to the increments dK, dL, dE of capital K, labor L and energy E by the equation

$$\frac{dQ}{Q} = \alpha \frac{dK}{K} + \beta \frac{dL}{L} + (1 - \alpha - \beta) \frac{dE}{E} \ \& \ C. \tag{1.1}$$

$\alpha = \alpha\,(K, L, E)$ and $\beta = \beta\,(K, L, E)$ are the elasticities of production. We have used the Wicksell-Johnson Theorem and assume constant returns of scale, which is justified, if all factors of production are taken into account. Then

$$0 < \alpha + \beta < 1.$$

The symbolically added quantity C in eq. (1.1) stands for creativity. It is the specifically human contribution to economic progress which cannot be made by any machine capable of learning. Creativity is responsible for new ideas, innovations and value decisions. Its working is unpredictable.

The equation of growth (1.1) can be considered as an extension and specification of the equation of growth of neoclassical theory, with the growth-potential "technological progress" being split into the mathematically accessible production factor energy and the bearer of the irrational forces "creativity".

2. The Production Factors

The production factors labor and energy are conveniently measured in energetic terms, i.e. work-calories per day or kilowatts. (Because of the rather similar structure of all human brains and nervous systems we do not discrimate labor with respect to information processing capabilities but assume the latter ones to be the same for all workers.)

The total of all machines in combination with all objects necessary for their protection and operation, e.g. factory buildings, foundations, pipe lines, cables etc., which have to be considered as integral parts of the machines, form the (physical) capital. Physical capital does physical work and processes information when it is actively employed in industrial production. This activity can be described and summarized by the concept of automation A which has been defined as [Kümmel, 1977]

> A = number of information units processed per unit time by machines and measured in "bits per second" multiplied by the physical work per unit time performed by machines and measured in kilowatts. (2.1)

Let us indicate the average degree of capital utilization during one economic time unit by $\eta, 0 < \eta \leqslant 1$. Then we can define physical capital K (including its part lying idle) by

$$A = \eta K. \tag{2.2}$$

This technical definition of capital allows to measure it in terms of work performance and information processing which are specific to its role in industrial production.

The capital unit, which we call 1 ATON, is the same as that of automation:

$$1 \ \text{ATON} = 1 \ \text{kW} \cdot \kappa \ \text{kB/sec},$$

where κ is an average equivalence factor of work performance and information processing.

Consistent with and a consequence of that is to define and measure the industrial production Q by the quantities of energy and processed information which have gone into its generation. The unit of Q is

$$1 \text{ ENIN} = 1 \text{ kWh} \cdot \zeta \text{ kB},$$

with ζ being another equivalence factor.

3. System Characteristics and Growth Intervals

Empirically the assumption seems to be well justified that creativity is not working permanently but rather in thrusts. When creativity is at rest, i.e. $C = 0$, we have a growth interval. Each growth interval is characterized by a set of system characteristics whose role is analogous to that of the equations of state in thermodynamics. Creativity-surges, with the associate changes of system characteristics, mark the beginning and end of growth intervals. There are two classes of growth intervals: A) physico-technological and B) socio-economic ones.

A) Physico-technological characteristics are:
A1) The energetic efficiency of instrumental capital.
A2) The average ATON/ENIN ratio of capital, which measures the ratio of capital's work performance and information processing capability to the energy and information processing that was required for the generation of the capital stock.
A3) The mean economic service life of instrumental capital.
A4) The position of the limits to growth in K, L, E-space.
B) The socio-economic characteristics are formed by the extremum principles which control the input of the production factors with respect to their quantity and their relation to each other. They are:
B1) Cost minimization. This principle can be completely operationalized [*Kümmel*, 1980] and determines the relative magnitudes of $K, L,$ and E.
B2) Profit maximization, or output maximization, or output optimization (according to the economic philosophy prevailing in a system). Any of these principles determines the absolute magnitudes of $K, L,$ and E.

4. The Elasticities of Production

A fundamental supposition of this theory is that within a growth interval with $C = 0$ production Q is a unique function of K, L, E because of the causal-deterministic nature of the technical processes involved in industrial production. As a consequence the dQ of the equation of growth

$$dQ = \alpha \frac{Q}{K} dK + \beta \frac{Q}{L} dL + (1 - \alpha - \beta) \frac{Q}{E} dE, \tag{4.1}$$

is also a total differential,

$$dQ = \left(\frac{\partial Q}{\partial K} \right)_{L,E} dK + \left(\frac{\partial Q}{\partial L} \right)_{K,E} dL + \left(\frac{\partial Q}{\partial E} \right)_{K,L} dE, \tag{4.2}$$

and its integral $Q(K, L, E)$ does not depend upon the path of integration in K, L, E-

space. The mathematical condition for this is that the second order mixed derivatives of Q with respect to the production factors are independent of the order of differentiation:

$$\frac{\partial^2 Q}{\partial L \partial K} = \frac{\partial^2 Q}{\partial K \partial L}, \frac{\partial^2 Q}{\partial E \partial L} = \frac{\partial^2 Q}{\partial L \partial E}, \frac{\partial^2 Q}{\partial K \partial E} = \frac{\partial^2 Q}{\partial E \partial K}. \tag{4.3}$$

Combining eqs. (4.1) – (4.3) we obtain a set of linear partial differential equations for the elasticities of production:

$$K\frac{\partial \alpha}{\partial K} + L\frac{\partial \alpha}{\partial L} + E\frac{\partial \alpha}{\partial E} = 0, \tag{4.4a}$$

$$K\frac{\partial \beta}{\partial K} + L\frac{\partial \beta}{\partial L} + E\frac{\partial \beta}{\partial E} = 0, \tag{4.4b}$$

$$L\frac{\partial \alpha}{\partial L} = K\frac{\partial \beta}{\partial K}. \tag{4.4c}$$

These equations represent the integrability conditions for the equation of growth. Their origin is the same as that of the Maxwell relations in thermodynamics. The most general solutions of eqs. (4.4a) and (4.4b), obtained by the method of the characteristic basis curves [Kamke], are

$$\alpha = u\left(\frac{L}{K}, \frac{E}{K}\right), \beta = v\left(\frac{L}{K}, \frac{E}{K}\right) \tag{4.5}$$

with u and v being any continuous differentiable functions of their arguments, which satisfy also eq. (4.4c). These functions are uniquely determined by boundary conditions which fix β on a surface in K, L, E-space that has not more than one point in common with any characteristic basis curve. For α we then only need to know its values on a suitable boundary curve.

However, these boundary conditions are not yet known. On the other hand we know something about the structure and asymptotic properties α and β should have, from technical and economical considerations. For instance, in α labor L and energy E should add, because they can substitute each other according to the First Law of Thermodynamics. Furthermore, in a combination of much capital with little labor and energy an increase of K contributes little to an increase of production, because there are not sufficient quantities of L and E without which capital cannot be productive. Thus we must have

$$\alpha = \alpha\left(\frac{L+E}{K}\right) \tag{4.6}$$

and

$$\lim \alpha \to 0 \tag{4.7}$$

$$\frac{L+E}{K} \to 0.$$

The simplest function satisfying these conditions is

$$\alpha = a_0 \frac{L+E}{K}. \tag{4.8}$$

The elasticity of production of labor, β, should vanish, if the industrial system would approach the state of total automation, when no worker and employee would be needed any more in production and administration. In this state only the factors capital and energy would be active. The energy E_t required for the totally automated generation of Q by the fully employed capital K_t (Q) is technically determined and is proportional to K_t (Q):

$$E_t = c_t K_t (Q),$$
(4.9)

and β must have such a form that

$$\lim \beta \to 0$$
$$E \to E_t$$
(4.10)
$$K \to K_t.$$

The simplest β which meets this requirement and satisfies the integrability conditions with the simple α of eq. (4.8) is

$$\beta = a_0 L \left(\frac{c_t}{E} - \frac{1}{K} \right).$$
(4.11)

With these elasticities of production the equation of growth within a growth interval becomes

$$\frac{dQ}{Q} = a_0 \frac{L+E}{K^2} dK + a_0 \left(\frac{c_t}{E} - \frac{1}{K} \right) dL + \left[\frac{1}{E} - a_0 \left(\frac{1}{K} + c_t \frac{L}{E^2} \right) \right] dE.$$
(4.12)

It includes all technical progress related to an increased use of energy and the corresponding quantitative and qualitative changes of K. If creatitivty improves the energetic efficiency of physical capital, this can be taken into account by a corresponding linear reduction of the constant c_t.

5. Integration of the Equation of Growth

The characteristic basis curves of the differential equations (4.4) for α and β are straight lines, on which α and β are constant. Integration of the equation of growth along these characteristic basis curves therefore yields Cobb-Douglas Production Functions (CDPF). Since every point in K, L, E-space can be reached on such a straight line, the magnitude of industrial production in all points of production factor space can be read off the complete set of CDPF

$$Q = Q_0 \left(\frac{K}{K_0} \right)^{u(L_0/K_0, E_0/K_0)} \left(\frac{L}{L_0} \right)^{v(L_0/K_0, E_0/K_0)} \left(\frac{E}{E_0} \right)^{(1-u_0-v_0)},$$
(5.1)

if we know all its values Q_0 on a surface Σ of initial points K_0, L_0, E_0 which separates the origin from the rest of factor space.

The boundary condition "Q_0 on Σ" is not known. Therefore, in general we would have to integrate the equation of growth piecewise from one K, L, E-point to the other. However, for all paths of growth, that do not deviate too much from a straight line, approximate solutions can be obtained by allowing the exponents of the CDPF (5.1) to vary with K, L, E while keeping fixed the initial point K_0, L_0, E_0 with Q_0. Thus, an approximate solution of the equation of growth (4.12) with the simple elasticities of production (4.8) and (4.11) is

$$Q = Q_0 \left(\frac{K}{K_0} \right)^{a_0((L+E)/K)} \left(\frac{L}{L_0} \right)^{a_0 L(c_t/E - 1/K)} \left(\frac{E}{E_0} \right)^{1-a_0(E/K + c_t L/E)}, \qquad (5.2)$$

if

$$\left| \ln \frac{KE_0}{K_0 E} \right| \ll 1, \quad \left| \ln \frac{LE_0}{L_0 E} \right| \ll 1 \qquad (5.3)$$

holds.

6. Economic Development in the Federal Republic of Germany in the Years 1970–78

Let us calculate the industrial production of Germany on the basis of the empirically known production factors and compare it with the actually generated gross national product (GNP).

We assume that i) during the time 1970–78 creativity was at rest economically in Germany; ii) the German GNP is proportional to the industrial output Q, and the values of Q and K in terms of the technical units ENINs and ATONs are proportional to their values as given in DM (after subtraction of inflationary enhancements); iii) the average value of labor is 0.038 kW per industrial worker (1200 kcal/day averaged over one year of 231 working days). Most of the data are taken from the 1980 statistics of the Institut der deutschen Wirtschaft [1980]. The basis year is 1970. For this year we have:

$$Q_0 = 679 \ 10^9 \ \text{DM} \qquad L_0 = 3.17 \ 10^5 \ \text{kW}$$
$$K_0 = 1416.74 \ 10^9 \ \text{DM} \quad E_0 = 1.37 \ 10^8 \ \text{kW}. \qquad (6.1)$$

We use the approximate production function (5.2). The conditions (5.3) of its validity are satisfied during the time-span 1970–78, with the possible exception of 1975, when $\ln (KE_0/K_0 E) = 0.32$. The parameters a_0 and c_t are determined from the economic data of 1971 and 1972 to be

$$a_0 = 5285 \ \text{DM/kW},$$
$$c_t = 0.0190 \ \text{kW/DM}. \qquad (6.2)$$

Fig. 1 compares the real growth of production with the calculated one and shows the relative magnitudes of the production factors K, L, E. It demonstrates the strong coupling of energy and economic growth during the years 1970–78. (E is only the energy used in industry.)

Agreement of theory with reality is rather good. Nevertheless the theory has to be tested further by applying it to other industrial systems and to different time intervals before a judgement can be made about the range of its validity. Presently it may perhaps be justified to have some confidence that the considerations developed so far are free of fundamental flaws.

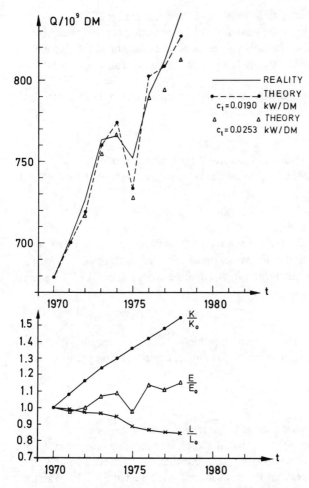

Fig. 1: Growth of production and of the production factors in Germany.

7. Limits to Growth

Energy produces material goods and wealth. A limited availability of energy, therefore, constitutes a serious limit to industrial growth. But let us assume that we can generate energy in abundancy. Then we must observe that energy also generates pollution: The energy powered, non-quasistatic industrial processes pour out a continuous flow of entropy and this entropy flow grows with increasing energy use. This is an inevitable consequence of the Second Law of Thermodynamics. It has been shown recently [*Kümmel*, 1977] that the rise of entropy within an economic system is equal to the system's environmental pollution. There are three forms of environmental pollution: chemical, radioactive, and thermal ones. Chemical and radioactive pollution can be abated technologically. But if for their reduction earth internal energy sources are used, thermal pollution inevitably increases, again because of the Second Law of Thermo-dynamics. A detailed consideration of the various forms of pollution is given elsewhere [*Kümmel*, 1980]. Here, for the sake of simplicity, let us be as optimistic as the Second Law allows us to be and assume, that we only have to deal with pollution in its most benign form, the thermal one.

Phenomenological thermodynamics tells us that the minimum increase of a system's entropy S is

$$dS = \frac{\delta q}{T},$$ (7.1)

if the system receives the heat δq at the temperature T (quasistatically).

The concentration of environmental pollution has been defined [*Kümmel*, 1977, 1980] as

$$U = \frac{1}{R} \frac{dS}{dt}$$ (7.2)

where R is the space of the economic system and $(dS)/(dt)$ is the time change of entropy.

The mayor part of the energy used in industrial production is transformed into heat as a consequence of the Second Law. Therefore, if we combine eqs. (7.1) and (7.2), we can put

$$\frac{\delta q}{dt} = E'$$

in a good approximation, where E' is our production factor "rate of energy input", plus the power used up outside industry. In terms of this factor, environmental pollution is larger than (or at best equal to)

$$U_{th} = \frac{1}{R} \frac{E'}{T}$$ (7.3)

and increases directly with E'. T is the average temperature of the atmosphere.

If the input of artificially generated heat into the biosphere exceeds a few per mills of the power radiated from the sun onto earth, we must fear that world climate will be changed. *V. Buttlar* [1975] estimates that the critical limit is reached at $3 \cdot 10^{14}$ Watts. This limit is also called the "heat barrier". This heat barrier will inhibit further industrial growth, when the damages from uncontrolled changes of world climate will outweigh the benefits humanity can derive from a further growth of production of material goods. Thus the concentration of environmental pollution (in the most optimistic case), has a critical value of the order of magnitude

$$U_c = \frac{1}{R_E} \frac{3 \cdot 10^{14} \text{ Watts}}{T}$$ (7.4)

where R_E is the space of earth's biosphere.

The impact of the approach of the heat-barrier is softened by thermal radiation of heat into interplanetary space. We can describe this by a purification rate U_0.

With that we introduce the growth-limiting pollution function

$$p(U) = \left[\exp\left(\frac{U - U_c}{U_0}\right) + 1 \right]^{-1} (e^{-U_c/U_0} + 1),$$ (7.5)

see Fig. 2.

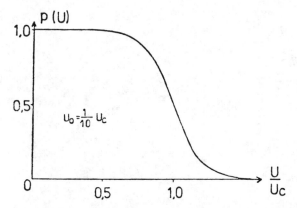

Fig. 2: The pollution function p (U) vs. the ratio of the degree of pollution U to the critical value U_c

As far as the finiteness of the natural resources of raw-materials on earth and the resulting growth-limiting consequences are concerned, we observe that recycling of the industrial products can in principle avoid any shortage of raw-materials so long as the mean economic service life τ of the industrial products does not exceed the time $1/\nu$, after which they have to be fed again into the recycling process. If $1/\nu$ becomes less than τ, i.e. if you recycle a product before its economic service life has expired, recycling does not make sense. In an overall way this situation is described by the recycling function

$$\theta\,(1-\nu\tau) = \quad \text{for} \quad \begin{matrix} 1 & \tau < 1/\nu \\ \\ 0 & \tau > 1/\nu. \end{matrix} \qquad (7.6)$$

With the growth limiting functions (7.5) and (7.6) the equation of growth becomes

$$\frac{dQ}{Q} = \left\{ \alpha\frac{dK}{K} + \beta\frac{dL}{L} + (1-\alpha-\beta)\frac{dE}{E} \right\} p\,(U)\,\theta\,(1-\nu\tau)\,\&\,C. \qquad (7.7)$$

Figure 3 shows estimates of the time when the "heat barrier" will be reached according to different rates r of the increase of the energy input. We see that even under the present most optimistic assumptions the thermodynamic limit to industrial growth is not very distant in the future, if industrial growth and the effect of all technologies involved are restricted to the space of earth's biosphere. We may describe this situation by the law of diminishing returns in ecological form:

"If technological progress is limited to earth-bound technology, the additional input of the production factor energy causes an increase of production. However, after a certain point of time the additional return of an additional energy unit will decrease. This decrease is due to the fact, that the additional energy unit is being combined with a continuously diminishing magnitude of space still capable of absorbing pollution."

Therefore, steady industrial growth is possible only, if the space of the economic system expands. (In eq. (7.3) despite of an increasing E', U may stay below its critical value U_c, if R increases sufficiently rapidly.)

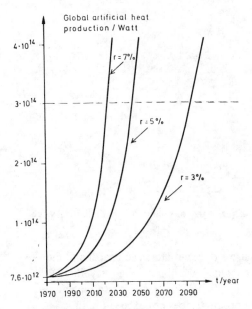

Fig. 3: Artificial heat production and approach of the "heat barrier" for different rates r of the increase of global energy use

8. Space Industrialization

"Surmount the limits to growth by growing into space." This may sound like science fiction at first, but by the work of *Glaser* [1977] of the Arthur D. Little Inc. and *O'Neill* [1978] of Princeton University space industrialization has been shown to be technically feasible and economically profitable.

Glaser has designed (and patented) solar power satellites (SPS) which will be located in geostationary orbit, permanently 36000 km above the same points on the surface of the earth. They will radiate solar power in the form of microwaves to receiving antennas on earth which convert the microwaves to electricity. Each satellite-antenna system delivers 5000 to 10000 Megawatts at busbar. Solar power satellites are subject to hearings in the US Congress, and studies of them are being made by the Department of Energy and NASA. The leading US aerospace firms have formed the SUN SAT Energy Council in order to promote SPS.

O'Neill proposes to use SPS as the economic workhorse to pull industry out into space. He and his collaborators have worked out detailed plans, how space manufacturing facilities, habitats with earth-like conditions for an increasing permanent work-force in space, and SPS can be built mainly from extraterrestrial materials — taken from the moon and the asteroids — with the help of solar power.

The required transportation system would consist of the Space Shuttle and an electrodynamic mass driver (EMD), prototypes of which have been and are being built at Princeton and MIT. The EMD receives its energy from the sun and can be used as the rocket-engine of space freighters, and as a catapult on the moon which ejects lunar material into space where it is collected and brought to the space manufacturing facilities. Powered by solar energy the space factories reproduce themselves and build solar power satellites. The energy delivered to earth by the SPS pays back the estimated initial investment cost of about 60 Billion $ within approximately 20 years. Figure 4 shows the most recently published investment and earnings scenario.

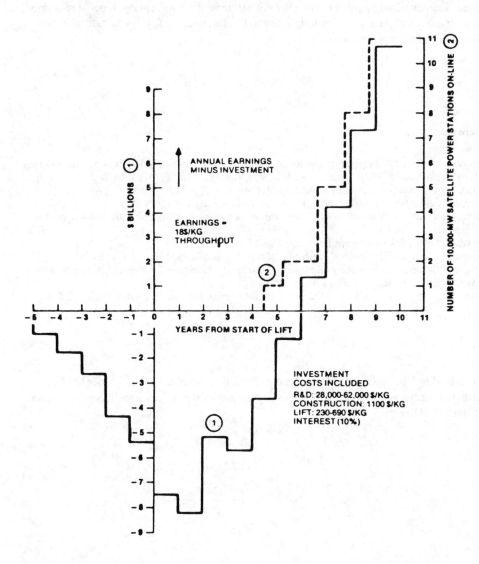

Fig. 4: Investment and earnings scenario for space industrialization ① and growth of the number of space manufactured 10000 MW solar power satellites ② , according to *O'Neill* [1978]. The "ignition point" is the time when earnings exceed investment, i.e. the sixth year from start of lift.

The space industrial system grows exponentially after the "ignition point" has been reached. This could be by the end of the century, if the legislative initiatives in US Congress like the House Concurrent Resolution 451 by Representative Olin Teague and "The High Frontier Feasibility Act" of Senator Williams will stimulate massive political and financial support for space industrialization not only in the US but also in other western industrialized countries. Then the energy dependent and energy supported economy could continue its growth for long times in the future and carry the industrial civilization beyond the bounds of earth.

References

Binswanger, H.C., and *E. Ledergerber*: Bremsung des Energiezuwachses als Mittel der Wachstumskontrolle. Wirtschaftspolitik in der Umweltkrise. Ed. by J. Wolff. Stuttgart 1974, pp. 107f.

Buttlar, H.v.: Umweltprobleme. Physikalische Blätter **31**, 1975, pp. 145f.

Glaser, P.E.: Solar Power from Satellites. Physics Today, February 1977, 30–38.

Institut der deutschen Wirtschaft: 1980-Zahlen zur wirtschaftlichen Entwicklung der Bundesrepublik Deutschland. Köln 1980.

Kamke, E.: Differentialgleichungen II. Leipzig 1962, 1–27.

Kümmel, R.: Energie und Wirtschaftswachstum. Konjunkturpolitik **23**, 1977, 152–173.

–: Growth Dynamics of the Energy Dependent Economy. Mathematical Systems in Economics, Vol. 54. Königstein/Ts. and Cambridge, Mass. 1980.

O'Neill, G.K.: The Low (Profile) Road to Space Manufacturing. Astronautics and Aeronautics, Special Section, March 1978.

Note added in proof: Recently the output of West German and U.S. industries has been calculated for the years from 1960–1978. Deviations of theory from reality are in general less than 5%. (Energy, in the press).

Economic Theory of Natural Resources. ©Physica-Verlag, Würzburg–Wien, 1982.

Growth Models with Restrictions Concerning Energy Resources: An Attempt to Identify Critical Parameters and Structural Features

Wolfgang Ströbele

1. Introduction

1.1 The Question Delt with

In the last ten years lots of models have been developed in order to analyse the question whether in the long run the economy is threatened by doom. The possible causes for a breakdown were discussed on both sides of the production process: Either a shortage of essential input resources or too much pollution in relation to the natural self-cleaning cycles were identified as origins of a possible doom. More or less this discussion has led to a moderately optimistic point of view concerning the long term growth prospects. As main weapons against doom economists trust upon technological progress and substitution of severely exhaustible resources by others and/or by reproducible capital.

In the following paper the discussion centres on the question:

- Which consequences for the possibility of long term economic growth can be derived from the fact that we use finite stocks of energy resources?

More specific: What can we learn from economic theory of exhaustible resources to cope with this question? And which hints on highly sensitive parameters can be obtained from different energy-scenarios?

1.2 Energy, Negentropy and the 2. Law of Thermodynamics

In the last consequence the economic problem results from the 2. Law of thermodynamics: Since all ordered structures which incorporate a certain negentropy follow an irreversible trend of decay towards increasing entropy, we need some energy input to compensate for this increasing entropy.[1]

In figure 1 the economic process is shown embedded into a flow of low to high entropy. The possible sources of low entropy are solar energy in its various forms (1) which in particular includes all work done by plants and animals and use of fuels from finite

---

[1] What is needed, is the ability to do useful work. Since 1 kJ in form of warm water (in an environment, which is only little cooler) does not represent the same source of negentropy as 1 kJ of electricity, there is a severe problem, how to measure the appropriate "amount of energy". Usually energy demand in the northern industrial societies differs very much with respect to the needed quality of energy: In Germany about 50% of final energy demand are just for low temperature purposes, mainly heating of rooms and water.

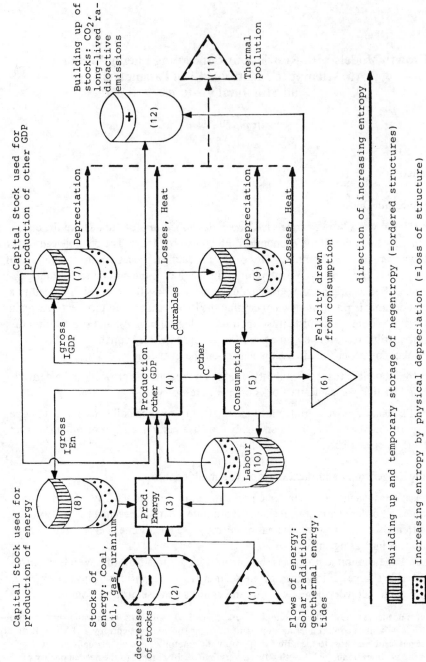

Fig. 1: Energy Use, Production, and Increasing Entropy

stocks (2). The latter are used as fossil fuels in large scale since about 200 years, i.e. since the beginning of industrialisation. Of course, extraction cost of one unit of fuel from stocks today is significantly smaller than the cost of harnessing the same unit from solar energy: otherwise there would not be an "energy-problem" (3).

The production process (4) and the consumption process (5) which produces "felicity" require a certain amount of energy for different tasks: transportation, warming of rooms, transforming materials etc. By elementary thermodynamic considerations one has to accept that for a given GDP (Y_0) which consists of a bundle of transportations, heated rooms, structured materials there exists an absolute minimum of energy which is required as an input. This yields the isoquants of figure 2 describing qualitatively the production function in (4).

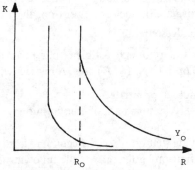

Fig. 2: Isoquants when R is energy input

The thermodynamic resource input R_0 is an ideal abstraction which could only be approximated if all processes worked infinitely slowly and under ideal energetic conditions avoiding any "unnecessary" loss of energy. Equivalently one could say: the quasistatic process that produces Y_0 requires an infinite amount of capital in order to get Y_0 in finite time. Transferring this micro concept to the macro level one ignores the following two possibilities of potential energy savings on the macro level:

− Structural change in the economy will influence the weights given to the different tasks and thereby move the thermodynamic minimum on the macro level.[2]
− Technical progress which replaces some tasks by others less energy consuming is excluded.[3]

From these two points considerable chances for medium-term energy policies can be derived, but they do not change the fundamental point: For a certain GDP (Y_0) there will always be an absolute minimum positive input of energy (R_0).

All inputs into the production process and consumption (7)−(10) and (1) and (2) are subject to entropic degradation, i.e.

---

[2] Although this influence could be of very great importance in the next decades, one has still to accept: Every GDP consists of some mixture of transformed materials, transported materials, communications etc. which puts a definite limit to the minimum amount of energy necessary for production of this GDP.

[3] Of course, this must not be mixed up with substitution processes in the framework of already known technologies. But even here there are limits set by natural laws which can at best be approximated roughly by the best imaginable technique.

- The stocks (7)–(9) have to be depreciated over time. An ever-lasting capital-stock of produced goods is a contradiction to the 2. Law of Thermodynamics.
- Labour (10) is in entropic equilibrium if a certain minimum consumption per capita is ensured.
- The energy inputs (1) and (2) are different: Use of (2) means entropic degradation within our system, whereas (1) comes to us due to an entropic increase outside the surface of the earth which we cannot control.

Since energy as such is not lost every energy input leads to an energy output mostly in the form of heat. This has to be radiated back into space (11). To avoid climatic changes there exists an upper limit for energy use additional to the natural energy flow on earth.[4]) Similarly there exists a limit for the cumulative use of fossil fuels (CO_2) and eventually for the cumulative use of nuclear power (long-lived radioactive emissions) (12).

1.3 Energy as an "Essential Resource"?

In traditional economic theory of exhaustible resources a resource R is called "essential", if either $f(K, 0) = 0$ or $\lim_{R \to 0} f_R(K, R) = \infty$. A revised definition given in *Dasgupta/ Heal* [1979] seems to be more appropriate:
A resource is essential if every feasible path of consumption necessarily declines to zero when $t \to \infty$.

This is equivalent to saying that doom of the economy is unavoidable if there is an essential resource. This definition better catches the following aspect of the problem: If in order to substitute for the dwindling resource society has to accumulate "almost all of production" to build up a very large capital stock of produced goods, such that "almost nothing remains for consumption" then this would not be a solution which one really is interested in. The traditional definition didn't take account of this problem appropriately.

If we remember the specific attributes of energy in the production process, energy fuels taken from fossil or nuclear stocks are a potential candidate for being an "essential resource". For a final judgement possible feasible paths have to be looked at.

2. Neoclassical Theory of Exhaustible Resources Applied to the Energy Problem

2.1 Basic Assumptions

- There is one produced good, which is universally used as capital and consumption good.
- There is no depreciation on capital stock.
- Maximize either the maximum sustainable consumption or the integral
$$\int_0^\infty U(C) \cdot e^{-\delta \cdot t} dt.$$
- Zero population growth is assumed. Whether there result some severe modifications by giving up this assumption is shortly discussed in section 2.3.

---

[4]) Since the relation of natural energy flows to human is about 15 000 : 1 today, there is no problem on a global scale. Locally, thermal pollution might require additional capital costs or cause climatic problems. The latter trouble cannot be avoided, until mankind prefers living near deserts where solar energy can be used without local and global problems of thermal pollution.

2.2 Doom of the Economy with Energy use Solely from Stocks

Assume no technical progress[5]), resource use solely from finite stocks and no extraction costs. Then the recommendation of neoclassical theory is: Substitute resource use by capital until a very small amount of the resource and a very large capital stock produce the same GDP. Since this recommendation depends heavily on the behaviour of the production function in the corners, one can as a first approximation analyse the problem by applying a CES-function. Then we have:

- $\sigma > 1$: The resource problem is trivial, since production can continue without using any input of R.
- $\sigma < 1$: The resource problem is unsolvable for an infinite time-horizon so that doom is unevitable.
- $\sigma = 1$: This special value of the elasticity of substitution defines the borderline between the trivial and the unsolvable case. Suppose $Y = K^{\alpha_1} \cdot R^{\alpha_2}$ with $\alpha_1 > \alpha_2$ and $\alpha_1 + \alpha_2 = 1$. As it is wellknown, there exists an optimal investment plan, which keeps the maximum feasible consumption constant: "A constant savings ratio of α_2 implies a sufficiently high rate of capital accumulation to overcome this dwindling resource use" [*Dasgupta/Heal*, 1979, p. 290]. Furthermore the Cobb-Douglas also allows for a formally simple treatment of technical progress.

In case of $\sigma = 1$ the recommendation can be translated into terms of entropy: Replace the diminishing negentropy of energy resources by accumulation of everlasting negentropy in the form of a produced capital-stock. From a thermodynamic point of view this is impossible. In other words: Since somewhere in the process of continuing substitution the elasticity of substitution σ is smaller than unity and if we approximate the production function in this area by a CES-function (which is then optimistic concerning substitution possibilities) the conclusion must be drawn: energy is an essential resource, as long as it is taken from finite stocks.

In particular, the still very popular widespread Cobb-Douglas function which *Robson* [1980] thinks to "capture the essence of the problem with depletable resources" must be ruled out for long-term energy analysis.

2.3 Growing Population: Some More Doom

The different analysis concerning the influence of a growing population on resource use patterns show the importance of

- resource augmenting technical progress[6]),
- rate of time preference δ and the rate of growth of population [cp. *Stiglitz*, p. 132],
- the behaviour of the production function in the corners [cp. *Ingham/Simmons*].

In case of energy some very simple conclusions can be drawn: A positive rate of popula-

---

[5]) That means, we have already a perfect book of blueprints of all different technologies, even if we do not use them today.

[6]) *Stiglitz* [1974, p. 128]. At best this can be interpreted as follows: Until the world reaches zero population growth some-where in the mid of the next century, we should hope that technical progress in energy use and energy production can compensate for increasing scarcity of fossil fuels.

tion growth draws nearer the date of doom, so that no qualitative change of the whole problem results so far. Of course, the number of people living in the world may be of great importance in the discussion of possible backstop-technologies. Both the feasibility of the backstop and the reachable level of consumption per capita will depend on this number[7]).

2.4 Backstop-Technologies for Energy

The concept of a backstop-technology was introduced by *Nordhaus* [1973] and has since then been discussed frequently. For reasons of theoretical precision it might prove helpful to differentiate the concept.

a) True, quasi and slow backstops

— A true backstop-technology is defined as a special production function for energy
   (see (1) – (3), (8) and figure 1) where the marginal capital-coefficient of every unit
   of energy is approximately constant and the resource flow can in principle be made
   very large and the resource will practically last forever.
— A quasi-backstop is defined by
   • constant marginal capital coefficient in the production of energy and a finite re-
     source stock which will be sufficient for several hundred years (coal, oil shale), or
   • an almost infinite resource-stock but increasing capital-costs in order to avoid
     thermal, CO_2 or radioactive pollution (coal, oil shale, nuclear fusion).
— A slow backstop-technology has a special characterization: The growth of usable energy resources R is not only determined by capital accumulation (8) but must be described by a formulae like $\dot{R} = \min(a \cdot I_R^{net}; b \cdot R)$ where b is some given technological parameter. Since under unfavourable conditions the resource path follows
   $R = R_0 \cdot e^{b \cdot t}$, both the parameter b and the initial endowment R_0 are then of
   crucial importance (breeder reactor).

In the energy field the only true backstop-technology is the use of solar energy.

For some centuries coal and oil-shale represent a quasi-backstop. Gas, oil and nuclear fuel burnt in light water reactors are only of medium term interest for several decades, about 100 years at the maximum.

Even the energy resource which is supposed to give infinitely lasting and very large energy supplies, namely nuclear fusion, is only a quasi-backstop: Since energy additional to the natural energy flows is a cause of thermal pollution, fusion energy cannot be made arbitrarily large without problems for the climate. Moreover it needs some rare chemicals (e.g. Li) and has also radioactive pollution.

The nuclear breeder reactor, which should play the role of a backstop-technology for energy is but a slow quasi-backstop. The amount of available energy can be described by

---

[7]) Today the world's energy use is about 9 – 9,5 TW and the population is 4 billion people. Harnessing solar energy in its various forms will yield 30 – 40 TW at a maximum. So even if specific energy uses can be reduced by 50 – 60%, solar energy could not be a backstop technology, if there are
more than 20 billion people in the world with an average standard of living twice as high as today.
Similar considerations for the case of a large scale breeder economy show, that a very deep change in
life styles and production will result from the switch to backstop technologies in the energy field.

the quantity of Pu-239. This Plutonium is generated in a slow breeding process in a reactor, where Uranium-238, which is available in very large quantities and which is almost useless in light water reactors, is transformed into the new "fuel" Pu-239. The main point is, that this transformation process takes time and is limited by technological parameters. Even if we already had a large-scale pool of well working breeders and reprocessing plants which also could fulfill the necessary safety and environmental standards, that would not make the breeder a true backstop. For practical purposes the hope is, that in the very long run, i.e. after the year 2100, the breeder will have reached an endowment with Pu-239, which makes it at least a quasi-backstop.

If one assumes constant population and a description of production possibilities in (4) by $Y = f(K, R)$, one can easily compare different backstop-technologies concerning their steady-state solutions. To derive the properties of a true backstop path the following model of solar energy will suffice. Thereafter this result will be confronted with the restrictions which can come up with a breeder technology.

b) Solar energy

$$R = \frac{1}{a} \cdot K_S$$

Usable solar energy = g (capital stock in solar energy production) (S0)

$$\dot{R} = \frac{1}{a} \cdot (I_S - \epsilon \cdot K_S)$$

Growth of solar energy = h (net investment in K_S) (S1)

$$\dot{K} = f(K, R) - I_S - \epsilon \cdot K - C$$

Net investment in productive capital-stock = GDP – energy investment – depreciation – consumption. (S2)

The meaning of equations (S0) – (S2) is evident. In the following it is easily shown, that under the assumptions of a true backstop-technology the determination of optimal growth paths leads to a formally well-known model. The limitation of the natural resource is only relevant insofar, as increasing resource input requires a proportionate increase of capital K_S. So at last we just have a model of optimal capital accumulation.

The usual Hamiltonian is given by (S3), from which characterizations of an equilibrium optimal path can be derived.

$$H = U(C) \cdot e^{-\delta \cdot t} + q \cdot e^{-\delta \cdot t} \cdot \{f(K, R) - I_S - \epsilon \cdot K - C\} +$$

$$+ r \cdot e^{-\delta \cdot t} \cdot \left\{ \frac{1}{a} \cdot I_S - \gamma \cdot R \right\} \tag{S3}$$

$$\hat{C} = \frac{f_K - \epsilon - \delta}{\eta(C)}$$

Ramsey-rule (S4)

$$q = \frac{1}{a} \cdot r$$

Price of the resource R is proportionate to the price of capital (S5)

$$\dot{q} = q \cdot (\delta + \epsilon - f_K) \tag{S6}$$

$$\dot{r} = r \cdot \left(\delta + \gamma - \frac{f_R}{a} \right) \tag{S7}$$

$$\hat{C} = 0 \Longleftrightarrow f_K = \epsilon + \delta \Longleftrightarrow \dot{q} = 0 \Longleftrightarrow \dot{r} = 0 \Longleftrightarrow$$

$$\Longleftrightarrow \frac{f_R}{a} = \gamma + \delta. \tag{S8}$$

A simple reformulation of the equations (S6) and (S7) gives us

$$\dot{q} = q \cdot \delta - q \cdot (f_K - \epsilon) \tag{S9}$$

and

$$\dot{r} = r \cdot \delta - q \cdot (f_R - a \cdot \gamma). \tag{S10}$$

Now everything is collected in order to describe the behaviour of our economy on the optimal path. We have two cases to distinguish:

i) The production function $f(K, R)$ shows constant or increasing returns to scale with respect to (K, R). The equation (S5) above allows to integrate the two factors of production to one new "integrated capital good" $(K; (1/a) \cdot K_S)$. For simplicity of the argument assume $f(K, R)$ being a homothetic production function. Then along the expansion path of the economy, a proportionate increase in K and R allows for an increase in production by at least the same percentage. The marginal productivities f_K and f_R are constant or increasing. To exemplify what can happen, let us assume, that the economy operates on the optimal path under such conditions that the production function in a neighbourhood of the expansion path may be approximated by a Cobb-Douglas function. This is not necessarily a contradiction to our arguments above, since here we are not forced to drive the substitution process into the "corners" of the production function. Instead it may be sufficient to have a locally reasonable representation around the expansion path.

The the production function is given by

$$f(K, R) = K^\alpha \cdot R^{1-\alpha} \quad \text{where } 0 < \alpha < 1. \tag{S11}$$

Let $U(C)$ be given by an isoelastic function, assume $\gamma = \epsilon$.

$$U(C) = \frac{1}{1-\eta} \cdot C^{1-\eta} \text{ where } \eta > 1 - \frac{\delta}{f_K - m} \text{ to ensure convergence.} \tag{S12}$$

Then we get by differentiation of (S5), use of (S11) and (S6) and (S7) an explicit formulae for f_K, which with (S4) gives:

$$\hat{C} = \frac{\alpha^\alpha \cdot ((1-\alpha)/a)^{1-\alpha} - \epsilon - \delta}{\eta}. \tag{S13}$$

Since the parameters α, ϵ, and δ are exogenously given, the question whether consumption increases or decreases over time along the optimal path depends heavily upon the capital-output-ratio a in energy production in relation to the other three parameters. The derivation of (S13) is very similar to that in *Heal* [1976].

For reasons of space and in order to make our argument concerning the different characters of backstops clearer we shall assume the second case, namely decreasing returns to scale in (K, R) in the production function.

ii) The assumption of decreasing returns can be justified by the assumption of zero population growth, which means that the "third factor of production" labour is omitted.

If then $F(K, R, L)$ shows constant returns to scale, then our assumption is not too heroic. Now there exists a solution of equation (S8), which will be denoted by an asterix. The general movement of the economy can be demonstrated in a simple figure. Let us assume, that the economy starts at point P in figure 3. Obviously the economy devotes too much of its capital stock to the production of GDP and too little capital to the production of solar energy. By assumption capital is malleable, so the first step is to move instantaneously into P'. Then the economy has reached the optimal path with a constant ratio of factor prices, so that it expands as long as the marginal ratings of future benefits $(q \cdot (f_K - \epsilon)$ and $q \cdot (f_R - a \cdot \gamma))$ are larger than the current benefit of one unit consumption $(q \cdot \delta$ and $r \cdot \delta)$. Starting with a capital stock below K^* and solar energy R smaller than R^*, the consumption is below C^* (which means that q is greater than q^*, since $U'(C) > U'(C^*)$). Along the optimal path C increases, until in P^* the economy reaches a point where it is indifferent between consuming one additional unit of GDP today or investing it into K and K_S.

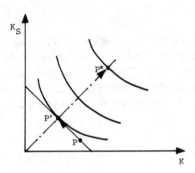

Fig. 3: Optimal path in the model with solar energy

So in this model there is no real restriction from the availability of the energy resource, as long as the parameters a and γ in relation to the productivity of energy are reasonably low. Empirically it is one of the main points discussed today whether a and γ can be made sufficiently small, so that solar energy will be a true backstop, allowing for a sufficiently high C^*.

Formally a true backstop technology can be characterised by a proportionate behaviour of the shadow prices for capital and the energy resource respectively. There are no physical limiting factors for the resource use but merely considerations concerning efficient and optimal accumulation of capital.

c) The breeder

In case of the breeder technology there are two logical possibilities: First, assume that nuclear fuel has been accumulated to such a large extent, that no physical restriction for the energy input results. This would make the breeder model similar to the solar energy model, at least as fas as one only concentrates on the energy input side. Since every use of energy additional to natural energy (i.e. solar, geothermal, tides) causes thermal pollution which might become a severe climatic problem if economic non-solar energy use reaches a significant share of natural energy flows, one has also to take into account limits on the energy "output" side, i.e. energy as thermal pollution of the atmosphere. If one assumes in a first step, that the "saturation point" of the economy (P^* in figure 3) lies well below such a critical energy use, the solar energy model would be formally good enough to describe what happens it there were plenty of nuclear fuel.

The second logical possibility of interest in connection with the breeder technology results from a specific aspect of this technology: Since the available amount of Pu-239 increases with the constant rate b, we can have a very long situation, where the initial endowments B_0 with Pu-239 and the effective breeding rate b put a severe technological restriction upon the available energy. This second case will be of interest in the first phase of a real breeder program. Since the transition period until an abundance of nuclear fuel will have been generated, is estimated in the order of magnitude of several decades or even centuries it is worth-while to analyse this case in an optimal growth context. Let us therefore analyse the behaviour of the economy in a formally similar way as in the solar model above. The equations are as follows:

$$B = \frac{1}{a} \cdot K_{B1}. \tag{B0}$$

Similar as in the case of solar energy the available energy is proportionate to the capital stock K_{B1}. In order to avoid thermal pollution and/or increasing health or safety risks connected with an increasing amount of nuclear waste there is a need for a second type of capital stock K_{B2} which grows more than proportionate to the amount B. Therefore the total gross investment for the nuclear power system is given by (B1):

$$I_B = \gamma \cdot a \cdot B + a \cdot b \cdot B + a \cdot b \cdot d \cdot B^2. \tag{B1}$$

Gross in-   depreciation + additional power plants +
vestment   additional capital investment to avoid environmental risk
in nuclear
plants

The parameters are almost self-explaining: a is the capital-output ratio of energy production, b is the effective breeding rate[8]. The parameter d is the reciprocal value of some small percentage of solar energy input on earth. The growth of available energy is determined by the breeding rate b:

$$\dot{B} = b \cdot B \text{ i.e. } B = B_0 \cdot e^{b \cdot t} \tag{B2}$$

$$\dot{K} = f(K, B) - I_B - \epsilon \cdot K - C. \tag{B3}$$

Equation (B3) is the standard relation describing the increase in capital stock. Here net investment equals GDP minus gross investment for nuclear plants, depreciation ($\epsilon \cdot K$) and consumption. As usual the Hamiltonian is given by

$$H = U(C) \cdot e^{-\delta \cdot t} + q \cdot e^{-\delta \cdot t} \{f(K, B) - a \cdot (\gamma \cdot B + b \cdot B \cdot (1 + d \cdot B)) -$$

$$- \epsilon \cdot K - C\} + p \cdot e^{-\delta \cdot t} \cdot b \cdot B \tag{B4}$$

[8]) The "effective breeding rate b" must not be mistaken for the breeding factor measured within the core of a breeder reactor. The first parameter is always smaller than the second, since additional time is required for the reprocessing process and the production of new nuclear fuel.
The numerical value of b is under favourable conditions about b = 0,02. Even if very significant technical progress could be reached in the breeder and the reprocessing technologies, b would not become larger than 0,03.

$$\hat{C} = \frac{f_K - \epsilon - \delta}{\eta\,(C)} \qquad\qquad \text{Ramsey rule} \qquad\qquad\qquad (B5)$$

$$\dot{q} = q \cdot (\delta + \epsilon - f_K) = q \cdot \delta - q \cdot (f_K - \epsilon) \qquad\qquad (B6a)$$

$$\dot{p} = p \cdot (\delta - b) + q \cdot (a \cdot (\gamma + b + 2 \cdot b \cdot d \cdot B) - f_B). \qquad (B6b)$$

In case that we neglect the additional investment for environmental preservation (i.e. set $d = 0$), we have as a special case:

$$\dot{p} = p \cdot \delta - q \cdot (f_B - a \cdot \gamma) + (q \cdot a - p) \cdot b. \qquad\qquad (B6c)$$

A comparison of the equations (S9) and (S10) with the equations (B6) shows the difference between a true and a slow backstop technology very clearly.

To make the argument clear, let the economy start in point P in figure 4. Again, there is too much of capital K compared with capital in energy production. The economy would wish to move into P', but there the initial endowment B_0 with Pu-239 is too small, so this allocation of capital would be inefficient. For this reason the economy could only move into point $\bar{P}'$. Compared with the optimal path without breeding restrictions (P' to P^*) in point $\bar{P}'$ we have $f_K\,(\bar{P}') < f_K\,(P')$ and $f_B\,(\bar{P}') > f_B\,(P')$.

Therefore at $t = 0$ the shadow price of capital falls more slowly than without a breeding restriction (Equations (S9) and (B6a)), the shadow price of energy falls faster (Equations (S10) and (B6c)). The last term in equation (B6b) is negative as long as the economy has not reached the optimal path $P' - \to P^*$. This can be easily explained by looking at the starting point $\bar{P}'$ and the final point P^*. In P^* we have: $p = a \cdot q$ and since the rates of decrease of the shadow prices $\dot{p}$ and $\dot{q}$ which are given by (B6), are as described above, we have $p > a \cdot q$ for all points which are not on the path $\bar{P}' - \to P^*$.

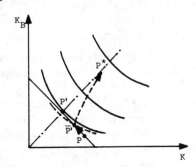

Fig. 4: Optimal path in the breeder model with a
      breeding restriction

This result is quite obvious in the framework of optimal growth theory: We have some scarce factor of production which cannot be increased by any economic means but which follows an exogenous growth path $B = B_0 \cdot e^{b \cdot t}$. So the economy has an economic evaluation of the more scarce factor B which is higher at the beginning than in a pure accumulation model.

This discussion is based upon the assumption that $f\,(K, B)$ shows decreasing returns to scale. If we have constant returns to scale the economy will be limited in its long term growth rate by the breeding rate b, which of course might be insufficient compared with the rate of time preference δ.

The conclusion is: The breeder is not a true backstop-technology; conversely, society has no chance on a possibly very long transition period to improve its available amount of energy by some investment measures.

Especially in case of a growing population one can draw the tentative conclusion: If society is forced to get its energy from a large-scale breeder program, then the growth rate of population must not exceed the breeding rate b. If the condition is met then the length of the transition period depends additionally upon the rate of time preference δ.

Since reasonable estimates of b are between $0{,}02$ and $0{,}03$[9]), the logical possibility, that the breeder could be a very slow backstop-technology for a very long time period, is also highly realistic. Especially by taking into account the population growth rate of about $0{,}02$ one must doubt the backstop characteristic of a breeder program.

d) Reflections on the transition period to a backstop-technology

Denote by T the moment, where the backstop-technology is used for the first time. The most elementary considerations to determine T are as follows:
If energy resources from fossil fuels have constant extraction costs b_1 and the same unit of energy produced by the backstop has a cost of b_2 (of course $b_1 < b_2$) then the following path of the market price q is efficient:

$$q_{fossil} = b_1 + p_0 \cdot e^{r \cdot t}, \qquad \text{where } r: \text{ rate of interest is a exogenously given constant.} \qquad (*)$$

Set p_0^* in formulae $(*)$ such that at $q_{fossil} = b_1 + p_0^* \cdot e^{r \cdot T} = b_2$ the whole finite stock of fossil fuel is used up. The backstop-technology is not used simultaneously with fossil fuel but will be kept in reserve until T [cp. *Dasgupta/Heal*, 1979, p. 176]. Behind this crude model there are a lot of assumptions and logical traps, so that this simple recommedation has to be modified in several points:

- If the substitute is produced with increasing costs then there is a transition period, where both fossil fuels and the substitute are used simulataneously [cp. *Sauter-Servaes*].
- If due to stock-effects fossil fuels are produced with increasing marginal extraction costs, it can be efficient to let a part of the stock unused in the earth.
- If capital goods are not homogeneous, there will be a transition period. Otherwise one would have a discontinuous jump in energy and production. A simple arbitrage argument can show that this would not be optimal.
- If we have technical progress which is generated in the process of using the substitute, then the backstop technology should not be introduced instantaneously at a switch point, but over a transition period. In the case of energy this point should be relevant concerning the training with a hydrogen-system or coal-gasification.
- If the backstop-technology is but a slow-backstop (breeder), then one needs a transition period in order to generate sufficient fuel.

---

[9]) These parameter values imply doubling times of nuclear fuel of 35–23 years.

— The most severe complication results from the change of factor prices which has to occur in the context of growth with changing weights of "scarcity" of the factors. Let us assume, that we have two resources oil and solar energy, which can be produced with a constant capital-output-ratio (in energy production) each, say b_{oil} and b_{sol}. In the first period only the cheaper resource oil is used. Since the price of oil includes a royalty, which increases over time, we have a substitution process in the production of our national product: the capital-resource ratio increases. Thus, the marginal productivity of capital falls (which as a consequence slows down the increase of the royalty). If the production function, which might be assumed as homogeneous in K and R, shows decreasing returns to scale, it can be shown, that a transition period will be efficient [Hanson]. During the transition period, the economy needs more and more capital per unit of energy, because $b_{oil} < b_{sol}$. The increasing "scarcity" of capital leads to an increase of the rate of interest, until the end of the transition period. There the finite stock of oil resource is finally used up and only solar energy will be used in the future. Therefore the rate of interest might well fall in the first period, increase during the transition period and then remain constant or fall first and remain constant then. (Compare the behaviour of the optimal path in figure 3).

This last mentioned type of complicated behaviour can only be analysed in the framework of an optimal-control model, that goes far beyond a partial equilibrium analysis.

Considering all these reservations one must expect a rather long transition period until the finite switch to the sole use of the backstop-technology is reached. And it might prove to be a very difficult task to model the optimal intertemporal decision process concerning consumption, investment, resource use etc. over these three phases (use of fossil fuels, transition period, sole use of the backstop) simultaneously. Although there are some very valuable contributions to deal with this question, there is still a large field for further theoretical and empirical work.

3. Energy Scenarios

3.1 Basic Assumptions

The technique of scenarios has become a very popular means of long-term planning in the energy field. "A scenario is a set of potential occurences which

— belong to a certain field of relevance (. . .);
— relate to a certain time period; and
— are connected by various kinds of relations (. . .) in such a way that an approximation to the whole set can be derived from a subset of basic hypotheses taken from if."
[Ducot/Lubben, p. 51.]

A typical energy-scenario has a set of exogenously given driving forces, which usually are assumed in several variants, in order to show the sensitivity of the results with respect to different (uncertain) paths of the driving forces. These driving forces determine energy-demand. In some scenarios it is just shown on a highly aggregated level as total energy demand or differentiated by two or three energy using sectors. In other scenarios there are more complicated structures: the different kinds of energy-use for low-temperature-heat, transportation, communication, etc. are described. The given path of energy demand is confronted with several possibilities of energy supply. The various fuels are chosen on the basis of either an optimization procedure or according to some ranking order by availability, environmental and safety criteria, social accepture etc.

The contribution of energy-scenarios can be seen in two points: Since there are no perfect future markets — as are assumed in the neoclassical theory, if it is applied to real problems in a competitive market economy — scenarios give benchmarks for decisions today. Secondly scenarios describe the transition periods to new energy systems and try to give an estimate of reasonable technical parameters involved.

Since most political institutions are interested in having a basis for long term planning and since the scenario technique offers a broad spectrum of possible futures it is plausible, that public discussions and the political planning process very often use some kind of energy-scenario. Therefore they deserve a closer inspection on the background of the theory of exhaustible resources.

3.2 The Nordhaus Model [cp. *Nordhaus*]

The Nordhaus model determines the path of energy supply that minimizes the total cost of the energy bill of society. The choice is made between different fuels with different prices. Energy demand is exogenously given. Assuming a backstop technology which Nordhaus expects to be the breeder in connection with hydrogen, he calculates the optimal structure of energy supply. Not included in the usable energy supply is solar energy. The switch to the backstop is postponed until after the year 2100. Since the breeder then should take over a very large part of energy supply within a short time span, and since — as is shown above — the breeder is only a slow quasi backstop technology, the Nordhaus model suffers from a severe shortcoming with respect to the power of its backstop technology.

3.3 The IIASA Scenarios [cp. *Sassin/Häfele; Häfele*]

"The IIASA-scenarios are defined by two basic development variables, population and gross domestic product. . . . In either scenario, population is assumed to grow to 8 thousand million in 2030 . . ." [*Häfele*, p. 22]. The world is devided into seven regions. For each region a growth path of GDP is assumed which is derived from assumptions on population growth and an improvement of GDP per capita. The relationship between GDP and final energy use is given by regionally different elasticities which generally follow a declining trend over time. The share of electricity in final energy use is assumed to reach 22 — 24% in 2030 in the industrialised regions (North America, Western Europe, Australia, Japan, Eastern Europe and Soviet Union etc.) and about 15% in the developing regions. This presupposes very large changes in the structure of energy use. For example, the share of electricity in West Germany 1980 is about 14 — 15%, which is already very high, since the "appropriate" applications of electricity, namely mechanic work, communication, lighting and some special high temperature applications, are within the range of 10%. The use of electricity for heat pumps and installations for solar energy use will increase, but it may be doubtful whether the assumptions made here in the

IIASA scenario will come true. Because of the increasing share of electricity and synthetic fuels the losses in energy conversion processes will increase more than proportionately. Therefore the corresponding use of primary energy will follow a steeper growth path than final energy use. The fundamental ideas behind the IIASA scenarios are sketched in figure 5.

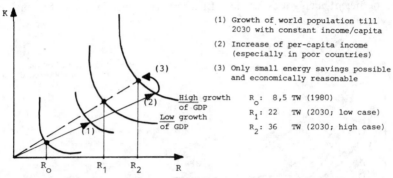

(1) Growth of world population till 2030 with constant income/capita

(2) Increase of per-capita income (especially in poor countries)

(3) Only small energy savings possible and economically reasonable

R_0: 8,5 TW (1980)

R_1: 22 TW (2030; low case)

R_2: 36 TW (2030; high case)

Fig. 5: The logic of the IIASA scenarios

In the year 2030 energy supply comes from oil/gas (+ 66 − 150% compared with today's figures), coal (+ 200 − 400%) and nuclear power (about 2200 power stations, 40 nuclear reprocessing plants of type Gorleben). The burning of fossil fuels will lead to a doubling of CO_2 in the atmosphere [*Häfele*, p. 22].

Investment to build up a sufficiently large capital stock for energy production has to be increased considerably compared with the shares of today. A long transition period till the finite switch on the backstop technologies (breeder, solar energy) is assumed.

The IIASA scenarios begin with such a large increase in energy demand, which is driven by population growth and improvement of GDP per capita as exogenous forces, that there is very little room left for any kind of optimisation procedure. Formally, the set of boundary conditions − i.e. to produce sufficient energy to meet the demand − does not leave very large margins for any optimisation. An estimate on the basis of technological informations will then be sufficient to calculate the structure of energy supplies.

3.4 The Scenario of the ÖKO-Institute [cp. *Krause/Bossel/Müller-Reißmann*]

The German ÖKO-Institute developed an energy scenario for the Federal Republic of Germany, which can stand as representative for similar arguments elsewhere in the circles of the ecologists [cp. *Lovins* or *Leach*].

Over the next fifty years German population will decrease and the growth rates of GDP per capita will also slow down compared with the past. Therefore the driving forces behind the energy demand, which are so important in the IIASA scenario are much less severe here. The situation gets even more open to several degrees of freedom by an energy strategy, which slows down energy demand considerably. This strategy is based upon four pillars:

− Energy saving by substitution of energy by capital. So the ÖKO-Institute assumes that the German economy is far away from the thermodynamic minimum in producing its GDP. Empirical evidence does support this assumption.

404

- development of new technologies on both the energy supply side and in energy use, i.e. technical progress.
- successive transition to energy supply from coal and solar energy, i.e. use of quasi and true backstop technologies.
- better fit of the quality of energy resources to the necessary quality in energy use, i.e. avoid inefficient energy uses, where "efficiency" is defined in terms of a rough net energy analysis.

The line of arguments is sketched in figure 6.

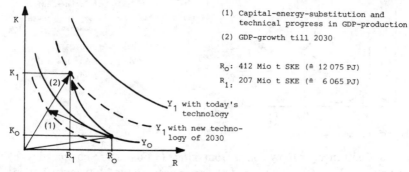

Fig. 6: The logic of the scenario of the ÖKO-Institute

If one takes the necessary investments in the IIASA scenarios over the next 50 years and calculates the estimated share of the Federal Republic of Germany, then one can compare this figure with the investments, which are assumed in the scenario of the ÖKO-Institute. The additional capital requirements prove to be about the same. Primary energy use in Germany is much lower than today in 2030. The decrease is almost 50%. The share of fossil fuels is about 70% below the value of today; renewable energy resources (sun, wind, water, wood and other plants, geothermal etc.) take a share of 40% of primary energy supplies.

4. Conclusions

In the following a summing up of the results obtained will be given. The question dealt with in this paper is formulated in section 1.1: Since economies of today use finite stocks of energy resources, are there some "real limits to growth" in the long run?

The *traditional answer* of neoclassical theory of exhaustible resources how to exploit a finite stock of non-renewable resources has its basis in the following: In the absense of technical progress compensate for the declining resource inputs by capital accumulation. In other words and energetic terms this means: Transform the stored negentropy from oil (gas or coal) into a new source of negentropy, namely the ever-lasting capital stock of machinery, buildings etc. This recommendation cannot be taken as relevant in the energy field: Technical progress has its definite limit in thermodynamic minima which are given by natural laws. Just as well, the substitution process cannot go indefinitely into the corners of the production function: the *elasticity of substitution* becomes less than one sooner or later.

Since energy taken from stocks is an essential resource, doom can only be avoided, if there is a *Backstop technology*. The concept of a backstop looks like a "key to paradise"[10]), but a closer inspection shows some necessary qualifications in the case of energy resources. If energy productivity is high enough in relation to the capital-output ratio in energy production and the depreciation rate of the equipment for harnessing solar energy, then the only true backstop technology will be solar energy. The breeder technology proves to be a slow backstop, and even a possibly "clean" fusion technology would have to respect the limits set by thermal pollution of the whole earth, so that it would be a quasi-backstop.

For all reasonable possibilities one has to accept a rather long *transition period* until a finite switch is made to the sole use of the backstop. In our analytical models we find some preliminary results. The traditional concept is either only a partial equilibrium concept or it applies a production function with constant returns, malleable capital etc., so that there is no transition period. Especially in case of the breeder, the transition to a true backstop characteristic will be very long, however.

If there is a backstop technology available, the increasing scarcity of the energy resources taken from stocks becomes a less severe problem. Consequently, the substitution process must no longer go far into the corners of the production function. The elasticity of substitution looses its dramatic significance. Nevertheless, the reachable level of per capita consumption depends heavily upon this parameter, population and the characteristic of the backstop.

The three chosen energy scenarios show a broad pattern of possible future growths paths. The Nordhaus model suffers from a sound technological background concerning the characteristics of a backstop technology, the IIASA scenarios and the scenarios of the ÖKO-Institute lack a precise economic background. The IIASA scenarios justify this shortcoming with the very little margins concerning future choices in the energy field; the ÖKO-Institute's scenario would argue, that it uses a broader pattern of social, environmental and economic criteria, which get lost in the simple minded economic objective functionals. The two most important variables, which determine our future possibilities in the energy field, will probably be population growth and improving the fate of the poor on the one side, and the realization of large scale energy savings especially in the ten most industrialised countries on the other hand. These variables will either cause a great pressure of time or give sufficient time to develop some possible technologies, which may take the role of a backstop. Both theoretical considerations and the results of the IIASA scenarios show, that the actual favourite backstop technology, the nuclear breeder, might well prove as a deadlock, at least, as far as the next 120 years are of concern.

References

Berndt, E.R.: Aggregate Energy, Efficiency and Productivity Measurement. Ann. Rev. Energy 3, 1978, 225–273.
Dasgupta, P.S., and *G.M. Heal*: The Optimal Depletion of Exhaustible Resources. Rev. of Econ. Studies (Symposium), 1974, 3–28.
–: Economic Theory and Exhaustible Resources. Cambridge 1979.

---

[10]) Or in order to repeat a well-known play upon words: a key to "fuel's **paradise**".

406

Ducot, C., and *G.J. Lubben:* A Typology for Scenarios. Futures **12** (1), 1980, 51–57.

Garg, P.C., and *J.L. Sweeney:* Optimal Growth with Depletable Resources. Resources and Energy **1**, 1978, 43–56.

Häfele, W.: IIASA's World Regional Energy Modelling. Futures **12** (1), 1980, 18–34.

Hanson, D.A.: Efficient Transitions from a Resource to a Substitute Technology in an Economic Growth Context. Journal of Econ. Theory **17**, 1978, 99–113.

Heal, G.M.: The relationship between price and extraction cost for a resource with a backstop technology. Bell Journal of Econ. **7**, 1976, 371–378.

Ingham, A., and *P. Simmons:* Natural Resources and Growing Population. Rev. of Econ. Studies **42**, 1975, 191–206.

Kemp, M.C., and *Ngo van Long:* On two folk theorems concerning the extraction of exhaustible resources. Econometrica **48**, 1980, 663–674.

Krause, F., H. Bossel and *K.-F. Müller-Reißmann:* Energie-Wende. Frankfurt 1980.

Leach, G.: A Low Energy Strategy for the United Kingdom. London 1978.

Lovins, A.B.: Sanfte Energie. Reinbek bei Hamburg 1978; German translation of "Soft Energy Paths", Harmondsworth 1977.

Nordhaus, W.D.: The Allocation of Energy Resources. Brookings Papers of Econ. Activity **3**, 1973, 529–576.

Robson, A.J.: Costly Innovation and Natural Resources. Internat. Econ. Rev. **21** (1), 1980, 17–30.

Sassin, W., and *W. Häfele:* Die Energiefrage und die zukünftige wirtschaftliche und politische Entwicklung. Alternativen der Energiepolitik. Ed. by D.J. Volkmann. Gräferlding/München, 1978, 19–47.

Sauter-Servaes, F.: Der Übergang von einer erschöpfbaren Ressource zu einem synthetischen Substitut. Erschöpfbare Ressourcen. Ed. by H. Siebert. Schriften des Vereins für Socialpolitik, N.F., Bd. 108, Berlin 1980, 245–257.

Stiglitz, J.: Growth with Exhaustible Natural Resources: Efficient and Optimal Growth Paths. Rev. of Econ. Studies, (Symposium), 1974, 123–137.

Ulph, A.M.: World Energy Models – A Survey and Critique. Energy Econ. **2** (1), 1980, 46–59.

Part V
Environment and Welfare

Economic Theory of Natural Resources. ©Physica-Verlag, Würzburg–Wien, 1982.

On Some Problems in the Formulation of Optimum Population Policies when Resources are Depletable

Swapan Dasgupta and *Tapan Mitra*[1])

1. Introduction

In recent years, considerable attention has been focused on the study of optimal deple-tion patterns of exhaustible resources. The existing models are mostly concerned with the possible mitigating effects of technological progress or capital accumulation in the growth process of economies facing exhaustible resource constraints [see, for example, *Dasgupta*, 1973; *Dasgupta/Heal; Solow; Stiglitz; Ingham/Simmons*, and others]. Population is as-sumed exogenous to these models, and the concern is with jointly solving the optimal de-pletion of an exhaustible resource, and optimal investment in augmentable capital goods.

The interrelationship between population policies, and depletion patterns of exhausti-ble resources has been studied by *Koopmans* [1973, 1974], who poses the problem as a trade-off between the survival time of a fixed population and its consumption rates. This line of analysis has been extended by *Lane* [1975], who allows the population itself to be a control variable, and also allows for a conservationist motive in the optimality exercise. Neither study includes the aspect of capital accumulation offsetting the effect of a (rapid-ly) depleting resource stock. However the study by *Lane* [1977] establishes a link between the interesting study of Koopmans, and the traditional literature on optimum population, without exhaustible resource constraints, studied by *Meade* [1955], *Dasgupta* [1969], *Lane* [1975], *Pitchford* [1974] and others.

In this paper, we attempt a systematic study of optimum population policies in a model in which capital, labor, and an exhaustible resource produce an output which can be consumed or accumulated as capital. The total stock of the resource is given, and the resource use over the (infinite) planning horizon must not exceed this stock. Population is "freely" controllable, and, so, like *Dasgupta* [1969], we are interested in "first-best solu-tions". Individual "Utility" is derived from consumption (per capita), and "Welfare" is individual utility times the population at each date. The reason for adopting this Classical Utilitarian view of "Welfare" is that with the alternative Average Utilitarian view, there does not even exist a Pareto-optimal program [see Proposition 3.1]. Furthermore, we fol-low *Meade* [1955] in assuming that when consumption of an individual is "low", his utili-ty is negative, when it is "high", his utility is positive. We show that this is a necessary condition for the existence of a Pareto-optimal program, with the Classical Utilitarian Welfare function [see Proposition 3.2]. Optimality is then defined in terms of the "maxi-

[1]) Research of the second author was partially supported by a National Science Foundation Grant.

misation" of the discounted or undiscounted sums of Welfares, by a suitable version of the "overtaking criterion".

We show that Optimal programs can be characterized in terms of a) the Ramsey Rule of capital accumulation, b) the Meade Rule of population, c) the Hotelling Rule of allocation of an exhaustible resource, and d) the transversality condition that the present value of capital and resource stocks converge to zero, over time [see Theorems 4.1–5.3].

We use this characterization to show that when future welfares are undiscounted, an optimal program does not exist, under a set of quite realistic assumptions [see Theorems 5.1 and 5.3]. This is a somewhat disturbing comment on the Classical Utilitarian view of welfare. We note that similar difficulties are also encountered, when exhaustible resources are not treated explicity [for example, in *Dasgupta*, 1969].

In Theorem 6.1, we show that when future welfares are discounted, an optimal program does exist. We note that the methods of proving the existence of an optimal program, in models where population is exogenous, and exhaustible resources are either absent [see *Gale; Brock; Brock/Gale*] or present [see *Dasgupta/Heal*], cannot be applied to our case. Similarly the methods used in models where population is controllable, but exhaustible resources are absent [see *Dasgupta*] also become inapplicable. Thus, our method of proof is new, although it borrows ideas, at several points, from the above stated "traditional methods".

While Theorem 6.1 might appear to lay at rest questions raised about the appropriateness of the Classical Utilitarian view of welfare [in the sense of Koopmans' "mathematical screening"], Theorem 7.1 raises fresh doubts. Here, we show that when future utilities are discounted, an optimal program must be an "extinction program". That is, it is optimal to have the extinction of the human race in finite time. We note that this result holds, even if there are feasible programs with stationary population, for whom "life is enjoyable" at each date [utility of individuals at various dates are bounded away from zero]. It seems that the Classical Utilitarian view places too small a "penalty" on the extinction of the economy, so that with resources depleting and the future being discounted, it is optimal not to have a "future" at all, beyond a finite time.

2. The Model

Consider an economy with a technology given by a production function, G, from R_+^3 to R_+. The production possibilities consist of capital input, K, exhaustible resource input, D, labor input, L, and current output $Z = G(K, D, L)$ for $(K, D, L) \geq 0$.

For simplicity, we will identify "population" with "labor input", at each date, and use the terms interchangeably. Capital will be assumed not to depreciate. Thus *total output*, Y, can be defined as $G(K, D, L) + K$ for $(K, D, L) \geq 0$. A *total output function, F* (from R_+^3 to R_+) can be defined by

$$F(K, D, L) = G(K, D, L) + K \qquad \text{for } (K, D, L) \geq 0. \tag{2.1}$$

The production function, G, is assumed to satisfy:

(A.1) *G is concave, homogeneous of degree one, and continuous for* $(K, D, L) \geq 0$; *it is continuously differentiable for* $(K, D, L) \gg 0$.

(A.2) *G is non-decreasing in K, D, L for* $(K, D, L) \geqslant 0; (G_K, G_D, G_L) \geqslant 0$ *for*
$(K, D, L) \gg 0.$

The initial capital and labor inputs, $\underset{\sim}{K}$ and $\underset{\sim}{L}$, and the initial available stock of the exhaustible resource, $\underset{\sim}{M}$, are considered to be historically given and positive. A feasible program is a sequence $\langle K, D, L, Y, C \rangle = \langle K_t, D_t, L_t, Y_t, C_t \rangle$ satisfying

$$
\left.
\begin{aligned}
&K_0 = \underset{\sim}{K}, \ L_0 = \underset{\sim}{L}, \ \sum_{t=0}^{\infty} D_t \leqslant \underset{\sim}{M} \\
&Y_t = F(K_t, D_t, L_t), \ C_t = Y_t - K_{t+1} \ \text{for} \ t \geqslant 0 \\
&(K_t, D_t, L_t, Y_t, C_t) \geqslant 0 \ \text{for} \ t \geqslant 0 \\
&L_t = 0 \ \text{implies} \ L_{t+1} = 0 \ \text{for} \ t \geqslant 1.
\end{aligned}
\right\}
\tag{2.2}
$$

Associated with a feasible program $\langle K, D, L, Y, C \rangle$ is a *sequence of resource stocks* $\langle M \rangle = \langle M_t \rangle$, given by

$$
M_0 = \underset{\sim}{M}, \ M_{t+1} = M_t - D_t \ \text{for} \ t \geqslant 0.
\tag{2.3}
$$

By (2.2), $M_t \geqslant 0$, and $M_{t+1} \leqslant M_t$ for $t \geqslant 0$.

A feasible program $\langle K, D, L, Y, C \rangle$ is called *positive* if $L_t > 0$ for $t \geqslant 0$. It is *interior* if it is positive and $(K_t, D_t) \gg 0$ for all $t \geqslant 0$. It is *regular interior* if it is interior, and $C_t > 0$ for $t \geqslant 0$.

For a positive program $\langle K, D, L, Y, C \rangle$ we denote, for $t \geqslant 0$,

$$
\left.
\begin{aligned}
&(K_t/L_t) = k_t; \ (D_t/L_t) = d_t \\
&(C_t/L_t) = c_t; \ (Y_t/L_t) = y_t.
\end{aligned}
\right\}
\tag{2.4}
$$

Preferences are represented by a *utility function*, u, from R_+ to R. The utility function is assumed to satisfy:

(A.3) *u is strictly increasing for* $c \geqslant 0$.
(A.4) *u is continuous and concave for* $c \geqslant 0$; *it is continuously differentiable for* $c > 0$.
(A.5) $u'(c) \to \infty$ *as* $c \to 0$.
(A.6) *There is* $0 < b < \infty$, *such that* $|u(c)| \leqslant b$ *for* $c \geqslant 0$.[2])

---

[2]) (A.6) is used only in proving the existence of optimal programs in the discounted case i.e. in Section 6. It may be noted that if there is an optimal program which is interior then from the Meade Rule (4.2 in p. 10) it follows that: $c_t u'(c_t) - u(c_t) = u'(c_t) F_{L_t} > 0$ or $u(c_t)/c_t < u'(c_t)$. Since under (A.7) there exists $\bar{c}$ such that $u(c)/c > u'(c)$ for $c > \bar{c}$ this means $u(c_t) < u(\bar{c})$ for all t. (A.6) guarantees that the utility sums along any feasible path is bounded above. Hence one can use the Cantor Diagonal process to establish existence of a program with largest utility sum as in Lemma 6.3 when the welfare function $W(C, L)$ is continuous. It may be noted that continuity of $W(C, L)$ at $C = 0$ or $L = 0$ (or alternatively defining $W(C, L)$ at $C = 0$ or $L = 0$ ensuring continuity) may be a problem when $u(c)$ is not bounded.

3. On Average and Classical Utilitarian Social Welfare Functions

It has been observed in the literature [see, for example, *Dasgupta*, 1969, p. 295] that if we take the index of social welfare to be the Average Utilitarian one [$V(C, L) = u(C/L)$], and formulate our criterion of optimality in terms of the sum of these welfares then there does not exist an optimal program. Quite apart from the ethical objections to the Average Utilitarian index, this consequence is considered to be a strong reason for rejecting it as a measure of social welfare. We feel that the case against adopting the Average Utilitarian index is further strengthened by showing that, under this valuation, even (interior) Pareto-optimal programs do not exist. We demonstrate this in Proposition 3.1.

In adopting the Classical Utilitarian index of social welfare [$W(C, L) = L u(C/L)$], it is assumed in addition that when the consumption rate of an individual is "low", his utility is negative; when it is "high", his utility is positive [see, for example, *Dasgupta*, 1969, p. 296]. We demonstrate (in Proposition 3.2) that a necessary condition for the existence of (interior) Pareto-optimal programs, under the classical Utilitarian valuation, is that the utility function, u, has the above-stated properties.

A *Classical Utilitarian welfare function*, $W(C, L)$, is defined by

$$W(C, L) = L u(C/L) \quad \text{for} \quad L > 0; \quad W(C, L) = 0 \quad \text{for} \quad L = 0. \tag{3.1}$$

An *Average Utilitarian welfare function*, $V(C, L)$, is defined by

$$V(C, L) = u(C/L) \quad \text{for} \quad L > 0. \tag{3.2}$$

Note that we leave $V(C, L)$ undefined for $L = 0$, as there is no "natural choice" for its value. The choice of $W(C, L) = 0$ for $L = 0$ makes W a continuous function of (C, L), for $(C, L) \geqslant 0$, under (A.4), (A.6). This is the reason for its choice in (3.1).

Clearly Pareto-Optimality and Optimality can be defined in terms of either of the valuations given by (3.1) and (3.2).

A feasible program $\langle K, D, L, Y, C \rangle$ is called *C-Pareto optimal* if there is no feasible program $\langle K', D', L', Y', C' \rangle$ satisfying $W(C'_t, L'_t) \geqslant W(C_t, L_t)$ for all $t \geqslant 0$, and $W(C'_t, L'_t) > W(C_t, L_t)$ for some t. A positive program $\langle K, D, L, Y, C \rangle$ is called *A-Pareto optimal* if there is no positive program $\langle K', D', L', Y', C' \rangle$ satisfying $V(C'_t, L'_t) \geqslant V(C_t, L_t)$ for all $t \geqslant 0$, and $V(C'_t, L'_t) > V(C_t, L_t)$ for some t.

To define optimality, we consider a discount factor, δ, where $0 < \delta \leqslant 1$, to be given. A feasible program $\langle K^*, D^*, L^*, Y^*, C^* \rangle$ is *C-optimal* if

$$\limsup_{T \to \infty} \sum_{t=0}^{T} \delta^t [W(C_t, L_t) - W(C_t^*, L_t^*)] \leqslant 0 \tag{3.3}$$

for every feasible program $\langle K, D, L, Y, C \rangle$. A positive program $\langle K^*, D^*, L^*, Y^*, C^* \rangle$ is *A-optimal* if

$$\limsup_{T \to \infty} \sum_{t=0}^{T} \delta^t [V(C_t, L_t) - V(C_t^*, L_t^*)] \leqslant 0 \tag{3.4}$$

for every positive program $\langle K, D, L, Y, C \rangle$.

Proposition 3.1: Under (A.1)–(A.6), *there is no interior A-Pareto-optimal program.*

Proof: Suppose, on the contrary, that there is an interior program $\langle K, D, L, Y, C \rangle$, which is A-Pareto optimal. Consider the sequence $\langle K', D', L', Y', C' \rangle$ given by:
$(K_0', D_0', L_0', Y_0') = (K_0, D_0, L_0, Y_0)$, $C_0' = C_0 + (1/2) K_1$; $(K_t', D_t', L_t', Y_t', C_t') = (1/2) (K_t, D_t, L_t, Y_t, C_t)$ for $t \geqslant 1$. Clearly $\langle K', D', L', Y', C' \rangle$ is an interior program. Now, $C_0' > C_0$ (since $K_1 > 0$), so $c_0' > c_0$, and $V (C_0', L_0') > V (C_0, L_0)$. Also, $C_t' = (1/2) C_t$, and $L_t' = (1/2) L_t$ for $t \geqslant 1$. So $c_t' = c_t$, and $V (C_t', L_t') = V (C_t, L_t)$ for $t \geqslant 1$. Hence, $\langle K, D, L, Y, C \rangle$ is not A-Pareto optimal. This contradiction establishes the Proposition. ‖

Remark: It is clear from Proposition 3.1 that there is no interior A-optimal program either, a fact which has been noted in the literature. In view of this, in the rest of the paper, we will be concerned only with the notions of C-Pareto optimality and C-optimality. Also, since there is now no scope for confusion, we will refer to these terms simply as Pareto optimality and optimality respectively.

We now proceed to consider the following additional assumption on u:

(A.7)   There is $0 < \underset{\sim}{c} < \infty$, such that $u (c) < 0$ for $0 \leqslant c < \underset{\sim}{c}$; $u (c) > 0$ for $c > \underset{\sim}{c}$; $u (\underset{\sim}{c}) = 0$.

Proposition 3.2: Under (A.1)–(A.6), if there exists an interior Pareto-optimal program $\langle K, D, L, Y, C \rangle$, then the utility function, u, satisfies (A.7).

Proof: Given (A.3), the utility function can be one of three types: (i) $u (c) < 0$ for $c \geqslant 0$; (ii) $u (c) \geqslant 0$ for $c \geqslant 0$; (iii) $u (c^1) < 0$ for some $c^1 \geqslant 0$, and $u (c^2) > 0$ for some $c^2 \geqslant 0$. If there is an interior Pareto optimal program $\langle K, D, L, Y, C \rangle$, we will show that cases (i) and (ii) cannot occur.

If case (i) occurs, we construct a sequence $\langle K', D', L', Y', C \rangle$ as follows:
$(K_0', D_0', L_0', Y_0') = (K_0, D_0, L_0, Y_0)$, $C_0' = C_0 + (1/2) K_1$; $(K_t', D_t', L_t', Y_t', C_t') = (1/2) (K_t, D_t, L_t, Y_t, C_t)$ for $t \geqslant 1$. Then, $\langle K', D', L', Y', C' \rangle$ is an interior program. Also, $C_0' = C_0 + (1/2) K_1 > C_0$, so $c_0' > c_0$, and $W (C_0', L_0') > W (C_0, L_0)$. Also, $C_t' = (1/2) C_t$, $L_t' = (1/2) L_t$ for $t \geqslant 1$. So $W (C_t', L_t') = (1/2) W (C_t, L_t) \geqslant W (C_t, L_t)$, since $u (c) < 0$ for $c \geqslant 0$. Hence $\langle K, D, L, Y, C \rangle$ cannot be Pareto-optimal, a contradiction. Thus, case (i) cannot occur.

If case (ii), occurs, then for $c \geqslant 0$, and $0 \leqslant \theta \leqslant 1$, $u (\theta c) = u [\theta c + (1 - \theta) 0] \geqslant \theta u (c) + (1 - \theta) u (0) \geqslant \theta u (c)$, since $u (0) \geqslant 0$. We construct a sequence $\langle K', D', L', Y', C' \rangle$ as follows: $(K_0', D_0', L_0', Y_0', C_0') = (K_0, D_0, L_0, Y_0, C_0)$; $(K_t', D_t', L_t') = (K_t, D_t, 2L_t)$ for $t \geqslant 1$, $Y_t' = F (K_t', D_t', L_t')$ and $C_t' = Y_t' - K_{t+1}'$ for $t \geqslant 0$. Then, $W (C_0', L_0') = W (C_0, L_0)$; also, for $t \geqslant 1$, $C_t' > C_t$, by (A.2), so $W (C_t', L_t') > L_t' u ((1/2) c_t) = 2L_t u ((1/2) c_t) \geqslant 2L_t (1/2) u (c_t) = L_t u (c_t) = W (C_t, L_t)$. Since $\langle K', D', L', Y', C' \rangle$ is clearly an interior program, so $\langle K, D, L, Y, C \rangle$ is not Pareto-optimal, a contradiction. Hence, case (ii) cannot occur.

Thus, case (iii) must occur. Since u is continuous, there is some $0 \leqslant \underset{\sim}{c} < \infty$, such that $u (\underset{\sim}{c}) = 0$. Since u is increasing, $\underset{\sim}{c} > 0$, and $u (c) < 0$ for $0 < c < \underset{\sim}{c}$; $u (c) > 0$ for $c > \underset{\sim}{c}$. ‖

In view of Proposition 3.2, we will assume that (A.7) holds, in the rest of the paper. Note that, under this additional assumption, there is $\tilde{c} > 0$, satisfying (i) $\underline{c} < \tilde{c} < \infty$, and (ii) $u(\tilde{c}) - u'(\tilde{c})\,\tilde{c} = 0$.

4. Characterization of Optimality

In this section, we will provide necessary and sufficient conditions for a positive program to be optimal. This characterization is used in Section 5 to examine the question of existence of an optimal program, when future utilities are undiscounted. It is also used in Section 7 to establish an asymptotic property of optimal programs, when future utilities are discounted.

For our purpose, we will assume that the three types of inputs are essential in production, and that the marginal product of the exhaustible resource is infinite at zero resource input.

(A.8) $G(0, D, L) = G(K, 0, L) = G(K, D, 0) = 0$

For $(K, L) \gg 0$, $G_D(K, D, L) \to \infty$ as $D \to 0$.

Furthermore, following *Mitra* [1978], we assume that the exhaustible resource is "important" in production, in the sense that the share of the resource in current output is bounded away from zero.

(A.9) $\beta \equiv \inf_{(K,D,L) \gg 0} [D\,G_D(K, D, L)/G(K, D, L)] > 0.$

Theorem 4.1: Under (A.1)–(A.9), *if a positive program* $\langle K, D, L, Y, C \rangle$ *is optimal, then*

(i)   *it is regular interior*

(ii) $u'(c_t) = \delta u'(c_{t+1}) F_{K_{t+1}}$ for $t \geq 0$ (4.1)

(iii) $[c_t\,u'(c_t) - u(c_t)] = u'(c_t) F_{L_t}$ for $t \geq 1$ (4.2)

(iv) $[F_{D_{t+1}} / F_{D_t}] = F_{K_{t+1}}$ for $t \geq 0$ (4.3)

(v)   a) $\lim_{t \to \infty} \delta^t u'(c_t) K_{t+1} = 0$; b) $\lim_{t \to \infty} M_t = 0$.   (4.4)

Proof: First, we establish that $C_t > 0$ for $t \geq 0$. Since $\langle K, D, L, Y, C \rangle$ is optimal, $C_t > 0$ for some t. If $C_t = 0$ for some period, then we can find a period s, such that either a) $C_s = 0$, $C_{s+1} > 0$, or b) $C_s > 0$, $C_{s+1} = 0$. Using (A.5), in either case, $\langle K, D, L, Y, C \rangle$ cannot be optimal, since $(L_s, L_{s+1}) \gg 0$. So, $C_t > 0$ for $t \geq 0$. By (A.8), $K_t > 0$ for $t \geq 0$.

We claim next, that $D_t > 0$ for $t \geq 0$. Clearly, $D_t > 0$ for some t. If $D_t = 0$ for some period, then we can find a period, s, such that either a) $D_s = 0$, $D_{s+1} > 0$, or b) $D_s > 0$, $D_{s+1} = 0$. In either case, $\langle K, D, L, Y, C \rangle$ cannot be optimal, by using (A.8), and $(K_s, L_s) \gg 0$, $(K_{s+1}, L_{s+1}) \gg 0$. Hence, $D_t > 0$ for $t \geq 0$. Thus, $\langle K, D, L, Y, C \rangle$ is a regular interior program, which is (i).

For $t \geqslant 0$, the expression

$$L_t \, u \, \{[F\,(K_t,\,D_t,\,L_t)-K]\,/\,L_t\} + \delta L_{t+1} \, u \, \{[F\,(K,\,D_{t+1},\,L_{t+1})-K_{t+2}]\,/\,L_{t+1}\}$$

must be maximised at $K = K_{t+1}$, among all $K \geqslant 0$, satisfying $K \leqslant F\,(K_t,\,D_t,\,L_t)$ and $F\,(K,\,D_{t+1},\,L_{t+1}) \geqslant K_{t+2}$. Using (i),

$$L_t \, u'\,(c_t)\,[-1/L_t] + \delta L_{t+1} \, u'\,(c_{t+1})\,[F_{k_{t+1}}/L_{t+1}] = 0$$

which yields (4.1) directly.

For $t \geqslant 1$, the expression $L \, u \, \{[F\,(K_t,\,D_t,\,L)-K_{t+1}]\,/\,L\}$ must be maximized at $L = L_t$, among all $L > 0$, satisfying $F\,(K_t,\,D_t,\,L) \geqslant K_{t+1}$. Using (i), we have

$$u\,(c_t) + L_t \, u'\,(c_t)\,\{[L_t\,F_{L_t}-C_t]/L_t^2\} = 0$$

which yields (4.2) immediately.

For $t \geqslant 0$, the expression

$$L_t \, u \, \{[F\,(K_t,\,D,\,L_t)-K_{t+1}]/L_t\} +$$
$$+ \delta L_{t+1} \, u \, \{[F\,(K_{t+1},\,D_t + D_{t+1} -D,\,L_{t+1})-K_{t+2}]/L_{t+1}\}$$

must be maximized at $D = D_t$, among all $D \geqslant 0$, satisfying $D \leqslant D_t + D_{t+1}$, $F\,(K_t,\,D,\,L_t) \geqslant K_{t+1}$, and $F\,(K_{t+1},\,D_t + D_{t+1} -D,\,L_{t+1}) \geqslant K_{t+2}$. Using (i), we get $L_t \, u'\,(c_t)\,[F_{D_t}/L_t] + \delta L_{t+1} \, u'\,(c_{t+1})\,[-F_{D_{t+1}}/L_{t+1}] = 0$ which yields, on simplification,

$$u'\,(c_t)\,F_{D_t} = \delta u'\,(c_{t+1})\,F_{D_{t+1}}. \tag{4.5}$$

Using (4.1) and (4.5) yields (4.3).

Clearly, there is no feasible program, $\langle K',\,D',\,L',\,Y',\,C' \rangle$ with $L'_t = L_t$ for $t \geqslant 0$, $C'_t \geqslant C_t$ for $t \geqslant 0$, $C'_t > C_t$ for some t. Hence, following the proof of Theorem 4.1 in *Mitra* [1978],

$$\lim_{t \to \infty} M_t = 0 \quad \text{and} \quad \lim_{t \to \infty} [K_{t+1}/F_{D_t}] = 0. \tag{4.6}$$

Note that by using (4.5) repeatedly we have

$$[u'\,(c_0)\,F_{D_0}]\,/\,F_{D_t} = \delta^t\,u'\,(c_t). \tag{4.7}$$

Using (4.6) and (4.7), we obtain (4.4). $\parallel$

Remarks: In Theorem 4.1, (4.1) is the well-known "Ramsey-rule" for optimal investment in the capital good. Similarly, (4.2) is the "Meade rule" for an optimum population [see *Meade*, p. 91; or *Dasgupta*, 1969, p. 299]. The marginal condition given by (4.3) is the "Hotelling rule" for optimal depletion of an exhaustible resource [see, for example, *Dasgupta/Heal*, p. 11]. Finally, (4.4) is the transversality condition that the present value of the capital and resource stocks converges to zero as t becomes indefinitely large. It should be noted that (4.1), (4.2), (4.3) are to be expected, as the relevant variables (capital, population and exhaustible resource use) are "freely" and independently controllable. The interesting difference, caused by the presence of exhaustible resources, is in (4.4). In the parallel exercise of optimum population without exhaustible resources, *Dasgupta* [1969, p. 298] notes that (4.1), (4.2) and (4.4) a) are sufficient conditions of optimality. Furthermore, these conditions are necessary when $0 < \delta < 1$. However, if $\delta = 1$ [the discount rate is zero] then (4.4) a) is generally not necessary. In the present exercise, irrespective of the value of δ, (4.4) is a necessary condition of optimality of a positive program.

Theorem 4.2: Under (A.1)–(A.9), *if a regular interior program* $\langle K, D, L, Y, C \rangle$ *satisfies* (4.1)–(4.4), *then there is a price sequence* $\langle p, q, \omega \rangle$, *with* $(p_{t-1}, q_t, \omega_t) \geqslant 0$ *for* $t \geqslant 0$, *such that*

$$\delta^t W (C_t, L_t) - p_t C_t + \omega_t L_t \geqslant \delta^t W (C, L) - p^t C + \omega_t L$$
$$\text{for } (C, L) \geqslant 0, t \geqslant 0 \tag{4.8}$$

$$p_t Y_t - p_{t-1} K_t - q_t D_t - \omega_t L_t \geqslant p_t Y - p_{t-1} K - q_t D - \omega_t L$$
$$\text{for } (K, D, L) \geqslant 0, Y = F (K, D, L), t \geqslant 0 \tag{4.9}$$

$$q_t = q_{t+1} \qquad \text{for } t \geqslant 0 \tag{4.10}$$

$$\lim_{t \to \infty} [p_{t-1} K_t + q_t M_t] = 0. \tag{4.11}$$

Proof: Define (p_{t-1}, q_t, ω_t) as follows:

$$p_t = \delta^t u' (c_t), \quad q_t = u' (c_0) F_{D_0}, \quad \omega_t = p_t F_{L_t} \qquad \text{for } t \geqslant 0 \tag{4.12}$$
$$p_{-1} = p_0 / F_{K_0}.$$

For $L > 0, C \geqslant 0, W (C, L)$ is a concave differentiable function of (C, L). Also, $(\partial W / \partial C) = u' (c)$ and $(\partial W / \partial L) = u (c) - cu' (c)$. So, for $C \geqslant 0, L > 0$, we have

$$\delta^t W (C, L) - \delta^t W (C_t, L_t) \leqslant \delta^t u' (c_t) (C - C_t) + \delta^t [u (c_t) - c_t u' (c_t)] (L - L_t)$$

$$= \delta^t u' (c_t) (C - C_t) - \delta^t u' (c_t) F_{L_t} (L - L_t)$$

$$\text{[using (4.2)]}$$

$$= p_t (C - C_t) - \omega_t (L - L_t)$$

$$\text{[using (4.11)]}.$$

Rearranging terms yields (4.8), for $C \geqslant 0, L > 0$. Note that $\delta^t W (C_t, L_t) = \delta^t u' (c_t) C_t + \delta^t [u (c_t) - c_t u' (c_t)] L_t$ since $W (C, L)$ is homogeneous of degree one for $C \geqslant 0, L > 0$. Hence, $\delta^t W (C_t, L_t) - p_t C_t + \omega_t L_t = 0$. Thus, if $C \geqslant 0$, and $L = 0$, (4.8) is true trivially, since $W (C, L) = 0$. Thus, for $C \geqslant 0, L \geqslant 0$, (4.8) is established.

For $(K, D, L) \geqslant 0$, we have

$$F (K, D, L) - F (K_t, D_t L_t) \leqslant F_{K_t} (K - K_t) + F_{D_t} (D - D_t) + F_{L_t} (L - L_t).$$

Multiplying through by p_t, and using (4.1), (4.3), (4.12),

$$p_t F(K, D, L) - p_t F(K_t, D_t, L_t) \leq p_{t-1}(K - K_t) + q_t(D - D_t) + \omega_t(L - L_t).$$

Rearranging terms gives us (4.9) for $(K, D, L) \geq 0$, $Y = F(K, D, L)$. Note that since F is homogeneous of degree one, so $F(K_t, D_t, L_t) = F_{K_t} K_t + F_{D_t} D_t + F_{L_t} L_t$. Hence $p_t F(K_t, D_t, L_t) = p_{t-1} K_t + q_t D_t + \omega_t L_t$. Thus, if $(K, D, L) \geq 0$, and $(K,D,L) >> 0$, then by (A.8), $G(K, D, L) = 0$, and (4.9) is trivially true, since $p_t < p_{t-1}$ by (4.1). Thus, for $(K, D, L) \geq 0$, $Y = F(K, D, L)$, (4.9) is established.

Finally, using (4.4), and noting from (4.12), that q_t is constant over time, (4.10), (4.11) follow. ‖

Remark: Theorem 4.2 provides a competitive price characterisation of an optimal program.

Theorem 4.3: *Under* (A.1)–(A.9), *if a feasible program* $\langle K, D, L, Y, C \rangle$ *has associated with it a price sequence* $\langle p, q, \omega \rangle$, *with* $(p_{t-1}, q_t, \omega_t) \geq 0$ *for* $t \geq 0$, *satisfying* (4.8), (4.9), (4.10), (4.11), *then* $\langle K, D, L, Y, C \rangle$ *is optimal.*

Proof: Let $\langle K', D', L', Y', C' \rangle$ be a feasible program. Using (4.8), we write for $t \geq 0$

$$\delta^t W(C'_t, L'_t) - \delta^t W(C_t, L_t) \leq p_t(C'_t - C_t) + \omega_t(L_t - L'_t)$$

$$= p_t Y'_t - p_t K'_{t+1} - \omega_t L'_t - p_t Y_t + p_t K_{t+1} + \omega_t L_t$$

$$= [p_{t-1} K'_t + q_t D'_t + \omega_t L'_t - p_{t-1} K_t - q_t D_t - \omega_t L_t] +$$

$$+ [p_t Y'_t - p_{t-1} K'_t - q_t D'_t - \omega_t L'_t] - [p_t Y_t - p_{t-1} K_t - q_t D_t - \omega_t L_t]$$

$$- p_t K'_{t+1} - \omega_t L'_t + p_t K_{t+1} + \omega_t L_t$$

$$\leq [p_{t-1} K'_t + q_t D'_t + \omega_t L'_t - p_{t-1} K_t - q_t D_t - \omega_t L_t]$$

$$- [p_t K'_{t+1} + \omega_t L'_t - p_t K_{t+1} - \omega_t L_t] \qquad \{\text{by (4.9)}\}$$

$$= p_{t-1}(K'_t - K_t) - p_t(K'_{t+1} - K_{t+1}) + q_t(D'_t - D_t).$$

Hence, $\sum_{t=0}^{T} \delta^t [W(C'_t, L'_t) - W(C_t, L_t)] \leq p_T[K_{T+1} - K'_{T+1}] + q_0 [\sum_{t=0}^{T} D'_t - \sum_{t=0}^{T} D_t]$

by using (4.10). Note that $\sum_{t=0}^{T} D'_t = \underset{\sim}{M} - M'_{T+1}$, and $\sum_{t=0}^{T} D_t = \underset{\sim}{M} - M_{T+1}$, so we have

$$\sum_{t=0}^{T} \delta^t [W(C'_t, L'_t) - W(C_t, L_t)] \leq p_T K_{T+1} + q_0 M_{T+1} = p_T K_{T+1} + q_{T+1} M_{T+1}$$

$\{\text{using (4.10)}\}$. Hence, using (4.11), $\langle K, D, L, Y, C \rangle$ is optimal. ‖

5. The Nonexistence of Optimal Programs when Future Welfares are Undiscounted

In this section, we examine the question of existence of an optimal program when future welfares are not discounted. We show that, under one of two alternative additional assumptions, there does not exist an optimal program. One assumption is that there is a feasible program with constant population, which can produce a (current) output sequence bounded away from zero. The other is that the share of capital in current output is bounded away from zero.

Neither of these assumptions is terribly unrealistic. In fact, if these assumptions are *not* satisfied, the model becomes somewhat uninteresting. Specifically, if the first assumption is not satisfied, there does not seem to be too much point in sticking to an infinite-horizon model. If the second assumption is violated, the role of capital accumulation in off setting the exhaustible resource factor is not captured properly, as capital is treated as "unimportant" in production. But the consequence of *either* of these assumptions is that there does not exist an optimal program, which is somewhat disturbing, if one adopts the "mathematical screening" viewpoint of Koopmans.

We note, however, that the result is not totally unexpected, since in exercises on optimum population without exhaustible resources, a similar difficulty is encountered by *Dasgupta* [1969].

Lemma 5.1: Under (A.1)–(A.9), and $\delta = 1$, if $\langle K, D, L, Y, C \rangle$ is an optimal program, then

$$\sum_{t=0}^{T} W(C_t, L_t) \text{ is convergent.} \tag{5.1}$$

Proof: If $L_t = 0$ for some $t = T$, then $L_t = 0$ for $t \geqslant T$, and $W(C_t, L_t) = 0$ for $t \geqslant T$. In this case (5.1) is trivial.

Otherwise $L_t > 0$ for $t \geqslant 0$. In this case $\langle K, D, L, Y, C \rangle$ is a positive program which is optimal. Hence, by Theorems 4.1, 4.2, there is a price sequence $\langle p, q, \omega \rangle$, with $(p_t, q_t, \omega_t) \geqslant 0$ for $t \geqslant 0$, such that (4.8)–(4.11) hold. Using the homogeneity of degree one, of W and F, we then have

$$W(C_t, L_t) = p_t C_t - \omega_t L_t = p_t Y_t - p_t K_{t+1} - \omega_t L_t$$

$$= [p_t Y_t - p_{t-1} K_t - \omega_t L_t - q_t D_t] + [p_{t-1} K_t - p_t K_{t+1}] + q_t D_t$$

$$= [p_{t-1} K_t - p_t K_{t+1}] + q_t D_t = [p_{t-1} K_t - p_t K_{t+1}] + q_0 D_t.$$

So

$$\sum_{t=0}^{T} W(C_t, L_t) = [p_{-1} K_0 - p_T K_{T+1}] + q_0 \sum_{t=0}^{T} D_t$$

$$= [p_{-1} K_0 - p_T K_{T+1}] + q_{T+1} [\underset{\sim}{M} - M_{T+1}].$$

The right-hand side converges by (4.11), as $T \to \infty$, so the left-hand side converges too. In fact, $\sum_{t=0}^{\infty} W(C_t, L_t) = p_{-1} \underset{\sim}{K} + q_0 \underset{\sim}{M}$. This establishes (5.1).   ‖

Now we consider the following additional assumption:

(A.10) *There is a feasible program $\langle \bar{K}, \bar{D}, \bar{L}, \bar{Y}, \bar{C} \rangle$ with $\bar{L}_t = \underset{\sim}{L}$ for $t \geqslant 0$, and*
$$\inf_{t \geqslant 0} G(\bar{K}_t, \bar{D}_t, \bar{L}_t) > 0.$$

For necessary and sufficient conditions on G, such that (A.10) is satisfied, see *Cass/Mitra* [1979].

Theorem 5.1: *Under (A.1)–(A.10), and* $\delta = 1$, *there does not exist an optimal program.*

Proof: Let $\inf_{t \geqslant 0} G(K_t, D_t, L_t) \equiv d > 0$. Clearly, $\langle \bar{K}, \bar{D}, \bar{L}, \bar{Y}, \bar{C} \rangle$ is an interior program.

Define $u((\underset{\sim}{c} + \tilde{c})/2) = e$. Then $e > 0$. Let J be a positive integer such that $[J\beta d / \underset{\sim}{L}] \geqslant$ $\geqslant [\underset{\sim}{c} + \tilde{c}]$. Choose $0 < \lambda < 1$, such that $(1/\lambda) \geqslant 2^J$.

Define a sequence $\langle K, D, L, Y, C \rangle$ as follows: $(K_0, L_0, D_0, Y_0) = (\bar{K}_0, \bar{L}_0, \bar{D}_0, \bar{Y}_0)$; $K_t = \lambda \bar{K}_t, D_t = \bar{D}_t, L_t = \lambda \bar{L}_t = \lambda \underset{\sim}{L}$ for $t \geqslant 1$, $Y_t = F(K_t, D_t, L_t)$ for $t \geqslant 1$; $C_t = Y_t - K_{t+1}$ for $t \geqslant 0$. Clearly, $C_0 > \bar{C}_0 \geqslant 0$. We will show that $C_t > 0$ for $t \geqslant 1$, so $\langle K, D, L, Y, C \rangle$ is a feasible program. We check this fact with the following calculations.
For $t \geqslant 1, G(K_t, D_t, L_t) = G(\lambda \bar{K}_t, \bar{D}_t, \lambda \bar{L}_t) = \lambda G[\bar{K}_t, (\bar{D}_t/\lambda), \bar{L}_t] \geqslant$

$$\geqslant \lambda G(\bar{K}_t, 2^J \bar{D}_t, \bar{L}_t) = \lambda \sum_{j=1}^{J} [G(\bar{K}_t, 2^j \bar{D}_t, \bar{L}_t) - G(\bar{K}_t, 2^{j-1} \bar{D}_t, \bar{L}_t)] + \lambda G(\bar{K}_t, \bar{D}_t, \bar{L}_t).$$

Now for $J \geqslant j \geqslant 1$, we have $G(\bar{K}_t, 2^j \bar{D}_t, \bar{L}_t) - G(\bar{K}_t, 2^{j-1} \bar{D}_t, \bar{L}_t) \geqslant$ $(1/2) G_D [\bar{K}_t, 2^j \bar{D}_t, \bar{L}_t] 2^j \bar{D}_t \geqslant (1/2) \beta G[\bar{K}_t, 2^j \bar{D}_t, \bar{L}_t] \geqslant (1/2) \beta d$. Hence, for $t \geqslant 1$, $G(\bar{K}_t, 2^j \bar{D}_t, \bar{L}_t) - G(\bar{K}_t, \bar{D}_t, \bar{L}_t) \geqslant (1/2) J \beta d$. Thus, for $t \geqslant 1$, we have

$$C_t = G(K_t, D_t, L_t) + K_t - K_{t+1}$$

$$= \lambda G(\bar{K}_t, (\bar{D}_t/\lambda), \bar{L}_t) + \lambda \bar{K}_t - \lambda \bar{K}_{t+1}$$

$$\geqslant \lambda G(\bar{K}_t, \bar{D}_t, \bar{L}_t) + (1/2) \lambda J \beta d + \lambda \bar{K}_t - \lambda \bar{K}_{t+1}$$

$$= \lambda \bar{C}_t + (1/2) \lambda J \beta d > 0.$$

Since, for $t \geqslant 1, C_t \geqslant (1/2) \lambda J \beta d$, so $c_t \geqslant [J\beta d / 2\underset{\sim}{L}]$, and $u(c_t) \geqslant e$ for $t \geqslant 1$. So $L_t u(c_t) \geqslant \lambda \underset{\sim}{L} e$ for $t \geqslant 1$. Thus, as $T \to \infty$, $\sum_{t=0}^{T} W(C_t, L_t) \to \infty$.

If there is an optimal program, $\langle K^*, D^*, L^*, Y^*, C^* \rangle$, then by Lemma 5.1, $\sum_{t=0}^{\infty} W(C_t^*, L_t^*)$ is convergent. But since $\langle K, D, L, Y, C \rangle$ is a feasible program with $\sum_{t=0}^{T} W(C_t, L_t) \to \infty$ as $T \to \infty$, so $\langle K, D, L, Y, C \rangle$ could not be optimal. $\|$

We now consider an alternative additional assumption:

(A.11) $\alpha \equiv \inf_{(K,D,L) \geqslant 0} [K G_K(K, D, L)/G(K, D, L)] > 0$.

(A.11) states that the share of capital in current output is bounded away from zero. [By (A.9), $\alpha < 1$].

Theorem 5.2: *Under (A.1)–(A.9), (A.11), and* $\delta = 1$, *there does not exist an optimal program.*

Proof: Define $g(K) = G(K, 1, 1)$ for $K \geqslant 1$. Then $g'(K) = G_K(K, 1, 1)$, and $[Kg'(K)/g(K)] = [K G_K(K, 1, 1)/G(K, 1, 1)] \geqslant \alpha$. So $[g'(K)/g(K)] \geqslant [\alpha/K]$, and

$(d/dK) [\log g (K)] \geqslant (d/dK) [\log K^{\alpha}]$. For $x \geqslant 1$, we have $\int_1^x (d/dK) [\log g (K)] dK \geqslant$
$\int_1^x (d/dK) [\log K^{\alpha}] dK$. So $\log g (x) - \log g (1) \geqslant \log x^{\alpha} - \log 1^{\alpha} = \log x^{\alpha}$, and
$\log g (x) \geqslant \log [g (1) x^{\alpha}]$. Then $g (x) \geqslant g (1) x^{\alpha}$ for $x \geqslant 1$, and $G (K, 1, 1) \geqslant g (1) K^{\alpha}$ for
$K \geqslant 1$. Define $\lambda = 1 + [\alpha/2 (1 - \alpha)]$. Choose $0 < \theta < 1$, such that

$$\sum_{t=1}^{\infty} [\theta \underset{\sim}{K}/t^{\lambda}] \leqslant \frac{1}{2} \underset{\sim}{M}.$$

Define a sequence $\langle K, D, L, Y, C \rangle$ as follows: $K_t = \underset{\sim}{K}$ for $t \geqslant 0; D_0 = (1/2) \underset{\sim}{M}$,
$D_t = [\theta \underset{\sim}{K}/t^{\lambda}]$ for $t \geqslant 1; L_0 = \underset{\sim}{L}, L_t = [\theta \underset{\sim}{K}/t]$ for $t \geqslant 1; C_t = G (K_t, D_t, L_t)$ for $t \geqslant 0$;
$Y_t = F (K_t, D_t, L_t)$ for $t \geqslant 0$. Clearly, $\langle K, D, L, Y, C \rangle$ is a feasible program.

Now, for $t \geqslant 1$, we have $C_t = G (K, [\theta \underset{\sim}{K}/t^{\lambda}], [\theta \underset{\sim}{K}/t]) \geqslant G (\theta \underset{\sim}{K}, [\theta \underset{\sim}{K}/t^{\lambda}], [\theta \underset{\sim}{K}/t])$
$= \theta \underset{\sim}{K} G (1, [1/t^{\lambda}], [1/t]) = [\theta \underset{\sim}{K}/t^{\lambda}] G (t^{\lambda}, 1, t^{\lambda-1}) \geqslant [\theta \underset{\sim}{K}/t^{\lambda}] G (t^{\lambda}, 1, 1) \geqslant [\theta \underset{\sim}{K}/t^{\lambda}]$
$t^{\alpha\lambda} g (1) = g (1) \theta \underset{\sim}{K} t^{(\alpha\lambda-\lambda)}$. Hence $c_t \geqslant [g (1) \theta \underset{\sim}{K} t^{[(\alpha-1)\lambda+1]}/\theta \underset{\sim}{K}] = g (1) t^{[1+(\alpha-1)\lambda]}$.
By definition of λ, $1 + (\alpha - 1) \lambda = (\alpha/2)$. So, $c_t \geqslant g (1) t^{(\alpha/2)}$ for $t \geqslant 1$. So there is
$T_1 < \infty$, such that for $t \geqslant T_1$, $c_t \geqslant (\underset{\sim}{c} + \tilde{c})/2$. Hence for $t \geqslant T_1 u (c_t) \geqslant$
$\geqslant u ((\underset{\sim}{c} + \tilde{c})/2) = e$, say [clearly, $e > 0$]. And so, for $t \geqslant T_1$, $W (C_t, L_t) \geqslant [\theta \underset{\sim}{K} e/t]$. Hence
$\sum_{t=0}^{T} W (C_t, L_t) \to \infty$ as $T \to \infty$. If there is an optimal program $\langle K^*, D^*, L^*, Y^*, C^* \rangle$ then
$\sum_{t=0}^{\infty} W (C_t^*, L_t^*)$ is convergent, by Lemma 5.1. Since $\langle K, D, L, Y, C \rangle$ is a feasible program,
and $\sum_{t=0}^{T} W (C_t, L_t) \to \infty$ as $T \to \infty$, so $\langle K^*, D^*, L^*, Y^*, C^* \rangle$ cannot be optimal. $\quad \|$

Remark: If $G (K, D, L) = K^{\alpha} D^{\beta} L^{\gamma}$, with $(\alpha, \beta, \gamma) \geqslant 0$, $\alpha + \beta + \gamma = 1$, then (A.10) is
satisfied if and only if $\alpha > \beta$. Thus, in the Cobb-Douglas case, (A.10) implies (A.11).

6. The Existence of an Optimal Program when Future Welfares are Discounted

The main result of this section is that, when future welfares are discounted, an optimal
program exists.

Readers familiar with the literature on optimum population will recognize that the
traditional methods of proving the existence of an optimal program break down, when

population is "freely" controllable.[3]) Specifically, given any t, and $M(t) < \infty$, one can find a feasible program with $L_t > M(t)$. Thus, the essential "boundedness" property of the relevant variables, which is exploited heavily in traditional methods [see, for example, *Gale; Brock; Brock/Gale* and others] to arrive at an optimal program as a limit of a convergent (sub)sequence of feasible programs, is not available.

Dasgupta [1969] solves the problem by constructing a particular stationary program (stationary in per-capita magnitudes), and checking that it satisfies the sufficient conditions of optimality of the sort discussed in Section 4. This is in the context of a model without exhaustible resources. When such resources are present, even this clever device is lost, as programs stationary in per-capita magnitudes do not satisfy the appropriate "marginal conditions" of Section 4. [Note that if K_t, D_t, L_t are all growing or decreasing at the same rate, then the marginal products of all three factors must be constant over time; but the "Hotelling Rule" (4.3) demands that the marginal product of the resource be increasing.]

Our method retains the spirit of the traditional (Ramsey) device, though in execution it appears different. We separate feasible programs into two categories: "good" and "bad". "Good" programs are those for which population does not grow "too fast" [in a manner made precise in the definitions below]; "bad" programs are feasible programs which are not "good".

We show that if a feasible program is bad, there is a good program which is "better". There *is* a good program; and, in the class of good programs, there is a "best" program. This is then shown to be an optimal program.

In order to simplify our existence proof (which is still quite elaborate), we assume in this section that the production function is Cobb-Douglas:

(A.12) $G(K, D, L) = K^\alpha D^\beta L^\gamma$, where $(\alpha, \beta, \gamma) \geqslant 0$, and $(\alpha + \beta + \gamma) = 1$.

We assume throughout, of course, that $0 < \delta < 1$. Given (A.12), we denote the expression $[(\underset{\sim}{K}^{1-\alpha}/\underset{\sim}{L}^\gamma) + \underset{\sim}{M}^\beta]^{1/1-\alpha}$ by E. Given any feasible program $\langle K, D, L, Y, C \rangle$ we denote

$$A_t = \sum_{s=0}^{t} L_s^{(\gamma/1-\beta)} \qquad \text{for } t \geqslant 0.$$

---

[3]) We have assumed throughout this paper that population can be controlled arbitrarily that is no bounds are imposed on the rate of growth of population per period. If there are such bounds then the existence question in Section 6 becames easier to handle using standard methods since definite bounds are available on the variable L_t in each period. One would suspect that in this case optimal paths would exist where these constraints are binding in some periods (see the literature on population growth without exhaustible resources where population is arbitrarily variable and where there are constraints on its rate of growth, *Dasgupta* [1969] and *Lane* [1977].

If population control is assumed costly in terms of resources or consumption then it introduces additional elements in the problem which forms a subject of enquiry beyond the scope of the present paper. Since in the case where population is costlessly controlled, along an optimal path in the discounted case, $L_t = 0$ after finite time, it is tempting to conjecture that a similar behaviour would occur when population control is costly with the decline in population taking place at a slower pace possibly happening only in the limit over an infinite horizon. The analysis of the case where population control is costly and is constrained within limits may be an interesting subject of future enquiry.

Lemma 6.1: Under (A.12), if $\langle K, D, L, Y, C \rangle$ is a feasible program, then

$$K_{t+1} \leqslant E A_t^{(1-\beta)/(1-\alpha)} \qquad \text{for } t \geqslant 0 \tag{6.1}$$

$$C_t \leqslant E A_t^{(1-\beta)/(1-\alpha)} \qquad \text{for } t \geqslant 0. \tag{6.2}$$

Proof: Consider the feasible program $\langle \bar{K}, \bar{D}, \bar{L}, \bar{Y}, \bar{C} \rangle$ given by $\bar{K}_0 = \underset{\sim}{K}, \bar{D}_t = D_t, \bar{L}_t = L_t$ for $t \geqslant 0; \bar{K}_{t+1} = \bar{Y}_t = F(\bar{K}_t, \bar{D}_t, \bar{L}_t)$ for $t \geqslant 0$, and $\bar{C}_t = 0$ for $t \geqslant 0$. Then $\bar{K}_{t+1} \geqslant K_t$ for $t \geqslant 0$.

Now, for $t \geqslant 0$, we have $\bar{K}_{t+1} - \bar{K}_t = \bar{K}_t^\alpha \bar{D}_t^\beta \bar{L}_t^\gamma$, so that $\bar{K}_{t+1}^{1-\alpha} - \bar{K}_t^{1-\alpha} \leqslant \bar{D}_t^\beta \bar{L}_t^\gamma = \bar{D}_t^\beta [\bar{L}_t^{\gamma/(1-\beta)}]^{1-\beta}$. Using Holder's inequality, we have for $T \geqslant 0$,

$$\bar{K}_{T+1}^{1-\alpha} - \bar{K}_0^{1-\alpha} \leqslant [\sum_{t=0}^{T} \bar{D}_t]^\beta [\sum_{t=0}^{T} \bar{L}_t^{\gamma/(1-\beta)}]^{1-\beta} \leqslant \underset{\sim}{M}^\beta \bar{A}_T^{1-\beta}$$

or,

$$\bar{K}_{T+1}^{1-\alpha} \leqslant \bar{K}_0^{1-\alpha} + \underset{\sim}{M}^\beta \bar{A}_T^{1-\beta} \leqslant E^{(1-\alpha)} \bar{A}_T^{(1-\beta)}.$$

So $\bar{K}_{t+1} \leqslant E \bar{A}_t^{((1-\beta)/(1-\alpha))}$ for $t \geqslant 0$. Since $K_{t+1} \leqslant \bar{K}_{t+1}$ for $t \geqslant 0$, so (6.1) follows. Also $C_t \leqslant Y_t \leqslant \bar{Y}_t = \bar{K}_{t+1}$ for $t \geqslant 0$, so (6.2) follows. ‖

Before proceeding further we introduce some notation. Denote $\beta/(1 - \alpha)$ by μ; $(1 - \beta)/(1 - \alpha)$ by η; $(1 - \alpha)/\beta$ by ν. Since we are dealing with the discounted case, we are given $0 < \delta < 1$. Choose $\lambda > 1$, so that $\theta \equiv \lambda^\nu \delta < 1$. [Then $\lambda\delta < 1$ also.] Note that $a \equiv \sum_{t=0}^{\infty} ((t + 1)^\eta/\lambda^t)$ is convergent. Denote $[2aE/\underset{\sim}{c}]$ by h, and $[h^\nu b/(1 - \delta)]$ by $\hat{A}$ [where b is given by (A.6)]. Note that $\hat{B} \equiv \sum_{t=0}^{\infty} [\lambda^\nu \delta]^t$ is convergent. Denote λ^ν by π; $\hat{D} = [\underset{\sim}{c} u'(\underset{\sim}{c})/2]$. Define $Q = \max [\{2\hat{A}/(1 - \theta)\hat{D}\}, 2h^\nu, \underset{\sim}{L}]$.

For any feasible program $\langle K, D, L, Y, C \rangle$, we define a sequence $t(n)$ as follows. Let $t(0) = 0$; for $n \geqslant 0$; define $\Omega(n + 1) = \{t \geqslant t(n) : L_t > L_{t(n)}\}$, and if $\Omega(n + 1)$ is non-empty, $t(n + 1) = \min \Omega(n + 1)$. If the set $\Omega(n + 1)$ is empty for some $n = \bar{n}$, $t(\bar{n} + 1) = \infty$, and $t(n)$ is undefined for $n > \bar{n} + 1$.

Lemma 6.2: Under (A.3)–(A.6), (A.12), if $\langle K, D, L, Y, C \rangle$ is a feasible program and $n \geqslant 0$, such that $t(n)$ and $t(n + 1)$ are defined, then for $t(n) \leqslant S \leqslant t(n + 1) - 1$,

(i) $L_{t(n)}^\mu \leqslant h\lambda^{t(n)}$ implies $\sum_{t=t(n)}^{S} \delta^t W(C_t, L_t) \leqslant \hat{A} \theta^{t(n)}$

(ii) $L_{t(n)}^\mu > h\lambda^{t(n)}$ implies $\sum_{t=t(n)}^{S} \delta^t W(C_t, L_t) \leqslant -\hat{D} \delta^{t(n)} L_{t(n)}.$

Proof: To prove (i), note that for $t(n) \leqslant t \leqslant t(n + 1) - 1, \delta^t L_t \leqslant \delta^{[t-t(n)]} \delta^{t(n)} L_{t(n)} \leqslant h^\nu [\delta\lambda^\nu]^{t(n)} \delta^{[t-t(n)]}$. Hence, for $t(n) \leqslant S \leqslant t(n + 1) - 1$, we have

$$\sum_{t=t(n)}^{S} \delta^t W(C_t, L_t) \leqslant h^\nu [\delta\lambda^\nu]^{t(n)} b \sum_{t=t(n)}^{S} \delta^{[t-t(n)]} \leqslant \theta^{t(n)} h^\nu b/(1 - \delta) = \hat{A} \theta^{t(n)}.$$

To prove (ii), we write for $t(n) \leqslant t \leqslant t(n+1) - 1$, $\delta^t L_t u(c_t) = \delta^t L_t [u(c_t) - u(\underset{\sim}{c})]$. So $\delta^t L_t u(c_t) \leqslant \delta^t L_t u'(\underset{\sim}{c})(c_t - \underset{\sim}{c}) = \delta^t u'(\underset{\sim}{c})[C_t - \underset{\sim}{c} L_t]$. Then for $t(n) \leqslant S \leqslant t(n+1) - 1$, we have

$$\sum_{t=t(n)}^{S} \delta^t L_t u(c_t) \leqslant u'(\underset{\sim}{c}) \sum_{t=t(n)}^{S} \delta^t C_t - \underset{\sim}{c} u'(\underset{\sim}{c}) \sum_{t=t(n)}^{S} \delta^t L_t. \tag{6.3}$$

Now, for $t(n) \leqslant t \leqslant t(n+1) - 1$, we have by Lemma 6.1, $\delta^t C_t \leqslant \delta E A_t^{\eta} = \delta^t E [\sum_{i=0}^{t} L_i^{(\gamma/1-\beta)}]^{\eta} \leqslant \delta^t E [\sum_{i=0}^{t} L_{t(n)}^{(\gamma/1-\beta)}]^{\eta} = \delta^t E (t+1)^{\eta} L_{t(n)}^{(\gamma/1-\alpha)}$. Thus, for $t(n) \leqslant S \leqslant t(n+1) - 1$, we have

$$\sum_{t=t(n)}^{S} \delta^t C_t \leqslant E L_{t(n)}^{(\gamma/1-\alpha)} \sum_{t=t(n)}^{S} \delta^t (t+1)^{\eta} \leqslant E L_{t(n)}^{(\gamma/1-\alpha)} (\delta\lambda)^{t(n)} a.$$

Using this information in (6.3), we have

$$\sum_{t=t(n)}^{S} \delta^t L_t u(c_t) \leqslant u'(\underset{\sim}{c}) a E L_{t(n)}^{(\gamma/1-\alpha)} (\delta\lambda)^{t(n)} - \underset{\sim}{c} u'(\underset{\sim}{c}) \delta^{t(n)} L_{t(n)}$$

$$= u'(\underset{\sim}{c}) \left[a E L_{t(n)}^{(\gamma/1-\alpha)} (\delta\lambda)^{t(n)} - \frac{1}{2} \underset{\sim}{c} \delta^{t(n)} L_{t(n)} \right] - \hat{D} \delta^{t(n)} L_{t(n)}$$

$$\leqslant -\hat{D} \delta^{t(n)} L_{t(n)}. \qquad \|$$

We call a feasible program $\langle K, D, L, Y, C \rangle$ *good* if $L_t \leqslant Q \pi^t$ for $t \geqslant 0$; we call it *bad* if it is not good.

Lemma 6.3: Under (A.3)–(A.6), (A.12), if a feasible program $\langle K, D, L, Y, C \rangle$ is bad, then there is a feasible program $\langle K', D', L', Y', C' \rangle$ which is good, such that

$$\lim_{T \to \infty} \sup \sum_{t=0}^{T} [\delta^t W(C_t, L_t) - \delta^t W(C_t', L_t')] \leqslant 0. \tag{6.4}$$

Proof: Since $\langle K, D, L, Y, C \rangle$ is bad, there is some t for which $L_t > Q\pi^t$. Let N be the first period this happens. Then, $N > 1$, and $L_{N-1} \leqslant Q\pi^{N-1} < Q\pi^N < L_N$. So, there is $n > 0$ such that $t(n) = N$. There are now two cases to consider: (i) $t(n+1) = \infty$, (ii) $t(n+1) < \infty$.

In case (i), by Lemma 6.2, $\sum_{t=t(n)}^{S} \delta^t W(C_t, L_t) < 0$ for all $S \geqslant t(n)$. Define a sequence $\langle K', D', L', Y', C' \rangle$ as follows: $(K_t', D_t', L_t', Y_t', C_t') = (K_t, D_t, L_t, Y_t, C_t)$ for $t < t(n)$, $(K_t', D_t', L_t', Y_t', C_t') = 0$ for $t \geqslant t(n)$. Then $\langle K', D', L', Y', C' \rangle$ is a feasible program which is good. Also since $\delta^t W(C_t', L_t') = 0$ for $t \geqslant t(n)$, so (6.4) is satisfied.

In case (ii), by Lemma 6.2, $\sum_{t=t(n)}^{t(n+1)-1} \delta^t W(C_t, L_t) \leqslant -\hat{D} \delta^{t(n)} Q \pi^{t(n)} \leqslant -2\hat{A}\theta^{t(n)}/(1-\theta)$. Now, for $S \geqslant t(n+1)$, we have by Lemma 6.2, $\sum_{t=t(n+1)}^{S} \delta^t W(C_t, L_t)$

$$\leqslant \sum_{i=n+1}^{\infty} \hat{A}\,\theta^{t(i)} \leqslant \hat{A}\,\theta^{t(n+1)}/(1-\theta).$$ So, for $S \geqslant t\,(n)$, we have $\sum_{t=t(n)}^{S} \delta^{t} W\,(C_{t}, L_{t})$

$\leqslant -\hat{A}\,\theta^{t(n)}/(1-\theta)$. Define a sequence $\langle K', D', L', Y', C' \rangle$ as follows:
$(K'_{t}, D'_{t}, L'_{t}, Y'_{t}, C'_{t}) = (K_{t}, D_{t}, L_{t}, Y_{t}, C_{t})$ for $t < t\,(n)$, and $(K'_{t}, D'_{t}, L'_{t}, Y'_{t}, C'_{t}) = 0$ for $t \geqslant t\,(n)$. Clearly $\langle K', D', L', Y', C' \rangle$ is a feasible program which is good. Also, since $\delta^{t} W\,(C'_{t}, L'_{t}) = 0$ for $t \geqslant t\,(n)$, so (6.4) is satisfied.   ‖

Lemma 6.4: Under (A.3)–(A.6), (A.12), *there is a good program.*

Proof: Define a sequence $\langle K, D, L, Y, C \rangle$ as follows: $K_{t} = \underset{\sim}{K}$, $L_{t} = \underset{\sim}{L}$, $D_{t} = \underset{\sim}{M}/2^{t+1}$, $Y_{t} = F\,(K_{t}, D_{t}, L_{t})$, $C_{t} = G\,(K_{t}, D_{t}, L_{t})$ for $t \geqslant 0$. Then $\langle K, D, L, Y, C \rangle$ is a feasible program which is good.   ‖

Lemma 6.5: Under (A.3)–(A.6), (A.12), *there is a good program* $\langle K^{*}, D^{*}, L^{*}, Y^{*}, C^{*} \rangle$ *such that*

$$\limsup_{T \to \infty} \sum_{t=0}^{T} \delta^{t}\,[W\,(C_{t}, L_{t}) - W\,(C^{*}_{t}, L^{*}_{t})] \leqslant 0 \tag{6.5}$$

for every good program $\langle K, D, L, Y, C \rangle$.

Proof: For any good program $\langle K, D, L, Y, C \rangle$, $\sum_{t=0}^{T} \delta^{t} \mid W\,(C_{t}, L_{t}) \mid \leqslant \sum_{t=0}^{T} (\delta\pi)^{t}\,Qb$

$\leqslant [Qb/(1-\delta\pi)] \equiv H$. Hence $\sum_{t=0}^{\infty} \delta^{t} W\,(C_{t}, L_{t})$ is absolutely convergent, so $\sum_{t=0}^{\infty} \delta^{t} W\,(C_{t}, L_{t})$

is convergent, with $\sum_{t=0}^{\infty} \delta^{t} W\,(C_{t}, L_{t}) \leqslant H$.

Let $\Lambda = [\sum_{t=0}^{\infty} \delta^{t} W\,(C_{t}, L_{t}) : \langle K, D, L, Y, C \rangle$ is a good program]. By Lemma 6.4, Λ is non-empty. Also, each element of Λ must be $\leqslant H$. Define $w = \sup \Lambda$; then $w \leqslant H$.

Clearly, there is a sequence $\langle K^{i}, D^{i}, L^{i}, Y^{i}, C^{i} \rangle$ of good programs, such that $\sum_{t=0}^{\infty} \delta^{t} W\,(C^{i}_{t}, L^{i}_{t}) \geqslant w - (1/i)\,[i = 1, 2, \ldots]$. Define $X_{0} = \underset{\sim}{K}$; $X_{t+1} = G\,(X_{t}, \underset{\sim}{M}, Q\pi^{t}) + X_{t}$ for $t \geqslant 0$. Then, if $\langle K, D, L, Y, C \rangle$ is a good program, $(K_{t}, M_{t}, L_{t}, Y_{t}, C_{t}) \leqslant (X_{t}, \underset{\sim}{M}, Q\pi^{t}, X_{t}, X_{t})$ for $t \geqslant 0$. Hence there is a subsequence j of i, such that for each $t \geqslant 0$, $(K^{j}_{t}, M^{j}_{t}, L^{j}_{t}, Y^{j}_{t}, C^{j}_{t}) \to (K^{*}_{t}, M^{*}_{t}, L^{*}_{t}, Y^{*}_{t}, C^{*}_{t})$ as $j \to \infty$. Defining $D^{*}_{t} = M^{*}_{t} - M^{*}_{t+1}$, it is easy to check that $\langle K^{*}, D^{*}, L^{*}, Y^{*}, C^{*} \rangle$ is a feasible program and it is a good program.

We claim that $\sum_{t=0}^{\infty} \delta^{t} W\,(C^{*}_{t}, L^{*}_{t}) = w$. Otherwise, by definition of w, there is $\epsilon > 0$, such that

$$\sum_{t=0}^{\infty} \delta^{t} W\,(C^{*}_{t}, L^{*}_{t}) \leqslant w - \epsilon.$$

Pick T such that $\sum_{t=T}^{\infty} (\delta\pi)^{t}\,Qb < \epsilon/4$. Pick J large enough so that for $j \geqslant J$,

$$\mid \sum_{t=0}^{T} \delta^t W\,(C_t^j,\,L_t^j) - \sum_{t=0}^{T} \delta^t W\,(C_t^*,\,L_t^*)\mid < \epsilon/4.$$

Then, for $j \geqslant J$, we have

$$w - (1/j) \leqslant \sum_{t=0}^{\infty} \delta^t W\,(C_t^j,\,L_t^j) = \sum_{t=0}^{T} \delta^t W\,(C_t^j,\,L_t^j) + \sum_{t=T}^{\infty} \delta^t W\,(C_t^j,\,L_t^j) \leqslant$$

$$\leqslant \sum_{t=0}^{T} \delta^t W\,(C_t^*,\,L_t^*) + (\epsilon/4) + (\epsilon/4) = \sum_{t=0}^{\infty} \delta^t W\,(C_t^*,\,L_t^*) -$$

$$- \sum_{t=T}^{\infty} \delta^t W\,(C_t^*,\,L_t^*) + (\epsilon/2) \leqslant [w - \epsilon] + (\epsilon/4) + (\epsilon/2) = w - (\epsilon/4).$$

So $(1/j) \geqslant (\epsilon/4)$ for $j \geqslant J$, a contradiction. Hence, our claim is established. Then (6.5) follows by the definition of w.   ‖

Theorem 6.1: Under (A.3)–(A.6), (A.12), *there exists an optimal program.*

Proof: Consider the program $\langle K^*, D^*, L^*, Y^*, C^* \rangle$ whose existence is established in Lemma 6.5. We claim that this is an optimal program.

For, consider any feasible program $\langle K, D, L, Y, C \rangle$. Either this is good or bad. If it is good, then (6.5) holds. If it is bad, then there is a good program $\langle K', D', L', Y', C' \rangle$ such that (6.4) holds. Hence,

$$\lim_{T \to \infty} \sup \sum_{t=0}^{T} \delta^t\,[W\,(C_t,\,L_t) - W\,(C_t^*,\,L_t^*)] \leqslant$$

$$\lim_{T \to \infty} \sup \sum_{t=0}^{T} \delta^t\,[W\,(C_t,\,L_t) - W\,(C_t',\,L_t')] +$$

$$\lim_{T \to \infty} \sup \sum_{t=0}^{T} \delta^t\,[W\,(C_t',\,L_t') - W\,(C_t^*,\,L_t^*)] \leqslant 0$$

by using Lemmas 6.3 and 6.5. Hence, in either case,

$$\lim_{T \to \infty} \sup \sum_{t=0}^{T} \delta^t\,[W\,(C_t,\,L_t) - W\,(C_t^*,\,L_t^*)] \leqslant 0.$$

This establishes our claim.   ‖

7. Optimality and the Extinction of the Economy

We have shown in Section 5, that under quite realistic assumptions, there does not exist an optimal program when future welfares are undiscounted. While this has been a discomforting result, we have noted that a similar feature is observable in optimal population exercises, even in the absence of exhaustible resource constraints. Furthermore, as in the study of optimum population [without exhaustible resources] by *Dasgupta* [1969], we have been able to establish the existence of an optimal program when future welfares are discounted. Thus, at this stage, the model of production and the Classical Utilitarian objective function may be said to have stood the "mathematical screening" of Koopmans, provided we agree to discount future welfares.

In this section we discover, however, that the discounted case has a disturbing aspect to it also. Namely, optimal programs *must be* extinction programs. This means that it is optimal (in the discounted case) to have a zero population from a certain time period onwards. This result is true independent of whether or not there is a feasible program, with positive stationary population, such that the per-capita consumption at each date generates a utility bounded away from zero. If there is such a feasible program and one finds it optimal to become extinct in finite time, then the Classical Utilitarian objective (with discounting) surely places too small a penalty on the extinction of the human race. This could be viewed as an unsatisfactory aspect of the objective. One might argue that the problem arises because we define $W(C, L) = 0$ rather than $W(C, L) = -\infty$ when $L = 0$. But it is very difficult to justify a discountinuity at $L = 0$ in the objective function, when everywhere else, it is continuous. Furthermore, with this discountinuity we might encounter the problem of nonexistence of an optimal program even in the discounted case: notice that if $W(C, L)$ is not continuous everywhere, the existence proof of Section 6 breaks down.

Thus, with the result of this section, we have doubts whether the Classical Utilitarian objective is the appropriate one to use in studying optimum population policies when resources are exhaustible.

Our result should be contrasted with that obtained by *Koopmans* [1974]. An optimal program in the Koopmans exercise is an extinction program, but this is to be expected since there is no aspect of capital accumulation in his model to offset the depletion of resources, and to produce a feasible program, with a utility sequence bounded away from zero. In our model, not only is there the capital accumulation aspect, but capital is smoothly substitutable for the exhaustible resource. Then, with a substitution condition of the type proposed in *Cass/Mitra* [1979], (A.10) will be satisfied. This, in turn, will ensure that there is a feasible program with positive stationary population, and a utility sequence bounded away from zero. However, it will *still* be optimal for the economy to become extinct, according to our result.

We define a feasible program $\langle K, D, L, Y, C \rangle$ to be an *extinction program* if there is an integer $T < \infty$, such that $L_t = 0$ for $t \geq T$.

Theorem 7.1: Under (A.1)–(A.9), (A.11), if $\langle K, D, L, Y, C \rangle$ is an optimal program, then it is an extinction program.

Proof: Suppose on the contrary that $L_t > 0$ for $t \geq 0$. Then $\langle K, D, L, Y, C \rangle$ is a positive program, which is optimal. We will now proceed to prove a number of claims, which lead ultimately to a contradiction.

(i) c_t *cannot converge to zero, as $t \to \infty$*. Otherwise, there exists N_1 such that $c_t < \underset{\sim}{c}$ for $t \geq N_1$. Construct a sequence $\langle K', D', L', Y', C' \rangle$ as follows: $(K'_t, D'_t, L'_t, Y'_t, C'_t) = (K_t, D_t, L_t, Y_t, C_t)$ for $t < N_1$, $(K'_t, D'_t, L'_t, Y'_t, C'_t) = 0$ for $t \geq N_1$. Clearly $\langle K', D', L', Y', C' \rangle$ is feasible. Since $W(C'_t, L'_t) = 0$ for $t \geq N_1$, while $W(C_t, L_t) < 0$ for $t \geq N_1$, so $\langle K, D, L, Y, C \rangle$ could not be optimal, a contradiction.

(ii) G_{K_t} *cannot converge to zero as* $t \to \infty$. Otherwise, there exists N_2, such that
$G_{K_t} \leqslant (1-\delta)/(2\delta)$ for $t \geqslant N_2$. Then, by Theorem 4.1, we have
$$u'(c_t) = u'(c_{t+1}) \delta (1 + G_{K_{t+1}}) \leqslant u'(c_{t+1}) \delta [1 + (1-\delta)/(2\delta)] = u'(c_{t+1})\{(1+\delta)/2\}$$
for $t \geqslant N_2$. Hence $u'(c_t) \to \infty$ as $t \to \infty$, and $c_t \to 0$ as $t \to \infty$. This contradicts (i).

(iii) $G_{D_t} \to \infty$ *as* $t \to \infty$.

Note that by Theorem 4.1, G_{D_t} is increasing with t, so if $G_{D_t} \nrightarrow \infty$ as $t \to \infty$, there is
$A < \infty$, such that $G_{D_t} \to A$. By (4.3), we have $G_{D_{T+1}} = G_{D_0} \prod_{t=0}^{T} (1 + G_{K_{t+1}})$. So
$\prod_{t=0}^{\infty} (1 + G_{K_{t+1}}) < \infty$, and $\sum_{t=0}^{\infty} G_{K_{t+1}} < \infty$. This implies that $G_{K_{t+1}} \to 0$ as $t \to \infty$, which
contradicts (ii).

(iv) $[G_{K_t}/G_{D_t}] \to 0$ *as* $t \to \infty$.

We have $G_{K_t}/G_{D_t} \leqslant F_{K_t}/F_{D_t} = 1/F_{D_t} = 1/G_{D_{t-1}} \to 0$ as $t \to \infty$ using (4.3) and (iii).

(v) $[D_t/K_t] \to 0$ *as* $t \to \infty$.

By using (A.11), $\alpha \leqslant \{[G_{K_t} K_t]/G(K_t, D_t, L_t)\} / \{[G_{D_t} D_t]/G(K_t, D_t, L_t)\} =$
$= [G_{K_t}/G_{D_t}][K_t/D_t]$. By (iv) $[G_{K_t}/G_{D_t}] \to 0$ as $t \to \infty$, so $K_t/D_t \to \infty$ as $t \to \infty$. That is,
$[D_t/K_t] \to 0$ as $t \to \infty$.

(vi) $G_{L_t} \to 0$ *for a subsequence of* t. Otherwise, there is $\theta > 0$, such that $G_{L_t} \geqslant \theta$ for
all t. This means that
$$\theta \leqslant G_{L_t} \leqslant \frac{G(K_t, D_t, L_t)}{L_t} = G\left(\frac{K_t}{L_t}, \frac{D_t}{L_t}, 1\right). \tag{7.1}$$
Consequently $[K_t/L_t] \to \infty$ as $t \to \infty$. For if $[K_t/L_t] \leqslant \hat{Q} < \infty$ for a subsequence of t, then
$[D_t/L_t] = [D_t/K_t][K_t/L_t] \leqslant [D_t/K_t]\hat{Q} \to 0$ for this subsequence, by (v). So
$G(K_t/L_t, D_t/L_t, 1) \to 0$ for this subsequence, which violates (7.1). Hence $(K_t/L_t) \to \infty$ as
$t \to \infty$, and $[L_t/K_t] \to 0$ as $t \to \infty$.

Now, $G_{K_t} \leqslant \{G(K_t, D_t, L_t)\}/K_t = G(1, D_t/K_t, L_t/K_t)$. Since $[D_t/K_t] \to 0$ as $t \to \infty$,
by (v), and $(L_t/K_t) \to 0$ as $t \to \infty$, so $G_{K_t} \to 0$ as $t \to \infty$. This contradicts (ii).

Thus (vi) is established. We now denote $(1+\delta)/2$ by λ; $(1-\delta)/2\delta = e$. Define
$S = \{t \geqslant 0 : \delta F_{K_{t+1}} \geqslant \lambda\}$; $S' = \{t \geqslant 0 : \delta F_{K_{t+1}} < \lambda\}$.

(vii) S *and* S' *each contain an infinite number of elements.*
If S contains a finite number of elements then there is N_1 such that for $T \geqslant N_1$, $t \in S'$.

So for $t \geqslant N_1$, $u'(c_t) < \lambda u'(c_{t+1})$. So $u'(c_t) \to \infty$ as $t \to \infty$, and $c_t \to 0$ as $t \to \infty$, which contradicts (i).

If S' contains a finite number of elements then there is N_2 such that for $t \geqslant N_2$, $t \in S$. So for $t \geqslant N_2$, $F_{K_{t+1}} \geqslant [\lambda/\delta]$, and $G_{K_{t+1}} \geqslant \{(1+\delta)/2\delta\} - 1 = (1-\delta)/2\delta = e$. So $e \leqslant G_{K_{t+1}} \leqslant \{G(K_{t+1}, D_{t+1}, L_{t+1})\}/K_{t+1} = G(1, D_{t+1}/K_{t+1}, L_{t+1}/K_{t+1})$. By (v), $[L_{t+1}/K_{t+1}] \to \infty$ as $t \to \infty$; so, $(K_{t+1}/L_{t+1}) \to 0$ as $t \to \infty$. Now, $(D_t/L_t) = (D_t/K_t)(K_t/L_t) \to 0$ as $t \to \infty$, since $(K_t/L_t) \to 0$ as $t \to \infty$, and (v) holds. Also, $(K_t/L_t) \to 0$ as $t \to \infty$, so $G(K_t/L_t, D_t/L_t, 1) \to 0$ as $t \to \infty$. Hence, $c_{t+1} \leqslant$ $\leqslant G(K_{t+1}/L_{t+1}, D_{t+1}/L_{t+1}, 1) + K_{t+1}/L_{t+1} \to 0$ as $t \to \infty$. This contradicts (i). Thus (vii) is established.

Choose $\epsilon > 0$, such that $G[1, \epsilon, (4/\underline{c})] \leqslant e$, and $G[(\underline{c}/4), (\epsilon \underline{c}/4), 1] \leqslant (\underline{c}/4)$. Choose $\widetilde{N}$ such that for $t \geqslant \widetilde{N}$, $(D_t/K_t) < \epsilon$.

(viii) If $t > \widetilde{N}$, $t \in S$, then $c_{t+1} \leqslant [\underline{c}/2]$.

For $t > \widetilde{N}$, $t \in S$, $\delta F_{K_{t+1}} \geqslant \lambda$, so $G_{K_{t+1}} \geqslant e$. So, $e \leqslant G_{K_{t+1}} \leqslant$ $G(1, D_{t+1}/K_{t+1}, L_{t+1}/K_{t+1}) \leqslant G(1, \epsilon, L_{t+1}/K_{t+1})$, and $(L_{t+1}/K_{t+1}) \geqslant [4/\underline{c}]$. Hence, $[K_{t+1}/L_{t+1}] \leqslant [\underline{c}/4]$, and $c_{t+1} \leqslant \{G(K_{t+1}, D_{t+1}, L_{t+1}) + K_{t+1}\}/L_{t+1} \leqslant$ $\leqslant G(\underline{c}/4, (\epsilon\underline{c})/4, 1) + \underline{c}/4 \leqslant (\underline{c}/2)$. Choose $\overline{N} > \widetilde{N}$, such that $\overline{N} \in S$.

(ix) If $t \geqslant \overline{N}$, then $c_{t+1} \leqslant [\underline{c}/2]$.

Suppose, on the contrary, there is some $t \geqslant \overline{N}$, such that $c_{t+1} > [\underline{c}/2]$. Consider $t = \tau$ to be the first period this happens. Then τ is not in S, by (viii). So, $\tau \in S'$; also, $\overline{N} \in S$, so $\tau > \overline{N}$. Now,

$$u'(c_\tau) = \delta F_{K_{\tau+1}} u'(c_{\tau+1}) < \lambda u'(c_{\tau+1}) < u'(c_{\tau+1}).$$

So $c_\tau > c_{\tau+1} > [\underline{c}/2]$. But since $\tau - 1 \geqslant \overline{N}$, and $c_\tau > (\underline{c}/2)$, so τ is not the first period $(\geqslant \overline{N})$, for which $c_{\tau+1} > [\underline{c}/2]$, a contradiction.

(x) $\langle K, D, L, Y, C \rangle$ is not optimal.

By (ix), $W(C_t, L_t) < 0$ for $t \geqslant \overline{N} + 1$. Construct a sequence $\langle K', D', L', Y', C' \rangle$ as follows: $(K'_t, D'_t, L'_t, Y'_t, C'_t) = (K_t, D_t, L_t, Y_t, C_t)$ for $t < \overline{N} + 1$; $(K'_t, D'_t, L'_t, Y'_t, C'_t) = 0$ for $t \geqslant \overline{N} + 1$. Since $W(C'_t, L'_t) = 0$ for $t \geqslant \overline{N} + 1$, so $\langle K, D, L, Y, C \rangle$ is not optimal.

By (x), $\langle K, D, L, Y, C \rangle$ must be an extinction program. ‖

References

Brock, W.A.: On Existence of Weakly Maximal Programmes in a Multi-Sector Economy. Review of Economic Studies 37, 1970, 275–280.

Brock, W.A., and D. Gale: Optimal Growth under Factor Augmenting Progress. Journal of Economic Theory 1, 1969, 229–243.

Cass, D., and *T. Mitra*: Persistence of Economic Growth Despite Exhaustion of Natural Resources. 1979, mimeo.

Dasgupta, P.S.: On the Concept of Optimum Population. Review of Economic Studies 36, 1969, 295–318.

– : Some Recent Theoretical Explorations in the Economics of Exhaustible Resources. Systems Approaches and Environmental Problems. Ed. by H.W. Gottinger. Göttingen 1973, 193–214.

Dasgupta, P.S., and *G. Heal*: The Optimal Depletion of Exhaustible Resources. Review of Economic Studies, Symposium on the Economics of Exhaustible Resources, 1974, 3–28.

Gale, D.: On Optimal Development in a Multi-Sector Economy. Review of Economic Studies 34, 1967, 1–18.

Ingham, A., and *P. Simmons*: Natural Resources and Growing Population. Review of Economic Studies 42, 1975, 191–206.

Koopmans, T.C.: Some Observations on "Optimal" Economic Growth and Exhaustible Resources. Economic Structure and Development. Ed. by Bos, Linemann and de Wolff. Amsterdam 1973.

– : Proof for a Case where Discounting Advances the Doomsday. Review of Economic Studies, Symposium on the Economics of Exhaustible Resources, 1974, 117–120.

Lane, J.S.: On the Ramsey-Meade Problems under Endogenous Population Growth. Review of Economic Studies 42, 1975.

– : On Optimum Population Paths. Berlin 1977.

Meade, J.E.: Trade and Welfare. Oxford 1955.

Mitra, T.: Efficient Growth with Exhaustible Resources in a Neoclassical Model. Journal of Economic Theory 17, 1978, 114–129.

Pitchford, J.D.: Population in Economic Growth. Amsterdam 1974.

Solow, R.M.: Intergenerational Equity and Exhaustible Resources. Review of Economic Studies, Symposium on the Economics of Exhaustible Resources, 1974, 29–45.

Stiglitz, J.F.: Growth with Exhaustible Natural Resources: Efficient and Optimal Growth Paths. Review of Economic Studies, Symposium on the Economics of Exhaustible Resources, 1974, 123–137.

Economic Theory of Natural Resources. © Physica-Verlag, Würzburg–Wien, 1982.

The Performance of Neoclassical-Econometric Models in Measuring Natural Resource Substitution with Environmental Constraints

Michael Hazilla, Raymond J. Kopp, and *V. Kerry Smith*[1])

1. Introduction

Attempts to measure the prospects for natural resource substitution have increased dramatically over the last five years.[2]) In large part, these studies were motivated by the recognition that the importance of limitations to natural resource availability for production activities depends on whether it is possible, within these processes, to substitute other factor inputs for the scarce, resource inputs. Indeed, *Solow* [1974] has developed a similar argument in formulating judgments on the importance of natural resources to the maintenance of society's well-being.[3]) While there are a number of substantive issues which bear on the applicability of his argument for an aggregate economy in the real world, they are not of direct concern to the motivation for our paper.[4]) Rather, Solow's argument is important because it has heightened the existing interest in the measurement of the prospects for natural resource substitution.

The purpose of this paper is to consider the effects of an important class of problems for the measurement of input substitution using conventional neoclassical econometric models. Estimates of the features of production technologies have increasingly relied upon dual representations of these technologies. Thus, their empirical models have incorporated an assumed behavioral framework along with the prior specification of the broad features of the technology (i.e., the definition of factor inputs and outputs, etc.). This approach implies that the properties of the estimates will depend both on how well the general technology has been described (i.e., whether the specific neoclassical functional

[1]) Kopp and Hazilla are Fellows in Quality of the Environment Division, Resources for the Future, and Smith is a Professor of Economics at the University of North Carolina at Chapel Hill. The authors wish to acknowledge the financial support of the National Science Foundation (under project NSF-C-ERS77-15083), the Electric Power Research Institute (project RP 1475-1) and the Andrew W. Mellon Foundation.

[2]) Examples of these studies include the work by *Humphrey/Moroney* [1975], *Berndt/Wood* [1975], *Moroney/Trapani* [1979], *Fuss* [1977] and others.

[3]) Of course, Solow was not the only one to develop these arguments. *Dasgupta/Heal* [1974] developed them formally in a special issue of the *Review of Economic Studies* devoted to problems arising in the allocation of exhaustible resources as well as their role in neoclassical growth models. More recently, *Stiglitz* [1979] and *Dasgupta/Heal* [1979] have reviewed this literature.

[4]) See *Smith/Krutilla* [1979] for a discussion of these issues and citations to the literature relevant to them.

form is a good approximation to the underlying technology) and on the accuracy *and* the completeness of the maintained behavioral framework.

As a practical matter, most behavioral descriptions of the firm's production choices abstract from many "real-world," nontechnological constraints that can impinge upon the feasible input choices made by the firm. Since duality theory relies on a complete description of the factors influencing choice patterns in order to infer (from the firm's actions) the nature of the technology, these omissions can be important. To the extent there are additional constraints (beyond the neoclassical production function) to a firm's input selections, dual representations of the production technology must acknowledge them. Equally important, we must consider what type of information is available for estimating such amended models. This last issue is one of the direct concerns of our analysis.

Often these additional constraints arise outside the market so we cannot rely upon records of market transactions for the information to characterize the exact features of each constraint. Indeed, the information available is frequently drawn from secondary sources and quite incomplete. Our experiments will demonstrate that these limitations can have significant effects on our ability to estimate substitution elasticities. The specific example we have used involves the effects of different types of information on the nature and severity of existing residual discharge constraints facing a hypothetical firm. While our intention is to use this case to illustrate a broader set of issues, it should be noted that constraints on emissions of effluents are likely to be among the most important additional constraints facing firms that utilize large amounts of natural resources as raw materials inputs.[5]

Our methodology is experimental and follows earlier analyses of properties of neoclassical models in estimating the nature of input associations in the presence of input and technology aggregations [see *Kopp/Smith*, 1980b, 1981]. One of the most important attributes of the approach is our assumption that the true technology is best characterized by an engineering framework that is consistent with the physical laws governing the transformation of materials inputs into the desired outputs.[6] To meet these requirements we have selected a large scale process analysis model for a basic oxygen furnace steelmaking plant developed by *Russell/Vaughan* [1976] as part of the industry studies program at Resources for the Future.

While the environmental economics literature abounds with theoretical models of producer generated externalities, these models structure the technology of residual generation and dispersal in an oversimplified format.[7] As a consequence, the distinct role of treatment and by-product recovery activities, as a separate set of production processes that transform the character of industrial effluents and can generate usable by-products, is often overlooked.[8] This oversight is especially important when it is recognized that the separation of residual generation and treatment activities may be important to the form

---

[5] For a discussion of a subset of these industries in relationship to the research activities of the industry studies program at Resources for the Future see *Bower* [1975].

[6] This argument is developed in analytical terms in *Marsden/Pingry/Whinston* [1974] and in terms of our experimental approach in *Kopp/Smith* [1980b].

[7] For a review of most of these models see *Fisher/Peterson* [1976] and *Baumol/Oates* [1975].

[8] A notable exception to this approach can be found in *Cowing's* [1976] analysis of the effects of environmental regulation in the presence of rate-of-return regulation.

of the information assumed to be available on residual discharge constraints. Section 2 develops, in simple terms, these arguments using a neoclassical production framework with appropriate amendments to reflect these issues. Using this model it is possible to identify each of five different levels of information an analyst might have available on the residuals discharge constraints facing a firm. These differences lead to distinct specifications of the firm's behavioral function (a neoclassical cost function in our case) and with them a potential for variation in each model's ability to discern input associations with the same data set.[9])

In the third section of this paper we outline the design of our experiments and criteria used to judge the performance of the neoclassical models. Section 4 presents the results and evaluates them with specific attention given to the features of the engineering model that are important to their interpretation. In the last section we summarize the implications of the analysis.

2. A Neoclassical Model of Production and Residuals Discharge Constraints

Consider a group of organized production activities (a firm) which employs a set of factor inputs, purchased in competitive markets, to produce a marketable output and a residual (effluent) discharge. The firm is assumed to minimize total factor cost subject to a given level of output and a specified production technology. Let the transformation function for this firm be

$$f(Q, R, x_1, \ldots, x_n) \geq 0 \tag{2.1}$$

where Q is output, R is the discharged residual, and $x_i \geq 0$, $i = 1, \ldots, n$ factors of production. f is nondecreasing in x_i, nonincreasing in Q, R, continuous and quasi-concave. The firm faces the added environmental constraint $R \leq R^*$. The firm's optimization problem becomes

$$\text{Min: } \sum_{\substack{x \\ i=1}}^{N} p_i x_i \tag{2.2}$$

$$\text{Subject to: } f(Q^*, R, x_1, \ldots, x_n) \leq 0$$
$$R \leq R^*.$$

The Kuhn-Tucker necessary conditions are:

$$p_i - \lambda \, \partial F/\partial x_i \leq 0 \qquad i = 1, \ldots, n \tag{2.3}$$

$$f(Q^*, R, x_1, \ldots, x_n) \leq 0 \tag{2.4}$$

$$R - R^* \leq 0 \tag{2.5}$$

$$\Sigma x_i \, (p_i - \lambda \, \partial F/\partial x_i) = 0 \tag{2.6}$$

$$\lambda f(Q^*, R, x_1, \ldots, x_n) = 0 \tag{2.7}$$

---

[9]) An alternative interpretation of our objective can be developed in terms of a specification error analysis. That is, the definitions for different types of information on residual discharge constraints and their incorporation within neoclassical cost functions, simply provide the background rationale for alternative specifications of a neoclassical cost function.

$$\mu (R - R^*) = 0 \tag{2.8}$$

$$x_i \geqslant 0, \ i = 1, \ldots, n, \ \lambda, \ \mu \geqslant 0 \tag{2.9}$$

where Q^* is the given level of output, p_i is the price of the i-th factor and λ, μ are Lagrangian multipliers.

Given the properties of f the Kuhn-Tucker necessary conditions are also sufficient.

We assume production occurs in an efficient manner thus (2.3) is satisfied as a strict equality. If each x_i is employed at positive levels (2.3) holds as an equality. If (2.5) holds as an equality then the environmental constraint on discharged residuals is binding on the firm's cost minimization and $\mu > 0$. If (2.5) holds as an inequality $\mu = 0$ and the constraint is not binding. This implies that the discharge constraint level R^* is a parameter in the optimal factor demand equations only when the constraint is binding. If the constraint is not binding the Lagrangian multiplier vanishes and R^* is not passed to the cost function. The upshot of this is the level of the constraint, not the level of discharge, belongs in the cost function and only belongs in the cost function when the constraint is binding.

In practice, U.S. (and several other industrialized nations, see *Haveman* [1977] for further discussion) statutory discharge constraints can differentially impact firms — depending on their production activities and the nature of their technologies. Thus, it is entirely reasonable to expect that such constraints may not be binding for some firms within an industry. Equally important, the differences may arise because of variations in other conditions facing these firms (i.e., different factor prices, or desired output levels). As a consequence, an ideal information set concerning environmental constraints would identify both the statutory level of the constraint and whether it was binding for each firm. Of course, actual data sets rarely include this type of information. This example illustrates one way for the level of informational detail to influence the specification of a neoclassical cost function.

We begin our analysis of these issues with a general statement of a neoclassical cost function based on the model above. For the sake of illustration we temporarily assume that the discharge constraints are binding. Following much of contemporary practice in production modeling, we have assumed that this cost function can be adequately approximated with a transcendental logarithmic specification (TRANSLOG).[10] Throughout our analysis we assume constant returns to scale. Equation (2.10) presents the TRANSLOG cost function model.

$$\ln C = \alpha_0 + \sum_1^n \alpha_i \ln P_i + \beta_Q \ln Q^* + .5\beta_{QQ} (\ln Q^*)^2 + \mu_R \ln R^* + .5\mu_{RR} (\ln R^*)^2$$
$$\tag{2.10}$$
$$+ \frac{1}{2} \sum_i^n \sum_j^n \gamma_{ij} \ln P_i \ln P_j + \sum_i^n \rho_i \ln P_i \ln Q^* + \omega \ln Q^* \ln R^* + \sum_i^n \Theta_i \ln P_i \ln R^*.$$

Constant returns to scale, linear homogeneity in input prices, and symmetry imply the following sets of linear restrictions on the parameters.

---

[10]) The properties of the translog specification have been discussed in a number of sources. Two notable examples are *Christensen/Jorgenson/Lau* [1970] and *Binswanger* [1974].

$$\sum_{1}^{n} \alpha_i = 1 \qquad \sum_{i}^{n} \gamma_{ij} = 0 \qquad \rho_i = 0 \qquad \omega = 0 \tag{2.11}$$
$$\text{for all } i$$

$$\beta_Q = 1 \qquad \beta_{QQ} = 0 \qquad \sum_{i}^{n} \Theta_i = 0 \qquad \gamma_{ij} = \gamma_{ji}.$$

Applying Shephard's lemma to (2.10) we derive a set of cost share equations. These relationships provide, for our purposes, all the information needed to describe the technology.

$$\frac{\partial \ln C}{\partial \ln P_i} = \alpha_i + \sum_{j}^{n} \gamma_{ij} \ln P_j + \Theta_i \ln R^*. \tag{2.12}$$

While the parameters of systems of cost share equations of the form given in (2.12) can be estimated with a variety of techniques (i.e., restricted SUR, IZEF), we have utilized a full information maximum likelihood estimator.[11]

Given prior information on discharge constraints for each observation (i.e., whether they hold as equalities or inequalities), Equation (2.12) can be modified by incorporating an interactive binary variable, V, which takes on the value of unity when the constraint is binding and zero otherwise. Such a model is given as Equation (2.13). It reflects the Kuhn-Tucker complementary slackness conditions on the relevant parameters to the neoclassical cost function when environmental constraints are differentially binding across firms in a given sample.

$$\frac{\partial \ln C}{\partial \ln P_i} = \alpha_i + \sum_{j}^{n} \gamma_{ij} \ln P_j + \Theta_i V \ln R^*. \tag{2.13}$$

Models specified in a form similar to (2.13) require complete information on the discharge constraints. *A priori* one would expect that they would yield the best estimates of *Allen* [1938] partial elasticities of input substitution. However, as we noted earlier, in practice, we rarely have such complete information. Thus, it is important to examine the effects of departures from this ideal model. To meet this task we have constructed four informational "scenarios," each with decreasing informational content regarding the discharge constraints. They can be detailed as follows:

1) No information on the nature of the statutory discharge constraints, only the quantities of discharged residuals are known. With this model one would be forced to assume that the discharge constraint was binding for all firms and that actual discharges equalled the constraint level. This form implies Equation (2.14) as the appropriate specification for the i-th factor's cost share.

$$\frac{\partial \ln C}{\partial \ln P_i} = \alpha_i + \sum_{j}^{n} \gamma_{ij} \ln P_j + \Theta_i \ln R. \tag{2.14}$$

---

[11]) The computational algorithm used to estimate the various cost share models is based on *Snella* [1978]. This general FORTRAN program is a modification of the widely known NLFIML program written by *Deaton* [1974]. The maximum likelihood estimator maximizes by definition the density function of the shares as a function of the parameters. As the distribution of the errors is degenerate, we have deleted the last share and maximized the logarithm of the likelihood function based on eight share equations. This procedure is equivalent to the widely used iterative Zellner efficient estimation technique.

2) No information on levels of constraint or levels of actual discharges; however, the severity of the discharge constraint can be ordered. Under this scenario the analyst is assumed to know that a discharge constraint faces the firm and that the severity of the constraint can be categorized for each firm as "mild," "somewhat severe," or "very severe." This classification might be based on the reduction in emissions implied by the constraint relative to unconstrained practices. Here we might assume that dummy variables could be used to control for the constraint and models based on Equation (2.15) would be estimated.

$$\frac{\partial \ln C}{\partial \ln P_i} = \alpha_i + \sum_j^n \gamma_{ij} \ln P_j + \sum_j^3 d_i V_j \qquad (2.15)$$

where the dummy variables V_1, V_2, V_3 stand for mild, somewhat severe and very severe constraints. The dummies are measured against the base state of a nonbinding constraint.

3) No information on constraint levels, or actual discharge levels. However, we assume that an ordinal index, akin to a time trend, for the severity of the constraint can be constructed. We assume that this model treats the index in a fashion similar to non-neutral technological change, using a time trend. It is equivalent to the assumption that $d_3 = 1.5d_2$ and $d_2 = 2d_1$ from the previous model. Equation (2.16) details the form for the cost share equation relevant to this case.

$$\frac{\partial \ln C}{\partial \ln P_i} = \alpha_i + \sum_j^n \gamma_{ij} \ln P_j + tT \qquad (2.16)$$

where T corresponds to the index of the severity of the discharge constraints.

4) It is not known that constraints exist. Here the analyst is forced to ignore the prospects for environmental constraints in the specification of the cost function. Thus, the relevant cost share equation becomes:

$$\frac{\partial \ln C}{\partial \ln P_i} = \alpha_i + \sum_j^n \gamma_{ij} \ln P_j. \qquad (2.17)$$

3. Experimental Methods Using Engineering Process Models

A. Conceptual Overview

Our frame of reference for this analysis maintains that the most appropriate interpretation of neoclassical production models is as approximations to the engineering activities that comprise any particular production technology [see *Marsden/Pingry/Whinston; Kopp/Smith*, 1980a, for further discussion]. Accordingly, we have used a large scale, process analysis model to describe the "true" production technology for our experiments. The model is of an integrated iron and steel plant using a basic oxygen (BOF) steelmaking furnace. It is one of a set of process analysis models for steel plants developed by *Russell/Vaughan* [1976]. Figure 1 provides a general schematic outline for the Russell-Vaughan steel models. In our present application we consider only BOF plants.

Since the process model was constructed to estimate industrial effluents, it was designed to take explicit account of heat and materials balances at each processing stage of the technology. It is a cost minimizing linear programing model with a fixed productive capacity (i.e., 2,000 short tons of finished shapes per day). The product mix of ingots, semi-finished shapes and strip is held constant for all of our experiments.

The BOF technology is the "dirtiest" of the three major steelmaking practices in the United States. It is a hot metal process that has limited ability to vary the composition of the metal practice in the steelmaking furnace (i.e., the ratio of molten iron to scrap), since the hot metal serves as the primary source of the heat used in refining the molten iron to molten steel. Thus, we can expect that the cost minimizing responses of this technology will be quite sensitive to residual discharge constraints.

B. Experimental Design

Our experiments involve repeated solutions of the model using alternative sets of factor prices and residual discharge constraints. Each solution constitutes a data point for the econometric estimation of the alternative neoclassical cost functions described earlier. While the general logic of the process is straightforward, there are several aspects of its application that should be highlighted. First, we have identified two types of capital equipment – production related and residual treatment and by-product recovery related capacities. As we noted above, the productive capital (i.e., plant and equipment) is held fixed for all of our experiments. Thus, we are describing the performance of neoclassical models in estimating an *ex post* technology. The treatment and recovery equipment is allowed to vary.

Second, our estimation requires a manageable set of factor inputs and therefore limits the detail with which we can represent the variable factor inputs. This constraint is potentially important because one of the mechanisms for increasing the inherent detail of a process model is through the classification of inputs according to their characteristics. Within the Russell-Vaughan model there are a substantial number of types of coal, iron ore, scrap, and other inputs. We have reduced these inputs to nine aggregate factors – iron ore, coal, fuel oil, natural gas, scrap, labor, maintenance, discharge controlling capital, and all other operating inputs. To insure consistent aggregation we invoke the composite commodity theorem [see *Diewert*] and vary the prices of all the constituent elements within each input class proportionately in all the experiments.[12])

---

[12]) Table A2 in the Appendix defines the specific levels of the discharge restrictions. The input prices are set as multiples of the 1973 levels. These multiples are given as follows:

Input	Low (L)	High (H)
Natural Gas	.27	1.73
Coal	.27	1.73
Fuel Oil	.27	1.73
Iron Ore	.67	1.33
Scrap	.22	1.78
Labor	.59	1.41
All Other Operating Inputs	.50	1.50
Maintenance	.59	1.41
Pollution Abatement Capital	.50	1.50

Tab. 1

Table A1 provides a tabular description of the experimental design for the sample solutions.

Our sample is composed of two types of solutions: (1) the optimal solutions in response to alternative specified values for each of the factor prices, with no residual discharge constraints present; and (2) the optimal solutions when discharge constraints are varied with given prices. The structure of each sample is illustrated in Table 1A in the Appendix. The solutions associated with alternative specified values for the factor prices were derived by varying each price individually from a base level (the 1973 values) to a low and high value (designated L and H in Table 1A). These limits were defined on the basis of two considerations: a) the monthly variation in the comparable wholesale price index for the factor from 1967 to 1975; and b) the potential for bias in approximating the piecewise-linear cost surface due to what *Griffin* [1981] refers to as the nondifferentiability of the production surface. Since these limits are different multiples of the base prices for several of the factor inputs we also include solutions with all factors at their low and high prices. Thus, we have twenty-one solutions due to price variation alone.

Constraints on atmospheric and waterborne residuals were each varied as a unit (because of the physical interdependencies between members in each class) over low, medium, and high levels of restrictions. These levels are defined in terms of increments over the minimum technically feasible emission levels. Equations (3.1) through (3.3) define the levels for the constraints.

$$C_{Lj} = TM_j + .70\,(D_{BOFj} - TM_j) \tag{3.1}$$

$$C_{Mj} = TM_j + .30\,(D_{BOFj} - TM_j) \tag{3.2}$$

$$C_{Hj} = TM_j \tag{3.3}$$

where:

C_{kj} = constraint at level k $(k = L, M, H)$ for discharges into the air (A) or water (W), $j = A, W$.

TM_j = minimum technically feasible discharge level for j, $j = A, W$.

D_{BOFj} = discharge level of the BOF plant (the dirtiest technology) to receptacle j.

The intermediate discharge constraint corresponds approximately to the 1977, U.S. Environmental Protection Agency BPTCA (Best Practicable Technology Currently Available) and the high constraint to the 1983 BATEA (Best Available Technology Economically Achievable). These constraint levels were considered for atmospheric and waterborne residuals individually for each of three price levels (base, low, and high) for all of the factors, thereby providing eighteen additional solutions. Each solution reports the optimal expenditures on each of the nine factors and the levels of residual discharges.

C. The Criteria for Evaluating the Econometric Estimates

Before turning to the results of our analysis there is one technical issue arising from the need for a standard of comparison for judging the quality of the estimates derived with the five cost functions. The process analysis models are not smooth neoclassical descriptions of the technology and therefore do not offer indexes comparable to the *Allen* [1938] partial substitution elasticities. Substitution in the process models arises because different mixes of process vectors are utilized in response to changes in the relative factor prices. It is necessary, nonetheless, to develop some gauge of the accuracy of in-

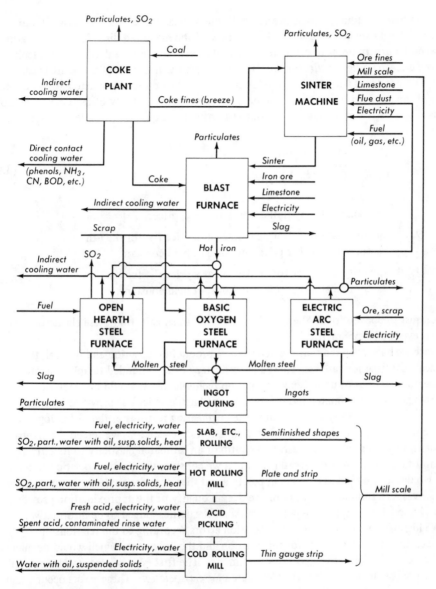

Fig. 1: Schematic Overview of Russell-Vaughan Model
   Source: *Russell/Vaughan* [1976, p. 22]

dexes based on the neoclassical models. In contrast to Monte Carlo studies, we cannot compare the estimated elasticities from our alternative neoclassical models to a set of "true" values of these parameters. Rather, we must evaluate the judgments that would be made concerning prospects for substitution using a neoclassical model in comparison to the actual substitution possibilities present in the underlying engineering model. Therefore, it has not been possible to judge, explicitly, the accuracy of the magnitude of substitution that is estimated to be present with the neoclassical elasticities. Instead, our focus has been directed to gauging the accuracy of the measured direction of association between inputs. In order to estimate the actual directions we have defined and calculated *derived arc elasticities of substitution* (to distinguish them from traditional arc elasticities). These indexes will consistently designate the actual direction of association between pairs of inputs. Their magnitudes will be quite sensitive to a variety of factors and cannot be used as a basis for judging the neoclassical estimates. Equation (3.4) defines this elasticity.

$$\sigma_{ij}^A = \frac{1}{C_{j2}} \cdot \frac{[(Q_{2i} - Q_{1i})/(Q_{2i} + Q_{1i})]}{[(P_{2j} - P_{1j})/(P_{2j} + P_{1j})]} \tag{3.4}$$

where:

C_{j2} = cost share of the j-th factor input at P_{2j} prices.

Q_{2i} = quantity of i-th factor demanded at a price P_{2j} for the j-th factor and all other prices and output held constant.

Q_{1i} = quantity of i-th factor demanded at a price P_{1j} for the j-th factor and all other prices and output held constant.

In contrast to conventional Allen partial elasticities of substitution these elasticities will not necessarily be symmetric.

Since we have assumed that the neoclassical production function and its dual, the neoclassical cost function, are best viewed as summary devices intended to approximate the engineering features of underlying production technologies, it would be a pointless exercise to analyze the estimated input associations (Allen elasticities) provided by a neoclassical model which poorly approximated the engineering features of the technology. Thus, before we begin the analysis of estimated substitution elasticities we screen the estimated elasticities with a significance test. If the ratio of an estimated elasticity to its estimated asymptotic standard error is greater than two we consider the input association to be one that would be regarded as credible in practice and therefore designate the estimate as *informative*. As a summary measure of the overall quality of the approximation provided by each model we employ the percent of Allen elasticities judged to be informative.

We identify two types of input association errors according to the relationship between the "true" prospects for substitution and the judgments which would be made on the basis of informative neoclassical estimates. The first type of error (and what will be regarded as the most serious) is designated *false association*. These errors occur when neoclassical estimates of the Allen elasticities of substitution lead to a conclusion that is directly opposite to the actual substitution between two inputs. For example, if two inputs are judged (using the neoclassical estimates) to be complements when they are actually substitutes in the underlying technology, this error is recorded. The second type of error is designated *nonassociation*. It arises when the neoclassical model provides an informative Allen elasticity when there is no clear underlying association between the inputs. For example, if the derived arc elasticity between inputs i and j is positive when the price of input i is increased but negative when it is decreased and the Allen elasticity between i and j is informative, an error of nonassociation results.

In summary, our evaluation calls for the estimation of each of five models, varying in their treatment of residual discharge constraints, using the same sample of solutions to the R-V process analysis model. These estimates are screened using our approximate significance "test" and a set of *informative* estimates identified. Since these judgments can change with the point of evaluation of the elasticities we selected two cases: a) elasticities evaluated at the solution values for the base prices; and b) elasticities evaluated at the mean cost shares. The resultant sets of estimates are then evaluated to judge whether they agree with the "true" nature of the input associations for each factor pair.

4. Analysis of Model Results

Tables 2 through 4 summarize our findings. In what follows we have identified each of the five econometric models developed in Section 2 as follows: 1) the price model (2.11), 2) the continuous severity constraint model (2.10), 3) the discontinuous severity constraint model (2.9), 4) the residual discharge model (2.8), and 5) the binding constraint model (2.7). As we noted earlier, each model was estimated using samples of thirty-nine solutions to the R-V model of a BOF plant (twenty-one without discharge constraints and eighteen with constraints).

Table 2 summarizes the implications of improvements in the nature of the information on residual discharges for the elasticity estimates evaluated at the mean cost shares. It seems clear that taking account of the discharge constraints improves the ability of the neoclassical model to precisely estimate the input elasticities. Based on the estimates evaluated at the mean cost shares this improvement seems to be completely realized once the potential for a differential severity in the constraints is recognized within a fairly flexible format (i.e., the discontinuous discharge constraint model). There appears to be some reduction in the proportion of informative estimates with our "ideal" model. However, there is no increase in the number of input association errors with the estimates.

Model	Percent of Elasticities Estimated Precisely	Nonassociation Errors	False-Association Errors
1. Price Model	44.4	Coal-Gas Coal-Oil	Gas-Oil Gas-Ore
2. Continuous Severity Constraint Model	48.8	Coal-Gas Coal-Oil	Gas-Oil Gas-Ore
3. Discontinuous Severity Constraint Model	53.3	Coal-Gas Coal-Oil	Gas-Oil Gas-Ore
4. Residual Discharge Model	55.5	Maint-Coal Coal-Gas	Gas-Oil
5. Binding Constraint Model	51.1	Coal-Gas Coal-Oil	Gas-Oil

Tab. 2: Model Performance: Elasticities Calculated at Sample Mean Cost Shares

The record is more clearcut with Table 3 when the elasticities are evaluated using the cost shares corresponding to the 1973 base prices. In this case none of the models exhibit the most severe association error and improvement in the proportion of informative estimates is consistent with the quality of the information incorporated in the model. There is, however, an additional attribute of the sample point used in the calculations reported in Table 3. The solution corresponds to the base prices together with the most severe constraints on water residual discharges. Had we selected the base price without the constraints, as given in Table 4, the record would be less clearcut.

Model	Percent of Elasticities Estimated Precisely	Nonassociation Errors	False-Association Errors
1. Price Model	37.7	Coal-Oil	None
2. Continuous Severity Constraint Model	44.4	Coal-Oil	None
3. Discontinuous Severity Constraint Model	46.6	Coal-Oil	None
4. Residual Discharge Model	48.8	None	None
5. Binding Constraint Model	51.1	Coal-Oil	None

Tab. 3: Model Performance: Elasticities Calculated at Base 1973 Prices in the Presence of Severe Constraints on Water Residual Discharges

Model	Percent of Elasticities Estimated Precisely	Nonassociation Errors	False-Association Errors
1. Price Model	24.4	None	None
2. Continuous Severity Constraint Model	33.3	None	None
3. Discontinuous Severity Constraint Model	37.7	None	None
4. Residual Discharge Model	44.4	Maint-Coal	None
5. Binding Constraint Model	35.5	None	None

Tab. 4: Model Performance: Elasticities Calculated at Base 1973 Prices, No Discharge Constraints

These findings serve to highlight the significance of the point of evaluation of our estimates. The Appendix to this paper reports the informative estimates for each input pair, model, and point of evaluation. Inspection of these more detailed findings indicates a second important feature of our results. The specific features of the technology, as summarized by the Allen partial elasticities of substitution can vary appreciably across sample points.

A striking example of this is the own Allen elasticity of substitution for discharge reducing capital. When evaluated at the base 1973 price, with no discharge constraints present, the value of the elasticity is -326, indicative of a very elastic price response. When evaluated at the sample mean cost shares the elasticity falls to -215; and when evaluated at the base 1973 prices with discharge constraints present, the elasticity falls to -69. The substantial variation in model performance and measured features of the underlying technology across data points is amplified in our results due to the considerable input disaggregation of our data and the fact that the technology underlying our plant is well defined. With aggregate studies using actual data, such as the work of *Berndt/Wood* [1975, 1979], the reported characteristics of the underlying technology remained fairly constant across data points. If our results can be generalized, then the trend toward greater input and technology disaggregation, as exemplified by the *Jorgenson/Fraumeni* [1980] model, may well require a more detailed analysis of elasticity estimates rather than placing reliance on estimates calculated using the sample mean cost shares.

Overall, our findings indicate that the model containing the most information (i.e., the binding constraint model, Equation (2.7)) produced the best approximation of the technology when the elasticities were evaluated at base prices with discharge constraints. However, the residual discharge model (Equation (2.8)) which neglected the differential relevance of information on residual discharge constraints performed comparably to our ideal model. Indeed, at some data points and with selected elasticities the estimates were superior. There is a clear advantage to incorporating information on the prospect for residual discharge constraints in as flexible a manner as possible. It is unlikely that the information in practice will be consistent with the demands of our ideal model. Nonetheless, our findings would suggest that the losses in terms of the quality of our substitution elasticity estimates associated with more limited knowledge of the constraints may not be great.

5. Summary

Applications of duality theory in production modeling have largely abstracted from the possibility that nonmarket constraints may influence the nature of a firm's input choices. As a consequence, it is reasonable to expect that our attempts to estimate the nature of input associations using dual behavioral models will be affected by how these constraints are treated in the models' specifications. This paper has addressed these questions explicitly in an experimental framework that assumes an engineering process analysis model is representative of the technology that is typically described with neoclassical models.

Our analysis began with an outline of a simple analytical production model that incorporated: a) multiple marketable outputs, b) multiple nonmarketable residual outputs, c) multiple intermediate inputs, d) by-product recovery and residual treatment activities, and e) residual discharge constraints. On the basis of this theoretical model we developed an "ideal" specification for a neoclassical cost function that explicitly incorporates the effect of environmental regulation, together with input prices. Since implementation of the ideal model requires considerable information on discharge constraints, we also considered four models, each with progressively less information on the constraints. Based on our experimental analysis, it is clear that the measurement of input associations can be significantly impacted by a recognition of these nonmarket constraints. However, it may not be necessary to have ideal information on all the constraints to the firm's actions. If our findings are representative, the improvement in the quality of the estimates may well be marginal after some minimum level of discrimination between the type and severity of the constraints has been incorporated in the model. Of course, we should acknowledge our evaluation criteria has largely been qualitative — focusing on the direction of input association and not the estimation of a specific "true" index of input substitution.

These conclusions are consistent with the earlier analysis of *Kopp/Smith* [1980b] and further reinforce the need for neoclassical models to take more explicit account of the technical features of the production activities these structures seek to summarize.

References

Allen, R.G.D.: Mathematical Analysis for Economists. London 1938.

Baumol, W.J., and *W.E. Oates*: The Theory of Environmental Policy. Englewood Cliffs, N.J. 1975.

Berndt, E.R., and *D.O. Wood*: Technology, Prices and the Demand for Energy. Review of Economics and Statistics 57, 1975, 259–268.

– : Engineering and Econometric Interpretations of Energy-Capital Complementarity. American Economic Review 69, 1979, 342–354.

Binswanger, H.P.: A Cost Function Approach to the Measurement of Elasticities of Factor Demand and Elasticities of Substitution. American Journal of Agricultural Economics 56, 1974, 377–386.

Bower, B.T.: Studies in Residuals Management in Industry. Economic Analysis of Environmental Problems. Ed. by E.S. Mills. New York 1975.

Christensen, L.R., D.W. Jorgenson and *L.J. Lau*: Conjugate Duality and the Transcendental Logarithmic Production Function. Unpublished paper presented at the Second World Congress of the Econometric Society, Cambridge, England, 1970.

Cowing, T.G.: The Environmental Implications of Monopoly Regulation: A Process Analysis Approach. Journal of Environmental Economics and Management 2, 1976, 207–223.

Dasgupta, P., and *G. Heal*: The Optimal Depletion of Exhaustible Resources. Review of Economic Studies, Symposium on the Economics of Exhaustive Resources, 1974, 3–28.

– : Economic Theory and Exhaustive Resources. Cambridge, Mass. 1979.

Deaton, A.S.: Models and Projections of Demand in Post-War Britain. London 1974.

Diewert, W.E.: A Note on Aggregation and Elasticities of Substitution. Canadian Journal of Economics 7, 1974, 12–20.

Fisher, A.C., and *F.M. Peterson*: The Environment in Economics: A Survey. Journal of Economic Literature 14, 1976, 1–33.

Fuss, M.A.: The Demand for Energy in Canadian Manufacturing. Journal of Econometrics 7, 1977, 89–116.

Griffin, J.M.: Pseudo Data Estimation with Alternative Functional Forms. Advances in Applied Micro-Economics, Vol. 2. Ed. by V. Kerry Smith. Greenwich, Conn. 1981.

Haveman, R.H.: Employment and Environmental Policy: A State-of-the-Art Review and a Suggested Approach. OECD working paper, Paris, Organization for Economic Cooperation and Development, February 1977.

Hudson, E.A., and *D.W. Jorgenson*: U.S. Energy Policy and Economic Growth, 1975–2000. The Bell Journal of Economics and Management Science, 1974, 461–514.

Humphrey, D.B., and *J.R. Moroney*: Substitution Among Capital, Labor, and Natural Resource Products in American Manufacturing. Journal of Political Economy 83, 1975, 57–82.

Jorgenson, D.W., and *B.M. Fraumeni*: Substitution and Technical Change in Production. Presented at the International Symposium on Natural Resources and Production, Karlsruhe, Federal Republic of Germany, June 1980.

Kopp, R.J., and *V.K. Smith*: Environmental Regulation and Optimal Investment Behavior: A Micro-Economic Analysis. Regional Science and Urban Economics 10, 1980a, 211–224.

– : Measuring Factor Substitution with Neoclassical Models: An Experimental Evaluation. Bell Journal of Economics 11, 1980b, 631–655.

– : Measuring the Prospects for Resource Substitution Under Input and Technology Aggregations. Modeling and Measuring Natural Resource Substitution. Ed. by E.R. Berndt and B. Field. Cambridge, Mass. 1982.

Marsden, J., D. Pingry, and *A. Whinston*: Engineering Foundations of Production Functions. Journal of Economic Theory 9, 1974, 124–140.

Moroney, J.F., and *J.M. Trapani*: Options for Conserving Nonfuel, Nonrenewable Resources in the United States. Unpublished paper, Tulane University, 1979.

Russell, C.S., and *W.J. Vaughan*: Steel Production: Processes, Products and Residuals. Baltimore 1976.

Shephard, R.W.: Theory of Cost and Production Functions. Princeton 1970.

Smith, V.K.: The Evaluation of Natural Resource Adequacy: Elusive Quest or Frontier of Economic Analysis? Land Economics 56, 1980, 257–298.

Smith, V.K., and *J.V. Krutilla*: Resource and Environmental Constraints to Growth. American Journal of Agricultural Economics 61, 1979, 395–408.

Smith, V.K., and *W.J. Vaughan*: Some Limitations of Long-Run Production Modeling with Pseudo Data. Journal of Industrial Economics 28, 1979, 201–207.

– : The Implications of Model Complexity for Environmental Management. Journal of Environmental Economics and Management 7, 1980, 182–208.

Snella, J.J.: A Program for Nonlinear Multivariate Regression-GCM. Econometrica 46, 1978, p. 481.

Solow, R.M.: The Economics of Resources or the Resources of Economics. American Economic Review Proceedings 64, 1974, 1–14.

Stiglitz, J.E.: A Neoclassical Analysis of the Economics of Natural Resources. Scarcity and Growth Reconsidered. Ed. by V.K. Smith. Baltimore 1979.

Appendix

Tab. 1A: Price Variation and Residual Constraint Table

		Solution Numbers																																						
		1	2	3	4	5	6	7	8	9	10	11	12	13	14	15	16	17	18	19	20	21	22	23	24	25	26	27	28	29	30	31	32	33	34	35	36	37	38	39
Inputs																																									
Nat. Gas		L	H																								L	L	L	H	H			H	H	L	L	L	H	H
Coal				L	H																																			
Fuel	B					L	H																																	
Ore	A							L	H																															
Scrap	S									L	H																													
Labor	E											L	H																											
All Other														L	H																									
Maint.																L	H																							
Capital																		L	H								L	L	L	H	H	H	H	L	L	L	L	H	H	H
Constraints																																								
Water[1]																					2	3	4				2	3	4	2	3	4	2	3	4	2	3	4	2	3
Air[1]																							2	3	4															4

[1]) Identification numbers 2, 3, 4 refer to discharge constraints identified as equations (3.1), (3.2), (3.3), respectively, in the text.

Tab. 2A: Levels of Discharge Constraints: Basic Oxygen Furnace

Residual	LOW	MED	HIGH
Water			
BOD	9335.5	4260.1	447.0
OILS	5396.0	2505.0	340.5
PHENOLS	1119.2	510.6	14.2
AMMONIA	2531.4	1163.0	68.4
SUS. SOLIDS	8370.9	3981.1	688.8
HEAT	9408.9	4095.2	100.4
Air			
SO_2	18236.3	14342.9	11507.9
PARTICULATES	11513.1	6824.9	734.9

Inputs	Maint.	Capital	Coal	Gas	Oil	Ore	Scrap	Labor	Other
Maint.	-.363	–	–	–	–	.257	–	–	–
Capital		-215.0	–	–	-118.8956	.614	2.301	–	8.1763
Coal			-2.452	200.4943[1]	18.155[1]	–	–	-.346	.292
Gas				–	-4296.483[2]	-95.0842[2]			
Oil					-430.376	.830	–	6.517	–
Ore						–			
Scrap							-15.851		
Labor								-.460	
Other									-1.316

[1] Nonassociation error
[2] False association error

Tab. 3A: Price Model, Allen Elasticities of Substitution Calculated at Sample Mean Cost Shares

Inputs	Maint.	Capital	Coal	Gas	Oil	Ore	Scrap	Labor	Other
Maint.	-.337	–	–	–	–	–	–	–	–
Capital		-326.980	–	–	–	.645	2.071	–	10.8521
Coal			-2.461	–	–	–	–	–	.369
Gas				–	–	–			
Oil					–	–			
Ore						-.823			
Scrap							-15.654		
Labor								-.444	
Other									-1.377

Tab. 4A: Price Model, Allen Elasticities of Substitution Calculated at Base Case Solution

Inputs	Maint.	Capital	Coal	Gas	Oil	Ore	Scrap	Labor	Other
Maint.	-.334	–	–	–	–	.256	–	–	–
Capital	–	-69.558	-.398	–	1.241	–	–	–	3.937
Coal	–	–	-2.121	–	4.083[1]	.533	2.216	-.867	–
Gas	–	–	–	–	–	–	–	–	–
Oil	–	–	–	–	-27.606	–	–	1.898	1.237
Ore	–	–	–	–	–	-.836	.727	–	–
Scrap	–	–	–	–	–	–	-14.704	–	–
Labor	–	–	–	–	–	–	–	–	–
Other	–	–	–	–	–	–	–	–	–

[1]) Nonassociation error

Tab. 5A: Price Model, Allen Elasticities of Substitution Calculated at Severe Water Constraint Solution

Inputs	Maint.	Capital	Coal	Gas	Oil	Ore	Scrap	Labor	Other
Maint.	-.353	–	–	–	–	.239	–	–	–
Capital	–	-206.334	–	166.150[1]	98.3168	–	–	–	7.618
Coal	–	–	-2.474	–	17.790[1]	.667	2.199	-.344	.277
Gas	–	–	–	–	-3893.061[2]	-85.860[2]	–	–	–
Oil	–	–	–	–	-407.152	–	–	5.585	–
Ore	–	–	–	–	–	.854	–	.300	–
Scrap	–	–	–	–	–	–	-15.451	–	–
Labor	–	–	–	–	–	–	–	-.417	.198
Other	–	–	–	–	–	–	–	–	-1.300

[1]) Nonassociation error
[2]) False association error

Tab. 6A: Continuous Severity Constraint Model, Allen Elasticities of Substitution Calculated at Sample Mean Cost Shares

Inputs	Maint.	Capital	Coal	Gas	Oil	Ore	Scrap	Labor	Other
Maint.	−.326	–	–	–	–	–	–	–	–
Capital		−310.009	–	–	–	–	–	–	10.086
Coal			−2.479	–	–	.694	1.987	−.225	.356
Gas				–	–	–	–	–	–
Oil					–	–	–	–	–
Ore						−.848	.729	.282	–
Scrap							−15.322	–	–
Labor								−.400	.204
Other									1.361

Tab. 7A: Continuous Severity Constraint Model, Allen Elasticities of Substitution Calculated at Base Case Solution

Inputs	Maint.	Capital	Coal	Gas	Oil	Ore	Scrap	Labor	Other
Maint.	−.323	–	−.368	–	1.148	.238	–	–	–
Capital		−68.301	1.948	–	− 4.475	–	–	–	3.708
Coal			−2.155	–	4.018[1]	.597	2.120	−.864	–
Gas				–	–	–	–	–	–
Oil					−27.116	−.860	–	1.747	1.156
Ore							.784	–	–
Scrap							−14.475	–	–
Labor								–	–
Other									−.940

[1]) Nonassociation

Tab. 8A: Continuous Severity Constraint Model, Allen Elasticities of Substitution Calculated at Severe Water Constraint Solution

Inputs	Maint.	Capital	Coal	Gas	Oil	Ore	Scrap	Labor	Other
Maint.	-.357								
Capital		-210.602	3.430		-104.887	.245	2.251	-.350	7.635
Coal			-2.461	182.975[1]	17.994[1]	.644			.278
Gas					-4067.567[2]	-89.368[2]			
Oil					-417.434	.846		5.926	
Ore							.679		
Scrap							-15.645		
Labor								-.429	.192
Other									-1.298

[1]) Nonassociation
[2]) False association

Tab. 9A: Discontinuous Severity Constraint Model, Allen Elasticities of Substitution Calculated at Sample Mean Cost Shares

Inputs	Maint.	Capital	Coal	Gas	Oil	Ore	Scrap	Labor	Other
Maint.	-.331								
Capital		-318.310	4.065			.217	2.030	-.231	10.109
Coal			-2.469			.672			.357
Gas									
Oil									
Ore						-.839	.703	.286	
Scrap							-15.483		
Labor								-.413	.198
Other									-1.360

Tab. 10A: Discontinuous Severity Constraint Model, Allen Elasticities of Substitution Calculated at Base Case Solution

Inputs	Maint.	Capital	Coal	Gas	Oil	Ore	Scrap	Labor	Other
Maint.	-.327	–	-.384	–	1.188	.244	–	–	–
Capital		-68.915	2.140	–	-4.838	1.324	–	–	3.715
Coal			-2.136	–	4.054[1]	.569	2.169	-.873	–
Gas				–					
Oil					-27.333	–	–	1.802	1.177
Ore						-.851	.763	–	–
Scrap							-14.586	–	–
Labor								–	–
Other									-.938

[1] Nonassociation

Tab. 11A: Discontinuous Severity Constraint Model, Allen Elasticities of Substitution Calculated at Severe Water Constraint Solution

Inputs	Maint.	Capital	Coal	Gas	Oil	Ore	Scrap	Labor	Other
Maint.	-.3234	–	.1656[1]	–	–	.155	–	–	.291
Capital		-159.989	–	–	–	5.254	8.401	4.038	6.117
Coal			-1.603	-6130.	–	.273	1.749	–	.403
Gas				90.740[1]	-1430.040[2]	–			–
Oil					–	–	–	–	4.265
Ore						-.574	1.023	.156	-.338
Scrap							-15.009	–	–
Labor								-.362	.432
Other									-1.572

[1] Nonassociation
[2] False association

Tab. 12A: Residual Discharge Model, Allen Elasticities of Substitution Calculated at Sample Mean Cost Shares

Inputs	Maint.	Capital	Coal	Gas	Oil	Ore	Scrap	Labor	Other
Maint.	-.296	–	.230¹)	–	–	.123	–	–	.288
Capital		-219.894	–	–	–	7.037	10.392	-6.082	8.025
Coal			-1.766	–	–	.331	1.616	–	.468
Gas				–	–			–	–
Oil					–			–	–
Ore						-.558	1.021	–	-.341
Scrap							-14.957		
Labor								-.344	.436
Other									-1.625

¹) Nonassociation

Tab. 13A: Residual Discharge Model, Allen Elasticities of Substitution Calculated at Base Case Solution

Inputs	Maint.	Capital	Coal	Gas	Oil	Ore	Scrap	Labor	Other
Maint.	-.2922	–	–	–	.617	.154	–	–	.218
Capital		-61.628	–	–	–	2.580	3.121	-1.143	3.094
Coal			-.822	–	–	–	1.700	-.377	–
Gas				–				–	–
Oil					-18.271	1.027	–	.779	1.511
Ore						-.591	1.017	–	-.413
Scrap							-14.224		
Labor									.315
Other									-1.257

Tab. 14A: Residual Discharge Model, Allen Elasticities of Substitution Evaluated at Severe Water Constraint Solution

Inputs	Maint.	Capital	Coal	Gas	Oil	Ore	Scrap	Labor	Other
Maint.	−.353	—	—	—	—	.247	—	—	—
Capital		−207.347	3.153	—	101.126	.656	—	—	7.574
Coal			−2.469	173.966[1]	17.812[1]	—	2.224	−.343	.276
Gas				—	−3923.8[2]	−89.370[2]	—	—	—
Oil					−412.284	—	—	5.817	—
Ore						−.851	—	.304	—
Scrap							−15.474	—	—
Labor								−.428	.193
Other									−1.299

[1] Nonassociation
[2] False association

Tab. 15A: Binding Constraint Model, Allen Elasticities of Substitution Evaluated at Sample Mean Cost Shares

Inputs	Maint.	Capital	Coal	Gas	Oil	Ore	Scrap	Labor	Other
Maint.	−.327	—	—	—	—	.218	—	—	—
Capital		−311.980	—	—	—	—	—	—	10.026
Coal			−2.474	—	—	.683	2.007	.224	.355
Gas				—	—	—	—	—	—
Oil					—	—	—	—	—
Ore						−.845	—	.286	—
Scrap							−15.342	—	—
Labor								−.411	.199
Other									−1.360

Tab. 16A: Binding Constraint Model, Allen Elasticities of Substitution Evaluated at Base Case Solution

Inputs	Maint.	Capital	Coal	Gas	Oil	Ore	Scrap	Labor	Other
Maint.	-.324	1.005	-.374	–	1.167	.246	–	–	–
Capital		-68.447	2.010	–	-4.630	1.332	2.143	–	3.691
Coal			-2.146	–	4.022[1]	.583		-.863	–
Gas				–	–	–			
Oil					-27.224	.791	–	1.784	1.170
Ore						-.857	.749	–	–
Scrap							-64.489	–	–
Labor								–	–
Other									-.939

[1] Nonassociation

Tab. 17A: Binding Constraint Model, Allen Elasticities of Substitution Evaluation at Severe Water Constraint Solution

Economic Theory of Natural Resources. ©Physica-Verlag, Würzburg–Wien, 1982.

Optimal Economic Growth and the Environment

Mikuláš Luptáčik and *Uwe Schubert*

1. Introduction

The improvement of environmental quality has become an important objective in the framework of economic and social policy in the industrialized world. It is often claimed that some of the goals of economic policy are in a trade-off relation, implying that better levels of one goal variable must, cet. par., be "paid for" by lower levels of another. A similar decision dilemma can be encountered when decisions about economic growth (in terms of increases of GNP) and environmental quality (in terms of ambient residuals' concentration) have to be made. This position, mainly based on the "spaceship earth concept" [*Boulding*] is not universally accepted, however. There may even be a complementarity between these goals, as we have to consider that improvements of environmental quality can often be achieved by means of expenditure for pollution abatement. These expenditures then are a part of the "national budget" (national income), the overall growth of which facilitates environmental policy. This can only happen, at the cost of other components of national income, however, i.e. productive investment and consumption.

All these expenditures have different effects over time. Consumption only has a one period effect, while investment leads to the accumulation of capital and hence the widening of productive capacity in the future. The expenditure for pollution abatement can have different effects, depending on the nature of the strategy chosen.

Before we turn to a brief discussion of some of the instruments and strategies of environmental policy, let us just state the objective of this paper. The few introductory comments should already highlight the complex decision problem about the optimal allocation of scarce resources having very different impacts on the welfare of an economic system over time. It is our goal to contribute to the clarification of some of the controversial issues briefly outlined above by investigating optimal policies in different situations, such as the economic development level, state of the art in abatement technology, etc.

Let us now briefly review some of the possibilities that are open for environmental policy [*Siebert; Schubert; Freeman/Haveman/Kneese*]. First we must distinguish between "residuals concentration" (a stock variable) and "emissions" (the corresponding flow variable) (technical details see below in Section 2). To improve environmental quality, an inverse function of residuals concentration, either the flows can be controlled ("*emissions control*") or the stock of residuals in the environment can be reduced ("*stock control*").

In the framework of this paper we will be dealing with the problems of the control of emissions only. A few comments should also be made about the possibilities to change technology in the direction of less waste generating production processes. Such technical progress can come about by investment into R & D, in which case funds will have to be allocated to these activities. An approach dealing with this aspect was adopted by *Mastenbroek/Nijkamp* [1976], so our analysis will not expound this subject any further.

The paper, which is an extension of *Forster* [1977] and of some previous work done by the authors [*Luptáčik/Schubert*, 1979a, 1979b] will proceed by first introducing, in Section 2, the components of an aggregated growth model step by step and discussing briefly the assumptions underlying the postulated relations.

Section 3 is devoted to deriving the various propositions for optimal rules of the allocation of funds to the control variables. This will be achieved by applying Pontrjagin's Maximum Principle to our growth model.

In Section 4 the conditions for a stationary state and its economic interpretation will be given.

Section 5 attempts to investigate some of the stability properties of the suggested optimal policies.

2. A Model of Optimal Economic Growth and Environmental Quality

Let us first clarify the goals of economic and environmental policy. On the one hand it is increases in the level of consumption (C) that make an economy better off, on the other environmental pollution (W), rising levels of which deteriorate the quality of living. As usually, we postulate the existence of a welfare function (U), defining the rates of trade-off between these two welfare indicators:

$$U = U(C, W); \; U_C = \frac{\partial U}{\partial C} > 0, \; U_{CC} < 0, \; C > 0;$$
$$U_W < 0, \; U_{WW} < 0, \; W > 0, \; U_{CW} \leqslant 0 \tag{1}$$
$$U_{CC} U_{WW} - U_{CW}^2 \geqslant 0.$$

The starting point of our analysis is hence a strictly concave welfare function, where the marginal utility of consumption is positive but at a decreasing rate, the marginal utility of environmental pollution is negative and falling.

Let us further postulate, to facilitate the derivation, that the slope of the welfare function as C approaches zero is infinity, to ensure that no optimal policy will entail a zero level of consumption.

$$\lim_{C \to 0} U_C (C, W) \to + \infty, \quad \text{for all } W > 0.$$

Furthermore we have to postulate:

$$W \geqslant 0 \text{ (negative pollution is physically impossible)}. \tag{2}$$

To be able to make a rational decision, future welfare levels have to be discounted, thus calculating the present value in utility terms of all future levels of consumption and environmental quality

$$V = \int_0^T e^{-\rho t} U(C, W)\, dt. \tag{3}$$

T is the time horizon of the planning authority and ρ the interest rate, where $\rho = \dot{\alpha}/\alpha$ and α is the discount rate. In our analysis we will always consider $T \to \infty$.

Consumption goods have to be produced, so there are technological constraints on the level of attainable consumption levels. For simplicity we assume that GNP denoted by Y is only produced by capital (K);

$$Y = F(K), \tag{4}$$

with $F'(K) > 0$, $F''(K) < 0$ and $F(0) = 0$. The production function described hence, is strictly concave, the marginal productivity of capital is positive, but falling and you cannot produce "anything with nothing".

This convential production function has to be extended, however, to be able to analyse problems of environmental pollution. From the point of view of physics, production is nothing but a transformation process of materials for which the physical law of the "conservation of mass" must be valid. The total mass of inputs (raw materials, energy, etc.) must be equal to the total mass of outputs, in our case, useful "economic" goods for consumption, investment and pollution abatement purposes, and waste. The technological constraint on the consumption level attainable is hence a "transformation relation", involving all inputs and outputs. We will postulate that this implicit production relation can be separated into two parts — a production function (as above) and an "emission function".

Let emissions emanating from the productive sector be E_Y:

$$E_Y = \epsilon_1 Y, \ \epsilon_1 > 0. \tag{5}$$

ϵ_1 is the emission rate reflecting a part of the technology which is used to produce Y, the aggregate bundle of goods and services in the economy. This emission rate, as briefly mentioned in the introduction, can change, when new technologies are applied (or there is a new consumption and production structure; this consideration will be neglected in our aggregate model). A similar argument can be used to describe the emissions generated by consumption in the household sector.

$$E_C = \epsilon_2 C, \ \epsilon_2 > 0. \tag{6}$$

The emission rate ϵ_2 then reflects the average "consumption technology" prevalent in the model economy.

There is a third source of emissions we still have to take into account. The capital stock of an economy (K) depreciates, whatever cannot be recycled becomes waste mostly in the form of solid waste (E_K) [Mäler].

Let the rate of capital depreciation β be a constant, and $\bar{\epsilon}_3$ be a constant emission rate, indicating that part of the depreciated capital stock that has potentially harmful effects.

$$E_K = \bar{\epsilon}_3 \beta K = \epsilon_3 K; \ \bar{\epsilon}_3, \epsilon_3, \beta > 0. \tag{7}$$

Let us next investigate the relation between emissions and the ambient environmental quality, or rather its inverse, the level of residuals concentration that can be measured in the various receiving media (air, water, land). Emissions are flows per unit of time which are deposited in a receiving medium where they accumulate. In this non-spatial analysis we have to neglect the diffusion process of these waste particles potentially creating different levels of pollution at different points in space and time. Furthermore, we will also abstract from possible "synergistic effects", where these residuals are transformed in the receiving medium itself, thus altering their quality, a fact, which strictly speaking, makes their "adding-up" infeasible.

A part of the stock of residuals is, however, transformed by natural processes into "harmless" materials, which are "recycled" into nature's stock of "ecological capital".

To summarize then, our analysis pertains only to such residuals which have a negative effect on welfare, other wastes, which may very well come about in the productive and consumption process will not be considered (this, however, makes the explicit introduction of the "conservation of mass" constraint impossible).

Turning now to environmental policy, and its effects, we must distinguish between the different strategies mentioned in the introduction. Let us, as indicated, consider only policies to control emissions. Looking at equations (5) and (6), we can see that a reduction of total production and/or consumption leads to decreasing emissions ("decrease throughput" strategy).

Technological changes can lead to a decrease in the emission rates ("new technology" strategy). Abatement processes can be installed to transform potentially harmful residuals into harmless, or even useful ones ("recycling"), or to transfer residuals to another receiving medium (e.g. water purification leads to solid waste in the form of sludge, etc.). In an aggregate model, this implies that besides the reduction of residuals achieved by nature, an "artificial" transformation process is interpolated. The change of the stock of residuals takes the following form:

$$\dot{W} = (\epsilon_1 Y + \epsilon_2 C + \epsilon_3 K) - (\delta W + Ab), \delta \geq 0; \tag{8}$$

where δ is the rate of natural "self cleansing" and Ab is the level of the abatement activity. This level of abatement can be achieved via a transformation process which requires some current expenditures (e.g. labour costs) and/or it may require investment expenditures in purification plants, which accumulate over time, increasing the abatement capacity of the abatement activities. Let current abatement expenditures be of the magnitude A per unit of time. Total abatement is then a function of A (similar to a production function):

$$Ab = G(A) \tag{9}$$

with $G'(A) > 0, G''(A) < 0, G(0) = 0$.

If this strategy is chosen the residuals accumulation process has the following form (from (8) and (9)):

$$\dot{W} = \epsilon_1 Y + \epsilon_2 C + \epsilon_3 K - G(A) - \delta W$$
$$= \epsilon_1 F(K) + \epsilon_2 C + \epsilon_3 K - G(A) - \delta W. \tag{10}$$

If, however, these expenditures have the character of investments we obtain:

$$\dot{W} = \epsilon_1 Y + \epsilon_2 C + \epsilon_3 K - H(K_A) - \delta W$$

and $\dot{K}_A = I_A$ neglecting abatement capital depreciation, where K_A is the stock of abatement capital and I_A the flow of abatement investment.

This case will, however, not be analyzed in the framework of this paper [see *Luptáčik/Schubert*, 1979b].

As mentioned above, we will consider capital as the only production factor in our production function (4). This capital stock is changed by investment, we hence obtain the following stock-flow relationship:

$$\dot{K} = \frac{dK}{dt} = I - \beta K, \; \beta > 0. \tag{11}$$

Furthermore, we must observe the national accounting constraint that total expenditures for consumption, investment and abatement are equal to the total national product.

$$Y = C + I + A \text{ or } F(K) - C - I - A = 0. \tag{12}$$

Assuming further that investment and "abatement goods" are irreversible, we must have:

$$I \geqslant 0, A \geqslant 0.$$

Let us summarize our trade-off problem between consumption and environmental quality in the next section as a problem of optimal control theory.

3. Optimal Allocation Patterns

3.1 A Summary of the Mathematical Model

Let us first briefly summarize the mathematical model we are going to use to derive rules for the optimal allocation of consumption, investment and abatement expenditures. The formal planning problem is to

$$\max_{C,A} V = \int_0^\infty e^{-\rho t} U(C, W) \, dt \text{ with } \rho > 0 \tag{13}$$

subject to:

$$\dot{K} = F(K) - C - A - \beta K \text{ by using } F(K) - C - A = I, \tag{14}$$

$$\dot{W} = \epsilon_1 F(K) + \epsilon_2 C + \epsilon_3 K - G(A) - \delta W, \tag{15}$$

$$W(0) = W_0, \; W(\infty) \text{ free} \tag{16}$$

$$K(0) = K_0, \; K(\infty) \text{ free}$$

$$A \geqslant 0$$

$$W \geqslant 0. \tag{17}$$

We are dealing with a problem of optimal control with 2 control (C and A) and 2 state variables (K and W).

Let us next formulate the Lagrange-function which we need for our further derivations:

$$L = U(C, W) + p_1(F(K) - C - A - \beta K) + p_2(\epsilon_1 F(K) +$$
$$+ \epsilon_2 C + \epsilon_3 K - G(A) - \delta W) + sA + r(\epsilon_1 F(K) + \epsilon_2 C +$$
$$+ \epsilon_3 K - G(A) - \delta W) \tag{18}$$

where p_1 and p_2 are the co-state variables and s and r are the Lagrange-multipliers.

3.2 Pontrjagin's Maximum Principle and Optimal Expenditures Patterns

What are the rules the planner postulated in our model should follow to ensure the maximum discounted value of the stream of future utilities accrueing from consumption and environmental quality?

Applying Pontrjagin's Maximum Principle we obtain:

$$\frac{\partial L}{\partial C} = U_C - p_1 + p_2 \epsilon_2 + r\epsilon_2 = 0 \tag{19}$$

hence

$$p_1 = U_C + (p_2 + r)\epsilon_2 \tag{20}$$

$$\frac{\partial L}{\partial A} = -p_1 - p_2 G'(A) + s - rG'(A) = 0$$
$$- (p_2 + r) G'(A) + s = p_1 \tag{21}$$

hence

$$p_2 = -\frac{p_1}{G'(A)} + \frac{s}{G'(A)} - r$$

$$s \geqslant 0, \quad sA = 0$$

$$r \geqslant 0, \quad rW = 0 \text{ and } r\dot{W} = 0. \tag{22}$$

The general rule that should be followed then is that

> marginal social benefits = marginal social costs

in all planning periods.

In our case (19) and (21) imply:

Proposition 1a: The marginal utility of consumption (U_C) has to be equal to its production cost (p_1) minus the environmental cost which is due to the extra unit of consumption causing emissions. If, however, the environment is still clean ($r > 0$, $W = 0$) the environmental costs of consumption are increased by the marginal social value of a clean environment.

Proposition 1b: The value of the marginal contribution of abatement expenditure has to be equal to the marginal cost of producing an extra unit of abatement equipment. This contribution to social welfare is diminished if abatement expenditure occurs in a state of a clean environment ($rG'(A)$) and raised by an extra premium (s) if the economy is leaving a state of no abatement at all ($A = 0$).

Is investment (and production) always useful and is more pollution always bad in terms of social welfare?

Let us take a look at the signs of the shadow prices (p_1 and p_2) of investment and emissions. Using (20) and (22) we obtain

$$p_1 = U_C \frac{G'(A)}{G'(A) + \epsilon_2} + \frac{s\epsilon_2}{G'(A) + \epsilon_2} > 0$$

and

$$p_2 = -\frac{U_C}{G'(A) + \epsilon_2} - r + \frac{s}{G'(A) + \epsilon_2} \gtrless 0$$

under the assumptions of our model.

This leads to the following corollary of proposition 1:

Corollary 1a: The marginal social value of capital investment is always positive, as there are always useful ways of spending the extra income produced by a larger capital stock, i.e. consumption and/or abatement expenditures can be raised.

Corollary 1b: The marginal social value of pollution is always negative when there is abatement in the system (i.e. $A > 0$ and therefore $s = 0$). Leaving a clean environment is always penalized extra (by an amount of r), which makes the marginal social disutility of pollution even worse. Only if the social cost of starting to abate is very high, (s is large and $A = 0$) could extra pollution actually be valued positively. In other words, the social benefit from the increase of consumption outweights the corresponding social environmental cost.

3.3 Changes in the Social Values of Capital and Environmental Quality

The social values of capital and environmental quality change as capital and residuals' accumulation occurs over time. At each planning period a decision has to be taken about how much extra product should be invested and used for production purposes or should be left for the next generations (which can be thought to be ready to pay an interest rate on the capital stock passed on to them).

Analogously we can think of environmental quality as a resource stock which is valued by the future generations, for which they are ready to pay an interest rate (for both stocks being equal to the rate of interest ρ).

Applying the maximum principle again, we obtain:

$$-\frac{\partial L}{\partial K} = \dot{p}_1 - \rho p_1 = -(F'(K) - \beta) p_1 - (\epsilon_1 F'(K) + \epsilon_3)(p_2 + r) \tag{23}$$

$$-\frac{\partial L}{\partial W} = \dot{p}_2 - \rho p_2 = -U_W + \delta p_2 + r\delta. \tag{24}$$

These expressions can be transformed to yield – according to Arrow's Interpretation [*Arrow*, p. 95] – the familiar equilibrium relation for investment in capital goods: the sum of capital gains and marginal productivity should be equl to the interest on the investment. Making use of (21) and (22), we have (under the assumption $A > 0$);

$$\rho = \frac{\dot{p}_1}{p_1} + \left(1 - \frac{\epsilon_1}{G'(A)}\right) F'(K) - \left(\frac{\epsilon_3}{G'(A)} + \beta\right) \tag{25}$$

and (under the assumption $W > 0, A > 0$):

$$\rho = \frac{\dot{p}_2}{p_2} - \frac{U_W}{U_C} (G'(A) + \epsilon_2)) - \delta. \tag{26}$$

In our case this relation can be read as follows:

Proposition 2a: The interest rate paid for leaving a unit of capital for the future has to be equal to the return on capital if it is used; this return consists of the "net marginal product", (some of the product has to be used to clean up the emissions (ϵ_1) caused by the increase in production) $(1 - \epsilon_1/(G'(A))) F'(K)$, minus the social cost of capital depreciation (i.e. the replacement and the environmental cost of depreciation) and the relative changes in the value of the capital stock over time $(\dot{p}_1/p_1)$.

Proposition 2b: Owing the next generations an extra unit of environmental quality costs an interest rate of ρ in all periods. This cost has to be equal to the cost of increasing pollution now, implying a loss of utility evaluated at the marginal utility of consumption foregone weighted with the environmental net effect of consumption. This cost is mitigated by the rate of natural regeneration capacity (δ).

3.4 Can Consumption Grow, when Abatement Expenditures Grow and when will Abatement Expenditures Grow over Time?

In each period there is a trade-off relation between consumption and abatement expenditure (cet. par.) implied by the national income constraint (12). Is it still possible that over time, as more resources are spent on abatement ($\dot{A} > 0$), that consumption (C) can still grow?

To find the answer, let us first use equations (20) and (22). In order to sharpen the analysis of this section we assume $A > 0$, $W > 0$ and $U_{CW} = 0$. We have

$$p_1 = U_C \frac{G'(A)}{G'(A) + \epsilon_2}. \tag{27}$$

Differentiation of (27) with respect to time yields:

$$\frac{\dot{p}_1}{p_1} = \frac{U_{CC}}{U_C} \dot{C} + \frac{G''(A)}{G'(A)} \dot{A} - \frac{G''(A)}{G'(A) + \epsilon_2} \dot{A}.$$

We denote by $\sigma(C) = -C(U_{CC}/U_C) > 0$ the elasticity of the marginal utility of consumption and by $\sigma(A) = -A[G''(A)]/[G'(A)] > 0$ the elasticity of the marginal efficiency of pollution abatement. Using (25) for $\dot{p}_1/p_1$ we obtain:

$$\frac{\dot{C}}{C} = -\frac{1}{\sigma(C)}\left[\rho - \left(1 - \frac{\epsilon_1}{G'(A)}\right)F'(K) + \beta + \frac{\epsilon_3}{G'(A)} + \right.$$

$$\left. + \left(\frac{\sigma(A)}{A} + \frac{G''(A)}{G'(A) + \epsilon_2}\right)\dot{A}\right].$$

Then for $\dot{A} > 0$, we can write:

$$\dot{C}\begin{Bmatrix}=\\<\\>\end{Bmatrix}0 \text{ if } \rho + \left(\beta + \frac{\epsilon_3}{G'(A)}\right) + \underbrace{\left(\frac{\sigma(A)}{A} + \frac{G''(A)}{G'(A) + \epsilon_2}\right)\dot{A}}_{>0}\begin{Bmatrix}=\\>\\<\end{Bmatrix}$$

$$\begin{Bmatrix}=\\<\\>\end{Bmatrix}\left(1 - \frac{\epsilon_1}{G'(A)}\right)F'(K). \tag{28}$$

This leads to:

Proposition 3a: Consumption can only grow on the optimal path if the marginal environmental consequences of this increase (i.e. the decreased value of the environment for the next generation plus the environmental cost of capital accumulation and the abatement cost due to increases in consumption) for a given increase of abatement expenditure A are less than the net marginal product.

From relation (28) it is easy to see that consumption can grow only if $G'(A) > \epsilon_1$. In other words, if the net marginal product is positive. In the opposite case ($\epsilon_1 > G'(A)$) it is always optimal (for $\dot{A} \geqslant 0$) to decrease consumption.

Let us next make use of (22) again (under the assumption $A > 0$, $W > 0$) to find:

$$\frac{p_1}{p_2} = -G'(A).$$

Taking logs and differentiating with respect to time yields:

$$\frac{\dot{p}_1}{p_1} - \frac{\dot{p}_2}{p_2} = -\sigma_A \frac{\dot{A}}{A}.$$

Therefore

$$\dot{A}\begin{Bmatrix}=\\<\\>\end{Bmatrix}0 \text{ if } \frac{\dot{p}_2}{p_2}\begin{Bmatrix}=\\<\\>\end{Bmatrix}\frac{\dot{p}_1}{p_1}.$$

Proposition 3b: Abatement expenditure has to grow on the optimal path as long as the growth rate of the marginal social value of environmental quality exceeds the growth rate of the marginal social value of capital accumulation.

By substitution of (25) and (26) for $\dot{p}_1/p_1$ and $\dot{p}_2/p_2$ and some rearranging we get

$$\dot{A}\begin{Bmatrix}=\\<\\>\end{Bmatrix}0 \text{ if } \delta + \left(1 - \frac{\epsilon_1}{G'(A)}\right)F'(K)\begin{Bmatrix}=\\<\\>\end{Bmatrix} - \frac{U_W}{U_C}(G'(A) + \epsilon_2) + \frac{\epsilon_3}{G'(A)} + \beta.$$

This corresponds to the rule that abatement expenditure has to grow as long as the net marginal product exceeds the social cost of this capital accumulation, i.e. the marginal cost of pollution control in terms of foregone consumption $(- U_W (G'(A) + \epsilon_2)$, divided by marginal utility of consumption (U_C) plus the social cost of depreciation $(\epsilon_3/(G'(A)) + \beta)$. Nature's "present" in the form of regenerative capacity can be deducted from this social cost.

4. The Stationary State

Let the change of the state variables approach 0 (i.e. $\dot{K} = \dot{W} = 0$), i.e. let the stocks become constant, there is no more growth in the system (stationary state).

It can be shown [*Arrow*, Proposition 9] that under some — not very strong — assumptions the solution, which converges to an equilibrium, constitutes an optimal path. The equilibrium conditions imply:

Proposition 4a: In the stationary state the net marginal product must be equal to the interest rate plus the social cost of capital depreciation.

Setting $\dot{K} = \dot{W} = \dot{p}_1 = \dot{p}_2 = 0$, it is easy to show after some transformations, that:

$$F'(K^\infty) \left(1 - \frac{\epsilon_1}{G'(A^\infty)}\right) = \rho + \beta + \frac{\epsilon_3}{G'(A^\infty)}.$$

From this formulation we can easily derive the following corollary (as $F'(K) > 0$):

Corrollary 2: In the stationary state the marginal reduction of emissions due to the abatement process must exceed the emission rate.

As $F'(K^\infty) > 0$, $(1 - \epsilon_1/(G'(A^\infty))) > 0$, as $\rho + \beta + \epsilon_3/(G'(A^\infty)) > 0$, this implies that $G'(A^\infty) > \epsilon_1$.

Furthermore we get, by setting $\dot{p}_2 = 0$, that (for $W > 0$, hence $r = 0$):

$$-\frac{U_{W^\infty}}{\rho + \delta} = \frac{U_{C^\infty}}{G'(A^\infty) + \epsilon_2} \quad \text{or} \quad U_{C^\infty} = -\frac{U_{W^\infty}(G'(A) + \epsilon_2)}{\rho + \delta}.$$

This leads to:

Proposition 4b: In the stationary state the net marginal utility of consumption has to be equal to the marginal utility of environmental quality discounted by the interest rate augmented by natures' rate of benevolence.

Alternatively, we could interpret $(- U_{W^\infty}(G'(A^\infty) + \epsilon_2)/\rho + \delta)$ as the utility gained from devoting an additional unit of output to pollution control. It must equal the marginal cost of pollution control in terms of foregone consumption.

It is further easy to derive that in the stationary state gross investment consists only of replacement $(I^\infty = \beta K^\infty)$ and total emissions are equal to total "abatement", natural and artificial:

$$\epsilon_1 F(K^\infty) + \epsilon_2 C^\infty + \epsilon_3 K^\infty = G(A^\infty) + \delta W^\infty.$$

5. Stability Analysis

Now the following question turns up: In our model with infinite horizon, does the optimal solution converge to a steady state as time tends to infinity?

The convergence question is as important for dynamic economics as the stability analysis is for static economics.

Results on the convergence question are virtually non-existent for problems with more than one state variable except for the case where future utilities or payoffs are not discounted. *Brock/Scheinkman* [1977] developed a new set of results on the convergence question, and demonstrated their usefulness for dynamic economic theory by applying them to models of optimal accumulation of capital by profit-maximizing firms in the face of adjustment cost. A restriction on the use of the Brock-Scheinkman results, is that work so far has been confined to problems in which the control region is unbounded. This means that there are no results for models with bounded control regions for which control variables may switch between values on the boundary of the control set and from values on the boundary to values in the interior.

In this part of our paper we try to apply the results by *Brock/Scheinkman* [1977] to our model of optimal economic growth and environment.

We denote by $\underline{k} = (k_1, k_2) = (K, W)$ the vector of state variables and by $\underline{x} = (C, A)$ the vector of control variables, $\underline{p} = (p_1, p_2)$ are the shadow prices. *Brock/Scheinkman* [1977, p. 190] prove under the assumption of concavity of function $U(\underline{k}, \dot{\underline{k}})$ the following

Lemma 1: The shadow price p can be written as $p(\underline{k})$ and the matrix $\partial p/\partial \underline{k}$ is negative semi-definite and symmetric at each $\underline{k}$ where it exists. It exists almost everywhere.

Now we consider the system of ordinary differential equations in the plane (the "reduced form"):

$$\dot{k}_1 = H_{p_1}(p_1(\underline{k}), p_2(\underline{k}), k_1, k_2) = H_{p_1}(\underline{p}, \underline{k}) \equiv F_{21}(\underline{k})$$

$$\dot{k}_2 = H_{p_2}(\underline{p}, \underline{k}) \equiv F_{22}(\underline{k}) \tag{*}$$

$$\underline{k}(0) = \underline{k}_0.$$

The Jacobian matrix of F_2 is

$$J_{F_2} = H_{11}\frac{\partial^2 V}{\partial \underline{k}^2} + H_{12}$$

where $\dfrac{\partial \underline{p}}{\partial \underline{k}} = \dfrac{\partial^2 V}{\partial \underline{k}^2}$ and $H_1 = \dfrac{\partial H}{\partial \underline{p}}; H_2 = \dfrac{\partial H}{\partial \underline{k}}.$

Hsu/Meyer [1968, p. 164] proved the following theorem:

Lemma 2: If the trace $J_{F_2}(\underline{k})$ does not change sign for all $\underline{k}$, then there are no limit cycles for (*).

It can now be proved [*Brock/Scheinkman*, 190–193]:

Lemma 3: Let A, B be two 2×2 real matrices that are symmetric; A positive definite and B negative definite, then

(i)   trace $(AB) < 0$.

If only semi-positive definiteness and semi-negative definiteness holds, then

(ii)   trace $(AB) \leqslant 0$.

If neither A nor B is 0 and trace $(AB) = 0$, then

(iii) A and B are both singular.

Theorem 1: Assume that there is a bound $M(\underline{k}_0)$ such that

$$\| \underline{k}(t/\underline{k}_0) \| \leqslant M(\underline{k}_0)$$

For all $t \geqslant 0$. Also assume $V''(k) \neq 0$, H_{11} positive definite, and trace $H_{12}(\underline{k}) \leqslant 0$, then $\underline{k}(t/\underline{k}_0) \to \underline{k}^{\infty}$, $t \to \infty$, when $\underline{k}^{\infty}$ is a rest point of (*).

Now we apply these results to our model under the assumption $A > 0$, $W > 0$ and $U_{CW} < 0$.

We have

$$\frac{\partial H}{\partial p_1} \equiv H_{p_1} = F(K) - C(\underline{p}, \underline{k}) - A(\underline{p}, \underline{k}) - \beta K$$

and

$$\frac{\partial H}{\partial p_2} \equiv H_{p_2} = \epsilon_1 F(K) + \epsilon_2 C(\underline{p}, \underline{k}) + \epsilon_3 K - G(A(\underline{p}, \underline{k})) - \delta W$$

$$H_{12} = \begin{vmatrix} \dfrac{\partial H_{p_1}}{\partial K} & \dfrac{\partial H_{p_1}}{\partial W} \\[2ex] \dfrac{\partial H_{p_2}}{\partial K} & \dfrac{\partial H_{p_2}}{\partial W} \end{vmatrix} = \begin{pmatrix} F'(K) - \dfrac{\partial C}{\partial K} - \dfrac{\partial A}{\partial K} - \beta & -\dfrac{\partial C}{\partial W} - \dfrac{\partial A}{\partial W} \\[2ex] \epsilon_1 F'(K) + \epsilon_2 \dfrac{\partial C}{\partial K} + \epsilon_3 - G'(A)\dfrac{\partial A}{\partial K} & \epsilon_2 \dfrac{\partial C}{\partial W} - G'(A)\dfrac{\partial A}{\partial W} - \delta \end{pmatrix}$$

$$H_{11} = \begin{pmatrix} \dfrac{\partial H_{p_1}}{\partial p_1} & \dfrac{\partial H_{p_1}}{\partial p_2} \\[2ex] \dfrac{\partial H_{p_2}}{\partial p_1} & \dfrac{\partial H_{p_2}}{\partial p_2} \end{pmatrix} = \begin{pmatrix} -\dfrac{\partial C}{\partial p_1} - \dfrac{\partial A}{\partial p_1} & -\dfrac{\partial C}{\partial p_2} - \dfrac{\partial A}{\partial p_2} \\[2ex] \epsilon_2 \dfrac{\partial C}{\partial p_1} - G'(A)\dfrac{\partial A}{\partial p_1} & \epsilon_2 \dfrac{\partial C}{\partial p_2} - G'(A)\dfrac{\partial A}{\partial p_1} \end{pmatrix}.$$

To complete the computations, we must derive

$$\frac{\partial C}{\partial p_1}, \frac{\partial A}{\partial p_1}, \frac{\partial C}{\partial p_2}, \frac{\partial A}{\partial p_2}, \frac{\partial C}{\partial K}, \frac{\partial A}{\partial K}, \frac{\partial C}{\partial W}, \frac{\partial A}{\partial W}.$$

We have

$$p_1 = \frac{U_C G'(A)}{G'(A) + \epsilon_2} \text{ and } p_2 = -\frac{p_1}{G'(A)} = -\frac{U_C}{G'(A) + \epsilon_2}$$

or

$$p_1 (G'(A) + \epsilon_2) = U_C G'(A) \quad p_2 (G'(A) + \epsilon_2) = - U_C.$$

Using the implicit function theorem we obtain:

$$|J| = \begin{vmatrix} -U_{CC} G'(A) & p_1 G''(A) - U_C G''(A) \\ \\ U_{CC} & p_2 G''(A) \end{vmatrix} = -U_{CC} p_2 G''(A) G'(A) - \\ - \{U_{CC}(p_1 - U_C) G''(A)\} > 0$$

and

$$\frac{\partial C}{\partial p_1} < 0, \frac{\partial A}{\partial p_1} < 0.$$

The levels of consumption and abatement expenditures are a decreasing function of p_1. If the shadow price fore capital is increasing, it is optimal to increase the capital investment and decrease the consumption and abatement expenditure.

$\partial C/\partial p_2 > 0$, the level of consumption is an increasing function of p_2. This means that if the (negative) shadow price for environmental quality is increasing (the negative implications of environmental deterioration are smaller) the consumption can increase.

$\partial A/\partial p_2 < 0$, the level of abatement expenditure is a drecreasing function of the shadow price for environmental quality p_2. If the negative implications of the environmental deterioration are smaller, it is optimal to decrease the abatement expenditure.

$\partial C/\partial W < 0$, the level of consumption is a decreasing function of the level of pollution. Finally

$$\frac{\partial A}{\partial W} = 0, \frac{\partial C}{\partial K} = 0, \frac{\partial A}{\partial K} = 0.$$

It is easy to show that H_{11} is symmetric and positive definite. It can also be shown that the optimal solution starting from $\underline{k}_0 = (K_0, W_0)$ denoted by $\underline{k} (t/\underline{k}_0)$ is bounded (diminishing returns and depreciation bound capital stock; the marginal utility of pollution is negative and decreasing).

At the steady state,

$$F'(K^\infty) = \frac{G'(A^\infty) (\rho + \beta) + \epsilon_3}{G'(A^\infty) - \epsilon_1}$$

so that (at the steady state)

$$\text{trace } H_{12} = G'(A^\infty) \rho + \epsilon_3 + \beta \epsilon_1 - \left(\epsilon_2 \frac{U_{CW}}{U_{CC}} + \delta \right) (G'(A^\infty) - \epsilon_1).$$

Using Theorem 7 by *Brock/Scheinkman* [1977, 201–202] we formulate the following

Proposition 5: If a) at the steady state $\underline{k}^\infty$

$$\text{trace } H_{12} \equiv G'(A^{\infty})\, \rho + \epsilon_3 + \beta\epsilon_1 - \left(\epsilon_2 \frac{U_{CW}}{U_{CC}} + \delta\right)(G'(A^{\infty}) - \epsilon_1) < 0,$$

and b) there is a closed curve Γ containing the steady state such that

$$\underline{\dot{k}} = H_{\underline{p}}\, (\underline{p}\,(\underline{k}), \underline{k})$$

'points inward' on Γ, then, the steady state is *locally asymptotically stable* (except for hairline cases).

The condition b) is saying that $\dot{k}_i > 0$ if k_i is small enough and $\dot{k}_i < 0$ if k_i is large enough.

The condition in a) is more likely to hold if the regeneration rate (δ) is high and the lower the capital depreciation-emission rate (ϵ_3) and the interest rate are, etc.

References

Arrow, K.J.: Applications of control theory to economic growth. Mathematics of the decisions sciences. Ed. by G.B. Dantzig and A.F. Veinott. Providence, R.J. 1968.

Boulding, K.E.: The economics of the coming Spaceship Earth. Environmental Quality in a Growing Economy. Ed. by H. Jarrett. Baltimore 1966.

Brock, W.A., and *J.A. Scheinkman*: The global asymptotic stability of optimal control with applications to dynamic economic theory. Applications of Control Theory to Economic Analysis. Ed. by J.D. Pitchford and St. J. Turnovsky. Amsterdam−New York−Oxford 1977, Essay 8, 173−205.

Forster, B.A.: On a one state variable optimal control problem. Consumption-pollution trade-offs. Applications of Control Theory to Economic Analysis. Ed. by J.D. Pitchford and St. J. Turnovsky. Amsterdam−New York−Oxford 1977, Essay 2, 35−56.

Freeman, A.M., R.M. Havemen, and *A.V. Kneese*: The Economics of Environmental Policy. New York 1973.

Hsu, J., and *A. Meyer*: Modern control principles and applications. New York 1968.

Luptáčik, M., and *U. Schubert*: Optimale Investitionspolitik unter Berücksichtigung der Umwelt: Eine Anwendung der Kontrolltheorie. Operations Research Verfahren 35. Meisenheim 1979a, 271−282.

−: Optimal investment policy in productive capacity and pollution abatement processes, an extension of the Ramsey model. Paper presented at the Third European Congress on Operations Research. Amsterdam, 9−11 April 1979b.

Mastenbroek, A.P., and *P. Nijkamp*: A spatial environmental model for an optimal allocation of investments. Environmental Economics, Vol. 2: Methods. Ed. by P. Nijkamp, Leiden 1976.

Mäler, K.G.: Environmental economics. A theoretical Inquiry. Baltimore 1974.

Schubert, U.: Instrumente des Umweltschutzes. Institut für Höhere Studien Wien, Wien 1974.

Siebert, H.: Ökonomische Theorie der Umwelt. Tübingen 1978.

Economic Theory of Natural Resources. ©Physica-Verlag, Würzburg–Wien, 1982.

Applied Welfare Indicators and the
Economics of Exhaustible Resources

George McKenzie

1. Introduction

In the past, many economists writing on the subject of exhaustible resources have utilized the concept of consumer surplus as the benefit function to be evaluated [e.g. *Hotelling, 1931; Manne*]. Unfortunately, as is well-known, this measure, first proposed by Dupuit in 1844, is fraught with difficulties. However, many economists have doggedly refused to abandon consumer surplus procedures, largely on the grounds that no suitable alternative exists. Fortunately, this is no longer the case. In this paper, I propose to develop a simple computational procedure for accurately approximating welfare variations. The method represents an extension of the procedures discussed by *Pearce* and myself [1976, 1982a].

2. The Basic Problem

The basic assumption made by those utilizing consumer surplus procedures is that there exist *known* demand functions associated with an *unknown* consumer preference system.[1] In principle it ought to be possible to retrieve the preference system from the demand functions by finding a suitable integrating factor, otherwise known as the marginal utility of money. However, there are two problems:

(i) The integrating factor may not be capable of expression in terms of elementary mathematical functions;

(ii) Even in those circumstances where the factor is capable of expression in terms of elementary functions, it may be extremely difficult to identify except by a tedious trial and error procedure.

Consumer surplus methods evade this issue by assuming that consumer preferences are such that the integrating factor is independent of the variables under consideration. As is well-known this imposes severe restrictions on the form of consumer preferences [cf. *Samuelson*]. In order to set the stage for the solution technique proposed in this paper, it is helpful to examine some of the difficulties arising in the aforementioned work of Hotelling and Manne.

---

[1] I shall assume that all individuals in the society under discussion possess identical preferences and that the distribution of income remains constant. In practice, however, it will be necessary to identify the effects of any resources policy upon different groups. Since the objective of this paper is to discuss the properties of alternative benefit functions, the above problem will not be discussed. For further details, the reader is referred to *McKenzie* [1982].

Consumer's Surplus

Obviously, it is necessary to take into account the intertemporal aspects of designing policies for the allocation of exhaustible resources. Indeed, this is how the problem is formulated by Hotelling. However, since no points of principle are involved, we may for the sake of simplicity carry out our analysis in terms of its one period analogue. This heuristic device is followed by Manne. Both he and Hotelling utilize inverse demand functions to calculate their consumer's surplus or benefit function. We shall write these as follows:

$$p_i = p_i (X_1, \ldots, X_k; X_{k+1}, \ldots, X_s, Y) \qquad i = 1, \ldots, s \tag{1}$$

where commodities 1 to k are those which are "renewable" whereas commodities X_{k+1} to X_s are exhaustible. The variable p_i represents the price of the i-th commodity and $Y = \sum_i^s p_i X_i$ is total expenditure. In essence, the inverse demand functions described by (1) may be interpreted as planning equations since they indicate the prices required to clear all markets, given total expenditure and the level of outputs which may have been chosen by some Planning Board. A full discussion of the properties of these equations if given by *Pearce* [1964]. However, for the purposes of our subsequent discussion, it is sufficient to note that the inverse demand functions may be written in terms of the derivatives of the underlying utility function, $U = U(X_1, \ldots, X_k; X_{k+1}, \ldots, X_s)$ as follows:

$$p_i = Y \left[\frac{\partial U / \partial X_i}{\sum_j^s (\partial U / \partial X_j) X_j} \right] . \tag{2}$$

The consumer's surplus indicator may then be defined as

$$\Delta CS = \int \sum_j^s p_j \, dX_j . \tag{3}$$

The well-known difficulty with (3) is that it is not path-independent. By constrast, we know that

$$\Delta U = \int_c \sum_j^s \frac{\partial U}{\partial X_j} dX_j = \int_c \sum_j^s \lambda p_j \, dX_j \tag{4}$$

is path independent since $\partial^2 U / \partial X_i \, \partial X_j = \partial^2 U / \partial X_j \partial X_i$. The difference between (3) and (4) is that in the latter formulation we have incorporated an integrating factor equal to the marginal utility of money,

$$\lambda = \lambda (X_1, \ldots, X_s, Y). \tag{5}$$

In constrast, the consumer's surplus formulation (3) assumes that λ remains constant or independent of the variable changes being evaluated.[2] For (3) to be path independent

---

[2] As *Samuelson* [1943] pointed out, at least one variable (e.g. Y) must be assumed to remain constant.

and hence capable of serving as a welfare indicator it must be the case that

$$\frac{\partial p_i}{\partial X_j} = \frac{\partial p_j}{\partial X_i} \qquad i = 1, \ldots, s. \tag{6}$$

In the context of consumer surplus analysis, this condition was first pointed out by *Hotelling* [1938]. [3])

It implies that all preferences must be homothetic [cf. *Pearce*].

The implications of (6) can be made to appear somewhat less restrictive in the following special case. Assume:

(a) Consumer preferences are additively separable between renewable and non-renewable commodities, viz.

$$U = U(\emptyset_1(X_1, \ldots, X_k) + \emptyset_2(X_{k+1}, \ldots, X_s)). \tag{7}$$

(b) The Planning Board, referred to above, holds constant the quantities of all renewable commodities, $X_1, \ldots, X_k$;

(c) The function $\emptyset_2$ containing the non-renewable commodities is homothetic (i.e., for $i = K + 1, \ldots, s$).

Then it is the case that the symmetry condition (6) is fulfilled. It implies that the income elasticities for all non-renewable commodities are identical but not necessarily equal to one. This is the approach adopted by Manne.

3. The Money Metric

The need to resort to such restrictive assumptions as these can be avoided by making use of the following facts.

Fact 1: Associated with any preference system there exists an equivalence function:

$$E = E(U, p) \tag{8}$$

where E indicates the expenditure required to sustain the level of satisfaction U given the vector of prices $p = (p_1, \ldots, p_s)$. [4])

Fact 2: Let the vector p^0 represent the vector of base period prices. Then E is an increasing, monotonic transformation of U and hence is a utility indicator in its own right. This is the "money-metric". [Cf. *Samuelson.*]

Fact 3: As a consequence of Fact 2, application of Roy's Identity enables the set of demand functions associated with (8) to be written as

---

[3]) The inverse demand function (2) and the integrability conditions (6) should not be confused with those derived by *Antonelli* in [1886]. A full-comparison is provided in *McKenzie* [1982].

[4]) Equation (8) should not be confused with the compensation function:

$$H = E(U^0, p)$$

which indicates the level of expenditure required to sustain a given base level of satisfaction U^0 but on the basis of any vector of prices. In general, H is not independent of U^0 and hence cannot serve as an ordinal metric welfare indicator.

$$X_i = -\frac{\partial E/\partial p_i}{\lambda} \quad i = 1, \ldots, s \tag{9}$$

where λ equals $\partial E/\partial Y$, the marginal utility of money.

Fact 4: As *Pearce* and I [1976] have shown, given base prices, the equivalence function or money-metric exhibits the following properties:

$$\lambda(Y, p_0) \equiv 1 \tag{10}$$

$$\frac{\partial^j \lambda}{\partial Y^j}(Y, p_0) \equiv 0 \quad j = 1, \ldots, \infty. \tag{11}$$

Fact 5: Since the money-metric (8) is a utility indicator, it is possible to express it in terms of a line integral which is path independent:

$$\Delta E = Y^1 - Y^0 + \int_c \Sigma \frac{\partial E}{\partial p_i}(Y^1, p) \, dp_i. \tag{12}$$

Note that when Y is varied first, we are able to utilize Fact 4 in carrying out the calculation implied by (12).

Fact 6: A useful path of integration to apply to (12) is the one suggested by *Willig* [1979]. In the case of three commodities this may be written:

$$\begin{aligned}
\Delta E = Y^1 - Y^0 &- \Delta E_1(p_1^0, p_2^0, p_3^0, Y^1) \\
&- \Delta E_2(p_1^1, p_2^0, p_3^0, Y^1) \\
&- \Delta E_3(p_1^1, p_2^1, p_3^0, Y^1)
\end{aligned} \tag{13}$$

where

$$\Delta E_1(p_1^0, p_2^0, p_3^0, Y^1) = -\int_{p_1^0}^{p_1^1} \lambda(p_1^0, p_2^0, p_3^0, Y^1) X_1(p_1^0, p_2^0, p_3^0, Y^1) \, dp_1 \tag{14}$$

$$\Delta E_2(p_1^1, p_2^0, p_3^0, Y^1) = -\int_{p_2^0}^{p_2^1} \lambda(p_1^1, p_2^0, p_3^0, Y^1) X_2(p_1^1, p_2^0, p_3^0, Y^1) \, dp_2 \tag{15}$$

$$\Delta E_3(p_1^1, p_2^1, p_3^0, Y^1) = -\int_{p_3^0}^{p_3^1} \lambda(p_1^1, p_2^1, p_3^0, Y^1) X_3(p_1^1, p_2^1, p_3^0, Y^1) \, dp_3. \tag{16}$$

In other words, first let us vary total expenditure. Since no price variations have occurred, it is still the case that (10) and (11) hold. Thus no adjustments to ΔY are required. The next step is to allow p_1 to vary and hence to calculate ΔE_1, *given the new level of total expenditure* Y^1. This result is then added to ΔY. Then we calculate ΔE_2, given both Y^1 and the new level of p_1 and so forth in a step-by-step, recursive path. It should be noted that although this path of integration is that suggested by Willig, he does fail to take into account the function λ.

4. Two Numerical Procedures

The above facts enable us to formulate two numerical procedures for calculating the money-metric from information contained in consumer demand functions. The first is less accurate but enables us to establish clearly the relationship between this discussion and that contained in the 1976 paper by Pearce and myself. There we showed that it was possible to express any well-behaved preference function in terms of a Taylor series expansion that required only information about the consumer demand functions. All reference to the marginal utility of money can be eliminated by making use of the conditions described in Fact 4 above. This same approach will now be used as the basis for the first numerical method.

Method I. This involves expressing each of the integral expressions contained in equation (14) – (16) in terms of Taylor series expansions, each evaluated at the appropriate variable values. The first decision that must be made is the order of the expansion. In the following discussion I have arbitrarily chosen to express each integral by means of a fourth-order Taylor series. Of course, a higher order series would lead to more accurate results. In general, the derivatives involved are as follows:

$$U1(i) = \frac{\partial E}{\partial p_i} = -\lambda X_i \tag{17}$$

$$U2(i) = \frac{\partial^2 E}{\partial p_i^2} = -\frac{\partial \lambda}{\partial p_i} X_i - \lambda \frac{\partial X_i}{\partial p_i} \tag{18}$$

$$U3(i) = \frac{\partial^3 E}{\partial p_i^3} = -\frac{\partial^2 \lambda}{\partial p_i^2} X_i - 2 \frac{\partial \lambda}{\partial p_i} \frac{\partial X_i}{\partial p_i} - \lambda \frac{\partial^2 X_i}{\partial p_i^2} \tag{19}$$

$$U4(i) = \frac{\partial^4 E}{\partial p_i^4} = -\frac{\partial^3 \lambda}{\partial p_i^3} X_i - 3 \frac{\partial^2 \lambda}{\partial p_i^2} \frac{\partial X_i}{\partial p_i} - 3 \frac{\partial \lambda}{\partial p_i} \frac{\partial^2 X_i}{\partial p_i^2} - \lambda \frac{\partial^3 X_i}{\partial p_i^3}. \tag{20}$$

General forms for the derivatives of λ are easily expressed in terms of the procedure outlined in *McKenzie/Pearce* [1976]. These are shown in column 3 of Table 1. For the *first* "integration" implied by the path described in Fact 6 (i.e. equation (14)); the calculation is particularly simple. By making use of Fact 4 the several derivates of λ can be expressed in terms only of the derivatives of the consumer functions (cf. column 4 of Table 1). These in turn enable equations (17) – (20) to be calculated so as to provide an approximation to (14):

$$\Delta E_1 \approx U_1 \Delta p_1 + \frac{1}{2} U_2 (\Delta p_1)^2 + \frac{1}{6} U_3 (\Delta p_1)^3 + \frac{1}{24} U_4 (\Delta p_1)^4. \tag{21}$$

Although this is a fourth-order approximation, information about the derivatives of the demand function is required only up to the third-order.

The calculation of the remaining integrals in (13) is slightly more difficult. Since p_1 has varied, the marginal utility of money will have changed from its initial values and hence we can no longer make direct use of Fact 4. However, we can approximate the new value of λ and its derivatives with respect to income by means of Taylor series expansions that make use of the available information about the demand function, viz.

Derivative	Symbol	General Form	Form Taken for First Integration
$\dfrac{\partial \lambda}{\partial p_i}$	B1	$-\lambda \dfrac{\partial X_i}{\partial Y} - X_i \dfrac{\partial \lambda}{\partial Y}$	$-\dfrac{\partial X_i}{\partial Y}$
$\dfrac{\partial^2 \lambda}{\partial p_i \partial Y}$	B2	$-2\dfrac{\partial \lambda}{\partial Y}\dfrac{\partial X_i}{\partial Y} - \lambda \dfrac{\partial^2 X_i}{\partial Y^2} - X_i \dfrac{\partial^2 \lambda}{\partial Y^2}$	$-\dfrac{\partial^2 X_i}{\partial Y^2}$
$\dfrac{\partial^2 \lambda}{\partial p_i^2}$	B3	$-\dfrac{\partial X_i}{\partial p_i}\dfrac{\partial \lambda}{\partial Y} - \dfrac{\partial \lambda}{\partial p_i}\dfrac{\partial X_i}{\partial Y} - \lambda \dfrac{\partial^2 X_i}{\partial Y \partial p_i} - X_i \dfrac{\partial^2 \lambda}{\partial Y \partial p_i}$	$\left(\dfrac{\partial X_i}{\partial Y}\right)^2 - \dfrac{\partial^2 X_i}{\partial Y \partial p_i} + \dfrac{\partial^2 X_i}{\partial Y^2} X_i$
$\dfrac{\partial^3 \lambda}{\partial p_i \partial Y^2}$	B4	$-3\dfrac{\partial^2 \lambda}{\partial Y^2}\dfrac{\partial X_i}{\partial Y} - 3\dfrac{\partial \lambda}{\partial Y}\dfrac{\partial^2 X_i}{\partial Y^2}$ $-\lambda \dfrac{\partial^3 X_i}{\partial Y^3} - X_i \dfrac{\partial^3 \lambda}{\partial Y^3}$	$-\dfrac{\partial^3 X_i}{\partial Y^3}$
$\dfrac{\partial^3 \lambda}{\partial p_i^2 \partial Y}$	B5	$-2\dfrac{\partial^2 \lambda}{\partial p_i \partial Y}\dfrac{\partial X_i}{\partial Y} - \dfrac{\partial \lambda}{\partial p_i}\dfrac{\partial^2 X_i}{\partial Y^2} - \lambda \dfrac{\partial^3 X_i}{\partial Y^2 \partial p_i}$ $-2\dfrac{\partial \lambda}{\partial Y}\dfrac{\partial^2 X_i}{\partial Y \partial p_i} - \dfrac{\partial X_i}{\partial p_i}\dfrac{\partial^2 \lambda}{\partial Y^2}$ $-X_i \dfrac{\partial^3 \lambda}{\partial Y^2 \partial p_i}$	$2\dfrac{\partial^2 X_i}{\partial Y^2}\dfrac{\partial X_i}{\partial Y} + \dfrac{\partial X_i}{\partial Y}\dfrac{\partial^2 X_i}{\partial Y^2} - \dfrac{\partial^3 X_i}{\partial Y^2 \partial p_i}$ $+2\dfrac{\partial X_i}{\partial Y}\dfrac{\partial^2 X_i}{\partial Y \partial p_i} - X_i \dfrac{\partial^3 X_i}{\partial Y^3}$
$\dfrac{\partial^3 \lambda}{\partial p_i^3}$	B6	$-\dfrac{\partial^2 \lambda}{\partial p_i^2}\dfrac{\partial X_i}{\partial Y} - 2\dfrac{\partial \lambda}{\partial p_i}\dfrac{\partial^2 X_i}{\partial Y \partial p_i}$ $-\lambda \dfrac{\partial^3 X_i}{\partial Y \partial p_i^2} - \dfrac{\partial^2 X_i}{\partial p_i^2}\dfrac{\partial \lambda}{\partial Y_i} - 2\dfrac{\partial X_i}{\partial p_i}\dfrac{\partial^2 \lambda}{\partial Y \partial p_i}$ $-\dfrac{\partial X_i}{\partial p_i}\dfrac{\partial^2 \lambda}{\partial p_i \partial Y} - X_i \dfrac{\partial^3 \lambda}{\partial Y \partial_i^2}$	$-\dfrac{\partial X_i}{\partial Y}\left(\left(\dfrac{\partial X_i}{\partial Y}\right)^2 - \dfrac{\partial^2 X_i}{\partial Y \partial p_i} + X_i \dfrac{\partial^2 X_i}{\partial Y^2}\right)$ $+2\dfrac{\partial X_i}{\partial Y}\left(\dfrac{\partial^2 X_i}{\partial Y \partial p_i}\right) - \dfrac{\partial^3 X_i}{\partial Y \partial p_i^2}$ $-X_i[B5] + 2\dfrac{\partial X_i}{\partial p_i}\dfrac{\partial^2 X_i}{\partial Y^2}$

Tab. 1

$$\frac{\partial \lambda}{\partial Y}(p_1^1, p_2^0, p_3^0, Y^1) = \frac{\partial \lambda}{\partial Y}(p_1^0, p_2^0, p_3^0, Y^1) + \frac{\partial^2 \lambda}{\partial Y_1 \partial p_1}(p_1^0, p_2^0, p_3^0, Y^1)(\Delta p_1)$$

$$+ \frac{1}{2}\frac{\partial^3 \lambda}{\partial Y \partial p_1^2}(p_1^0, p_2^0, p_3^0, Y^1)(\Delta p_1)^2 \qquad (22)$$

$$\frac{\partial^2 \lambda}{\partial Y^2}(p_1^1, p_2^0, p_3^0, Y^1) = \frac{\partial^2 \lambda}{\partial Y^2}(p_1^0, p_2^0, p_0^3, Y^1) + \frac{\partial^3 \lambda}{\partial Y^2 \partial p_1}(p_1^0, p_2^0, p_3^0, Y^1)\Delta p_1 \qquad (23)$$

$$\frac{\partial^3 \lambda}{\partial Y^3}(p_1^1, p_2^0, p_3^0, Y^1) = \frac{\partial^3 \lambda}{\partial Y^3}(p_1^0, p_2^0, p_3^0, Y^1). \qquad (24)$$

Since $(\partial^3 \lambda)/(\partial Y^3)(p^0, Y^1)$ is zero, this derivative will always take up this value irrespective of the level of prices and expenditure. Effectively this means that we are approximating ΔE by a function which possesses the property that the third and higher-order derivatives of the marginal utility of money with respect to expenditure are always zero.

Equations (22) – (24) may now be used as a basis for determining new values of $B1 - B6$ and these in turn for new values of $U1 - U4$ so as to enable an approximation of the second integral. This pattern of calculations may then be repeated in recursive fashion until all price variations have been accounted for. Although at first glance the above manipulations are tedious, they are also repetitive and hence can easily be translated into a simple computer programme. The key, as can be seen from the above outline, is that we do not require any cross-price effects. These have been automatically taken into account via the chosen path of integration. Hence the computations are considerably simpler than those involved in the generalised Taylor series expansion originally devised by Pearce and myself.

Method II. Since the above Taylor series approach is based on derivatives evaluated at the initial price/quantity situation, there is the possibility that for large price changes or for particularly "sensitive" functions, a very high order expansion may be required before an acceptable approximation is obtained. A technique that utilised information over part or all of the range or price variation would thus seem to be preferable to the one just discussed. One possibility which requires no more information than that utilised in the previous exercise involves the introduction of Simpson's Rule.

Let us begin again with the integral described by equation (14). If we start from the initial set of prices, the problem is to calculate the area under the curve describing marginal money metric utility $\partial E/\partial p_i$ is a function of p_i. This may be achieved by adopting a two-step approximation procedure. First, provided that E has a continuous fifth derivative then the integral

$$\Delta E_1 = \int_{p_i^0}^{p_i^2} \frac{\partial E}{\partial p_i} \, dp_i$$

may be written exactly as:

$$\Delta E = \frac{p_1^1 - p_1^0}{6} \left[\frac{\partial E}{\partial p_1} (p_1^0) + 4 \frac{\partial E}{\partial p_1} (p_1^m) + \frac{\partial E}{\partial p_1} p_1^1 \right]$$

$$+ \frac{(p_1 - p_1^0)^5}{2880} \frac{\partial^5 E}{\partial p_1^5} (p_1^c) \tag{25}$$

where $p_1^m = (p_1^1 + p_1^0)/2$ and p_1^c lies between p_1^1 and p_1^0. This formula is known as *Simpson's Rule.* The first three terms on the right-hand side of (25) form the basis for an approximation. The last term involving the fifth derivative $(\partial^5 E)/(\partial p_1^5) (p_1^c)$ is not known since we do not know the value of p_1^c.

Unfortunately, we cannot apply Simpson's Rule in a straightforward manner to the problem at hand since we do not possess an exact representation of the function $\partial E/\partial p_1 = -\lambda X_1$. We do know the functional form for X_1 but do not, of course, know λ. However, in the spirit of the previous section we may utilise a third-order Taylor series to approximate the values of λ required to calculate the *Simpson's Rule* approximation. Thus to approximate (25) we calculate

$$\Delta E_1 \approx -\frac{p_1^1 - p_1^0}{6} (\hat{\lambda} (p_1^0) X_1 (p_1^0) + 4 \hat{\lambda} (p_1^m) X_1 (p_1^m) + \hat{\lambda} (p_1^1) X_1 (p_1^1)). \tag{26}$$

Since our initial situation is one where all prices are at their base values, we know that $\hat{\lambda}\,(p_1^0) = 1$. We may then utilise a third-order Taylor series approximation for $\hat{\lambda}\,(p_1^m)$, viz:

$$\hat{\lambda}\,(p_1^m) = 1 + \frac{\partial \lambda}{\partial p_1}\,(p_1^0)\left(\frac{\Delta p_1}{2}\right) + \frac{1}{2}\frac{\partial^2 \lambda}{\partial p_1^2}\,(p_1^0)\left(\frac{\Delta p_1}{2}\right)^2 + \frac{1}{6}\frac{\partial^3 \lambda}{\partial p_1^3}\,(p_1^0)\left(\frac{\Delta p_1}{2}\right)^3$$

$$(27)$$

and similarly for $\hat{\lambda}\,(p_1^1)$:

$$\hat{\lambda}\,(p_1^1) = \hat{\lambda}\,(p_1^m) + \frac{\partial \lambda}{\partial p_1}\,(p_1^m)\left(\frac{\Delta p_1}{2}\right) + \frac{1}{2}\frac{\partial^2 \lambda}{\partial p_1^2}\,(p_1^m)\left(\frac{\Delta p_1}{2}\right)^2 +$$

$$+ \frac{1}{6}\frac{\partial^3 \lambda}{\partial p_1^3}\,(p_1^m)\left(\frac{\Delta p_1}{2}\right)^3 .$$

$$(28)$$

A similar procedure may now be followed to evaluate the additional integrals in equation (13). As in Method I approximations for the marginal utility of money and its several derivatives can be obtained by a Taylor series approximation.

An important virtue of this approach is that it enables us to see quite clearly the relationship between the approximation described by (26) and the calculation of consumer surplus. In general, the integral expression for the latter, may not be capable of expression in terms of elementary functions. In such situations, however, a numerical representation of consumer surplus is possible. If this is based on a Simpson's Rule calculation such as we have previously discussed, we obtain:

$$\Delta CS_1 \approx \frac{p_1^1 - p_1^0}{6}\,[X_1(p_1^0) + 4\,X_1\,(p_1^m) + X_1\,(p_1^1)].$$

$$(29)$$

A comparison of (29) with (26) reveals that the factors $\hat{\lambda}\,(p_1^0)$, $\hat{\lambda}\,(p_1^m)$ and $\hat{\lambda}\,(p_1^1)$ act as coefficients which correct for the inherent error in the consumer surplus method.

The results of this section can be summarized by the following algorithm:

Algorithm

Input: 1. A set of n consumer demand functions and their derivatives with respect to prices and total expenditure. (These functions must be consistent with the theory of consumer behaviour.)
2. A set of observations on n prices (p_i^0) and quantities demanded (X_i^0) for an arbitrarily chosen base period.
3. A set of observations on n prices (p_i^1) and quantities demanded (X_i^1) for a period different than the base period.
4. Initial values of the marginal utility of money and its derivatives up to the third order:

$$\lambda = 1$$

$$\frac{\partial^i \lambda}{\partial Y^i} = 0 \quad i = 1,2,3.$$

Output: A monetary value representing the variation in the equivalence function associated with a change in prices and total expenditure from base to new levels.

Method: 1. Calculate λ for $p_i^m = p_i^0 + \dfrac{\Delta p_i}{2}$ and $p_i^1 = p_i^0 + \Delta p_i$ using the Taylor Series method (equations (27) and (28)).

2. Calculate the change in the equivalence function ΔE_i for commodity i by the Simpson's Rule method (equation (26)).

3. Repeat steps 1 and 2 for all n, utilizing the value of λ (p_i^1) as the starting point for the $i + 1$ iteration.

4. Sum all ΔE_i and $\Delta Y = (\Sigma p_i^1 X_i^1) - (\Sigma p_i^0 X_i^0)$ to obtain the change in the equivalence function.

5. Difficulties Involved in Determining Errors Bounds

Unfortunately, it is difficult to undertake any evaluation of the errors involved in the two procedures discussed above. These will depend upon a) the initial values assumed by the variables, b) the magnitude of their variation and c) the functional form of the system of demand functions. Since we do not know the exact functional form of λ, the marginal utility of money, it is not possible to establish any procedures for determining error bounds. A more detailed discussion of the issues involved is discussed in *McKenzie* [1982]. More complex procedures, such as those developed by *Vartia* [1978] are available but these lack the computational simplicity that consumer surplus advocates desire. Further, it is reasonable to conjecture on the basis of extensive simulations, such as those reported in the next section, that the errors associated with Method II are likely to be negligible.

6. An Example

Experiments with situations where the cost-of-utility functions are known confirms that the procedures discussed in this chapter are highly accurate. In addition, there is one situation where we know the exact value of the cost-of-utility even though we cannot express the result in terms of elementary functions. Since the money-metric is homogeneous of degree zero in prices and total expenditure, any proportional change in these variables will leave the welfare indicator unaffected. Since we do not need to know an exact functional form to ascertain this result, it becomes a useful bench mark for carrying out simulations designed to ascertain the likely magnitudes of approximation errors. Consider the following example.

Let us suppose that consumer preferences are described by *Houthakker*'s indirect addilog function [1960]:

$$U = \Sigma a_i \left(\frac{Y}{p_i}\right)^{b_i}. \tag{30}$$

The first thing to note is that the money metric associated with (30) cannot be expressed in terms of an elementary function except when all the b_i are equal. However, changes in the money metric can be calculated via the numerical procedures just discussed. If we maximise (30) subject to the budget constraint, we obtain a set of demand functions of the form:

$$X_i = \frac{a_i b_i Y^{b_i} p_i^{(b_i-1)}}{\Sigma a_i b_i Y^{(b_i-1)} p_i^{-b_i}}. \tag{31}$$

Inspection of (31) reveals that it cannot be integrated in terms of an elementary function to obtain a consumer surplus measure. It should be emphasized that these two properties of the indirect addilog are not peculiar to it. Indeed, *most* preference functions will not admit to simple functional representations of either consumer's surplus of the money metric.

Let us now suppose that the parametric specification of (31) is as follows. The initial level of income is assumed to be 3000 and this is spent on ten commodities whose initial prices all equal one. In addition

$a_i = 1$	$a_2 = 1, \ldots, 10$
$b_1 = .19$	$b_6 = .09$
$b_2 = .13$	$b_7 = .08$
$b_3 = .12$	$b_8 = .07$
$b_4 = .11$	$b_9 = .06$
$b_5 = .10$	$b_{10} = .05$

In Table 2 are shown the result of several examples using the two methods discussed in this paper. In addition, a consumer's measure based on the indirect addilog is also calculated via Simpson's Rule. The "path of calculation" is analogous to that utilised for the money metric. (The path chosen is the same as that recently suggested by *Willig* [1979].)

Case	Method I	$\dfrac{\text{error}}{Y_0}$	Method II	$\dfrac{\text{error}}{Y_0}$	Consumer's Surplus	$\dfrac{\text{error}}{Y_0}$
I $Y = 3900$ $p_i = 1.3 \ (i = 1, \ldots, n)$	9.83	—	0.15	—	−126.672	.04
II $Y = 2100$ $p_i = .7 \ (i = 1, \ldots, n)$	7.25	—	2.12	—	−154.239	.05
III $Y = 2700$ $p_i = 1 + (-1)^i \,(.3)$ $(i = 1, \ldots, n)$	73.35	—	65.45	—	41.13	.01

Tab. 2

Cases I and II may be used as rough indicator of the error bands associated with any range of variable change which is plus or minus 30 per cent of the initial level of expenditure and prices. In both instances the true change in money-metric utility is zero. The errors associated with the second method are the smallest and indeed are virtually negligible as a proportion of initial expenditure. The errors associated with Method I are also small, but not as small as Method II since only information about a particular set of prices and expenditure is utilised in the Taylor series expansion. In contrast, Method II uses information over the whole range of the price variation. As we might expect, the errors associated with consumer's surplus are definitely not close to zero ranging between four and five percent of initial total expenditure.

For a third test of the robustness of the proposed methods, a more complex price variation was examined. This involved a 30 per cent cut in p_1, a 30 per cent rise in p_2, a 30 per cent cut in p_3 and so forth. In addition, it was assumed that income fell from 3000 to 2700. As a proportion of national income the errors associated with all three are small although here again that associated with consumer's surplus is the largest. As a percentage of the true value of money metric utility 65.45, however, Method I is in error by 12 per cent whereas the consumer's surplus measure has an error of 37 per cent. No appreciable error arises from using Method II.

It should be emphasised that these examples are designed merely to illustrate the robustness of Method II and to a lesser extent the accuracy of the first method. Obviously the nature of any calcuations will depend on the complexity of the problem under consideration. In the past most cost-benefit analysts have tended to evaluate projects within a partial equilibrium framework. The danger with that approach is that secondary effects involving price and expenditure variations tend to be neglected. However, within the framework discussed here these are easily and accurately capable of computation.

7. Conclusions

In the past most economists have resorted to the use of consumer's surplus techniques in their attempts to assess the monetary gains or losses associated with alternative economic policies. This has been true whether one was considering policies designed to husband the consumption of scarce resources or such other objectives as assessing the social costs of monopoly or tariff protection. On all counts, however, the money metric provides a superior basis for such assessments. It is ordinal and can be calculated from the parameters of ordinary demand functions. The object of this paper has been to provide a numerically and economically straightforward procedure for computing this metric.

References

Antonelli, G.B.: Sulla teoria matematica della economia politica. Pisa 1886; English translation "On the Mathematical Theory of Political Economy" J.S. Chipman et al. Preferences, Utility and Demand. New York 1971, 332–364.
Hildebrand, F.B.: Introduction to Numerical Analysis. New York 1974.

Hotelling, H.: The Economics of Exhaustible Resources. Journal of Political Economy **39**, 1931, 137–175.

–: The General Welfare in Relation to Problems of Taxation and of Railway and Utility Rates. Econometrica **6**, 1938, 242–269.

Houthakker, H.S.: Additive Preferences. Econometrica **28**, 1960, 62–87.

Manne, A.S.: ETA: A Model for Energy Technology Assessment. Bell Journal of Economics 7, 1976, 379–406.

McKenzie, G.W.: Measuring Gains and Losses. Journal of Political Economy **84**, 1976, 641–646.

–: Consumer's Surplus Without Apology: A Comment. American Economic Review **69**, 1979, 465–468.

–: New Methods for Measuring Economic Welfare. Cambridge 1982.

McKenzie, G.W., and *I.F. Pearce*: Exact Measures of Welfare and the Cost of Living. Review of Economic Studies **43**, 1976, 465–468.

–: Welfare Measurement – A Unification. American Economic Review **72**, 1982.

Pearce, I.F.: A Contribution to Demand Analysis. Oxford 1964.

Samuelson, P.A.: Constancy of the Marginal Utility of Income. Studies in Mathematical Economics and Econometrics. Ed. by O. Lange, F. McIntyre, and T.O. Yntema, Chicago 1942.

–: Complementarity – An Essay on the 40th Anniversary of the Hicks-Allen Revolution in Demand Theory. Journal of Economic Literature **12**, 1255–89.

Vartia, Y.O.: Efficient Methods of Measuring Welfare Change and Compensated Income in Terms of Market Demand Functions. Keskustelvaiheta Discussion Papers, No. 20. The Research Institute of the Finnish Economy, Helsinki 1978.

Willig, R.D.: Consumer's Surplus Without Apology: Reply. American Economic Review **69**, 1979, 469–474.

Economic Theory of Natural Resources. ©Physica-Verlag, Würzburg–Wien, 1982.

A Linear Model for the Determination of
Pollution Control Cost in Industry

Otto Rentz

1. The Problem

During the past decade there came into existence a series of reasons why industry should have the opportunity to determine the investment and/or cost caused by pollution control activities. In some cases such data are even required by law, e.g. by the "Environmental Statistics Law" [Gesetz über . . .] in the Federal Republic of Germany, which however up to now refers to pollution control investment only. Reasons for the evaluation of pollution control cost data can be seen — just as a matter of example — in the framework of tax relief by accelerated depreciation for pollution control equipment, in the context of requirements of authorities for further control activities, which especially under retro-fit conditions are also subject to economic considerations in many countries, then such data are needed on behalf of social accounting purposes and others more. But also with numerical optimization problems of pollution control activities, very often an extreme lack of reliable data on a micro-economic basis could be observed. For example if an optimal level of pollution control is intended to be determined numerical information on the relevant cost functions is required.

However there are some major reasons why the determination of these cost was not easily feasible in the past:

— On accounts the relevant data were mixed up with e.g. production data in the framework of the companies' accounting systems without a possibility of easy access to a break down to e.g. production and pollution control shares. On the other hand there had not been the need for such a break down in the past as long as pollution control discussion had not become so stringent.
— There are several (practical) problems to partition the total investment and/or cost and to associate the different parts with activities such as
  — production
  — pollution control
  — labour protection
  — infra structure

and other activities of a company, because the same technical device may have been installed and operated for more than one of the above-mentioned purposes. In some sense we have a similar problem as with the determination of the unit cost for co-products. These problems have been outlined by a series of industrial [Guidelines] listed in chapter 5.

2. The State of the Art in Industry

The actual state of the art with regard to the determination of pollution control cost in industry can be outlined briefly as follows [Rentz]:

Pollution control investments cannot be derived from balance sheets as there is no information on the actual uses of the different items. The same is valid for informations on the cost from profit and loss acounts.

However in the main pollution relevant industries such as the chemical industry, the iron & steel industry, power generation etc. there is usually a detailed accounting system based on in-plant cost centres (accounting departments) available. Because only by the actual use of equipment in the cost centres (in situ!) it can be decided whether the equipment is used for pollution control purposes or not any efforts to determine pollution control costs have to start with an analysis of the cost centre costs.

In practice there will be three types of cost centres:

- Cost centres without any pollution control activities, e.g. pure production centres.
- Pure pollution control cost centres, e.g. big waste water treatment facilities.
- Mixed cost centres, in which at least both: production and pollution control are effected.

Practically the number of mixed centres is considerable as it is not usual to install new cost centres for integrated or even added-on pollution control technologies. E.g. in a steel plant with a total of 700 cost centres there are 113 mixed centres and only 32 pure pollution control cost centres.

Actual industrial procedures for the determination of pollution control cost therefore start by analysing in situ the cost flow into each cost centre; this means in detail

- if c_{oj} [CU/UT] is a cost item flow from outside the plant system into cost center $j \in I$, then a pollution control share $pcc_{oj}: 0 \leqslant pcc_{oj} \leqslant c_{oj}$ is estimated.
- if $m_{ij} \cdot p_i$ [CU/UT] is the flow of a cost item from inside the plant system, the quantity m_{ij} delivered from centre i to centre j with the according price (= unit cost) p_i, a ratio $\gamma_{ij}: 0 \leqslant \gamma_{ij} \leqslant 1$ is estimated as pollution control induced; e.g. the total energy cost of centre j which might be $m_{i'j} \cdot p_{i'}$, is split up into a share $\gamma_{i'j} m_{i'j} p_{i'}$ for pollution control and a share $(1 - \gamma_{i'j}) p_{i'}$ for non-pollution purposes, mainly production.

The total pollution control cost K then are calculated by summarizing over the set of cost centres I

$$K = \sum_{j \in I} \sum_{o \in O} pcc_{oj} + \sum_{j \in J} \sum_{i \in I} \gamma_{ij} m_{ij} p_i. \tag{1}$$

In addition to these cost special cost items have to be estimated which cannot be derived "automatically" by checking the cost input of each cost centre account in situ, e.g. increased raw material cost due to higher raw material qualities to be able to meet a certain emission standard. A practical example would be the use if low sulfur heavy oil fractions instead of high sulfur oil to meet a given emission standard for SO_2 without or with smaller flue gas desulfurization facilities.

However the estimate (1) includes two systematic errors:

— If we have cost centres in series with pollution control activities in preceding stages which simultaneously produce output for pollution control purposes to subsequent cost centres, via the prices p_i (= unit cost) some cost ratios will be recorded several times, thus leading to a systematic overestimate of the pollution control cost.

— Again if we have cost centres in series where preceding centres are pure production centres (or mixed centres) and where one or several subsequent centres are mixed centres (or pure pollution control centres) then only the *direct* pollution cost/investments in these subsequent centres are recorded in spite of the fact that preceding centres have to provide *production capacity* which is needed in subsequent centres for pollution control, thus leading to a systematic under-estimate of the pollution control investment.

To avoid these two systematically built-in errors the following linear model (chapter 3) is developed.

3. Development of a Linear Model for the Determination of Pollution Control Investment/Cost

We shall use the following definitions:

K	[CU/UT]	Total pollution control cost
c_{oj}	[CU/UT]	Flow of cost item o from outside the plant system[1]) to centre $j \in I$
pcc_{oj}	[CU/UT]	Direct pollution control induced cost share of c_{oj}; $0 \leqslant \text{pcc}_{oj} \leqslant c_{oj}$.
m_{ij}	[Qu/UT]	Flow of goods from centre i to centre j: $i, j \in I$
p_i	[CU/Qu]	Unit cost associated with m_{ij}
γ_{ij}	[−]	Pollution control induced ratio of m_{ij}; $0 \leqslant \gamma_{ij} \leqslant 1$
$\widetilde{m}_i$	[Qu/UT]	Total output of cost centre $i \in I$
$\widetilde{\widetilde{m}}_i$	[Qu/UT]	Total output of cost centre $i \in I$ in a production system without any pollution control
m_i	[Qu/UT]	Output of centre $i \in I$ to be delivered outside the plant system (e.g. to the market)
I		Index set of cost centres
O		Index set of cost items from outside the plant system
IN	[CU]	Total investment for pollution control activities
in_j	[CU]	Investment cost centre j
pci_j	[CU]	Direct pollution control investment cost centre j
CU		Currency unit
UT		Unit time
Qu		Quantity units.

Defining Leontief coefficients for the given production system

$$u_{ij} := m_{ij} / \widetilde{m}_j$$

---

[1]) For formal reasons we also consider the capital cost and similar cost items ("fixed" cost as depreciation, interest, repair and maintenance etc.) as special c_{oj}; $o \in O$, $i \in I$.

we obtain an algebraic balance system

$$\tilde{m}_i - \sum_j u_{ij}\,\tilde{m}_j = m_i;\, i, j \in I. \tag{2}$$

In the same way we define a new balance system for a production system *without* any pollution control activity:
With

$$\bar{u}_{ij} := \bar{m}_{ij}/\tilde{m}_j = \frac{(1 - \gamma_{ij})\, m_{ij}}{\tilde{m}_j} = (1 - \gamma_{ij})\, u_{ij}$$

we obtain

$$\bar{\tilde{m}}_i - \sum_j \bar{u}_{ij}\,\bar{\tilde{m}}_j = m_i,\ i, j \in I \tag{3}$$

for a given production level m_i with $\bar{u}_{ij} \leqslant u_{ij}$. Provided systems (2) and (3) have a solution, in general system (3) will require a smaller input (because of $\bar{u}_{ij} \leqslant u_{ij}$) and the difference in the systems' inputs may be considered as pollution control induced.

If we define for n cost centres square $n \times n$-matrices $U := (u_{ij})$, $\bar{U} := (\bar{u}_{ij})$, $\Gamma := (\gamma_{ij})$,

$$\Xi := \begin{pmatrix} 1, 1, \dots \dots, 1 \\ \dots \dots \dots \dots \\ 1, 1, \dots \dots, 1 \end{pmatrix},$$

then $\mathbf{R}^{n+}$-vectors $c := (\sum_o c_{o1}, \sum_o c_{o2}, \dots, \sum_o c_{on})$, $\mathrm{pcc} := (\sum_o \mathrm{pc}_{o1}, \sum_o \mathrm{pc}_{o2}, \dots, \sum_o \mathrm{pc}_{on})$, $m := (m_1, \dots, m_n)$, $\tilde{m} := (\tilde{m}_1, \tilde{m}_2, \dots, \tilde{m}_n)$, $\bar{\tilde{m}} := (\bar{\tilde{m}}_1, \dots, \bar{\tilde{m}}_n)$, with the unity matrix E we can rewrite (2) as

$$\tilde{m} - U\tilde{m} = m \Rightarrow \tilde{m} = (E - U)^{-1} \cdot m \tag{2}$$

and (3) as

$$\bar{\tilde{m}} - \bar{U}\bar{\tilde{m}} = m \Rightarrow \bar{\tilde{m}} = (E - \bar{U})^{-1} m \tag{3}$$

with $\bar{U}$ calculated by means of the product by elements of matrices from

$$\bar{U} = U \otimes (\Xi - \Gamma).\ ^2)$$

---

[2]) Matrix Γ can be used to classify cost centres in the sense of chapter (2). For a pure (direct!) non-pollution control centre *all* the γ_{ij} in the corresponding row/column of Γ will be 0. For a pure pollution control centre there will hold $m_{ij} > 0 \Rightarrow \gamma_{ij} = 1$, the corresponding row/column of Γ including only 0 and 1 and for a mixed centre on the input side there will exist a least one $\gamma_{ij} > 0$ (the corresponding row of Γ including at least one $\gamma_{ij} > 0$) and $\exists\, m_{ij} \colon \gamma_{ij}\,(m_{ij}) < 1$.

It should be noted that for pure pollution control centres on the output side the physical flow of masses/energies is adverse to the economic flow of goods.

The existence of a solution to system (2) has been proven in literature already many times.[3] However system (3) might not have a solution due to the existence of pure pollution control centres: for these will be $\gamma_{ij} = 1$; therefore the corresponding row/column in $\bar{U}$ will include only O.

To overcome this problem we have to rearrange the matrix $\bar{U}$

$$\bar{U} = \begin{pmatrix} \bar{U}_{11} & | & O \\ ---- & + & ---- \\ O & | & O \end{pmatrix}$$

resulting in a new system:

$$\tilde{\bar{m}} - \bar{U}_{11} \cdot \tilde{\bar{m}} = m \Rightarrow \tilde{\bar{m}} = (E - \bar{U}_{11})^{-1} \cdot m \tag{4}$$

with $\tilde{\bar{m}} \in \mathbf{R}^{Rg(\bar{U}_{11})}$, and where the dimension of U_{11} corresponds to the total number of cost centres minus the number of pure pollution control centres.

It can be also shown easily that system (4) will have non-negative solution $\tilde{\bar{m}} \geqslant 0$ for a given non-negative demand level m, too.[4]

From (4) and (2) we can derive the change of the total output of each cost centre due to pollution control activities $\Delta m_j := \tilde{m}_j - \tilde{\bar{m}}_j$. The changes of output Δm_j can be associated with changes of the necessary primary inputs c_{oj} in such a way that the direct share of pollution control cost in c_{oj}: pcc_{oj}, is increased by an indirect share caused by production for pollution control purposes in other centres, the pollution control cost of centre $j \in I$ then being

$$k_j = \sum_o pcc_{oj} + \left(\sum_o c_{oj} - \sum_o pcc_{oj}\right) \frac{\Delta \tilde{m}_j}{\tilde{m}_j}.$$

For a pure pollution control centre c_{oj} is equal to pcc_{oj} so that for such a centre the second term is equal to zero. The total pollution control cost K then follow as

$$K = \sum_I \sum_O pcc_{oj} + \sum_I \left(\sum_o c_{oj} - \sum_o pcc_{oj}\right) \frac{\Delta \tilde{m}_j}{\tilde{m}_j} \tag{5a}$$

or more general

$$K = \sum_I \sum_O pcc_{oj} + \sum_I \left(\sum_o c_{oj} - \sum_o pcc_{oj}\right) \cdot f(\Delta \tilde{m}_j). \tag{6a}$$

Respectively we receive for the pollution control investment

---

[3] If we consider the cost centre system as a directed graph with the cost centres as a set V of vertices and the flow of cost items as edges, then for

a) $(\forall X: X \in \mathbf{P}(V) \wedge X \neq \emptyset) \, (\exists m_{ij} > 0 \vee c_{oj} > 0: v_j \in X \wedge v_i \notin X$
$\Rightarrow \exists m_{ij} > 0 \vee m_i > 0: v_i \in X \wedge v_j \notin X)$
b) $(\forall v_v \in V) \, (\exists m_{iv} \vee c_v > 0)$

there will exist a non-negative price-system p_i, $i \in I$, and a non-negative solution to (2) [see *Kistner/Luhmer; Rosenblatt; Münstermann; Hadley; Solow; Markowski* et al.; *Rentz; Hawkins/Simon*].

[4] See preceding footnote.

$$IN = \Sigma \ \text{pci}_{oj} + \Sigma \ (in_j - \text{pci}_j) \ \frac{\Delta \widetilde{m}_j}{\widetilde{m}_j} \tag{5b}$$

or

$$IN = \Sigma \ \text{pci}_{oj} + \Sigma \ (in_j - \text{pci}_j) \cdot \widetilde{f}(\Delta \widetilde{m}_j). \tag{6b}$$

4. Discussion and Application of the Model

The investment/cost calculated according equation (5a, 5b) provide a linear ex post break down of the total investment/cost based on the capacity used/required. The investment/cost IN/K cannot provide an answer to the question to which extent a production system could be "cheaper" if there would be no need for pollution control. An answer to this question would have to be based on cost centre cost functions and would have to consider especially economies of scale, too (6a, 6b) which might be provided by adequate functions $f(\Delta \widetilde{m}_j)$ and $\widetilde{f}(\Delta \widetilde{m}_j)$ according equations (6a) and (6b) respectively.

At present there is no information available on the numerical difference between the "correctly" calculated values for IN/K according equations (5a) and (5b), and the approximative values calculated according equation (1). However for a big steel manufacturer such a comparison will be carried out in the near future so that after that empirical study at least a result in the form of a case study will be available.

References

Betriebswirtschaftlicher Ausschuß des Verbandes der Chemischen Industrie e.V.: Erfassung und Verrechnung der Aufwendungen für den Umweltschutz in der Chemischen Industrie. Der Betrieb, H. 42, Okt. 1973.

Betriebswirtschaftliches Institut der Eisenhüttenindustrie: Entwurf der Richtlinien für die Erfassung der Betriebskosten in Zusammenhang mit dem Umweltschutz. Düsseldorf, August 1974.

Bundesverband der Deutschen Industrie e.V.: Entwurf einer Anleitung zur Bestimmung und Erfassung der Betriebskosten für den Umweltschutz in der Industrie. Bundesverband, Köln, Juli 1978.

Gesetz über Umweltstatistiken, in: Bundesgesetzblatt Teil I, 1974, 1938–1941.

Guidlines: VDI 3800 „Kostenrechnung für Anlagen und Maßnahmen zur Emissionsminderung", Gründruck Düsseldorf 1977, Weißdruck 1979.

Hadley, G.: Linear Algebra. Reading 1965.

Hawkins, D., and *H.A. Simon*: Note: Some Conditions of Macroeconomic Stability. Econometrica 17, 1949, 245–248.

Kistner, K.-P., and *A. Luhmer*: Die Dualität von Produktionsplanung und Kostenverrechnung bei komplexen Produktionsstrukturen. ZfB 47, 1977, 767–786.

Kommission der Europäischen Gemeinschaften: Entwurf einer Empfehlung des Rates an die Mitgliedstaaten betreffend Verfahren zur Berechnung der Umweltschutzkosten der Industrie. KOM (77) 630 endg., Brüssel 8.12.1977.

Markowski, H. et al.: Zur praktischen Durchführung von Produktionsplanung und Kostenrechnung bei komplexen Produktionsstrukturen – Anmerkungen zu K.P. Kistner und A. Luhmer: Die Dualität von Produktionsplanung und Kostenverrechnung bei komplexen Produktionsstrukturen. ZfB 48, 1978, 381–388.

Mineralölwirtschaftsverband e.V.: Erfassung der Umweltschutz-Betriebskosten in der Mineralölwirtschaft, (E). Hamburg 1978.

Münstermann, H.: Unternehmensrechnung. Wiesbaden 1969.

Rentz, O.: Techno-Ökonomie betrieblicher Emissionsminderungsmaßnahmen, Berlin 1979.

Rosenblatt, D.: On linear models and the graphs of *Minkowski Leontief* matrices. Econometrica **25**, 1957, 325–338.

Solow, R.: On the structure of linear models. Econometrica **20**, 1952, 29–46.

VGB Techn. Vereinigung der Großkraftwerksbetreiber e.V.: Kostenrechnung für Einrichtungen zum Umweltschutz im Kraftwerksbereich (E). Essen 1978.

Economic Theory of Natural Resources. ©Physica-Verlag, Würzburg–Wien, 1982.

Negative Externalities, Environmental Quality and the Transformation Space[1]

Horst Siebert

The purpose of this paper is to analyze the properties of the transformation space of an economy with private goods, environmental quality, and negative externalities. The property of the transformation space determines the level of permissible decentralization [*Laffont*]. If nonconvexities prevail, only milder forms of decentralization (such as taxation instead of artifical markets) are permitted for optimal allocation results; or, as *Baumol/Oates* [1975, p. 103] point out, "prices may give the wrong signals — directing the economy away from the social optimum."

Technological externalities are defined as interrelations between economic activities outside the market system. Let y_i represent the output of activity i (or an output vector) such as production quantities or utility, let x_i represent an input to activity i (or an input vector) and let y_j and x_j denote the output and input of activity j, so that

$$y_i = \pi_i (x_i, x_j, y_j). \tag{1}$$

Then, a negative externality exists if $\partial y_i/\partial x_j < 0$ or $\partial y_i/\partial y_j < 0$. We may have negative externalities in production (output of activity i and inputs in activity j or output of activity j) or in consumption (utility from consumption activity of individual i and input [or output] of consumption activity of individual j). Furthermore, externalities may exist between consumption and production activities.

When externalities exist, the two basic propositions of welfare economics can no longer be established. This result is due to the fact that externalities cause nonconvexities to arise. In this paper we will analyze the problem to what extent the introduction of externalities will affect the convexity condition. We can show that the introduction of some aspects of externalities still allows the concavity of the transformation space. Also, the paper generates some insight into the question what type of externalities may destroy the concavity of the transformation space.

The starting point of the analysis is that in the literature on technological externalities, the technological systems were not discussed through which economic activities are

[1]) This paper was written in the Sonderforschungsbereich 5 "Allocation policy in market economies" sponsored by the Deutsche Forschungsgemeinschaft. The author acknowledges support from the Center of Energy Policy Research and the Energy Laboratory at the Massachusetts Institute of Technology. He received helpful comments to a first draft from F. Dudenhöffer, H. Gebauer, H. Meder, S. Toussaint, and two anonymous referees.

linked. Such systems are ground-water systems, river systems, meteorological systems or other natural and environmental media.[2]) The innovation of environmental economics consists in explicitly considering these systems and introducing intervening variables between different activities that explain the technological links. This procedure has an important advantage: By introduction intervening variables such as emissions, pollutants ambient in the environment and environmental quality we get new starting points for economic policy. For instance, we are able to fix a target in terms of environmental quality by defining the tolerable quantity of pollutants. And we are also able to indicate the policy instruments to be used such as emission taxes or pollution rights (defined as a permissible quantity of emissions) not yet known to the Pigouvian analysis (1920). Also, some type of externality may exist, and the convexity condition may not be violated.

In the following analysis, we consider an economy with two private outputs and a public good: environmental quality. Production generates pollutants, and pollutants ambient in the environment determine environmental quality. Pollutants in the environment also have a negative effect on output. Each sector or a government agency can abate pollutants. The abatement of pollutants uses up resources and consequently competes with resource use in production. In this context, the concavity of the transformation space may be destroyed by the negative effect of pollutants on production. Also, we introduce a convex emission function for each firm.

In Section I, the assumptions for our analysis are specified. In Section II, we study the properties of the transformation space. Whereas in Section II the production function is concave, we consider nonconvexities in the production function and their possible influence on the transformation space in Section III. In the appendix, we establish some of the formal properties of the transformation space.

I. Assumptions

A 1. Output Q depends on resource input R and on the quantity of pollutants S ambient in the environment. In order to keep the model as simple as possible, we assume only one type of resource. We have declining marginal productivities of the resource and a negative impact of pollutants on output. With a higher level of pollution, the impact increases in absolute terms. In order to simplify the presentation, we assume that the production function is seperable in R and S. Diagram 1 shows the production function

$$Q^i \leqslant F^i (R^i, S)$$

$$F^i_R > 0, F^i_{RR} < 0; F^i_S < 0, F^i_{SS} < 0; F^i_{RS} = F^i_{SR} = 0. \tag{2}$$

---

[2]) Another system linking economic activities is the social system. For instance, in a developing country a firm with high technical knowledge may have a positive effect on the labour force in a region and thus on other firms located in the area. This technological effect runs via the social system.

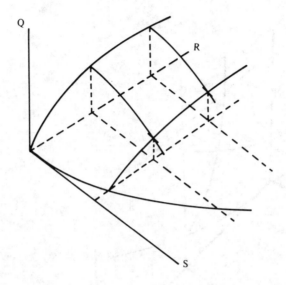

Diagram 1

The production function is concave.[3]) Since pollutants reduce output, increasing pollutants require more resources if a given output is to be maintained.[4])

The production function 2 defines an inverse

$$R^i = \phi^i (Q^i, S) \tag{2i}$$

that can be interpreted as an input requirement function for alternative Q^i, S. Since we make use of this function in our argument, the properties of the input requirement function are of interest to us. These properties are completely determined by the properties of the production function. Diagrammatically, the input requirement function is obtained by turning the production function around the S-axis in Diagram 1 by 90 degrees. Diagram 2a shows the input requirement function. For convenience of interpretation, the same function is shown in Diagram 2b.

---

[3]) We have $d^2Q < 0$ since in the Hessian determinant

$$H: \begin{vmatrix} F_{RR} & F_{SR} \\ F_{RS} & F_{SS} \end{vmatrix}$$

$|H_1| < 0$ and $|H_2| = F_{RR} F_{SS} - F_{RS} F_{SR} > 0$ for $F_{RS} = 0$.
This property also holds for the isoquant $Q^i = 0$ so that the output space is limited by a convex function $R^i = \phi^i (0, S)$.

[4]) The assumption of seperability implies that for a cut through the production surface for given S, F_S remains constant for all R. Similarly F_R is constant for all S, if R is given.

492

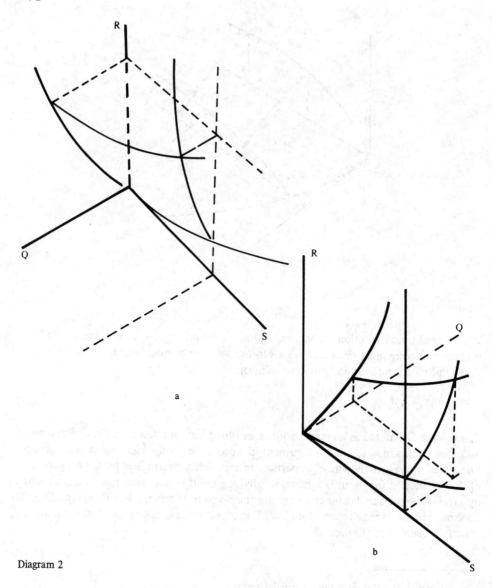

Diagram 2

The properties of the input requirement function can be determined as follows. Take the total derivative of the production function, rearrange it into

$$dR^i = \frac{1}{F_R^i} dQ^i - \frac{F_S^i}{F_R^i} dS \qquad (2ii)$$

and compare it with the total derivative of Equation (2i)

$$dR^i = \phi^i_Q \, dQ^i + \phi^i_S \, dS. \tag{2iii}$$

Then, we have

$$\phi^i_Q = \frac{1}{F^i_R} > 0$$

$$\phi^i_S = -F^i_S \, \phi^i_Q - \frac{-F^i_S}{F^i_R} > 0.$$

Taking the second total derivative[5]) of the input requirement function and the production function we establish

$$\phi^i_{QQ} = -\frac{F^i_{RR}}{(F^i_R)^3} > 0$$

$$\phi^i_{SS} = -\frac{F^i_{SS} \, (F^i_R)^2 + F^i_{RR} \, (F^i_S)^2}{(F^i_R)^3} > 0$$

$$\phi^i_{QS} = \frac{F^i_{RR} \, F^i_S}{(F^i_R)^3} > 0.$$

A 2. Production generates pollutants S^{pi} as a joint product. For purposes of simplification, there is only one type of pollutants. It is assumed that pollutants emitted rise proportionally or progressively with output

$$S^{pi} = H^i \, (Q^i) \text{ with } H^i_Q > 0, H^i_{QQ} \geqslant 0. \tag{3}$$

A 3. Resources may also be used for abatement purposes. Let S^r indicate the quantity of pollutants reduced in the economy. The abatement function is given by

$$S^r \leqslant F^r \, (R^r) \text{ with } F^r_R > 0, F^r_{RR} < 0. \tag{4}$$

---

[5]) The total derivative of Equation (2iii) is

$$d^2R = \phi_{QQ} \, dQ^2 + \phi_{SS} \, dS^2 + 2\phi_{QS} \, dQdS. \tag{I}$$

The total derivative of Equation (2ii) is (with $F_{RS} = F_{SR} = 0$)

$$d^2R = -\frac{F_{RR}}{F^2_R} \, dRdQ - \frac{F_{SS} \, F_R}{F^2_R} \, ds^2 + \frac{F_{RR} \, F_S}{F^2_R} \, dRdS.$$

Substituting Equation (2iii) for dR we have

$$d^2R = -\frac{F_{RR}}{F^3_R} \, dQ^2 - \frac{(F_{SS} \, F^2_R + F_{RR} \, F^2_S)}{F^3_R} \, ds^2 + 2\frac{F_{RR} \, F_S}{F^3_R} \, dQdS. \tag{II}$$

From Equations (I) and (II), the properties for ϕ_{QQ}, ϕ_{SS} and ϕ_{QS} follow.

The abatement function describes a technology that prevents pollutants from entering the environment. Alternatively, we can introduce an index i and assume a technology to reduce pollutants that is specific to each sector.

A 4. Net emissions or pollutants ambient in the environment are defined as emissions produced minus emissions abated. A diffusion function is not explicitly introduced.

$$S = \Sigma S^{pi} - S^r. \tag{5}$$

A 5. The resource can be used for production and abatement. Resource endowment is given.

$$R^1 + R^2 + R^r \leqslant \bar{R}. \tag{6}$$

A 6. The public good: environmental quality U, is determined by the quantity of pollutants ambient in the environment (S)

$$U = G(S) \text{ with } G' < 0, G'' \leqslant 0. \tag{7}$$

Note that equation (7) may be understood as a linear transformation ($G'' = 0$), but it may also be understood as damage function in a physical sense ($G'' < 0$). If equation (7) is interpreted as a linear transformation, then environmental quality is defined in terms of pollutants ambient in the environment. If equation (7) is interpreted as a damage function, the stock of pollutants negatively affects environmental quality, that is, the stock of pollutants influences such variables as the height of trees, abundance of natural systems, ecological equilibria etc.

II. Properties of the Transformation Space

Inserting Equations (2i), (3), (4), (5) and (6) into Equation (7) we have

$$U = G\left[\Sigma H^i (Q^i) - F^r \{\bar{R} - \Sigma \phi^i (Q^i, G^{-1} (U))\}\right]. \tag{8}$$

If we leave the damage function (7) out of consideration, Equation (8) reduces to

$$S = \Sigma H^i (Q^i) - F^r \{\bar{R} - \Sigma \phi^i (Q^i, S)\}. \tag{8'}$$

Equations (8) and (8') describe two different versions of the transformation space. We now discuss the properties of these equations. We consider three different cases, namely i) $F_S = 0$ and $G'' < 0$, ii) $F_S < 0$ and $G'' < 0$ and iii) $F_S < 0$ and $G'' = 0$.

Case 1. As a frame of reference, consider a case where $F_S^i = 0$ and $G'' < 0$. Then the transformation space has the property shown in Diagram 3 [*Siebert*, 1978, 1981].

At a zero production in both sectors, the maximal environmental quality ($0A$) is reached, so to speak the natural original condition. Let $Q^2 = 0$ and expand production of commodity 1. Then one can imagine such a resource allocation (R^1, R^r) at which all pollutants occuring in the production of 1 are abated (distance AG). Analogously, AH indicates those production quantities of commodity 2 for $Q^1 = 0$ at which the environmental quality remains at a maximum. Except for the curve GH, the horizontal ceiling represents a situation with maximal environmental quality and underemployment.

Expand production of commodity 1 at point G for $Q^2 = 0$ by one unit. Then the quantity of emissions increases progressively due to $H^1_{QQ} > 0$. Because environmental quality decreases overproportionally with emissions, environmental quality has to fall overproportionally as consequence of the expanded production of commodity 1. With an increase in production of commodity 1, additional resources are used in production that have to be withdrawn from abatement. Therefore, the quantity of emissions abated falls (and environmental quality declines). We even know that due to every further input unit withdrawn from abatement, the emissions not abated increase overproportionally. This is explained by the decreasing marginal productivities in abatement. Finally, the law of declining marginal returns demands that every further unit of commodity 1 produced requires an increasing resource input. Consequently, for a movement from G to B the quantity of pollutants has to increase progressively because inputs are reallocated from abatement to the production of commodity 1, and the environmental quality has to decrease progressively. The curve GB is concave. A similar reasoning holds for the curve HC and other cuts through the transformation space. We can establish that the transformation space is concave for $F^i_S = 0$ [*Siebert*, 1978, 1981]. Note that the projection of BC into the $Q^1 - Q^2$ plane is the traditional transformation curve $Q^1 = \pi(Q^2)$ without taking into account environmental quality.

Proposition 1: If there is no negative productivity effect of the stock of pollutants on production, i.e., $F^i_S = 0$, the transformation space is concave for $G'' < 0$ as well as $G'' = 0$.

Compare this result with an intuitive reasoning for a Pigouvian type concept of externalities between production and consumption as specified in equation (1). In a Pigouvian world one would expect prima vista that the externality distroys the convexity conditions. This, however, does not hold.

Case 2. Consider now the case where pollutants ambient in the environment affect output negatively, i.e., $F^i_S < 0$ and $G'' < 0$. Note that point G is identical to Diagram 3. This is due to the fact that at G, the level of pollution is zero and there cannot be a negative effect on output. Moving from G and increasing Q^1 (Diagram 4), output is reduced by the negative productivity effect so that the transformation space $[F^i_S < 0]$ lies inside the transformation space $[F^i_S = 0]$. With a reduction of environmental quality (or an increase in pollutants), the curve $G\tilde{B}$ (diagram 4) will have a stronger curvature than curve GB (Diagram 3). If the negative effect of pollutants is large enough, the transformation space will bend inward. The slope $\partial U / \partial Q^i$ becomes positive due to a stronger impact of pollutants on output. From Equation (3) in the appendix we have

$$\frac{\partial U}{\partial Q^i} \lesseqgtr 0 \Leftrightarrow \phi^1_S + \phi^2_S \lesseqgtr \frac{1}{F^r_R}. \tag{9}$$

On the right side of Equation (9), the term $1/F^r_R$ specifies the input requirement for reducing one unit of pollutants. Note that from $S^r = F^r(R^r)$ and the inverse $R^r = F^{r-1}(S^r)$, we have $dR^r/dS = 1/F^r_R$ (inverse function rule). Consequently, $1/F^r_R$ denotes the input requirement for reducing one unit of pollutants. On the left side of

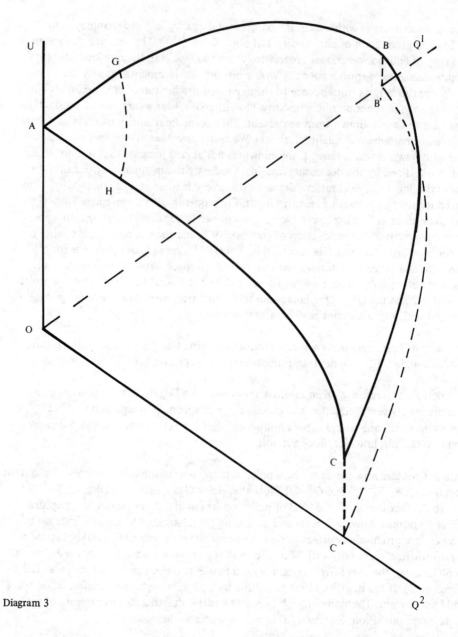

Diagram 3

Equation (9), the term $\phi_S^1 + \phi_S^2$ specifies the inputs required to compensate for the negative productivity effect of one unit of pollutants on output ($\phi_S^1 + \phi_S^2$). If resources are less productive in abating one unit of pollutants than in compensating its negative effect, the transformation space has a negative slope. If, however, it requires more resources to compensate the negative effect of one unit of pollutants in production than it requires resources to abate one unit of pollutants, the slope of the transformation space is positive.

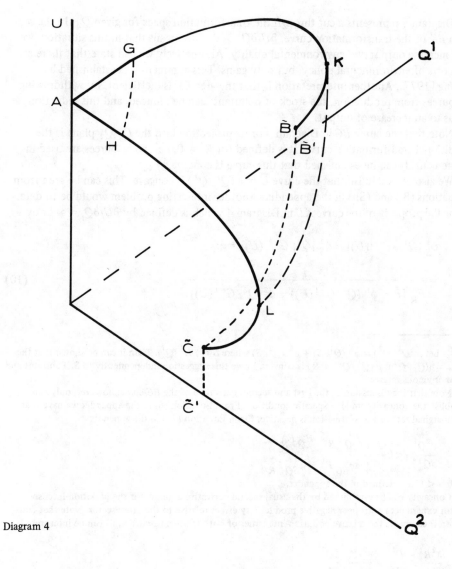

Diagram 4

Diagram 5

Diagram 5 represents a cut through the transformation space for given Q_2. In the section $\widetilde{B}K$ of the transformation curve, $\partial U/\partial Q^1 > 0$. This means that in this situation, we can increase output *and* environmental quality. Alternatively we can state that there are no costs of environmental policy, but only gains. This argument was established by *Pethig* [1977]. Another interpretation is that the area $\widetilde{B}K$ is inefficient. By withdrawing resources from production, the stock of pollutants can be reduced, and this reduction leads to an increase of output.

Note that the curve $\widetilde{B}C$ in Diagram 4 or its projection into the Q_1-Q_2-plane is the traditional transformation curve. It is defined for $R^r = 0$, i.e., no resources are used in abatement. It can be established that this curve is concave.[6]

We also can establish that the curve $\bar{U} = \pi(Q^1, Q^2)$ is concave. This can be seen from Equations (8i) and (8ii) in the appendix. Another interesting problem would be to determine the property of the curve KL in Diagram 4 which is defined by $\partial U/\partial Q_i = \infty$ or by

$$\phi^1_S [Q^1, G^{-1}(U)] + \phi^2_S [Q^2, G^{-1}(U)] =$$

$$= \frac{1}{F^r_R [\bar{R} - \phi^1(Q^1, G^{-1}(U)) - \phi^2(Q^2, G^{-1}(U))}. \tag{10}$$

---

[6]) Let $\rho(Q^1, Q^2) = \phi^1(Q^1, S) + \phi^2(Q^2, S)$ where $S = \Sigma H^i(Q^i)$. Than it can be shown that the set $Z = \{(Q^1, Q^2): \rho(Q^1, Q^2) \leq \bar{R}\}$ is convex. I owe this suggestion independently to S. Toussaint and an anonymous referee.

Note that the discussion of the first and second derivative of the $\widetilde{B}\widetilde{C}$ curve, however, only can establish the concavity under a specific condition. From Equation (6) in the appendix we have that the marginal rate of transformation is negative. From Equation (7ii) in the appendix

$$\frac{d^2 Q^1}{dQ^{2^2}} < 0 \Leftarrow \begin{cases} H^1_Q F^1_R \lessgtr H^2_Q F^2_R & \text{i)} \\ \alpha\phi^1_{SQ} F^1_R \gtrless \phi^2_{SQ} F^2_R & \text{ii)} \end{cases}$$

with $\alpha < 1$. α is defined in the appendix.

Concavity can be established by the usual second derivative argument if the pollution-intensive sector experiences a stronger negative productivity effect relative to the other sector. Note that condition i) compares the relative pollution-intensities of both sectors. Condition ii) can be interpreted as

$$\alpha \frac{\partial^2 R^1}{\partial S \partial Q^1} \frac{\partial Q^1}{\partial R^1} > \frac{\partial^2 R^2}{\partial S \partial Q^2} \frac{\partial Q^2}{\partial R^2}.$$

This expression tells us how many resources are needed to compensate the negative productivity effect arising from using one unit of the resource in production. The condition states that the pollution-intensive Sector 1 needs more resources to compensate the negative productivity effects of pollutants (per unit of resources used in production).

According to this approach, the transformation curve $\widetilde{B}\widetilde{C}$ will be concave if the pollution-intensive sector experiences a strong negative productivity effect. This means, that the pollution-intensive sector hurts itself. If, however, Sector 1 is the pollution-intensive sector and if Sector 2 experiences a high negative productivity effect of pollutants, $d^2 Q^1/dQ^{2^2} < 0$ cannot be established. This result points into the direction of the analysis of *Baumol/Oates* [1975]. They can show in a different model that if a parameter denoting the intensity of a negative externality is strong enough, the transformation space may not be concave.

From the discussion in section 1. iii) of the appendix we cannot establish that the transformation space is concave. Also, if we look at a cut $GK\tilde{B}$ in Diagram 4 through the transformation space we cannot establish a negative second derivative for the section $K\tilde{B}$ (compare the discussion of Equation (4) in the appendix). Consequently, we have:

Proposition 2. With a negative productivity effect ($F_S^i < 0$) and a negative effect on environmental quality ($G'' < 0$), the concavity of the transformation space cannot be established. However, a truncated part of the transformation space is concave.

It is apparent that the relevance of nonconvexities depends on the magnitude of $| F_S |$. If $| F_S |$ is relatively small, a large part of the transformation space is concave.

Case 3. If we only consider the set $X := \{Q^1, Q^2, S\}$, than we can establish that the set X is convex (compare the discussion in section 1.i)) of the appendix. The set X is not influenced by the damage function G and its properties. We can also show that the set $Y := \{Q^1, Q^2, U\}$ is convex if G is interpreted as a linear relationship, i.e., if $G'' = 0$ (see section 1. ii)) of the appendix.

Proposition 3. With a negative productivity effect ($F_S^i < 0$), the transformation space is concave for $G'' = 0$.

All three propositions can be summarized in the following statement.

Proposition 4. The concavity of the transformation space can be established if the negative effect of the stock of pollutants relates to the private goods or the public goods only. It cannot be established, if the negative productivity effects influences both private production *and* the public good environmental quality.

Note that in this section we have assumed that all individual functions in the model are concave so that the model is defined by a set of concave functions. Yet, the overall relationship specified by this set of relationships produces convexity only under special conditions. Compared to a world with a more intuitive Pigouvian interpretation of externalities such as in equation (1), we can show that some type of externalities do not destroy the convexity condition.

III. Nonconvexities in the Production Function

In Equation (2) it was assumed that $F_{SS}^i < 0$ so that the production function is concave. This assumption implies that the negative productivity effect of additional pollutants increases (in absolute terms). It may be more realistic that with an increasing stock of pollutants, F_S^i decreases in absolute terms. The first unit of pollutants has done already such a damage that the damage of an additional unit of pollutants will be smaller. This assumption implies $F_{SS}^i > 0$, i.e., the production function shown in Diagram 1 is no longer concave (compare Diagram 6).

From

$$\phi_{SS} = -\frac{F_{SS} F_R^2 + F_{RR} F_S^2}{F_R^3} \gtrless 0,$$

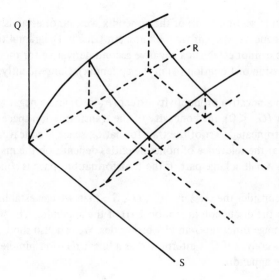

Diagram 6

we can see that $\partial^2 U/\partial Q^{i^2} > 0$ (Equation (4) in the appendix) cannot be ruled out. In Diagram 7 the transformation curce is shown for the one-commodity case, i.e., for $Q^2 = 0$. The curve GB illustrates the case $F_S = 0$. If $F_S < 0$ and $F_{SS} > 0$, we cannot rule out that the transformation curve $G\tilde{B}$ is convex. This result seems to be consistent with the analysis of nonconvexities by *Baumol/Oates* [1975]. Note that $|F_S|$ is relatively large for a small stock of pollutants and becomes smaller for a larger quantity of pollutants. Consequently, nonconvexities may arise relatively early in the game. Therefore, the idea to truncate a concave section of the transformation curve may not be too helpful for the analysis [compare assumption A 2.5 in *Pethig, 1979*].

The transformation curve may have the form shown in Diagram 7. Whereas in the case of a concave production function we can establish the concavity of the transformation curve $\tilde{B}\tilde{C}$ for $R' = 0$ (no abatement), we now cannot establish the concavity of $\tilde{B}\tilde{C}$ (compare equation (7i) in the appendix).

Note that from Equations (8i) and (8ii) in the appendix we have that a cut through the transformation space for $\bar{U}$ or $\bar{S}$ is concave, even if $F_{SS} > 0$.

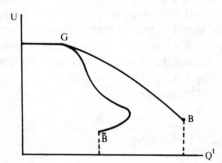

Diagram 7

The result of this section may be summarized in

Proposition 5. If the production function is not concave, the concavity of the transformation space cannot be established. Only a truncated part of the production function is concave. But this truncated part may be relatively small since non-convexities may arise "early in the game".

IV. Summary

The paper shows that the property of concavity of the transformation space varies with the assumptions on the negative effect of the stock of pollutants. The propositions discussed are summarized in Table 1.

Proposition	Production function $(i = 1, 2)$	Damage function	$X := \{Q^1, Q^2 S\}^7)$	$U = \zeta (Q^1, Q^2)^{\ 8})$
1.	Concave; $F_S^i = 0$	$G'' < 0$	Convex	Concave
2./3.	Concave; $F_S^i < 0$	$G'' < 0$	Convex	Not concave Truncated part concave
		$G'' = 0$	Convex	Concave
5.	Not concave; $F_S^i < 0$	$G'' < 0$	Not convex	Not concave Truncated part concave

Tab. 1

If the production function is not concave, the transformation space will not be concave. Concavity in the individual functions of the model is not sufficient to establish the concavity of the transformation space. If the stock of pollutants has a negative effect on private goods only or on the public good only, concavity can be established. If the negative effect influences both private and public goods, concavity cannot be shown.[9])

Appendix

1. i)   It can be shown[10]) that set $X := \{Q^1, Q^2, S\}$ is convex. Define the function ψ

$$\psi (Q^1, Q^2, S) = \phi^1 (Q^1, S) + \phi^2 (Q^2, S) + F^{r-1} (H^1 (Q^1) + H^2 (Q^2) - S)$$

---

[7]) The set X is defined in the appendix.
[8]) Function ζ is implicitly defined in equation (8).
[9]) We have not analyzed the case in which $G'' < 0$, $F_S^i < 0$ and $F_S^i = 0$ for $i \neq j$.
[10]) I owe this proof to S. Toussaint.

and define the set

$$X := \{(Q^1, Q^2, S): \psi(Q^1, Q^2, S) \leqslant \bar{R}\}. \tag{1}$$

In order to show that X is a convex set we establish the convexity of the function ψ.

Since ϕ^i is convex, we have

$$\phi^i [\lambda Q^i + (1-\lambda)\tilde{Q}^i, \lambda S + (1-\lambda)\tilde{S}] \leqslant \lambda \phi^i(Q^i, S) + (1-\lambda)\phi^i(\tilde{Q}_i, \tilde{S}).$$

Since H^i is convex, we have

$$H^i(\lambda Q^i + (1-\lambda)\tilde{Q}^i) \leqslant \lambda H^i(Q^i) + (1-\lambda)H^i(\tilde{Q}^i).$$

Due to $d(F^r)^{-1}/dS^r = 1/F_R^r > 0$ and $d^2(F^r)^{-1}/dS^{r^2} = -F_{RR}^r/(F_R^r)^3 > 0$, we have

$$(F^r)^{-1}[\sum_i H^i(\lambda Q^i + (1-\lambda)\tilde{Q}_i) - (\lambda S + (1-\lambda)\tilde{S})] \leqslant$$

$$(F^r)^{-1}[\sum_i (\lambda H^i(Q^i) + (1-\lambda)H^i(\tilde{Q}^i)) - (\lambda S + (1-\lambda)\tilde{S})] =$$

$$(F^r)^{-1}[\lambda(\sum_i H^i(Q^i) - S) + (1-\lambda)(\sum_i H^i(\tilde{Q}_i) - \tilde{S})] \leqslant$$

$$\lambda(F^r)^{-1}(\sum_i H^i(Q^i) - S) + (1-\lambda)(F^r)^{-1}(\sum H^i(\tilde{Q}^i) - \tilde{S}).$$

It follows that

$$\phi[\lambda(Q^1, Q^2, S) + (1-\lambda)(\tilde{Q}^1, \tilde{Q}^2, \tilde{S})] \leqslant$$
$$\lambda\psi(Q^1, Q^2, S) + (1-\lambda)\psi(\tilde{Q}^1, \tilde{Q}^2, \tilde{S}) \leqslant \bar{R}$$
if $\psi(Q^1, Q^2, S) \leqslant \bar{R}$ and $\psi(\tilde{Q}^1, \tilde{Q}^2, \tilde{S}) \leqslant R$.

Consequently, X is convex.

ii) If the damage function is linear, we have

$$G^{-1}(\lambda U + (1-\lambda)\tilde{U}) = \lambda G^{-1}(U) + (1-\lambda)G^{-1}(\tilde{U}) = \lambda S + (1-\lambda)\tilde{S}$$

if $S = G^{-1}(U)$ and $\tilde{S} = G^{-1}(\tilde{U})$.

Therefore the set

$$Y := \{(Q^1, Q^2, U): \psi(Q^1, Q^2, S) \leqslant \bar{R}\} \tag{2}$$

is convex, if $G(S)$ is linear.

iii) If $G'' < 0$, the convexity of Y cannot be established. Then
$(d^2(G^{-1}))/(dU^2) = -G''/(G')^3 < 0$ and $G^{-1}(U)$ is concave. That implies that
$G^{-1}(\lambda U + (1-\lambda)\tilde{U}) \geqslant \lambda G^{-1}(U) + (1-\lambda)G^{-1}(\tilde{U})$ and
$$\phi^i[\lambda Q^i + (1-\lambda)\tilde{Q}^i, G^{-1}(\lambda U + (1-\lambda)\tilde{U})] \geqslant$$
$$\phi^i[\lambda Q^i + (1-\lambda)\tilde{Q}^i, \lambda G^{-1}(U) + (1-\lambda)G^{-1}(\tilde{U})].$$
Thus, $\phi^i(Q^i, G^{-1}(U))$ is no longer a convex function of Q^i and U.

2. An alternative approach is to analyze whether for Equation 8 we can establish that $d^2 U < 0$. For this we have to show that the Hessian matrix is negative definite, i.e., that $| H_1 | < 0$ and $| H_2 | > 0$. The result $| H_2 | > 0$ cannot be established since the expression is too complex. However, some results allow an economic interpretation. We have

$$\frac{\partial U}{\partial Q^1} = \frac{-G' \, (H_Q^1 + F_R^r \, \phi_Q^1)}{F_R^r \, (\phi_S^1 + \phi_S^2) - 1} = G' \frac{dS}{dQ^1} = -\frac{A_1}{B} \tag{3}$$

with $A_i = G' \, (H_Q^i + F_R^r \, \phi_Q^i) < 0$

$B = F_R^r \, (\phi_S^1 + \phi_S^2) - 1$

$$\frac{\partial^2 U}{\partial Q^{1\,2}} = -\frac{1}{B^2} \left\{ -BG' \, F_{RR}^r \left[\frac{A_1}{BG'} \, (\phi_S^1 + \phi_S^2) - \phi_Q^1 \right]^2 \right.$$

$$+ \frac{A_1^2}{G'} \left[\frac{-G''}{G'} + \frac{F_R^r \, (\phi_{SS}^1 + \phi_{SS}^2)}{B} \right]$$

$$\left. + BG' \, (H_{QQ}^1 + F_R^r \, \phi_{QQ}^1) \right\}. \tag{4}$$

Equations (3) and (4) define the properties of the curve $GK\tilde{B}$ and $HL\tilde{C}$ in Diagram 4. From Equation (3) we have

$$\frac{\partial U}{\partial Q^1} < 0 \Leftrightarrow B < 0.$$

In this case, Equation (4) yields $(\partial^2 U)/(\partial Q^{1\,2}) < 0$. If, however, $B > 0$, $(\partial^2 U)/(\partial Q^{1\,2}) > 0$ cannot be ruled out, i.e., beneath the curve KL in Diagram 4 non-convexities may prevail.

3. The curve $\tilde{B}\tilde{C}$ or its projection onto the Q_1-Q_2-plane (Diagram 4) is the traditional transformation curve. This curve is characterized by the property that no resources are used for abatement so that $R^r = 0$. Therefore we have

$$\bar{R} = R^1 + R^2$$

$$\bar{R} = \phi^1 \, [Q^1, H^1 \, (Q^1) + H^2 \, (Q^2)] + \phi^2 \, [Q^2, H^1 \, (Q^1) + H^2 \, (Q^2)] \tag{5}$$

$$\frac{dQ^1}{dQ^2} = -\frac{\phi_Q^2 + H_Q^2 \, (\phi_S^1 + \phi_S^2)}{\phi_Q^1 + H_Q^1 \, (\phi_S^1 + \phi_S^2)} < 0 \tag{6}$$

$$\frac{d^2 Q^1}{dQ^{2\,2}} = -\frac{1}{(\phi_Q^1 + aH_Q^1)} \left\{ \phi_{QQ}^2 + b\phi_{QS}^2 + aH_{QQ}^2 + eH_Q^2 \right.$$

$$\left. -\frac{(\phi_Q^2 + a \, H_Q^2)}{(\phi_Q^1 + a \, H_Q^1)} \left(\phi_{QQ}^1 \frac{dQ^1}{dQ^2} + b\phi_{QS}^1 + aH_{QQ}^1 \frac{dQ^1}{dQ^2} + eH_Q^1 \right) \right\} \tag{7}$$

where

$$a = \phi_S^1 + \phi_S^2 > 0$$

$$b = H_Q^1 \frac{dQ^1}{dQ^2} + H_Q^2$$

$$c = \phi_{QS}^2 + \phi_{QS}^1 \frac{dQ^1}{dQ^2}$$

$$e = \phi_{SQ}^1 \frac{dQ^1}{dQ^2} + \phi_{SQ}^2 + b (\phi_{SS}^1 + \phi_{SS}^2).$$

Define

$$n = \phi_Q^1 + aH_Q^1 > 0.$$

Then, Equation (7) can be simplified into

$$\frac{d^2 Q^1}{dQ^{2^2}} = -\frac{1}{n} \left\{ \phi_{QQ}^1 \left(\frac{dQ^1}{dQ^2} \right)^2 + \phi_{QQ}^2 + a \left[H_{QQ}^1 \left(\frac{dQ^1}{dQ^2} \right)^2 + H_{QQ}^2 \right] \right.$$
$$\left. + 2bc + b^2 (\phi_{SS}^1 + \phi_{SS}^2) \right\}. \tag{7i}$$

We have the following condition

$$\frac{\partial^2 Q^1}{\partial Q^{2^2}} < 0: bc \geqslant 0 \text{ or sgn } b = \text{sgn } c \text{ or } b = 0 \text{ or } c = 0. \tag{7ii}$$

Equation (7ii) is satisfied if conditions (7iii) and (7iv) are given

$$b = H_Q^1 \frac{dQ^1}{dQ^2} + H_Q^2 < 0 \text{ if } H_Q^1 F_R^1 > H_Q^2 F_R^2 \tag{7iii}$$

$$c = \phi_{QS}^1 \frac{dQ_1}{dQ_2} + \phi_{QS}^2 < 0. \tag{7iv}$$

Equation (7iv) is given, if

$$\frac{\phi_{SQ}^2}{\phi_{SQ}^1} = \frac{\phi_{QS}^2}{\phi_{QS}^1} < -\frac{dQ^1}{dQ^2} = \frac{\phi_Q^2 + H_Q^2 (\phi_S^1 + \phi_S^2)}{\phi_Q^1 + H_Q^1 (\phi_S^1 + \phi_S^2)}.$$

Define

$$\alpha = \frac{1 + H_Q^2 F_R^2 (\phi_S^1 + \phi_S^2)}{1 + H_Q^1 F_R^1 (\phi_S^1 + \phi_S^2)}$$

with $\alpha < 1$ if $H_Q^1 F_R^1 > H_Q^2 F_R^2$.

The condition (7iv) is given if

$$\frac{\phi^2_{SQ}}{\phi^1_{SQ}} < \alpha \frac{F^1_R}{F^2_R} \tag{7v}$$

or

$$\frac{\partial^2 R_2}{\partial S \partial Q_2} \frac{\partial Q_2}{\partial R_2} = \phi^2_{SQ} F^2_R < \alpha \frac{\partial^2 R_1}{\partial S \partial Q_1} \frac{\partial Q_1}{\partial R_1} = \alpha \phi^1_{SQ} F^1_R. \tag{7vi}$$

4. Consider $\bar{U} :=$ constant so that due to $S = G^{-1}(U)$ also S is constant. Then we have from

$$\phi^1(Q^1, \bar{S}) + \phi^2(Q^2, \bar{S}) + (F')^{-1}[H^1(Q^1) + H^2(Q^2) - \bar{S}] = \bar{R} \tag{8}$$

that

$$\frac{dQ^1}{dQ^2} = -\frac{H^2_Q + F^r_R \phi^2_Q}{H^1_Q + F^r_R \phi^1_Q} < 0 \tag{8i}$$

$$\frac{d^2 Q^1}{dQ^{2^2}} = -\frac{1}{(H^1_Q + F^r_R \phi^1_Q)} \left\{ H^1_{QQ} \left(\frac{dQ^1}{dQ^2}\right)^2 + H^2_{QQ} \right.$$

$$- F^r_{RR} \left[\phi^2_Q - \phi^1_Q \frac{dQ^1}{dQ^2} \right]^2$$

$$\left. + F^r_R \left(\phi^1_{QQ} \left(\frac{dQ^1}{dQ^2}\right)^2 + \phi^2_{QQ} \right) \right\} < 0. \tag{8ii}$$

References

Baumol, W.J.: On Taxation and the Control of Externalities. American Economic Review **62**, 1972, 307–322.

Baumol, W.J., and D.F. Bradford: Detrimental Externalities and Nonconvexity of the Production Set. Economica **39**, 1972, 160–176.

Baumol, W.J., and W.E. Oates: The Theory of Environmental Policy. Englewood Cliffs N.J., 1975.

Laffont, J.-J.: Decentralization with Externalities. European Economic Review 7, 1976, 359–375.

Pearson, Ch.: International Trade and Environmental Controls: Comment. Weltwirtschaftliches Archiv **111**, 1975, 562–564.

Pethig, R.: Die gesamtwirtschaftlichen Kosten der Umweltpolitik. Zeitschrift für die gesamte Staatswissenschaft **133**, 1977, 322–342.

–: Umweltökonomische Allokation mit Emissionssteuern. Tübingen 1979.

Pigou, A.C.: The Economics of Welfare. London 1920.

Rockafeller, R.T.: Convex Analysis. Princeton N.J., 1970.

Schlieper, U.: Externe Effekte, Handwörterbuch der Wirtschaftswissenschaften zugleich: Neuauflage des Handwörterbuches für Sozialwissenschaften, Bd. 2, Stuttgart–New York; Tübingen; Göttingen–Zürich, 1980, 254–530.

Siebert, H.: Externalities, Environmental Quality and Allocation. Zeitschrift für Wirtschafts- und Sozialwissenschaften **2**, 1975a, 17–32.

–: Resource Withdrawal, Productivity Effect and Environmental Policy: Comment. Weltwirtschaftliches Archiv **111**, 1975b, 569–572.

–: Ökonomische Theorie der Umwelt. Tübingen 1978.

–: Economic Theory of Environmental Allocation. To be published in: The Environment and Natural Resources. Ed. by P. Kent. Oxford 1980.

–: Economics of the Environment. Lexington, Mass., 1981.

Siebert, H., and *A. Antal-Berthoin*: The Political Economy of Environmental Protection. Greenwich, Conn., 1979.

Siebert, H. et al.: Trade and Environment. A Theoretical Inquiry. Amsterdam 1980.

Starrett, D.: Fundamental Nonconvexities in the Theory of Externalities. Journal of Economic Theory **4**, 1972, 180–199.

Part VI
Energy-Modeling and Methodology

Economic Theory of Natural Resources. © Physica-Verlag, Würzburg–Wien, 1982.

Energy Substitution with Partially Fixed Factor Proportions

Klaus Conrad

The objective of this paper is to propose an approach in production economics which incorporates the aspect of substitutability in the neoclassical theory as well as the aspect of partially fixed factor proportions in the Walras-Leontief approach. In contrast to Leontief production functions we assume that only fractions of the input quantities are related in fixed factor proportions and that therefore, in contrast to the neoclassical theory, only fractions of the input quantities are disposable for substitution. In order to take into account this aspect we separate the quantity of an input into a bounded part and into an unbounded one:

$$v_i = \bar{v}_i + \tilde{v}_i \qquad i = 1, \ldots, n,$$

where v_i is the quantity of the factor of production i, $\bar{v}_i$ is the quantity of i, bounded by the usage of the remaining $n - 1$ inputs, and $\tilde{v}_i$ is the disposable quantity of i.

From the workers of a firm a crane-driver and a crane are bound inputs, from fuel input technically determined fuel consumption and machinery are bound inputs, and with capital, labor and energy as inputs we regard a truck, a truck-driver and the minimal possible fuel consumption as bound inputs. In general however, not the total quantity of an input is bound by other inputs with fixed proportions, but a fraction is unbound and disposable for substitution. It is this fraction which is relevant for a reallocation of inputs if relative factor prices change. If the energy price increases, the maintenance of the machinery will be improved (an additional worker) and truck drivers drive slower (working over-time or less milage per day). However, this substitution effect can primarily be observed with respect to the unbound component of an input; bound factors like machinery, the stock of trucks, or truck drivers are not objects of a substitution decision; they will be replaced either simultaneously or not at all as one more unit is linked to high costs due to bound inputs (an additional truck driver requires an additional truck). In case of a higher energy price the disposable energy input will therefore be the one which will be reduced. Furthermore, other inputs are bound to energy so that their reallocation will also influence energy consumption.

To take into account this aspect we next assume that the bounded part of input i depends with fixed factor proportions on the disposable input quantities of the other factors:

$$\bar{v}_i = \sum_{j \neq i} \alpha_{ij} \tilde{v}_j, \quad \alpha_{ij} \geq 0, \qquad i = 1, \ldots, n. \tag{2}$$

If the disposable quantity of input j is raised by one unit, the quantity α_{ij} of input i is needed simultaneously. Therefore, α_{ij} is the quantity of input i which is bound by one unit of input j. Substituting (2) in (1), we obtain:

$$v_i = \sum_{j=1}^{n} \alpha_{ij} \, \tilde{v}_j \text{ and } \alpha_{ii} = 1, \qquad i = 1, \ldots, n. \tag{3}$$

If the disposable part of input j is increased by one unit, this increases the total quantity of input j by just this unit and all other inputs i ($i = 1, \ldots, n, i \neq j$) by the quantities α_{ij}. An additional worker, for instance, needs an equipped working place, uses energy and must be equipped with specific inputs to become productive. Therefore, in the relationship of the production process, described by the matrix $A = (\alpha_{ij})$, the j-th column indicates which quantities α_{ij} of the inputs i ($i = 1, \ldots, n$) are required if the input j is increased by one unit. Looking at the rows of A, or (3) respectively, each element indicates the part of input i which will be bound by one unit of the other inputs whereas $\tilde{v}_i$ (for $j = i$) is the conventional part which enters, together with the remaining $\tilde{v}_j$ from relations analogous to (3), the transformation process of the substitutive elements of all inputs. If now the price of input i increases, we observe a direct effect in terms of a cost-minimizing reallocation of $\tilde{v}_1, \ldots, \tilde{v}_n$ by using less of input i and its complements and more of its price-substitutes. The new factor allocation has however, according to (3), also an indirect effect on v_i, because the substitution between the disposable input quantities entails bounded input quantities.

Therefore, with a higher price of input i all those inputs j_0 will become relatively more expensive whose α_{i,j_0} are high. This means that those inputs will be substituted too, which require a lot of input i.

One might ask how the case $\tilde{v}_i = 0$ in (3) has to be interpreted. This only means that the factor i is completely bound by other factors of production. It will be needed if output grows but it is not an input which will be considered with respect to decisions for substitution. If all $\tilde{v}_i$ are zero, then according to (3) all v_i are zero and this implies that an approach with possibilities for substitution has to be rejected in favor of a pure approach with fixed factor proportions which has to be solved by activity analysis. In contrary, if A is the unit matrix, the pure approach with substitution is the appropriate one.

We conclude that for saving inputs (energy) one can not simply reduce the quantity v_i because without knowing which inputs are bound to energy and to which extent, input saving might result in serious interruptions of the production process. The objective to reduce the quantity v_i (energy) can be achieved, if at all, by reducing the substitutive, disposable part $\tilde{v}_i$ and by choosing at the same instant an input combination $(\tilde{v}_1, \ldots, \tilde{v}_n)$, which reduces v_i and which minimizes costs. We next replace the quantities v_i in the cost minimizing approach by the partitioning given in (3). Instead of

$$\min \left\{ \sum_i q_i \, v_i \mid x = H(v_1, \ldots, v_n) \right\} \tag{4}$$

we write

$$\min \left\{ \sum_i q_i \sum_i \alpha_{ij} \, \tilde{v}_j \mid x = H\left(\sum_i \alpha_{1j} \, \tilde{v}_j, \ldots, \sum_j \alpha_{nj} \, \tilde{v}_j \right) \right\}$$

or

$$\min \left\{ \sum_j \tilde{q}_j \, \tilde{v}_j \mid x = F(\tilde{v}_1, \ldots, \tilde{v}_n) \right\} \tag{5}$$

where

$$\tilde{q}_j := \sum_i \alpha_{ij}\, q_i \text{ and } \alpha_{jj} = 1, \quad j = 1, \ldots, n. \tag{6}$$

The cost price $\tilde{q}_j$ consists of the own price q_j and of additional costs, which arise because the input of one unit of the disposable quantity of factor j implies jointly the input of bounded parts of the remaining inputs $i = 1, \ldots, n$ with costs $\alpha_{ij}\, q_i$ per unit of $\tilde{v}_j$. The essential feature of (5) is, that the price q_j is no more the true decision variable for carrying out the substitution process, but the cost price $\tilde{q}_j$. The economic reason for that is that an increase in the relative price for crude oil with respect to coal or natural gas does not simply mean to substitute coal or gas for oil, but requires to evaluate all relevant costs which accrue in conjunction with the realisation of the substitution.

It is easy to show that under our linear transformation $F(\tilde{v})$ is a well-behaved production function if $H(v)$ is well-behaved.

Lemma 1: If $x = H(v)$ is a monotonically increasing and concave function in v and $v = A\tilde{v}$, then $x = F(\tilde{v})$ with $F(\tilde{v}) := H(A\tilde{v})$, is a monotonically increasing and concave function in $\tilde{v}$.

The proof is given in the appendix.

The necessary conditions for a minimum of (5) are:

$$\tilde{q}_j = \lambda F_{\tilde{v}_j}(\cdot) \qquad j = 1, \ldots, n \tag{7}$$

$$x = F(\tilde{v}_1, \ldots, \tilde{v}_n)$$

where λ is the Lagrange multiplier. By substituting the cost-minimizing factor demand functions $\tilde{v}_j = f_j(\tilde{q}_1, \ldots, \tilde{q}_n; x)$ $(j = 1, \ldots, n)$ into (3) we obtain the cost-minimizing input quantities $v_1, \ldots, v_n$ with respect to $\tilde{q}_1, \ldots, \tilde{q}_n$. The cost function with respect to the cost prices is:

$$K(\tilde{q}_1, \ldots, \tilde{q}_n; x) = \sum_j \tilde{q}_j f_j(\tilde{q}_1, \ldots, \tilde{q}_n; x).$$

The analogue to *Shephard's* [1953] Lemma holds:

Lemma 2:

$$\frac{\partial K(\tilde{q}; x)}{\partial \tilde{q}_i} = \tilde{v}_i \tag{8}$$

$$\frac{\partial K(\tilde{q}; x)}{\partial q_i} = v_i \qquad i = 1, \ldots, n. \tag{9}$$

Proof: Shephard's Lemma holds for any positive prices, therefore also for $\tilde{q}$. Differentiation of the cost function with respect to q_i implies:

$$\frac{\partial K(\tilde{q}_1, \ldots, \tilde{q}_n; x)}{\partial q_i} = \sum_{j=1}^n \frac{\partial K(\cdot)}{\partial \tilde{q}_j} \frac{\partial \tilde{q}_j}{\partial q_i} = \sum_{j=1}^n \tilde{v}_j \alpha_{ij} = v_i$$

because of (8) and the definition (6) and (3). We also note:

Lemma 3: The cost function $K(\tilde{q}; x)$ is linear homogeneous and concave in the prices $\tilde{q}$ and q, respectively.

The proof is given in the appendix.

We next rewrite (9) in terms of cost-shares:

$$\frac{v_i q_i}{K(\cdot)} = q_i \frac{\partial \ln K(\tilde{q}; x)}{\partial q_i} \tag{10}$$

and suggest (10) for econometric estimation of the parameters of the cost function and the weights α_{ij}. In principle, one could choose as functional form of a cost function any well-behaved cost function or an approximation (i.e. translog). Of advantage is the simplest case, namely a cost function of the Cobb-Douglas type (henceforth CD) wich implies that the corresponding production function $F(\tilde{v}_1, \ldots, \tilde{v}_n)$ is also of the CD-type. However, an approach with cost prices and bounded inputs does not result in simple measures of the degree of substitutability like in the conventional CD case where the elasticity of substitution is unity and all inputs are price substitutes. It can be shown that even under the CD-assumption variable elasticities of substitution and complementary relations are possible.

Under the assumption of a homothetic production function of the CD type the cost function can be factorized as follows:

$$\ln K(\tilde{q}; x) = \ln f(x) + \alpha_0 + \sum_j \gamma_j \ln \tilde{q}_j \quad \text{where } \sum_j \gamma_j = 1. \tag{11}$$

Because of (10):

$$w_i := \frac{q_i v_i}{K} = q_i \left(\sum_j \frac{\gamma_j}{\tilde{q}_j} \alpha_{ij} \right). \tag{12}$$

One has to keep in mind that according to the definition of $\tilde{q}_j$ there appears a column of the matrix A in each denominator of the components of the sum, and these denominators are the same in all equations. In general, the cost shares are not constant — inspite of the CD-assumption. Only if A is a unit matrix, all shares are constant, because in this case all inputs are disposable and the usual CD-approach is under consideration. For a cost share to be constant, say $w_k = \gamma_k$, the k-th row and column have to be zero except for the element on the diagonal. This means that the k-th input is not strictly bound by any other input (k-th row) and also no other factor will be partially bound by the use of factor k (k-th column). In this case we have $v_k = \tilde{v}_k$ and $q_k = \tilde{q}_k$, that is, input k is a disposable and substitutable input with no extra cost if used.

The Allen partial elasticities of substitution (AES) between input i and j can be computed from:

$$\sigma_{ij} = \frac{K(\partial^2 K(\cdot))/(\partial q_i \partial q_j)}{(\partial K/\partial q_j)(\partial K/\partial q_i)}. \tag{13}$$

With the cost function (11) and the shares (12) the AES are

$$\sigma_{ij} = 1 - \frac{q_i q_j \sum_k ((\gamma_k/\tilde{q}_k^2) \alpha_{ik} \alpha_{jk})}{w_i w_j}. \tag{14}$$

The AES are related to the price elasticities of demand for factors of production ϵ_{ij}:

$$\epsilon_{ij} = \sigma_{ij} \, w_j = w_j - \frac{q_i q_j \sum_k ((\gamma_k/\tilde{q}_k^2) \, \alpha_{ik} \, \alpha_{jk})}{w_i}. \tag{15}$$

If $i = j$ and i a completely disposable input (i-th row and column of A are unit vectors), we obtain $\epsilon_{ii} = \gamma_i - 1$, the usual CD-result. If i and j are completely disposable inputs (i-th and j-th row and column are unit vectors) we obtain $\epsilon_{ij} = \gamma_j$, that is, the CD-result for price substitutes. Furthermore, we observe $\epsilon_{ii} \leqslant 0$ because of the concavity of the cost function which implies $\sigma_{ii} \leqslant 0$ according to (13) and $\epsilon_{ii} \leqslant 0$ according to (15). In spite of the CD-approach not all inputs have to be price substitutes. If in (15) the positive first term w_j is compensated by the negative effect of the second term both inputs are complements. If the elements α_{ij} and α_{ji} in the i-th and j-th row of A are big, that is, input i and j are used intensively if input j or input i, respectively, is increased by one unit, then i and j are complements with high probability as the negative term tends to be large. It should be mentioned that the unity in (14) is due to the CD-approach and that the negative term implies that the elasticity of substitution is always less than one. Our approach of taking into account additional factor costs in deciding to substitute reduces the ease of substitution.

The concept of a bound and a disposable part of an input with the corresponding concept of the cost price and the market price of an input permits therefore a generalization of the CD-approach.

Finally, the quantities of the disposable inputs can be determined if A is regular:

$$\tilde{v} = A^{-1} v.$$

Appendix

Proof of Lemma 1:

$$\frac{\partial F}{\partial \tilde{v}_j} = \frac{\partial H}{\partial \tilde{v}_j} = \sum_i \frac{\partial H}{\partial v_i} \frac{\partial v_i}{\partial \tilde{v}_j} = \sum_i \frac{\partial H}{\partial v_i} \alpha_{ij} \geqslant 0 \text{ as } \frac{\partial H}{\partial v_i} \geqslant 0.$$

Ouput increases more with respect to the disposable quantity than with respect to one unit of the total quantity. For proofing concavity we write the production function as $-x = -H(v)$ where $-H(v)$ is convex in v.

The second order partial derivatives of $-x = -F(\tilde{v})$ take the form

$$\frac{-\partial^2 F}{\partial \tilde{v}_j \, \partial \tilde{v}_k} = \sum_i \sum_k \alpha_{ij} \frac{-\partial^2 H}{\partial v_i \, \partial v_k} \alpha_{kj} = A^T B A$$

where the Hessian matrix $B = ((-\partial^2 H)/(\partial v_i \, \partial v_k))$ is positive semidefinite. As A is a non-singular matrix, $A^T B A$ is positive semidefinite and $-F(\tilde{v})$ konvex in v, that is, $F(\tilde{v})$ concave in $\tilde{v}$.

Proof of Lemma 3:
The linear homogeneity is obvious, and with respect to the concavity it is known [Shephard, 1953] that a cost function of the type $K(\tilde{q}; x)$ is concave in $\tilde{q}$.

514

For proofing $K(\tilde{q}; x)$ to be concave in q we have to show that:

$$K(\tilde{q}(q^3); x) \geqslant \mu K(\tilde{q}(q^1); x) + (1 - \mu) K(\tilde{q}(q^2); x)$$

where $q^3 = \mu q^1 + (1 - \mu) q^2$, $0 < \mu < 1$.

$$\begin{aligned}
K(\tilde{q}(q^3); x) &= \sum_j \tilde{q}_j(q^3)\, \tilde{v}_j^3 = \sum_j \sum_i \alpha_{ij}\, q_i^3\, \tilde{v}_j^3 \\
&= \mu \sum_j \sum_i \alpha_{ij}\, q_i^1\, \tilde{v}_j^3 + (1 - \mu) \sum_j \sum_i \alpha_{ij}\, q_i^2\, \tilde{v}_j^3 \\
&= \mu \sum_j \tilde{q}_j(q^1)\, \tilde{v}_j^3 + (1 - \mu) \sum_j \tilde{q}_j(q^2)\, \tilde{v}_j^3 \\
&\geqslant \mu \sum_j \tilde{q}_j(q^1)\, \tilde{v}_j^1 + (1 - \mu) \sum_j \tilde{q}_j(q^2)\, \tilde{v}_j^2
\end{aligned}$$

which proof the proposition as $\tilde{v}^1$ and $\tilde{v}^2$ are cost-minimizing input vectors with respect to $\tilde{q}(q^1)$ and $\tilde{q}(q^2)$, respectively.

References

Shephard, R. W.: Cost and Production Functions. Princeton 1953.
−: The Theory of Cost and Production Functions. Princeton 1970.

Economic Theory of Natural Resources. ©Physica-Verlag, Würzburg–Wien, 1982.

Two-Factor and Multi-Factor Trade-Offs in Energy Conservation

Willem van Gool

This paper explores methodologies for analyzing decisions and trade-offs in policy analysis. For two-factor trade-offs, such as between energy and capital in energy conservation, the method called cost-energy dynamics (CED) is presented. CED combines the basic principles of physics, engineering and economics into a framework with which to design policy. CED can be used to determine the cost of a certain level of conservation, and the optimum allocation of government subsidies.

When the trade-offs involve many factors some of which cannot be directly compared, the use of an acceptability function is proposed. This acceptability function is analogous to the Fermi-Dirac statistics for describing the behavior of a system of particles. It appears possible to evaluate each factor according to its acceptability, then to combine these individual acceptabilities for an overall assessment index. An example involving the trade-offs between coal, oil, natural gas and conservation for the future of a country called N'Oilandia is presented.

1. Introduction

The postwar period 1945–1970 can be characterized by well-defined objectives in many countries. Rebuilding destructed societies and achieving rapid industrialization were often the main objectives. This development was accompanied by visible benefits, such as better medical care, increased social amentities, more education opportunities and more leisure time.

But there are negative effects, and they were already visible in the sixties. The gap in living standards between industrialized and non-industrialized nations became larger. The increasing scale of most industrial operations removes the average citizen further away from the decision process. The environmental impacts of industrial production became unacceptable on many locations. In 1972, it also became obvious that inexpensive oil was no longer available to large-scale industrialization.

Many studies have been devoted to the possible outcome of society's future. There are considerable differences between solutions suggested by engineers, sociologists, and economist, etc. The engineer sees possibilities for abundant energy – such as solar and breeders – coupled with large scale recycling of critical materials, improving efficiency by automatization of industrial processes, etc. This solution requires decisions to be made by small groups of highly qualified people. Economists assume continued economic growth with an adaptation to high energy prices. The social sciences evaluate possibilities for decentralization of the decision processes.

In analyzing the possible consequences of these proposed solutions we need theories and models. Traditionally, economic models are used to evaluate quantities such as national income or disposable personal income which are often used as indicators for wealth and economic well-being. Some economic models cannot be used for situations complete-ly different from what happened in the past, since economic theory alone cannot derive causal relationships between technical parameters.

Besides economic factors other factors like the environment suggest the need for inte-grating technical, social and economic knowledge. It is possible to distill from the dif-ferent long term speculations those factors which do not depend much on unpredictable elements.

Much data can be derived from the basic assumption that the world will strive for an acceptable existence of say 6 to 10 billion inhabitans (6×10^9 to 1×10^{10}). This fixes a minimum requirement for the necessary amount of food, materials and transport to be used annually.

Analysis along this line [see *Goeller/Weinberg*] have shown that the availability of use-ful energy is a basic requirement: fulfilling this condition the required food and materials can be produced. Here it is assumed that the social structure would be such that this production is desired and permitted. Thus, certain industrial processes will always be required. This paper deals with the minimum amount of energy required to produce cer-tain commodities. The interaction between such energy and the capital is analyzed. This one-to-one relationship is also later extended to pairs of factors such as employment and air pollution, energy and material. Finally, the simultaneous trade-offs between factors are examined.

2. Time Dependence of Energy Analysis

The need for interdisciplinary studies is illustrated by following the development of energy analysis in recent years.

When, since 1973, the oil shortage problem became obvious to the public at large, the typical technical reaction was to search for other forms of primary energy. Thus, many studies were devoted to coal, solar, waves, tides, fusion, and geothermal energy. The general conclusion was that there is enough energy, particularly in the long term (say 50 years from now) when the realization of these techniques are not constrained by the existing capital stock and the present unwieldy social structure.

The next question was how to introduce these alternative energy sources. Two prob-lems arose preventing a fast relief from the oil pressure: the capital and the time required to reach an appreciable displacement of the present oil and gas. Still, a period of 30 years might be long enough to provide the necessary capital.

No solution for the very short term was clearly available. When substitution of energy supply sources is not possible, one turns to the possibility of decreasing the demand. The conservation issue got top priroity.

Again the approach to conservation started along the technical path. The energy re-quired for the final function (the energy service) is compared to the energy available in the carrier or in the resources and large savings seems to be possible. However, the mini-mum energy requirement for final service is based upon an equilibrium concept. This means that the service is rendered at a zero speed, whereas the services in modern society are required with high velocities (transport, annual production volume of materials and food, etc.). High velocities together with low local velocity densities can be obtained by increasing the size of equipment. This again suggests the possibility of increasing the capital investment in order to reduce the annual energy requirement for fulfilling a certain energy service at a fixed velocity. The availability of capital was considered to be a polical issue in the technical analyis. [Am. Inst. of Phys.] This is in line with the idea that the resource constraint is not really severe if one could drive the substitution process infinitely into the corners of the isoquants. This is generally assumed in some economic models, but the empirical evidence or theoretical foundation for such a confidence is poor.

Note that the concepts energy use (per year), time to perform the service and capital available for conservation occur concurrently in the evaluation of both new energy supplies and conservation.

Recently, we developed an approach that might reconcile concepts originating from different sciences [*van Gool,* 1978b]. The annual energy requirement can be decreased by either lowering the annual demand for materials, commodities and services or by rendering the required energy service more efficiently. The first possibility often corresponds to a change in lifestyle. We do not analyze this option here, chiefly because voluntary change of lifestyle does not seem to be presently a driving force in industrialized nations. Thus, the analysis is concentrated on the scond possibility: how can we perform the energy services more efficiently? This implies that we maintain the annual production rate of aluminum, food, etc. Then the time problem is eliminated to a certain extent and the analysis of capital investment versus used energy (process energy) predominates for large scale industrial processes. In the economic description, this trade-off occurs as an isoquant of the production function with capital and energy as parameters. Isoquants based upon variations which occured in the past might be available, but new technology or changes outside the scope of the experience of the past can be implemented in the theory in a very general description only.

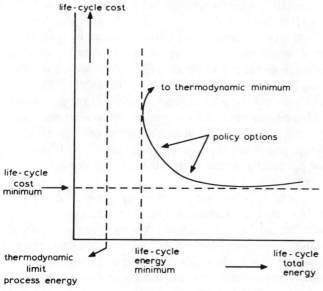

Fig. 1: Life-cycle cost and energy along the conservation path.

At this point knowledge from other sciences and engineering can be useful. It is recog-zed that capital investment will require energy and materials. Thus, we can analyze the life-cycle energy (process energy plus invested — or embodied — energy.) as a function of the changes in equipment leading to a lower energy use. It is also possible to consider the total money cost over life, including both investment cost and cost for process energy. Having gone through this ecercise of cost engineering one can finally present the life-cycle cost versus the life-cycle energy use along the conservation path. Figure 1 illustrates the general pattern.

Several important conclusions are obtained from this analysis [*Phung*, 1980a, b]. The life-cycle energy minimum is higher than the value corresponding to the thermodynamic limit which was used in many analyses to estimate the ultimate limit of conservation policy. It is not even useful to go all the way to the energy minimum, since the last amount of energy saved becomes infinitely expensive. On the other hand the first amount of energy saved when one brings the system towards the cost minimum is very inexpensive. Both life-cycle cost and life-cycle total energy are composed of two components, which leads to the turning away from the asymptotes when one tries to reach the limits. A very simple example is when one puts additional insulation material on a well insulated wall. The energy loss through the wall will decrease slightly, but one does not recover during lifetime of the application the energy that was used to produce the insulation material. One neither recovers the cost of the additional material.

A careful interpretation of embodied energy is required when the time dependence of conservation policy is analyzed. Embodied energy is generally less than 10% of the life-cycle energy. However, the embodied energy has to be invested fully before process en-ergy is used or saved. The energy necessary for the investment might not be available once an energy emergency situation exists. In non-emergency situations the net energy effect of a continuous conservation program might be negative in the beginning of the program. The payback time in energy is the critical parameter — this factor is not favourable for certain solar energy installations [*van Gool*, 1978b].

It is stressed that life-cycle cost is not a simple concept. It is influenced by many fac-tors, such as the effective cost of money, effective income tax rate, depreciation schedule, energy cost escalation, and others. For examples of the use of life-cycle cost in comparing technological options, see *Phung* [1979, 1980a, 1980b] and *Harnett/Phung* [1979].

The engineering data on which the analysis is based suggests the use of energy consum-ing unit operations, (rather than industrial sectors), for aggregation of conservation op-tions. Using five unit operations covering 70% of the industrial energy use in the USA, preliminary data for 1980 leads to an estimate capital requirement of $ 81 \times 10^9$ for the first 10% energy saving beyond the cost minimum, whereas the next 10% requires $ 305 \times 10^9$.

Detailed results have been reported elsewhere and a short survey is given in Appendix 1. It is stressed that the marginal investments increase along the conservation path. Whereas the process energy continues to decrease, the total life-cycle energy — including the embodied energy — goes through a minimum (see Figure 2). Continuing the decrease of the process energy might lead to a situation in which the savings on total energy be-come zero ro even negative (which means that more energy has gone into the conserva-tion measures than can be recovered from the process).

In this section it was suggested that long term analyses of the energy situation in the world can be based upon energy analyses; but medium term analysis has to take into account at least capital and energy simultaneously. Going to the implementation of conservation and supply policy, more trade-offs have to be considered for short-term actions. Environmental inputs differ for the conservation options, and other traditional economic quantities – employment, trade balance, etc. – determine the short term possibilities of energy policy. Different policies can be followed and a system is needed to evaluate favourable and unfavourable effects to a different nature. This is one of the basic problems in decision science. Some ideas are presented in the next section.

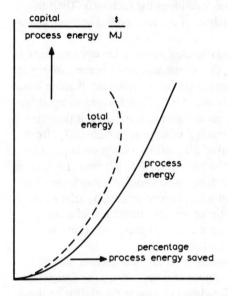

Fig. 2: Percentage saving in process energy and in total energy along the conservation path

3. Handling of Uncomparable Effects

The theory of multi criteria decision problems goes through rapid developments [*Starr/Zeleny*]. The mathematical analysis of optimization methods is relevant to unravel condition, limitations, etc.

In this paper we start from engineering methods, and experimental facts, to arrive at a generalized optimization procedure. Two stages are considered: the trade off between two factors and the simultaneous trade-off of several factors.

Above we dealt with the trade-off between capital and energy along the conservation path. This path can be described as the locus of capital – energy design points when the energy consumed by the equipment is decreased in the direction of the thermodynamic limit. Simple power functions between capital or energy and a characteristic parameter for the change of equipment are used (see Appendix 1 for further details). These power functions are useful as a first approximation of a generally non-linear relationship. This approximation is also valid over a certain range when the energy — capital relationship is other than a power function.

Obviously, there are considerable difficulties when data of unit operations have to be aggregated for the total industrial production. Conventional statistics does not supply the necessary information. Other changes might occur, such as materials substitutions, other transport modes, etc. A more detailed discussion has been given elsewhere [*van Gool*, 1980].

These cases might require descriptions other than the one used in this paper. The major problem is to establish first whether a general theory can be developed using functions simple but general enough to represent the general features of the trade-offs. Therfore, we continue to use the power functions in the analysis of the relationship between essential quantities and design parameters.

For example, it is interesting to evaluate the relationship between the environmental impact and the use of process energy. Decreasing the annual amount of process energy for a certain production, will decrease the thermal impact on the environment. Pushing this to a theoretical limit, the capital required for the equipment will increase exponentially, (see section 2). This steep capital increase means investments in materials and thus the environmental burdens. Another example is the removal of sulphur dioxide (SO_2) from stack gases. Generally, the decrease of the amount of SO_2 left in stack gases requires investments on a logarithmic scale as a function of the percentage SO_2 left over. Thus, going from 10% to 1% might increase the investment with the same factor as going from 1% to .1% SO_2. However, the last step gives only a slight improvement in the SO_2 release, but concomitantly introduces a large burden to the atmosphere due to the manufacturing of the abatement equipment. This suggests the existence of an optimum pollution level beyond which an extra abatement effort yields negative effects.

Similar trade-offs between energy and environment are found when leaner energy resources are used. Witness the high investments required for collecting solar energy or for extracting the dilute uranium in the ocean. The classic technique for evaluating these effects is the inversed matrix method of Leontieff [*Bullard/Penner/Pilati; Muller*]. Presently, there is not enough data available to quantify all these effects, although research is quite active in developing techniques and acquiring the essential data. The general power relationships described earlier appears useful.

Following the time scale backwards from long term design (energy only) through medium term implementation (energy, capital and environment) to the necessary policy decisions, it is obvious not two-factor, but multi-factor trade-offs are involved. Reallocations of capital among the domestic sector, the industry, and the government can affect employment opportunities, trade balance, political independency, and more, in addition to the factors already under consideration.

There appears to be no good method for analyzing exactly the causal relationship between many factors. Still they enter the decision process, either explicitly or implicitly, and modeling research has to take into account of such, in order to be of value as a policy tool.

We offer the following proposal for discussion. It is noted that whenever a group of people has to judge a controversial subject, the establishment of a limit (say unemployment rate, amount of sulfur dioxide in the atmosphere) can give rise to the maximum amount of unsatisfaction, since 50% of the group thinks the limit is too high and the other half thinks it is too low. It is obvious that the results of modeling in which such limits are used are open to criticism and rejection. Therefore it is important in modeling to use limits or boundaries which are acceptable to a large majority — say 90% — of the people involved. Now it seems easier in the described situation to get agreement on limits which are either acceptable or are unacceptable to 90% of the decision-makers. One might consider the question whether or not 85% or 95% should be used instead of 90%, whatever it is, it really is a practical problem rather than a critical issues.

Taking 10% and 90% acceptability limits leads to two important observations. First, a large majority supports the choices. This is important since democracies face large problems when large minorities (say between 35% and 50%) oppose basic issues. Secondly, there will always be some people or some groups opposing any limit. There is no judgement involved whether or not the small fraction of people with disagreeing opinion is right. Modeling has to imitate or to predict the decision processes which are based upon majority opinions — sometimes they are right, sometimes wrong.

A question arises about the selection of the groups which have to decide about the acceptability limits: these can be quite different depending on the issue under discussion. Compare, for example, the unemployment rate, the trade balance, and the amount of carbon dioxide (CO_2) in the atmosphere. For unemployment rate both the trade unions and the employers are involved, but since social benefits are involved, society or government has also a say. The question of how far and how long the trade balance can be negative, has to be answered primarily by macro economists, although society exercises some influence. Obviously, none of these groups can say anything, based on their experience, about the acceptability of 400 or 500 ppm CO_2 in the atmosphere: one has to consult the small group of independent scientists working in this field. It is stressed that social science studies are required to settle the selection of the groups within the aims of model making.

Assuming now that the mechanisms to establish the 10% and 90% acceptability limits can be developed, two other problems must be solved: Firstly, the construction of the acceptability function for each of the factors under discussion, and secondly, the construction of the overall acceptability function for all factors together. A proposition for the acceptability function of factor i is given by the equation:

$$A_i = \frac{1}{1 + e^{(T-T_{0.5})/C}} \tag{1}$$

in which T is a function of the sizes of the factor under consideration, $T_{0.5}$ and C are constants.

Given the values $T_{0.9}$ and $T_{0.1}$ for which the acceptabilities 0.9 and 0.1 have been established, the constants follow from

$$T_{0,5} = \frac{1}{2}(T_{0.1} + T_{0.9}) \tag{2}$$

and

$$C = \frac{T_{0.1} - T_{0.9}}{2 \ln 9} = 0.228 (T_{0.1} - T_{0.9}). \tag{3}$$

522

Fig. 3. shows the behaviour of this function for $T_{0.9} = 4.0$, $T_{0.1} = 16.0$ and for $T_{0.9} = 8.0$, $T_{0.1} = 12$. Both sets have $T_{0.5} = 10.0$, but one has a C value of 2.736 and the other, 0.9120.

The proposed acceptability function has many interesting features. The tails behave exponentially, that is

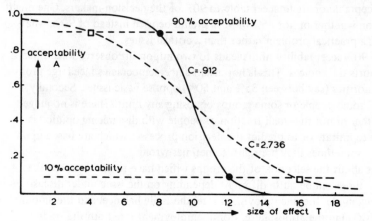

Fig. 3: Acceptability function for two values of parameter C

$$A \approx e^{-T/C} \text{ for } T \gg T_{0.5}. \tag{4}$$

On the other hand, the acceptabilities approach unity for $T \ll T_{0.5}$. They are to be described by the unacceptability U

$$U = 1 - A = \frac{1}{1 + e^{-(T-T_{0.5})/C}} \tag{5}$$

which can be approximated, when $T \ll T_{0.5}$, by

$$U \approx e^{T/C} \cdot e^{-T_{0.5}/C} \qquad (T \ll T_{0.5}). \tag{6}$$

The function T of the size S of the effect has to be specified for each of the factors. In some situations T will be proportional to S, whereas in other cases the relationship $T \sim \ln S$ might be more appropriate. The logarithmic relationship can be useful when S (the size) is large, since the subjective perception of changes is logarithmic rather than absolute in this situation. For example, the change from 100 nuclear reactors in operation to 200 is of importance to policy, whereas a change to 95 or 105 plants will not affect policy appreciably.

At the lower end of the scale, the approximation is

$$U \sim e^{T/C} \sim e^{\ln S/C} \sim S^{1/C}. \tag{7}$$

Thus, for small values of S, an absolute change is felt appreciably (for example, the increase from one plant to three in a certain region).

It is also noticed that a large value of $T_{0.1} - T_{0.9}$ leads to a high value of C. Now the large range between acceptability and unacceptability means a lack of knowledge or a controversy about the problem. When we know and agree on everything, the 0.1 and 0.9 levels of acceptability would coincide, leading to low values of C and a step function for the acceptability. Research and development, technology transfer and social consensus can narrow the range between acceptability and unacceptability.

This behaviour of the acceptability function suggests analogies in other fields of science, viz. the statistical thermodynamics [*Reif*]. There the behaviour of a system of particles is described without accounting for specific properties of each particle. Under certain conditions the probability of the existence of a state is described with the Fermi-Dirac statistics, leading to a formulae equivalent to the definition of the acceptability A (eq. 1). In this statistics the parameter C is identified with the temperature of the system. A high temperature corresponds to a high disorder and lack of information about the detailed situation of each particle. The use of formula 1 to describe the possible outcome for acceptability is therefore, not quite accidently. Recently, *Kümmel* [1980] used the same function to describe a pollution function.

The acceptability function can be compared to the values used by the U.S. Department of Energy (DOE) for ranking research and development opportunities. After screening proposals for compliance with the objectives of DOE, the remaining proposals are evaluated on the basis of a number of factors. The following example will demonstrate the relationship between the two.

In assessing the impact scale for the value of energy savings, the following scale is used:

Range R (in 10^6 \$)	Value
$R > 1000$	8
$1000 > R > 100$	4
$100 > R > 10$	2
$10 > R$	1

Comparing both systems, it seems reasonable to set the 90% acceptability limit at 1000 ($\times$ 10^6 \$) and the 10% acceptability limit at 10 ($\times$ 10^6 \$). Then the acceptability function is known. We can plot the discontinuous judgement of ranges against the continuous acceptability function (Fig. 4).

In the next section, we will examine the question of combining acceptability functions.

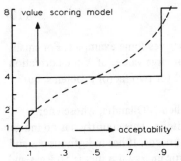

Fig. 4: Comparing two assessment systems.

It is not suggested here that the use of the acceptability function can solve all problems in daily life. A condition for the use of the function is that the size scale covers at least a certain number of units to be useful (say, for example, from 1–10). In many nations discussions about the nuclear program deal with a choice between zero and one or between one and two nuclear plants. The proposed function is not useful in these situations. However, when a nation has five nuclear plants and the discussion concerns the extension to 8, 10 or 12 plants, the use of the function becomes more meaningful, Given in this case it will be necessary to split the problem in a number of detailed questions, such as the available spcae with low-density population, the question how much radioactive waste can be handled, etc. In these cases the sizes of the different factors are relevant. A fundamental decision to stop all nuclear plants cannot be discussed with the proposed function.

In spite of this limitation it is pointed out that the dimension of the nuclear debate is not representative for the present energy supply situation in many nations. Often the energy supply is large based upon oil, gas, coal, etc., and the real situation requires many decisions which are not of the bang-bang type. In these cases then all of the acceptability functions might be helpful.

4. Acceptability of a Multifactor System

Assume a system with N factors each giving rise to an acceptability A_i, $(i = 1, N)$. Several methods were used to define the total acceptability A_t of the system, for example

$$A_t = \frac{1}{N} \sum_{i=1}^{N} A_i \tag{8}$$

and

$$A_t = \left[\prod_{i=1}^{N} A_i \right]^{1/N} = \prod_{i=1}^{N} A_i^{1/N}. \tag{9}$$

These procedures, however, do not reflect the fact that when one factor has a very low acceptability, then the overall acceptability must also be low. This can be reflected by multipling the acceptability with a function that decreases as the acceptability A_i becomes low. The following equation has useful properties

$$A_t = \prod_i A_i^{1/N} [1 - \exp\{-A_i/(0,2 - A_i)N\}]. \tag{10}$$

The correction term is applied only for $A_i < 0.2$. Table 1 gives some examples. For small values of N the correction is somewhat weak, whereas for large values of N the correction is somewhat heavy. This procedure is probably not useful for two factor problems, but is quite attractive for the multi-factor ones.

Let's consider a fictitious West European Country, called N'Oilandia, whose energy futures depend on a few parameters and four decision criteria. This country has no indigenous oil and coal, thus has to import all the oil and coal it needs. It has indigenous gas and is selling gas to several neighbouring countries. Its domestic energy use mix is 50% gas and

	Case 1	Case 2	Case 3	Case 4	Case 5
	0.19	0.90	0.15	0.20	0.10
	0.19	0.90	0.15	0.20	0.20
	0.19	0.10	0.15	0.30	0.30
	–	–	–	0.40	0.40
	–	–	–	0.50	0.50
	–	–	–	0.60	0.60
	–	–	–	0.70	0.70
	–	–	–	0.80	0.80
	–	–	–	0.90	0.90
N	3	3	3	9	9
A_t (uncorrected)	0.190	0.433	0.150	0.448	0.418
A_t (corrected)	0.189	0.123	0.038	0.448	0.044

Tab. 1: Values of Geometrically Averaged and Weighted Acceptability as a Function of the Number of Factors

50% oil at a total level of 2.8×10^9 GJ per year. The imported amount of oil in 1978 is 1.4×10^9 GJ or about 33 million ton of oil per year. The BNP growth is at 3% per year and the annual energy use also grows at 3% per year after accounts have been made for conservation on the one hand and economic growth on the other. Therefore, within 10 years, the annual energy need increases by 34%, to a total of 3.76×10^9 GJ in 1978. Now, the government of N'Oilandia wants to decrease the use of domestic gas consumption by 10% from 1.40×10^9 GJ/yr. to 1.26×10^9 GJ/yr. Thus, it has to find a solution for $3.76 \times 10^9 - 1.26 \times 10^9 = 2.50 \times 10^9$ GJ/yr. Since N'Oilandia does not want new nuclear reactors in that period, the choice is between import of oil, import of coal or conservation. This leaves only two fractions to be chosen, since the third makes up for the total required amount.

Below we shall evaluate the possibilities using a four-factor decision criterion (details are reported in Appendix 2).

4.1 Government Income

By taxes and duties the government earns income from the oil import which is about 80% of the world price or crude. The income is less with coal, at 50%, since government policies are to stimulate its use. On the other hand, at a 20% subsidy to conservation investment, the government spends money without direct income. Combining these three cases, the total government income is

$$G = p_o \times 47.8 \times 10^6 \times f_o + p_c \times 42.6 \times 10^6 \times f_c - [(1 - 0.831 \times f_b)^{-0.3} - 1] \times 3.2 \times 10^9 \tag{11}$$

in which f_o, f_c and f_b are respectively the fractions oil import, coal import and conservation with

$$f_o + f_c + f_b = 1. \tag{12}$$

p_o and p_c are import prices for oil and coal in Dfl/ton. N'Oilandia happens to use Dutch Florins as currency (2 Dfl. = 1 US $). Using $p_o = 450$ Dfl/ton and $p_c = 150$ Dfl/ton the government income runs from 22×10^9 Dfl ($f_o = 1$) to -2×10^9 Dfl (for $f_b = 1$). Acceptability limits are set on 10×10^9 Dfl ($T_{0.9}$) and zero ($T_{0.1}$).

4.2 Energy Effect on the Trade Balance

The amount of money paid out to foreign nations for oil and coal is

$$I = p_o \times 59.8 \times 10^6 \times f_o + p_c \times 85.3 \times 10^6 \times f_c \text{ (Dfl)}. \tag{13}$$

The acceptability limits are based upon the increased export in the assumed growth situation. Part of it can be spend in buying fuel, but the traditional import structure cannot be changed considerably at once. The following values are used: $T_{0.9} = 10 \times 10^9$ Dfl and $T_{0.1} = 20 \times 10^9$ Dfl (Appendix 2).

4.3 Environmental Burden

Only SO_2 is considered. The annual production of 500×10^6 kg SO_2 has been considered as a limit, but many consider it as too high. Therefore 400×10^4 kg SO_2 is used as the $T_{0.9}$ limit. Perhaps a certain increase cannot be avoided, but around 800×10^6 kg SO_2 per year no acceptability can be expected ($T_{0.1}$). Furthermore, it is assumed only 75% of the sulfur in oil and 50% of the sulfur in coal will reach the atmosphere. The result is

$$SO_2 = f_c \times s_c \times 853 + f_o \times s_o \times 898 \ (10^6 \text{ kg}) \tag{14}$$

in which s_c and s_o are the sulfur concentrations in coal and oil.

4.4 Limitation to Oil Import

N'Oilandia is involved in an international cooperation aiming at a reduction of their total oil use. A reduction from the present use of 33×10^6 ton oil per year to 25×10^6 ton oil per year 10 years later, will probably meet a positive international response ($T_{0.9} = 25 \times 10^6$). An increase to 45×10^6 ton oil per year would certainly meet a high resistance ($T_{0.1} = 45 \times 10^6$). The imported amount follows from

$$O_i = 59.8 \times 10^6 \times f_o \text{ (tons of oil per year)}. \tag{15}$$

The four decision criteria are evaluated upon their acceptabilities T_1 to T_4, and the total acceptability T is determined with the method discussed earlier. The result is plotted in Fig. 5. The maximum acceptability is found for 60% conservation and 40% oil ($T = 0.87$). However, the maximum is rather flat and viewing the few parameters that were considered, it might be better to take the area representing T values above 0.80 as an indication where the optimum combinations occur. Then a mix of 40% conservation, 30% oil, and 30% coal is also acceptable. One can also use the plot to exclude certain areas. $T < 0.30$ occurs for oil $> 60\%$ or coal $> 80\%$ or conservation $< 20\%$ and $> 80\%$. Note that, conservation is treated here as a resource. At the maximum acceptability point, the role of natural gas is not 2.5×10^9 MJ but only 1.0×10^9 MJ. Then the total energy use is 2.4×10^9 MJ, which is lower than the 1978 value.

Of course, it is not intended to establish policy on basis of this example. Although data and assumptions are quite reasonable, the limited number of decision factors must be considered.

```
         OIL
          0
         0  0
        0  0  0
      18  5  0  0
     57 47 25  1  0
    79 71 59 47  7  0
   87 84 78 68 54 12  2
  84 86 85 81 72 59 15  3
 73 78 81 82 80 73 62 17  3
19 58 70 74 76 76 71 62 19  4
 3  6 13 30 66 69 69 66 60 21  4
CONSERVATION                COAL
```

Fig. 5: Total acceptability in the trade-off between coal, oil, and conservation.

5. Concluding Remarks

This paper explores methodologies for analyzing decisions and trade-offs in policy analysis. For two-factor trade-offs, such as between energy and capital in energy conservation, the method called cost-energy dynamics (CED) is presented. CED is based on a combination of physical, engineering and economic principles. The formulations and approximations are very general and give reasonable estimates when applied to some typical situations. CED can be used to design a rational conservation policy and to find an optimum allocation of government subsidies.

When the trade-offs involve many factors some of which cannot be directly inter-compared, we suggest an acceptability function. It seems possible to evaluate each factor according to its acceptability and to combine these individual acceptabilities for an over-all index. An example involving three factor criteria in the trade-offs between coal, oil, natural gas and conservation is given.

Acknowledgment

The author acknowledges Mr. C.P. van Driel for the calculations, Dr. R.W. Gilmer (Institute for Energy Analysis, Oak Ridge, Tennesse) for his constructive remarks and Dr. D.L. Phung (also at I.E.A.) for an extensive revision of this paper.

Appendix 1: Cost Energy Dynamics: a Summary

Cost Energy Dynamics (CED) was developed recently at the Institute for Energy Analysis (Oak Ridge, Tennessee, U.S.A.) in cooperation with Dr. Doan Phung. The objective was to analyse industrial conservation policy with capital, process energy, and time as parameters as trade-off components. The CED formulation is based on basic principle of physics, engineering and economics. Several reports available on CED and related subjects. Some salient properties of CED are summarized below.

Conservation of energy involves anything that leads to lower energy use. Since the energy use is not constant, a reference situation must be described in order to formulate a conservation policy. Cost-energy dynamics is developed for industrial production. Thus, the method using a decreased demand — for example by changing lifestyle — to decrease the energy use, is not a part of CED. Neither are the easy housekeeping measures which involve no costs.

CED deals with the trade-offs between decreasing process energy and increasing investments in order to achieve such saving. The trade-off is effected at the level of unit operations where energy is actually consumed. Examples of these unit operations are furnaces where oil and coal are burnt. In some cases the heat is used directly (for example, melting of silica to make glass); as in others, an intermediate energy carrier is formed (electricity, steam, hydrogen, etc.) and additional equipment is involved in rendering the (final) energy service (transport of materials, evaporation, etc.).

Basic physical laws point to increasing energy losses with increasing process intensity. This intensity depends on equipment design; for example, the amount of heat transferred per second through $1 \, m^2$ surface, the amount of liquid pumped per second through $1 \, m^2$ pipe diameter, the amount of chemicals reacting per second per m^3 reactor volume, etc.

For most operations one can determine which changes are necessary to decrease the process intensity and thus to a lower energy loss. For example, increasing the heat transfer surface is needed to keep the total heat transferred the same. The locus of configuration versus energy saving constitutes the conservation path.

When we use D as a generalized parameter indicating the size of equipment corresponding to a constant production volume rate, we have in principle

$$E_p = E_p^0 + \gamma \cdot D^{-\alpha} \tag{I-1}$$
$$C_i = C_i^0 + R \cdot D^\beta. \tag{I-2}$$

Here E_p is the process energy used per year and C_i the cost per year for the invested capital. E_p^0, C_i^0, γ, R, α and β are constants used for adaptation to the problem under investigation. The formulas have been found to apply to a number of unit operations. They are useful in most cases, although the theoretical realtionship might be different for some situations.

Important are the constants E_p^0 and C_i^0. Very often the capital required for the equipment is linear on a log-log plot when the size of the equipment is changed. Then C_i^0 can be taken zero in the range of D under consideration. When installation costs are important C_i^0 might become important. This will happen when a combination of many small efforts is considered. Thus, when we apply formula (I-2) to levels of aggregation much higher than that of the energy-using equipment, the constant C_i^0 becomes more important.

The constant E_p^0 is more fundamental: it represents the energy required to run the operation even when the process intensity approaches zero. It occurs in the literature as the required Gibbs Free Energy, the Exergy and the Availability. There are two ways to express the fact that for certain operations the constant E_p^0 is fundamentally different from zero. Either one corrects the process energy and applies the formulae for the corrected value $E_p - E_p^0$ or one uses Eq. (I-1) as such, which complicates the mathematics somewhat.

CED allows equations (I-1) and (I-2) to apply both in the case of money or in the case of energy. Thus, multiplying Eq. (I-1) with the price of process energy gives the money cost for process energy. Combination with Eq. (2) leads to the total cost for the process and the cost optimum can be derived. Correspondingly, Eq. (I-2) can be converted to an equation representing the energy involved in the capital investment: combination with Eq. (I-1) leads to the energy optimum. In the Cost energy Dynamics formulation, appropriate corrections are introduced for discounting taxes, lifetime of the equipment, etc. The "invested" (or embodied) energy is important in the dynamic analysis of conservation policy [*van Gool*, 1978b].

Another observation is important to link CED to the more common economic analysis. Eliminating D from Eqs. (I-1) and (I-2) leads to a relationship between the process energy and the capital cost along the conservation path. Since the production rate has been assumed constant, this relationship represents an isoquant of the production function using capital cost and process energy as production factors. It is interesting to observe that a Cobb-Douglas function is obtained when both E_p^0 and C_i^0 are taken as zero. The exponent in that equation is equal to $c = -\beta/\alpha$. This is important since c can be found from engineering data rather than from statistical analysis of historical data.

It was suggested above that E_p^0 will not be zero for certain processes. Application of the theory by using $E - E_p^0$ will still lead to the Cobb-Douglas production function. It can be shown that the relationship between E_p and C_i will lead to a CED production for $E_p \neq 0$.

The importance of this approach is obvious. If economic analysis of technically oriented phenomena is based on historical data, it is difficult to predict long term developments, given future technological changes are sometimes different from historical experiences. This is exactly the situation we are facing in the structural changes of the energy supply. The method of CED is helpful in translating the engineering analysis into quantities relevant to economic analysis. A more complete description has been given in quoted references.

Finally, it follows from Eq. (I-1) and (I-2) that a change in the process energy E_p with respect to some reference state is related to the change ΔC_i in the cost for capital by the equation

$$\frac{\Delta E_p}{E_p - E_p^0} = 1 - \left(1 + \frac{\Delta C_i}{C_i - C_i^0}\right)^{-1/c}. \tag{I-3}$$

The overall value of c for the US situation has been estimated to be between 3.2 and 3.5. With the assumption $E_p^0 = 0.2\,E_p$ and $C_i^0 = 0.2\,C_i$, the following equations are obtained:

$$\frac{\Delta E_p}{E_p} = 0.8\left[1 - \left(1 + 1.25\,\frac{\Delta C_i}{C_i}\right)^{-0.30}\right] \tag{I-4}$$

and

$$\frac{\Delta C_i}{C_i} = 0.8\left[\left(1 - 1.25\,\frac{\Delta E_p}{E_p}\right)^{-0.30} - 1\right]. \tag{I-5}$$

These equations have been used in the example in the main text to estimate the cost for capital required to obtain a certain saving of the process energy.

Appendix II: The Simple Economy of N'Oilandia

The quanties occuring in this example are for illustration of the use of the acceptability function only. Although the similarity of the economy and other relevant topics between N'Oilandia and the Netherlands in 1978–1980 is not an accident, the results should not be taken seriously. It is stressed that the choice of the $T_{0.1}$ and $T_{0.9}$ in the proposed method is made by groups of experts. Their selection in this example has been made by the author for demonstration purposes. Changes in prices and interest rates have been neglected to avoid unnecessary complications in this illustration. As in all forms of analysis of the future, the expected or estimated changes must be taken into account when the theory is applied to real situations.

The first criterion deals with the government income from the energy business. In this simplified example, the range of such income is between Dfl 22×10^9 (oil only) to minus Dfl 2×10^9 (conservation only). What is acceptable? This question has to be settled by economists and politicians. Obviously, nearly every government wants more income to carry out its many programs. However, there are beneficial aspects of more conservation (less income) such as less pollution and less political dependence. The first factor is judged separately in this analysis in a simplified form (SO_2, see the third criterion). Thus, we must not include the environmental factor here to avoid double counting, That leaves — in this version — only the political dependence as a trade-off to the government income.

The above discussion leads to an important principle: specifying as many factors as possible makes the judgement on each of them more independent from the rest. In this case we put an income for the government at Dfl 10×10^9 as an upper limit ($T_{0.9}$) for the trade-off between the desire to increased income and the political independence, whereas a zero income is considered to be highly unacceptable to the government. These judgements are also based on considerations such as institutional constraints which cannot be changed overnight.

The second factor deals with the trade balance. First it is observed that import and export are about Dfl 150×10^9 in 1978. The imported oil was valued at about Dfl 16.5×10^9 of which about one half was consumed domestically (the remainder was exported). Thus, about 5% of the import was paid to the exporting countries for oil. With this data, the judgement was that the limits for oil imports move between 5% and 10% of the export. This export is growing in agreement with the assumed economic growth. So it was assumed that Dfl 10×10^9 is acceptable ($T_{0.9}$) and Dfl 20×10^9 becomes unacceptable ($T_{0.1}$).

In the third criterion, the amount of sulfur dioxide (SO_2) produced and released by the fuels is used as a criterion for the environmental burden. The policy design takes an annual production of 500×10^6 kg SO_2 as an upper limit, but the present values are probably higher. Assuming 1% sulfur in the 1978 deomstically used oil, the amount of SO_2 would be 669×10^6 kg SO_2. However, the crude oil is processed and sulfur is removed partially. When we assume that about 25% of the sulfur in 1% sulfur oil does not reach the atmosphere, the oil import and the SO_2 production in 1978 are in rough agreement. To get the same heating value, more coal than oil must be used. Thus, even when coal with 1% sulfur is used, stricter conditions have to be applied. Therefore, it is assumed that 50% of the sulfur in this coal does not come into the atmosphere. Finally it was judged that an annual production of 400×10^6 kg SO_2 will be acceptable $(T_{0.9})$, whereas a doubling will not be tolerated $(T_{0.1})$.

The last criterion concerns the size of the oil import. The international pressure is to decrease the oil import within the EEC and the IEA. Thus, a decrease from the present (1978) domestic use of about 33×10^6 tons of oil per year to 25×10^6 tons of oil per year will meet international approval $(T_{0.9})$. There are, however, reasons for an increased import of oil, but if is estimated that an increase to 45×10^6 tons of oil would meet strong disapproval in the international incorporation $(T_{0.1})$.

References

American Institute of Physics; Efficient Use of Energy. A/P Conference Proceedings No. 25, 1975.

Bullard, C.W., P.S. Penner and *D.A. Pilati*: Net Energy Analysis: Handbook for Combining Process and Input-Output Analysis, Resources and Energy 1, 1978, p. 267.

Goeller, H.E., and *A.M. Weinberg*: The Age of Substitutability. A Strategy for Resources. Ed. by M. Goldsmith, H. Waalwijk and N. Wiedenhof. Amsterdam 1977.

Gool, W. van: Limits to Energy Conservation in Chemical Processes. Report ORAU-IEA-78-6(M), Institute for Energy Analysis, Oak Ridge, Tenn., USA, 1978a.

–: Fundamental Aspects of Energy Conservation Policy. Report ORAU/IEA-78-20(M), Institute for Energy Analysis, Oak Ridge, Tenn., USA, 1978b, Also published in Energy, The International Journal 5, 1980, 429–444.

–: Constraints on Energy Conservation. Physics Today, March, 1979a, p. 9.

–: Thermodynamic Aspects of Energy Conservation. Workshop on Second Law of Thermodynamics, George Washington University. August 14–16, 1979b. Energy, The International Journal 5, 1980, 783–792.

Gool, W. van, and *D.L. Phung*: On Industrial Energy Conservation Policy: The Trade-Off Between Energy Savings and Additional Investments. Materials and Society 4, 1980, p. 471.

Harnett, R.M., and *D.L. Phung*: Three Modes of Energy Cost Analysis: Then-Current, Base-Year, and Perpetual-Constant Dollar. Energy Systems and Policy 3, 1979, p. 61.

Kümmel, R.: Growth Dynamics of the Energy Dependent Economy. Königstein/Ts. 1980.

Muller, F.: Energy and Environment in Interregional Input-Output Models. Gravenhage 1979.

Phung, D.L.: Selection of Discount Rates in Energy Cost Analysis Using Discounted Cash Flow (DCF) and Revenue Requirement (RR) Methodologies. Energy Systems and Policy 3, 1979, p. 145.

Phung, D.L., et al.: Assessment of Industrial Energy Conservation by Unit Processes. Report ORAU/IEA-80-4 (14), 1980.

Phung, D.L., and *W. van Gool*: Cost Energy Dynamics. Second Annual Conference on Industrial Energy Conservation Technology and Exhibition, Houston (Texas), 1980b.

Reif, F.: Fundamentals of Statistical and Thermal Physics. New York 1965.

Starr, M.K., and *M. Zeleny* (Eds.): Multiple Criteria Decision Making. Amsterdam 1977.

Economic Theory of Natural Resources. ©Physica-Verlag, Würzburg–Wien, 1982.

The Global Energy Problems and Japanese Crisis Management Policies

Shinichi Ichimura[1])

1. Three Possible Courses for Energy Situations

There are three possible courses of development for global energy situations in the 1980's. The first is the one in which the oil price will kepp on rising in real terms so that oil-importing countries must slow down their growth rates to cope with resultant domestic inflation and unfavorable balance of payments. But in this course the serious disruptions of oil supply does not occur, and even the slacking demand and supply conditions are conceivable at a time of recessions. This is the most peaceful course of probable events for which ordinary economic policies should be considered adequate. If one can really believe in the possibility of this course only, then no serious crisis management policies are needed. The second course is similar to the first, except that once or several times the disruption of oil supply like the one caused by Iranian situation in 1979 takes place. Then, the world market of oil will be seriously shocked, and the oil price and supply will be seriously disturbed. The extent of disturbance seems very uncertain. This is the situation of uncertainty and swing which is the most probable to occur according to most experts' opinions.[2])

The third course is the situation in which a serious disruption of oil supply, at least over three months or longer, takes place and the oil market is thrown into complete confusion. This is the situation of crisis. In this case it is almost certain that some military action is going to be undertaken by some country. Some experts in the U.S. seem to think that the disruption over 6 months leads inevitably to war. Even in the second course, however, there may appear a serious political and military threat under some circumstances. The first course described as the peaceful one may also implies a serious situation to some countries, if not to Japan or big powers. A number of LDC's may be badly affected, so that the internal economic and social instability may bear even an international repression. Hence, in all cases it is highly desirable for any responsible government to prepare a set of policies so that it may be able to meet such serious situations. The so-called crisis management policies are necessary to meet this requirement.

---

[1]) This paper is based on *Ichimura/Fujime* [1980] and *Ichimura* [1980a, 1980b]. It was written down when the author held a visiting professorship at the Institut für Gesellschafts- und Wirtschaftswissenschaften der Universität Bonn.

[2]) The best analysis of Japanese Energy crisis management policies before the socond oil crisis is given by Nomura Research Institute [1979]. This report gives the results of a survey on 32 experts on the likely situation in the 80th. Some of these survey results are quoted in § 6,

The crisis management policies must be always coordinated with other, ordinary economic policies, so that this discussion on crisis management need to proceed in balance with those on fiscal and monetary policies in the first course. The crisis management policies must always consider the socio-economic and political implications of oil crisis and the requirement of national security.

2. Geopolitics of Oil, Food, Industrialization and Arms Trade

There are several reasons why the oil problem is particularly colored by politics. Firstly the oil and gas resources are concentrated so much in the Middle East which is such a "volatile, unstable and crisis-prone Area". The countries in the area are not populous and do not always need to increase the oil production with increasing demand. The regional distribution of oil supply according to the latest comprehensive study by *Nehring* [1978], is given by Table 1. The economics indicators of Middle Eastern countries are shown in Table 2.

Region	Assured	Potential	Total	%
North America	1.798	1.000 ~ 2.000	2.800 ~ 3.800	16.5
South America	684	520 ~ 920	1.200 ~ 1.600	7.0
West Europe	246	250 ~ 450	500 ~ 700	3.0
East Europe and SU	1.024	630 ~ 1.230	1.650 ~ 2.250	9.8
Africa	756	450 ~ 940	1.200 ~ 1.700	7.4
Middle East	5.099	3.500 ~ 6.300	8.600 ~ 11.400	49.6
Asia and Oceania	508	540 ~ 12.880	1.050 ~ 1.550	6.7
Total	10.115	6.880 ~ 12.880	17.000 ~ 23.000	100.0

Source: *Nehring* [1978]

Tab. 1: Regional Distribution of Oil Supply (100 billion of Barrels)

The Middle East borders on USSR, so that in emergency it may be swept away by one stroke. Such a possibility must be kept in mind. In general, the geopolitics of resource distribution must be analyzed with great care [*Conant*], and it is related not only to such a critical conflict between superpowers but also to various confrontations between USSR and USA, North-South problems, multipurpose usage of oceanic space and border conflicts among different countries. It is normal, therefore, that bilateral confrontations and potential conflicts on the ways of establishing the regional framework in all the areas from the Aege Sea to the South China Sea are receiving an intense attention.

Secondly the economic power of the US as a core of stabilizing forces in the world has relatively receded, and her dependence on imported oil suddenly increased in the 1970's. Table 3 dramatically demonstrates the fact with the figures of major countries. The US dependence on imports is equally serious regarding other mineral resources. Table 4 shows one projection in this and next decade. Surprisingly the US depends already 50% on imported iron ore.

	Polit. System,	Popul. '70,	Export '70,	Import '70,	GNP '70
1. Irak	military	9.4	1.099	509	28.6
2. Iran		28.7	2.354	1.658	128.0
3. Saudi Arab.	Monar.	7.3	2.360	750	29.3
4. Kuweit	Const. Monar.	0.7	1.581	625	23.5
5. Egypt	Repub.	33.3	162	778	64.0
6. Syria	Repub.	6.1	203	360	16.6
7. Turkey	Repub.	35.2	578	577	128.9
8. Arab. Emer	Tribal	0.2	–	–	–
9. Yemen	Repub.	5.7	4*	32	2.5
10. Lebanon	Repub.	2.8	172	577	15.0
11. Jordan.	Const. Monar.	2.3	34	184	5.6
12. Bahren	Tribal	0.2	42*	122	–
13. Qadar	?	0.1	–	–	–
14. Ohman	Monar.	0.8	–	–	–
15. South Jemen	Repub.	1.5	140*	227	1.5
16. Afganistan	Military	17.0	86	73	0.1
17. Israel	Repub.	3.0	130	1.431	48.0

1) Pop. million; Export and Import million US $; GNP 0.1 bill. $; *are for 1969
2) Information is for 1970–1972
3) Needless to say, Iranian situation completely changed.

Tab. 2: Economic Indicators of ME countries

	'60	'70	'75	'77
USA	19.0	24.4	40.2	49.1
Japan	98.5	99.6	99.8	99.8
West Germany	83.5	94.2	95.7	96.4
UK	99.8	99.9	98.5	68.6
France	93.6	97.2	99.1	99.2
Italy	93.7	96.9	99.0	99.0
Canada	45.0	36.5	34.3	32.5

Source: OECD: Energy Balances

Tab. 3: Degree of Dependence on Imported Oil

Since many of the trade-partners are mainly developing countries, she must be more careful in dealing with LDC's and the security of trading lanes. All these resource problems require the US to take the cautious considerations of the interdependence among friendly industrialized countries, oil-producing countries and resource supplying LDC's. Despite the declining importance of American relative position in the world economy, the US policies to cope with these situations are of vital importance to Japan as well as any

	50	70	85	2000	Main Suppliers		LDC
Bauxite	64	85	96	98	Jamaica	53.5	
					Surinam	27.4	88.2
					Guyana	7.3	
Copper	31	?	34	56	Peru	23.2	37.9
					Chile	14.7	
Iron Ore	8	30	55	67	Venezuela	30.6	30.6
Manganese	88	95	100	100	Gabun	26.3	55.5
					Brasil	18.8	
					Zaire	10.4	
Tin	77	?	100	100	Malaysia	64.3	96.5
					Thailand	23.3	
					Bolivia	8.9	
Tungsten	?	50	87	97	Peru	12.0	
					Thailand	9.0	39.2
					Bolivia	18.0	

Source: *Brown*

Tab. 4: The United States' Dependence on Imported Mineral Resources and their Supplies

Western country, and their policies must very carefully be coordinated with the US policies.

Thirdly, the oil crisis occured along with three other fundamental disequilibria in the world economy: a) disequilibrium between food and population, b) disequilibrium of aggregate demand and supply demonstrated by secular trend to inflation, c) disequilibrium between demand and supply of international currency. These four disequilibria are fundamental because they are closely related to the institutions and structure of the world economy now. Their solution seems to require the institutional reform in each country as well as the international system. The policies to cope with the oil crisis must be examined not only in its own light but also in view of the effects on the other fundamental problems. Often the causes which make the solution of these four problems difficult are common and interrelated, so that the solution of one problem may contradict with or facilitate the solution of other problems.

Fourthly, the oil crisis has affected also the countries in the Communist bloc the same way as the West [Lee/Ricky]. Almost all the Socialist countries are dependent on the oil imported from the Soviet Union, so that they have been suffering from the higher oil prices. Solidarity of socialism did not prevent the Soviet from charging the Eastern Europe countries the world market price. They are suffering from inflation and staggering growth. This may be affecting in turn the Soviet economy. The Soviet economy, however, seems to benefit more from the higher price of oil as an oil-exporting country and her power of influence has increased in the Middle East as well as Eastern Europe. The CIA report [1977] has pointed out the possible decline of oil production in the Soviet Union around 1985, which has been denied by the Soviet authorities. They admit, however, that the location of new oil fields is moving to the north-east and the cost of explorations is increasing. It is conceivable, therefore, that she may not be able to supply oil to Eastern Europe as much as they want. For this reason conflicts between Eastern Europe and the Soviet Union may increase in the 80's.

The Soviet Union and Eastern Europe have other weaknesses; the shortage of food, the slow-down of industrial growth and the increasing dependence on Western capital market. From 1973 to 1976 the Soviet Union and East European countries borrowed more than 7 billion dollars, and the amount in early 80's is expected to be more on the annual average. If these loans are not available, the growth rates of Socialist economies must pace down.

All these and other considerations must be taken together to evaluate the changes in geopolitics of the world economy, and the economic and other policies must be prepared to overcome the difficulties imposed by oil crisis. The general picture of some changes is summarized by Table 5.

	Energy	Food	Industry	Arms
1. USA	−	+	0	+
2. USSR	+	−	−	+
3. Canada	+	+	0	+
4. West Europe	−	0	+	+
5. Japan	−	−	+	0
6. Australia	+	+	−	0
7. China	+	−	−	0
8. East Europe	−	−	−	−
9. OPEC	+	−	−	−
10. Non. oil prod. LDC	−	−	−	−

* +, −, 0 means favorable, infavorable, no change due to the oil crisis.

Tab. 5: Changes in Economic Power related to security

As for energy, USSR, Canada, Australia and China as well as OPEC became very advantageous, but except for USA, Canada and Australia all the countries have serious problems in food supply. USSR and China are steadily importing more than 10 million ton of grains every year. Other Socialist countries, Western Europe, Japan and non-oil-producing LDC's suffer from the high price and shortage of energy and food alike, but Western Europe and Japan can cope with the situation by exercising their industrial strength. Non-OPEC LDC's whether they are in the free world or in the Communist bloc, are truely "have-not" and must seriously be affected by oil crisis.

One peculiar effect of oil crisis is the increased importance of arms trade. Due to the internal and international instability, most OPEC countries are greatly interested in their national securities, so that the countries with the capacity to export the armaments obtain the effective leverage in dealing with OPEC's. Table 5 gives an assessment of overall changes in these matters in the 70's. The crisis management policies of any country must respond to such changes in the future as well as in the past.

3. The Roles of Majors and OPEC

There are some special aspects of the demand and supply of oil. The first is the fact that oil-supply countries are not homogeneous. Most of them belong to OPEC, but some do not, as US, UK, USSR, Mexico, *etc.* do not. The second is that even among OPEC members, their national interests are not congenial. It was proved by the fact that at a time of Middle Eastern War Libia, Algeria, and Iraq did not practise the oil embargo. Furthermore, there are enough number of countries like Iran, Iraq, Algeria, Libia, Indonesia, Nigeria, Venezuela, Peru, Ecuador which have large populations and suffer from low percapita income, so that even with a sharp rise in price they do not restrict but maintain the production levels, and thereby obtain the necessary foreign exchange to import the industrial materials and equipments and wish to step up the pace of industrialization. Hence the oil price is more significantly affected by the production and pricing policies of the OPEC members with high percapita income like Saudi Arabia, Kuwait, Union of Arab Emirates, Qatar. For these two reasons the policies of diversifying the sources of supply must aim at keeping a proper balance among these three types of oil suppliers: non-OPEC countries, poor and large OPEC countries and rich and small OPEC countries.

The third is that the so-called Majors are playing a very significant role in explorations, crude oil supply, refinery and distribution. The share has declined sharply as Table 6 shows. As a result, Majors have decreased the supply to the companies not affiliated with them. In emergency, Majors may adapt their own distribution policies which may or may not coincide with the national policies of their home countries. At the time of the second oil crisis, they seem to have behaved as Table 7 demonstrates.

	1970		1975		1978	
1 BP	3,868	16,5	833	3,1	400	1,3
2 Shell	2,913	12,4	1,303	4,8	351	1,1
3 Exxon	3,909	16,7	1,995	7,3	1,161	3,7
4 Mobil	1,223	5,2	516	1,9	504	1,7
5 Saucal	1,882	8,0	1,274	4,7	1,306	4,6
6 Texaco	1,981	8,5	1,407	5,2	1,435	4,8
7 Gulf	2,256	9,6	676	2,5	118	0,4
8 CFP	1,108	4,7	447	1,6	327	1,1
Sub-Total	19,140	81,7	8,451	27,5	5,611	18,8
Others	3,736	16,0	2,045	6,7	1,691	5,7
Oil Co. Total	22,876	97,7	10,496	34,2	7,302	24,5
OPEC, Gov.	538	2,3	16,659	61,3	22,503	75,5
Total	23,414	100,0	27,155	100,0	29,805	100,0

Source: OPEC statistics

Tab. 6: Major's Interest Share in OPEC Crude Oil Production (10^3 B/D, %)

Clearly the internal disposal became dominant, and the share of Majors in the total supply to the free world declined from 67% in 1974 to 64% in 1979. But it is still nearly half so that its importance should not be underestimated.

	1974			1979		
	Crude Oil Supply	Intern'l Disp'l	Outside Sales	Crude Oil Supply	Intern'l Disp'l	Outside Sales
BP	4,440	2,100	2,270*	3.015	2,000	733
Shell	5,917	4,873	891*	4,259	4,242	17
Gulf	2,700	1,957	749	1,970	1,765	230
Exxon	6,367	5,138	1,189	4,453	4,427	26
Mobil	2,462	2,060	402	1,967	2,049	
Texaco	4,507	3,060	1,447	3,422	2,788	634
Saucal	3,815	2,134	1,462*	3,272	2,205	1,070
Total	30,208	21,361	8,375	(22,361)	19,476	(2,710)
		(0,71)	(0,28)		(0,87)	(0,12)
Majors' share	0.67			· 0.46		

Source: *Middle Eastern Economy*, Feb. 1980

Tab. 7: Changes in Major Supply Capacities (/,000 B/D)

(1) Outside sales are estimated as the same as crude oil supply *minus* internal disposal, except that those with * are actual.
(2) The internal disposal in 1979 and 1978 are assumed equal.
(3) The figures of B's crude oil supply and the outside sales are estimates on the basis of those in (source).
(4) The crude oil supply by Majors include the crude oil obtained with the proper right *plus* the one repurchased from OPEC and the oil obtained in the US.

In view of this trend, Japanese government is trying to increase, as it should, the percentage of DD (Direct Deals) and GG (Government to Government) oil dealings and decrease the share of Majors from 72% an 1972 down to far less than half. Already Japanese Shosha (trading companies) and other foreign independents are playing the role that the sales departments of Majors used to perform. One of criterions that the Majors may adopt in allocating the crude oil in emergency seems to allot each subsidiary with due consideration of their share of capital in each corporation. Since the capital share in Japanese subsidiaries is 50%, they may encounter severer restrictions at the time of disruptions.

Nevertheless, it is considered wise to keep as friendly relations with Majors as possible and not to compete unnecessarily by establishing Japanese Majors, because they are still keeping good terms with most OPEC countries and will do so also in the future. Moreover, the high price of oil has brought them an enormous amount of profit, which must be invested in further explorations of oil fields whereever possible or development of oil substitutes. Thus their importance as suppliers of liquid fuels is very unlikely to decrease much further. It has been recognized, therefore, that the best policies are to maintin the friendly competition with them.

The fourth is that the marginal market called the spot market plays a significant role in adjusting the oil price quickly to the demand and supply conditions in the world. The characteristics of this market needs a careful analysis, but it will not be discussed here.

4. The Two Oil Crises in 1973—1974 and 1978—1979

It is well-known that the oil price at the time of Teheran Agreement in February 1973 was $ 2.18 P/B but now after the OPEC meeting Caracus about $ 30.— with considerable variations as is shown by Table 8. In the first oil crisis the rise in oil price from January 1973 to January 1974 was from 2.59 to 11.65; namely, 9.06 dollars or 4.5 times, whereas in the second oil crisis the price rise from January 1979 to January 1980 was from 13.34 to 30.00 dollars; namely, 16.66 dollars or 2.2 times. The mulitplication ratio is less in the second crisis, but the absolute amount of increase is greater. Hence, the absolute amount dollars needed to pay the oil imports almost doubled. This is the reason why so many oil importing countries are suffering from the unfavorable balance of payment in 1980.

	Dec. 1978	Feb. 1980	Δp	Feb. 1980 / Dec. 1978
Arabian-Light	12.70	26.00	13.30	2.05
Dae-Kei	13.20	32.33	19.13	2.45
Sumatra-Light	13.55	29.50	15.95	2.18
Iranian-Light	12.81	31.00	18.19	2.42
Suetena	13.90	34.72	20.82	2.50

Tab. 8: The Price Increase in Main Crude Oils

In the case of Japan, she imports about 5 million barrels a day, so that the annual payment for oil imports can be estimated 24.3 billion dollars for 13.33 dollars P/B, 54.8 billion dollars for 30 dollars P/B. The gap is indeed 30.5 billion dollars. Unless Japanese exports of manufactured goods can increase within reasonable time, her balance of payments mut remain unfavorable for several years. In the case of the US, her recent imports are 7 million barrels per day, so that 42.59 billion dollars additional payment is necessary for the same amount of oil. Both countries must face the difficult problem of controlling the oil cost push inflation combined with the unfavorable balance of payments. This is the situation somewhat similiar to those experienced by many countries in early postwar years. The answer to overcome the difficulties is a proper combination of austerity, saving, increase in productivity, sound fiscal policy, tight money supply, and when necessary, foreign loans (recycling oil money). There is no easy way out, as there was not throughout the postwar years. Still with the vivid memories of postwar hardships, the Japanese government and people seem to have handled the oil crisis very well, particularly the second oil crisis. Table 9 compares the changes in the prices of various categories of commodities at the time of two oil crises. As the commodities are those produced in the later stages of manufacturing their rate of inflation seems particularly less.

	1979.4 ~ 1980.3	1973.10 ~ 1974.9
Average WPI	22.8	30.6
Domestic goods	16.2	25.3
(industrial)	(16.7)	(24.7)
Export	18.4	39.0
Import	82.1	79.7
(Exchange Rate)	(3.5)	(1.3)
Crude Material	73.7	71.9
Intermediate goods	26.6	29.0
Finished goods	6.0	22.3
Cap. goods	3,1	24.7
Cons. goods	7.2	20.9
CPI	8.0	21.9

Tab. 9: Inflations After Two Oil Crisis

This implies that the impact of imported oil price increase has been absorbed by the labour productivity increase in almost all sectors, and the restrained rise of money wage accepted by the labor unions. One important aspect of the successful control of inflation in Japan seems to have something to do with the tight money policy in the second oil crisis to be contrasted with the policies in the first crisis. Table 10 demonstrates this fact.

	Money	Price	GNP
1973	22.7	11.7	5.3
1974	11.9	24.5	−0.2
1975	13.1	11.8	3.6
1976	15.1	9.3	5.1
1977	11.4	8.1	5.3
1978	11.7	3.8	5.2
1979	11.5	3.6	5.5
1980	8.5	8.0	5.0

Tab. 10: The Performance of Japanese Economy Supply, Price-Level and GDP Growth Rates (%)

The contrast in two oil crises is remarkable particularly if one remembers that the disruption of oil supply in the first crisis was not so serious *expost*. Table 11 and 12 clearly proves that there was really no serious shortage of oil in the Japanese economy. Yet such a high inflation occurred in 1974, resulting in *minus* growth for the first time in postwar years. A coordinated set of economic policies could have tided over the oil shocks much more smoothly than in the second oil crisis, although the unfavorable balance of payments might have persisted a little longer, and recycling oil money would be a more important matter to consider now and in the future. These experiences prove that the crisis management policies must be well coordinated with ordinary economic policies.

	1973				1974		
	Sept.	Oct.	Nov.	Dec.	Jan.	Feb.	Mar.
Saudi Arabia	100	96.2	71.0	79.7	90.6	84.8	98.0
Kuwait	100	90.0	73.1	74.6	82.4	75.0	81.6
Iraq	100	104.1	102.5	107.5	108.0	95.3	106.9
UAE	100	103.2	85.6	78.1	92.6	87.8	113.6
Qatal	100	95.4	77.6	76.2	86.6	78.0	89.5
Libia	100	109.3	78.4	81.1	93.2	80.6	86.3
Iran	100	106.7	103.7	108.3	108.8	98.8	109.3

Source: Petroleom Economist, May 1974

Tab. 11: Supply Conditions in ME countries in the first oil crisis

	1973				1974		
	Sept.	Oct.	Noc.	Dec.	Jan.	Feb.	Mar.
Saudi Arabia	(4,680)	94.7	92.8	102.5	102.5	104.8	131.7
Kuwait	(2,332)	66.9	74.7	72.6	84.3	111.2	91.4
Neutral Count.	(1,231)	93.6	85.3	118.0	83.5	88.1	119.5
Iraq	(–)	–	–	(22)	(163)	(337)	(347)
UAE	(3,001)	101.9	82.1	82.8	90.6	65.4	95.0
Iran	(7,780)	109.1	98.5	87.8	96.1	63.9	74.1
ME Total	(19,735)	97.5	90.3	92.9	94.0	83.0	98.1
SEA	(4,176)	107.5	104.0	127.6	106.4	98.0	114.0
Africa	(913)	60.8	70.8	144.2	56.7	43.7	70.2
Total	(25,352)	97.8	91.3	99.8	93.6	83.3	99.0

* Figures in parentheses are absolute quantities in 10^3 Kl.

Tab. 12: Japanese Imports from ME countries and others (%/Sept.)

5. Cost-Benefit Analysis in Peace-time and Crisis

The demand structure for oil is very different between US and Japan; for instance, in 1972.

	Industry (%)	Transportation (%)	Others (%)
US	39	32	29
Japan	63	21	16

More than half of oil consumption is gasoline and jet fuel in the US. Nevertheless it is not completely unreasonable for the US to aim at self-sufficiency. The fundamental idea behind the oil policies to the Carter administration seems to reduce the dependence on imported oil by sacrificing considerably the economic calculation. The crisis management policies can be also conceived along this line.

There is, however, another line or thinking on energy policies. Even in the US, dependence on imported oil, some observe, may not be so bad as all the protectionist policies required to reduce dependence, because they weaken the long-run efficiency of the US economy which is the real basis of American strength. Crisis management policies along this line may be rather different from the one along the first. Since the energy policies of the US government in practice can not ignore the national security apsects in crisis, the first line of thinking tends to prevail. Then the premium actually paid for the sake of security must be clearly recognized and accepted by the American people. This argument holds, more or less, European countries and Japan, where cost and benefit of economic effiency and national security is the crucial problem in the context of oil crisis.

Needless to say, national security does not justify the unlimited or extremely large amount of premium to be paid in peace-time. It is required to determine the appropriate amount of premium for the sake of national security in view of conceivable courses of events described at the outset of this paper.

Five main sondierations may be mentioned here.

1. A criterion, such that it can offer the true cost of energy as a scarce resource in the 80's, including the premium for national security and can be a basis of national calculation for consumers and suppliers, must be offered.
2. The policies to be adopted according to a certain criterion must be examined in the light of their impact on the vulnerability of the US economy at the time of oil supply disruptions.
3. The policies required to put a criterion into practice may cause the unfair distribution of income or inconvenience in living conditions. Such an aspect of social justice can or can not be compensated pecuniarily or otherwise. The Devices to mitigate the unfavorable effects in emergency may have an unusual importance.
4. A proposed criterion for policy recommendations must be carefully reexamined in view of its long term implications on restructuring of manufacturing industries and desirable division between the public and private sectors.
5. The various policies to overcome the energy crisis must be examined from the viewpoint of environmental problems. CO_2 problems related to coal liquefaction is a well-known example.

The most fundamental consideration is the first point. The most straight-forward application of such a criterion would be to take the market value of oil as a cost for security. If, therefore, the expenses needed to produce an oil substitute equivalent to a barrel of crude oil exceeds 30 dollars, it impairs the economic efficiency of the national economy to the extent. That excess must be justified on some other ground like those listed above from 2 to 5. Most economists accept this view even when OPEC sets the price for political reasons, so long as the price prevails in the world market. It is harder, however, how one can evaluate the benefit of security. The practical approach recommended is to examine the policies that can be done with the cost given by the prevailing import price and evaluate the benefit to be achieved. One of typical views along this line is expressed by a group of energy experts at MIT as follows [*Jakoby*]:

a) Energy crisis management must try to achieve a good balance between economic policy objectives and political objectives.

b) It is desirable to reduce the oil import or accelerate the reduction, but the cost of effecting the necessary policies should not exceed the world market price of imported oil.

c) The reduction of oil import does not automatically increase the national security.

d) Undertaking the projects of developing synthetic fuels with the cost more than the price of imported oil will lead to a waste of resources, inflation and the unsustainable industrial structure. This weakens the competitive strength of national economy and reduces the national security in the long run.

6. Typology of Oil Supply Disruptions

The so-called oil crisis seems to imply two phenomena: (1) the secular trend in adjusting the industrial and consumption structure in response to the exhaustion of oil resources; and (2) the sudden and short-lived disruptions of oil supply from major suppliers due to socio-economic or political causes. The first phenomenon seems to persist until some new energy can completely replace oil, and it is the continuous long-term trend, to which most of the foregoing arguments apply. But crisis may occur suddenly, and certain policies must be ready to meet the situations when they come. The crisis management policies in the common sense means the type of policies which are the policies only in emergency for a short period. After a while, when the conditions become normal again, the temporary policies adopted for emergency will be remedied. The crisis in this sense may be classified as four types shown in Table 13. The critical situations market with * lead to energy crisis. How the critical conditions particularly in the Middle East affects the supply of oil depends on the regional distribution of each country's import of oil, which is shown by Table 14.

Economic	Social	Political	Military
*1. Oil Supply Disruption	1. Nuclear accidents	1. Economic Conflicts with US or EC	1. SU's military invasion of nearby countries
2. Food Supply Disruption	2. Earthquake	2. Soviet Threat or Blackmail	2. China-Soviet Confrontion
*3. Uranium Supply Disruption	3. Terrorism	* 3. Resource Supplier's Blackmail	3. Civil Wars in SEA countried
4. Intril Monetary Panik	4. Pollution	4. Tension in Korean, Peninsula	* 4. ME wars
*5. Economic Blocade	5. Contagious Disease	5. Nuclear Proliferation	5. Korean War
6. Depression	6. Psychological Panic	6. Political Instability in SFA Count.	

Source: Japan National Research Institute [1979]

Tab. 13: Four Types of Crises

		USA	Germany	France	UK	Italy	Japan
Oil in Primary Energy		42.3	45.0	65.2	45.5	70.6	74.0
Oil Import %		42.6	94.7	99.3	88.0	98.9	99.7
Total Import 10^6 MT		297.2	99.2	121.1	86.3	100.6	229.6
Main Suppliers % Share	1	Saudi Arab. 20.4	Libia 21.1	Saudi Arab. 36.3	Iran 26.3	Saudi Arab. 27.0	Saudi Arab. 30.7
	2	Nigeria 18.1	Iran 19.5	Iraq 13.9	Saudi Arab.	Libia 16.8	Iran 20.1
	3	Iran 9.5	Saudi Arab. 19.2	Iran 12.1	Kuwait 21.3	Iraq 15.5	Indonesia 12.0
	4	Indonesia 8.9	Algeria 10.6	Abudabi 8.3	Iraq 14.9	Iran 14.4	Abudabi 11.1
	5	Libia 8.6	Nigeria 9.2	Nigeria 6.3	Katal 6.8	USSR 8.1	Kuwait 6.6
	6	Algeria 7.1	Abudabi 7.0	Algeria 3.9	OECD 5.8	Egypt 3.7	Other EE 4.4
	7	Canada 6.2	USSR 3.4	Kuwait 3.6	Other ME 5.0	Other ME 3.4	Neutral 4.2
	8	Venezuela 5.7	OECD 2.0	Libia 2.6	Nigeria 4.5	Algeria 2.5	Other ME 3.4
	9	Abudabi 5.5	Iraq 1.8	Katal 2.4	Libia 4.3	Abudabi 1.6	Iraq 2.9
	10	Trinidad 1.7	Other ME 1.8	OECD 2.3	Abudabi 4.3	Katal 1.3	China 2.6
Regional Dependence	ME	38.0	51.5	81.3	82.0	70.2	79.3
	Afr.	35.8	41.6	14.4	8.1	20	1.4
	Other	26.2	6.9	4.3	9.9	8.9	19.3

Source: IEA Oil Statistics (1976) and others.

Tab. 14: OECD Countries Oil Imports and Suppliers Shares

France and Japan are most vulnerable to the disruption of oil supply from the Middle East.

These disruptions can be caused for a number of reasons listed in Table 13, but it is useful for the purpose of analysis and policy considerations to distinguish between the disruptions due to the damages of physical facilities or hardwares for oil production and shipment and those due to the malfunctioning of administrative system or softwares to control and manage the physical facilities and personnel. The former facilities include oil fields and exploratory facilities, pipe-lines, tanks, harbors, shipping facilities and lanes, refinery or liquefaction factories *etc.* The latter include all kinds of administrative or institutional systems, facilities and personnel engaged in production, transportation, export, import of petroleum and its related products. Oil crisis occurs if one or both of these systems are damaged. It is also possible, however, that with both systems properly maintained oil crisis occurs. Thus, four cases can be distinguished.

Physical facilities Institutions	maintained	damaged
maintained	A	C
damaged	B	D

Case A is exactly the oil crisis in 1973. They are primarily caused by the politico-economic strategies of OPEC and can be managed within some resonable time. Case B is like the one caused by Iranian coup, and may not be manageable in a short time. Since the physical facilities are difficult to maintain without using them all the time, this case may shift to D, if the administrative system does not recover its function in time. Japanese Petro-chemical Plant in Iran is the case in point. Case C happens mainly due to some accidents. Those in the springs of 1977 and 1978 are the real examples. Case D is the most catastrophic one and may lead to a major war. A careful survey of expert opinions was conducted in Japan early July, 1978. The following results are probably the most authoritative views then and are of great interest.

Question A: Will oil supply disruption occur?

	Within 2 to 3 years	Before 1990
1. Almost certainly occur	0	1
2. Very Probable	0	6
3. Probable	12	12
4. 50–50	7	6
5. Improbable	12	5
6. Very Improbable	7	2
7. Almost certainly not	0	0
	32	32

Question B: How much disruption of oil is likely to be made?

Answers

1. 10 %	2	6. 60 %	3
2. 20 %	13	7. 70 %	0
3. 30 %	8	8. 80 %	0
4. 40 %	2	9. 90 %	0
5. 50 %	3	10. 100 %	1
			32

Question C: Which country is likely to experience a domestic instability leading to disruption of oil supply? (% of replies)

	Answer
Saudi Arabia	50
Kuwait	75
UAE	34
Iraq	38
Neutral Zone	20
Indonesia	25
China	38

Clearly Iran was recognized as a most unstable country, and China is still considered as unstable as Iraq. Policies must be always prepared to cope with the development in each case.[3] A critical issue is how long the disruption will last. This was asked to experts in the same survey and the answers for Case A to D are as follows.

Question D: How long will the disruption of oil supply last in each case?

months	Case A	B	C	D
1	4	2	5 0	0
2	3	8	3	0
3	10	7	12	4
4	5	3	1	1
5	0	0	1	1
6	6	10	6	8
7	0	0	0	0
8	1	0	0	2
longer	2	2	3	17
	32	32	32	32

The impact of crisis may be analyzed in three aspects: 1. economic, 2. social, 3. security. It is also important to pay attention to the time pattern of crisis and the available information on the nature and degree of crisis.

The economic effects of oil supply disruption are not limited to the demand adjustment to the shortage of oil. The overall readjustment of production, employment and price-wage adjustments will be required to administer the national economy under the conditions of energy shortage. If the disruption becomes serious and elongated, the economic conditions become almost like war-time.

The social effects are primarily the matter of distribution of income and sharing inconveniences mentioned as point 3. The shortage of daily necessities may cause social restlessness or confusions. If the situation becomes more serious, then it may be regarded as a matter of political security similar to the matter of national security in wartime. The crisis management policies must be contrived in accordance with the needs of the different degrees of critical situations.

---

[3] These policies are briefly discussed in Nomura Research Institute [1979].

The time pattern of energy crisis is unlikely to be so abrupt as the first oil crisis, and the information of critical conditions likely to occur tends be known beforehand, because now the communication between OPEC countries and consumers countries is far better than before. Indeed, the improvement in information alone contributes a great deal to cope with the crisis, and ignorance and uncertainty of the events to occur amplify the effects of crisis on the economy more violently through the psychological anxieties than they really do when the likely events are anticipated well.

7. A likely Course of Emergency and Policies

In preparing the crisis management policies the most likely type of crisis and its degree of seriousness must be assumed; otherwise, any policy prescriptions will not be possible. Several authorities [see Nomura Research Institute; *Levy; Deese*] have given their judgements which may be summarized as follows:

1. New discovery of oil fields in Alaska and North Sea cannot force the fall of oil price, because OPEC can take it into their consideration in setting the oil price and production amount.
2. Iranian production is very unstable, so that unless Saudi Arabia increases its production with some other gulf states, when necessary, the price may rise again in the near future. But it is more likely that the gulf states operate the production lines near the capacity levels and thereby keep the real price of oil fairly steady after the second oil crisis.
3. Although it is possible that some countries like Libya, Nigeria or Indonesia may take steps to raise the oil price due to the need of improving their economic conditions, the major ME countries may be more concerned with the hyperinflation going on in the US and other industrialized countries so that recycling oil money may face the difficulty and not be profitably and safely reinvested. As Table 15 shows, the amount of oil money estimated by Morgan Trust and others is as much as 119.2 billion dollars at 1978's end. In addition, the oil revenue is estimated 188 billion $ in 1979, 276 billion $ in 1980, and oil money is expected to go up to 214 and 304 billion $ in 1979 and 80. Major gulf states are naturally concerned with the inflation in the US and Europe. Indeed, it may be conceivable to experience a steady decline in real terms and go up again in the latter half of the 1980's.
4. It has become recognized that too rapid industrialisation causes social disorder. OPEC will reconsider their development plan from the viewpoints of employment-creation, foreign exchange reserve, contributions to development capacities and people's education. This would probably slow down the pace of growth rate, increase the bargaining power of industrialized countries and make the OPEC policies more moderate at least from the economic point of view.
5. Industries to be developed in ME cannot obtain the international competitive capacities for several decades, so that OPEC cannot have the alternative sources of foreign exchange in the years to come. They will try to sustain the steady flow of oil supply. Hence, the industralized countries must consider properly the justifiable interests of gulf states and, in exchange with the proper price of oil, offer a cooperation to foster

the establishment of industries, their management, and training of engineers and bureaucrats. The transfer of technology must be achieved step by step.

These are the lines of likely events to take place in ME and between OPEC and OECD. The crisis management policies must be formulated, while keeping in mind these situations.

	1973	1977	1978
Saudi Arabia	43.4	424.0	358.0
Iran	41.0	213.0	205.0
Iraq	38.4	96.0	98.0
Venezuela	26.7	61.0	56.0
Kuwait	19.0	89.0	92.0
Nigeria	22.0	96.0	82.0
Libya	23.0	89.0	86.0
UAE	9,0	90.0	80.0
Indonesia	9,5	57.0	56.0
Algeria	9.0	43.0	50.0
Qatar	4.1	20.0	20.0
Gabon	–	6.0	5.0
Equadore	–	5.0	9.0
OPEC total	225.1	1.289.0	1.192.0
% of world trade	3.9	11.5	9.1
oil money	–	1.630.0	1.620.0

Tab. 15: OPEC's Oil Money (100 million $)

8. Crisis Management Policies

Policies to meet the needs at a time of crisis can be divided into several kinds. The first is the policies to avoid the occurance of crisis. It aims at doing the best by all means to keep the steady flow of oil supply from any possible disruptions. Main policies are listed:

I. *Avoidance of crisis:*
1. strenghtening the economic ties and friendly international relations with oil supplying countries,
2. promotion of D/D, G/G deals,
3. effort to stabilize the purchase and taking-back of delivered oil,
4. establishment and maintenance of friendly and steady dealings with majors,
5. cooperation with other main oil importers and cooperative bargaining with OPEC,
6. stabilization and cooperation of oil supplies among consuming countries,
7. promotion of own explorations of new fields.

The second kind is the policies to reduce the risky effects of crisis by diversifying the causes of such impacts. They are listed below:

II. *Diversification of risks:*
1. decrease the dependence on oil as a primary source of energy,
2. diversify the supply sources of oil,

550

3. diversify the sources of energy and try to obtain other energies,
4. develop the domestic sources of energy,
5. try to develop more flexible systems of switching the types of energy in emergency,
6. establish the industrial structure less dependent on energy,
7. develop the energy-saving technologies.

The third is the policies to make the preparations beforehand for the possible effects of crisis. These are the policies to mitigate the impact of crisis.

III. Preparation for preserving the capacities to meet the needs in emergency
1. increase the strategic (emergency) reserves by stock-piling oil substitutes (like uranium ores for nuclear power stations),
2. participation in international cooperation system for emergency,
3. ensure the alternative sources of supply or stock-piles abroad,
4. preserve the domestic supply of oil.

When crisis comes, the unfavorable effects on GDP and its distribution are unavoidable. There are a number of ways to minimize the effects which are as follows:

IV. Minimization of effects on GDP in emergency
1. improve the capacity of obtaining information on oil market and supply conditions,
2. improve the capacity of forecasting the impacts on national economy due to supply disruption,
3. maintain the best distributive capacity for oil,
4. demand control and rationing,
5. policies to maintain appropriate distribution among consumers and producers,
6. socio-economic measures for maintaining income distribution undisturbed.

All these policies involve some cost which must be compared with the benefit for national security as discussed in section 5. It should also be noticed that a distinction can be made between the cost of preparation and the cost to be incurred actually when crisis comes. The more preparation has been made, the less the actual cost will be. The relations may be shown by the following diagram. The total cost should be minimized if the level of security, for example expressed in terms of the time period to keep the oil supply unchanged – can be chosen to minimize the cost of crisis management at P. Bayond this point P, the benefit of security must be greater to justify the higher cost. The marginal benefit curve may be increasing at the diminishing rate as the level of security increases, so that the net benefit may be maximized at the point of intersection of the two curves.

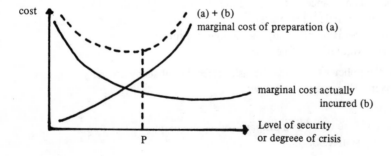

cost

(a) + (b)
marginal cost of preparation (a)

marginal cost actually
incurred (b)

Level of security
or degreee of crisis

P

9. Strategic Emergency Stocks and their Problems

For a country like Japan that depends almost exclusively on imported oil, the only way to mitigate the shock of supply disruption is to reserve the strategic stocks. The Japanese government passed a law called "Petroleum Reserve Law" in April, 1976 and made it a legal duty for oil companies as a whole to stockpile the 90 days consumption equivalent of crude oil by March, 1980. This was achieved earlier and more than required. But as the rate of daily consumption increases, the amount of strategic reserves must increase also. Japan Oil Association estimates that the additional stocks needed from 1972 to 1985 are about 53.1 mill. kl. The financial burden of this stockpiling cannot be underestimated. The total cost including the expenses for land, tanks and oil itself is about 4 trillion Yen (18.2 bill. $). This is the cost for security imposed by law, and it is annually about 1 billion $ in 1980 price.

The effective days during which the normal economic conditions can be maintained cannot be simply calculated by an arithmetic: namely, if 50% of imported oil is cut, then 90 days stocks guarantee 180 days of normal economic conditions. There are some stocks which can never be used; the oil on the way to Japan is likely to be used oil consumption steadily increases. Assuming the unusuable part as 10%, oil on tankers to Japan as 20 days worth, and the rate of increase in demand as 4.5%, the available oil for given stocks of X days worth is:

$$(1 - 0.1)(X + 20) C,$$

where C is the daily rate of consumption in previous years. Dividing it by this year's daily consumption $1.045\ C$, the number of day Y for which stocks can be avoidable is given as

$$Y = 0.9 (X + 20)/1.045.$$

If the percentage of oil import reduction is a, the same Y for given a is: $Y = = 0.861 (X + 20)/a$. Table 16 gives this Y and a for reasonable figures:

a/x	90	120	150	180
10	947	1.206	1.464	1.722
20	474	603	732	861
30	316	402	488	574
40	236	301	366	431
50	189	241	293	344

Tab. 16: Effects of Strategic Reserves

Needless to say, similar tables can be calculated under several hypotheses.

In crisis, the rate of consumption may have to be reduced. But the more reserves a country has the less the reduction of consumption will be. Table 17 shows under the same hypothesis as table 16 how much reduction of consumption can be avoided if strategic reserves are 120, 150 and 180 days worth rather than 90 days.

a/x	120	150	180
10	2.2	3.5	9.5
20	4.3	7.0	9.0
30	6.4	10.6	13.5
40	8.6	14.2	18.0
50	10.8	17.8	22.5

Tab. 17: Avoidable Percentage in Oil Consumption

If the economy has only 90 days worth stocks, then it must save 22.52 of consumption at a time of 50% disruption in order to consume the same amount of oil as the normal rate for 180 days. Thus it is highly desirable to study how much conservation of energy can be achieved without affecting the economic welfare, because the cost involved in increasing stockpiles of oil is really enormous and in the case of Japan to find an appropriate space on land is very difficult.

9. The Present State of Emergency Laws in Japan

It is needless to say that any kind of government intervention into the market requires some legal bases. With no detailed explanations, these laws and their policy implications are presented here.

I. *Demand side:*
1. Consumption control
   a) Optimization of Petroleum Demand and Supply Law (OPDS)
      (It demands to prepare various statistics but not adequate enough for large corporations)
   b) Electric Power Company Law
      (Household electricity supply lines cannot be controled)
2. Rationing of oil
   a) OPDS
      (It permits rationing or petroleum and petro products. System for LPG is not appropriate)
3. Price Control
   a) Emergency Policy for People's Living Law
   b) Price Control Law
      (Both are the laws carried over from war-time but permits the government to set the standard price.)
4. Energy saving
   a) Energy Conservation Law
      (Newly passed in October 1979. The government is entitled to force the private corporations to substitute other fuels for oil)

II. *Supply side:*
1. Strategic reserve

a) Petroleum Reserve Law
   (No regulations to decumulate stocks in crisis)
2. Information on stocks
   a) OPDS
      (Information on oil demand, supply, and stocks are required. They are monitored well. They are not linked with international distribution or exchange)
3. Fair trade
   a) OPDS
   b) Law to Prohibit Cornering and not Selling
      (In 1973 the law was enforced to oil companies and gas stations)
4. Development of oil substitutes
   a) Law to Develop Oil Substitutes
      (This is the new law to be passed in the near future and establishes a new agency called "New Energy Development Organization" and thereby promote the development of new sources of energy and synthetic fuels).

References

Brown, L.R.: World without Border. New York.

CIA: The International Energy Situation: Outlook to 1985. April 1977.

Conant, M.: Geopolitics of Energy. Westview Press, 1978.

Deese, D.A.: Energy: Economics, Politics and Security. International Security, Winter 1979/80.

Ichimura, S.: Economic Security. Peace and Security for Japan. Ed. by S. Eto et al. Tokyo 1980a.

−: Energy Problems and National Security Policies. Toyo Keizai Shinpo Weekly, August 1980b.

Ichimura, S., and *K. Fujime*: Oil Energy Problems and National Security. Institute for Peace and Security, Tokyo 1980.

Jakoby, H.D. et al.: Energy Policy and the Oil Problem. A Review of Current Issues. Energy Laboraty Working Paper No. MIT-EL 79-046, Sept. 1979.

Japan National Research Institute: Kokusai Kankyo No Henka To Nippon No Taioo. (Changes in International Situations and Japan's Response-proposals for the 21st Century. Tokyo 1978.

Lee, J.R., and *J.R. Ricky*: Soviet Oil Development. Soviet Economy in Time of Changes, US Congress, Joint Economic Committee, Oct. 1979.

Levy, W.J.: Foreign Affairs. Winter, 1978/79.

Nehring, R.: Giant Oil Fields and World Oil Resources. Rand Corporation, June 1978.

Nomura Research Institute: A Comprehensive Study of Energy Crisis Management in Japanese. Tokyo 1979.

Economic Theory of Natural Resources. ©Physica-Verlag, Würzburg–Wien, 1982.

Energy Policy Oriented Modeling Concerning Restricted Energy Availability

Peter Jansen

Introduction

Factors, mainly influencing energy demand, are

— economic growth as represented in GDP growth rates;
— growth pattern within the economy, that is, i.e. slow growth of the energy intensive basic industries, higher growth of the service-sector (that is a changing basket, of consumer goods and an internationally changing distribution of production);
— trends especially of some energy intensive consumption areas, i.e. saturation of individual transportation needs, or of home space heated;
— energy conservation measures (rational use of energy) that is improving the ratio of useful to delivered energy;
— choice of energy conversion technologies, effecting the choice and efficient use of primary energy carriers including solar energy and other renewables, nuclear energy, coal, oil and gas.

Some technologies in the conversion and end use sector may substitute others and so allow for substitution of one energy carrier by another or for conservation of energy. Given upper limits of availability of certain energy carriers, the optimal and under economic, political and public acceptance restricted, that is admissible substitution rates for technologies may dictate the maximum possible energy services, and finally the maximum achievable economic growth.

Normally prices are said to influence the substitution processes and growth patterns. Efforts mostly were undertaken, therefore, to model these relationships, especially to show the market behavior in reactiion to predictions of the energy prices.

This can be done in two principal ways. One is to simulate price reactions by catching historical behaviour in econometric functions. These can either directly link energy prices with energy consumption (you use so called energy elasticities), broken down for the major energy consuming areas, or the technical coefficients simulating the major economic sectors are functions of the energy price. The second principal way is to offer modelwise all reasonable technological alternatives with their energyprice dependent cost structure and to choose a cost optimal path, restricted by technology lifetime and perhaps some principal market penetration inertias. Elasticities, then, may be derived from those resulting paths as they are derived in the real world.

On the other hand, energy prices are closely governed by the match and dismatch of energy supply and demand and therefore they are itself governed by a reality which one might have tried to model primarily. The market is too complex to endogenize this part of the problem and in addition political aspects influencing the prices, of which we had much experience recently, add.

So, it is not only impossible to model the price path but it also is difficult to predict the price development, which should be the input to the first kind of models.

In addition energy policy itself was highly involved in measures aside the price mechanisms since ever or energy policy used the price mechanisms aritficially only, to reach various normative goals. It starts with all measures to influence economic growth, to stabilize employment or to cope with inflation — and we can see easily that those measures at the end influence the energy needs. It continues in subsidizing certain technologies, imposing a certain behavior to the consumer or certain properties (norms) to energy equipments or assuring supply by treaties. So this very energy policy which overrides price governed modeling is it which needs modeling in order to be best advised. Apparently this must be a different kind of modeling.

To predict the economy's response to energy prices is one thing, and it is of such difficulty that one might even stop it. It is still more difficult to predict the price trace itself. But it is another thing, to ask, what the energy system should look like to obviously reduce the unsecurities of supply. To look at that you need no explicit price models and you need not to predict most uncertain market parameters, especially prices. Rather you have to paint energy respective economy and technology futures which you are content with; and then you may use price influencing or the whole set of other political measures to control the development path. This does not mean a centrally planned economy, it only means to use the instruments of a free market economy according to what an energy policy was ment for, if you want any, if you have any. The set of measures may even be not known completely in advance, but evolves as the reality deviates from the derived path and readjustment seems necessary. But it is important that you know what way the development should go and which one is an undesirable one.

Some sets of measures may as well be undesirable. On the other hand development paths or measures, you are content with, may be manyfold. In any case you must know a broad set of possible, consistent energy futures in order to make up your mind about them and to deduce a policy. In a second step then, when judging alternative futures or sets of measures, prices and their social trade offs may be of interest, but it more adequately corresponds to their vagueness, to pay attention to them in the secondary, judgemental step only, than in the first, in the modelling step.

These are the reasons that in the following we present an energy-economy model, which traces the physical interrelationships between economic growth, consumer behaviour, technology choices and energy needs and do not pay attention to price elasticities. According to the argumentation above we nevertheless believe that this model helps to evaluate energy policies in an economy's context. The model mainly adresses the impacts and the possible consequences of restricted availability of certain energy carriers, which, we think, is one of the main reasons that energy policy has got that broad attention, it actually has.

Confronted with an incomplete market, with not early enough foresight on the scarcity of goods because of high delay times in the circulation of information and implementation of new technologies, with much policy involvement and opaque economic structures calls primarily to enlighten what "could be" if a policy would somewhat succed. This implies a lot of assumptions on very different modeling levels. The degree of detailisation heavily depends on the degree of competence of those who want to be adivised. It makes no sense to disaggregate more than the ability of the user goes to judge the assumptions; to judge the assumptions is part of the preconditions to judge the results of a modeling effort. And judgement is all we are struggling for because we know that projections are meaningless, but policy means influence and we must know what to influence and what for.

The model to be described below was built to serve a parliament commission in the FRG. The degree of detailisation was governed by the possibility to influence certain parameters politically. A politician can not dictate the consumer basquet or the development of a certain industry, but he may influence the trend to less basic industries needed or more, to more services used or less. A politician cannot specify the appliances used in households but he can ease the use of advanced technologies or hinder it. To elaborate on the potential given for different political environments, it might be necessary to describe specific technologies, but they only serve as pars pro toto. And with respect to the accuracy one may bear in mind what Oskar Morgenstern said: "Economics is a one or two digit science".

The Model

A model of the energy system should cope with three aspects of systems

— the hierachical aspect
  A system has to be well defined against its environment. Influences from or to the environment are treated exogenously. The elements of the system may itself be systems, that is subsystems with elements on a lower hierarchical level. The subsystem for nuclear power activities in an energy system for example may be designed for minimal uranium needs, though the system on the next hierarchical level may minimize oil imports and so dicdate the nuclear power needs.

— the structural aspect
  The element of a system (subsystems of a system, elements of a subsystem) are interrelated. The relations may be of different type. For example a relation may connect specific industrial activities with consumers' comfort, the growth of basic industries with GDP growth or the demand of energy for heating appliances with the technologies supplying that energy. The relations between the elements constitute the structure of the system, it may have positive and/or negative feed back loops.

— the functional aspect
  At some lower hierarchic level it may not be necessary from a problem solving point of view, to further break down the structure of an element (subsystem) but merely to regard the elements as "black boxes" with inputs and outputs, these are those relations which would be exogenous, if the black box would again be treated as a subsystem. These inputs and outputs are the sinks and sources of the relations. For example a nuclear power station produces electricity (output) and needs uranium (input),

or a electric heat pump needs electricity and environmental heat (two inputs) to produce residential heat (output), or a raffinery needs crude oil (input) to produce several outputs. So, inputs and outputs may be n-tupels.

Between the outputs and inputs time delays may take place. All this constitutes a dynamic system.

The model to be described, copes with all three aspects in a very easy way. It is up to the user to identify hierarchies and to build up and change structures only by defining elements (technologies) and their inputs and outputs. The details of a subsystem 'nucelar energy' for example might be described by a large number of technologies, simulating the structure of various fuel cycles, which are introduced. They may culminate in one artificial technology "nuclear energy" which may be the only link to the rest of the energy system. It is furtheron also up to the user which aggregation level the element (technology) represents in defining its inputs and outputs. The model automatically connects the corresponding inputs and outputs and thus generates the structures and hierarchies. It should be noted, that it is a special advantage of the model, not to be fixed in structures and the degree of detailisation by the coding process but to let it open to the user to create the corresponding structure, corresponding to the intention represented by the "black boxes" and the "relations" indicated by the inputs and outputs of the black boxes. In this way the complexity of the model used does not exceed the complexity the user is able to cope with, when requalifying the results, judging what he did and evaluating a policy. That is more important than usually considered.

Let T be a set of technologies constituting a system, with x_t the activity level of the technology $t \in T$. Let P be a set of production factors with $b_{p,t}$ the quantitiv realization of the production factor $p \in P$ at the technology $t \in T$. We say p is an input to the technology t if $b_{p,t} < 0$ and an output from the technology t if $b_{p,t} > 0$. A technology with only outputs simulates exogenous parameters. The basic equation now which constitutes the system, is

$$(\forall p \in P): (\sum_{t \in T} b_{p,t} \cdot x_t = 0).$$

That is, the total System is described by technologies t, $t \in T$, and its inputs

$$b_{p,t} < 0, p \in P$$

and outputs

$$b_{p,t} > 0, p \in P.$$

This constitutes the complete structure of the system, its hierarchies and degree of detailisation.

The user of the model needs not to paint the complicated structure of the energy system explicitly, nor has the programmer to do this. It is only the definition of technologies and these input and output n-tupels — that is the individual knowledge about the different facts in an energy system (in an aggregation the user likes) — which constitute the structure.

In fact, the equations are more complicated and supplemented. The model is able to cope with time dependent activity levels and the following additional aspects:

- to obey technologies lifetime
- to restrict the technologies build up rates or installations (activity levels), if desired
- to care for inventories, i.e. the initial plutonium needs of power stations or the energy-"investment" for insulation measures
- to calculate year by year and cumulated material balances (book keeping), i.e. for uranium needs, and to apply restrictions to these, if desired
- to obey lead and/or lag times to material flows (inputs and/or outputs) of technologies
- to retrofit the properties of a technology (that is the quantitative realisation of the inputs and outputs).

Clearly the solutions of that system of equations may be manifold and it is necessary to guide which to choose. This calls for a goal function.

The goal function might be

$$G = \sum_{p \in P_g} g^p \cdot B^p, P_g \subset P.$$

It is recommended that the weights g^p differ such strongly, that the hierarchical aspect is observed, that is, priority one may be to minimize oil import, priority two to minimize natural uranium needs, whatever the demand for nuclear energy is. Or, when a certain lower oil-import level is reached, to minimize coal production may be an additional third priority goal. This is a kind of lexicographical ordering which is closer to real thinking than is theoretically assumed. If some special goals are set to specific technologies an artificial exogenous relation can be built up and be treated similarly.

One of the interesting variants is, to give upper resource limits and to maximize the economic growth (given the consumer's energy-wise behaviour and the structural changes in industry).

One word to the structural changes in industry. Industrial sectors can be treated as technologies and their inputs and outputs may be treated in the common I/O way. But it is difficult to project the technical coefficients of such an I/O matrix. We prefered to break down the industry with respect to energy intensivness only, energy needs being inputs and outputs being their contribution to the GDP. Their individual growth behaviour is coupled to the GDP growth by some general equations, representing principal trends one may think to be probable. One of those trends is, that the basic industries grow only half as quick as the rest of the industry. There are several reasons for this assumption, and if a corresponding scenario seems good, one may decide to support this assumption by actual policy, that is day by day decisions according to the actual deviations. But one also can investigate what would happen, if the basic industry would grow as fast as the GDP or would not grow at all. Similar assumption are possible for the services and treated by the user in a fashion as all other technologies are treated, where inputs and outputs guarantee the way, they are crosscoupled and coupled to the energy sector and the GDP.

Clearly it would be possible to treat monetary aspects the same way or to define those inputs and outputs, that create an economic I/O submodel. In any case it is the flexibility to the user's intention and to model this intention as easy as possible that led to that general "black box" structure of the code.

An Application

We have modelled the FRG energy system for the above mentioned parliament commission by defining 90 different black boxes (technologies) with their inputs and outputs. Different lifetimes and introduction dates and rates guarantee for a time-dependent behaviour of the system, switching from a today's technology mix, to some optimal mix lateron. Calculations were made for three time steps, one for 1980, which simulates the present situations, one for 2030 which simulates a long term optimal equilibrium, given the free choice between certain new technologies, and one for the year 2000, dependent on the admissible introduction rates of new technologies and the time delays of restructuring old technology mixes in the direction of the long term optimal equilibrium.

2030 represents not more than scenario-wise a consistent energy-economy picture of what could be and what was assumed to be principal possible. Derived from that and the today's reality, the results for 2000 give a picture, which allows to judge the different scenarios and then to derive, which way is preferable and what therefore should be the policy of the next years.

All subsequent assumptions are explained in detail in the report of the above mentioned government commission (see reference). The scope of this paper forbids to repeat those details.

Starting with the government's offical energy projection of 1977, a nearly historical 3.3%/year average GDP growth up to the year 2000 was assumed, together with moderate improvements in the rational use of energy, corresponding to the present price induced trends. Again in estimating present trends services were assumed to grow 30% faster than GDP and the basic industry only half. The official assumptions were furtheron that 75 GWe nuclear capacity could be working in 2000 and that domestic coal production increases by 40%. This leads to an oil and gas demand of about the same as today (280 Mio to SKE/yr) and adds up to 600 Mio to SKE primary energy needs in 2000 compared to 400 today. Implicitely it is necessary to enlarge electricity production considerably, especially to support direct electric heating systems. Though, as a result, the elasticity between economic and energy growth is already down at 0.55, compared to the historical 1, it is evident that neither the nuclear capacity, nor the oil imports can reasonably be assured.

When reducing the oil and gas imports in 2000 to the 1970 level of about 190 Mio to SKE/yr and the nuclear capacity to 40 GWe in the year 2000, that is 2 GWe of new orders per year beginning now, we must double the rates of improving the rational use of energy and lower the GDP growth to 2%/year. In this scenario the energy needs growth only slightly, no over-proportional growth of electricity may take place, coal switches from electricity generation to oil substitution in the industrial sector. The elasticity here is down at 0.15.

Beyond 2000 the elasticity between economy and energy cuts back again to 0.65. With further substitution of oil and gas (2030 half of today) by slightly enlarging the coal supply (2030 160 Mio to SKE/yr) and trippling nuclear energy availability (120 GWe in 2030) only 1.1%/yr GDP growth is managable (Faktor 3 per caput in 2030 compared to 1970!).

The energy conservation measures may be characterized by 1/3 conservation in the average, 60% in home heating (including sun) and 50% in private cars for the year 2030. Enhancing these measures to 80% in home heating and 50% over all, and assuming that the energy intensiv basic industries don't grow at all, leads to the possibility to renounce nuclear energy.

In case coal availability would be only 125 Mio to SKE/year all the time in both scenarios, that is stay constant instead of growing to 145 in 2000 and 160 in 2030, the poșible growth rates are reduced to 1.5%/year before 2000 and 0.8%/year thereafter, or together with the enhanced conservation, one might use 25 GWe of nuclear power in order to hold the previous growth rates of 2%/year respective 1.1%/yr. Each 10 Mio to SKE oil less in the year 2000 reduces the growth possibilities of the GDP by 0.3%/yr.

What can be seen is clearly that the traditional projection cannot be achieved. Even the reduced growth szenario has several difficulties to overcome, that is

− to put through the conservation goals
− to get acceptance for the nuclear power addition
− to guarantee the oil and gas demand, still necessary
− to manage the growing domestic coal production
− to cope which the unemployment problem, that is to limit the growth or productivity.

A pragmatic strategy in the context of those scenarios may be (the sequence indicating priorities):

1. Not to enhance economic and productivity growth beyond the necessary minimum for social stability and international competitivness.
2. To damp the growth of energy intensiv basic industry and to enhance their production in the 3. world.
3. To conserve as much energy as possible and to orient efforts at a not growing energy demand, including a not growing electricity demand.
4. To substitute oil by coal especially in high efficiency fields like coal for industrial process heat (not so much for gasification or liquefaction) aiming a reduction rate in oil and gas of 2%/year.
5. To enhance domestic coal production as much as possible.
6. To use surplus coal to produce electricity.
7. To use nuclear power for the rest of electricity need.

It should be mentioned that the lower economic growth rates may coincide with lower worker's productivity and therefore not cause additional unemployment problems, as a stringent energy conservation policy may need additional work forces.

With the priority-strategy, given above, nuclear power will be installed as it is necessary mainly dependent on the conservation success, if growth rates, oil and gas goals and coal enhancement work as planned.

In case the situation with oil gets more severe or conservation is less or growth rates are higher, or coal cannot be produced as planned, then correspondingly more nuclear energy is necessary.

With low growth rates, effective conservation, relaxed oil market (still 2% substitution per year) and increase of coal availability no additional nuclear power stations may by necessary.

These many conditions need testing. A responsible policy therefore strengthens all efforts mentioned but in addition does not weaken the potential use of nucelar energy. Only the reality itself will show wether we do not need it on a long term.

What is necessary, is subtile market observation and reacting on changed situations with probed scenario runs as yardsticks. Thus, with the example of the FRG, the role of modeling, its chances and limits should be apparent. They don't say the trend and are no projections but guide the priorities as what aspects a politician should give attention to and which actual developments are reasonable and which not.

Reference

Bericht über den Stand der Arbeit und die Ergebnisse der Enquête-Kommission „Zukünftige Kern-energie-Politik" des 8. Deutschen Bundestages. Deutscher Bundestag, 8. Wahlperiode, Drucksache 8/4341, Bonn, Juni 1980.

Economic Theory of Natural Resources. ©Physica-Verlag, Würzburg–Wien, 1982.

Resource Extraction under Imperfect Information

Günter Menges

1. Introduction

The author has (jointly with *Kofler* [1976, 1978, 1979a, b, 1980a, b]) developed methods of dealing with decision making problems under uncertainty when some information regarding the probability distribution over states is known but the exact distribution is unknown. In the present paper it is shown how such problems may arise in the economics of extraction of resources and where such methods may be fruitfully applied.

Uncertainty may be with respect to the location of deposit in possible sites. The probabilities of its occurrence in the different sites may be known to lie within certain limits but the exact values are unknown. Given data regarding costs associated with extraction policies under each state of nature (actual occurrence of deposit in some site) this can be viewed as a two person game, with the strategies for nature, the other player, being the possible probability distributions satisfying the given constraints. The solution concept used is of the minimax variety. It is shown how such problems can arise in different ways in this context as for instance reagrding decisions to generate more information.

Both referees ask: Why is a minimax solution considered appropriate in this context where nature need not appear as an hostile opponent selecting strategies to inflict the maximum possible damage to the decision maker? The answer is: The minimax type of solution is certainly only one among others. Another one which may be fruitfully applied is the principle of *c*-optimality as developed by *Kuss* [1980]. The minimax type however is the (only) one motivated by *caution* on the part of the extractor. Application of the minimax type avoids unnecessary high costs and hence avoids — among other risks — the danger of the extractor firm to go bankrupt before a drilling is successful. What is better than caution vis à vis uncertainty? Nature need indeed not appear as hostile. But the optimal search of exhaustible resources may be *like* a game against a hostile opponent, if the true state is unknown. This however, is not the main point of the paper. The main ideas of the paper are rather:

1) Exploitation of all information available, (according to the quality and nature of data),
2) Retaining of the minimax type of solution only to the extent of the ever remaining uncertainty,
3) Deciding not only about search as such but also about the possible procurement of additional information.

Insofar, the game-theoretical analogy is limited; it is further restricted since the mixing of strategies can not appear reasonable. Nature may be uncertain and therefore may motivate the searcher (and researcher) to behave with caution. But mother nature *is* in fact not hostile. Or?

2. The "Model"

Gilbert's article [*Gilbert*] indicated to me that the problem of resource extraction is a genuine one, if not to say the most characteristic one of optimal search under imperfect information at least in the sense of linear partial information (LPI)[1]. I want to try and make this clear by using a simple example of resource extraction.

Let us consider a piece of land which is supposed to hold a deposit. We distinguish four cases:

1) The correct location is known. We are not at all interested in this case of complete knowledge.
2) The exact probability distribution over the piece of land is known. In statistical decision theory, this case is called risk or Bernoulli case. We call it the case of complete information: it is one of the two limiting cases of LPI.
3) Nothing at all is known about the probability distribution over the piece of land. In statistical decision theory, this is the case of null-information or of minimax. We call it the case of complete ignorance; it is the second of the two limiting cases.
4) A little is known about the probability distribution over the piece of land, i.e. more than nothing and less than exact knowledge. This case, completely neglected in the literature until the book by *Kofler* and myself [1976] appeared, is the case of imperfect or partial information[2].

The incompleteness of information can have different causes and can occur in different forms. We do not treat the causes here, and among the many possible forms I shall consider one which on the one hand, has some theoretical advantages, and on the other hand, has very many possible applications. It is the form of weak partial ordering.

Let L be the piece of land with a subdivision into subsections L_1, L_2 and L_3.

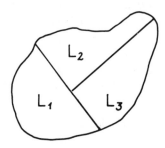

Fig. 1: Piece of land with three sections and one deposit

---

[1]) In this paper I will not consider the generalization of the LPI concept, called SPI (stochastic partial information); see, however, *Kofler/Menges* et al. [1980b].

[2]) *Rothschild* [1974] studied a similar problem [cp. last formula on p. 694]. He considered the case of a prior be known on the distribution simplex.

Instead of the probability density over L (complete information) it is only known that

$$p_1 \leqslant p_2 \leqslant p_3, \tag{1}$$

where p_1 is the probability that the deposit is in sections L_1, p_2 that it is in L_2, and p_3 that it is in L_3.

The expression $p_1 \leqslant p_2 \leqslant p_3$ is called a linear partial information. It is called partial for obvious reasons; it is called linear because the restrictions regarding one element or more of the vector $p = (p_1, p_2, p_3)$ are given in linear form (if they are not given in linear form, then the problem becomes more complicated, but can — in general — nevertheless be solved).

Examples of linear partial information

$$p_2 \leqslant 0.3, p_1 + p_3 \geqslant 0.7$$
$$p_1 = p_2, p_3 = 1 - 2p_1$$
$$p_2 = 0.4, p_1 + p_3 = 0.6.$$

In practical work, people often think information of this kind is nearly or even totally useless. This is not true. In order to show the degree in which uncertainty is reduced by an LPI of the form (1) and to prepare for more sophisticated considerations, we ask for the set of admissible distributions $p = (p_1, p_2, p_3)$ in the LPI-case (1).

Geometrically, the set of possible distributions is given by the triangle ABC in Fig. 2. Each point of ABC is a possible distribution, the whole triangle represents the case of complete ignorance. The LPI (1) reduces the set of possible distributions to the new triangle GEC.

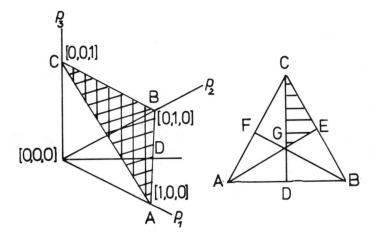

Fig. 2: The information triangles

Now, one can see the high degree by which an LPI of form (1) reduces the uncertainty, namely from *ABC* to *GEC*.

Actually we can concentrate all considerations upon the vertices *G*, *E* and *C* themselves if we accept the following interpretation together with a certain principle:

Interpretation: The resource extraction is a game of the searcher against nature. Where information is given, the searcher tries to maximize his utility expectation; when no information is given, the searcher behaves cautious.

Principle: The searcher meets the uncertainty of nature by applying the Min*E*max-principle (which is the minimax-principle confined to the ever remaining uncertainty). In other words: The searcher plays a game against nature only where nature is uncertain ("as if" nature where hostile).

In Fig. 2, the possible states of nature are confined to the triangle GEC, and nature's "best" point is one of the three vertices G, E, or C, depending on the utility matrix.

In *algebraic* form, an LPI is a system of linear inequalities and equations regarding the elements of the probability vector $p = (p_1, \ldots, p_n)$. We want to find those distributions which satisfy the inequalities. An important theorem says that a solution of a system of k inequalities in n variables is a vertex iff n restrictions are fulfilled as equations. G is a vertex since it satisfies

$$p_1 = p_2$$
$$p_2 = p_3$$
$$p_1 + p_2 + p_3 = 1.$$

We will now write down the restrictions corresponding to the LPI: $p_1 \leqslant p_2 \leqslant p_3$; they are

$$
\left.
\begin{aligned}
&((1))\ p_1 \geqslant 0 \\
&((2))\ p_1 \leqslant p_2 \quad (\to p_2 \geqslant 0) \\
&((3))\ p_2 \leqslant p_3 \quad (\to p_3 \geqslant 0) \\
&((4))\ p_1 + p_2 + p_3 = 1.
\end{aligned}
\right\}
\qquad (1')
$$

One can easily realize that the three relevant vertex distributions are

$$C:\ 0,\quad 0,\quad 1$$

$$E:\ 0,\quad \frac{1}{2},\quad \frac{1}{2}$$

$$G:\ \frac{1}{3},\quad \frac{1}{3},\quad \frac{1}{3}$$

The matrix

$$
M = \begin{bmatrix} 0 & 0 & \frac{1}{3} \\[2mm] 0 & \frac{1}{2} & \frac{1}{3} \\[2mm] 1 & \frac{1}{2} & \frac{1}{3} \end{bmatrix}
$$

is called vertex matrix of the LPI (1); it contains all relevant information about the probabilities. The generalization to more than three states is straightforward; for a finite number of states M has the following form

$$
M = \begin{bmatrix}
0 & 0 & \cdots & \dfrac{1}{n} \\[2mm]
0 & \cdot & \cdots & \dfrac{1}{n} \\[2mm]
\cdot & \cdot & \cdots & \cdot \\[2mm]
\cdot & \dfrac{1}{2} & & \cdot \\[2mm]
1 & \dfrac{1}{2} & \cdots & \dfrac{1}{n}
\end{bmatrix} .
\tag{2'}
$$

3. The Information Problem

Usually in resource extraction as in other practical problems, the information problem is linked with and only preliminary, to a decision problem. A typical one is the decision to screen in a particular area, either A_1, A_2, or A_3 (to screen first or to screen at all). *Gilbert* tells that in the United States "outlays on these information generating activities have been on the order of 20 percent of drilling costs in recent years" [1977, p. 250]. It is therefore quite justified, to make the information generating process a decision problem of its own. If we want to do this, we need an information measure.

Both tasks, the solution of the *screening* decision problem and the solution of the *information* decision problem can be accomplished by the Min$E$max-principle. For that to be demonstrated, we need a somewhat more formal treatment.

Let A be the set of possible decisions, either procedural ones regarding information or final ones regarding the drilling or screening.

Let Z be the set of possible states and Ω the set of probability distributions on Z. We confine ourselves the finite sets

$$A = \{a_i \mid i = 1, \ldots, m\}$$
$$Z = \{z_j \mid j = 1, \ldots, n\}$$

with measure space $(Z, \text{Pot } (Z))$. Pot (Z) is the power set of Z.

Every probability distribution $p = (p_1, \ldots, p_n)$ on $(Z, \text{Pot } (Z))$ is uniquely defined by $p_j = p\,(z_j); j = 1, \ldots, n$.

Ω is part of a set S of discrete probability distributions admitted where S is the distribution simplex

$$
S = \{p \in \mathbf{R}^n \mid p \geqslant 0, \ \sum_{i=1}^{n} p_i = 1\}.
\tag{3}
$$

If the information about Ω ($\Omega \subseteq S$) is given in the form of ordinal measurement

$$
p_{i_1} \leqslant p_{i_2} \leqslant \ldots \leqslant p_{i_n} \quad \text{(LPI)}
\tag{4}
$$

where $\{i_1, \ldots, i_n\}$ is a certain permutation of the index set $\{1, \ldots, n\}$, then by the information (4) a convex polyhedron in S is generated which corresponds to LPI.

The possible vertices of the convex polyhedron are given by the column vectors of the vertex matrix (2').

On $A \times Z$, a real-valued, bounded cost function

$u: A \times Z \to \mathbf{R}$ is given.

Finally the decision problem DP reads

$$\text{DP: } (\{a_i\}, \{z_j\}; \text{LPI}, [u_{ij}]; i = 1, \ldots, m, j = 1, \ldots, n). \tag{5}$$

For the set of all distributions p admitted by LPI a cost matrix is to be defined by attaching a cost expectation or risk $\bar{u}$ to every possible coincidence of an action with a distribution p admitted by LPI.

$$\bar{u}: A \times \text{LPI} \to \mathbf{R}; a_i \in A, p \in \text{LPI}$$

$$\bar{u}(a_i, p) = \sum_{j=1}^{n} u_{ij} p_j = E(a_i, p).$$

The decision model (5) has become an uncertainty model of the kind

$$(\{a_i\}, \text{LPI}, \bar{u}; i = 1, \ldots, m). \tag{6}$$

This model finds a proper solution by the Min$E$max-principle which says:
Given the decision problem

$$(A, Z, \text{LPI}, [u_{ij}]), \text{ then } a_{i*} \text{ is min}E\text{max-optimal if} \tag{7}$$

$$\max_{p \in \text{LPI}} E(a_{i*}, p) = \min_{a_i \in A} \max_{p \in \text{LPI}} E(a_i, p). \tag{8}$$

It goes over to the Bernoulli type of solution if LPI contains only one element (complete information); it goes over to Wald's minimax type of solution if the LPI contains all points of the distribution simplex S (complete ignorance).

If the LPI is of type (4), i.e. given in the form of a complete weak ordering, it can be shown that the application of the Min$E$max-principle reduces to the application of the minimax principle to the matrix

$$E = [u_{ij}] \cdot M. \tag{9}$$

The elements of E are $E_{ij} = E(a_i, p)$.

4. Screening Costs

As an example we consider the screening costs in a two-area model, with LPI:
$p_1 \leqslant p_2$.

The costs to screen in:

area 1 first, then in area 2: $c_1 + c_{12}$.
area 2 first, then in area 1: $c_2 + c_{21}$.

c_1 represents the cost of screening in area 1 only, c_{12} the costs of screening in area 2 after having screened in area 1. Correspondingly, c_2 represents the costs of screening in area 2 only, c_{21} the costs of screening in area 1 after having screened in area 2.

The screening decision matrix reads as follows:

		deposit is in fact in area 1 Z_1	area 2 Z_2
action a_1 :	screen first in area 1, if successful: stop, if not, screen in area 2	c_1	$c_1 + c_{12}$
action a_2 :	screen first in area 2, if successful: stop, if not, screen in area 1	$c_2 + c_{21}$	c_2

By post-multiplying this cost matrix by M we get the Matrix E

$$E = \begin{bmatrix} c_1 & c_1 + c_{12} \\ c_2 + c_{21} & c_2 \end{bmatrix} \begin{bmatrix} 0 & \frac{1}{2} \\ 1 & \frac{1}{2} \end{bmatrix}$$

$$= \begin{bmatrix} c_1 + c_{12} & c_1 + \frac{1}{2} c_{12} \\ c_2 + c_{21} & c_2 + \frac{1}{2} c_{21} \end{bmatrix}.$$

The vector of row maxima is

$$\begin{bmatrix} c_1 + c_{12} \\ c_2 + c_{21} \end{bmatrix}.$$

In order to obtain the minimal element of this vector we have to know the relations between the four cost factors. If $c_1 = c_2$ and $c_{12} = c_{21}$ (but $c_1 \neq c_{12}$) then to this problem there is no solution; it makes no difference, then, which is the first to be screened.

If $c_1 = c_2$, but $c_{12} \neq c_{21}$, then the comparison of c_{12} and c_{21} determines the decision. On the other hand, if $c_{12} = c_{21}$, but $c_1 \neq c_2$, then the comparison of c_1 and c_2 determines the decision.

If $c_1 = c_2 = c_{12} = c_{21} = c$, we get

$$c \begin{bmatrix} 1 & 2 \\ 2 & 1 \end{bmatrix} \begin{bmatrix} 0 & \frac{1}{2} \\ 1 & \frac{1}{2} \end{bmatrix} = c \begin{bmatrix} 2 & 1.5 \\ 1 & 1.5 \end{bmatrix}.$$

Here, the first row is dominated by the second, and therefore the decision is in favour of a_2. There is no need to apply the Min$E$max-principle. The solution by the dominance criterion is natural; a_2 is chosen because of the LPI: $p_1 \leqslant p_2$. One can easily verify that this result is a general one for an arbitrary finite number of actions, and of states, and for any LPI (of form (4)).

E.g., for the three-area-case, by which we started, we get for identical costs c of screening of one area:

deposit is in fact in area

action	screening sequence	L_1	L_2	L_3
a_1	1 2 3	c	$2c$	$3c$
a_2	1 3 2	c	$3c$	$2c$
a_3	2 1 3	$2c$	c	$3c$
a_4	2 3 1	$3c$	c	$2c$
a_5	3 1 2	$2c$	$3c$	c
a_6	3 2 1	$3c$	$2c$	c

$$= [u_{ij}]$$

Post-multiplying $[u_{ij}]$ by the corresponding vertex matrix M we get

$$E = c \begin{bmatrix} 3 & 2.5 & 2 \\ 2 & 2.5 & 2 \\ 3 & 2 & 2 \\ 2 & 1.5 & 2 \\ 1 & 2 & 2 \\ 1 & 1.5 & 2 \end{bmatrix}$$

Here, all rows are dominated by others, except the last one. Thus, the dominance principle identifies a_6 as optimal. It is the action which requires to screen in the most probable area, viz. L_3 first, then in the second probable area, viz. L_2, and finally in L_1.

This result is certainly not of a revolutionary kind but it gives a decision-theoretical motivation for a procedure which is apparently rational or vice versa, viz. shows the intuitive rationality of a decision-theoretical procedure.

We shall later on turn to cases which are not quite as obvious.

5. Information Measurement

First, I want to take up the previously mentioned problem of information measurement.

To every possible action $a_i \in A$ we attach a value $V(a_i)$ which represents the maximal cost expectation (risk) in row i ($i = 1, \ldots, n$)

$$V(a_i) = \max_j E_{ij}. \tag{10}$$

For the optimal $a_{i*} \in A$ this value $V(a_{i*})$ amounts to

$$V(a_{i*}) = \min_i V(a_i) = \min_i \max_j E_{ij}. \tag{11}$$

We symbolize $V(a_{i*})$ simply by V and give it an index 0: V_0 is called the semantic information of a given decision situation 0; for reasons of simplicity it is the decision situation with no information about the state probabilities at all. Then, an LPI (or a new one) is given. Again, we determine $V(a_{i*})$, for the new decision situation and call it V_1. The semantic information of the LPI, I (LPI) is then the difference

$$I \text{ (LPI)} = V_0 - V_1. \tag{12}$$

It has to be compared with the measurement cost regarding V_1.

It is also possible to consider a sequence of LPI's and then to have a sequence V_0, $V_1, V_2 \ldots$ of the semantic information of the LPI's. And so on.

I would now like to go on to present an example where the LPI, called LPI_2, is not given in the form of an ordering but in form of intervals. Again, we consider three regions L_1, L_2, L_3 where one deposit is to be supposed, with corresponding probabilities p_1, p_2, p_3.

Experts judge these probabilities in the form of the following intervals

$$LPI_2 : \begin{cases} p_1 \in [0.225; \ 0.5] \\ p_2 \in [0.25; \ \ 0.75] \\ p_3 \in [0.5; \ \ \ 0.8]. \end{cases}$$

We want to find the vertex matrix of this LPI_2. Now, since the minima add up to 0.975, no probability can assume a value greater than its minimum plus 0.025.

Therefore the maxima are

0.25   for p_1

0.275   for p_2

0.525   for p_3.

In all, there are only 3 (not 6) vertices, and the vertex matrix M is

$$M = \begin{bmatrix} 0.25 & 0.225 & 0.225 \\ 0.25 & 0.275 & 0.25 \\ 0.5 & 0.5 & 0.525 \end{bmatrix}.$$

Let the cost matrix be given, as before, then $[u_{ij}] \cdot M = E$ leads to a matrix E in which the last row dominates all others. This last row, belonging, to a_6, is

1.75 c 1.725 c 1.70 c.

The solution of the decision problem is as before (screening sequence 3 2 1) but: Is the LPI_2 more informative than the previous LPI (4), which we now call LPI_1?

The answer:

$$V_1 = V(a_6 \mid LPI_1) = 2 c$$
$$V_2 = V(a_6 \mid LPI_2) = 1.75 c.$$

If we call the additional (semantic) information of LPI_2, as compared to LPI_1, by $I(LPI_1 \rightarrow LPI_2)$, we get

$$I(LPI_1 \rightarrow LPI_2) = V_1 - V_2 = 0.25 c.$$

Although a_6 is the optimal action in both cases, by the amount of $0.25\,c$ the LPI_2 is more informative than the LPI_1.

By the methods presented so far it is also possible to use LPI's of different orders, actually a hierarchy of LPI's.

By an LPI of higher order and with the help of the semantic information I (LPI) one can also measure the conditional information, given another information, e.g. the conditional information about a certain area, A, given information about another area, B.

6. Evaluation of Experimental Results

Another possibility presumably very useful in resource extraction problems is the evaluation of experimental results. I shall indicate this possibility by another simple two-area example, with two actions, a_1 to drill first in L_1, and a_2, to drill first in L_2. The probability of a deposit being either in L_1 or L_2 is p_1 and p_2, resp., and the information about p_1 and p_2 is given in interval form as follows

$$\text{LPI}^{(1)}: p_1 \in \left[\frac{1}{9}, \frac{7}{9}\right], p_2 = 1 - p_1.$$

The vertex matrix of this decision problem is

$$M = \frac{1}{9} \begin{bmatrix} 1 & 7 \\ 8 & 2 \end{bmatrix}.$$

Pre-multiplying by the simple cost matrix $c \begin{bmatrix} 1 & 2 \\ 2 & 1 \end{bmatrix}$ gives the decision matrix

$$E = \frac{c}{9} \begin{bmatrix} 17 & 11 \\ 10 & 16 \end{bmatrix}$$

which identifies $16\,(c/9)$ as saddle point and a_2 as optimal action.

The company wants to improve the decision situation by core drillings. In order to make the old $\text{LPI}^{(1)}$ receptive for experimental results we split the intervals into symmetrical halves

$$\text{LPI}_1^{(1)}: p_1 \in \left[\frac{1}{9}, \frac{4}{9}\right], p_2 = 1 - p_1;$$

$$\text{LPI}_2^{(1)}: p_1 \in \left[\frac{4}{9}, \frac{7}{9}\right], p_2 = 1 - p_1.$$

Now, a series of core drillings is carried out whose results speak in favour of the second interval $\text{LPI}_2^{(1)}$ to contain the true probability. Let π_1 be the probability of $\text{LPI}_1^{(1)}$ to be true and π_2 of $\text{LPI}_2^{(1)}$, then we have another LPI, one of higher order, which we call $\text{LPI}^{(2)}$.

$$\text{LPI}^{(2)}: \pi_1 \leqslant \pi_2.$$

Let this ordering be the only information emanating from the core drillings. It, nevertheless, changes the situation completely. According to a certain transition theorem we can reduce the two level LPI to a single-level one, whose vertex matrix is

$$M = \frac{1}{18} \begin{bmatrix} 5 & 14 \\ 13 & 4 \end{bmatrix}.$$

Pre-multiplying it again by the simple cost matrix

$$c \begin{bmatrix} 1 & 2 \\ 2 & 1 \end{bmatrix} \text{ yields}$$

$$E = \frac{c}{18} \begin{bmatrix} 31 & 22 \\ 23 & 32 \end{bmatrix}$$

which identifies 31 ($c/18$) as Min$E$max point and not a_2 but a_1 as optimal action.

The value I of experimentation can be determined by a comparison of the semantic information before and after experimentation:

$$I = \frac{c}{18} = 16 \frac{c}{9} - 31 \frac{c}{18},$$

a comparatively small[3]) amount for a complete change to the better decision.

In the planning stage (ex ante analysis) the information $\pi_1 \leqslant \pi_2$ is of course only a possible or hypothetical one. The drillings may show $\pi_1 > \pi_2$ as well. Therefore, in ex ante analysis the second possibility has to be considered as well. Maybe, an LPI of higher degree, saying e.g. "$\pi_1 \leqslant \pi_2$ is more likely than $\pi_1 > \pi_2$", is given, and this information can be used. And so on.

Hierarchies of LPI's also enable to evaluate information, to evaluate the evaluation. In problems of resource extraction, this possibility is pretty important, since there are different experts on different decision levels. Their judgements, knowledge and experimental results can be brought together, even if they are of a very disparate and heterogenous kind, like — on a lower decision level — results of seismic testing, aerial surveys, core screenings, core drillings and so on. Technological, traffic economic, political aspects etc. can be added at higher levels of decision.

It goes without saying that the LPI-methodology is also applicable to the probability distribution of returns, either separately or in connection with all the problems mentioned before.

7. Behaviour Towards Risk

A particular problem in this context is the behaviour of the firms towards risk. In the case of risk neutrality no additional difficulty comes up, but in the cases of risk averting

---

[3]) Compared with the cost level ($22/18 \, c$ to $32/18 \, c$) and compared with the cost differences ($22/18 \, c$ to $31/18 \, c$, $23/18 \, c$ to $32/18 \, c$).

or risk preferring one has – in addition to the Luce-Raiffa axioms – to guarantee a certain property, we call it axiom 7, which says virtually:

For a given LPI, to every action $a_i \in A$ a lottery, called LPI-lottery, is attached, which maximizes risk within the LPI. With the property, an action a_1 dominates another action a_2 then and only then if, within the given LPI, the maximal risk connected with a_1, $V(a_1)$, is not greater than the maximal risk $V(a_2)$; $V(a_i) = \max_i E(a_i); i = 1, 2$:

$$a_1 \text{ dom } a_2 \Leftrightarrow \max_{LPI} E(a_1) \leqslant \max_{LPI} E(a_2). \tag{13}$$

An action $a^* \in A$ is optimal if, within the LPI, the maximal risk is minimal among all actions, not dominated by others. In want to make this clear by modifiying the three-area example with two decisions, a_1 and a_2, say to make a certain reservation contract or not.

	p_1	p_2	p_3
	z_1	z_2	z_3
a_1	e_4	e_1	e_6
a_2	e_3	e_5	e_2

The outcomes are $e_1, \ldots, e_6$. The firm's preference ordering is $e_1 \succsim e_2 \succsim \ldots \succsim e_6$. The following indifference statements reflect the firm's risk behaviour:

$$e_2 \sim \left(\frac{3}{5} e_1, \frac{2}{5} e_6 \right)$$

$$e_3 \sim \left(\frac{2}{5} e_1, \frac{3}{5} e_6 \right)$$

$$e_4 \sim \left(\frac{1}{5} e_1, \frac{4}{5} e_6 \right)$$

$$e_5 \sim \left(\frac{1}{5} e_1, \frac{4}{5} e_6 \right).$$

By setting $u(e_1) = 1$ und $u(e_6) = 0$ we get the following outcome matrix in the form of utilities:

$$[u_{ij}] = \begin{bmatrix} 0.2 & 1 & 0 \\ 0.4 & 0.2 & 0.6 \end{bmatrix}.$$

Post-multiplying this utility matrix by the vertex matrix of the LPI: $p_1 \leqslant p_2 \leqslant p_3$ yields

$$E = \begin{bmatrix} 0 & 0.5 & 0.4 \\ 0.6 & 0.4 & 0.4 \end{bmatrix}.$$

The column vector of the row maxima is $\begin{bmatrix} 0.5 \\ 0.6 \end{bmatrix}$. The minimal element of it is 0.5, thus

identifying the action a_1, to drill, as optimal for the given partial information and for the given risk behaviour of the firm.

References

Gilbert, R.J.: Resource extraction with differential information. The American Economic Review. Papers and Proceedings **67**, 1977, 250–254.

Kofler, E., and *G. Menges*: Entscheidungen bei unvollständiger Information. Berlin–Heidelberg–New York 1976.

–: Linear stochastic structuring of indeterminate decision matrices. Pioneering Economics. International Essays in Honour of Giovanni Demaria. Edited by T. Bagiotti and G. France. Padova 1978, 691–699.

–: Lineare partielle Information, "fuzziness" und Vielziele-Optimierung. Proceedings in Operations Research **8**. Ed. by K.-W. Gaede et al. Würzburg–Wien 1979a, 427–434.

–: Über unscharfe Mengen (nicht im Sinne Zadehs). Statistische Hefte **20**, 1979b, 237–249.

–: Prognosen bei partieller Information. Zeitschrift für Wirtschafts- und Sozialwissenschaften **100**, 1980a, 1–17.

Kofler, E., G. Menges et al.: Stochastische partielle Information (SPI). Statistische Hefte **21**, 1980b, 160–167.

Kuss, U.: C-optimale Entscheidungen. Statistische Hefte **21**, 1980, 261–279.

Rothschild, M.: Searching for the lowest price when the distribution of prices is unknown. The Journal of Political Economy **82**, 1974, 689–711.

Economic Theory of Natural Resources. ©Physica-Verlag, Würzburg–Wien, 1982.

IIASA Energy Modeling and Long-Term Scenarios

Hans-Holger Rogner

National and Regional energy studies mainly concentrate on the short- to medium-term aspects of the energy problem. Supply shortages, ever increasing energy prices and their impacts on economic development, balance of payments, are the focus of these studies. The approach of the Energy Systems Program of the International Institute for Applied Systems Analysis has to be seen as a complement to these detailed investigations. The transition from today's fossil fuels to a more advanced and eventually sustainable energy supply system became the central issue of this Program. Furthermore, energy is not only of regional or national importance. It has a global perspective. Economic growth and prosperity have been based to a large extent on cheap and easily manageable energy sources. The aspirations of the developing parts of the world to industrialize call for increasing quantities of inexpensive energy supply. This paper presents the general approach to the energy transition up to the year 2030, the mathematical models involved and summarizes two scenarios of global energy demand and supply.

Industrialization, economic growth, and the prosperity of the northern part of the globe have been based to a large extent on an adequate energy supply system. The build-up of an industrialized infrastructure is a dynamic process with various stages of maturity. Thus, the energy supply system had to keep pace with the needs of dynamically developing economic structures. In the middle of the last century, the world energy supply system was mainly based on wood, covering a market share of roughly 70%. The introduction of heavy machinery in production processes, the world-wide expansion of markets for goods and services and the increasing importance of the transportation system called for a new type of fuel with a higher energy density, with easier transportability and better storage conditions. Coal, endowed with such characteristics, consequently started to substitute wood. Similar substitutions should follow in the cases of oil and gas as the northern economies' industrialized structures matured. Figure 1 shows the decline and rise of the market shares of various types of primary energy sources for the world. The substitution processes given appear to follow some remarkable regularity. It suggests that the time required for any energy technology to become a substitute for another one, is about constant, irrespective of the industrial maturity of the economy. According to Figure 1 it takes about 50 to 60 years for any new energy carrier to increase its market share from 1% to 50% [*Marchetti/Nakicenovic*]. Since the events in the seventies, it has become celar that the global energy system has reached the threshold of another significant structural change. The world runs out of cheap, easily manageable fossil fuels while the global demand for such fuels seems ever growing.

Firstly, the same fuels that enabled the economies of the northern part of the globe to mature are now required in increasing quantity to satisfy the developing regions' aspirations to industrialize.

578

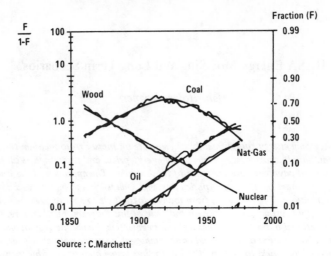

Source : C.Marchetti

Fig. 1: Global primary energy substitution. Logarithmic plot of the transformation F/(1-F) where F is the fractional market share. Smooth lines are model estimates of historical data; jagged lines are historical data; straight lines show the logistic model substitution paths

Secondly, the industrialized regions will also require more energy in order to sustain their economic growth and not to run into stagnation or depression. The gap in energy consumption between the developed and developing regions is in the same order as that in per capita income. Unlike the past, when the technological substitution process of fuel wood to coal and later oil and gas, has provided the use of inexpensive, abundant and easy-to-use energy resources, the coming substitutes will be increasingly more constrained through higher costs, resource depletion and environmental constraints.

At present, roughly 70% of the world population belongs to developing regions, consuming only about 16% of the global commercial demand (see Figure 2). All this points to the truly global nature of the world's energy system.

The Energy Systems Program at IIASA began its activities to study future global energy demand and supply having in mind this uneven distribution of per capita energy consumption between the northern and the southern hemisphere. The long-term dynamics of the energy system shown by the market penetration analysis [*Marchetti/Nakicenovic*] mentioned earlier dictate a planning horizon of at least 50 years, thus capturing the dynamic development of the global energy system and its structural changes at large. An investigation as complex as this one covering a planning horizon from 1980 to 2030 has problems of its own, however. The world's energy demand, its resources and its technological know-how are not uniformly distributed.

Moreover, the evolution of energy demand is expected to be quite dissimilar in world regions whose evolution over time differs largely in terms of the economic, social and demographic structures. For IIASA's energy study [Energy Systems Program Group of the International Institute for Applied Systems Analysis, Wolf Häfele, Program Leader]

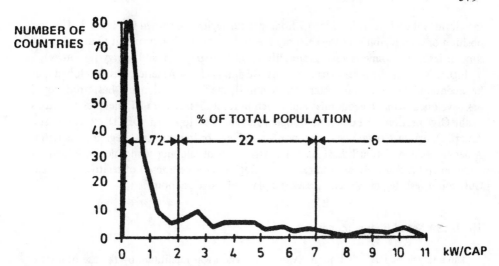

Fig. 2: Per Capita Energy Consumption, an uneven Distribution

THE SEVEN WORLD REGIONS ANALYZED IN THE STUDIES OF THE INTERNATIONAL INSTITUTE FOR APPLIED SYSTEM ANALYSIS, LAXENBURG, AUSTRIA

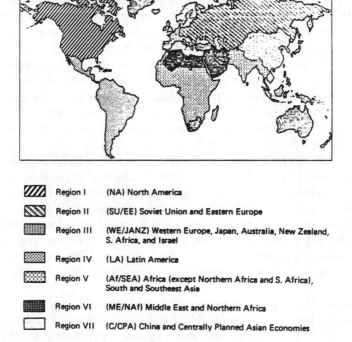

Region I   (NA) North America

Region II   (SU/EE) Soviet Union and Eastern Europe

Region III (WE/JANZ) Western Europe, Japan, Australia, New Zealand, S. Africa, and Israel

Region IV   (LA) Latin America

Region V   (Af/SEA) Africa (except Northern Africa and S. Africa), South and Southeast Asia

Region VI   (ME/NAf) Middle East and Northern Africa

Region VII (C/CPA) China and Centrally Planned Asian Economies

Fig. 3: The IIASA world regions

the world is therefore divided into 7 homogenous regions as shown in Figure 3. The composition of each region is not necessarily based on geographical proximity but reflects similarities in economic infrastructure, lifestyle, demographics, and energy resources.

Figure 3 shows the seven world regions. Region I, North America, has developed market economies and is rich in resources. Region II, the Soviet Union and Eastern Europe, has developed planned economies and is rich in resources. Region III, member countries of the Organisation for Economic Cooperation and Development (OECD, except North America), has developed market economies and is poor in resources. Region IV is Latin America. Region V, South East Asia and Africa, has developing economies with high population and is relatively poor in resources. Region VI is composed of relatively oil-rich Gulf countries; Region VII comprises the planned Asian economies.

The IIASA Set of Energy Models

The analysis of IIASA's Energy Systems Program was facilitated by the use of a set of mathematical models serving as an analytical tool. However, long-term projections of energy demand and supply can be made only in the light of mutually consistent assumptions on future population growth, economic activity, availability of energy, materials and other resources with some perception of technological innovation as well as in the wake of various physical, social and environmental constraints. All this predetermined information has been summarized into scenarios so as to serve as the principal input to the set of models. In Figure 4, a schematized sequence of the relevant models and their interaction is shown, wherein the scenario inputs are indicated by non-rectangular boxes. The main scenario definitions concern the future evolution of world population, economic activity, technical progress and changes in lifestyles. Two distinct scenarios for seven world regions were selected labeled "high" and "low", indicating a kind of reasonably expectable range of future global economic growth. The population growth, however, is common to both scenarios. The study undertaken by IIASA relied on the projections of *Keyfitz* [1977] that envisage the overall population growth from 4 billion in 1975 to 8 billion by the year 2030. This is quite a conservative estimate of the population growth rates dominated by a general decline of the global population growth reaching an asymptotic level beyond the year 2030 (i.e. replacement level of fertility is assumed by 2015 for developing regions). Since the models are not "hard-wired", consistency checks are carried out on the information flow between the models in each step of iteration. Human judgement therefore examines the input and output of the models at all steps.

In general, one should note that the scenario assumptions are not an end in themselves. The model approach as shown in Figure 4 is highly iterative. The given set of scenario assumptions leads to qualitative and quantitative results which feed back to modify the initial scenario assumptions eliminating internal inconsistencies until a consistent picture evolves.

Before turning to the general discussion of the IIASA set of energy models it is appropriate to mention some of the major problems and shortcomings in the methodological approach underlying this long-term evaluation of global energy strategies. The global component immediately points to the lacking availability of adequate and comparable

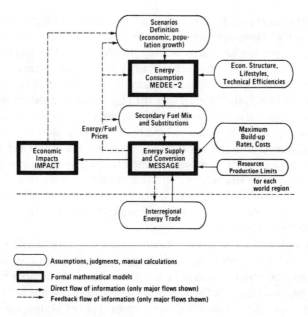

Fig. 4: IIASA's set of energy models: a simplified representation

data for seven world regions. For some countries in a region excellent data sources were outdone by very poor ones of other countries. In addition to the availability of national data the difficulties of a correct aggregation had to be handled. Thus the methodology, i.e. the kind of models and their structure chosen — common to all regions — was highly influenced by the data problem. Therefore, the design and the development of practical, robust and quasi non-data intensive models (in an econometrical sense) rather than methodological sophistication was in the forefront. Further, various limitations originate from the length of the time horizon considered. Over a period of 50 years it is impossible to take into account for relative price changes and interpret their impacts on related economic variables such as demand structures etc. Consequently, the analysis focussed as much as possible on technological relations and pure cost considerations, i.e. in terms of 1975 US-$ (see MESSAGE and IMPACT). Many of the technological relations, functions, and data are exogenously determined within the scenario setup, especially their evolution over time. Thus individuals' jugdements of the future enter the models at various stages explicitly including the individuals' own biases. By means of an iterative application of the models and the consistency checks between each step it was attempted to cut such biases to a minimum.

The first model in this loop, MEDEE [*Lapillonne*] is an accounting algorithm for evaluating energy demand implied by the given economic and lifestyle scenarios. Special consideration in this model is given to the speed of introduction of energy conservation measures. The demand analysis is broken down into three major parts: energy needs for transportation, industries and the household/service sector. The transportation module distinguishes mainly between passenger and freight transportation and between urban and intercity traffic. Domestic freight transportation is a function of GDP contribution of various economic sectors such as agriculture, mining, manufacturing and the energy sectors. The allocation of various modes of transportation, such as air, rail, truck, water, or the energy intensity per ton/km has to be exogenously specified serving as further scenario parameters. Passenger transportation and its energy needs are calculated from data on urban and rural population, average distances travelled, load factors, and assumed energy intensities. The industry module uses the split of value added among the economic sectors mentioned above. Together with the energy intensity per unit of dollar value added the energy demand in the industrial sectors are broken down into demands for electricity (for lighting, motive power and so on) thermal uses (space and water heating, low/high temperature heat, steam generation and furnace operation) as well as motor fuel in nonstationary uses. Whenever substitution processes are possible, for example between electricity and liquid fuels in space heating, the specification of penetration rates of various technologies, such as district heat, heat pumps, soft solar and insulation standards, has to be done by the modeler.

In the household/service sector, main consideration was given to space heating which presently accounts for the major share of energy consumption in this sector in the developed regions. Improved insulation in newly constructed buildings will reduce this type of energy demand significantly. The model therefore distinguishes between single home units and apartment houses including different types of heating facilities. Energy demand for water heating, cooking, air conditioning, electrical appliances are calculated from exogenously given annual consumption rates, ownership fractions, family size, and efficiency improvements. Figure 5 gives a schematic description of the MEDEE model. The final energy demand for the various kinds of fuels is then the ultimate outcome from this model serving as an input to the energy supply model MESSAGE. MESSAGE [*Agnew/Schrattenholzer/Voss*] is a dynamic linear programming model with the objective of exploring the cost optimal supply of the energy demand determined by MEDEE. The model considers a number of primary energy sources and their associated conversion technologies ranging from traditional fossil fuels to central solar and nuclear breeding technologies (see Figure 6). Energy resources are specified in various categories according to cost of extraction, quantity and quality of resources, and location of the deposits. Build-up rates for new energy production technologies, capacities and production restrictions serve as further constraints in this model. The central issue of MESSAGE is to evaluate various "what if" considerations on exogenous assumptions concerning energy resource availability, extraction and conversion technologies and related costs, import curtailments and so on. The objective function minimizes the sum of discounted costs of fuels, of maintenance/operation and capital costs to meet the energy demand over the total planning horizon. An optimal energy supply strategy then contains capacity needs for domestic energy production as well as the energy import requirements in quantitative terms. The next model in this loop, IMPACT, uses the optimal energy supply strategy and calculates the corresponding direct and indirect capital requirements for such a strategy. IMPACT [*Kononov/Por*] is a dynamic input/output model, which explicitly accounts for lags between the start of investment and the putting into operation of production capacities. Further, the model takes into consideration material consumption for the capacity expansion of the energy system. A schematic description of IMPACT is given in Figure 7.

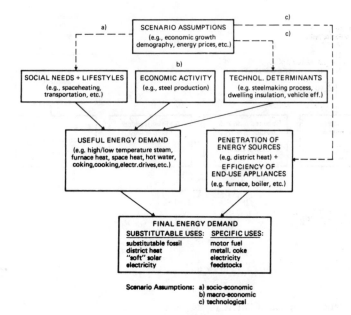

Fig. 5: Schematic description of MEDEE-2

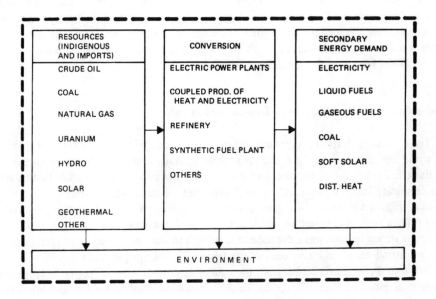

Fig. 6: Schematic description of MESSAGE

584

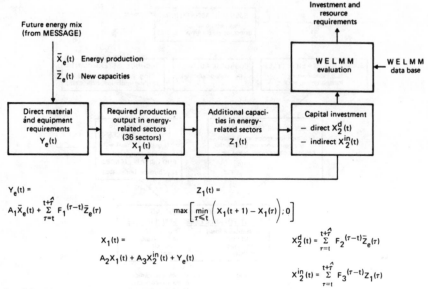

$Y_e(t) =$

$$A_1 \bar{X}_e(t) + \sum_{\tau=t}^{t+\hat{T}} F_1^{(\tau-t)} \bar{Z}_e(\tau)$$

$Z_1(t) =$

$$\max\left[\min_{\tau \leqslant t} \left(X_1(t+1) - X_1(\tau) \right); 0 \right]$$

$X_1(t) =$

$$A_2 X_1(t) + A_3 X_2^{in}(t) + Y_e(t)$$

$$X_2^d(t) = \sum_{\tau=t}^{t+\hat{T}} F_2^{(\tau-t)} \bar{Z}_e(\tau)$$

$$X_2^{in}(t) = \sum_{\tau=t}^{t+\hat{T}} F_3^{(\tau-t)} Z_1(\tau)$$

Fig. 7: Schematic description of IMPACT

Having applied all three models to the seven world regions, the energy import requirements as well as the energy export possibilities of various regions can be identified (see
the bottom of Figure 4). Obviously, in a first iteration, it is unlikely to achieve a balanced
interregional energy trade account. Therefore, it was necessary to revise the initial assumptions and reiterate the loop several times until a globally consistent picture emerged. By
the same token, the scenario assumptions concerning, for example, economic growth
rates or maximum oil production levels are not simply inputs but have to be considered
as part of the results of this modeling effort.

Global Economic Growth, Energy Demand and Supply

The ulitmately derived projections of Gross Domestic Product (GDP) growth rates for
all world regions show a gradual decline with time. Many factors are likely to contribute
to this trend (including social and institutional) but the two most important factors are
the decreasing trend in population growth rates and the increasing scarcity of basic resources. Figure 8 gives the GDP growth rates for different world regions disaggregated
over certain periods for the high and low scenarios. These GDP projections implicitly
assume a strong link between the economic growth in the developing regions and that in
the industrialized world on account of the trade relationships [Hicks et al.].

Between the industrialized regions the economic growth rates of Region II range above
those of Regions I and III. This is due to the relative lower initial level of absolute Gross
Domestic Product in Region II. Similar to the developing regions it was assumed that

	HISTORICAL		LOW SCENARIO			
	1950-1960	1960-1975	1975-1985	1985-2000	2000-2015	2015-2020
I (NA)	3.3	3.4	3.1	2.0	1.1	1.0
II (SU/EE)	10.4	6.5	4.5	3.5	2.5	2.0
III (WE/JANZ)	5.0	5.2	3.2	2.1	1.5	1.2
IV (LA)	5.0	6.1	4.7	3.6	3.0	3.0
V (Af/SEA)	3.9	5.5	4.8	3.6	2.8	2.4
VI (ME/NAf)	7.0	9.8	5.6	4.6	2.7	2.1
VII (C/CPA)	8.0	6.1	3.3	3.0	2.5	2.0
WORLD	5.0	5.0	3.6	2.7	1.9	1.7
I + III	4.2	4.4	3.1	2.1	1.3	1.1
IV + V + VI	4.7	6.5	5.0	3.8	2.9	2.6

	HISTORICAL		HIGH SCENARIO			
	1950-1960	1960-1975	1975-1985	1985-2000	2000-2015	2015-2030
I (NA)	3.3	3.4	4.3	3.3	2.4	2.0
II (SU/EE)	10.4	6.5	5.0	4.0	3.5	3.5
III (WE/JANZ)	5.0	5.2	4.3	3.4	2.5	2.0
IV (LA)	5.0	6.1	6.2	4.9	3.7	3.3
V (Af/SEA)	3.9	5.5	5.8	4.8	3.8	3.4
VI (ME/NAf)	7.0	9.8	7.2	5.9	4.2	3.8
VII (C/CPA)	8.0	6.1	5.0	4.0	3.5	3.0
WORLD	5.0	5.0	4.7	3.8	3.0	2.7
I + III	4.2	4.4	4.3	3.4	2.5	2.0
IV + V + VI	4.7	6.5	6.3	5.1	3.9	3.5

Fig. 8: Real growth rate of GDP (% year)

technology transfer from Regions I and III and the catching up aspirations of the centrally planned economies allow Region II to accomplish higher but steadily declining economic growth rates than those of Regions I and III.

In general one may conclude that the economic activity in the high scenario allows
for a notable improvement of the developing countries' share in total world output,
whereas in the low scenario the goal of the New Economic Order can most likely not be
reached. Although the per capita GDP growth rates of the developing Regions IV–VII,
the economic development gap of those of the developed ones, I–III, is not substantially
narrowed, especially not in the low scenario.

Final Energy Growth (%/yr)

	1950-1975	HIGH		LOW	
	1950-1975	1975-2000	2000-2030	1975-2000	2000-2030
I (NA)	2.7	1.4	1.1	0.8	0.5
II (SU/EE)	5.2	2.5	1.8	2.2	1.0
III (WE/JANZ)	4.3	2.6	1.2	1.7	0.7
IV (LA)	6.8	5.6	3.3	4.3	2.8
V (Af/SEA)	6.7	5.9	3.7	4.7	2.9
VI (ME/NAf)	10.4	7.0	3.5	5.8	2.3
VII (C/CPA)	10.8	4.7	3.2	3.1	2.1
WORLD	4.3	3.0	2.2	2.1	1.4

Final Energy (TW)

	1950	1975	HIGH		LOW	
	1950	1975	2000	2030	2000	2030
I (NA)	0.96	1.87	2.63	3.67	2.26	2.64
II (SU/EE)	0.36	1.28	2.39	4.14	2.17	2.95
III (WE/JANZ)	0.55	1.59	3.04	4.38	2.39	2.99
IV (LA)	0.05	0.26	1.01	2.64	0.73	1.66
V (Af/SEA)	0.05	0.25	1.06	3.17	0.80	1.88
VI (ME/NAf)	0.01	0.11	0.58	1.64	0.43	0.87
VII (C/CPA)	0.03	0.39	1.23	3.20	0.85	1.59
WORLD	2.01	5.74	11.93	22.83	9.64	14.57

Fig. 9:   Final energy growth rates and in absolute terms

The corresponding final energy demand in absolute terms and in growth rates is given in Figure 9. The final energy demand growth rates given in the high scenario lie well below the historically observed rates. Declining economic activity and overall improvement of the ratio of final energy to GDP are mainly responsible for this tendency. However, there still exist significant dissimilarities in the energy intensiveness in various regions. In Figure 10, final energy per unit of GDP is plotted against GDP per capita.

The developed Regions I, II and III show a gradually decreasing energy input as per capita income increases. Input factors to the production processes are used rather efficiently on account of a developed industrial infrastructure and technical progress. The situation in developing regions is converse. The need to industrialize in these regions requires an overproportionally greater amount of energy than the operation of an already existing infrastructure.

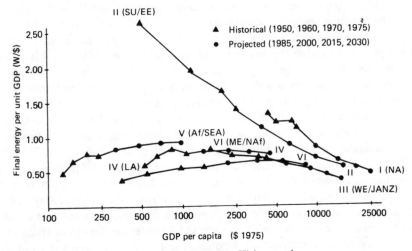

Fig. 10: Energy intensiveness versus per capita income – High scenario

On the other hand, one may derive from Figure 10 that the build-up of an economic infrastructure has been completed when a per capita income of about $2000 in 1975 terms has been reached. This range of per capita income corresponds to the maximum values of the final energy intensity of about .8–1.0 W/$ in 1975 terms.

Which types of energy characterize the future global energy demand? In Figure 11, the relative distribution of secondary energy demand will continuously be dominated by liquid fuels. The problems caused by this sustained demand for liquids will be seen when demand and supply have to be balanced.

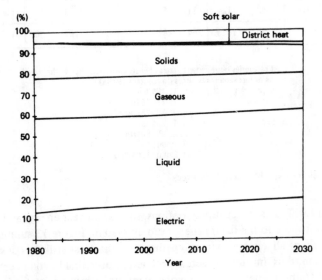

Fig. 11: Global secondary energy demand – High scenario

Before going into the assessment of future energy supply strategies one also has to look into the potential energy resources situation. For a period of as many as 50 years, this is quite a hazardous undertaking. Indeed, one has to anticipate considerable additions to the energy reserves and resources commonly used today, even more since advanced technological developments are likely to open up new avenues. Further, today's non-conventional fossil fuels such as shale oil or tar sands might in due course turn into conventional fuels as the general energy price level continues to rise at its present rates.

The ultimately recoverable fossil fuel resources are summarized according to distinct cost categories in Figure 12. The aggregates of the resources estimated in this figure are about 3 times higher than the numbers usually reported. However, this is readily understandable since the non-conventional fossil fuel resources are included in these estimates. The transition or structural change in the energy sector is not only a transition from fossil to non-fossil energy technologies, but also a transition from for example, today's oil resources to the exploitation of shale oil which may call for mining operations at a scale similar to that required for coal. In general one should note that the exploitations of fuels belonging to the more expensive cost categories do not only cause larger costs, but also cause enormous ecological and environmental impacts.

RESOURCE	COAL (TWyr)		OIL (TWyr)			GAS (TWyr)			URANIUM (10^3 tU)	
COST CATEGORY	I	II	I	II	III	I	II	III	I	II
I (NA)	174	232	23	26	125	34	40	29	1920	1500
II (SU/EE)	136	448	37	45	69	66	51	31	n.e.	4140
III (WE/JANZ)	93	151	17	3	21	19	5	14	793	2087
IV (LA)	10	11	19	81	110	17	12	14	56	3544
V (AF/SEA)	55	52	25	5	33	16	10	14	311	5269
VI (ME/NAF)	<1	<1	132	27	n.e.	108	10	14	78	1524
VII (C/CPA)	92	124	11	13	15	7	13	14	n.e.	1980
WORLD	560	1019	264	200	373	267	141	130	3158	20044

* Cost categories represent estimates of costs either at or below the stated volume of recoverable resources (in constant 1975 $).
  For oil and natural gas: cat. 1: 12$/boe
     cat. 2: 12–20$/boe
     cat. 3: 20–25$/boe
  For coal: cat. 1: 25$/ton
     cat. 2: 25–50$/ton
  For uranium: cat. 1: 80$/kgU
     cat. 2: 80–130$/kgU

Fig. 12: Ultimately recoverable energy resources

Apart from fossil fuels, other supply options, such as nuclear energy and renewable resources will contribute to the future energy supply system. Figure 13 summarizes the resource potentials of all energy sources together with the most striking constraints in their exploitation, thus limiting the actual production potential beyond certain levels. The renewable forms of energy, such as wood plantations, hydropower, windpower, geothermal energy, and so on have an infinite resource potential. Technical considerations, however, limit the annual exploitation of such forms of energy to about 14TWyr/yr. This number is further reduced to about half this value and considers practically realizable production in the wake of social, environmental, economic and other constraints. There are schools of thought that consider that the actual potential of renewable resources may be 50 to 70% over the numbers given here. In fact, more in depth analysis and study are required before this controversy is settled.

	PRODUCTION (TWyr/yr)	RESOURCE (TWyr)	CONSTRAINTS
RENEWABLES			
WOOD	2.5	∞	ECONOMY – ENVIRONMENT
HYDRO	1–1.5	∞	ECONOMY – ENVIRONMENT
TOTAL	6–(14)	∞	ECONOMY – (NATURE)
OIL AND GAS	8–12(?)	1000	ECONOMY – ENVIRONMENT – RESOURCES
COAL	10–14(??)	2000(?)	SOCIETY – ENVIRONMENT – ECONOMY
NUCLEAR			
BURNER	12 for 2020	300	RESOURCES
BREEDERS	<17 by 2030	300 000	BUILDUP RATES – RESOURCES
FUSION	2–3 by 2030	300 000	TECHNOLOGY – BUILDUP RATES
SOLAR			
SOFT	1–2	∞	ECONOMY – LAND – INFRASTRUCTURE
HARD	2–3 by 2030	∞	BUILDUP RATES – MATERIALS

Fig. 13: Summary of energy resources, production potentials and constraints

Nuclear energy is limited to 300 TWyr resource-wise if no reprocessing, advanced converters and fast breeder reactors are introduced, which can multiply the resource availability by a factor of 1000. The resource estimates of Figures 12 and 13 and their practically realizable potential serve as an input to the detailed and quantified energy supply strategies made for each region. What production levels are actually achieved by the year 2030 will depend on the time of introduction of new technologies, their cost economics relative to major technologies in use and the dynamics of market penetration as well as on political considerations and societal acceptance. The optimum distribution of primary energy sources in the year 2030 in the world supply system is shown in Figure 14. It should be noted that the share of oil in primary energy supply has decreased from about 45% in 1975 to about 18% in 2030 in both scenarios, whereas the share of liquid fuels in the final energy demand has remained practically constant. The decrease of oil was offset by synthetic fuel production from coal liquefaction and coal gasification. This high demand for synthetic fuels to replace oil reduces the availability of coal as a primary fuel, mainly in combustion for electricity generation.

Consequently, nuclear power has to take over the electricity generation. The use of nuclear energy, therefore, increases from 6% in 1975 to about 20% in the year 2030. At the same time, the share of coal, excluding the use in liquefaction decreases by about the same amount as the increase in the share of nuclear power while the total percentage of

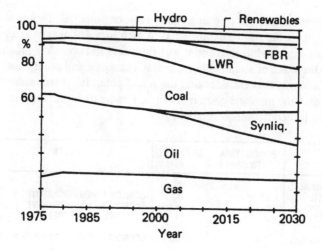

Fig. 14: Global primary energy – High scenario, 1975–2030

coal use remained fairly constant. Hydropower and gas maintain their relative market shares while renewables, here presented by solar, do not influence the global energy supply situation before the year 2030. Figure 15 summarizes the global energy supply strategy in absolute numbers. The high scenario total is 36TWyr/yr and the overall energy requirement of the low scenario is 22TWyr/yr. The actual distribution of various primary energy sources in physical units is characterized by significant consumption increases in all available sources. According to Figure 14, the relative share of oil decreases but in absolute terms, for example in the high scenario, oil requirements nearly double over the next 50 years.

In absolute terms 6.8TWyr/yr of oil is roughly compared with the world energy consumption in 1970. Further, the oil in the year 2030 is quite different from the cheap, clean and easily manageable fuels of the early 70s. 6.8TWyr/yr include shale oil, tar sands and enhanced recovery in increasing shares whose extraction is costly, involving enormous ecological and environmental impacts. Coal in the high scenario reaches the incredible amount of 12TWyr/yr in the year 2030 compared to 2.26TWyr/yr in 1975. One should bear in mind that the scenario of 12 billion tons of annual production appears feasible by definition but does not consider political, social and environmental aspects. If coal production does not seem advisable, one must embark upon alternatives.

For instance, by deploying allothermal coal liquefaction instead of autothermal coal liquefaction as assumed in the high and low scenario, which might cut down the coal input for liquefaction to about 30%, might be one alternative. In such a configuration, nuclear power or hard solar would have to provide the necessary hydrogen, for example, by way of electrolysis. According to Figure 13, the nuclear potential is about 17TWyr/yr but the high scenario allocates only 8TWyr/yr. This indicates that there is still a certain amount of flexibility in the energy supply system as it is anticipated.

Two supply scenarios – Global primary energy by source, 1975–2030 (TWyr)yr)

	1975	HIGH SCENARIO		LOW SCENARIO	
		2000	2030	2000	2030
OIL	3.62	5.89	6.83	4.75	5.02
GAS	1.51	3.11	5.97	2.53	3.47
COAL	2.26	4.95	11.98	3.93	6.45
LWR	0.12	1.70	3.21	1.27	1.89
FBR	0.00	0.04	4.88	0.02	3.28
HYDRO	0.50	0.83	1.46	0.83	1.46
SOLAR	0.00	0.10	0.49	0.09	0.30
OTHER	0.21	0.22	0.81	0.17	0.52
TOTAL	8.21	16.84	35.65	13.59	22.39

Global primary energy by region (TW)

	1975	HIGH		LOW	
		2000	2030	2000	2030
I (NA)	2.65	3.89	6.02	3.31	4.37
II (SU/EE)	1.84	3.69	7.33	3.31	5.00
III (WE/JANZ)	2.26	4.29	7.14	3.39	4.54
IV (LA)	0.34	1.34	3.68	0.97	2.31
V (Af/SEA)	0.33	1.43	4.65	1.07	2.66
VI (ME/NAf)	0.13	0.77	2.38	0.56	1.23
VII (C/CPA)	0.46	1.44	4.45	0.98	2.29
	8.21	16.84	35.65	13.59	22.39

Fig. 15: Global primary energy by source and region

Global Energy Trade

How do these supply schemes affect the allocation of resources between various regions, especially the allocation of oil. The global balance between liquid fuel demand and supply will continue to depend on the oil reserves of the Middle East. According to Figure 16, the liquid fuel production outside the Middle East is by no means sufficient to meet the demand for liquids in the market economies. The oil production outside Region VI is highly characterized by a consequent transition from conventional to non-conventional oil resources as well as to coal liquefaction. In spite of the fact that demand for liquid fuels is reserved only for premium uses, the slow market penetration rates for

592

nonconventional and synthetic fuel technologies limit their capacity build-up. The insufficient domestic supply of liquid fuels is essentially critical in Regions III and V due to
lacking domestic fuel resources. Therefore, Region VI continues to play the role as the
world's major oil supplier. Beyond the year 2000 it will even be the only one (see Figure
17). In the high scenario, Region I (North America) must achieve autonomy in its oil
economy. Autothermal coal liquefaction enables Region III to diminish its oil imports
from 1.2TWyr/yr to less than .7TWyr/yr by the year 2030. Region IV is self-sufficient
while Region V turns into an oil-importing region. The determinant factor in the supply
schemes and trade flows is the oil production limit in Region VI assumed at a maximum
level of 33 million barrels a day. Other production ceilings however might be considered.

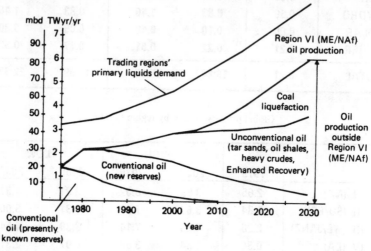

Fig. 16: Oil supply and demand, 1975–2030, World, excluding centrally planned economies –
High scenario

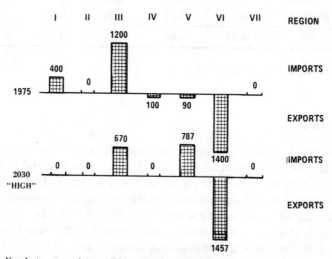

Fig. 17: Oil trading between regions – High scenario, 1975–2030

Concluding Remarks

Having seen the picture of world energy demand and supply over the next 50 years one may now once again take a look at the stock of fossil fuel resources. How much of these resources have been consumed in the two scenarios and what is left for future use? As shown in Figure 18, we have not run out of stock even in the case of the high scenario and have consumed only 69% of conventional oil, 40% of the conventional gas and 72% of category I coal.

	Total Resource Available (TWyr)	Total Consumed	
		(TWyr)	(%)
Oil			
conventional (cat. I + II)	464	317	68
unconventional (cat. III)	373	4	1
Natural Gas			
conventional (cat. I + II)	408	199	49
unconventional	130	0	
Coal			
cat. I	560	341	61
cat. II	1019	0	0

Fig. 18: Cumulative uses of fossil fuels, 1975–2030 – High scenario

The unconventional gas has not been touched at all and only 2% of category II coal and 1% of unconventional oil, which perhaps one should not call oil, have been tapped. Thus, from about 3000 TWyr of fossil fuels resources, more than 2000TWyr will still be available for use for the years after 2030. The transition phase which sets in at the turn of the century will therefore continue beyond the year 2030 and the running out phenomenon of fossil fuels will occur only in the latter half of the next century.

Balancing demand and supply on a global basis requires the use of all supply and demand opportunities. Energy conservation, coal, oil, gas as well as nuclear and alternatives have to be used extensively. No option can be excluded a priori.

****

The considerations in this paper are based on the seven year study of the Energy Systems Program at IIASA. Roughly 150 research scholars participated in this study which has been summarized in the book entitled "Energy in a Finite World – A Global Systems Analysis". This paper is the author's interpretation of the study preceding the publication of the above mentioned book.

594

References

Agnew, M., L. Schrattenholzer and *A. Voss*: A Model for Energy Supply Systems Alternatives and Their General Environmental Impact. WP-79-6. Laxenburg, Austria 1979.

Energy Systems Program Group of the International Institute for Applied Systems Analysis, Wolf Häfele, Program Leader. Energy in a Finite World – A Global Systems Analysis. Cambridge, Mass. 1981.

Hicks, N.L., et al.: A Model of Trade and Growth for the Developing World. Eur. Econ. Rev. 7, 1978, 239–255.

Keyfitz, N.: Population of the World and Its Regions 1975–2050. WP-77-7. Laxenburg, Austria 1977.

Kononov, Y., and *A. Por*: The Economic IMPACT Model. RR-79-08. Laxenburg, Austria 1979.

Lapillonne, B.: MEDEE-2: A Model for Long-Term Energy Demand Evaluation. RR. 78-77. Laxenburg, Austria 1978.

Marchetti, C., and *N. Nakicenovic*: The Dynamics of Energy Systems and the Logistic Substitution Model. RR-79-13. Laxenburg, Austria 1979.

Economic Theory of Natural Resources. ©Physica-Verlag, Würzburg–Wien, 1982.

Gaming: A New Methodology for the Study of Natural Resources

Ingolf Ståhl

1. Introduction

Gaming – the actual playing of games in order to study a game situation – has a long tradition in the military field. It has also been successful within education. In particular there has, since the middle of the 1950's, been a large increase in computer supported games for management education.

Only during the last decade, however, has there been any extensive application of operational gaming, i.e., gaming as an aid to decision-makers, in the civilian field.

Many of these applications have been in corporations or government agencies and have not been reported on, but several such cases have come to our attention through personal contacts. Others have been in socialist countries and have not been reported on in the English language.[1]

Looking through some of the standard bibliographies on gaming [e.g. *Cruikshank/ Telfer; Gibbs; Horn/Cleaves; Rohn; Smit* etc.] one finds that only a very small fraction of the games is devoted to the study of natural resources. Most of these games were constructed in the 1970's. It should, however, be stressed that almost all of these games have a purely educational purpose, often directed towards students at the high-school or college level.

Only a handful of games seem to have a strong research or operational purpose. These are also of a quite recent date [*Birr et alia; Kumata et alia; Leijendeckers* etc.]. It hence, appears justified to regard operational gaming as quite a new method in the field of study of natural resources.

However, it appears to be reasonable to assume that operational gaming is an appropriate method for the study of various problems connected with natural resources. This follows first of all from the fact that gaming appears to be a very suitable complement to game theory, when analysing strategical decision problems. In particular it appears that gaming can be used as an "acid test" to game theoretical models aimed at helping decision-makers. Since, as witnessed by many of the papers in this volume, game theoretical models are of interest for decisions in the field of natural resources, gaming then also has a role to play in the testing of these models.

The idea behind this "acid test" is the use of gaming as a screening process to give "green" or "red light" for models that one wants to use for decisions in reality. The cost

---

[1] At the International Institute for Applied Systems Analysis we are also working on surveys of how gaming has been applied to actual cases of decision making, as well as making a special survey of gaming in the socialist countries.

of using an inappropriate model can be very high, while gaming experiments are inexpensive, in particular if they are of a fairly small size. If one, hence, by a row of gaming experiments can stop inappropriate models this would in most cases be a profitable venture.

In an experimental situation one can in most cases, to a large extent, adjust the rules of the games, for example, the pay-offs, the information available, the means of communication etc., to fit the "institutional assumptions" of the game theoretical model. There is in general a much smaller difference between the game theoretical model and the game used in gaming experiments than between the game theoretical model and the complex real situation. Because of this it is in general more likely that people will behave (or can be influenced to behave) according to the game theoretical model in the gaming experiment than in reality. This implies that if one, in a series of gaming experiments, has found that a specific group of people, e.g., decision makers, have not behaved or have not wanted to behave in line with the game theoretical model in the gaming exercise, there are reasons to have great doubt that they would behave according to the game theoretical model in the complex real situation. In such a case one is generally better advised to go back to question the fundamental behavioral assumptions of the game theoretic model than trying to apply this model directly in reality.[2]

Gaming appears to have a use in natural resources studies also for purposes other than the testing of models. Here, among others, we shall mention:

a) forecasting
b) scenario-generation
c) answering "what if questions".

Forecasting refers to the case that one tries to use gaming as a method to predict what would actually happen in reality. The question of validity is obviously much more problematic in this case than in the case above of the "acid test", since we have a much greater discrepancy between the institutional assumptions of the game and the corresponding set up in the real decision situation.

Scenario generation can be regarded as a type of less ambitious "forecast". The result of the gaming experiments can be thought of as one of several possible outcomes in reality. The result is then mainly of interest for further discussions, possibly regarding what further investigations should be carried out.

The answering of "what if" – questions focusses on the experimental possibilities of gaming. By keeping everything else regarding the gaming set up constant and only changing *one* significant variable, e.g., the amount of information supplied, between two series of gaming experiments, one can study the effect of the difference as regards this important variable. Two things should be stressed. Firstly, since one generally would have to use different players in the different experiments, many experiments as well as careful random choice of players is needed for excluding the possibility that differences in the personal characteristics of the players rather than differences in the experimental variable is the cause of differences between the results of the two series of gaming experiments.

---

[2] A further discussion of the problems of using gaming for the acid test of game theoretical models is presented in Sĭahl [1980a]. Here we also discuss instances where further experiments are needed before rejection of the game theoretical model.

Secondly, we have the same kind or problem of validity as mentioned above, when we want to apply the "what if answers" to the real decision situations. Gaming should, therefore, also in this context mainly be seen as a complement to other methods by, e.g., providing a basis for discussions regarding further research efforts.

Having given this background indicating something about the relevance, as well as the problems, of gaming in the study of natural resources, we can proceed to look at the two games of the present research program at IIASA, the International Institute for Applied Systems Analysis at Laxenburg near Vienna in Austria.

Since this institute has a tradition of dealing with the problems of natural resources, particularly water and energy, it is not surprising that both games deal with such issues: One with cost allocation in water projects and the other with CO_2-emissions and coal trade.

Furthermore, since the institute is an international one with 17 member nations from both East and West the research as regards both games has an international focus. The water cost allocation game has been played in five different countries; the CO_2-emission and coal trade game deals with the global problem of how coal burning in one country might affect the climate of all countries on the globe.

2. Game on Cost Allocation in Water Resources

Game Theoretic Analysis

We shall first introduce the game theoretical model that we have aimed at testing by the use of gaming.

The background is the following: In Sweden, six blocks of municipalities in Southwestern Skane have a choice of strategy as regards their long term water planning. Such a municipality block[3]), henceforth simply called municipality, can either solve its water supply problem on its own, or it can join together with another municipality to do it more cheaply. In fact, it can join together with several municipalities, up to the grand coalition involving all six municipalities. Due to "economies of scale", there are in most cases, cost savings when municipalities join together and the grand coalition leads to the lowest total costs.

The question is now, how costs should then be allocated. The cost allocation problem arises from the fact that the fixed costs of construction of the plant cannot be assigned to the municipalities in any unique way. One can only propose various principles on which such allocations should depend. Suitable principles can be found, e.g., in game theory. Some such principles have been discussed in connection with other IIASA research [*Young/Okada/Hashimoto, 1980*].

The first principle is that the parties form the most efficient coalition, the grand coalition, N.

---

[3]) Although in reality there are 18 municipalities in this region, it was found practical and realistic to group these into six units which for this purpose can be regarded as acting as independent municipalities. It is sufficient to note here that the symbols A, H, K, L, M and T denote the main municipalities in each group, with L denoting the university town Lund and M. Malmö, the largest city in the region. For details, see *Young/Okada/Hashimoto* [1980].

The theory then focusses on how the parties shall divide these costs of the grand coalition, called c (N). We shall hence determine the payments made by a party i:

x_i for $i = 1, \ldots, 6$.

We next introduce the "full cost principle", implying that total costs should be covered, leaving no surplus and no loss to any third party. We hence demand that:

$$\sum_{i=1}^{6} x_i = c\ (N).$$

For determining these payments x_i, we first introduce the "individual rationality" principle, implying that no municipality shall pay a higher cost than it would have to pay if it were to fulfill its water needs completely on its own. Calling the cost that a municipality i occurs when going alone, i.e., its "going alone cost", for c (i), we require that

$x_i \leqslant c$ (i)   for $i = 1, \ldots, 6$.

Furthermore, we add the "group rationality principle," implying that the sum of payments made by the members of every coalition which is smaller than the grand coalition, should not be larger than the cost that this coalition incurs if it is working on its own. We hence require that:

$$\sum_{i \in S} x_i \leqslant c\ (S)$$

for every coalition S, which is smaller than the grand coalition. This implies, for instance, that the coalition consisting of parties 1, 2, and 3 would not agree to paying x_1, x_2, x_3, if the payment $x_1 + x_2 + x_3$, is higher than the total costs would be to these three parties if they only formed the three-party coalition 123.

The set of all allocations satisfying the principles stated above, are said to constitute "*the core*". In some cases, this core might not exist; in many cases, like the one studied in this concrete case, it exists, but is in no way unique.

There are several ways of obtaining a unique allocation within the core. In this case, three are discussed: The Nucleolus, the Weak Nucleolus and the Proportional Nucleolus.[4]

The basic idea behind obtaining a unique solution is by decreasing the costs of different subcoalitions by introducing hypothetical subsidies. One then looks for the smallest subsidy or subsidy rate, ϵ, which still allows for the principles above to hold.

Hence we seek to minimize ϵ under the restriction of

$$\sum_{i=1}^{6} x_i = c\ (N)$$

adding as regards the subcoalitions one further set of restrictions, which we more generally write as

$$\sum_{i \in S} x_i \leqslant f\ (c\ (S),\ \epsilon) \text{ for every } S.$$

f (c (S), ϵ), varies for the different methods in the following manner.

---

[4] The terms are those used in Young/Okada/Hashimoto and do not necessarily correspond to terms generally used in other game theoretical literature.

For the Nucleolus

$$f(c(S), \epsilon) = c(S) - \epsilon,$$

i.e. each coalition is given the same subsidy.

For the Weak Nucleolus

$$f(c(S), \epsilon) = c(S) - |S| \epsilon;$$

i.e., each coalition gets a subsidy which depends on the number of members in the coalition.

For the Proportional Nucleolus

$$f(c(S), \epsilon) = c(S) - [c(S) - \sum_{i \in S} c(i)] \epsilon.$$

In this case there is a constant subsidy rate but the subsidy rate is proportional to the *savings* that the coalition leads to, compared to everyone being on his own.

A fourth solution concept based on game theory, but not necessarily within the core, was also discussed: The Shapley Value. One way of representing this value is the following: The grand coalition is formed step by step; first one party joins together with another party to form a two-party coalition. Then one more party is added to form a three-party coalition, and then another party is added to form a four-party coalition, etc., until finally the grand coalition is formed. There are many ways or orders in which such a procedure can take place, depending on which party "signs up" first, and which party "signs up" next. For each order, a party joining a coalition is thought only to pay the incremental costs, $c(S) - c(S - i)$, (i.e., the difference between the cost of the new coalition and the cost of the one he joins). The Shapley Value for each party is then the party's *average* payments, computed over all coalition formation orders.

Finally, a fifth method is presented. A modified version of the Separable Cost-Remaining Benefits (SCRB). This method has been developed specifically for practical use in water resource planning. We define the marginal cost for a party $c'(i)$ as $c(N) - c(N - i)$, i.e. the marginal cost of being the last to join the *grand coalition*. Next the "remaining benefit" $r(i)$ is defined as $= c(i) - c'(i)$, i.e., the difference between the cost if the municipality goes alone and its marginal costs. The payment made by party i is then computed as:

$$x_i = c'(i) + [r(i) / \sum_{j=1}^{N} r(j)] [c(N) - \sum_{j=1}^{N} c'(j)]$$

i.e., marginal cost *plus* its share of the non-allocated costs, where the share is set in relation to the party's share of remaining benefits.

On the basis of real cost data regarding the actual situation in Southern Sweden, a cost table was computed for each of the possible coalitions that these six municipality groups could form. The results are in Table 1 below, where costs are specified in millions of Swedish Crowns.

On the basis of this data, the allocations were computed according to the five procedures discussed above, and also on the basis of population and demand. These cost allocations in millions of Swedish Crowns are given in Table 2.

Comparing these two tables, it can first of all be seen that the allocations based on population and demand violate the principle of *individual* rationality, for example for *M*, who on his own can get away with 20.81 (see. Table 1).

A	21.95	AHK	40.74	AHKL	48.95
H	17.08	AHL	43.22	AHKM	60.25
K	10.91	AHM	55.50	AHKT	62.72
L	15.88	AHT	56.67	AHLM	64.03
M	20.81	AKL	48.74	AHLT	65.20
T	21.98	AKM	53.40	AHMT	74.10
		AKT	54.85	AKLM	63.96
AH	34.69	ALM	53.05	AKLT	70.72
AK	32.86	ALT	59.81	ALMT	73.41
AL	37.83	AMT	61.36	HKLM	48.07
AM	42.76	HKL	27.26	HKLT	49.24
AT	43.93	HKM	42.55	HKMT	59.35
HK	22.96	HKT	44.94	HLMT	64.41
HL	25.00	HLM	45.81	KLMT	56.61
HM	37.89	HLT	46.98	AKMT	72.27
HT	39.06	HMT	56.49	AHKLM	69.76
KL	26.79	KLM	42.01	AHKMT	77.42
KM	31.45	KLT	48.77	AHLMT	83.00
KT	32.89	KMT	50.32	AHKLT	70.93
LM	31.10	LMT	51.46	AKLMT	73.97
LT	37.86			HKLMT	66.46
MT	39.41				
				AHKLMT	83.82

Tab. 1: Total cost of each possible coalition

	A	H	K	L	M	T
Population Proportional	10.13	21.00	3.19	8.22	34.22	7.07
Demand Proportional	13.07	16.01	7.30	6.87	28.48	12.08
SCRB	19.54	13.28	5.62	10.90	16.66	17.82
Shapley Value	20.01	10.71	6.61	10.37	16.94	19.18
Nucleolus	20.35	12.06	5.00	8.61	18.32	19.49
Weak Nucleolus	20.03	12.52	3.94	9.07	18.54	19.71
Proportional Nucleolus	20.36	12.46	3.52	8.67	18.82	19.99

Tab. 2: Allocations in Millions of Swedish Crowns

Furthermore, the SCRB and the Shapley Value procedures can be criticized because none of them satisfied the principle of group rationality. Let us look at the coalition HKL. According to the SCRB procedure, HKL shall together pay 29.80 and according to the Shapley Value 27.69. Should they not join the grand coalition, but remain satisfied with the three-party coalition HKL, they would only have to pay the cost of this coalition, or 27.26. Hence, neither the SCRB nor the Shapley Value belong to the core.

Hence only the three types of core solution remain. The choice between these methods is based on other general principles.

One is the so-called *monotonicity principle,* that if total costs go down, no one should be charged more, and if total costs go up, no one shall pay less. It can next be shown that the Nucleolus violates this principle in this game. If, for example the costs of the grand coalition *increased* from 83.82 to 87.82 K's payment according to the Nucleolus would *decrease* from 5.00 to 4.51.

Choosing finally between the Weak Nucleolus and the Proportional Nucleolus, Young/Okada/Hashimoto favor the Proportional Nucleolus, since the Weak Nucleolus does not fulfill another principle: A player who never contributes to any cost savings when joining with other parties or coalitions, should *not* realize any cost savings above his go alone costs.

Rules of the Game

On the basis of this work, in particular on the basis of the table depicting the total cost of each possible coalition, a game has been constructed. The game involves some transformation of the money amount, e.g., single crowns instead of millions of crowns.

In the game there are six players. By lottery, each player is assigned the role of the representative if one of the six municipalities: A, H, K, L, M or T. Next, the players are seated around a small table.

The idea is that each municipality will now try to solve its water supply problem as cheaply as possible by entering into a coalition with some other municipality or municipalities. When forming a coalition, the players reach an agreement on how much each of the participants in the formed coalition shall pay of the total cost of the whole coalition.

Should a municipality not enter into a coalition with any other municipality, it will pay that sum in Table 1 which represents what each municipality would be obligated to pay if acting alone. By acting skillfully both during the formation of coalitions and during the allocation of the total costs within the coalition, each player can get away with a lower payment, in some cases, a considerably lower one.

As soon as a coalition has been formed and an agreement has been reached as to the allocation of the total costs of this coalition among its members, they register the coalition with the game leader. He will record the names of the coalition participants, as well as the payment each of them would make toward the total costs of the coalition. Once a coalition has been registered, its content, i.e., the participants and the cost allocation, is announced to all participants of the game.

A coalition does not come into force, however, until a certain time (e.g., 15 minutes) has elapsed since its registration, and then, only provided that none of its members has been registered in another coalition during this period. Hence a player can leave one coalition and join another in order to decrease the amount of his payment. Furthermore, a coalition dissolves by registering a new coalition with additional members.

Once a coalition has come into force, each of its members "pays" the game leader the amount agreed upon at the time of the registration. The game can either be played by using real money (e.g. single crowns instead of millions of crowns in table 1) or using completely ficticious money.[5])

The game continues in this way until all participants are members of a coalition which has come into force (with the possible exception of a single "leftover" participant). Should the game continue more than 90 minutes from the time of its start, it will be brought to an end and the coalitions registered but not broken, will come into force.

The Playing of the Game

The game has up to now been played sixteen times, in five different countries, and with both real decision makers, researchers and doctoral students, as shown in table 3.

Game	Location	Types of Players
1	Sweden	Water planners in Skane
2	Italy	Regional planners in Tuscany
3,4	IIASA, Austria	Swedish doctoral students of economic geography
5,6,7	IIASA, Austria	Young Scientists from eight countries
8	Poland	Water planners
9	Poland	Researchers and Doctoral students in planning
10	Bulgaria	Water planners
11	Bulgaria	Researchers in planning and management
12,13	Bulgaria	Students in Management Development Program
14	Sweden	Regional planners in Northern Sweden
15,16	Sweden	Doctoral students of economics (15) and business administration (16)

Tab. 3: Location and types of players

Due to the fact that the game, including instructions, can be run in a couple of hours, it has not been any major problem to obtain suitable subjects to play the game. For example, it should be mentioned that the first game was played with Swedish water planners mainly from the involved municipalities.

The experimental set up varied somewhat from experiment to experiment. Eleven of the sixteen games were played with a purely predictive aim, while the remaining games were adjusted somewhat to allow also for some kind of more direct testing of the normative purpose of the models.

---

[5]) While preferring to use real money, we had for administrative reasons, to give a prize to only the "best player" in some games. Since the amounts of real money was fairly small and the players were in general well motivated, this difference did not appear to have played any major role in the results. See *Ståhl* [1981a].

In three of these games the players were, before the playing of the game, given a one hour lecture on the game theoretic analysis, presented above. In two of these games (games 5 and 6) each player obtained a "consultant's report", suggesting he should argue for one specific method and outlining the main arguments for this method. Each player got a different report to argue for[6]), in general that method which happened to be the most favorable for him, e.g., the Shapley value for player H, the proportional nucleolus for player K, etc.

In the remaining game (game 7), the parties had to specify their distribution for two cost levels for the grand coalition, both 83.82 and 87.82. This was done in order to focus the attention of the players on the monotonicity principle, which, as noted above, played an important role in the game theoretic analysis. This two-cost-level approach was also used in another game, (game 4), in which, however, we did not give the players any game theory.

In another game (game 15), the parties started the game with a sealed bid auction, based on a model suggested by Young. Each party was initially told only his own go alone costs and that the cost of the grand coalition was roughly 100. He could then make a sealed bid to a government agency stating how much he would be willing to pay in order to be included in some kind of coalition. The agency would then look at each of the coalitions in table 1; compute the surplus of this coalition as the difference between what the parties in this coalition were willing to pay according to the sealed bids and the actual costs of this coalition (in table 1): select that coalition which led to the highest surplus and announce which parties would be included and obtain water at the costs they had bid. Those not included paid their go alone costs. This "auction" procedure took place more than once, since we allowed players to reconsider. By repeated bidding the parties could improve their savings. Those not included in one round could bid more

Game	A	H	K	L	M	T
1	21.15	9.70	6.00	9.10	18.37	19.50
2	20.81	9.55	6.10	8.88	18.72	19.77
3	18.15	12.77	8.10	13.25	12.90	18.65
4	18.56	13.79	6.75	8.00	17.66	19.05
5	18.65	10.38	6.60	9.18	19.21	19.80
6	21.02	9.85	6.29	9.15	17.83	19.68
7	20.65	10.84	4.67	9.65	18.42	19.59
8	18.80	10.19	5.80	9.42	19.81	19.80
9	19.02	10.54	5.98	9.94	19.78	18.56
10	19.23	10.63	6.82	9.81	18.10	19.23
11	17.87	12.56	8.10	11.80	15.40	17.99
12	16.79	14.08	7.90	10.18	18.91	19.50
13	21.95	13.50	5.50	8.26	20.81	21.98
14	19.50	10.50	6.00	9.50	18.82	19.50
15	19.75	10.66	7.99	8.99	16.75	19.75
16	18.89	8.27	6.90	12.09	19.41	18.23

Tab. 4: Game Results

---

[6]) All methods in table 2, except allocating costs in proportion to population, were used. See Ståhl [1981a].

in order to be included in the next round. Those included could bid less, hoping to still be included but save more money. The auction was in this case broken up after six rounds. Then all players were included. The players could then either jointly agree on this distribution of costs or negotiate a new agreement like in the other games. With the agency's surplus significant, the players started such a negotiation.

Another difference in the experimental set up was that in eight of the games (games 2, 10-16) information was given concerning both water demand and population, in seven games (games 3-9), information was given only on water demand and in one game (game 1), no data was given on either of these.

The results, i.e., the players' final payments in the 16 games are summed up in Table 4.

In order to see how well the theoretical allocations fit these experimental values, we have used three measures of difference:

1) The sum of absolute differences. With T_i as the theoretical value and E_i as the experimental value for party i, the measure is:

$$\sum_{i=1}^{6} |T_i - E_i|.$$

2) The sum of the squared differences, i.e.,

$$\sum_{i=1}^{6} (T_i - E_i)^2.$$

Compared to measure 1, this gives a higher relative weight to large discrepancies.

3) The sum of the relative squared differences, i.e., of the squared differences after dividing each difference by the theoretical value, i.e.,

$$\sum_{i=1}^{6} (T_i - E_i)^2 / T_i.$$

The idea behind this measure is that a difference is more important if it is relatively large in comparison with the "expected" value.

For all games we have calculated these measures for each of the seven methods of distribution earlier presented, for example in table 2. We have then for each game ranked the methods, regarding one method as better than another, if it has a lower value for at least two different measures.[7]) We then give the best method the rank 1 and the worst the rank 7.

We can now summarize the findings from all sixteen games in table 5, in which we present the average difference measures as well as the average ranking values.

We have in this table also given the difference measures for the case when we used the outcome in the Swedish game as a predictor of what would happen in the other games. Since this measure is meaningless in the Swedish game, we have not included this measure in the average ranks.

The most striking outcome to be seen in table 5 is how far away the actual performance is from allocations according to demand or population. The reason is not that the play-

---

[7]) Although we could theoretically get a problem of intransitivity this has fortunately not happened in any of these games.

ers ignored this data; in fact, in more than half of the games there were strong efforts to base the cost distribution on either demand or population. It was, however, not possible to obtain an agreement on such allocations for any larger coalitions, because individual rationality would then be violated. In fact individual rationality, i.e., that a municipality will not accept higher costs than its go-alone costs, appeared as a very valid principle. In all 16 games there were only three instances when a violation of this principle was close. In games 3, 4 and 13, each involving students, distributions involving a violation of this principle were about to be registered. At each instance, however, when the game leader asked whether all parties agreed, the distribution proposal was retracted.

	Average Rank	1	2	3
Shapley Value	1.75	7.26	13.67	1.06
Swedish Game		7.16	17.36	1.42
Nucleolus	2.00	7.97	17.26	1.69
Weak Nucleolus	3.31	8.74	21.65	3.01
SCRB	3.62	9.99	23.12	1.80
Prop. Nucleolus	4.31	9.93	25.74	3.96
Demand	6.00	32.90	244.86	15.00
Population	7.00	52.60	616.83	47.23

Tab. 5: Average difference measures for sixteen games

The second fact to be observed in the table is that among the game theoretic methods the difference measures are larger for the methods which were favored in the game theoretic analysis mentioned above. The Proportional Nucleolus preferred in this analysis is at the bottom among these methods, while the Shapley Value, which is not even in the core, is at the top, slightly ahead of the Nucleolus, which although in the core, violates the monotonicity principle.

In this connection it should be mentioned that the solution was outside the core in 10 of the 16 games. Of the six games with the solution in the core,[8] three were the games when the players had obtained information about the game theoretic analysis *prior* to the playing. One might hypothesize that the core concept is more valid as a normative concept than as a predictive concept. It should, however, be noted that even in these three "normative" experiments the Shapley Value fared better than the Proportional Nucleolus.

The question then naturally arises why the players did not play more in line with the game theoretically "best" solution. One important reason seems to be the fact that in all sixteen games the parties did *not* form the grand coalitions directly without first forming some smaller coalition(s). In many games, a two or three party coalition was first formed and then a five party coalition, before the forming of the grand coalition. The actual coalition formation procedure was thus more in line with the Shapley Value, implicitly assuming a step by step build up of the grand coalition, than with the Core solutions, which do not take any gradual coalition formation into account.

---

[8] In two of these games the solution lay exactly on the boundary of the core.

It is furthermore of importance to mention that we found no obvious differences in results between different countries. The difference between different types of players (planners with experience, students with no practical experience etc.), seemed more important.[9] For instance, in both the game in Italy and in Poland, the outcome of the Swedish game was the best predictor and in the game with the Bulgarian water planners the Swedish game was the second best predictor, only slightly behind the Shapley Value.

This does not rule out that the actual negotiation process appeared quite different in different countries, e.g., as regards the amount of arguments exchanged etc.

The difference in behavior that appeared to exist between, for example, planners and students with little experience of the actual kind of problem, indicates that it might be well worth the extra cost to involve as far as possible "real decision makers" when one wants to use gaming as a test of models ultimately aimed at aiding real decisions.

3. CO_2-Emission and Coal Trade Game

At IIASA, there has been considerable research in the field of energy. Among the many topics covered are the future use of coal and the relation between carbon dioxide emission from the combustion of coal and changes in climate.[10] One question is, what would be the effects on the climate if the CO_2 contents in the atmosphere were doubled?

Some of the research has indicated that such a doubling of CO_2 might take place a little more than half a century from now, due mainly to the possible rapid increase in the combustion of coal. It could possibly lead to a general increase of global temperature of a couple of degrees, leading, e.g., to a substantial change in conditions for agricultural production in some countries. It should, however, be stressed that there is a great uncertainty both regarding how much coal will be combusted and what the effects will be of various levels of CO_2 emissions.

A project with a new focus on these two issues has recently been started at IIASA: Carbon and Climate gaming.[11]

The project is a joint effort by Jesse Ausubel, John Lathrop, Jennifer Robinson and the author. This section of the paper relies heavily on the input of the other members of this team.

The project aims at producing two games: One board game with a wide educational purpose and one computer game.

At least in its more developed stages, the computer game will be a research tool intended to raise and to give some very preliminary answers to specific questions about the CO_2 issue. For example, will potentially threatening levels of CO_2 be created or not? What is a likely range of total accumulated CO_2 emissions? If created, what kind of a global market does a CO_2 problem presuppose? Will it be possible for the big coal producing nations to form and enforce some sort of cartel? As the atmospheric CO_2

---

[9] This is discussed further in, e.g., *Ståhl* [1980c].

[10] For example, see Energy in a Finite World, a report in two volumes by the Energy Systems Program Group of IIASA. For specific information on CO_2 see *Williams* [1978] and on coal see *Grenon* [1979].

[11] A more detailed overview of this project is given in *Ausubel/Lathrop/Ståhl/Robinson* [1980].

content increases, will the interest become stronger in control strategies and will strategies of reducing carbon extraction, trade or emissions be preferred? An important question is whether there are institutional scenarios (treaties, cartels and so forth) which will help to avoid the "Tragedy of the Commons" outcome of the CO_2 problem.

Obviously, the answers to these questions will be dependent on the specific character of the game, including the data base used. However, the game will be oriented toward indicating what scenarios are more likely given various information and institutional arrangements. The questions and the tentative answers will be intended mainly to serve as a basis for future discussions both with regard to what kind of research is most urgently needed and which outcome scenarios are acceptable to various interested groups.

The computer game focuses on coal, trade and many countries.

Why Coal: The main cause of the problem in the long run as regards the release of carbon dioxide is the burning of coal. Coal is likely to account for two-thirds or more of the emissions in a scenario of serious climatic change. In fact, present estimates of total resources of oil, gas, coal, and other forms of carbon indicate that atmospheric carbon dioxide levels regarded by some experts as critical (for example, a doubling of the present level within the next century) can only be reached by very substantial burning of coal. Other carbon resources are simply not available in large enough quantities. Because coal plays this critical role in the CO_2 issue, it is logical to begin game development with emphasis on coal.

Why Trade? About 80% of the coal deposits of the world are in the hands of three big countries: The USSR, the USA and China. Thus, in discussing possibly dangerous levels of CO_2, one can conclude in theory that if these three large players do not export any coal and also keep their own coal combustion low, a severe CO_2 emission problem will not arise. However, by far the largest part of future potential coal combustion lies in the world outside of these three players. Much of this coal would come from imports over a long period of time. Hence, the main CO_2 emission threat arises from scenarios, like the one that can be projected from the recent MIT World Coal Study, where roughly a tenfold increase in world coal trade is envisaged. The trade in coal is also of interest in connection with different schemes of international cooperation to reduce or prevent CO_2 emissions. The possibility for the larger countries to limit supplies of coal either on the world market or to specific countries can give "teeth" to attempts at enforcing international trade in coal. This feature is important when discussing whether coal prices will be cartelistic and thus high, discouraging the use of coal, or more formed by competition and thus cost-based, possibly leading to a rapid increase in combustion. The game will attempt to capture the essential aspects of a world coal market as it relates to the CO_2 problem while avoiding the considerable complexities of a detailed market simulation.

Why Many Countries? The computer game will try to represent a world where many countries, acting independently, affect the problem. The first reason for this is that a major portion of energy consumption will be taking place outside of the three big countries in a great many smaller countries. These can act independently and use this independence to their own advantage. Secondly, even if the three big players account for around 80% of total coal resources, the resources of some smaller holders are large from an absolute point of view. Around a dozen countries have probable resources that alone could lead to a level of emissions of the same size as total global emissions during the whole of the last decade. Ultimately, one would probably wish to include about twenty countries of different sizes to catch fully the strategic problem. If we limit ourselves to only a handful of actors in all phases of development of the game, we would exclude certain scenarios where international cooperation is impeded by the actions of several relatively small countries.

The playing of this game would take place both at IIASA and outside IIASA, first with scientists, and then with visitors in connection with IIASA workshops on related topics, such as energy policy, environmental protection, etc. Outside of IIASA, the game would be played with interested groups of people from government, industry and academic communities of various countries.

In order to have the computer game played frequently with such persons engaged in energy policy it must be of a convenient duration, for example three hours. Allowing for about ten rounds in a game, each round, therefore, calls for only a small number of decisions by each player. The actions of each player at each round of the game include mainly a coal extraction decision, a coal trade decision (supply or demand), a decision on the total amount of energy consumed and carbon combusted (implying a certain level of CO_2 emission), and a decision relating to emission control.

After market clearing calculations at the end of each round, players are informed about the price of coal, their status as regards coal extraction and coal trade, total CO_2 emission in the world, as well as their present "welfare" measured in the form of an index. In the early stages of the game, welfare would be largely a function of the size of coal combustion. In the later stages of the game, however, effects of global environmental change would begin significantly to affect in varying ways the welfare of individual players, depending on the accumulated level of atmospheric CO_2.

An important part of the construction of the game is the modeling of how coal costs develop in different countries. It is important that the players consider these forecasts to be reasonable. Hence it has appeared suitable to construct a man-computer dialogue system by which a player, perhaps playing the role of his own country, can construct his own new cost function or modify an existing one. This dialogue system is described in Ståhl [1980d]. A similar procedure is foreseen, for example, for determining how the short-run welfare of a country depends on the amount of coal combusted.

The construction of the computer-based game is to take place in several stages. In the first versions of the game there would only be human players involved. Since the game has to be administratively simple only a limited number of human players can participate. Thus, less than ten countries can be studied in such a manual game. This limitation causes an important problem, since, as noted above, we are ultimately interested in studying a world with many more countries acting independently. A preliminary plan for taking care of this problem is to design a game which can take advantage of the computer's capacity to simulate additional players. This computer-based game might thus have the following form. It would include the three big countries (USSR, USA, China) and four smaller countries. The roles of these seven countries would be played by humans. Besides this, the playing of some ten or more countries would be simulated by the computer. These "robot players" would act partly in the way that the four smaller-country human players acted in previous games.

References

Ausubel, J., J. Lathrop, I. Ståhl and *J. Robinson*: Carbon and Climate Gaming. Working Paper IIASA Laxenburg, 1980.

Birr, M. et alia: REMUS (Rechnergestütztes Entscheidungsmodell für Umweltsimulation). Ottobrunn 1977.

Cruikshank, D.R., and *R.A. Telfer*: Simulations and Games: An ERIC Bibliography. Washington 1979.

Grenon, M. (Ed.): Future Coal Supply for the World Energy Balance. Oxford 1979.

Gibbs, G.E. (Ed.): Handbook of Games and Simulation Exercises. London 1979.

Horn, R.E., and *A. Cleaves*: The Guide to Simulations/Games for Education and Training, 4th Edition. Lexington, Mass. 1980.

IIASA Energy Systems Program Group: Energy in a Finite World. Vls. 1 and 2. Cambridge 1981. 1981.

Kumata, Y., et alia: An Approach to the Evaluation of Alternative Programs for the Nuclear Power Plant Construction Using the Gaming Simulation. Papers at the meeting of Association of City Planning. Japan 1975, 72–78. (In Japanese.)

Leijondeckers, I.P.: The Solar Boiler Sequence Dilema. Papers at the International Symposium on Non-Technical Obstacles to the Use of Solar Energy. Brussels 1980.

Rohn, W.E.: Literatur-Liste über Planspiel-Veröffentlichungen. Wuppertal 1980.

Smit, P.: Bibliografie rond Operationele Spielen. Utrecht 1975.

Ståhl, I.: A Gaming Experiment on Cost Allocation in Water Resources Development. Working Paper IIASA, Laxenburg, 1980a.

–: The Application of Game Theory and Gaming to Conflict Resolution in Regional Planning. Working Paper IIASA, Laxenburg 1980b.

–: Cost Allocation in Water Resources-Two Gaming Experiments with Doctoral Students. Working Paper IIASA, Laxenburg 1980c.

–: An Interactive Model for Determining Coal Costs for a CO_2-game. Working Paper IIASA, Laxenburg 1980d.

–: Cost Allocation in Water Resources – Three Gaming Experiments with Young Scientists at IIASA. Working Paper IIASA, Laxenburg 1981a.

Ståhl, I., R. Wasniowski and *I. Assa*: Cost Allocation in Water Resources – Six Gaming Experiments in Poland and Bulgaria. Working Paper IIASA, Laxenburg 1981b.

Young, H.P.: Cost Allocation and Demand Revelation in Public Enterprises. Working Paper IIASA, Laxenburg 1980.

Young, H.P., N. Okada and *T. Hashimoto*: Cost Allocation in Water Resources Development – A case study of Sweden. Working Paper and Research Report IIASA, Laxenburg 1979 and 1980.

Williams, J. (Ed.): Carbon Dioxide, Climate and Society. Oxford 1978.

World Coal Study: COAL-Bridge to the Future. Cambridge, Mass. 1980.

Economic Theory of Natural Resources. ©Physica-Verlag, Würzburg–Wien, 1982.

Energy-Macro-Modeling in the Federal Republic of Germany

Götz Uebe

1. Introduction

As in other countries there has been quite an effort to model the role of energy in the Federal Republic of Germany. In addition to those models which I will review or cite here, there are additional models presented in this volume (by Jansen, Jorgenson-Frameni, Kümmel), and models published late in 1980, such as in Voss-Schmitz, e.g. Mischke (Battelle model), Schmitz (Jülich model). These are not reviewed in detail. However, most of the points of the paper to follow can be found in these later publications, too, provided there is documentation.

In order to obtain a feeling for the huge literature and the very many models I have prepared a printout from our bibliography of macro-models [*Uebe/Huber/Fischer*] referring to the keyword energy (Appendix 1). This is a subset of work only with respect to energy, namely macro and quantitative, formal empirical work. Even with this restriction there are more than 170 references. With respect to the Federal Republic of Germany there are considerably less references, approximately 60 (Appendix 2). However, even for a brief review there are a dozen or so distinct models. Differently from an approach such as Charpentier's or Kline's energy models are not presented on a tabular basis. The purpose is to review energy model-building *ideas* across models. Secondly and differently from an apparant mainstream thinking energy models proper cannot be considered to be *the* center of focus per se. Energy models must be seen against the total background of macro modeling. Thirdly energy models in this author's view do not deserve scientific attention just because they are big, discussed by very articulate proponents or used politically. Obviously the plain size of the energy modeling effort deserves a review. However, even more important is the well-known factual background of the OPEC price rounds, the exhaustion of energy resources (?), the economic implications of energy problems, economic feedbacks into energy, etc., etc. . .

The ideas to be presented are

(i)   some ad hoc theorizing using a brief look at some time series,
(ii) a short description of the energy balances, and related analyses,
(iii) the outline of two basic model types:
      – the input-output model,
      – the simulation type model,
(iv) a review of some model realizations of these two types.

612

2. The Income Elasticity Approach

For the Federal Republic, e.g. seen against the U.S., energy modeling is different with respect to two distinct characteristics: First, factually there is practically no domestic energy source, except for coal. Secondly, the facts in energy relations are different: there is no "iron link" between energy and income (as it is called in the most recent book by Koreisha and Stobaugh) such as

$$E = f(Y) \tag{1}$$

$$\epsilon := \frac{dE}{E} \frac{Y}{dY} \tag{2}$$

(E energy flows, Y national income, ϵ a constant elasticity).

What is known for the total economy, e.g. by Hoffmeyer and Neu, and what is plotted in figure 1, there is no constant elasticity of energy with respect to income. Using whatsoever fancy statistical specification, for the total economy the above link could not be corroborated. A different picture arises for individual sectors of the economy for which Kriegsmann has been able to find significant, yet very much distinct elasticities. The only

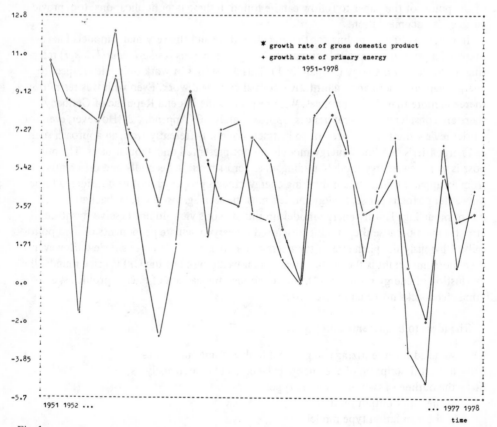

Fig. 1

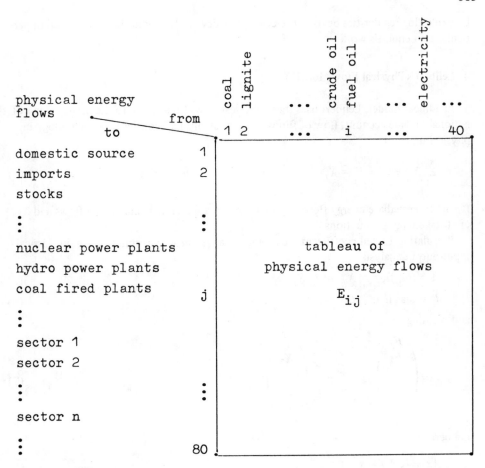

Fig. 2: A simplified energy balance

conclusion supportable is of utmost precautiousness. Possibly there is a sectoral meaning-ful summary measure such as (1)–(2). However, aggregation may blur the results, i.e. one must turn to the details.

3. The Energy Balance

One such detailed structure has been for many years the well established compilation of energy balances. For the Federal Republic they have been built by the "Arbeitsgemein-schaft" since the early seventies. I.e. one considers a set of physical energy flows

$$((E_{ij})) \quad \begin{matrix} (i = 1, 2, \ldots, I \approx 80; \ i \text{ primary energy sources)} \\ (j = 1, 2, \ldots, J \approx 40; \ j \text{ secondary energy sinks).} \end{matrix} \qquad (3)$$

Surprisingly, or considering figure 1, not so surprisingly, these flows are quite unstable. It seems to be very difficult to establish a smoothly developing sequence of such tables, by exploiting regularities beyond the descriptive device. This point has been raised in particular by Lehbert's work.

4. Lehbert's Physical Flow Model[1])

In a linear model, Lehbert uses these physical flows (in analogy to the money flows of national income account, flow of funds etc.) to establish a Leontief-type technology in physical units:

$$\sum_{j=1}^{n} X_{ij} + L_i + F_i = X_i \qquad (i = 1, 2, \ldots, n), \ n = 8. \tag{4}$$

X_{ij} are intermediate energy flows, L_i are losses, F_i are final demand energy flows and X_i are total energy productions.

Postulating a fixed coefficient technology — a well proven assumption e.g. in classical input-output-analysis —

$$A = ((a_{ij})); \qquad X_{ij} := a_{ij} X_j \tag{5}$$
$$\hat{l} = \text{diag}\,(l_i); \qquad L_i := l_i X_i \tag{6}$$

and defining

$$f := \begin{pmatrix} F_1 \\ F_2 \\ \vdots \\ F_n \end{pmatrix}; \qquad x := \begin{pmatrix} X_1 \\ X_2 \\ \vdots \\ X_n \end{pmatrix}. \tag{7}$$

Lehbert obtains

$$Ax + \hat{l}x + f = x \tag{8}$$

respectively

$$x = (I - A - \hat{l})^{-1} f \tag{9}$$

i.e. a model completely corresponding to usual input-output analysis. However, the empirical final result (9), to be used for forecasting and policy analysis (by varying f, respectively any coefficient of A and/or $\hat{l}$) is not satisfactory. Lehbert's analysis clarifies a number of valuable points:

(1)   All data problems which are well known for national income accounts, flow of funds or any other large body of statistical aggregates in money terms are re-encountered,

(2)   The coefficients $(A, \hat{l})$ are not of reasonable constancy. At least for the Federal Republic there are no such tight engineering facts. Energy models are much richer than such a model can depict. Even if there is a computerized projection of energy balances such as in Lenhardt et alii, such descriptive devices must be augmented:

---

[1]) The derivation of an equivalent model is given by Nordhaus (1977, p. 241).

(3) Energy modeling must be related to total macro-economic models in general. It can only be understood against the background of macro-modeling in total. Neglect of this embedding, which one may call a myopic energy model type, may be the source of the only result, which we know is true, i.e. energy modeling has been generally wrong for orders on magnitude with exceptions. (See e.g. the review of Gately or Henize.)

5. Some German Economy Wide Energy Models (Input-Output-Analysis)

The energy sector is part of the economy and not even a large part. Hence for the Federal Republic one has to be aware of the economy wide models (Appendix 3). There are about 100 models, small, medium and large, Keynesian monetarist, input-output, simulation, econometric, etc., and in very few of them energy is even mentioned. Basically there are about 10 models in which energy is modeled explicitly. (Table 1, a first subset; for the remainder see 9.)

The basic approach is Leontief's fundamental (difference) equation

$$A_t x_t (+ B_t \Delta x_t) + f_t = x_t \tag{10}$$

where the interindustry matrix is partitioned into energy and non-energy sectors:

$$A := A_t = \begin{pmatrix} A_{11t} & A_{12t} \\ \hline A_{21t} & A_{22t} \end{pmatrix} \quad \begin{matrix} \} & \text{Energy sectors} \\ \\ \} & \text{Non-energy sectors.} \end{matrix} \tag{11}$$

Obviously the distinction is a data problem. The applications of high disaggregation are (i) one shot affairs, with no follow up studies (e.g. Bonhöffer, Britschkat), or (ii) they are based on quite old input-output tables (see e.g. Pestel) or (iii) they are combined with model-building approaches of doubtful validity (see below section 9). The second distinction is constancy of the interindustry coefficient. The system differs corresponding whether the A-Matrix is constant or not. For the non-constant case, two subcases can be distinguished

$$A = \begin{cases} A_t & A \text{ is a matrix function of time} & (12.1) \\ \\ A(x) & A \text{ is systematically adjusted by the endogenous} & (12.2) \\ & \text{structure of the remainder of the model.} \end{cases}$$

Subcase (12.1) may be based on observed trends, and/or the good (or not so good) judgment of the model builder. For the more interesting subcase (12.2), there are only two applications, the Chemical Industry Study and the Conrad replica of the Hudson Jorgenson model.

6. The Chemical Industry Study

This model is a system of (linked) sectoral submodels, which is a lucid illustration a) how energy modeling pervades total relations of an industry and b) how various techniques can (must) be combined to obtain a proper modeling.

The model consists of

(i) a system dynamics model of capital formation, which determines investment, depreciation and technical progress.

$$\dot{y}_1 = f(y_1, x_1, a_1) \tag{13}$$

(ii) an LP of "optimal" product mix

$$c_2' y_2 \Rightarrow \text{Min}$$

$$\text{s.t. } A_2 y_2 = b_2 \tag{14}$$

$$y_2 \geqslant 0$$

where the coefficients of (14) are determined by (13), i.e.

$$c_2 = c_2(y_1)$$

$$b_2 = b_2(y_1) \tag{15}$$

$$A_2 = A_2(y_1)$$

(iii) a model solution dependent interindustry matrix and an economy wide input-output model, i.e. (10), where

$$A = (A_{.1} A_{.2} \ldots A_{.n}) \tag{16}$$

and each individual column is possibly generated by (14)

$$A_{.i} = A_{.i}(y_2) \qquad i \in \{1, 2, \ldots, n\} \tag{17}$$

(iv) an interactive linkage of submodels (i)–(ii)–(iii).

7. Conrad's Adaptation of the Jorgenson-Hudson Model of the U.S.

The approach is a complete economy wide econometric model with the centerpiece of fully endogenous interindustry coefficients, of the type

$$A = ((a_{ij})); \quad a_{ij} = (a_i + \sum_k b_{ik} \ln f_{kj} p_k) \frac{p_j}{f_{ij} p_i} \tag{18}$$

(a_i, b_{ik} constant coefficients, p_j prices to be determined by the full model, f_{kj} additional parameters of the model, see e.g. Conrad, Friede).

8. Energy Modeling as a Subcase of Input-Output-Analysis

Partitioning of sectors, time dependence of the interindustry matrix, adjustment of coefficients due to changes in the remainder of the model obviously can be seen as a general problem of interindustry analysis (Appendix 4).

author(s)	A-Matrix	number of sectors	number of energy sectors	type of Leontief system	determination of final demand	general structure of model
Bonhöffer, Britschkat	constant	97 (60+37)	37	static	exogenous	input-output
Pestel, Oest, Bauerschmidt (Henize) ISP-model	constant and/or A_t	19	1	static	exogenous (scenario)	input-output; system dynamics
Kononov, Voss	constant	31 (26+5)	5	dynamic	exogenous (scenario)	simulation; input-output
Brand, Jochem, Herz, et al.	constant and/or A_t	41	?	static	exogenous (scenario)	simulation; system dynamics
Dieckheuer, et al.	constant	12	1	dynamic part of econometric model	Keynesian econometric model	system of difference equations
Pfeiffer, et al. (Chemical Industry Study)	$A(x)$	56	3 (7)	dynamic	system of LP, system-dynamics model and input-output-model	
Conrad	$A(x)$	14 (9+5)	5	part of econometric model	econometric model, Hudson-Jorgenson replica	

Tab. 1: Some energy models based on Leontief's input-output-technique

Example 1: The adjustment of coefficients

How to change input-output coefficients has been an old topic in input-output analysis independent of energy problems, e.g. by a price dependent scheme independently proposed by Krelle-Frerichs and Kreijger

$$A = ((a_{ij})); \qquad a_{ij} = a_{ij0} \prod_{k=1}^{n} \left(\frac{p_k}{p_j} \right)^{b_{kj}} . \tag{19}$$

Example 2: Static versus dynamic input-output models

Energy models may be static input-output models, i.e. those in which the capital matrix term in (10) in brackets drops out (e.g. Bonhöffer-Britschkat). However, an apparently static formulation

$$Ax_t + f_t = x_t \tag{10}'$$

combined with a remainder of the model, say

$$x_t = Gx_{t-1} + Hf_t \tag{20}$$

(G and H matrices) may produce a dynamic model (e.g. Dieckheuer, The Chemical Industry Study):

$$x_t = AGx_{t-1} + (AH + I)f_t. \tag{21}$$

(21), however, corresponds to (10) solved for x:

$$x_t = -(I - A_t - B_t)^{-1}x_{t-1} + (I - A_t - B_t)^{-1}f_t. \tag{22}$$

I.e. total input-output-analysis is applicable.

9. Some German Economy wide Energy Models (Simulation Models)

A second emphasis in energy modeling — partly overlapping with that based on input-output-analysis — has been on the energy conversion problem.

The basic string of reasoning is as follows: Primary energy (E_1) is converted into secondary energy (E_2), and secondary energy is converted into tertiary energy (E_3), respectively sectoral energy "requirements". Energy modeling must describe all energy flows, say those of the energy balance and detail the summary relation (1). Hence one starts with a sectoral production function

$$F_j = F_j(\ldots, E_{3j}, \ldots) \tag{23}$$

defines

$$\frac{F_j}{E_{3j}} =: f_{3j} \tag{24}$$

and introduces into the model a relation

$$E_{3j} = f_{3j}F_j. \tag{25}$$

I.e. a typical statement of such models is:

$$\frac{\text{Energy}}{\text{requirements}} = \frac{\text{Factor}}{\text{intensity}} * \text{Product.} \tag{26}$$

Actually the model building effort usually does *not* start with (23), but with (26). The factor intensity is *not* formally derived from (23) and all desirable properties, which do belong into production theory are introduced more or less by a priori judgment by specifying a time path of f_{3j}. (See e.g. Bossel, Brand, Pestel, Rath-Nagel, Voss.) Secondly the energy requirements are computed "backwards" into primary energies, i.e.

$$\mathbf{R}^n \rightarrow \mathbf{R}^{n_1}: \quad E_3 := F(Y) \tag{27}$$

$$\mathbf{R}^{n_1} \rightarrow \mathbf{R}^{n_2}: \quad E_2 := S(E_3) \tag{28}$$

$$\mathbf{R}^{n_2} \rightarrow \mathbf{R}^{n_3}: \quad E_1 := T(E_2) \tag{29}$$

(F, S, T appropriately defined functions). In particular a linear chain of computations is popular

$$E_{3t} = F_t Y_t \tag{27}'$$

$$E_{2t} = S_t\, Y_t \tag{28$'$}$$

$$E_{1t} = T_t\, E_{2t}. \tag{29$'$}$$

Thirdly total conversion is part of an even larger model, usually a system dynamics (simulation) model

$$\dot{y} = f(y, x) \quad y \in \mathbf{R}^N, \quad x \in \mathbf{R}^K, \quad K \gg N \tag{30}$$

(y the vector of endogenous variables, including (27)–(28)–(29); x the vector of exogenous variables, parameters).

I.e. this kind of energy model is a colossal sequence of operations (see for a more detailed critique Koreisha-Stobaugh) to be analyzed by "scenarios" i.e. error and trial, to find out which of the x's determine the y's.

Again the energy sector has to be judged against the background of model building in toto. Recalling the often most acrimoniously debated factual content and structure of simulation models, this author does not want to join that contest with some more sweeping statements, except with three observations.

(i)   Considering the modest knowledge of all model builders about the true structure of past and present

(ii) recognizing the great uncertainty of the future, in particular, where structural changes will and have to be made as is typical of energy modeling

(iii) realizing the computational magnitude of (27)–(28)–(29), respectively (30) there does not seem to be any basis to place any confidence into these models per se.

10. Summary

The summary with respect to energy modeling for the Federal Republic is slightly frustrating:

(i)   There is no acceptable, i.e. well-established by reasonable ex ante forecasts or well proven policy advice — energy modeling

(ii) Energy modeling is as weak as macro modeling in general

(iii) The two basic model formats are
(1) the large general Leontief difference equation
(2) the large scale simulation model

(iv) Judging, highly subjectively, the above results, respectively non-results, the promise of improvement appears to be more with the first avenue of model building.

References

References (distinct form the references referring to the problem area "energy")

Randers, J.: Elements of the System Dynamics Method. Cambridge, Mass. 1980.

Uebe, G., G. Huber, and *J. Fischer*: A selected bibliography of macro-econometric models. 3rd microfiche edition, Technical University Munich, April 1980.

Abbreviations

Abbreviations of journals listed in appendices 1, 2, 4.

AER/S	American Economic Association, Papers and Proceedings
BEM	The Bell Journal of Economics and Management Science
CEB	Cahiers Economiques de Bruxelles
COR	Computers and Operations Research
EA	Economie Appliquée
EER	European Economic Review
EMM	Ekonomika I Matematiceskie Metody
JJER	The Journal of Japan Economic Research
OR	Operations Research
WA	Weltwirtschaftliches Archiv
WW	Wirtschaftswissenschaft
ZN	Zeitschrift für Nationalökonomie
ZS	Zeitschrift für die gesamte Staatswissenschaft

Appendix 1: References referring to the keyword "energy" (exclusive "W-Germany")

Agnew, M., L. Schrattenholzer, and *A. Voss*: A Model for the Energy Supply Systems Alternatives and their General Environmental Impact. Internationales Institut für Angewandte Systemanalyse, Laxenburg, Österreich 1979.

Al-Bashir, F.S.: A Structural Econometric Model of the Saudi Arabian Economy, 1960–1970. New York 1977.

Anders, H.D., and *H. Schilar*: Internationales Seminar zur Anwendung von Modellsystemen in der Planung. WW **23**, 1975, 1846–1851.

Aronofsky, J.S., A.G. Rao, and *M.F. Shakun*: Energy Policy. Amsterdam 1978.

Avi-Itzhak, B.: Experience with the Stanford Pilot Energy/Economic Model. Technion, Israel Institute of Technology, Haifa, Israel, and Stanford University, 1978.

Bager, G., and *L. Szabo*: A System of Models for Medium-Term Planning in Hungary. United Nations ECE/EC.AD.11, 1975, 112–144.

Bagiotti, I., and *G. Franco*: Pioneering Economics. International Essays in Honour of Giovanni Demaria. Padova 1978.

Barker, T.S. (ed.): Economic Structure and Policy with Applications to the British Economy. London 1976.

Basile, P.S.: The IISA Set of Energy Models: Its Design and Application. Internationales Institut für Angewandte Systemanalyse, Laxenburg, Österreich 1980.

Basile, P.S., and *C.L. Wilson*: Energy Supply-Demand Intergrations to the Year 2000, Global and National Studies. Cambridge, Mass. – London 1977.

Behling, D.J.J., and *R. Dullien*: A Combined Linear Programming and Econometric Systems Analysis of the Relation between Energy, Growth and the Economy. Brookhaven National Laboratory 21281, 1976.

Behling, D.J.J., et al.: The Long-Term Economic and Environmental Consequences of Phasing Out Nuclear Electricity. Modeling Energy-Economy Interactions: Five Approaches. Ed. by C.J. Hitch. Resources for the Future, Washington, D.C. 1977, 46–134.

Benenson, P. (ed.): Conference on Energy Modeling and Forecasting. Berkeley, Calif. 1975.

Bernanke, B., and *D.W. Jorgenson*: The Integration of Energy Policy Modeling. COR **2**, 1975, 225–249.

Bossel, H.: Energy Supply System: Simulation Model, Results, and Evaluation. Institut für Systemtechnik und Innovationsforschung (ISI), Karlsruhe 1974.

– : System Analysis on Programmable Pocket Calculators. Concepts and Tools of Computer-Assisted Policy Analysis, Vol. 3. Ed. by H. Bossel, 1977, 432–456.

Brain, P.: The Institute Multi-Purpose Model: An Outline. The Australian Economic Review **3**, 1977, 47–64.

Buckler, M.B., D. Gilmartin, and *T.C. Reimbold*: The Inforum Model. Advances in Input-Output Analyses, Ed. by K.R. Polenske and J.V. Skolka. Cambridge, Mass. 1976, 297–327.

Bürstenbinder, J.: Simulationsmodell für die Entwicklung des Energiesektors unter Berücksichtigung von Umweltproblemen und Kostengesichtspunkten. Energiemodelle für die Bundesrepublik Deutschland. Ed. by C. König. Basel–Stuttgart 1977, 135–159.

Carter, A.P.: Energy, Environment, and Economic Growth. BEM **5** (2), 1974, 578–592.

Charpentier, J.P.: A Review of Energy Models. No. 1 – May 1974, IIASA Publications, July 1974.

– : Overview on Techniques and Models used in the Energy Field. Energiemodelle für die Bundesrepublik Deutschland. Ed. by C. König. Basel–Stuttgart 1977, 229–259.

Cherif, M., and *Y. Guillaume*: Les Energies Douces et la Lutte Contre le Chomage en Belgique: un Exemple d'Application de la Méthode Input-Output. CEB **81**, 1979, 3–17.

Cherniavsky, E.A.: Linear Programming and Technology Assessment. Brookhaven National Laboratory, Upton, N.Y. 1975.

Cherniavsky, E.A., L.L. Juang, and *H. Abilock*: Dynamic Energy System Optimization Model. Brookhaven National Laboratory, Upton, N.Y. 1977.

Cole, H.S.D., et al.: Models of Doom, A Critique of the Limits of Growth. New York 1973.

Connolly, T.J., G.B. Dantzig, and *S.C. Parikh*: The Stanford Pilot Energy/Economic Model. Department of Operations Research, Stanford University, California 1977.

– : The Stanford Pilot Energy/Economic Model. Advances in the Economics of Energy and Resources. Vol. 1, The Structure of Energy Markets. Ed. by R.S. Pindyck. Greenwich, Conn. 1979.

Cook, E.: The Flow of Energy in an Industrial Society. Scientific American **225** (3), 1971, 135–144.

Dantzig, G.B., T.J. Connolly, and *S.C. Parikh*: The Stanford Pilot Energy/Economic Model. EPRI RA-626, Project 652-1, Interim Report, Vol. 1, Electric Power Research Institute, 1978.

Dantzig, G.B., and *S.C. Parikh*: Pilot Model for Assessing Energy-Economic Options. Pioneering Economics. International Essays in Honour of Giovanni Demari. Ed. by I. Bagiotti and G. Franco. Padova 1978, 271–276.

Deam, R.J.: World Energy Supply Analysis. Energy Research Unit, Queen Mary College, University of London 1973.

Deutsch, E.: A Decision Model under Risk and Uncertainty Emphasizing the Energy Policy. Models and Decision Making in National Economies. Ed. by J.M.L. Janssen, L.F. Pau and A. Straszak. Amsterdam 1979, 127–129.

Dickler, R.: Zum Stand der Energiesystem-Analyse in den USA. Argumente in der Energiediskussion, Energiebedarf und Energiebedarfsforschung. Ed. by H. Matthöfer. Villingen 1977, 290–333.

Freeman, D., et al. (eds.): A Time to Choose. Cambridge, Mass. 1974.

Glickman, N.J.: Econometric Analysis of Regional Systems, Explorations in Model Building and Policy Analysis. New York 1977.

Goreux, L.M., and *A.S. Manne* (eds.): Multi Level Planning, Case Studies in Mexico. Amsterdam 1973.

Gottinger, H.W.: Structural Characteristics of Economic Models. A Study in Complexity. Universität Bielefeld, Mimeograph No. 72, 1978.

Greenleaf, R.W. (ed.): Structural Change and Current Problems Facing Regulated Public Utilities. Graduate School of Business, Indiana University, Indianapolis 1975.

Grenon, M.: An Approach to Comparing Long-Term Global Energy Strategies. Energy Policy. Ed. by J.S. Aronofsky, A.G. Rao and M.F. Shakun. Amsterdam 1978, 21–35.

Griffin, J.M.: The Effects of Higher Prices on Electricity Consumption. BEM **5** (2), 1974, 513–539.

Grunwald, V.: Der Energiebedarf Thailands. Eine ökonometrische Modellstudie. Frankfurt/Main–Bern–Cirencester/U.K. 1980.

622

Guillaume, H.: Compatibility between Sectoral and Global Approaches. United Nations ECE/EC.AD. 11, 1975, 199–207.

Guillaume, Y.: Modelisation du Systeme Energetique Belge. Présentation des Principaux Axes de Recherche et d'un Premier Modèle d'Essai, CEB **78**, 1978, 141–182.

Häfele, W., and *A. Makarov*: Modeling of Medium and Long-Range Energy Strategies. IIASA Workshop on Energy Strategies, Conception and Embedding. Schloss Laxenburg, Mimeograph, 1977.

Häfele, W., and *A.S. Manne*: Strategies for a Transition from Fossil to Nuclear Fuel. International Institut for Applied Systems Analysis. IIASA-Research Report 74–7, Laxenburg, Austria 1974.

Häfele, W., and *H.H. Rogner*: Energie – Die globale Perspektive. Angewandte Systemanalyse **1** (2), 1980, 57–67.

Häfele, W., and *L. Schrattenholzer*: Modelle für Energiebedarf und -verbrauch in weltweitem Rahmen. Energiemodelle für die Bundesrepublik Deutschland. Ed. by A. Voss and K. Schmitz. Köln 1980, 23–34.

Halvorsen, R.: Econometric Models of U.S. Energy Demand. Lexington, Mass. – Toronto 1978.

Hanada, M.: Simulation of Oil Supply Constraint. Bank of Japan, Tokyo, Oct. 16, 1979.

Hanssmann, F.: Energiemodelle kritisch gesehen. Energiewirtschaftliche Tagesfragen **26** (6), 1976.

– : Modelle zur Energieplanung – Eine kritische Betrachtung. IBM Sympsium – Ökonometrische Modelle und Systeme, Bad Neuenahr, Sept. 14–16, 77, 1977. Reprint in Ökonometrische Modelle und Systeme. Ed. by F. Schober and H.D. Ploetzeneder. München–Wien 1978, 249–259.

Hausman, J.A.: Project Independence Report: An Appraisal of U.S. Energy Needs up to 1985. BEM **6** (2), 1975, 517–551.

Hicks, N.L.: A Model of Trade and Growth for the Developing World. EER 7, 1976, 239–255.

Hirshfeld, D.S.: Management Science Issue: Matching Energy Models to Energy Issues. OR-MS-Today 7 (2), 1980, p. 12.

Hitch, C.J. (ed.): Modeling Energy-Economy Interactions: Five Approaches. Resources for the Future. Washington, D.C. 1977.

Hoffman, K.C.: The United States Energy System – A Unified Planning Framework. Ph.D. Dissertation. Polytechnic Institute of Brookly, 1972.

– : Coupled Energy System-Economic Models. Conference on Energy Modeling and Forecasting. Ed. by P. Benenson. Berkeley, Calif. 1975.

– : A Systems Approach to Energy Resource Planning. Energiemodelle für die Bundesrepublik Deutschland. Ed. by C. König. Basel–Stuttgart 1977, 27–44.

– : Energy Modeling – Perspectives and Policy Application. Energy Policy. Ed. by J.S. Aronofsky, A.G. Rao and M.F. Shakun. Amsterdam 1978, 5–20.

Hoffman, K.C., and *E.A. Cherniavsky*: Interfuel Substitution and Technological Change. Brookhaven National Laboratory, BNL 18919, Upton, N.Y. 1974.

Hoffman, K.C., and *D.W. Jorgenson*: Economic and Technological Models for Evaluation of Energy Policy. BEM 8, 1977, 444–446.

Hoffmeyer, M., and *A.D. Neu*: Zu den Entwicklungsaussichten der Energiemärkte. Die Weltwirtschaft, Heft 1, 1979, 154–182.

Hogan, W.W.: Energy Policy Models for Project Independence. COR **2**, 1975, 251–271.

– : Energy and the Economy. Energy Modeling Forum, Inst. Energy Stud., Stanford University 1977.

Hogan, W.W., and *A.S. Manne*: Energy-Economy Interactions: The Fable of the Elephant and the Rabbit. Modeling Energy-Economy Interactions: Five Approaches. Ed. by C.J. Hitch. Resources for the Future, Washington, D.C. 1977, 247–277.

– : Energy-Economy Interactions: The Fable of the Elephant and the Rabbit. Advances in the Economics of Energy and Resources. Vol. 1, The Structure of Energy Markets. Ed. by R.S. Pindyck. Greenwich, Conn. 1979, 7–26.

Hogan, W.W., J.L. Sweeny, and *M.H. Wagner*: Energy Policy in the National Energy Outlook. Energy Policy. Ed. by J.S. Aronofsky, A.G. Rao and M.F. Shakun. Amsterdam 1978, 37–62.

House, P.W., and *J. McCleod*: Large-Scale Models for Policy Evaluation. New York 1977.

Houthakker, H., and *M. Kennedy*: The World Petroleum Model. Cambridge, Mass. 1974.

Hubbert, M.K.: The Energy Resources of the Earth. Scientific American **225** (3), 1971, 61–70.

Hudson, E.A., and *D.W. Jorgenson*: Economic Analysis of Alternative Energy Growth Patterns. Report to the Energy Policy Project, Ford Foundation. A Time to Choose. Ed. by D. Freedman et al. Cambridge, Mass. 1974a, 493–511.

— : Tax Policy and Energy Use, Fiscal Policy and the Energy Crisis. 93rd Congress, 1st and 2nd Sessions, Committee on Finance, U.S. Senate, 1974b, 1681–1694.

— : U.S. Energy Policy and Economic Growth, 1975–2000. BEM **5**, 1974c, 461–541.

—.: U.S. Energy Policy and Economic Growth, 1975–2000. Harvard Institute of Economic Research, Discussion Paper No. 372, 1974d.

— : Projections of U.S. Economic Growth and Energy Demand. Structural Change and Current Problems Facing Regulated Public Utilities. Ed. by R.W. Greenleaf. Graduate School of Business, Indiana University, Indianapolis 1975, 75–128.

— : Tax Policy and Energy Conservation. Econometric Studies of U.S. Energy Policy. Ed. by D.W. Jorgenson. Amsterdam 1976, 7–94.

— : Energy Policy and U.S. Economic Growth. AER/S **68**, 1978, 118–123.

Huggins, J.: An Annual Econometric Forecasting, Model of the State of Florida. Ph.D. Dissertation. The Florida State University, 1975.

Ichimura, S.: Japanese Energy Crisis Management Policies. Kyoto University, Japan, and University of Bonn, Germany, 1980, Mimeograph, July 1, 1980.

Intriligator, M.D. (ed.): Frontiers of Quantitative Economics. Amsterdam 1971.

Jansen, P.J.: Decision under Several Objectives. Department of Operations Research, Systems Optimization Laboratory. Technical Report SOL 77-20, Stanford University, 1977.

Janssen, J.M.L., L.F. Pau, and *A. Straszak* (eds.): Models and Decision Making in National Economies. Amsterdam 1979.

Jorgenson, D.W.: The Role of Energy in the U.S. Economy. National Tax Journal **31**, 1978, 209–220.

— (ed.): Econometric Studies of U.S. Energy Policy. Amsterdam 1976.

Joskow, P.L.: America's Many Energy Futures – A Review of Energy Future, Energy: The Next Twenty Years, and Energy in America's Future. BEM **11** (1), 1980, 377–398.

Joskow, P.L., and *M.L. Baugham*: The Future of the U.S. Nuclear Energy Industry. BEM **7** (1), 1976, 3–32.

Kader, A.A.: The Role of the Oil Export Sector in the Economic Development of Iraq. Ph.D. Dissertation. West Virginia University, 1974.

Kantorovich, L., and *T.C. Koopmans*: Problems of Application of Optimization Methods in Industry. Federation of Swedish Industries, Stockholm 1976.

Keeny, S.M., et al.: Nuclear Power Issues and Choices. Report of the Nuclear Energy Policy Study Group. Cambridge, Mass. 1977.

Kennedy, M.: An Economic Model of the World Oil Market. BEM **5** (2), 1974, 540–577.

— : A World Oil Model. Econometric Studies of U.S. Energy Policy. Ed. by D.W. Jorgenson. Amsterdam 1976, 95–176.

Klein, L.R.: Supply Constraints in Demand Oriented Systems. An Interpretation of the Oil-Crisis. ZN **34**, 1974, 45–56.

— : Econometric Policy Formation through the Medium of Econometric Models. Frontiers of Qualitative Economics. Ed. by M.D. Intriligator. Amsterdam 1977, 765–782.

— : Money in a General Equilibrium System: Empirical Aspects of the Quantity Theory. EA **31**, 1978, 5–13.

Klein, L.R., et al.: The Newsweek WEFA Forecast, Newsweek, October 4, 1976a, 44–58.

— : Applications of the Link System. In: Waelbroeck, ed., 1976b, 1–16.

— : World Economic Forecast, Newsweek, September 26, 1977, 30–43.

— : The Newsweek WEFA Forecast, Newsweek, September 25, 1978, 44–56.

Kline, D., and *M. Swift*: A Catalog of Energy Models. Energy Modeling Forum. Occasional Paper EMF OP 1.0, Stanford University, California 1978.

Kononov, Y.: Modelling of the Influence of Energy Development on Different Branches of the National Economy. International Institute for Applied Systems Analysis, Laxenburg, Austria, Mimeograph, 1976.

Kononov, Y., and *A. Voss*: Ermittlungen der Anforderungen alternativer Energieversorgungsstrategien an die Wirtschaft mittels Input-Output-Modellen. International Institute for Applied Systems Analysis, Laxenburg, Austria, Mimeograph, 1977.

– : Ermittlung der Anforderungen alternativer Energieversorgungsstrategien an die Wirtschaft mittels Input-Output-Modellen. Makroökonomische Input-Output Analysen und dynamische Modelle zur Erfassung technischer Entwicklungen. Ed. by J. Seetzen, R. Krengel, and G. von Kortzfleisch. Basel–Boston–Stuttgart 1979, 216–226.

Koopmans, T.C., et al.: Discussion. AER/S **68**, 1978, 124–130.

Koreisha, S., and *R. Stobaugh*: Appendix: Limits to Models. Energy Future. Report of the Energy Project at the Harvard Business School. Ed. by R. Stobaugh and D. Yergin. New York 1979, 234–265.

Kresge, D.T., et al.: Issues in Alaska Development. Seattle 1978.

Landsberg, H.H., et al. (eds.): Energy: The Next Twenty Years. Cambridge, Mass. 1979.

Lapillonne, B.: Medee 2: A Model for Long-Term Energy Demand Evolution. Internationales Institut für Angewandte Systemanalyse, Laxenburg, Österreich, 1978.

Lave, L.B.: What have we Learned from these Scenarios. Modeling Energy-Economy Interactions: Five Approaches. Ed. by C.J. Hitch. Resources for the Future. Washington, D.C. 1977, 278–303.

Longva, S., L. Lorentsen, and *O. Olsen*: Energy in a Multi-sectoral Growth Model. Statistisk Sentralbyra. Rapporter 80/1, Oslo 1980.

Lovins, A.B.: Sanfte Energie – Das Programm für die Energie- und Industriepolitische Umrüstung unserer Gesellschaft. Reinbek 1978.

Macavoy, P.W., and *R.S. Pindyck*: The Economics of the Natural Gas Shortage (1960–1980). Amsterdam 1975.

Maddala, G.S., W.S. Chern, and *G.S. Gill* (eds.): Econometric Studies in Energy Demand and Supply. New York–London 1978.

Manne, A.S.: On Linking Energeticos to Dinamico. Multi Level Planning. Case Studies in Mexico. Ed. by L.M. Goreux and A.S. Manne. Amsterdam 1973, 277–289.

– : ETA: A Model for Energy Technology Assessment. BEM 7 (2), 1976, 379–406.

– : ETA-Macro: A Model of Energy-Economy Interactions. Modeling Energy-Economy Interactions: Five Approaches. Ed. by C.J. Hitch. Resources for the Future, Washington, D.C. 1977, 1–45.

– : ETA-Makro: Model Vzaimodejstvija Energetiki I Ekonomiki. EMM **14** (5), 1978, 867–886.

– : International Energy Supplies and Demands. A Long Term Perspective. Energiemodelle für die Bundesrepublik Deutschland. Ed. by A. Voss and K. Schmitz. Köln 1980, 35–48.

Manne, A.S., R.G. Richels, and *J.P. Weyant*: Energy Policy Modeling: A Survey. OR **27** (1), 1979, 1–36.

Marchetti, C., et al.: The Dynamics of Energy Systems and the Logistic Substitution Model. Internationales Institut für Angewandte Systemanalyse, AR-78-1A/B/C, Laxenburg, Österreich, 1978.

Marcuse, W., et al.: A Dynamic Time Dependent Model for the Analysis of Alternative Energy Policies, Brookhaven National Laboratory, BNL 19406, Upton, N.Y. 1975.

MIT Energy Policy Study Group: The FEA Project Independence Report: An Analytical Review and Evaluation. MIT-EL 75-017, June 1975, Cambridge, Mass. 1975.

Müller-Reissmann, K.F., and *F. Rechenmann*: Cognitive Systems Analysis: An Interactive Program for the Modelling of Deduction. Concepts and Tools of Computer-Assisted Policy Analysis, Vol. 3. Ed. by H. Bossel. 1977, 482–537.

Murota, Y.: Survey of Energy Economic Models. Saitama University, 1979, 26–31 (in Japanese).

Neri, J.A.: An Evaluation of two Alternative Supply Models of Natural Gas. BEM 8 (1), 1977, 289–302.

Nordhaus, W.D.: The Allocation of Energy Resources. Brookings Papers Econ. Activity **3**, 1973, 529–576.

Norman, M., and *H.H. Rogner*: Potential GNP Model for the U.S. IIASA Workshop on Energy Strategies, Conception and Embedding, Schloss Laxenburg, Mimeograph, 1977.

Palma-Carillo, P.A.: A Macro-Econometric Model of Venezuela with Oil Price Impact Applications. Ph.D. Dissertation, University of Pennsylvania, Philadelphia 1976.

Parikh, S.C.: Progress Report on the Pilot Energy Modelling Project. Technical Report SOL 77-11, Department of Operations Research, Stanford University, California 1977.

− : A Welfare Equilibrium Model (WEM) of Energy Supply, Energy Demand, and Economic Growth. Technical Report SOL 79-3, Department of Operations Research, Stanford University, California, 1979.

Pindyck, R.S.: The Econometrics of Natural Gas and Oil. Energy Modeling. Surrey 1974a.

− : The Regulatory Implications of Three Alternative Econometric Supply Models of Natural Gas. BEM 5 (2), 1974b, 633–645.

− : International Comparisons of the Residential Demand for Energy. EER 13, 1980, 1–24.

− (ed.): Advances in the Economics of Energy and Resources. Vol. 1, The Structure of Energy Markets. Greenwich, Conn. 1979.

Polenske, K.R., and *J.V. Skolka* (eds.): Advances in Input-Output Analyses. Cambridge, Mass. 1976.

Quante, H.: Anforderungen an Energiemodelle aus der Sicht des Energieplaners in Politik und Wirtschaft. Energiemodelle für die Bundesrepublik Deutschland. Ed. by C. König. Basel–Stuttgart 1977, 263–265.

Reister, D.B., and *J.A. Edmonds*: A General Equilibrium Two-Sector Energy Demand Model. Modeling Energy-Economy Interactions: Five Approaches. Resources for the Future, Washington, D.C. 1977, 199–246.

Ridker, R.G., *W.D.J. Watson*, and *A. Shapanka*: Economic, Energy and Environmental Consequences of Alternative Energy Regimes. An Application of the RFF/SEAS Modeling System. Modeling Energy-Economy Interactions: Five Approaches. Resources for the Future, Washington, D.C. 1977, 135–198.

Rodberg, L.S.: Beschäftigungswirkungen beim Übergang zu einer alternativen Energiestruktur. Mitteilungen aus der Arbeitsmarkt- und Berufsforschung 13 (1), 1980, 15–38.

Rose, J., and *C. Bilciu* (eds.): Modern Trends in Cybernetics and Systems. Berlin–Heidelberg–New York 1977.

Rubida, K.W.: An Econometric Model of the Colorado Economy. Ph.D. Dissertation, University of Colorado, 1977.

Ruby, M., *R. Thomas*, and *P.L. Abraham*: The Economic Impact. Newsweek, May 2, 1977, 23–33.

Saito, M.: Impact of the Oil Price Rise on the Japanese Economy. Kobe University, Kobe, Japan, 1979 (Abstract, in Japanese).

Sassin, W.: Energy. Scientific American 243 (3), 1980, 107–110.

SAWA: Review of Energy Models. Kobe University, Kobe, Japan, 1979 (Abstract).

Schmitt, D., and *H. Suding*: Die Gemeinschaftsprognose der Institute, Charakter und Aussagewert. Energiemodelle für die Bundesrepublik Deutschland. Ed. by A. Voss and K. Schmitz. Köln 1980, 49–62.

Schober, F., and *H.D. Ploetzeneder* (eds.): Ökonometrische Modelle und Systeme. München–Wien 1978.

Schurr, S.H., et al.: Energy in America's Future. The Choices Before us. Baltimore–London 1979.

Shahshahani, M.A.: An Econometric Model of Development for an Oilbased Economy. The Case of Iran. Ph.D. Dissertation. University of Colorado, Mimeograph, 1976.

Shapiro, J.F.: OR Models for Energy Planning. COR 2, 1975, 145–152.

− : Decomposition Methods for Mathematical Programming/Economic Equilibrium Energy Planning Models. Energy Policy. Ed. by J.S. Aronofsky, A.G. Rao and M.F. Shakun. Amsterdam 1978, 63–76.

Sharp, J., *F. Shupp*, and *W. Perkins*: Energy Conservation and Induced Inflation. JEDC 2, 1980, 213–231.

Starr, C.: Energy and Power. Scientific American 225 (3), 1971, 37–49.

Stobaugh, R., and *D. Yergin* (eds.): Energy Future. Report of the Energy Project at the Harvard Business School. New York 1979.

Sweeny, J.L.: The Energy Modeling Forum: Past, Present and Future. Energiemodelle für die Bundesrepublik Deutschland. Ed. by A. Voss and K. Schmitz. Köln 1980, 147–167.

Taylor, L.D.: The Demand for Electricity: A Survey. BEM 6 (1), 1975, 74–110.

Tessmer, R.G., et al.: Coupled Energy System – Economic Models and Strategic Planning. COR **2**, 1975, 213–224.

Tintner, G., et al.: Ein Energiekrisenmodell. Empirica **2**, 1975, 125–164.

Uchida, M.: Denken Macro Model (1970 I – 1977 IV). Version 1979.8.17, No. 2. Central Research Institute of the Electric Power Industry, Tokyo, Mimeograph, 1979 (in Japanese).

UNCTAD: Trade Prospects and Capital Needs of Developing Countries. New York 1968, 318–339.

Uno, K.: Social Indicators and Macro-Economic Framework. JJER, No. 3, 1974, 28–51 (in Japanese).

Vakil, F.: An Econometric Model for Iran, Bank Markazi Iran, The Central Bank of Iran **11** (63), 1972, 115–120.

– : An Econometric Model for Iran. Estimated Structural Equations. Bank Makazi Iran, The Central Bank of Iran **11** (66), 1973, 633–655.

– : A Twenty Year Macro-Economic Perspective for Iran 1351–1371 (1972–1992). Plan and Budget Organization. Tehran 1974.

Voss, A.: Ansätze zur Gesamtanalyse des Systems Mensch – Energie – Umwelt. Eine dynamische Computersimulation. Basel–Stuttgart 1977a.

– : Methodische Probleme bei der Erstellung von Energiemodellen. Energiemodelle für die Bundesrepublik Deutschland. Ed. by C. König. Basel–Stuttgart 1977b, 267–269.

– : Anspruch und Wirklichkeit von Energiemodellen. Energiemodelle für die Bundesrepublik Deutschland. Ed. by A. Voss and K. Schmitz. Köln 1980, 15–21.

Voss, A., and *K. Schmitz* (eds.): Energiemodelle für die Bundesrepublik Deutschland. Köln 1980.

WAES: Energy Demand Studies: Major Consuming Countries. Workshop on Alternative Energy Strategies. Cambridge, Mass. 1976.

– : Energy Supply to the Year 2000: Global and National Studies. Workshop on Alternative Energy Strategies. Cambridge, Mass. 1977.

Webster, P.V.: Western World Supply/Demand and its Links with OPEC Economies. Models and Decision Making in National Economies. Ed. by J.M.L. Janssen, L.F. Pau and A. Straszak. Amsterdam 1979, 143–146.

Weizsäcker, C.F.von: Die Friedliche Nutzung der Kernenergie – Chancen und Risiken. Reihe Kern-Themen des Informationskreises Kernenergie. Bonn 1978.

Wilson, C.L.: Energy: Global Prospects 1985–2000. Report of the Workshop on Alternative Energy Strategies. New York 1977.

Withagen, C.: The Exploitation of Natural Gas in the Netherlands. An Exploration. Econometrie, AE 4/80. Universiteit van Amsterdam, Interfaculteit der Actuariele Wetenschapen en 1980.

Woodward, V.H.: Alternative Economic Environments. Economic Structure and Policy with Applications to the British Economy. Ed. by T.S. Barker. London 1976, 295–335.

Wright, B.D.: The Cost of Tax-Induced Energy Conservation. BEM **11** (1), 1980, 84–107.

Young, J.W., et al.: A Simulation Examining the Causalities Underlying Land, Agriculture, Transportation and Energy Relationships (Speculator). Modern Trends in Cybernetics and Systems. Ed. by J. Rose and C. Bilciu. Vol. 1. Berlin–Heidelberg–New York 1977, 485–506.

Appendix 2: References referring to the keyword "energy" and "W-Germany"

Bauerschmidt, R.: Systemanalyse technologischer Veränderungen unter Verwendung von Input-Output-Verfahren. Makroökonomische Input-Output Analysen und dynamische Modelle zur Erfassung technischer Entwicklungen. Ed. by J. Seetzen, R. Krengel and G. von Kortzfleisch. Basel–Boston–Stuttgart 1979, 197–213.

– : Das Energieversorgungsmodell des ISP. Energiemodelle für die Bundesrepublik Deutschland. Ed. by A. Voss and K. Schmitz. Köln 1980, 127–147.

Boeckels, L., *C. Krebsbach-Gnath*, and *J. Scharioth*: Risiko und Akzeptanzprobleme einer Energieunterversorgung – Battelle –. Deutscher Bundestag, 8. Wahlperiode, 1980, 1219–1398, Materialband 4, Drucksache 8/4341.

Bonhöffer, F., and *G. Britschkat*: Die Energiekosten-Studie des IFO-Institutes. Makroökonomische Input-Output Analysen und dynamische Modelle zur Erfassung technischer Entwicklungen. Ed. by J. Seetzen, R. Krengel and G. von Kortzfleisch. Basel–Boston–Stuttgart 1979, 167–196.

Bossel, H., P. von der Hijden, and *W. Hudetz*: An Interactive Program for Energy Policy Assessment. Concepts and Tools of Computer-Assisted Policy Analysis, Vol. 2. Ed. by H. Bossel, 1977, 355–391.

Bossel, H., et al.: Dialogprogramm zur Entwicklung und Überprüfung von Langfristkonzepten für das Energieversorgungssystem und Anwendung auf die Bundesrepublik Deutschland. Jülich, Kernforschungsanlage (Conf. 15), 1975.

– : Dialogprogramm zur Entwicklung und Überprüfung von Langfristkonzepten für das Energieversorgungssystem und Anwendung auf die Bundesrepublik Deutschland. Energiemodelle für die Bundesrepublik Deutschland. Ed. by C. König. Basel–Stuttgart 1977, 45–100.

– : Energy Policy Assessment using an Interactive Model Package. New Trends in Mathematic Modelling, 1978, 203–231.

Brand, P., et al.: Abschätzung der Folgen alternativer Strategien der Energiewirtschaft mittels Dynamischer Simulation in Kooperation mit den Interessengruppen (Technology Assessment), ISI-Projekt, Nor. 6026, 1975.

Breitenecker, M., and *H.R. Grümm*: Ein schematisches Ökonomiemodell und seine Resilienz. Energiemodelle für die Bundesrepublik Deutschland. Ed. by A. Voss and K. Schmitz. Köln 1980, 205–218.

Burchard, H.J.: Energiemodelle und Wirtschaftsordnung. Energiemodelle für die Bundesrepublik Deutschland. Ed. by C. König. Basel–Stuttgart 1977, 11–25.

CDU: Lebenswerte Zukunft, Wissenschaftliche Fachtagung zu Umwelt und Wachstum. Eine Dokumentation zur wissenschaftlichen Fachtagung der CDU am 1. und 2. März 1979, Bonn 1979.

Charpentier, J.P.: A Review of Energy Models, No. 1 – May 1974. IIASA Publications, July 1974.

Conrad, K.: Energieprojektionen mit einem ökonometrischen Makro- und Input-Output-Modell für die Bundesrepublik Deutschland. Berichte der Kernforschungsanlage Jülich (Conf. 15), Mimeograph, 1975.

Dieckheuer, G., U. Meyer, and *J. Schumann*: Ein dynamisches Input-Output-Modell zur simultanen Erklärung der Entwicklung von Mengen und Preisen, angewendet auf die Bundesrepublik Deutschland 1954–1967. Makroökonomische Input-Output Analysen und dynamische Modelle zur Erfassung technischer Entwicklungen. Ed. by J. Seetzen, R. Krengel and G. von Kortzfleisch. Basel–Boston–Stuttgart 1979, 73–104.

DIW, EWI, RWI: Die zukünftige Entwicklung der Energienachfrage in der Bundesrepublik Deutschland bis zum Jahre 1985 und deren Deckung – Perspektiven bis zum Jahre 2000. Deutsches Institut für Wirtschaftsforschung (DIW), Berlin 1978.

Döllekes, H.P.: Ein multisektorales Energie- und Umweltplanungsmodell. Energiemodelle für die Bundesrepublik Deutschland. Ed. by C. König. Basel–Stuttgart 1977, 207–228.

Drepper, F., R. Heckler, and *H.P. Schwefel*: Energieplanung mittels dynamischer Simulation und überlagerter Optimierung. DGOR-Jahrestagung 1980, Essen 1980, p. 96 (Abstract).

Egberts, G.: Kostenoptimale Entwicklungsperspektiven des Raumheizungssektors im Energieversorgungssystem der Bundesrepublik Deutschland. Angewandte Systemanalyse Nr. 12, Ph.D. Dissertation. Kernforschungsanlage, Jülich 1979.

Faude, D., P. Jansen, and *P. Klumpp*: Das Energiemodell SOPKA-E – Modellbeschreibung und Computer-Ausdrucke der Energiepfad-Berechnungen. Deutscher Bundestag, Enquete-Kommission zukünftige Kernenergie-Politik, 1980, Materialband 1, Drucksache 8/2628, 1–88.

Fendt, H.: Regionale Energieplanung. DGOR-Jahrestagung 1980, Essen 1980, p. 95 (Abstract).

Friede, G.: Preisabhängige Darstellung von Input-Koeffizienten der Bundesrepublik Deutschland. Makroökonomische Input-Output Analysen und dynamische Modelle zur Erfassung technischer Entwicklungen. Ed. by J. Seetzen, R. Krengel and G. von Kortzfleisch. Basel–Boston–Stuttgart 1979, 55–71.

Giesen, G., S. Rath-Nagel, and *D. Sievert*: Markal – Ein mehrperioden-LP-Modell des Energieversorgungssystems. DGOR-Jahrestagung 1980, Essen 1980, p. 96 (Abstract).

Gonschior, P. (ed.): Technologieeinsatz und wirtschaftlicher Strukturwandel als Problem für die Input-Output Analyse. Bericht: ASA-PW, 04/76, Köln 1976.

Hanssmann, F.: Überblick und Konzeption für ein regionales Energiemodell am Beispiel Münchens. AP, Heft 47, 1976, 20–22.

Hasenkamp, G., and *H.U. Opitz*: Eine kurzfristige Nachfrageanalyse für Energieprodukte durch Input/Output Tabellen für die Bundesrepublik Deutschland. Energiemodelle für die Bundesrepublik Deutschland. Ed. by A. Voss and K. Schmitz. Köln 1980, 63–67.

Henize, J.: A Critical Evaluation of the Pestel Deutschland-Modell. Gesellschaft für Mathematik und Datenverarbeitung. Interner Bericht, IPES.78.210, 1978.

Herz, H.: Probleme der Kopplung von Input-Output-Modellen mit anderen systemtechnischen Modell-ansätzen am Beispiel eines Energiemodells und eines Branchenmodells. Makroökonomische Input-Output Analysen und dynamische Modelle zur Erfassung technischer Entwicklungen. Ed. by J. Seetzen, R. Krengel and G. von Kortzfleisch. Basel–Boston–Stuttgart 1979, 285–291.

Jochem, E., et al.: Entwicklung eines Verfahrens zur Technikfolgenabschätzung (TA) mittels dynami-scher Simulation am Beispiel eines veränderten Mineralölangebots. Forschungsauftrag des BMFT Bonn. Institut für Systemtechnik und Innovationsforschung der FHG Karlsruhe, 1976.

Klauder, W.: Zu den Arbeitsmarktauswirkungen unterschiedlicher Energiestrukturen. Mitteilungen aus der Arbeitsmarkt- und Berufsforschung **13** (1), 1980, 1–14.

König, C. (ed.): Energiemodelle für die Bundesrepublik Deutschland. Basel–Stuttgart 1977.

Krallmann, H.: Die Kombination eines Branchen- und eines Input-Output-Modells im Bereich der chemischen Technik. Makroökonomische Input-Output Analysen und dynamische Modelle zur Er-fassung technischer Entwicklungen. Ed. by J. Seetzen, R. Krengel and G. von Kortzfleisch. Basel–Boston–Stuttgart 1979, 265–271.

Kriegsmann, K.P.: Energieverteuerung und sektoraler Strukturwandel als Determinanten des Energie-verbrauchs. Die Weltwirtschaft 1980, No. 1, 1980, 100–120.

Lehbert, B.: Vorschlag für ein Prognose- und Simulationsmodell des Umwandlungsbereichs der Energiewirtschaft in der Bundesrepublik Deutschland. WA **116**, 1980, 131–161.

Lenhardt, W., H.P. Schwefel, and *D. Sievert*: Ein Energieversorgungsmodell zur Langfristprognose der Umwandlungskapazitäten. Angewandte Systemanalyse Nr. 15. Kernforschungsanlage, Jülich 1979.

Liebrucks, W., H.W. Schmidt, and *D. Schmitt*: Die künftige Entwicklung der Energienachfrage in der Bundesrepublik Deutschland und deren Deckung. Perspektiven bis zum Jahre 2000. Gemein-schaftsprognose, 1978.

Matthöfer, H. (ed.): Argumente in der Energiediskussion. Energiebedarf und Energiebedarfsforschung **2**, Villingen 1977.

Mischke, H.: EG-Energiemodelle für die Bundesrepublik Deutschland. Energiemodelle für die Bundes-republik Deutschland. Ed. by A. Voss and K. Schmitz. Köln 1980, 89–125.

Müller-Reissmann, K.F., and *F. Rechenmann*: Cognitive Systems Analysis: An Interactive Program for the Modelling of Deduction. Concepts and Tools of Computer-Assisted Policy Analysis, Vol. 3. Ed. by H. Bossel. 1977, 482–537.

Nordhaus, D.W.: The Demand for Energy: An International Perspective. International Studies of the Demand for Energy. Ed. by D.W. Nordhaus. Amsterdam 1977, 239–285.

Oest, W.: Ein dynamisches sektoral disaggregiertes Wirtschaftsmodell für die Bundesrepublik Deutsch-land zur Abschätzung alternativer Entwicklungsmöglichkeiten. Berlin–München 1979.

Pestel, E., et al.: Das Deutschland-Modell. Herausforderung auf dem Weg ins 21. Jahrhundert. Stutt-gart 1978.

Pestel, R.: Einbettung von Energiemodellen in Gesamtmodelle und die Kopplung nationaler und glo-baler Modelle. Energiemodelle für die Bundesrepublik Deutschland. Ed. by C. König. Basel–Stutt-gart 1977, 261–262.

Pfeiffer, R., and *H. Lindner*: Untersuchung von Problemen der Rohstoffversorgung im Bereich der chemischen Technik mit variablen Input-Output-Koeffizienten. Makroökonomische Input-Output Analysen und dynamische Modelle zur Erfassung technischer Entwicklungen. Ed. by J. Seetzen, R. Krengel and G. von Kortzfleisch. Basel–Boston–Stuttgart 1979, 247–264.

Pindyck, R.S.: International Comparisons of the Residential Demand for Energy. EER **13**, 1980, 1–24.

Rath-Nagel, S.: Alternative Entwicklungsmöglichkeiten der Energiewirtschaft in der BRD. Untersuchung mit Hilfe eines Simulationsmodells. Basel–Stuttgart 1977.

Schmitt, D., and *H. Suding*: Die Gemeinschaftsprognose der Institute, Charakter und Aussagewert. Energiemodelle für die Bundesrepublik Deutschland. Ed. by A. Voss and K. Schmitz. Köln 1980, 49–62.

Schmitz, K.: JES-Jülicher Energiemodell-System. Ein Instrumentarium zur Analyse der Entwicklungsmöglichkeiten der Energiewirtschaft in der Bundesrepublik. Energiemodelle für die Bundesrepublik Deutschland. Ed. by A. Voss and K. Schmitz. Köln 1980, 69–87.

Schwieren, G., and *L. Trepte*: Risiko- und Akzeptanzprobleme einer Energieunterversorgung – Dornier –. Deutscher Bundestag, 8. Wahlperiode 1980, 1399–1594, Materialband 4, Drucksache 8/4341.

Seetzen, J., et al.: Systemanalytische Methoden zur Untersuchung technischer Entwicklungen. Programmleitung Angewandte Systemanalyse. Jahresbericht 1976, Anlagenband V. Köln 1977.

Seetzen, J., R. Krengel, and *G. von Kortzfleisch* (eds.): Makroökonomische Input-Output Analysen und dynamische Modelle zur Erfassung technischer Entwicklungen. Basel–Boston–Stuttgart 1979.

Strobel, M.G., and *H. Bossel*: Matching Man and Model: The "Guide" System for Interactive Model Handling. Concepts and Tools of Computer-Assisted Policy Analysis, Vol. 2. Ed. by H. Bossel, 1977, 309–354.

Trenkler, H.: Kritische Wertung von Energiemodellen. Energiemodelle für die Bundesrepublik Deutschland. Ed. by A. Voss and K. Schmitz. Köln 1980, 175–183.

Überhorst, R., et al.: Bericht der Enquete-Kommission – Zukünftige Kernenergie-Politik – über den Stand der Arbeit und die Ergebnisse gemäß Beschluß des Deutschen Bundestages. Deutscher Bundestag Bonn, 8. Wahlperiode, 1980, Drucksache 8/4341, 27.6.80.

Voss, A.: A Model Approach for Evaluating the Impact on the Economy of Different Energy Strategies. Technologieeinsatz und wirtschaftlicher Strukturwandel als Problem für die Input-Output Analyse. Ed. by P. Gonschior. Bericht: ASA-PW, 04/76, Köln 1976, 22–37.

Voss, A., et al.: Dynamische Energiemodelle als Planungs- und Entscheidungshilfe, dargestellt an einem Energiemodell für die Bundesrepublik Deutschland. Energiemodelle für die Bundesrepublik Deutschland. Ed. by C. König. Basel–Stuttgart 1977, 101–134.

Voss, A., and *K. Schmitz* (eds.): Energiemodelle für die Bundesrepublik Deutschland. Köln 1980.

Weizsäcker, C.F.von: Die friedliche Nutzung der Kernenergie – Chancen und Risiken. Reihe Kern-Themen des Informationskreises Kernenergie. Bonn 1978.

Appendix 3: Survey of macro-econometric models in chronological order

```
../.    CHRONOLOGICAL NUMBER OF MODEL
        (NUMBER OF FIBLIOGRAPHICAL IDENTIFICATION)
*       CHRONOLOGICAL NUMBER NOT YET ASSIGNED
EQU     NUMBER OF EQUATIONS, NUMBER OF ENDOGENOUS VARIABLES
STO     NUMBER OF STOCHASTIC EQUATIONS
DEF     NUMBER OF DEFINITIONS
        EQU = STO + DEF
MON     NUMBER OF ENDOGENOUS MONETARY VARIABLES
IO      NUMBER OF INPUT-OUTPUT SECTORS
EXO     NUMBER OF EXOGENOUS VARIABLES
PER     LENGTH OF PERIOD IN YEARS
        1/12    MONTHLY
        1/4     QUARTERLY
        1/2     SEMI-ANNUAL
        1       ANNUAL
        X.Y     X.Y YEARS

FAMILY OF MODEL
    EITHER
        NAME OF AUTHOR(S),PROPRIETARY INSTITUTION,ETC.
    OR
        TYPE OF MODEL ETC.
```

```
M     MONETARY MODEL
LP    LINEAR PROGRAM
NLP   NONLINEAR PROGRAM
CON   CONSISTENCY MODEL
SIM   SIMULATION MODEL
```

BLANK ENTRIES USUALLY DO NOT INDICATE THAT THERE ARE NO
FIGURES FOR THESE ENTRIES; GENERALLY THEY ONLY INDICATE
AN INCOMPLETE DESCRIPTION OF THE MODEL. ANY READER, WHO
CAN SUPPLY ADDITIONAL INFORMATION, IS INVITED TO DO SO.

W-GERMANY

NO.	AUTHOR(S)		EQU	STO	DEF	MON	IO	EXO	PER	MODEL
59/1	WAFFENSCHMIDT		16	12	4	1	0	7	1	
59/2	MENGES		4	4	0	0	0	2	1	
61/1	MENGES		7	5	2	0	0	5	1	
61/2	GUELICHER		14	7	7	0	0		1/4	
62/1	KOENIG-TIMMERMANN		19	14	5	2	0	23	1/2	
62/2	VON HOHENBALKEN-TINTNER		5	2	3	0	0	8	1	
62/3	BREMS		10	8	2	0	0		1	
63/1	GEHRIG		19	3	16	0	0	12	1	
			17	3	14	0	0	12	1	
			6	3	3	0	0	10		
	MISCHKE 1976		20	7	12	0	0		1	
64/1	SCHERF		4	4	0	0	0	7	1/4	
66/1	JAHNKE		16	12	4	0	0		1	
67/1	HANSEN		26	15	11	0	0	14	1	
68/1	WAFFENSCHMIDT		7	4	3	0	0	6		
69/1	KRELLE ET ALII	1969	70	34	36	0	0	0	1	BONN
	VERSION 2	1970	70	35	35	0	0	0	1	BONN
		1970	97	49	48	0	0	0	1	BONN
	VERSION 3	1971	100	53	47	0	0	0	1	BONN
	VERSION 4	1972	133	56	77	0	0	0	1	BONN
	VERSION 4	1972	130	56	74	0	0	0	1	BONN
	VERSION 5	1974	127	51	76	0	0	10	1	BONN
	VERSION 5	1978	130	50	80	0	0		1	BONN
	VERSION 8	1975	207	106	101	45	0	19	1(1/4)	BONN
	VERSION 8.1 1976		229	115	114	60	0	20	1(1/4)	BONN
	VERSION 8.2 1979		218	100	118	57	0	21	1(1/4)	BONN
	VERSION 9	1976	214	72	142		0	47	1	BONN
	VERSION 10 1976 CA		300	120	180	100	0	50	1(1/4)	BONN
	CONRAD-KOHNERT,VERSION 10 (21.7.1977)		190	104	86	68	0	41	1	BONN
	CONRAD-KOHNERT,VERSION 10 (APRIL 1979)		220	111	109	85	0	113	1	BONN
	CONRAD-KOHMERT,VERSION 10 (FEBRUARY 1980)		220	100	120	80	0		1	BONN
	FRERICHS ET ALII 1976 CA.		44	20	24	0	0	50	1	BONN,
			16*22	7*22	9*22	0	22	2*22		MODELL 22
	IN TOTAL		400	174	222	0	22	94	1	
69/2	LUEDEKE		48	28	20	0	0	21	1/4	LUEDEKE
	VON NATZMER, VERSION 2 1978		30	13	17	3	0	8	1/4	LUEDEKE
69/4	DUVAL ET ALII	5M+2N+1=(3M+2N)+(2M+1)				0	M	7M	1	BATTELLE
70/1	VAN DER WERF VERSION 1		38	16	22	0	0	18	1	VAN DER WERF
	BECKMANN- VERSION 2 UEBE		32	21	11	0	0	11	1	VAN DER WERF
	VAN DER WERF VERSION 3		24	15	9	0	0	19	1	VAN DER WERF
	VAN DER WERF VERSION 4		50	19	31	0	0	22	1	VAN DER WERF
	UEBE VERSION 5		15	11	4	0	0	6	1	VAN DER WERF
70/2	OTT		53	34	19	53	0		1/4	M,LUEDEKE
	KAU 1977		74	58	26	74	0		1/4	M,LUEDEKE
70/3	JAHNKE		37	22	15		0		1	
70/4	KERAN								1/4	ST.LOUIS
71/1	SCHNEEWEISS H.		6	3	3	0	0	2	1	SEE USA 54/1
71/4	GRINWIS-GUILLAUME		14	12	2	0	0	5	1	
73/1	KOENIG-GAAB-WOLTERS		31	20	11	31	0	37	1/4	M,VERSION 1

CONTINUATION

NO.	AUTHOR(S)	EQU	STO	DEF	MON	IO	EXO	PER	MODEL
		31	18	13	31	0	33	1/4	M,VERSION 2
73/2	POSER-HECHELTJEN	12	12	0	0	0	29	1/4	
*	INSTITUT FUER HOEHERE STUDIEN								
74/1	MARTIENSEN-SANDERMANN								M,BONN,69/1
	MARTIENSEN	47	35	12	47	0	28	1/4	M,BONN,69/1
	VERSION 1	88	55	33	88	0	53	1/4	M,BONN,69/1
	KRELLE, 1976 VERSION 2	CA 100	50	50	100	0	50	1/4	M,BONN,69/1
74/2	NIESSEN	22	22	0	0	0	21	1/4	
74/3	KRELLE-FLECK-QUINKE	398			0	37		1	BONN
74/4	MESAROVIC-PESTEL					0			WORLD 74/1
74/5	DE RIDDER-VERBAAN	36	24	12	5	0	16	1	SEE CPB
74/20	KAYA-ONISHI	48	26	22	0	0		1	WORLD 74/20
75/1	JAHNKE VERSION 05/02/75	137	39	98	34	0	82	1/2	BUNDESBANK
75/2	SPAHN	171	65	106	0	0	63	1/2	LITTAUER
75/3	KRELLE ET ALII	CA 1000				12		1	BONN
	FRERICHS-KUEBLER	CA 1300	1000	300		12		1	BONN
75/4	HANSEN-WESTPHAL	216	97	119	21	5		1/4	SYSIFO
	APRIL 1978	279	118	161	42	7		1/4	SYSIFO
75/5	DRAMAIS	47	30	17	2	7	-		EEC 75/1
75/6	RANUZZI DE BIANCHI	31	17	14	0	0	7	1	EURO
75/7	OECD							1/4	OECD
75/8	LAEUFER	1	1	0	0	0	4	1/4	ST.LOUIS
75/9	LEHMANN	CA 141	40	101	0	3(2)		1	SIM
75/10	RATH-NAGEL ET ALII	CA 1125	336	789	0	7(6)		1	SIM
75/11	BRAND-JOCHEM ET ALII					41		1	KARLSRUHE
75/12	CONRAD	20	7	13	5	(14)	33	1	SEE USA 74/12
		18	5	13	4	0	31	1	
76/1	MENGES ET ALII	21	14	7	0	0	11	1	SEE 70/1
76/2	BERNER-CLARK ET ALII	58	36	22	23	0	15	1/4	FRB, MCM
76/2	BERNER-CLARK ET ALII 1977	64	39	25	29	0	14	1/4	FRB, MCM
76/2	CLARK, NOVEMBER 21,1977	129	69	60	50	0	95	1/4	FRB, MCM
76/3	ARTUS	12	8	4	12	0	10	1/12 M	
76/4	PFEIFFER ET ALII	18				0		1	
		17				0	11	1	
	VERSION 1978	23	13	10	3	0	9	1	
76/5	BARTEN ET ALII,VERSION 1								COMET 1, 1972
76/5	BARTEN ET ALII,VERSION 2	62	30	32	0	0			COMET 2, 1976
76/6	DIECKHEUER	40	21	19	15	0	50	1/2	
76/8	FROWEN-ARESTIS	10	8	2	4	0	4	1/4	
76/9	MISCHKE VERSION 1 1976	84	28	56	1	0	20	1	
	BLEIMANN VERSION 2 1979	81	32	49	2	0	19	1	
76/10	SPRINGER					44		1/4	DRI
76/11	KOELLREUTER, VERSION 2 1976	19	15	4	0	0	24	1/4	BRD II
76/11	(PROGNOS) VERSION 3					0		1/4	BRD III
	VERSION 4 1978	45	32	13	4	0	50	1/4	BRD IV
76/12	REHM	13	13	0	12	0	8	1	
77/1	RAU ET ALII, VERSION 1	54	24	30	0	0	20	1/4	RWI-ESSEN
	VERSION 2	55	25	30	0	0	6	1/4	RWI-ESSEN
	VERSION 3	100	28	72	0	0	13	1/4	RWI-ESSEN
	VERSION 4	123						1/4	RWI-ESSEN
77/2	TEWES ET ALII	119	41	78	2	0	147	1/4	IWW-KIEL
	1980		55						IWW-KIEL
77/3	BONHOEFFER ET ALII	100	34	66	0	0	18	1/4	IFO-MUNICH
	SCHUELER-STOCK VERSION 2	75	23	52	0	0	16	1/4	IFO-MUNICH
	VERSION 3	100	30	70	0	0	38	1/4	IFO-MUNICH
77/4	JAHNKE	199	47	152	10	0	38	1/4	BUNDESBANK
	VERSION 13/11/77	197	63	134	78	0	47	1/4	BUNDESBANK
77/5	WOLTERS	6	5	1	0	0	2	1/4	
77/6	MUTH	33	17	16	1	0	13	1/4	IBM
77/7	WILLMS	14	11	3	4	0	4	1/4	SEE UK 76/6
77/8	PFEIFFER	17	12	5	2	0	11	1/2	
77/9	LAVEN	8	5	3	0	0	4	1	
77/10	EHLERS	124	62	62	0	0	36	1	SYSIFO
77/11	DOELLEKES ET ALII								LP
77/12	NUSCH	8	4	4	1	0	3	1/4	ST.LOUIS

NO.	AUTHOR(S)	EQU	STO	DEF	MON	IO	EXO	PER	MODEL
73/1	PESTEL ET ALII	ABOVE 1000			0	19		1	SIM
	OEST 1979	ABOVE 1000			0	19		1	SIM
78/2	HEILEMANN	45	33	12	0	(30)	13	1	
78/3	HEIKE ET ALII	125	46	79	9	0	41	1/4	
78/4	DIW BERLIN								UNPUBLISHED
78/5	SCHIPS	137	35	102	8	(11)	63	1/2	MEBA
78/6	DIECKHEUER	84	33	46	42	0	35	1/4	
78/7	DEWALD-MARCHON	1	1	0	0	0	3	1/4	ST.LOUIS
78/8	DE GRAUWE	11	4	7	11	0	10	1/4	M
73/10	MINK	9	7	2	3	0	3	1/4	
79/1	FRIEDRICH ET ALII	192	80	112	29	0	85	1/4	FREIBURG (LUEDEKE II)
79/2	WOLTERS	15	10	5	4,5	0	7	1/4	SEE 77/5
79/3	HENIZE ET ALII	ABOVE 1000							IAB, SIM
79/4	ARESTIS ET ALII	29	11	18	8	0	14	1/4	IMPERIAL COLLEGE
79/5	BLAZEJCZAK	193	71	122	7	0	63	1	DIW-BERLIN
79/6	DIECKHEUER ET ALII	114	35	29	0	12		1	
79/7	STEINHERR-MORELLE	11	7	4	0	0		1	
79/8	HUJER ET ALII	7	5	2	0	0	14	1/4	
79/20	KATO ET ALII	75	36	39	33	0	22	1/4	EPA-LINK
80/1	FONTANA	40	23	17	7	0	7	1	GERECON
80/2	NAGGL	86	77	9	1	0	120	1/4	
80/3	FAUDE ET ALII							1	LP, SIM
80/4	WESTPHAL ET ALII							1/4	EUROLINK
80/6	SCHMITZ ET ALII	ABOVE 1000							LESS, SIM JUELICH
*	IDW	100						1	IDW

W-GERMANY, REGIONAL MODELS

NO.	AUTHOR(S)	EGU	STO	DEF	MON	IO	EXO	PER	MODEL
76/13	MEISSNER ET ALII								HESSEN,SIM
78/9	THOSS-WIIK								FRANKFURT 4 REGIONS
79/9	CARLBERG								INPUT-OUTPUT

Appendix 4: References referring to the keywords "input-output" and "W-Germany"

Bauerschmidt, R.: Systemanalyse technologischer Veränderungen unter Verwendung von Input-Output-Verfahren. Makroökonomische Input-Output Analysen und dynamische Modelle zur Erfassung technischer Entwicklungen. Ed. by J. Seetzen, R. Krengel and G. von Kortzfleisch. Basel–Boston–Stuttgart 1979, 197–213.

Bezikofer, M.: The Link between GNP Components and Sector Production – An Input-Output Approach. Sysifo Research Memorandum No. 4. University of Frankfurt, University of Hamburg, 1976.

Blazejczak, J., et al.: Einfluß der Marktentwicklung auf die Durchsetzung des technischen Fortschritts: Ein kombiniertes System Dynamics-, Lineares Optimierungs- und Input-Output-Modell. Makroökonomische Input-Output Analysen und Dynamische Modelle zur Erfassung technischer Entwicklungen. Ed. by J. Seetzen, R. Krengel and G. von Kortzfleisch. Basel–Boston–Stuttgart 1979, 227–245.

Bonhöffer, F., and *G. Britschkat*: Die Energiekosten-Studie des IFO-Institutes. Makroökonomische Input-Output Analysen und Dynamische Modelle zur Erfassung technischer Entwicklungen. Ed. by J. Seetzen, R. Krengel and G. von Kortzfleisch. Basel–Boston–Stuttgart 1979, 167–196.

Britschkat, G.: Auswirkungen von Änderungen der Hauptdiagonalkoeffizienten auf die sektorale Bruttoproduktion. Makroökonomische Input-Output Analysen und Dynamische Modelle zur Erfassung technischer Entwicklungen. Ed. by J. Seetzen, R. Krengel and G. von Kortzfleisch. Basel–Boston–Stuttgart 1979, 145–149.

Carlberg, M.: Ein interregionales multisektorales Wachstumsmodell – dargestellt für die Bundesrepublik Deutschland. Studien zur Angewandten Wirtschaftsforschung und Statistik, Heft 7, Göttingen 1979.

Dieckheuer, G., U. Meyer, and *J. Schumann*: Ein dynamisches Input-Output-Modell zur simultanen Erklärung der Entwicklung von Mengen und Preisen, angewendet auf die Bundesrepublik Deutschland 1954–1967. Makroökonomische Input-Output Analysen und Dynamische Modelle zur Erfassung technischer Entwicklungen. Ed. by J. Seetzen, R. Krengel and G. von Kortzfleisch. Basel–Boston–Stuttgart 1979, 73–104.

Duval, A., E. Fontela, and *G. McNeill*: EXPLOR 80. A computable Model for Europe. Battelle Institute Geneva Research, Carouge-Geneva, Switzerland, Mimeograph, 1969.

Frerichs, W., and *K. Kübler*: Preis-, Fortschritts- und Kapazitätsabhänige Input-Output-Koeffizienten. Technologieeinsatz und wirtschaftlicher Strukturwandel als Problem für die Input-Output Analyse. Ed. by P. Gonschior. Bericht: ASA-PW, 04/76, Köln 1976, 54–74.

– : Allgemeiner Bericht über integrative Modelle. Argumente in der Energiediskussion, Energiebedarf und Energiebedarfsforschung. Ed. by H. Matthöfer. Villingen 1977a, 265–289.

– : Input-Output-Prognosemodelle für die Bundesrepublik Deutschland. ZS **133**, 1977b, 276–286.

Gehrig, G.: Ein interregionales Gesamtmodell für die BRD. IBM Symposium – Ökonometrische Modelle und Systeme, Bad Neuenahr, Sept. 14–16, 77, 1977. Reprint in Ökonometrische Modelle und Systeme. Ed. by F. Schober and H.D. Ploetzeneder. München–Wien 1978, 261–280.

Herz, H.: Probleme der Kopplung von Input-Output-Modellen mit anderen systemtechnischen Modellansätzen am Beispiel eines Energiemodells und eines Branchenmodells. Makroökonomische Input-Output Analysen und Dynamische Modelle zur Erfassung technischer Entwicklungen. Ed. by J. Seetzen, R. Krengel and G. von Kortzfleisch. Basel–Boston–Stuttgart 1979, 285–291.

Krallmann, H.: Die Kombination eines Branchen- und eines Input-Output-Modells im Bereich der chemischen Technik. Makroökonomische Input-Output Analysen und Dynamische Modelle zur Erfassung technischer Entwicklungen. Ed. by J. Seetzen, R. Krengel and G. von Kortzfleisch. Basel–Boston–Stuttgart 1979, 265–271.

Kreijger, R.G.: Production Functions and Interindustry Analysis. A monograph. To appear. Heidelberg–New York 1980.

Krelle, W., W. Frerichs, and *K. Kübler*: Ökonometrische Input-Output-Modellanalysen und -prognosen. Makroökonomische Input-Output Analysen und Dynamische Modelle zur Erfassung technischer Entwicklungen. Ed. by J. Seetzen, R. Krengel and G. von Kortzfleisch. Basel–Boston–Stuttgart 1979, 35–54.

Krelle, W., and *K. Kübler*: Input and Investment Functions in a Disaggregated Forecasting Model. University of Bonn, Mimeograph, 1977.

Krengel, R.: Ökonomische Strukturen der Zukunft. Institut für Zukunftsforschung, 1976, 117–133.

Lehbert, B.: Vorschlag für ein Prognose- und Simulationsmodell des Umwandlungsbereichs der Energiewirtschaft in der Bundesrepublik Deutschland. WA **116**, 1980, 131–161.

Matthöfer, H. (ed.): Argumente in der Energiediskussion, Energiebedarf und Energiebedarfsforschung **2**, Villingen 1977.

Oest, W.: Ein Disaggregiertes dynamisches Modell zur Analyse langfristiger Wirtschaftsentwicklungen in der Bundesrepublik Deutschland. Institut für Angewandte Systemforschung und Prognose E.V., ISP, 1979.

Pfeiffer, R., and *H. Kornprobst*: Die Erstellung variabler Input-Output-Koeffizienten mit Hilfe eines ökonometrischen und System-Dynamics-Submodells. Technologieeinsatz und wirtschaftlicher Strukturwandel als Problem für die Input-Output Analyse. Ed. by P. Gonschior. Bericht: ASA-PW/04/76, Köln 1976, 82–98.

Pfeiffer, R., and *H. Lindner*: Die Untersuchung von Problemen der Rohstoffversorgung im Bereich der chemischen Technik mit variablen Input-Output-Koeffizienten. ASA-Seminarbericht 77, Nr. 02, 1977.

– : Untersuchung von Problemen der Rohstoffversorgung im Bereich der chemischen Technik mit variablen Input-Output-Koeffizienten. Makroökonomische Input-Output Analysen und Dynamische Modelle zur Erfassung technischer Entwicklungen. Ed. by J. Seetzen, R. Krengel and G. von Kortzfleisch. Basel–Boston–Stuttgart 1979, 247–264.

634

Reyer, L., M. Koller, and *E. Spitznagel*: Beschäftigungspolitische Alternativen zur Arbeitslosigkeit, Voraussetzungen, Arbeitsmarktwirkungen und Kosten. Institut für Arbeitsmarkt- und Berufsforschung (IAB), Mimeograph, 1979.

Schintke, J.: Der Einfluß von Input-Koeffizientenänderungen auf die sektorale Bruttoproduktion. Makroökonomische Input-Output Analysen und Dynamische Modelle zur Erfassung technischer Entwicklungen. Ed. by J. Seetzen, R. Krengel and G. von Kortzfleisch. Basel–Boston–Stuttgart 1979, 127–144.

Seetzen, J., et al.: Systemanalytische Methoden zur Untersuchung technischer Entwicklungen. Programmleitung Angewandte Systemanalyse. Jahresbericht 1976, Anlagenband V, Köln 1977.

Seetzen, J., R. Krengel, and *G. von Kortzfleisch* (eds.): Makroökonomische Input-Output Analysen und Dynamische Modelle zur Erfassung technischer Entwicklungen. Basel–Boston–Stuttgart 1979.

Stobbe, A.: Volkswirtschaftliche Gesamtrechnung. Handwörterbuch der Wirtschaftswissenschaften (HDWW) 5, 1979, 368–405.

Stoewe, H.: Ökonometrie und makroökonomische Theorie. Stuttgart 1959.

Author Index

References referring to the keyword "energy" (exclusive "W-Germany"), to "energy" and "W-Germany", and to "input output" and "W-Germany" can be found on pp. 620–626, 626–629, and 632–634, respectively. The present index contains only authors whose names occur up to p. 619.

636

Subject Index

642

List of Contributors

Beckmann, Martin J.,
Institut für Statistik und Unternehmensforschung, Technische Universität München,
D–8000 München, Federal Republic of Germany

Bhattacharya, Gautam,
Department of Economics, University of Kansas, Lawrence, Kansas 66045, U.S.A.

Blackorby, Charles,
Department of Economics, University of British Columbia, Vancouver B.C. V6T 1W5, Canada

Breyer, Friedrich,
Alfred Weber-Institut, Universität Heidelberg, D–6900 Heidelberg, Federal Republic of Germany

Buchholz, Wolfgang,
Wirtschaftswissenschaftliches Seminar, Universität Tübingen, D–7400 Tübingen,
Federal Republic of Germany

Clark, Colin W.,
Department of Mathematics, University of British Columbia, Vancouver, B.C. V6T 1W5, Canada

Conrad, Klaus,
Lehrstuhl für Volkswirtschaftslehre und Statistik, Universität Mannheim, D–6800 Mannheim,
Federal Republic of Germany

Dasgupta, Swapan,
Department of Economics, University of Rochester, Rochester, N.Y. 14627, U.S.A.

Diewert, W. Erwin,
Department of Economics, University of British Columbia, Vancouver, B.C. V6T 1W5, Canada

Eichhorn, Wolfgang,
Institut für Wirtschaftstheorie und Operations Research, Universität Karlsruhe, D–7500 Karlsruhe,
Federal Republic of Germany

van Gool, Willem,
Department of Inorganic Chemistry, State University, Utrecht, NL–3522 AD Utrecht, Netherlands

Haas, Peter,
Institut für Statistik und Mathematische Wirtschaftstheorie, Universität Karlsruhe,
D–7500 Karlsruhe, Federal Republic of Germany

Hazilla, Michael,
Environment Division, Resources for the Future, Washington, D.C. 20036, U.S.A.

Hellwig, Klaus,
Universität Bielefeld, Postfach, D–4800 Bielefeld, Federal of Republic Germany

Henn, Rudolf,
Institut für Statistik und Mathematische Wirtschaftstheorie, Universität Karlsruhe,
D–7500 Karlsruhe, Federal Republic of Germany

Hild, Claus,
Institut für Statistik und Mathematische Wirtschaftstheorie, Universität Karlsruhe,
D–7500 Karlsruhe, Federal Republic of Germany

Höpfinger, Eckhard,
Kernforschungsanlage Jülich, D–5170 Jülich, Federal Republic of Germany

Ichimura, Shinichi,
Institute for Southeast Asian Studies, Kyoto University, Kyoto, Japan

Ingham, Alan,
  Department of Economics, University of Southampton, Southampton SO9 5NH, England

Jaksch, Hans Jürgen,
  Alfred Weber-Institut, Universität Heidelberg, D–6900 Heidelberg, Federal Republic of Germany

Jansen, Peter,
  Institut für Energiewirtschaft, Technische Universität Wien, A–1040 Wien, Austria

Kemp, Murray C.,
  School of Economics, University of New South Wales, Kensington, NSW 2033, Australia

Kogelschatz, Hartmut,
  Institut für Statistik und Mathematische Wirtschaftstheorie, Universität Karlsruhe,
  D–7500 Karlsruhe, Federal Republic of Germany

Kopp, Raymond J.,
  Environment Division, Resources for the Future, Washington, D.C. 20036, U.S.A.

Krelle, Wilhelm,
  Institut für Gesellschafts- und Wirtschaftswissenschaften, Universität Bonn, D–5300 Bonn,
  Federal Republic of Germany

Kümmel, Reiner,
  Physikalisches Institut, Universität Würzburg, D–8700 Würzburg, Federal Republic of Germany

Lewis, Tracy R.,
  Department of Economics, University of British Columbia, Vancouver, B.C. V6T 1W5, Canada

van Long, Ngo,
  Department of Economics, Australian National University, Canberra, ACT 2600, Australia

Luptáčik, Mikuláš,
  Institut für Unternehmensforschung, Technische Universität Wien, A–1040 Wien, Austria

McKenzie, George,
  Department of Economics, University of Southampton, Southampton SO9, 5NH, England

Melese, F.,
  Institut de Recherches Economiques, Université Catholique de Louvain, B–1348 Louvain-la-Neuve,
  Belgium

Menges, Günter,
  Institut für Statistik, Universität Heidelberg, D–6900 Heidelberg, Federal Republic of Germany

Mitra, Tapan,
  Department of Economics, State University of New York, Stony Brook, New York, U.S.A.

Müller, Gerhard O.,
  Institut für Angewandte Mathematik, Universität Heidelberg, D–6900 Heidelberg, Federal of
  Republic of Germany

Neumann, Klaus,
  Institut für Wirtschaftstheorie und Operations Research, Universität Karlsruhe, D–7500 Karlsruhe,
  Federal Republic of Germany

Nuske, Manfred,
  Institut für Entscheidungstheorie und Unternehmensforschung, Universität Karlsruhe,
  D–7500 Karlsruhe, Federal Republic of Germany

Pethig, Rüdiger,
  Fachbereich Wirtschaftswissenschaften, Universität Oldenburg, D–2900 Oldenburg, Federal
  Republic of Germany

Pflug, Georg,
 Institut für Wirtschaftswissenschaften, Universität Wien, A−1090 Wien, Austria

Reiss, Winfried,
 Alfred Weber-Institut, Universität Heidelberg, D−6900 Heidelberg, Federal Republic of Germany

Rentz, Otto,
 Fakultät für Wirtschaftswissenschaften, Universität Karlsruhe, D−7500 Karlsruhe, Federal
 Republic of Germany

Rogner, Hans-Holger,
 International Institute for Applied Systems Analysis, A−2361 Laxenburg, Austria

Sauter-Servais, Florian,
 Fakultät für Wirtschaftswissenschaften und Statistik, Universität Konstanz, D−7750 Konstanz,
 Federal Republic of Germany

Schäfer, Martin,
 Fachbereich Wirtschafts- und Organisationswissenschaften, Hochschule der Bundeswehr Hamburg,
 D−2000 Hamburg 70, Federal Republic of Germany

Schubert, Uwe,
 Institut für Raumordnung, Wirtschaftsuniversität Wien, A−1090 Wien, Austria

Schwefel, Hans Paul,
 Kernforschungsanlage Jülich, D−5170 Jülich, Federal Republic of Germany

Schweizer, Urs,
 Fakultät für Wirtschaftswissenschaften, Universität Bielefeld, D−4800 Bielefeld 1, Federal Republic
 of Germany

Schworm, William,
 Department of Economics, University of British Columbia, British Columbia V6T 1W5, Canada

Shephard, Ronald W.,
 Department of Industrial Engineering and Operations Research, University of California, Berkeley,
 California 94720, U.S.A.

Siebert, Horst,
 Lehrstuhl für Volkswirtschaftslehre und Außenwirtschaft, Universität Mannheim,
 D−6800 Mannheim 1, Federal Republic of Germany

Smith, V. Kerry,
 Department of Economics, University of North Carolina, Chapel Hill, N.C. 27514, U.S.A.

Spremann, Klaus,
 Fachbereich Wirtschaftswissenschaften, Univeristät Ulm, D−7900 Ulm, Federal Republic of
 Germany

Ståhl, Ingolf
 International Institute for Applied Systems Analysis, A−2361 Laxenburg, Austria

Ströbele, Wolfgang,
 Fachbereich 4, Wirtschaftswissenschaften, Johann-Justus-Weg 147, D−2900 Oldenburg,
 Federal Republic of Germany

Trautmann, Siegfried,
 Institut für Entscheidungstheorie und Unternehmensforschung, Universität Karlsruhe,
 D−7500 Karlsruhe, Federal Republic of Germany

Uebe, Götz,
 Fachbereich Wirtschafts- und Organisationswissenschaften, Hochschule der Bundeswehr Hamburg,
 D−2000 Hamburg 70, Federal Republic of Germany

Ulph, Alistair,
  Department of Economics, University of Southampton, Southampton SO9 5NH, England

von Ungern-Sternberg, Thomas,
  Institut für Gesellschafts- und Wirtschaftswissenschaften, Universität Bonn, D–5300 Bonn, Federal Republic of Germany

Weiserbs, Daniel,
  Institut de Recherches Economiques, Université Catholique de Louvain, B–1348 Louvain-la-Neuve, Belgium

Winckler, Georg,
  Institut für Wirtschaftswissenschaften, Universität Wien, A–1090 Wien, Austria

empirical economics

A Journal of the Institute for Advanced Studies

Managing Editor: E. Fürst, Vienna

Editorial Board: H. Abele, Fribourg — R.J. Ball, London — G. Basevi, Bologna — R. Bentzel, Uppsala — W. Driehuis, Amsterdam — W. Eichhorn, Karlsruhe — H. Fritsch, Wien — L. Johansen, Oslo — L.R. Klein, Philadelphia — H. König, Mannheim — W. Krelle, Bonn — R. Krengel, Berlin — P. Kukkonen, Helsinki — J. Lambalet, Lausanne — W. Leontief, New York — J. Mairesse, Paris — W. Oberhofer, Regensburg — K. Rothschild, Linz — M. Saito, Kobe — G. Schwödiauer, Bielefeld — H. Seidel, Wien — P. Sevaldson, Oslo — H. Theil, Chicago.

This periodical contains papers in the field of empirical economic research, using advanced statistical methods and tackling the economic problems of our time. Preference will be given to contributions in the fields of economic policy and control. **Empirical Economics** will have space devoted to studies of all industrialized countries, with special emphasis on the European communities. Publications in **Empirical Economics** contain analysis of data on a specific level of aggregation and will, therefore, not be concerned with pure microeconomic problems. Papers are written in English.

Empec is published **quarterly**. Subscription rate for volume 8/1983 is DM 158.—/ U.S.$ 63,20* postage additional. Volumes 1—7 are available, prices upon request.

* prices are subject to change without notice.

————————— **Physica-Verlag · Wuerzburg—Vienna** —————————

Place your order directly with:

Physica-Verlag · P.O. Box 5840
D—8700 Wuerzburg/Germany

for **U.S.** and **Canada:**
Physica-Verlag · P.O.Box 2007
Cambridge, Mass. 02139 / USA

games,
economic dynamics,
and time series analysis

A Symposium in Memoriam Oskar Morgenstern

Edited by
Manfred Deistler, Erhard Fürst, Gerhard Schwödiauer

1982. 398 pages. Paperbound. DM 140,–/U.S.$ 56,–*. ISBN 3 7908 0271 9.

(= IHS-Studies No. 2)

This volume contains the papers given in the symposium which the Institute of Advanced Studies in Vienna organized to honor the memory of the great economist Oskar Morgenstern. The deliberate heterogeneity of the topics represented in the volume reflects the wide range of Oskar Morgenstern's scientific interests without exhausting them. The three topics chosen for the symposium, however, seem to be the ones which had been closest to Oskar Morgenstern's heart. They are

Game Theory as a Tool of Economic Analysis
Expanding and Contracting Economies
Economic Time Series Analysis

The volume represents a stock-taking of the state of the art in these fields by leading games theorists, economists, and econometricians.

Authors are:
S.M. Berman, New York – *H.J. Blommestein*, Amsterdam – *W. Böge*, Heidelberg – *K. Borch*, Bergen – *G.C. Chow*, Princeton – *M. Faber*, Heidelberg – *D.M. Grether*, Pasadena – *W. Güth*, Cologne – *J.C. Harsanyi*, Berkeley – *A.C. Harvey*, London – *S. Heiler*, Dortmund – *T. Ichiishi*, Iowa City – *G.S. Maddala*, Gainesville – *M. Maschler*, Jerusalem – *O. Morgenstern* – *D. Pallaschke*, Bonn – *F.C. Palm*, Amsterdam – *G.D.A. Phillips*, Canterbury – *D. Reetz*, Berlin – *W. Reiss*, Hamburg – *P.M. Robinson*, Guildford – *J. Rosenmüller*, Bielefeld – *D. Schmeidler*, Tel-Aviv – *H. Schneeweiß*, Munich – *A. Schotter*, New York – *R. Selten*, Bielefeld – *G. Thompson*, Pittsburgh – *A. Wenig*, Bielefeld

* Prices are subject to change without notice.

———— **Physica-Verlag · Wuerzburg–Vienna** ————

Place your order directly with:

Physica-Verlag · P.O. Box 5840
D–8700 Wuerzburg/Germany

for **U.S.** and **Canada:**
Physica-Verlag · P.O.Box 2007
Cambridge, Mass. 02139 / USA